Special Edition

Using Microsoft™ Systems Management Server

que®

Special Edition

Using Microsoft™ Systems Management Server

Written by Tim Darby with

Lee Hadfield • Noelani Rodriguez

Special Edition Using Microsoft Systems Management Server

Library of Congress Catalog No.: 96-69953

ISBN: 0-7897-0820-5

98 97 96 6 5 4 3 2 1

Interpretation of the printing code: the rightmost double-digit number is the year of the book's printing; the rightmost single-digit number, the number of the book's printing. For example, a printing code of 96-1 shows that the first printing of the book occurred in 1996.

Screen reproductions in this book were created using Collage Plus from Inner Media, Inc., Hollis, NH.

Credits

PRESIDENT
Roland Elgey

PUBLISHER
Joseph B. Wikert

SENIOR TITLE MANAGER
Bryan Gambrel

EDITORIAL SERVICES DIRECTOR
Elizabeth Keaffaber

MANAGING EDITOR
Sandy Doell

DIRECTOR OF MARKETING
Lynn E. Zingraf

ACQUISITIONS EDITOR
Al Valvano

SENIOR EDITOR
Elizabeth A. Bruns

EDITOR
Gill Kent

PRODUCT MARKETING MANAGER
Kim Margolius

ASSISTANT PRODUCT MARKETING MANAGER
Christy M. Miller

STRATEGIC MARKETING MANAGER
Barry Pruett

TECHNICAL EDITORS
Matthew Brown
Tom Krause

TECHNICAL SUPPORT SPECIALIST
Nadeem Muhammed

ACQUISITIONS COORDINATOR
Carmen Krikorian

SOFTWARE RELATIONS COORDINATOR
Patty Brooks

EDITORIAL ASSISTANT
Andrea Duvall

BOOK DESIGNER
Ruth Harvey

COVER DESIGNER
Dan Armstrong

PRODUCTION TEAM
Stephen Adams
Debra Bolhuis
Kevin Cliburn
Jennifer Earhart
DiMonique Ford
Brian Grossman
Jason Hand
Steph Mineart
Casey Price
Erich Richter
Laura Robbins
Bobbie Satterfield

INDEXER
Tim Tate

Composed in *Century Old Style* and *ITC Franklin Gothic* by Que Corporation.

To my father, Rod Darby
T. Darby

This book is dedicated to the memory of Ferne Terhune.
L. Hadfield

About the Authors

Tim Darby is a Microsoft Certified Systems Engineer and has a B.S.E.E. degree from Rice University. He has 15 years' experience in PC systems design and integration. For the past four years, he has performed a variety of network design and integration efforts as part of PRC, Inc.'s Automated Patent System project for the U.S. Patent Office. He is currently performing network integration and system administration at Integra Technology International, Inc.

Lee Hadfield is a Senior Systems Engineer for Integra Technology International, Inc., a Microsoft Solution Provider and software developer. He has over ten years of PC networking experience, and currently heads the Network Integration Group for Integra's Solution Services Division located in Tucson, Arizona. Experienced with Novell, Lan Manager, and Windows NT, his work is currently focused around the Microsoft BackOffice family of server products. He holds both Microsoft Certified Systems Engineer and Novell Certified Netware Engineer certifications.

Noelani Rodriguez is a Microsoft Certified Trainer, public speaker and Webmaster for the Microsoft Certification Exam Resource Page on the Web. Although she is a graduate of Harvard in economics, data processing has proven to be one of her best loves.

Acknowledgments

This book would not have been possible without the generous support of Armand Sperduti and Mike Bernstein, who allowed me to use Integra's network for all of the examples and screen shots.

Thanks to Steve Wynkoop for all the valuable advice and for introducing me to Que.

Special thanks to Lee Hadfield, my friend and co-author, without whose help I would not have been able to finish this book.

T. Darby

I would like to acknowledge several people; including Elliot Masie and the Masie Center, for being a beacon of light in the industry, Kent Joshi, co-chairman of the Los Angeles chapter of National Association of Solution Providers, and Chiara Freedom, for typing faster than God and understanding my lousy sign language.

N. Rodriguez

Many people have helped make this book a reality and need to be thanked for their efforts. I'd like to start with Armand Sperduti, senior vice president of solution services at Integra Technology, for allowing me to take on this project. Without his approval I would not have been able to participate in the writing of this book. Both he and Mike Bernstein, chief executive officer of Integra Technology, were kind enough to let me use the company's SMS installation to illustrate most of the examples found in the text of this book. Thank you both for your help.

Next I'd like to thank Steve Wynkoop, a co-worker and the author of several Que publications, for putting me in touch with folks at Macmillian Computer Publishing. Thanks for having the confidence in me to recommend me to Que. I'd specifically like to thank Al Valvano, the Acquisitions Editor at Que, for allowing me the opportunity to work on this project. Also a big thanks to Elizabeth Bruns, Senior Editor at Que, for letting me get things submitted in the nick of time. I really appreciate it. My co-authors, Tim Darby and Lani Rodriquez also deserve many thanks for their contributions to this book. It would not have been completed without their help and hard work.

I'd like to thank my wife, Teresa for her encouragement and support during the project, thanks for not forgetting who I am. Finally I'd like to thank a few friends named Sam, Gordo, and Cowboy for keeping me company during the long hours of writing. They helped keep reality in check, and provided me with comic relief when I needed it most.

L. Hadfield

We'd Like to Hear from You!

As part of our continuing effort to produce books of the highest possible quality, Que would like to hear your comments. To stay competitive, we *really* want you, as a computer book reader and user, to let us know what you like or dislike most about this book or other Que products.

You can mail comments, ideas, or suggestions for improving future editions to the address below, or send us a fax at (317) 581-4663. For the online inclined, Macmillan Computer Publishing has a forum on CompuServe (type **GO QUEBOOKS** at any prompt) through which our staff and authors are available for questions and comments. The address of our Internet site is **http://www.mcp.com** (World Wide Web).

In addition to exploring our forum, please feel free to contact me personally to discuss your opinions of this book: I'm **avalvano@que.mcp.com** on the Internet.

Thanks in advance—your comments will help us to continue publishing the best books available on computer topics in today's market.

Al Valvano
Acquisitions Editor
Que Corporation
201 W. 103rd Street
Indianapolis, Indiana 46290
USA

Contents at a Glance

VII Appendixes

Contents

Introduction

Microsoft Systems Management Server version 1.2, or simply SMS, is a comprehensive, distributed, multi-site platform for taking inventory, auditing, distributing software, and configuring and troubleshooting the desktop and server machines in your organization, all from a single location. With SMS, Microsoft has addressed the seemingly insurmountable task of managing PCs operating with a variety of hardware configurations, operating systems, and applications, whether they're all in one building or spread out around the world. SMS achieves this by utilizing at least one Windows NT server PC at each of your company's sites to manage inventory and applications at the local site. A relational database at each site (SQL Server) stores information about the site, inventory information, and other SMS data. SMS uses its own network communications processes (called Senders) that take advantage of standard Windows NT networking services to communicate information among the sites. The difficult goal of centralized management is made possible by the ability to establish a communications hierarchy among all your site servers, with one server at the top acting as the central management point for all sites in your organization.

SMS is one of the Microsoft BackOffice applications, but it's not a stand-alone product. It runs on Windows NT Server, and it requires Microsoft SQL Server 4.21 or later for storing its site configurations and inventory information. If your network includes SNA connectivity, then SMS also requires that SNA server be installed.

For those of you not familiar with SMS, a history of the releases may help you see the direction SMS is heading. SMS 1.0 debuted in November, 1994. While this introduction was generally welcomed as being a big first step towards getting a handle on the complexities of managing client/server networks, there was clearly a lot of room for improvement—especially in the areas of interoperability and ease of use. There was also the perception that SMS locked you into a single vendor (Microsoft) solution. SMS 1.1, delivered in August, 1995, was designed to address those problems and more. SMS 1.1 improved on SMS 1.0 in the following areas:

- Ease of Use

  Predefined queries, prompted queries, the addition of a NOT condition for queries, and a faster query operation all added up to much less work in formulating queries on the SMS database. A software auditing database, and the ability to retrieve specific properties about files that comprise a given application, made software auditing and inventory a lot simpler.

- More Control

  SMS 1.0 mostly forced you to do things its way. SMS 1.1 gave more control to the administrator. The ability to adjust the percentage of each link's bandwidth that SMS is allowed to use to send instructions and data to remote sites is just one example. Improved Help Desk features, such as support for Windows 95, the ability to invoke the Windows diagnostics program on a Windows NT machine, and more client-side security options, provided much more flexibility in real-time troubleshooting. Customizable machine properties enabled administrators to tailor their views of the inventory database.

- Better Interoperability

  SMS 1.1 was designed not only to support the management of Windows 95 PCs, but to be the best migration and deployment tool for Windows 95. This release supported Windows NT 3.51 (both server and workstation versions) and SQL Server 6.0. IBM's OS/2 Warp was also supported, along with LAN Server 4.0. Finally, the Network Monitor was enhanced to recognize a number of additional network protocols.

SMS 1.2, the current version, provides further enhancements in all the above areas. Windows 95 clients gain access to shared network applications. Remote control and all the other Help Desk tools are now available for Windows NT workstation and Server. The software auditing database has been greatly expanded. Network Monitor recognizes many more network protocols. Third-party add-ons now have their own place in the Administrator program (the Options, Add-Ins menu). SNMP support increases interoperability with the other network management products. The improvements are discussed in more detail in Chapter 2, "What's New." ■

Who Should Read This Book?

The authors have tried to cater to both the seasoned administrator and the novice alike by presenting enough step-by-step examples to get you up and running, while assuming a certain level of systems knowledge. SMS, by its very nature, encompasses so many different areas of computing that it would be impractical to explore them all in depth. Familiarity with PC networking is assumed, for example, and SQL Server is covered only to the extent necessary to understand its relationship to SMS. You will likely benefit from this book if you are any one of the following:

- An administrator of a large network of PCs with a mix of operating systems and applications and a staff that is overworked trying to keep track of it all.
- Planning a new network or the expansion of a small one—and you want to be sure that good systems management is in place from the start.
- Experienced with Windows NT Server and familiar with PC networking concepts.
- A NetWare administrator who wants to explore the management possibilities of SMS in the NetWare environment or is planning to migrate to Windows NT Server.
- Already using a management product—and you want to see how SMS might complement that product or perhaps supplant it.

SMS has evolved to the point where it now interoperates with SNMP, and a number of vendors have built direct SMS links into their network management systems, so the perception of SMS as a Microsoft-only management solution is no longer accurate. Since SMS is built around an SQL Server database, you don't even have to rely totally on the SMS administrator program—you can use your favorite SQL query program.

Other Sources of Information for SMS

The amount of available information on SMS is relatively small. There are no books available and no periodicals devoted to SMS, although *BackOffice Magazine*, published by PennWell Publishing Company, provides some coverage of SMS, and *Special Edition Using BackOffice*, published by Que, is an excellent introduction to the BackOffice suite, including SMS. At this time, most of the information about SMS comes from Microsoft.

Microsoft TechNet

Microsoft publishes a monthly TechNet CD containing a wealth of technical information on SMS (and many other Microsoft applications), including the entire Microsoft Knowledge Base. You can buy an annual subscription to TechNet. Contact Microsoft for licensing and pricing details.

The Internet

Microsoft maintains a Web page devoted to SMS at its main Web site. Just point your Web browser to **http://www.microsoft.com** and select SMS from the pull-down list of products. In addition, Microsoft's public Internet news server (**msnews.microsoft.com**) contains the following SMS-oriented news groups:

- **microsoft.public.sms.admin**
- **microsoft.public.sms.inventory**
- **microsoft.public.sms.misc**
- **microsoft.public.sms.netmon**
- **microsoft.public.sms.rcdiags**
- **microsoft.public.sms.setup**
- **microsoft.public.sms.shareapps**
- **microsoft.public.sms.sitecomm**
- **microsoft.public.sms.swdist**
- **microsoft.public.sms.tools**

To access these, you'll need an NNTP-compliant news reader (Microsoft distributes one for free from its Web site, and there are other good ones available from various FTP sites on the Internet). You just configure your news reader to use **msnews.microsoft.com** as the address for the news server, make the connection, and subscribe to the above news groups. In addition, to the SMS groups, you'll find many others representing a variety of Microsoft applications. Access is free and the big benefit is that you can post questions and get answers from other users or even from Microsoft employees.

Another good Web site operated by Beverly Hills Software, **http://www.bhs.com**, specializes in maintaining current information on all the BackOffice applications, including SMS.

Microsoft Knowledge Base

The Microsoft Knowledge Base is available on the Microsoft Web site mentioned earlier and on the CompuServe online service (GO MSKB). This database contains known bugs and fixes (if available) and technical solutions to common questions.

How This Book is Organized

This book starts with the assumption that you don't know anything about SMS, and then follows a step-by-step approach that takes you from SMS concepts, through planning and installation of SMS sites, and on to managing your system and your SMS configuration. Part I gives you the basics on SMS capabilities, covering each of the important functional areas. Part II discusses the issues involved in planning and implementing your SMS sites, with emphasis on NT's domain structure and how domains fit into the SMS site picture. Part III gets down to the actual management operations available with SMS, including hardware and software inventory, software audit, software distribution, and so on. The real-time troubleshooting tools—Network

Monitor, Help Desk, and Remote Diagnostics—are discussed separately in Part IV. Part V shows you what's involved in managing your SMS configurations, and Part VI provides step-by-step real-world examples of selected topics from Parts I through V. Finally, we've included appendixes that cover SMS components, terminology, configuration files, data flow, NT and SQL server installation, software deployment, and third-party add-ons.

Part I, "Understanding SMS Capabilities," explores the basic concepts of each category of systems management provided by SMS.
Chapter 1, "Learning the Basics of SMS," describes the tasks that the systems management functions perform and how they work.

Chapter 2, "What's New," presents the new features in SMS version 1.2.

Part II, "Planning Your SMS Installation and Implementing the System," identifies the network issues that you need to be aware of when planning and implementing SMS, including NT domain and NetWare issues as well as physical network issues. Site installations and a variety of client installations are covered in detail.
Chapter 3, "Understanding Domains, Sites, and the SMS Hierarchy," explains NT domain concepts, SMS sites, and the components that make up a site, and shows how NT domains map to SMS sites.

Chapter 4, "Planning, Design, and System Requirements," begins with an overview of some planning and design methods that can be used when implementing SMS. The chapter covers the four basic phases of design starting with the system analysis and specification phase. After that, the design, implementation, and maintenance phases of the project are outlined and discussed. The last part of the chapter takes a look at the hardware and software requirements of the various SMS components.

Chapter 5, "Server Installation, Part I," outlines the setup and configuration of both Windows NT Server and SQL Server, which are prerequisites to the installation of the first SMS site server. The chapter will show you how to create the service accounts that are used by SMS and SQL, set up directory replication, and make changes to the SQL default configuration.

Chapter 6, "Server Installation, Part II," describes the installation of the first site server, followed by an explanation of the SMS setup events that take place during installation. The chapter continues with a discussion of the SMS Administration program and its role in the creation of logon, helper, and distribution servers. The chapter takes an in-depth look at the administrator functions used to create secondary sites, followed by an example of a secondary site installation. The last part of the chapter covers SMS integration with NetWare and Macintosh environments.

Chapter 7, "Installing Client Sites," deals with the SMS clients' components and their installation. The chapter starts with a look at the Use Automatically Configure Workstation Logon Scripts option, followed by a section on the manual configuration of workstation logon scripts in NT, LAN Manager, and NetWare environments. The chapter concludes with a discussion of Macintosh clients and what's required when adding them to the SMS system.

Part III, "Managing Your System with SMS," shows you how to collect hardware and software inventory, perform a software audit, distribute software, create shared network applications, and perform queries.

Chapter 8, "Using the SMS Administrator Program," demonstrates all the features of the System Administrator program, which is the primary means of configuring SMS and querying the database. This includes creating and managing packages, jobs, queries, machine groups, site groups, program groups, and alerts.

Chapter 9, "Collecting Hardware Inventory," describes hardware inventory collection and how to configure and manage it. Hardware inventory is installed automatically when you install clients.

Chapter 10, "Software Inventory and Audit," shows you how to configure SMS to collect software inventory and perform a software audit.

Chapter 11, "Software Distribution," examines the complex tasks of software distribution and application sharing, and how SMS has simplified them. You'll learn about the role that distribution servers play in the process, and you'll learn a lot about creating SMS jobs and packages.

Chapter 12, "Queries and Reports," discusses the creation of queries in SMS and the use of predefined queries. These can shorten your learning curve since you can use them as examples when you create your own. You'll find out how to use Crystal Reports to query and generate reports from the SMS database.

Part IV, "Remote Diagnostics and Troubleshooting," covers the excellent real-time analysis and troubleshooting tools that SMS provides.

Chapter 13, "Using Help Desk and Diagnostics on a Remote PC," explores the SMS Help Desk and Remote Diagnostics. Help Desk enables you to control a PC remotely on your network, initiate a remote chat session, transfer files, and even reboot the remote PC. Remote Diagnostics scans the CMOS and memory of the remote PC to provide a wealth of information about machine configuration, memory usage, and processes running on the remote PC.

Chapter 14, "Using the Network Monitor," demonstrates all the features of this impressive network monitoring tool. You'll see how to capture traffic on any network segment and even transmit some of this traffic back onto the network for simulation purposes.

Part V, "Managing SMS," focuses on the management of SMS itself. This includes adding and deleting sites, configuring SMS alerts and viewing events, troubleshooting SMS components, and ensuring fault tolerance.

Chapter 15, "Changing Your Site Configuration," looks at the procedures for making changes to your initial SMS implementation. Over time, you may need to add or move sites or you may decide to tweak your SMS configuration by adding helper servers. This chapter shows you how.

Chapter 16, "Monitoring the SMS Site," examines the event-reporting mechanisms that SMS uses and shows you how to configure alerts—conditions that SMS will monitor, performing the action you specify when a given condition occurs.

Chapter 17, "Troubleshooting SMS Components," provides troubleshooting techniques for all the servers involved in the operation of SMS, including NT server and SQL server.

Chapter 18, "Providing Fault Tolerance and Database Recovery," discusses techniques for providing backup and recovery of your SMS servers in case of failure.

Part VI, "Putting It All Together—A Step by Step Example," provides practical examples of the most important SMS features.

Chapter 19, "Installation Overview," demonstrates how to create both primary and secondary sites and install SMS clients.

Chapter 20, "Taking the Hardware and Software Inventory," shows examples of hardware and software inventory collection and software audit.

Chapter 21, "Sharing Applications," walks you through the processes of distributing a software package and sharing a network application. You'll see how to create the jobs and packages required and how to verify the jobs have run.

Chapter 22, "Retrieving System Data," provides examples of SMS queries and shows how to generate a report from a query using Crystal Reports.

Chapter 23, "Investigating Remote PC Problems," uses Help Desk and Remote Diagnostics to solve typical PC problems.

Chapter 24, "Investigating Network Problems," looks at typical situations where Network Monitor can help with network problems.

Chapter 25, "SMS Management Tasks," examines a variety of tasks that involve the management of your SMS configuration, including removing items from the system, monitoring events, configuring alerts, and troubleshooting.

Appendix A, "SMS Components and Terminology," provides a convenient reference for all the new terms that come with SMS.

Appendix B, "SMS System Files and Utilities," covers the details of the main SMS configuration files, as well as some of the important SMS utilities such as DBCLEAN.EXE.

Appendix C, "SQL Server Basics and Installing NT Services," provides the essentials of SQL Server and some of the NT services required by SMS.

Appendix D, "A Detailed Look at the Data Flow," illustrates the flow of data and instructions throughout the SMS system. This includes the services that are involved and where the data resides as it moves from server to server. Understanding the data flow can be a big help when SMS doesn't behave as expected.

Appendix E, "Deploying Software," looks at using SMS to deploy three popular software packages—Exchange, Windows 95, and Office 95.

Appendix F, "Third-Party Add-On Products for SMS," surveys the products other vendors have developed that work within the SMS administrator or operate as separate applications that integrate with SMS.

Conventions Used in This Book

This book assumes that you are already familiar with the graphical user interface used in Windows-based applications. Consequently, no attempt has been made to describe how to select or choose various options in the dialog boxes discussed throughout this book. Instead, the terms click, select, choose, highlight, activate, disable, and turn on/off have been used to describe the process of positioning the cursor over a dialog box element (radio button, check box, command button, drop-down list arrow, and so on) and clicking a mouse button. Those familiar with using the keyboard to select various dialog box options may relate this selection process to keystrokes instead of mouse clicks. Either method is equally acceptable.

Tips, notes, cautions, warnings, and troubleshooting annotations, used generously throughout the book, appear in specially formatted boxes to make this important information easier to locate. References to paragraph headings that have appeared previously in the book or that will follow later in the book are generally annotated as cross-references and appear near the text to which they pertain.

At times, you may be required to press keyboard keys in selected combinations to activate a command or cause a selected display window to appear. When these situations occur, you will see the key combinations described in a couple of different ways. When two or more keys need to be depressed simultaneously, a plus sign (+) is used to combine the keys. For example, if the Alt and Tab keys need to be pressed simultaneously, you would see the annotation Alt+Tab. Likewise, if the Ctrl and Y keys need to be pressed simultaneously, the annotation would be Ctrl+Y. When keys need to be depressed in a certain sequence with no intervening actions, a comma (,) is used as a separator. ●

PART I

Understanding SMS Capabilities

CHAPTER 1

Learning the Basics of SMS

The SMS Components

An SMS system can include site servers, logon servers, helper servers, distribution servers and others. We'll introduce all of the servers that SMS depends on.

The SMS Management Functions

You'll learn all the management functions that SMS performs. Additionally, you'll gain insight into how they are performed and some significant things you should be aware of.

The SMS Vocabulary

SMS brings with it a lot of new terminology, and terms you think you know may have slightly different meanings in SMS. This chapter will introduce many of the important terms. Appendix A, "SMS Components and Terminology," provides a complete glossary.

You already know that it takes a team of people to effectively manage a large network of PCs, so you shouldn't be surprised to learn that it takes more than a single program to automate those activities. SMS is actually a complex collection of programs that work together. Add to that the Windows NT Server and Microsoft SQL Server components that SMS relies on for security, communications, and data storage, then throw in the distributed server architecture that enables SMS to operate across a variety of network protocols and topologies, and the prospect of truly understanding SMS seems daunting. We show you that it's easy to understand if you break SMS down to its essential elements. This chapter gets down to the basics of what SMS is and what it does. This will provide a foundation for understanding the relationships between the various components provided in subsequent chapters which, in turn, gives you the tools you need to get your SMS system started and keep it humming along. ■

What is SMS?

Before we answer that question, let's answer the related question "What is systems management according to Microsoft?" Simply put, it's the following:

- Knowing exactly what hardware and software you've got on your machines.
- Updating or adding software to a machine or a group of machines.
- Easily obtaining answers to questions about machine configurations.
- Diagnosing and fixing problems on remote machines from your workstation.

Systems Management Server (SMS) is Microsoft's answer to the problem of managing networked PCs. It's a software tool set for extracting detailed information from networked computers and distributing data files, programs, and other types of information to those computers. It also includes tools that tackle network problems and remote machine problems. SMS relies fundamentally on two other pieces of Microsoft BackOffice to do its job—Windows NT Server and Microsoft SQL Server. NT Server provides SMS with an operating environment, file system, network communications, and security; SQL Server provides the relational database that stores most of the SMS-related data including SMS site configurations, job details, alerts, and machine inventories.

To build an SMS system, let's start with a PC running Windows NT Server and configured as either a primary or backup domain controller. Next, install SQL Server and the SMS site server software. You have now created the simplest SMS system. You can attach this server to a network of PCs and manage the network as a single site. This may be all you need, but the desire for good performance might require splitting large networks into multiple sites and managing those sites with multiple server machines. The distributed architecture of SMS enables it to divide the work among a number of server machines, allowing it to grow as your network grows.

SMS requires you to organize your network into a collection of one or more sites. "Site" is a key organizational concept in SMS, and you must create sites that enable you to achieve your administrative goals. In SMS, a site is a group of domains and computers consisting of one SMS site server, at least one Windows NT domain, optional NetWare domains, optional additional servers to share the management load with the site server, and the machines that you will be managing within that site. It is natural to think of sites in geographical terms (the Tucson site, for example), but you must also take into account the logical and physical layout of your entire network before creating your sites.

SMS also enables you to define a hierarchical organization for your sites, with a single site (called the central site) at the top of the hierarchy, and fanning out to child sites that can, in turn, be parents to other sites. Figure 1.1 shows the three types of SMS sites (central, primary, and secondary) and illustrates the way sites are made up of Windows NT domains. Note that a domain (domain "A" in this figure) can span several sites.

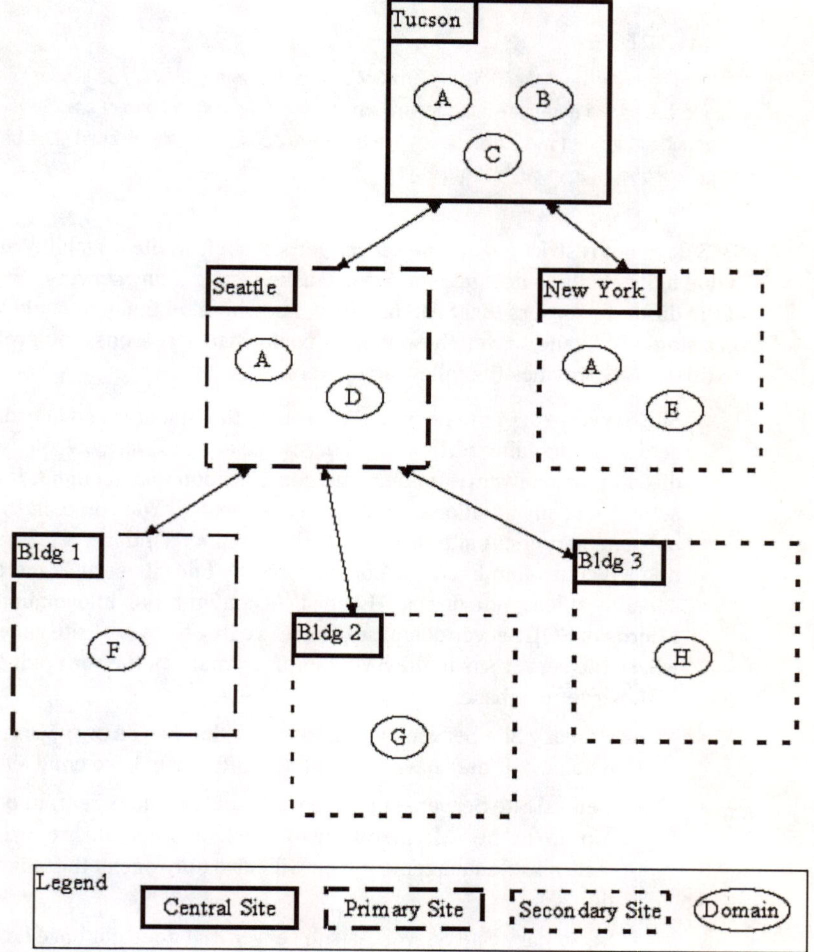

FIG. 1.1
An example of an SMS site hierarchy.

This hierarchy is not just an organizational convenience and it requires careful planning on your part. The hierarchy determines the actual flow of data through the SMS system. Child sites report configuration changes and SMS job progress reports to their parent sites, which forwards the information to their parents, and so on until it all reaches the central site. SMS jobs that originate from a given site may be sent to all of that site's child sites, to the children of those sites, and so on. SMS can create a great deal of data to be moved and stored, so it's important to plan ahead.

CAUTION

You must understand the impact of the SMS hierarchy on the disk space in your site servers. SMS actually replicates all the database information from each child site to its parent site. As you go up in the site hierarchy, more and more disk space is required to account for all the child sites below. The central site's disk must be large enough to store all the data for all the sites.

SMS does not restrict you to one server per site. In fact, the scalability and robustness of SMS is due to its ability to delegate its various tasks among many servers. As you read the list below of the different servers that SMS provides, keep in mind that you could host all these functions on a single SMS site server (however, for performance reasons, you probably wouldn't want to do this). SMS provides the following servers:

- Site Server—the fundamental SMS server that initiates and coordinates all SMS activities, including SMS logons, hardware and software inventory collection, software distribution, software auditing, and configuration management. It also coordinates the activities of any additional servers you've created. You could, in theory, do it all using only site servers. A site server must be running Windows NT Server configured as a domain controller. Each site contains exactly one site server, and therefore each site contains at least one domain. Each site's configuration information is stored in a Microsoft SQL Server database. There are three types of site servers, depending on where the server sits in the SMS hierarchy and whether or not it has its own Microsoft SQL Server database:
    - Primary Site Server—any site server that has its own Microsoft SQL Server database. It may have a parent site and it may have child sites.
    - Central Site Server—a primary site that has no parent. In other words, this is the top site in the SMS hierarchy to which all other sites report. If you want true centralized management, you will have only one of these in your entire organization.
    - Secondary Site Server—a site server that does not have its own SQL server database. It must have a parent site and it cannot have child sites, because it has no database to store their configurations. Its own configuration is maintained in the database of its parent site. Secondary sites are appropriate for locations that don't require local administration.
- Logon Server—a specialized SMS server that aids the site server by sharing the duty of validating logons from client computers. Normally, this server is a Windows NT Server, but for NetWare clients it must be a NetWare 3.1x file server or a NetWare 4.x file server running 3.1x bindery emulation. There can be as many logon servers as you need and you can use your existing backup domain controllers to perform this function, but you don't have to.
- Helper Server—a logon server to which you have additionally assigned one or more of the following site server services: Scheduler, Despooler, Inventory Processor, or Inventory Data Loader. As with the logon server, there can be more than one of these.

- Distribution Server—a server that acts as the destination for the source files for a software package that has been distributed via SMS. When a package installs on a client computer, the client computer looks to a local distribution server for the source files. It's preferable for this server to be a logon server, but it doesn't have to be. The distribution server is really just a file server. You can have as many of these as you need.
- Database Server—a server that contains the site database for a primary site. It is included here to make the point that the SQL server database that is associated with a primary site server need not reside on the same physical machine. SMS allows you to host the site database on a separate machine dedicated to running SQL Server. In fact, several primary sites can share the same database server.

Each SMS primary site stores its own configuration and the configurations for all sites below it in the hierarchy in a SQL server database. Therefore, if you want to administer a given site, you can do so by connecting to any primary site in the hierarchy from which it is descended. Of course, from the central site, you can manage everything.

SMS uses a service called a "sender" to make the communications links that forge the sites into a reporting chain. SMS provides three sender types: LAN sender, SNA sender, and Remote Access Service sender. The LAN sender is installed by default.

The SMS programs that do most of the work are Windows NT services. You can have a single NT server at each site, or several to share the load. These services can send data from site to site and perform queries and updates on the SQL server database(s). Each service has a specific role in SMS. Additionally, the client computers (a term we will use to refer to the servers and workstations you administer) run programs that are specifically designed to interact directly with SMS.

So far, we've just touched on the basic organization of SMS and we've thrown out some terminology that we haven't defined yet (SMS job, for example). The rest of this chapter will cover the tasks that SMS performs and will define terminology and concepts along the way. The organization of each topic will include a description of the task followed by a number of significant things to be aware of for that task.

The User Interface

We know you'll be tempted to skip this part and launch right into the functions that SMS performs—we understand, we're busy people too! But the SMS user interface has a different orientation from those of other Microsoft products, and it takes some getting used to. Chapter 8, "Using the SMS Administratior Program," will cover the interface in detail. For now, let's examine the main features.

The first thing you'll notice as you flip through the pull-down menus of SMS Administrator is that there don't seem to be any commands relating to jobs, packages, machines, or many of the other parts of SMS we'll be talking about later in this chapter. That's because the command set is designed to be generic enough to operate on any *object* in the SMS system. In SMS, any item that can be created or viewed in the Administrator Program is an object. Objects are stored in each site's SQL server database. This design allows the total set of commands to be fairly small, because the real work is done in the different dialog boxes that appear for each type of object that you work on.

Figure 1.2 shows the File menu, which you'll use often to create new objects, examine properties of existing objects, and execute queries. Figure 1.2 also shows the Packages window, one of the nine windows that the Administrator program provides for working with objects (Sites, Jobs, Queries, Alerts, Machine Groups, Site Groups, Program Groups, and Events are the other eight windows). The File menu is misnamed, because it opens and closes windows rather than files. Basically, the SMS Administrator Program is a database manipulation and query tool that is tied into the SMS database.

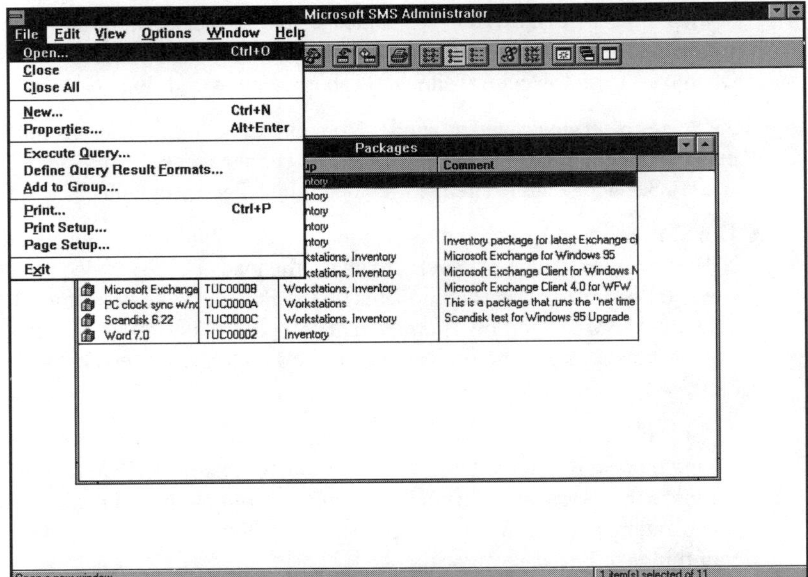

FIG. 1.2
The SMS command set is small.

Hardware Inventory

SMS collects and stores detailed hardware information for each computer in a site. This information includes CPU type, operating system, total RAM, total and free disk space, I/O ports, BIOS settings, network card, and so on. SMS provides a program called the Inventory Agent for each supported client operating system that executes on the client and collects the hardware information. Chapter 9, "Collecting Hardware Inventory," discusses the details of collecting hardware inventory from client computers. Figure 1.3 shows the hardware inventory window for a particular machine.

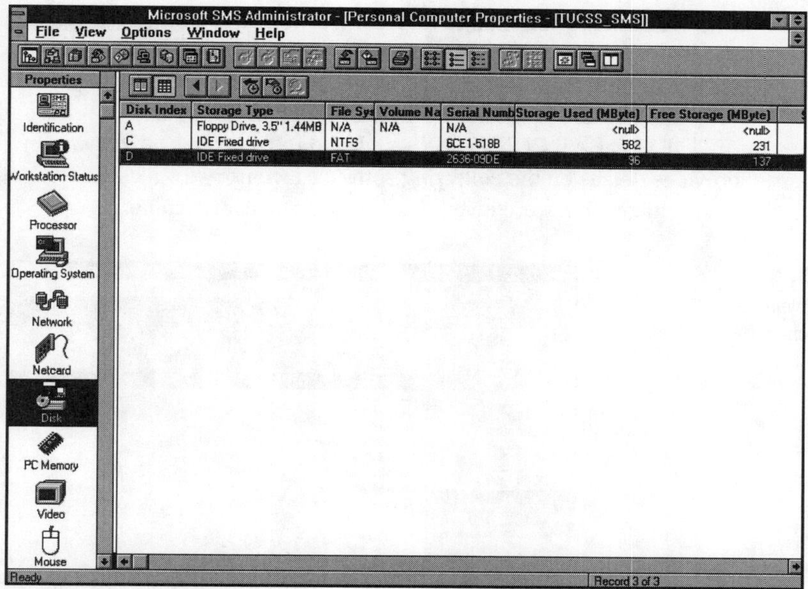

FIG. 1.3 The disk drives in machine TUCSMS1.

You should bear in mind the following:

- The client computer, not SMS, initiates the execution of the Inventory Agent. Therefore, to take hardware inventory on a regular basis, the Inventory Agent is typically set up to run from a login script or from AUTOEXEC.BAT.
- The items that the Inventory Agent scans for are predetermined by Microsoft and can't be changed. However, SMS does allow you to add your own items, and these will be picked up during the scan. SMS also supports the Desktop Management Interface standards being developed by the Desktop Management Task Force, so that when DMI-compliant PCs are added to your network, SMS will automatically recognize them and extract the information.
- The Inventory Agent's accuracy is impressive, but not perfect. If you have two identical network cards, it'll only find one. It sometimes reports incorrect processor speed. Microsoft is aware of the problems and is working to improve its accuracy.

Software Inventory

SMS can perform an inventory of software for each computer in a site. SMS identifies a given software package (Microsoft Word 7.0, for example) by using predefined or your own custom rules that describe a key file or group of files that belong to the package. Now here's where the terminology gets confusing. In order to describe a particular *software* package to SMS for inventory, you must create an *SMS Inventory* package using the SMS Administrator Program. An inventory package is a file (with extension .PDF) that contains the rules describing the *software* package you want to inventory. SMS has two other types of packages that you'll learn about shortly. In addition to finding files on client computers, SMS can, if you specify, copy particular files from the client computer and store them on the site server. This feature can be very valuable and is intended primarily for small configuration-related files (such as WIN.INI, AUTOEXEC.BAT, CONFIG.SYS, and so on). Chapter 10, "Software Inventory and Audit," provides details on the collecting software inventory from client computers. Figure 1.4 shows the packages that were inventoried on a particular machine.

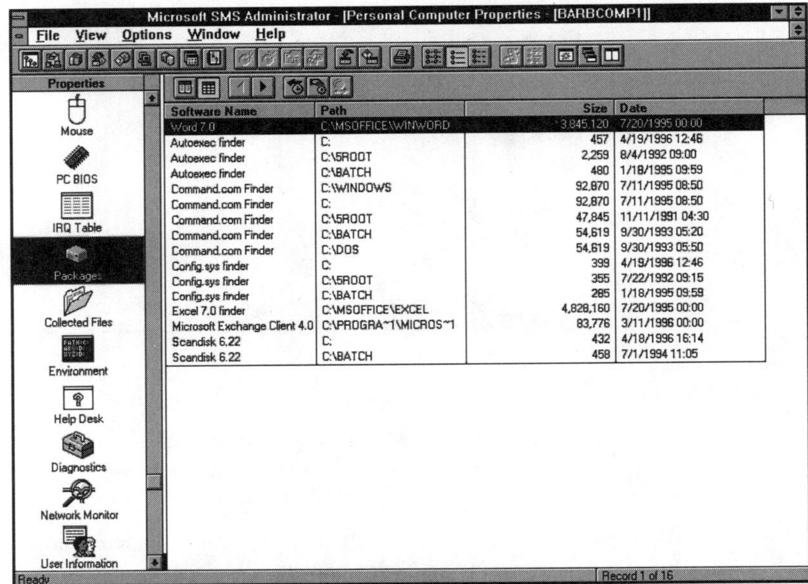

FIG. 1.4
Software found in machine BRIANCOMP.

You should bear in mind the following:

- The same Inventory Agent that performs the hardware inventory scan also performs the software inventory scan.
- SMS comes with many predefined software inventory package files for popular software packages.
- SMS includes a program that enables you to extract the essential identification information from an existing installation of a software package.
- Software inventory is designed to handle a relatively small number of packages. Microsoft recommends that you limit the number to less than 200.

Software Audit

SMS can perform a software audit for each computer in a site. Although software audit sounds very much like software inventory, and they perform similar tasks, they are separate functions in the SMS system. The basic difference is that the SMS software audit is a CPU-intensive operation that searches for over 4,500 packages, as opposed to software inventory's relatively small number of packages. Software audit also uses rules to identify software packages, but it doesn't require you to define an inventory package for each one. Instead, it uses a single file (with extension .RUL) to hold all of its rules. SMS requires you to create a package for it and schedule a time for the package to run, and that means you must create a job. An SMS job includes all the details necessary to deliver a particular package to the desired sites and clients at a given time. Software audit requires a "Run Command on Workstation" job. The other type of job that SMS provides, the "Share Package on Server" job, will be discussed later. Chapter 10, "Software Inventory and Audit," provides details on performing a software audit.

You should bear in mind the following:

- The same Inventory Agent that performs the software inventory scan also performs the software audit.
- SMS comes with a predefined audit rule file for popular software packages and a predefined package for the software audit itself.
- Software audit and software inventory have different roles. Table 1.1 summarizes the differences between the two.

Table 1.1 Comparison of Software Inventory and Software Audit

	Software Inventory	Software Audit
Scheduling	Runs periodically according to the settings in SMS Administrator (every logon or every N days).	Runs at a specific time defined in the job (it could be set to run after normal business hours, for example).
Target machines	Every computer in a site.	Only the machines or groups that you specify in the job.
Defining software packages	You must create an inventory package for each software package to be inventoried.	A single file contains all rules for all packages to be audited.
Collecting inventoried files	You can specify that inventoried files will be copied to the site server.	No provision for copying audited files to the site server.

Software Distribution

SMS can distribute software packages and software updates. You must create an SMS Workstation Package, which includes such details as the directory where the installation files are stored (typically a network share directory), the command line that runs the installation program, and the required client operating system. Then you must create a Run Command on Workstation job to specify the target computers and schedule the job. SMS handles the packaging and distribution of the source files to all designated sites and notifies each user that a package is available for installation. When the user gives the go-ahead, SMS automatically installs the software on that user's workstation. Chapter 11, "Software Distribution," provides details on performing software distribution via SMS. Figure 1.5 shows the setup dialog box for a workstation package.

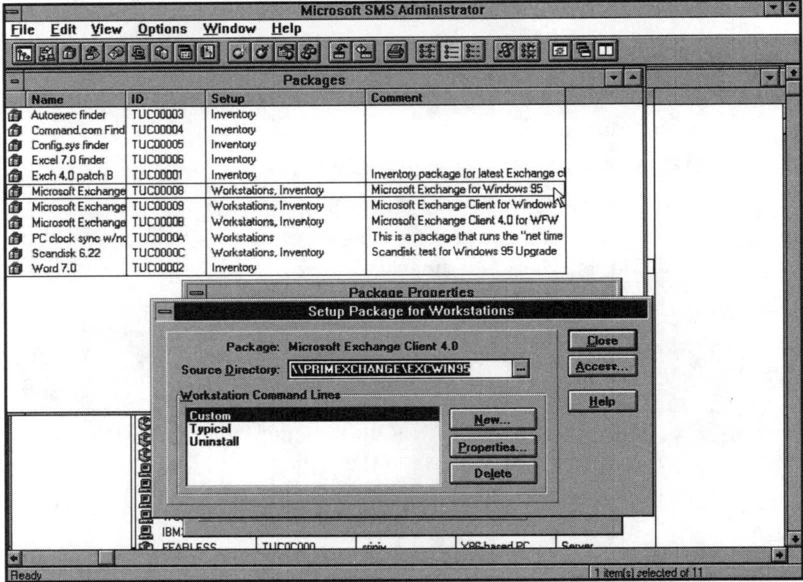

FIG. 1.5
Package properties for distributing Microsoft Office 95.

You should bear in mind the following:

- The files you distribute don't have to be software. They could be on-line corporate training manuals or the latest set of templates for in-house documentation. You don't even have to send any files—perhaps you just want to use this facility to run a command on each computer.
- As with other aspects of SMS, the user is in control. The user can delay or even skip the actual installation. However, if you define a mandatory installation, it can be delayed only until the date you specify, and then SMS takes over and installs the job without asking the user.

- SMS provides you with a large number of definitions for the distribution of popular software packages. This is important because it can be time-consuming to develop and test your own definitions and installation scripts.

Sharing a Network Application

SMS enables you to install network applications and specify that a given set of client computers can run these applications from a network shared directory. At first you might wonder how this is different from or better than simply installing the application manually and pointing client computers to the shared directory as you have done in the past. The benefit is that SMS brings true management for the first time to network applications. SMS will do the actual work of installing the application on the servers and shared directories you specify throughout your organization. SMS allows a given application to be shared from multiple servers within a site, and decides dynamically which server should be used for each client access. This provides fault tolerance and a simple form of load-balancing. SMS does this by creating special program groups in each Windows client's Program Manager using the Program Group Control program. When the user double-clicks the icon for a network application in one of these special program groups, SMS picks a server for the application and sends to the client the path to that server. SMS also ensures that only the client computers you specify have access to a given network application.

To instruct SMS to share a network application, you must first install the application to a network shared directory. Then you create a Sharing Package that includes many of the same details as the Workstation Package and also includes the name of the shared directory that the client computer will connect to in order to run the application. Finally, you create a Share Package on Server job, which identifies the sites and the distribution servers that are the destinations for the network application files. Chapter 11, "Software Distribution," provides details on sharing network applications via SMS. Figure 1.6 shows the Package Properties dialog box for a typical software application.

You should bear in mind the following:

- SMS provides you with a number of scripts that you can use to install many of the popular applications as network applications.
- A user can access the network application only through the SMS-created program groups. There is no way for the user to get to the application directly.
- Creating the program groups and distributing the files to the network servers are two distinct operations for the administrator. You need to be careful that you don't put the cart before the horse by providing the program groups to the users before the application has reached the servers.

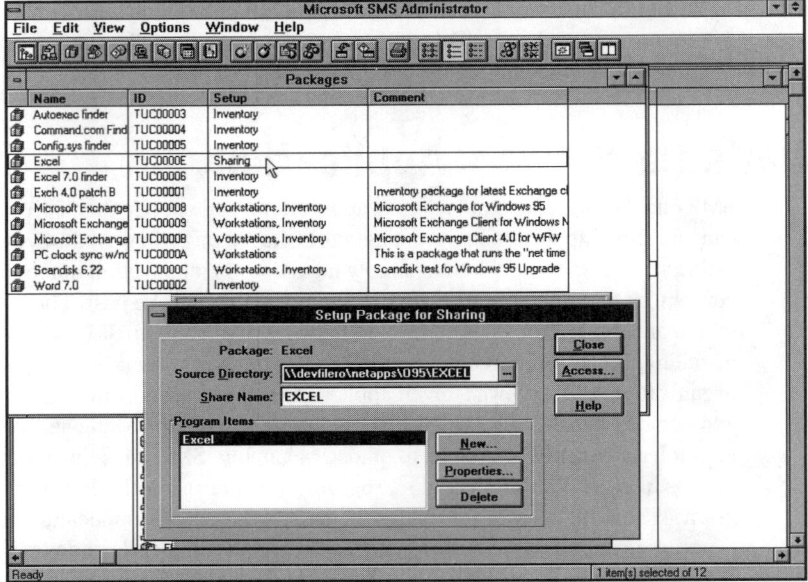

FIG. 1.6
Package properties for sharing Microsoft Excel.

Remote Support and Diagnostics

With the SMS Administrator program, you can use the Help Desk function to connect to a computer on the network and work on it remotely from your PC. You see the same screen the user sees, and the remote computer will respond to your keystrokes and mouse actions. It's just like being there. You can also obtain diagnostic information remotely. This includes a variety of dynamic information, such as memory structures, interrupt vectors, and many Windows-specific items that are all gathered in real time from the client computer. Figure 1.7 shows some of the diagnostic information you can obtain and figure 1.8 provides an example of the remote control feature.

For network-related problems, SMS provides the Network Monitor, a program that is capable of capturing all the packets on a given LAN segment and filtering them based on criteria you specify. Network Monitor understands the packet formats for a large variety of network protocols. Figure 1.9 shows the Network Monitor in action.

See chapter 13, "Using Help Desk and Remote Diagnostics on a Remote PC," and chapter 14, "Using the Network Monitor," for details on the use of these real-time analysis tools.

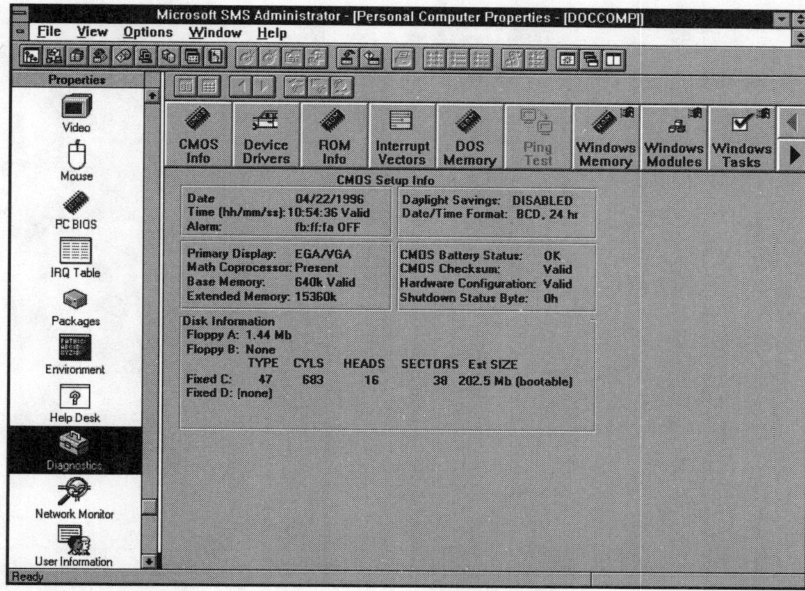

FIG. 1.7
Viewing the CMOS settings for machine GUEST_PC.

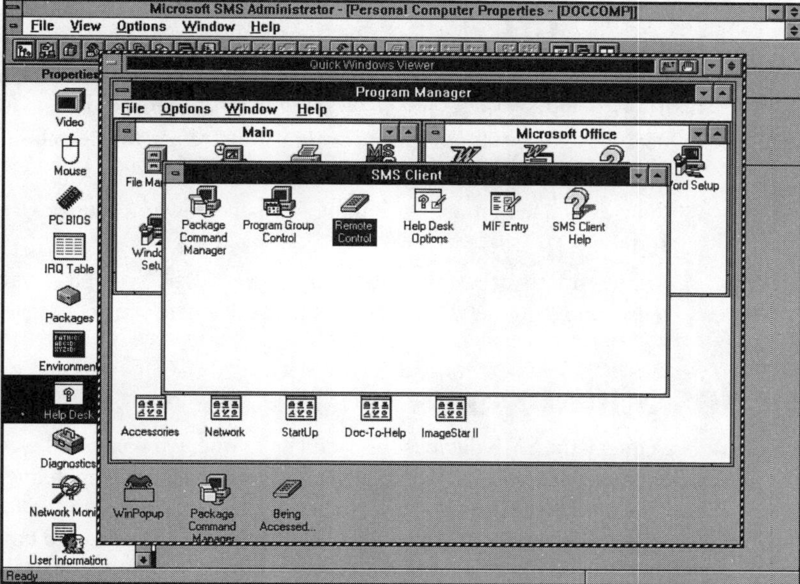

FIG. 1.8
Using Program Manager remotely on machine GUEST_PC.

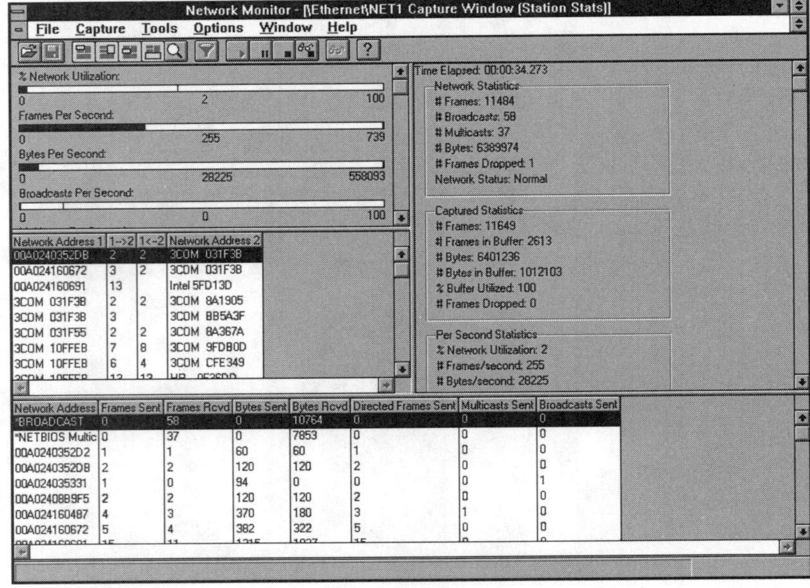

FIG. 1.9
Capturing packets with Network Monitor.

You should bear in mind the following:

- The user has ultimate control over remote access. The user must run a TSR and the remote control program to enable this access, and must also turn on the permissions. There is no way for someone to sneak in unless all of these are in effect. Make sure the user closes the remote control program and resets the permissions after a troubleshooting session.
- Your workstation must be running the same network protocol that user's computer is running.
- Although Network Monitor is a very powerful tool, you must have detailed knowledge of networking and network protocols to make any sense out of the information it gives you.

Queries and Reports

You can query the SMS database at each site or query the one at the central site. There are a number of useful predefined queries to choose from, or you can define your own. Query results can simply be viewed or they can be saved and used as a target for another SMS function. For example, a query could result in a list of machines that need to have a piece of software upgraded. This query result could be used as the target group for the software distribution function.

Reports can be generated and viewed or printed using the included Crystal Report Writer program, which has been customized for SMS. Chapter 12, "Queries and Reports," provides details on the creation of SMS queries and the use of the report generator. Figure 1.10 shows the Query window, which contains all the queries defined for the site.

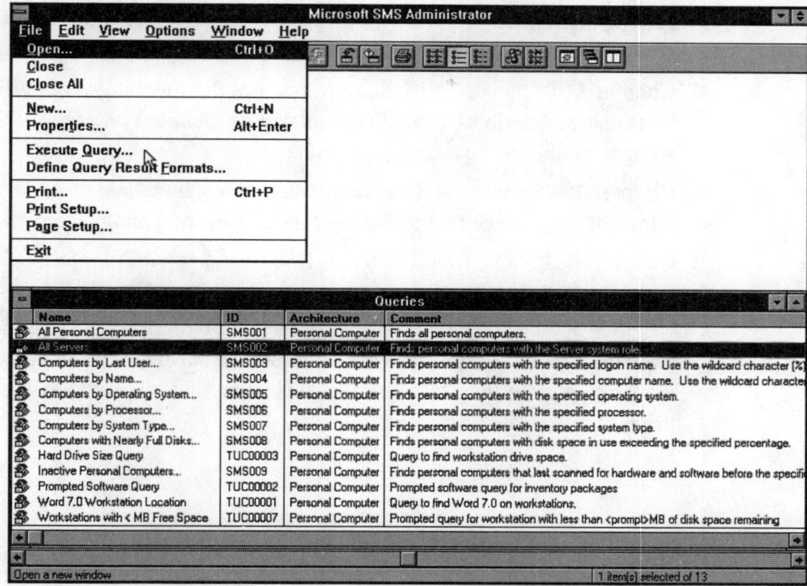

FIG. 1.10 Executing a selected query.

You should bear in mind the following:

- You can rely on the SMS query functions or you can dig even deeper into the database using any good SQL query generating program, such as Access or Excel.
- You must first run the included program SMSVIEW before you can access the SMS database with Crystal Report Writer or other external query programs.
- You can integrate the Microsoft Internet Information Server (IIS), which is now being bundled with Windows NT Server, with the SMS database to provide customized query capability to anyone on your corporate intranet with a compatible web browser.

From Here...

This chapter has given you a basic understanding of the management tasks that SMS can perform and some of the components that comprise SMS. You should now have an appreciation for the power and the scope of the management functions that SMS brings to the PC world for the first time. Later chapters will bring out the details of the SMS management functions and show you how to exploit the full power of SMS.

- Chapter 3, "Understanding Domains, Sites, and the SMS Hierarchy," is critical to understanding the organization of SMS and how its components are distributed.

- Chapter 9, "Collecting Hardware Inventory," shows you how to set up client computers running a variety of operating systems for collecting their hardware inventory.
- Chapter 10, "Software Inventory and Audit," introduces the key concepts of SMS package and SMS job, while showing you how to perform these functions. It also gives you guidance for proper usage of both functions.
- Chapter 11, "Software Distribution," covers the mechanics of getting applications out to your users, whether the applications will be installed on each workstation or installed on a network shared directory.
- Chapter 12, "Queries and Reports," shows you how to extract detailed and customized information from SMS and how to format this information into attractive reports.
- Chapter 13, "Using Help Desk and Diagnostics on a Remote PC," explains the tools you need to control a PC on the network and extract real-time diagnostic information while sitting at your management workstation.
- Chapter 14, "Using the Network Monitor," describes the vast array of network packet viewing and handling features that this valuable tool provides. It's arguably worth the price of the whole SMS package!

CHAPTER 2

What's New

New SMS Features

Version 1.2 includes new features that improve interoperability with other management platforms and extend all SMS management functions to Windows NT and Windows 95.

SMS Enhancements

Version 1.2 includes performance and usability enhancements in many areas including database maintenance, auditing, network monitoring, third-party add-on support, and reporting.

Although it's not a major upgrade of version 1.1, SMS 1.2 provides a number of enhancements and two much-hoped-for additions: remote control for Windows NT workstations, and program group control for Windows 95 workstations. The new support for Simple Network Management Protocol (SNMP) is a welcome addition for both administrators who rely solely on SMS and those who employ management stations from other vendors.

SMS is inherently dependent on two other BackOffice components, Windows NT Server and Structured Query Language (SQL) Server, and you must have the correct versions of those to ensure a successful installation. SMS 1.2 supports Windows NT server version 3.51 or later (with service pack 3 or later). SMS 1.2 still supports SQL Server version 4.21 or later. However, if you are using Windows NT 4.0, you must upgrade to SQL Server 6.5, since NT 4.0 does not support earlier versions of SQL Server. At the time of this writing, we are not aware of any new restrictions on the version of SNA server that you can use with SMS 1.2. ■

Windows NT Enhancements

Support for Windows NT machines was not up to par with the other Windows platforms in previous versions of SMS. SMS 1.2 corrects these deficiencies by providing Remote Control and an improved Inventory Agent.

Remote Control

The big news in SMS 1.2 is that the remote control features of SMS that supported other Windows clients are now available for Windows NT server and workstation version 3.51 or later. This includes all the features of both Help Desk and Remote Diagnostics. Additionally, under NT only, you can specify a list of administrators who are allowed to use the remote control features. As with the other SMS clients, the NT client has the ability to allow or disallow remote access. Chapter 13, "Using Help Desk and Remote Diagnostics on a Remote PC," shows how to obtain the remote diagnostics and use the remote control features.

Inventory Agent Service

The Windows NT Workstation Inventory Agent now runs as an NT Service instead of from a login script as it did in previous versions. This means that it now has the necessary privileges to perform a complete inventory of the workstation. Chapters 9 and 10, "Collecting Hardware Inventory" and "Software Inventory and Audit" describe how the SMS inventory functions work.

Windows 95 Enhancements

Enhancements related to Windows 95 include the addition of Program Group Control and Package Definition File (PDF) files for Office 95.

Program Group Control

Program Group Control dynamically builds special program groups and items on client computers. It's a necessary component for running shared applications from SMS distribution servers. Previously this was not available under Windows 95, and therefore Windows 95 users couldn't access shared applications. Chapter 11, "Software Distribution," covers program group control and its role in application sharing.

Office 95 PDF Files

SMS now includes Package Definition files for automated distribution of both the standard and professional versions of Microsoft Office 95. This includes versions 7.0, 7.0a, and 7.0b and the mini applications that go with Office. Chapter 11, "Software Distribution," shows you how to use PDF files to distribute applications.

SNMP

SMS now supports SNMP traps for network management. SMS treats SNMP traps as a new architecture, and you can query the traps and set SMS alerts on them, just as you can with other SMS architectures. This support has the following two components:

- Windows NT Events Translator—this software is an add-on to NT servers and workstations that translates Windows NT Events of your choosing to SNMP traps. These are standard SNMP traps that can be sent to SMS or to any SNMP-based network management station that receives traps. It requires NT 3.51 or later.
- SNMP Trap Receiver—using the Trap Receiver, SMS can receive SNMP traps from Windows NT machines configured to generate traps as well as any network device that is capable of sending an SNMP trap. You can specify criteria that SMS uses to decide which traps to accept.

Bigger Software Auditing Database

The SMS software auditing database, contained in the file AUDIT.RUL, has been expanded to include definitions for over 5,000 software applications. AUDIT.RUL is a text file that you can use as is or modify to add your own package definitions.

Improved Network Monitor

The SMS Network Monitor, already an invaluable tool for in-depth network analysis, includes a number of really useful additional features, as follows:

- Top User/Consumer—gives you an indication of which machine is using the most network bandwidth.
- Find Network Routers—analyzes network traffic and correctly identifies routers and their associated port addresses.
- Address Resolution—identifies the network address of any computer name that you enter using several different address resolution techniques.
- Protocol Distribution—identifies the different protocols in use on your network and ranks them according to how much bandwidth each is using.

Network Monitor also supports many more protocols, including Point-To-Point Tunneling Protocol (PPTP), Java, Network News Transfer Protocol (NNTP), Generic Routing Encapsulation (GRE), and Simple Mail Transfer Protocol (SMTP), and it has the ability to utilize any network card for network monitoring. Previously it could utilize only those network cards that could be placed in "promiscuous" mode. Chapter 14, "Using the Network Monitor," discusses all the features that this tool provides.

SMS Enhancements

SMS components have received a number of enhancements in version 1.2 which are detailed in the following sections.

Performance

The overall speed of both the server and client portions of SMS has improved.

Improved Database Maintenance

The SMS DBCLEAN utility, a program that lets you remove unused data from the SMS database, has received enhancements to the following functions:

- Delete selected PCs.
- Delete groups.
- Delete abandoned collected files.
- Display duplicate personal computers.
- Merge history for selected PCs.

The DBCLEAN utility is covered in detail in Appendix B, "SMS System Files and Utilities."

Access to Third-Party Add-Ins

You can run third-party integrated applications from the new Add-Ins menu item on the Options menu in the SMS Administrator. The default Add-In menu includes the following SMS and Windows NT tools:

- SMS Security Manager
- SMS Service Manager
- SMS Database Maintenance Utility
- SMS Sender Manager
- Event Viewer
- Server Manager
- User Manager
- Performance Monitor
- Event/Trap Translator

Client Mapping

You can now map client computers to an SMS domain/site combination. This means that you can allow SMS automatically to assign logon scripts in configurations that have multiple sites in one domain. You can also map a client computer to a specific server, which means you can choose the logon server if you have multiple domain controllers. Chapter 3, "Understanding

Domains, Sites, and the SMS hierarchy," discusses the Windows NT domain issues that relate to your SMS configuration.

Package Delivery to Distribution Servers

You can, via a registry setting, guarantee that a package that is intended to update files on a distribution server succeeds in overwriting the specified files. In previous releases, the update might fail if any of the files contained in the update was being used on a distribution server. The new server registry setting forces disconnection of any files that are in use. Chapter 11, "Software Distribution," describes the use of distribution servers for software distribution.

Group NOT for Queries

You can now negate a single query expression or a set of query expressions as a group using the Group NOT button in the Query Properties dialog box. Chapter 12, "Queries and Reports," shows you how to build SMS queries.

Sender Bandwidth Control

There is a new Sender Manager utility (accessed from the Administrator Options, Add-Ins menu) that enables you to control the percentage of bandwidth used for each site to which your server sends packages. For each site server, you can specify the link speed and the percentage of that speed to be used for sending packages. As the package is sent, the SMS dynamically computes a delay value that it uses to pause between transmittal of each packet that is part of the package. By inserting delays, it effectively reduces its usage of the link to the percentage specified in the Sender Manager. Part II, "Planning Your SMS Installation and Implementing the System," discusses the use of senders and how to configure them.

Improved Reporting

SMS includes Crystal Report Writer version 4.5 for retrieving information from the SMS database and printing reports. This version of Crystal Report Writer lets you create SMS reports in HTML format so you can put them up on your corporate web server. Chapter 12, "Queries and Reports," shows you how to create SMS reports.

From Here...

- Chapter 8, "Using the SMS Administrator Program," covers all the features of the SMS Administrator Program.
- Chapter 11, "Software Distribution," explains how application sharing works, and how to set up Program Control Groups to enable clients to access shared applications.

- Chapter 13, "Using Help Desk and Diagnostics on a Remote PC," shows you how to connect to a remote client, remotely control its keyboard and mouse, and collect a great deal of real-time information about the current state of the machine and the processes running on it.
- Chapter 14, "Using the Network Monitor," explores all the packet capturing features as well as the new discovery features of the Network Monitor tool.

PART II

Planning Your SMS Installation and Implemenating the System

CHAPTER 3

Understanding Domains, Sites, and the SMS Hierarchy

SMS is totally integrated with the Windows NT domain structure, so understanding the domain concept is very important. We don't plan to cover domain models to the extent that other fine references such as the Special Edition Using Windows NT book do, but we will point out the special considerations you need to be aware of when planning your SMS implementation. We'll start out with a refresher on the four domain models, then explore SMS sites and how they fit into a hierarchy, and finally we'll show you what to consider when planning your SMS sites, based on your domain structure, physical network, and any existing non-NT network operating systems you may have. ■

SMS Sites

We'll cover the different types of SMS sites and the servers and services that are required to manage a site. You'll see that SMS provides both flexibility and scalability in the way that it uses NT Server machines, and you'll see how the SMS hierarchical arrangement for multiple sites makes true centralized administration possible.

NT and Netware Domains

We'll look at the NT domains and trust relationships, since SMS sites consist of groups of domains. Additionally, SMS can use Netware servers as logon servers by grouping them into pseudo-NT domains.

SMS Support for Other Operating Systems

We'll also look at how SMS, in conjunction with NT Server's native networking capabilities, provides support for a variety of operating systems. And third parties are filling in the gaps for operating systems such as UNIX that aren't commonplace in the PC world.

Understanding Domains and Trust Relationships

A Windows NT Server Domain, according to Microsoft, is "a collection of computers that can recognize the same user accounts." While technically accurate, there's a lot more to the domain concept than just that. Physically, a domain is made up of one or more computers running Windows NT Server and capable of communicating with each other on a Local Area Network (LAN). One of these servers has the special role of primary domain controller, and any other servers that make up your domain have the role of backup domain controller. A domain contains a security account for each user who logs on to the domain, and each user can have access rights only on machines that are logged on to or are members of the domain.

If you have more than one domain, you will probably want certain users to have access to resources in domains other than the one they log on to. In order to give users access to another domain, you must establish a trust relationship from that domain to the one they normally log on to. A trust relationship is simply a link from one domain to the another that enables the "trusting" domain to grant access rights to user accounts that are located in the "trusted" domain.

The Windows NT Domain

Rather than attempt a concise definition, let's attack domains from the angle of what they do for you as a system administrator. A domain provides:

- Network Security

  There is a single database of users for each domain. The primary domain controller holds the master copy of the database and each backup controller contains a copy of the database. Any changes are automatically replicated to all backup domain controllers. The backup domain controllers provide redundancy in the event that the primary domain controller fails.

  SMS relies on NT domain security to grant different users different rights to the SMS database. SMS also tracks the domain that each machine belongs to and which user last logged on to a machine.

- Network Logon

  Users log on to the domain instead of a workgroup or an individual server. The advantage of a domain logon is that the user may be granted rights to any resource in the domain with a single logon. Windows NT and Windows 95 machines have access to the domain user accounts database and can grant rights to any files, directories, or printers that they own. This is a big improvement over the workgroup concept, where each machine must maintain its own security information. When a user logs on to a domain, he or she can be authenticated by any of the domain controllers. Backup domain controllers share the effort of logon processing with the primary domain controller.

  SMS has logon servers that are used to collect the hardware and software inventory from each client that logs on to one of the site domains. You'll probably want to configure your domain controllers as SMS logon servers, and SMS makes that easy to do.

- Ease of Administration

  Because all the user accounts are in one database, centralized management is possible. The administrator simply logs on to the domain with an account that has administrator privileges and manipulates the user account database with the User Manager for Domains program.

  SMS takes this a step further and allows you to organize your domains into sites. SMS management is performed at the site level, and you can manage all sites in your organization from the central site.

Trust Relationships

If I say that I trust you, then I've established a relationship that opens the door for a variety of interactions. For example, I might give you a key to my tool shed and let you borrow something whenever you want. But you don't implicitly get free rein in my house. This is the way NT trust relationships work. A trust relationship is a link between two domains that allows the trusting domain access to the user accounts database of the trusted domain. This extends the single logon feature of a domain to multiple domains, because a user can log on to the trusted domain and have access to files, directories, and printers in one or more trusting domains. Note that the trust relationship merely opens the door—the administrator for the trusting domain still has to let you in! The trust relationship is one-way only. If you want mutual trust, you must establish two trust relationships. The differences among the four domain models have to do entirely with how the trust relationships are set up.

Single Domain Model

Of course, the simplest network would have no trust relationships, so we'll start with that one. In the Single Domain model, you have one domain that contains all your user accounts and resources. You'll have one primary domain controller and one or more backup domain controllers (at least one for backup, and more for load-sharing, depending on how many users you have). The obvious advantages to the single domain model are simplicity and centralized management of both users and resources. As you'll see, SMS is a breeze to set up on this domain model, but it could be complicated if your domain is split by a Wide Area Network (WAN).

Master Domain Model

Perhaps your company has different departments that want control over their own resources, but you still want centralized management of user accounts. Then your network is a candidate for the Master Domain model. This model features a single domain, known as the master domain, and one or more "resource" domains. The master domain contains all the user accounts, and the resource domains contain only resources (shared directories and printers). You set up a trust relationship from each resource domain to the master domain. Users log in to the "trusted" master domain and use resources in the "trusting" resource domains. This model retains the centralized management of user accounts while enabling the flexibility in managing resources that a medium-to-large company requires. With SMS and multiple domains, you have to make decisions about which domains to include in each of your sites.

Multiple Master Domain Model

Suppose your company is so large that a single domain for user accounts just won't cut it. Then you go with the Multiple Master Domain model. This model splits your user accounts between two or more master domains. Other domains in this model are resource domains. Now your trust relationships really start to multiply, because each master domain must trust every other master domain, and each resource domain must trust every master domain. Why? Remember that NT trust relationships are not transitive. The fact that you set up domain A to trust domain B and domain B to trust domain C does not cause domain A to trust domain C. Therefore, if A is a resource domain and B and C are master domains, and you want users in B and C to get to resources in A, you've got to set up trust relationships between A and B and between A and C, regardless of the trust between B and C. Your master domains must all trust each other, so that you can log on as administrator in any of the master domains and be able to manage all the user accounts. The downside of this model is that you no longer have true centralized management, because your user accounts are split up among several domains.

Complete Trust Domain Model

What if you don't have or don't want a central administrator? Then you might opt for the Complete Trust Domain model. In this model, all domains are equal in the sense that they can each have user accounts and resources. Therefore, each domain has to trust all the others, making the number of trust relationships large even for a small number of domains. It's generally not recommended because it requires the most trust relationships of the four models and because you're putting faith in other system administrators, some of whom may not be as security-conscious as you.

SMS Sites and Site Components

SMS sees your network as a collection of one or more sites. You must have at least one, and SMS will ask you to name it during installation. Therefore, before you get to that point, it's a good idea to know exactly what it is you're creating. In this section, we'll describe in detail the three different type of SMS sites and the various servers that carry out SMS tasks within a site. We'll refer to figure 3.1 when discussing the different types of SMS sites.

Primary Site

Think of the primary site as an administrative site in the SMS hierarchy. The primary site has its own SMS database that stores all the SMS site configuration information and the data collected from client computers in the site. Additionally, the primary site's database contains all the information from all the sites below it in the hierarchy. In figure 3.1, Tucson and Seattle are examples of primary sites.

Create primary sites at each location where local management is required. Keep in mind that the primary site can manage all sites below it, so you'll want to place the primary sites at points where they're really needed.

FIG. 3.1
An SMS site hierarchy.

Tucson
A
B
C
Seattle
A
D
New York
A
E
Bldg 1
F
Bldg 2
G
Bldg 3
H

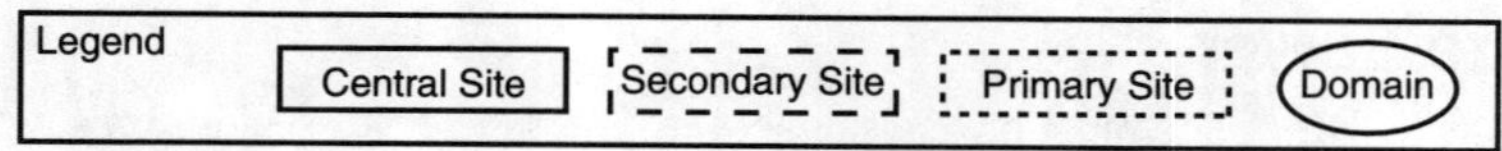

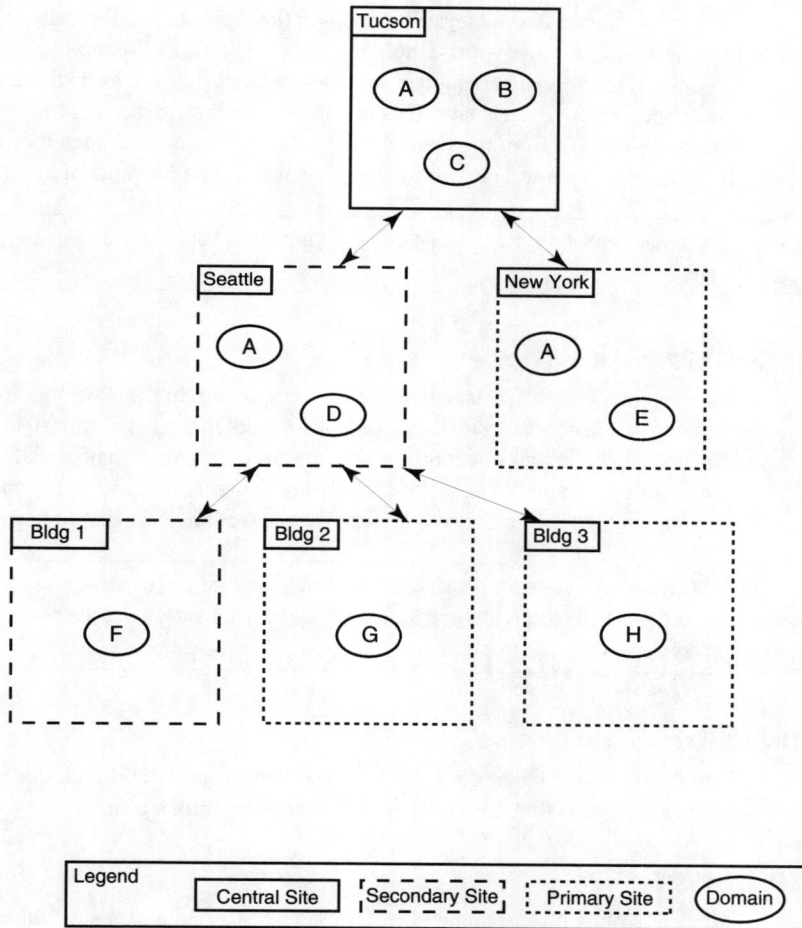

The primary site can appear at any place in the SMS hierarchy, but you should avoid placing primary sites where they're not needed (that is, where there is no administrator). Each primary site requires its own Structured Query Language (SQL) Server database and possibly a dedicated machine to host the database.

▶ **See** Appendix C, "SQL Server Basics and Installing NT Services," for info on SQL Server.

Primary sites on the same LAN can share an SQL Server machine for hosting their databases.

Central Site

The site at the top of the hierarchy is called the central site. It's really just a primary site that has no parent. In other words, there isn't a special installation option for creating a central site. Because of the way information automatically flows in SMS, everything from every site eventually collects at the central site. This is how SMS achieves true centralized management. Packages and jobs flow from the central site to all sites below, and inventory and status flow back up the chain to the central site. In figure 3.1, Tucson is an example of a central site.

Be sure your central site server's hard disk is big enough to hold all the data that your other sites generate.

Secondary Site

The secondary sites are at the bottom of each branch in the SMS hierarchy. You can't put any sites below a secondary site because it lacks an SQL Server database to store site information. You also can't manage a secondary site directly—you must manage it from its parent site. These sites give you the benefits of SMS site management without requiring a local administrator to manage them. In figure 3.1, New York and Bldg. 2 are examples of secondary sites.

Place secondary sites under primary sites depending on the types of packages and jobs you expect to send out from that primary site and the level of control you have given to the person managing that primary site.

Child Site

A child site is any site in the hierarchy that has a parent. This includes all secondary sites and any primary sites that are attached below another primary site.

Site Server

Every site must have a site server. The site server resides on a machine running Windows NT Server configured as either a primary or backup domain controller. The domain that the site server is in is called the site server domain. If the site is a primary site, you need to install Microsoft SQL Server (version 4.21a or later) prior to installing SMS. When you create a site server, SMS installs the following site services and components:

- Site Hierarchy Manager—a Windows NT service that watches for any changes in the site's configuration or the configurations of any of its subsites. If it detects a change, it creates a site control file and sends that file to the affected site.

- Site Configuration Manager—a Windows NT service that watches for the appearance of site control files and makes the proposed changes to the site's configuration.
- Inventory Agent—a Windows NT or OS/2 service that takes hardware and software inventory on SMS servers.
- Package Command Manager for Windows NT—a Windows NT service that installs packages on SMS servers.
- Bootstrap—this service is used for creating secondary sites. It is copied to the new site server and started. After starting, it installs a package containing all the files necessary to start up the secondary site.
- Systems Network Architecture (SNA) Receiver—a Windows NT service that works with the SNA Sender service to enable SNA communications between sites. It is started only if the SNA Sender service is installed at a site.
- SMS Executive—a component manager that starts the following SMS components. It reads the NT registry to decide which components to start depending on, whether the server is a site, logon, or helper server.
- Maintenance Manager—periodically checks the SMS files on all logon servers and replaces any that have been changed or deleted. It also performs the following functions:

  Collects the inventory on Netware servers, since there is no inventory agent for a Netware server

  Moves the raw files (.RAW files) created by the inventory agent from the logon servers to the site server

  Replicates Package Command Manager instruction files from the site server to all logon servers
- Inventory Processor—creates files called Delta-MIF files for each client computer by comparing each newly received RAW inventory file with the previous saved one and writing out only the changes to a Delta-MIF file.
- Site Reporter—periodically creates a system job to send Delta-MIFs (containing inventory, job status, or events) up to the parent site. It maintains a queue of Delta-MIFs, and the send is triggered when the queue reaches a length that is defined in the NT registry.
- Scheduler—prepares and manages the send requests that send the job files and instructions to a target site. It compresses necessary files and creates the set of instructions (despooler file) for running the job at the target site. Then it creates the send request. It can also manipulate the order in which send requests are processed by allowing high-priority jobs to be sent out before lower-priority jobs.
- Despooler—watches for jobs from the scheduler and processes them. It uses the accompanying instruction file to determine how to process the job, and decompresses the files if applicable.

- Inventory Data Loader—updates the SMS site database whenever a new Delta-MIF file arrives. Updates are made to inventory, event, user group, and job status information. In the event that the object to be updated is missing, the inventory data loader sends out a `resync` command which causes a full scan of that particular client computer. After updating the database, the inventory data loader forwards the Delta-MIF file to the Site Reporter, which sends the Delta-MIF file to the parent site, if one exists.
- Sender—enables site-to-site communication. Senders distribute packages, jobs, and inventory information throughout the SMS hierarchy, and they work on a point-to-point basis. When you define a sender for a site, you specify the type of sender you need and the address of the site to which it will connect. Senders are one-way links, so if you want two-way communications between site A and site B, you must set up two senders. There are six different types of senders (LAN, RAS async, RAS X.25, RAS ISDN, SNA batch, SNA interactive) for you to select from, depending on which network protocol you need to connect two sites.
- Applications Manager—maintains program group configuration information and package information at a site and replicates that information to all subsites. The applications manager is responsible for maintaining the Program Group Control database at each site.
- Alerter—performs SMS database queries that you have specified and takes an action if a query result satisfies the criteria you have specified for that alert. The four possible actions are Log an SMS Event, Log a Windows NT Event, Execute a Program, and Send a Message to a User or Computer on the LAN.

Logon Server

An SMS Logon server is a machine that performs SMS logons for users. During site installation, the logon servers are configured with the SMS files that client computers use each time a network logon occurs.

For Windows users, a logon server is typically a Windows NT domain controller, but it could be any NT server that is a member of one of the site domains. If you specify during site installation that SMS should automatically configure all logon servers, it will find all servers that are members of each domain in the site and configure them as logon servers.

For Netware users, the Netware file server that they normally log on to will be their logon server. Since Netware doesn't support Windows NT domains, SMS enables you to specify groups of one or more Netware file servers that it will treat like Windows NT domains for management purposes.

The SMS site server is your first logon server, and you can create additional logon servers to spread the load.

> **CAUTION**
> An SMS site server must manage its logon servers, so creating too many can cause more load on the site server due to management processing than you save by offloading the logon processing.

Helper Server

A Helper server is a logon server that can further reduce the burden imposed by SMS processing on your site server by taking over certain services from the site server. You can have only up to four helper servers, because there are only four services that can be transferred. Of the nine components that are controlled by the SMS Executive, the following four can be transferred to helper servers:

- Scheduler
- Despooler
- Inventory Processor
- Inventory Data Loader

Distribution Server

A Distribution server is a machine (normally a logon server) that is used as a network distribution point for a software application that will be installed on a client computer or run from a shared directory on the distribution server. Note that the distribution server does not have to be a logon server, in which case it is handled a little differently by SMS.

SMS Site and Domain Planning

SMS site planning is a key activity that involves many considerations, including your organizational structure, your administrative needs, the network topology, and NT domain structure. Keep in mind, as you create sites and build your hierarchy, exactly what it is you're trying to achieve. Your goals should be to:

- Simplify the administration of the enterprise.
- Automate as much as possible.
- Match your SMS site hierarchy as closely as possible to your organizational hierarchy.
- Anticipate future changes and growth.

Because SMS is so completely tied in to the Windows NT domain system, you must take into account your domain structure and any trust relationships you have when planning your SMS implementation. We will examine the NT domain models and highlight the important points to be aware of when you're planning your SMS installation. In this section, we'll assume that all your domains are connected by high-speed links. In the section "Considering the Network

Physical Structure," we'll discuss how your decisions might be affected by your physical network.

SMS Site Server Domain

Each site must contain at least one domain, known as the site server domain, which contains the site server. The site server domain could be your master domain, if you use that model, but it doesn't have to be. In fact, you may decide not to place your site server in the master domain because you don't want it to have the additional burden of processing user network logons. If you are using trust relationships, you'll want to have the site server domain trust your master domain(s), because your SMS service account will be located in a master domain. As you'll see, SMS allows you to be flexible in how you assign domains to sites, so you can focus on organizational and administrative criteria when assigning domains.

SMS Domains and Logon Domains

An understanding of how SMS deals with client computer logons will help you to make decisions on assigning domains to sites. In order for SMS to identify, configure, and inventory a client computer, that computer must either log on to a domain (let's call it LOGON) that is part of an SMS site (causing the NT SMS logon script to run), or that computer must connect to an SMS logon server in the domain LOGON and run SMSLS.BAT. In either case, the client computer will be added to the domain LOGON unless you have changed the SMSLS.INI file to cause the SMS domain of the workstation to be remapped. A key point here is that the logon domain of a workstation does not have to match its SMS domain. Indeed, from an administrative point of view, you may very well want to make sure these don't match, especially in the case of the master domain model, because most, if not all, of your machines will show up under the master domain icon in SMS Administrator. The following simple example should make this clear and reinforce the notion that SMS gives you a lot of flexibility when it comes to assigning domains to sites:

1. Workstation TEST01 logs on to domain MASTER (the master domain).
2. The SETLS program runs from an NT logon script and detects that the SMSLS.INI file has been modified to remap TEST01 to the TEST domain.
3. A connection is then made at random to one of the SMS logon servers in the TEST domain.
4. The inventory for workstation TEST01 is taken while connected to this logon server, and therefore TEST01 will be added to the site containing the TEST domain.

For a detailed discussion of the SMSLS.INI file and how to edit it to map your client computers to your SMS domains in a variety of different ways, see Appendix B, "SMS System Files and Utilities."

Site Planning and Domains

Domains are usually set up based on organizational or functional considerations. For example, you might have a FINANCE domain for accounting or a DEVELOP domain for your developers. In the master domain model, these would be set up as resource domains (domains containing servers that share printers and directories), and users would log on to a master domain, rather than logging on to these domains directly.

When you assign domains to sites, you should try to match your site hierarchy as closely as possible to the organizational hierarchy that you have already established with your domain structure. Having said that, there are some things to watch out for. Although SMS allows you to build an arbitrarily complex hierarchy, it's best to keep things as simple as possible. If you can get away with just one site, that's the optimal situation. We recommend that you try to avoid constructing more than two levels of sites below the central site. Due to the distributed architecture of SMS, and the fact that it potentially touches every computer in your organization, it's almost impossible to give out a set of definite recommendations, but the following are some considerations for assigning domains to sites:

- You must have a central site, and this site should be located where most of your domain and systems administration occurs. It's generally pretty obvious where your central site should be (typically at corporate headquarters).
- If you have a location with a full-time systems administrator, you should add the domains in that location to a primary site.
- If you have a group of domains that has no administrator or perhaps just a part-time administrator, you should add these to a secondary site and attach that site to a primary site that will manage them. The only difference between a primary site and a secondary site is that the secondary site doesn't have an SQL Server database to store its configuration.
- Consider placing each site server in a domain by itself, with no user accounts. This approach avoids the burden of processing user logons and makes troubleshooting somewhat easier. If you're dealing with a split domain, however, you'll want to follow Microsoft's recommendations for setting up SMS on a split domain, as described in the WAN section of this chapter.
- Be careful not to overload the site server. This can happen if you arbitrarily add all domains at a location to one SMS site, and the combined number of logon servers creates too much work for the site server. Each logon server places additional processing load on the site server. In each domain, the Primary Domain Controller (PDC) and every Backup Domain Controller (BDC) will be logon servers, and the total number of logon servers in a site will be the sum of the logon servers in all the domains in that site. You may want to split a proposed site into two or more just to keep down the number of logon servers in each site. Of course, this will depend on how powerful your site server is.

- Be careful not to overload your WAN links. SMS sends a separate job for each site you target (there is no forwarding of jobs). If you send a job to multiple sites at a remote location that is connected to the central site by a WAN link, SMS will send the job multiple times over that link. For that reason, try to keep the number of sites at each remote location to a minimum.

SMS and Trust Relationships

The various SMS services must be able to log on to all the domains in a site. You can take advantage of NT trust relationships to make this easy. If you are using one of the standard domain models (master, multiple master, or complete trust), just pick one of the account domains that all the other domains trust, and set up the SMS service account there. The SMS service account must be in the Local Administrators group and have the NT user right "Logon as a service" in each domain at the site.

If you have domains that don't trust the domain where your SMS service account is located, you'll have to create an SMS service account in each of those domains with the same user ID and password as your primary SMS service account. This will allow the various SMS services to log on to these domains.

Domains and Site-to-Site Communications

You don't need trust relationships to enable site-to-site communications. An SMS site communicates with another site by placing files in that site's SITE.SRV\DESPOOLR.BOX\RECEIVE subdirectory of the SMS_SITE share. Therefore, the LAN_SENDER must be able to log on to an account on the destination site that has at least NT Change rights on the above share and directory. The account that you specify as part of the LAN_SENDER address may be just the user name (TIMD, for example), in which case it will be authenticated by the destination site server domain. If you have trust relationships set up to point to an account domain (let's call it MASTER), you may specify a user from that domain using the form MASTER\TIMD. In order for this to work, the destination site server domain must trust MASTER.

Including Netware File Servers

Netware servers don't support Windows NT domains, yet they can still be set up as SMS logon servers. This is possible because SMS enables you to group one or more Netware servers into "Netware domains" for administrative purposes. A Netware domain is a group of Netware servers that is recognized and used only by SMS. Netware domains are completely invisible to Windows NT and Netware. After a server is included in a Netware domain, it can be configured as an SMS logon server and can handle SMS client logins. The Netware server should be configured as follows:

- The version of Netware must be 3.11 or 4.x with 3.11 bindery emulation enabled.

- An SMS service account must be created on the server with the same name and password as the one created under Windows NT. Additionally, this account must have Supervisor privileges on the server and must have all permissions on all volumes on the server.

Considering the Network Physical Structure

The physical layout of your network will influence your decisions regarding site location and domain mapping. With low-speed WAN links between your headquarters and remote locations, for example, you'll want to be sure that a site does not span a WAN link. This section will show you how to deal with that situation.

LAN Considerations

SMS is designed around the assumption that traffic within a site will all be on the same LAN. Don't violate this assumption! In your site planning, you'll want to make sure that all the domains you intend to add to a given site have high-speed access to the site server domain. If necessary, make the physical network changes before installing SMS. This section will cover network traffic considerations and other LAN-related issues.

WAN Considerations

SMS is designed to minimize traffic between sites, based on the assumption that sites are separate locations that are typically connected by relatively low-speed WAN links. For example, SMS compresses software packages before sending them from one site to another. In planning your SMS implementation, you should consider how much SMS traffic is likely to travel over WAN links and prepare for it in advance. You may find that you need to buy faster links. This section will cover network traffic considerations and other WAN-related issues.

Split Domains It's not uncommon to have one or more remote sites tied into a headquarters site by WAN links and routers. But if you're using one of the master domain models, you don't want each user logon to generate traffic on your expensive WAN link. The recommended NT Server solution is to place one or more backup domain controllers at each remote site, so that local domain logons are handled locally. This configuration is referred to as a "split domain" because your account domain is split over multiple sites. Of course, account database replication still occurs across the WAN, but you can control how frequently this occurs.

SMS accommodates a split domain, but you have to take certain steps when you install the servers. For instance, you can't let SMS automatically detect all logon servers, because SMS will find all your domain controllers over the WAN links and make them all part of the same site. Instead, you've got to decide on your remote sites and the domains to be included, and manually specify the logon servers for each site. You must set up SMS on a split domain as follows:

1. If you are using logon scripts, be sure that none of the sites in the domain are configured with the "Automatically Configure Logon Script" option. This means that you must manually assign logon scripts to clients. You must also set up replication at your primary domain controller and all backup domain controllers in order to replicate the script files.

You can use multi-select in the User Manager to assign scripts to a number of users at once.

2. Make sure that none of the sites in the domain is configured with the "Automatically Detect Logon Servers" option.
3. You must manually copy the following script files (see Appendix B, "SMS System Files and Utilities," for descriptions) into the SCRIPTS subdirectory of the REPL$ share on your primary domain controller (or whichever machine you are using for the export server):

   CHOICE.COM

   CLRLEVEL.COM

   DOSVER.COM

   NETSPEED.COM

   NETSPEED.DAT

   SETLS16.EXE

   SETLS32A.EXE

   SETLS32I.EXE

   SETLS32M.EXE

   SETLSOS2.EXE

   SMSLS.BAT

   SMSLS.CMD

   SMSLS.INI
4. Microsoft recommends that you set the Inventory False Logon limit on your primary domain controller to some number higher than the default of three. This is based on the scenario of a backup domain controller failing at a remote site. This would cause the primary domain controller to handle logon requests from that site, and SMS would detect that the site code on each client computer is different from the site containing the primary domain controller. After the default of three logon attempts, SMS would move the client computer to that site. Increasing the Inventory False Logon limit will help to prevent this from happening, but you should take into account the availability of the backup domain controllers at your remote sites.

SMS identifies machines in a split domain using a site/domain naming convention. Each client computer will have an assignment of the form "SSS:DDD" (where SSS is the 3-letter site code and DDD is the domain name, as shown in figure 3.2).

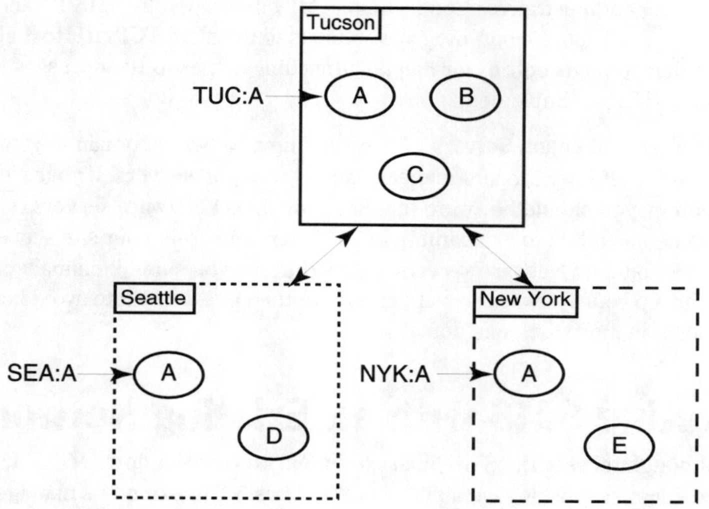

FIG. 3.2
Domain "A" is split across three sites.

Part II Ch 3

Most SMS tasks behave in a split domain the same way they do in a normal domain configuration. One important difference involves the distribution of packages. When sending a package out to the remote sites, you must create a separate job for each site. If you include all sites in the same job, the Package Command Manager and the Program Group Controller at each client computer will erroneously see servers from other sites in addition to their own.

Routers

This section will discuss the known issues related to running SMS on a routed network.

Remote Control and Transport Control Protocol and Internet Protocol (TCP/IP) Generally speaking, if your regular network activities are working, SMS will work too because it relies on the same NT network transports. The remote control feature, however, requires that SMS be able to locate a remote client computer using its network address. In a routed TCP/IP environment, you have two options. The recommended option is to set up Dynamic Host Configuration Protocol (DHCP) and Windows Internet Naming Service (WINS) servers to dynamically assign IP addresses and register computer names, respectively. This option requires very little ongoing administrative attention and is fully supported by SMS 1.1 and later versions. The other, much more labor-intensive option is to maintain TCP/IP Host files. The Host file is a text file that contains entries for mapping machine names to IP addresses and is a standard feature of any TCP/IP implementation.

Netware and Logon Servers When adding a Netware domain to your SMS site, you have the option of letting SMS automatically detect all logon servers. If your Netware network contains routers, you should be aware that SMS will detect Netware servers that are on different routed segments and up to a maximum of 16 router hops from your site server. Note that since SMS can autodetect Netware servers across routers, you should manually select servers if you want to group your Netware servers into more than one domain to avoid having the same servers appear in more than one domain.

Integrating SMS with an Existing Network

Although most of the SMS binaries run only under Windows NT, SMS takes advantage of the excellent networking capabilities of Windows NT to extend its management benefits to a variety of network operating systems. There are two basic issues. First, the client computer must be able to log on to SMS via its normal network logon. Second, SMS must be able to manipulate files and directories on the file server that the client logs on to. This section will describe what is required to enable SMS to interact with other network operating systems.

Netware

SMS logon servers can be installed on machines running Netware 3.1x or Netware 4.x (with 3.x bindery emulation). Each Netware server can be placed in its own Netware domain, or you can group multiple servers into domains, depending on how you want to manage different groups of users. Once you've configured your Netware domains, SMS can take over and automatically configure login scripts, or you can do it manually.

> **CAUTION**
>
> The "Use All Detected Servers" option causes SMS to detect all Netware servers within 16 router hops and place them in one domain. If you have already placed nearby servers in other domains, these servers will be mapped to two domains and you will have major configuration problems.

From the Netware user's point of view, nothing changes except that the SMS logon script runs when they log on to their preferred server.

Of course, your SMS server must be able to access the Netware servers, and that's where NT networking comes in. The component that makes this happen is NT's Gateway Services for Netware. You'll need to install and configure this if you don't already have it. Also, each Netware server must have an account with the same name and password as the SMS service account. These accounts must have Supervisor privileges and have all permissions on all volumes. Netware does not allow the user name and password to be the same (a good security practice, in general), so you'll have to change the password in NT if that's the way you set it up.

Gateway Services for Netware is included in the NT Server distribution. Perform the following steps to install it:

1. Open the Control Panel and double-click the Network icon. This brings up the Network dialog box as shown in figure 3.3.

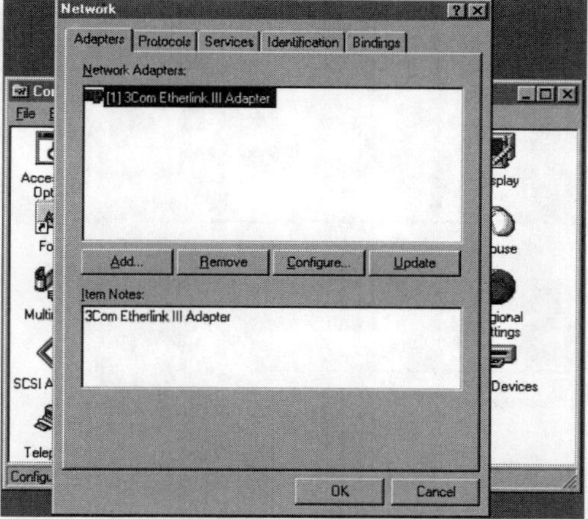

FIG. 3.3
Installing a network service.

2. In the Network dialog box, click the Services tab and then the Add... button. This brings up the Select Network Service dialog box as shown in figure 3.4.
3. Select Gateway (and Client) Services for Netware and click the OK button.
4. Windows NT Setup will prompt you for the path to the NT Server distribution files, as shown in figure 3.5. Enter the full path and click the Continue button.
5. NT will copy the appropriate files and return to the Network dialog box. Verify that NT Setup also installed the NWLink IPX/SPX Compatible Transport and NWLink NetBIOS by clicking the Protocols tab. Click the Close button to exit.
6. The NWLink IPX/SPX Properties dialog box appears, as shown in figure 3.6. Verify that the network adapter that connects to your Netware network is displayed in the Adapter selection box if your server has more than one adapter. You must select the frame type that your Netware network is using. You can let NT attempt to autodetect the frame type

by selecting the Auto Frame Type Detection option, or you can specify it by selecting the Manual Frame Type Detection option and clicking the Add... button. The choices for Ethernet are 802.2 (the default), 802.3, Ethernet II, and SNAP. Click the OK button to exit.

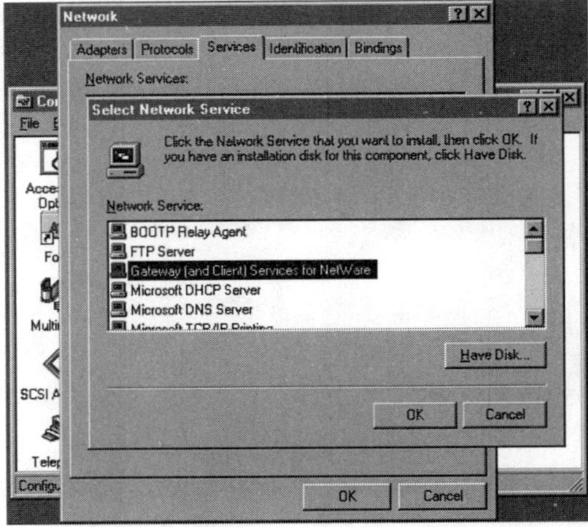

FIG. 3.4
Adding Gateway Services for Netware.

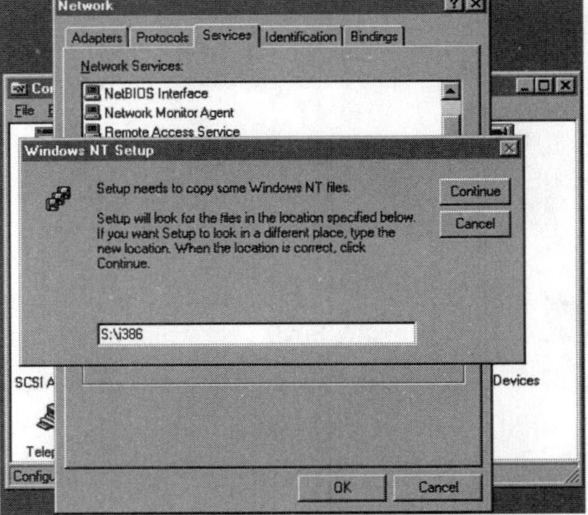

FIG. 3.5
Enter the full path to your NT files.

7. NT will offer to restart the machine. Click the Yes button. After NT has restarted, log on as Administrator.
8. NT will prompt you for your preferred server. Select it from the drop-down list and click OK to continue logging on. If the list is empty, then something is wrong with the installation. Be sure that the frame type you selected is correct.

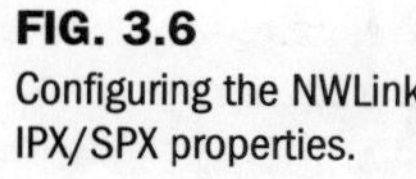

FIG. 3.6
Configuring the NWLink IPX/SPX properties.

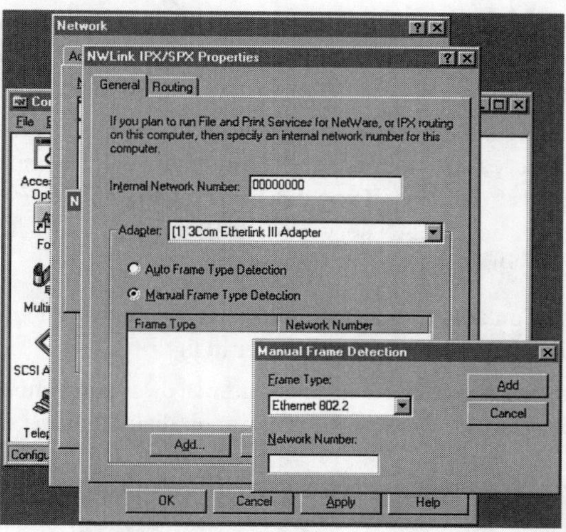

9. In Control Panel, you will find the GSNW icon. This application enables you to change your preferred server and make other configuration changes.

After installing the Gateway Services for Netware, you've got to make some changes on your Netware servers in order for SMS to use this gateway. You make these changes with the Netware SYSCON utility, which can be run on NT Server. You must perform the following steps on each Netware server:

1. Create the Netware group NTGATEWAY.
2. Create the SMS service account, as mentioned earlier.
3. Add the SMS service account to the group NTGATEWAY.
4. Using Netware Security Equivalencies, assign Supervisor privileges to the SMS service account.

Microsoft OS/2 and LAN Manager

SMS logon servers can be installed on machines running Microsoft OS/2 1.3x (and later) and Microsoft LAN Manager 2.1 (and later). When the SMS installs the server components, it installs the SMS inventory agent for OS/2. There are some differences between LAN Manager and NT Server concerning domains, browsers, and so on, that need to be considered when adding a LAN Manager domain to your SMS site. Specifically, you need to do the following:

- Create an SMS service account in each LAN Manager domain. This account must have the same name and password that your NT SMS service account has, and it must belong to the ADMINS group.

- Pay attention to the age of the SMS service account's password and the Maximum Password Age setting for your LAN Manager domain. If the SMS service account's password expires, SMS will be unable to access the domain.
- Configure your site server's computer browser service to include each LAN server domain. This is necessary because of the way that the NT computer browser service handles LAN server domains. If you don't do this, the SMS Site Configuration Manager may fail to enumerate the LAN server when adding it to your site. Perform the following steps to configure the computer browser service:
  1. Open the Control Panel and double-click the Network icon. This brings up the Network dialog box, as shown earlier in figure 3.3.
  2. Click the Services tab, select Computer Browser and choose the Configure button. This brings up the Browser Configuration dialog box, as shown in figure 3.7.

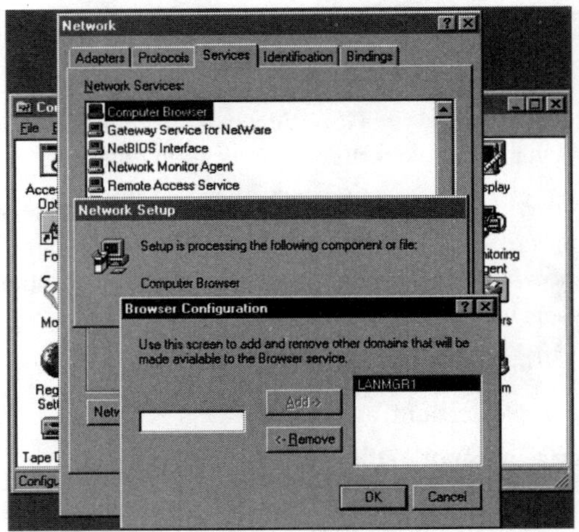

FIG. 3.7 Adding a non-NT domain to your computer browser.

  3. Enter the name of the LAN Manager domain and choose the Add button. Then choose the OK button to close the dialog box and choose OK again to close the Network dialog box.

IBM OS/2 and LAN Server

SMS logon servers can be installed on machines running IBM OS/2 2.x and IBM LAN Server 3.0 and 3.1. When the SMS installs the server components, it installs the SMS inventory agent for OS/2. There are some differences between LAN Server and NT Server concerning domains, shares, browsers, and so on that need to be considered when adding a LAN Server domain to your SMS site. Specifically, you need to do the following:

- Create an SMS service account in each LAN Server domain. This account must have the same name and password that your NT SMS service account has, and it must belong to the ADMINS group.
- Restore the SMS shares (SMS_SHR and SMS_SHRx) on each logon server at startup. This is necessary because LAN Server doesn't support persistent shares (shares that reappear after a reboot). The best way to do this is to add the appropriate "NET SHARE" commands manually to the OS/2 STARTUP.CMD file. Or, you can let the SMS Site Configuration Manager do this for you, but it won't happen until the next watchdog cycle.
- Ensure that the program SMSOS2AG.EXE has been added to STARTUP.CMD on each OS/2 client computer and that it is listed after the network startup commands on OS/2 2.x clients. This program is installed by SMS client setup; it enables Package Command Manager to use the network.
- Configure your site server's computer browser service to include each LAN Server domain. This is necessary because of the way that the NT computer browser service handles LAN server domains. If you don't do this, the SMS Site Configuration Manager may fail to enumerate the LAN server when adding it to your site. Perform the following steps to configure the computer browser service:
    1. Open the Control Panel and double-click the Network icon. This brings up the Network dialog box, as shown in figure 3.3.
    2. Click the Services tab, select Computer Browser and choose the Configure button. This brings up the Browser Configuration dialog box, as shown in figure 3.7.
    3. Enter the name of the LAN Server domain and choose the Add button. Then choose the OK button to close the dialog box and choose OK again to close the Network dialog box.
- If you want to have SMS automatically configure logon scripts, perform the following steps:
    1. In the Domain Properties dialog box, select the "Use All Detected Servers" option.
    2. Create the REPL$ share on the primary domain controller using the command "NET SHARE REPL$=C:\IBMLAN\REPL\EXPORT" and add this command to the file STARTUP.CMD.
    3. On the primary domain controller, create the directory "C:\IBMLAN\REPL\EXPORT\SCRIPTS."
    4. In the directory "C:\IBMLAN\REPL\EXPORT" on the primary domain controller, look for the file REPL.INI. If it exists, then don't do anything. If it's not there, then create it and insert the following entries:

       EXTENT=TREE
       INTEGRITY=FILE

5. In the [Replicator] section of the IBMLAN.INI file on the primary domain controller, make sure that these lines appear:

   REPLICATE=BOTH

   EXPORTPATH=C:\IBMLAN\REPL\EXPORT

6. In the [Replicator] section of the IBMLAN.INI file on the backup domain controllers, make sure that each backup domain controller is setup to import replicated files from the primary domain controller.
7. In the [Server] section of the IBMLAN.INI file for all domain controllers, add "replicator" to the SRVSERVICES line.
8. Restart the Replicator service on all domain controllers.

Macintosh

SMS uses Windows NT-based logon servers to support Macintosh clients. In addition to the normal SMS logon server installation, you must also install Windows NT Services for Macintosh (SFM) on each site server that needs to support Macintosh clients and you must install the Macintosh client components on each site server.

You can install the Macintosh components using the SMS setup program. These are not installed by default.

Perform the following steps to install Services for Macintosh:

1. Open the Control Panel and double-click the Network icon. This brings up the Network dialog box, as shown in figure 3.3.
2. In the Network dialog box, click the Services tab and then the Add... button. This brings up the Select Network Service dialog box, as shown in figure 3.4.
3. Select Services for Macintosh and click the OK button.
4. Windows NT Setup will prompt you for the path to the NT Server distribution files, as shown in figure 3.5. Enter the full path and click the Continue button.
5. NT will copy the appropriate files and return to the Network dialog box. Click the Close button to exit.
6. The Microsoft AppleTalk Protocol Properties dialog box appears, as shown in figure 3.8. You must set the Default Adapter, the Default Zone, and routing parameters, if applicable. Click the OK button to exit.

To complete the server preparations, you must add the Apple Installer file (provided by Apple Computer) to each primary site server that supports Macintosh clients or that has secondary sites supporting Macintosh clients. The Installer performs the task of installing the SMS files to a Macintosh client computer when the client computer connects to a logon server. Finally, you must create accounts for the Macintosh clients that you want to include in your inventory.

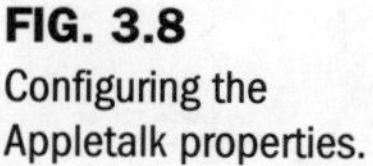

FIG. 3.8
Configuring the Appletalk properties.

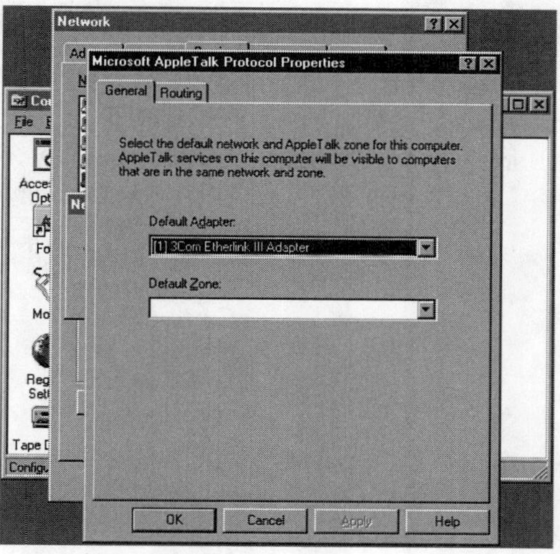

If you want to send packages to Macintosh clients, you have to take the following additional steps:

- Create your package source directory on an SFM volume. This is a special disk volume that emulates the Macintosh file system.
- Copy the source files from a Macintosh computer to the SFM volume. This is necessary to preserve all the Macintosh file attributes.
- Create an SFM volume on every distribution server that will be supporting Macintosh clients.

TIP In general, every component of the SMS system that needs to manipulate or copy Macintosh source files must have an SFM volume to store the files.

UNIX

Support for UNIX servers and clients comes from third-party vendors only. Table 3.1 lists some of the available products.

Table 3.1 Third-Party UNIX products for SMS

Company	Product	Phone	Product Description	Status	SMS Integrated
Distributed Technologies	PATHtracker	617-684-0060	Automatic asset discovery and management application.	Shipping	

continues

Part II Ch 3

Table 3.1 Continued

Company	Product	Phone	Product Description	Status	SMS Integrated
Computing Edge	Proxy Domain Services	206-788-4828	SMS add-on product to enable SMS to work better in Novell and UNIX environments. Custom programming also provided to ISV's and customers.	beta	yes
Digital Equipment Corporation	Polycenter AssetWorks	603-881-0390	Polycenter AssetWorks is a high-end inventory/reporting tool based on SMS; includes support for Unix and VMS clients.	shipping	yes

SNA

SNA is an IBM-developed communications protocol that is typically used to communicate with IBM mainframes and minicomputers. If you already have or are planning to have an SNA network in place, you can use it to connect your SMS sites. SMS supports SNA communications in either batch or interactive mode. An important requirement for connecting sites via SNA is that each site must have a Windows NT Server machine running Microsoft SNA Server. SNA relies on the Advanced Program-to-Program Communications (APPC) Logical Unit (LU) to make connections. An APPC LU represents a communication endpoint for a computer process with which you want to communicate. An SNA connection consists of a pair of LUs, one on the server computer and one on the client computer. In order to use SNA to connect a pair of SMS sites, you must do the following:

- Set up an SNA Server machine at each site.
- Define a local LU for each site.
- Decide whether you want to use batch or interactive mode for the connection. SMS supports a sender for each mode. Note that, unlike the other SMS senders, you can have only one of each per site.

If you are using your SNA network for terminals connecting to a host, you'll probably want to use batch mode, to lessen the impact of SMS traffic.

- Create the sender using the LU pair consisting of the local site's LU and the remote site's LU.

From Here ...

- Appendix B, "SMS System Files and Utilities," covers the contents of the SMSLS.INI file in detail. This file enables you to assign client computers to the domains you want them to appear in, no matter which domain they normally log on to.
- Chapter 15, "Changing Your Site Configuration," shows you how to make changes to your sites and domains after you've installed SMS.
- Chapter 19, "Installation Overview," takes you through a sample SMS installation.

CHAPTER 4

Planning, Design, and System Requirements

SMS implementation deserves careful planning if you intend on taking full advantage of its features while minimizing the installations impact on you're network. In the first part of this chapter, we'll discuss the planning process and point out some things you'll need to consider before implementing SMS. In the last part of the chapter, we'll go over the system requirements for each of the SMS System components.

Planning and design considerations for the implementation of SMS

This section will outline some fundamental tasks that should be considered prior to the deployment of SMS within your organization.

What the four basic phases of system design are

We'll start with an outline of the system analysis and specification phase, then continue on to discuss the design, implementation and maintenance phases of a project. You'll see how to use the design phases presented here to form your own implementation strategy for SMS.

The system requirements for servers and clients

In the last section of the chapter, we'll cover the hardware and software requirements of the SMS system. You'll see what operating systems and network types are supported by SMS and if any special requirements are needed to support them.

Choose a Planning Method

SMS is an extensive system that literally places files on all machines within its hierarchical structure. Before you install any of the SMS components, you'll need to plan the implementation very carefully in order to insure a smooth roll-out and to minimize the possibility of server and user downtime. Several methods of planning exist. Which method you choose will depend on your organization, it's structure, and your management's currently adopted method of information system implementation (if one exists).

Let's look at two planning methods that are widely recognized.

Microsoft Solutions Framework (MSF) is an approach developed by Microsoft to plan and deploy enterprise-wide business solutions with complex products such as SMS. MSF breaks the planning into four key areas, as follows:

- Business architecture—identifies the business need regardless of any application-specific solution to those needs.
- Application architecture—solutions to the business need are defined.
- Technology architecture—the technical aspects of implementing the desired solution are defined and implemented.
- Data architecture—describes a method for managing data. Usage and access patterns can be monitored to provide ongoing information on which to base decisions concerning data replication, distribution, or location.

Another methodical and consistent approach to system design and implementation that's widely used by the electronic information industry, and adopted by many IS departments, is a tool called the System Design Life Cycle (SDLC)

Many different variations of the design cycle exist, but they all eventually share some common phases. The extent to which each step is performed is determined by the individual needs of the project. The four basic phases in the evolution of system design are as follows:

- System analysis and specification
- Design
- Implementation
- Maintenance

The complete subject of MSF or SDLC could easily fill another book, and it's beyond the scope of this text to teach the theory of either. But we can take a quick look at the general steps involved within a design cycle, and discover what portions of the strategy may be beneficial to the design and implementation of SMS within your organization. Use this as a template for creating your own implementation. The object is to integrate SMS into your network (and organization) in the smoothest, most efficient way with as little impact on the user productivity as possible. Let's take a general look at each of the steps in the cycle; as we do, we'll see which ones you can take advantage of when planning the deployment of SMS.

System Analysis and Specification

This is the first phase of a new project, when the underlying business need is determined, project goals are identified, and resource requirements are evaluated. Now is also the time when members of the project team are chosen and asked to participate. Team members then divide the responsibilities and decide on a preliminary project schedule. Let's take a closer look at some of the tasks associated with this phase.

Determine the Underlying Business Need

Before you make any major change or addition to your corporate information system, you will have first determined an underlying business need for the change. In each case, the reasons for installing SMS are similar. You've determined that one or more of the following needs is relevant to your situation:

- You need up-to-date hardware and software inventory available for the accounting or other internal departments.
- You want to monitor software usage for license compliance.
- You want to cut the number of man-hours spent by support personnel manually installing software and updates on clients.
- You need to reduce man-hours spent by support personnel making trips to remote office locations for problem calls.
- You need real-time monitoring of network resource usage.
- You require automated warnings to support personnel when network problems occur.
- You need a method to monitor network bandwidth usage, so problems can be spotted and resolved before they manifest themselves as serious network communications failures.

Identify Project Goals

Once the business needs have been identified, the next step is to determine what end results or goals will satisfy those needs.

One of our goals is to eliminate or at least automate some of the mundane tasks associated with network support (such as hardware and software inventory), allowing the support personnel to concentrate on more important issues.

Another objective is to provide an effective set of tools for the support staff, so they can better monitor the use of network resources, provide better assistance to the users of the network, and anticipate network or resource problems before they cause user downtime. The eventual intent is to move from a repair mode of operation to a preventative mode of operation.

Of course, problems can still occur on any network system despite the best preventive measures. So another goal is to provide an alert mechanism for those times when problems do occur. It's much better if the system notifies the support staff, instead of the users providing the notification.

We can further refine these goals into more specific definitions that address the business needs in greater detail. In the our example, the following specific goals emerge:

- A method to provide administrative access to online software and hardware inventory information is needed.
- The ability quickly to create informational reports on network resources for management is required.
- The capability to distribute and monitor networked software applications centrally.
- Automated file distribution and update ability.
- Remote support and diagnostic ability for support personnel and systems administrators.
- The ability to monitor and alert support personnel to adverse network conditions.
- Network bandwidth and data flow monitoring from central or remote locations.

Identify the Constraints and Resource Requirements

Now you must determine if any constraints exist that would prevent you reaching any of the goals. Once they are identified, you can address each one on an individual basis. You must also determine what the resource requirements are, not only in terms of software and hardware, but also in terms of personnel, training, and technical expertise.

In small organizations, the requirements may be quite minimal. However, the reverse is usually the case when SMS is deployed on large, corporate networks with thousands of users.

Form a Project Team

In the framework of a design cycle, this is the point at which you would want to gather together specific members of your organization to form a project team. For a small business with a small number of support staff, the choice of project team members may be limited, and usually, if the implementation is small, a large project team is not needed.

But for a large installation, the efforts of several different members from different areas of your organization may be required. Following are some examples of the areas from which representative project team members should be drawn when the implementation of SMS within a large organization is being considered:

- Management—this person will provide the needed resources in the terms of personnel and project funding.
- Technical Services—responsible for planning the technical aspects of the design and integration into the current network system.
- Training—will provide input on any training issues that may arise as a result of the implementation.
- Logistics—plans the smooth roll-out of the system throughout the organization.

Design

The next phase of the design cycle deals with formulating some generic solutions needed to attain the goals that have been identified. You may be able to come up with several alternatives, or you may find your goals are unrealistic and need to be rethought. After deciding on one of the alternatives, this phase calls for the design of a specific solution.

For our solution, we know that Systems Management Server will meet the project goals. So we'll begin to plan the integration of SMS into the current network system by organizing the current network into SMS sites. To understand why we must organize the network into sites, let's take a short review of the "site" concept.

All SMS installations are based on the concept of individual sites. Each site is a logical grouping of domains that can be administered as a unit. Each site contains a site server that may (or may not) pass information to another site higher in the hierarchy. SMS is very flexible in respect to how you set up your sites. This allows you to pattern your SMS hierarchy after your company's organizational or departmental structure, if desired.

The basic requirement is that you have a domain structure (NT or LAN Manager) in place before implementing SMS. This structure can be any of the NT domain models discussed in Chapter 3, "Understanding Domains, Sites, and the SMS Hierarchy."

▶ For further information regarding the NT domain structure, different domain models, and site design considerations, see the sections entitled "Understanding Domains and Trust Relationships" and "SMS Site and Domain Planning" in Chapter 3, "Understanding Domains, Sites, and the SMS Hierarchy."

If you have multiple domains, you can combine them under a single site for SMS administrative purposes. Larger organizations can also group domains into several separate sites to allow more flexibility when assigning administrative responsibilities. Actually, several factors should be considered when combining domains into SMS sites, as follows:

- The need for multiple SMS administrators. Each will be responsible for a subset of the SMS system.
- The domain trust relationships that are currently in place on your network.
- The physical layout of your network. Do you have separate locations connected by WAN links?
- Do you want the SMS hierarchy to reflect your company's organizational structure?

The first site design we need to consider is the Central Site. The central site is a Primary Site that all other sites (or subsites) report to. A primary site has its own SQL server database. This SQL database contains information such as inventory, package, and status information on the primary site and all the other sites below it in the site hierarchy. You can have multiple primary sites within your SMS structure, but you will have only one central site. Administration of any site can be accomplished from the central site.

One of the factors that must be considered when planning the central site is potential for growth within the organization. Any additional sites added to your SMS hierarchy will end up forwarding all the information they collect to the central site. Since the SQL database at this site will contain information gathered from all other sites, you'll need to consider the disk resource requirements of the central site's SQL Server database and make sure you plan accordingly. You can use Table 4.1 to estimate the amount of drive space needed by the SMS database components on your site's SQL server.

Table 4.1 Disk Space Requirements for SMS Database Components

# of PCs	SMS Data Device Size	SMS Log Device Size	TempDB Size
250	5MB	5MB	20MB
500	10MB	5MB	20MB
1000	20MB	5MB	20MB
2000	40MB	8MB	20MB
5000	100MB	20MB	20MB
10000	200MB	40MB	40MB
20000	400MB	80MB	80MB
50000	1GB	200MB	200MB

For example, if your central site has 10,000 PCs, and you have another site reporting to it that has 10,000 PCs, you would need a central site SMS database on your SQL Server large enough to hold the information for 20,000 PCs. We'll take a look at exactly how to set up the database components later in this chapter.

Another major design consideration is the physical layout of your network. Do you have remote offices connected by slower WAN links? The current network may need to be documented (if this has not already been done) to help you determine the proper placement of SMS site servers throughout your organization. Carefully review the information found in the section entitled "Considering the Physical Network Structure" in Chapter 3, "Understanding Domains, Sites, and the SMS Hierarchy," before planning the placement of your sites. This information is key to preventing bottlenecks over slower WAN connections.

Once the design phase is completed, the actual implementation can begin in a phased manner, starting with a test group.

Implementation

Continuing to follow the general design cycle guidelines, we can now turn our attention to the actual implementation of SMS on your network. The actual implementation consists of installing site servers and connecting them in a hierarchy. But by far the most important task in implementing SMS is that of formulating a staged roll-out of the client components.

It's best to begin the roll-out using a select handful of users, preferably those users who would suffer the least impact in the event of problems. A test group of five to ten users is sufficient to start with. If this is not possible, you may want to consider setting up a test environment with one SMS server and a few client stations. This may be a good idea, even if you have an available test bed of users but you've never worked with SMS and would like to get familiar with the package before being put in the position of supporting it on a production network. If you don't have the resources to set up a test environment, and you don't have a test group to work with, install the server and configure yourself (or members of the IS staff) as the only client(s).

When you're comfortable with the operation of SMS you can start to expand the user base, a few clients at a time. This incremental approach to adding clients on the SMS system avoids two potential problems that can occur.

The first potential problem results in your network's bandwidth being exceeded due to a large number of client installations taking place simultaneously. As you will see, the client components are installed at a user station automatically the first time a user runs the SMS script or batch file. This causes the one-time download of several files over the network, and therefore may cause problems if 1,000 people are all loading the same files over the network from the same server at once. Besides overuse of network bandwidth, you could experience overload of the site server.

The other problem is dealing with the number of inquiries and support calls you or your IS staff can expect to receive from the users of your network at one time. Configuring SMS to configure login scripts automatically and install the client software on 1,000 user stations at once is sure to create a deluge of phone calls from users wondering what's being done to their system. Despite your best efforts to inform users of the impeding installation, its purpose, and how minimal the impact of the client components are on their workstations, you will still have those individuals who, for one reason or another, did not get the message. They will call IS support when the client components start to install themselves, usually reporting strange problems with their system. You can also anticipate some legitimate (and usually minor) problems to occur in a small percentage of the client installations.

Both of these potential problems can be minimized, if not eliminated, by using the phased cyclical approach when adding user machines to the SMS system, as follows:

- Start with a manageable number of users machines for the first group of installations. You may want to base the number of machines installed this first time on the capability and size of your IS support staff.
- Inform the users selected as members of the installation group that the next time they log on, SMS will automatically install its client components on their system.
- Manually configure the logon scripts of the first group to load the SMS components during user logon.
- Monitor your system's resources during the process of installing the client components; use this information as a baseline for further installations.

- Verify that all the targeted user machines have been added to the SMS inventory database. Determine the reason for any machines not being added, and remedy the situation.
- After successful completion of the first round of installations, continue with another (and possibly larger) group of user machines.
- Repeat the cycle until SMS has been deployed throughout your user base.

After the first few installation groups are completed, you should have a good idea on the problems to anticipate in subsequent installations. From here, you can adjust the size of the installation group or free up IS resources as needed.

From the support standpoint, the object is to deploy SMS as transparently as possible throughout your user base. If during an installation, problems occur that render a user's machine inoperable (highly unlikely, but possible), support personnel need to be available to remedy the situation. By limiting the number of client installations to predetermined groups of machines, you will avoid having you and your network overloaded in the event of an unforeseen problem.

Maintenance

The last phase of the design cycle doesn't have much to do with design at all. It is focused more on the upkeep and upgrade of the system. Usually, in the life of an information system, the cost of maintenance to the system will eventually outweigh the cost of a new system. When this happens, the design cycle comes full circle and starts all over again.

Fortunately, SMS gives us all the tools needed to monitor the network system, provide the upkeep, and even alert us to problems. It also give us a means to distribute software updates throughout the enterprise in a consistent and reliable way. SMS can actually be used to maintain itself.

After planning is completed, the initial site installation begins with the configuration of the hardware and software components needed to bring up the first SMS primary site server. First, the server's hardware is properly configured, then the installation process continues with the prerequisite setup and configuration of Microsoft NT Server and Microsoft SQL Server. We begin the installation process with a look at the system requirements for each of the SMS system components.

System Requirements

Before we begin our installation we must first insure that we have the appropriate system resources available to meet the system hardware and software requirements.

Site Server Requirements

Both primary and secondary site servers have the same basic requirements, with a couple of exceptions. The secondary server will not need access to a CD-ROM, nor will it need additional memory for the SQL Server. The site servers (both primary and secondary) have the following requirements:

- Windows NT Server version 3.5 or later.
- Primary Domain Controller (PDC) or Backup Domain Controller (BDC).
- Intel 486/66 or greater, DEC Alpha, or MIPS R4000 processor.
- Twenty-four megabytes (MB) of RAM, minimum for a site server. The recommended RAM requirement is 32MB for a primary site server that also contains the Microsoft SQL Server components. A minimum of 24MB of RAM is recommended for secondary site servers.
- NTFS-formatted drive with 100 to 500MB free space.
- Access to a CD-ROM for the primary site installation.

Keep in mind that these are the minimum requirements that should be considered. Providing an adequate processor in combination with enough memory and disk drive space is essential to the performance of your server, especially in large or active sites. Avoid problems and provide adequate hardware resources for your SMS servers, particularly a primary central site server that's also running SQL Server.

Real world implementation would call for a Pentium processor (not a 486 processor). If you're running Intel platforms, you'd also want to add enough memory to prevent excess paging to the disk drives—how much memory that's required for your particular hardware setup can best be determined by using Performance Monitor in conjunction with Windows diagnostics.

Multiple drive spindles can also be utilized to enhance server performance. Placing the system files along with the paging file on a separate drive spindle will eliminate seek time on the drives containing the SQL and SMS components.

Placing log files (which are sequentially written) on a drive that's FAT formatted can reduce disk drive head movement. The use of a drive array, especially a hardware array, will definitely improve performance. Drive arrays also add the safety net of fault tolerance to your system. Many even provide online replacement of failed drives without interruption to the server. Mirroring drives can add to performance by providing split seeks; mirroring also provides a reliable means of fault tolerance. Spanning hard drives with a single partition can limit excess drive activity, but it provides no fault tolerance. Having one of the spanned drives fail would force a restoration from backup—perhaps more of a problem than a benefit.

In addition to beefing up the hardware, you should insure you're running at least MS NT version 3.51 with the latest service packs installed. To insure the best performance, use the latest versions of the operating system that are available. The examples in this text are based on a system running MS NT version 4.0.

SQL Server

In addition to the requirements above, each primary site must have Microsoft SQL Server installed running a multiple-user version of SQL 4.21 or later. Depending on your situation, you can install MS SQL Server on the primary site server, or you can install SQL on a separate server to minimize load on the site server. Another option is to use an existing installation of SQL running at your site for the SMS database. This will also ease the load on the primary site server.

NOTE Do not run SQL Server on any PDC (Primary Domain Controller) that validates user logons for a large network. This could seriously impair the controller's ability to perform logon requests. In turn, the additional SQL services running on such a server may be affected. PDCs being used as SQL Servers with the boost (Boost SQL Server Priority) option set (in the SQL setup program) may be rendered inoperable by the use of such a configuration. This may even cause the PDC to crash. ■

As with the operating system, insure optimum performance by installing the latest available version of SQL when implementing your site. The installation and SQL configuration information contained in this text is based on MS SQL version 6.5.

Be aware that some restrictions may exist with respect to using later versions of SQL with older versions of the NT operating system or the SMS system. Before implementing a new version of SQL, review the information contained in the release notes.

The requirements currently established for SQL version 6.0 are as follows:

- Windows NT Server version 3.5. Version 3.51 or later recommended.
- Intel 486/66 or greater, DEC Alpha, or MIPS R4000 processor.
- 16MB of server memory as an absolute minimum. 32MB with 16MB dedicated to SQL Server if participation in directory replication is required as either a distribution server or a combined publication/distribution server.
- 60MB of drive space. More space is needed if the default size of the Master device is increased.
- 15MB of additional drive space is needed if installing the online manuals, but only 1MB if running the manuals from the installation CD-ROM.
- Upgrades to SQL version 6.0 from SQL version 4.2x require approximately 50MB of hard disk space.

Logon Servers

We learned in Chapter 3, "Understanding Domains, Sites, and the SMS Hierarchy," that logon servers are used by SMS to support the configuration, inventory, software distribution, and shared applications of the SMS clients in the logon (or account) domain the server resides in. Several network types and operating systems are supported for SMS logon servers. Table 4.2 lists the options available.

Table 4.2 SMS Logon Servers Are Supported by Several Operating Systems and Network Types

Network Type	Operating System	Comments
Microsoft NT version 3.1 and higher	Microsoft NT Server version 3.1 and higher	NTFS drive is required to support Macintosh clients

Network Type	Operating System	Comments
Microsoft LAN Manager version 2.1 and higher	Microsoft OS/2 version 1.3 or higher	
Novell NetWare version 3.1x	Novell NetWare version 3.1x	
Novell NetWare version 4.x	Novell NetWare version 4.x	Server must be running NetWare 3.x Bindery Emulation.
IBM LAN Server versions 3.0 and 3.1	IBM OS/2 2.x	

Helper Servers

Helper servers allow you to minimize the load on the primary site server. They do this by letting you offload up to four Executive Service processes (Scheduler, Despooler, Inventory Processor, and Inventory Data Loader) from the primary site server onto the helper server. The requirements for a helper server are as follows:

- Microsoft NT Server version 3.5 or higher
- Primary or backup domain controller
- Already configured as an SMS logon server
- An NTFS-formatted hard disk

Requirements for Providing NetWare Support

You must install the Gateway Service for NetWare on the site server if you want to support NetWare within your site. For instructions on installing the Gateway Service for NetWare, refer to the section entitled "Integrating SMS with an Existing Network" in Chapter 3, "Understanding Domains, Sites, and the SMS Hierarchy."

Requirements for Providing Macintosh Support

The following conditions must be met in order to support Macintosh clients:

- Windows NT Server version 3.1 or higher running the Windows NT Services for Macintosh (SFM).
- Windows NT Services for Macintosh (SFM) must be installed on the site server and any logon servers.

Note that SMS does not support clients using either the LAN Manager Services for Macintosh or NetWare for Macintosh.

For instructions on installing SFM, refer to the Microsoft Windows NT Server Services for Macintosh documentation.

Requirements for Sender Connectivity

Communication between sites can be accomplished using three general methods. Which method you use will primarily depend on the structure of your network. The three methods are as follows:

- NetBIOS-based transport protocols over an established LAN or WAN.
- Microsoft SNA Server Version 2.1 or higher using LU 6.2 links.
- Microsoft Remote Access Server (RAS) version 3.5 or higher utilizing NetBIOS-based transports over asynchronous, X.25, or ISDN connections.

LAN/WAN Requirements Communication between sites on the same LAN is accomplished using any NetBIOS-based transport protocol that's supported by NT. The three protocols typically used are as follows:

- NetBEUI
- TCP/IP
- IPX

Communication between sites on a WAN (where the servers are separated by routers) must use a protocol that can be routed, such as the following:

- TCP/IP
- IPX (limited)

Requirements for SNA and LU 6.2 Link Connectivity Both the sending and receiving site must have a Microsoft SNA Server (version 2.1 or higher) running in one of their SMS domains. The servers are then linked using LU (Logical Unit) pairs. LUs are ports into an IBM Systems Network Architecture network, typically a mainframe environment. SMS can utilize these ports as communications paths for SMS sites.

To make this work properly you must do the following:

1. Create an APPC (Advanced Program-to-Program Communications) local LU on the SNA server that will be used by the SNA Sender. This must be done at each SMS site.
2. Create a connection at between the sending site's own SNA Sender LU (local LU) and the receiving site's SNA Sender LU (remote LU). Create the connection at both communicating sites.

NOTE You can set up the LU pair for both connections using the #BATCH or #INTER mode; however, the mode you set up will determine the type of SNA Sender(s) you must install.

Remote Access Service (RAS) Communications Requirements Both the sending and receiving site must have Windows NT RAS Service version 3.5 or higher running in one of their domains. Each receiving site must have a user account that the sending site's RAS Sender can use at the destination site's "site" server.

NOTE The receiving site's phonebook entry type (Async, X.25, or ISDN) will determine which RAS Sender you must install.

SMS Client Requirements

The SMS System supports a wide variety of network clients, as shown in Table 4.3.

Table 4.3 Client Platforms Supported by SMS

Network Type	Operating System	Notes
Microsoft Windows NT Workstation version 3.1 and higher	Microsoft Windows NT Workstation version 3.1 and higher	1
Microsoft Windows 95	Microsoft Windows 95	
Microsoft LAN Manager version 2.1 and higher	Microsoft OS/2 version 1.3x	2
	IBM OS/2 version 2.x	3
	MS-DOS version 3.3 and higher	4
	Microsoft Windows version 3.1	4,8
	Microsoft Windows for Workgroups version 3.1x	5,8
	Microsoft Workgroup Add-On for MS-DOS	5
Microsoft Network Client for MS-DOS version 3.0	MS-DOS version 3.3 and higher	6
Novell NetWare 3.1x	MS-DOS	
	Microsoft Windows version 3.1	8
	Microsoft Windows for Workgroups version 3.1x	8
	Microsoft Workgroup Add-On for MS-DOS	
Novell NetWare 4.x	MS-DOS	7
Apple	Apple Macintosh System 7.x	
IBM LAN Server versions 3.0 and 3.1	IBM OS/2 version 2.x	

Table 4.3 Notes

Note 1. Client components may also be installed on NT Servers.

Note 2. Only the Inventory component is supported.

Note 3. Only Inventory is supported on OS/2 2.0 clients; OS/2 2.1 clients support Inventory, Package Command Manager, and MIF Entry.

Note 4. LAN Manager Basic is not supported; client must be running the LAN Manager Enhanced redirector.

Note 5. Basic redirector not supported on these clients; full redirector must be running.

Note 6. Client software provided with Windows NT Server.

Note 7. Server must be running 3.x Bindery Emulation Mode.

Note 8. Only the Windows Program Manager desktop shell.

From Here...

This concludes the chapter on SMS design and system requirements. In the upcoming chapters, we'll proceed with the implementation, starting with the installation of NT and SQL Server.

- Chapter 5, "Server Installation Part I," goes over the installation steps for both Windows NT Server and Microsoft SQL Server. This includes the setup of the Replicator service, and the various service accounts needed for SMS and SQL.
- Chapter 6, "Server Installation Part II," takes a look at the installation of both the primary and secondary SMS site servers. We'll examine the Administrator program and the role it plays in creating secondary sites. Later in the chapter, we look at the integration of both NetWare and Macintosh environments with SMS. In the last section of the chapter, we'll look at the SMS client components and the different ways to add clients to the system.

CHAPTER 5

Server Installation, Part I

How to install and configure Windows NT Server

We'll start with the step by step installation of Windows NT Server on the machine that will server as the SMS primary site server in our example. Our example will illustrate a NT Server version 4.*x* installation on an Intel platform.

What service accounts need to be created and how to do it

Next we'll set up the service accounts that will be used for the NT Replicator, SQL Server Executive, and SMS services. You'll see how to set them up, what user groups they need to be members of, and what special user rights they'll need to function properly.

The setup procedures for the NT Replication service

You'll need to setup the NT Replication service in order for the Automatically Configure Workstation Logon Scripts option of SMS to be implemented across a domain environment. SMS uses the NT Replication service to distribute the SMS logon component files to the logon servers within the domain. This chapter will show you how to setup and enable this service.

In this chapter we'll take a look at the prerequisite installation of Windows NT Server and Microsoft SQL Server. Both of these installations must be completed before the setup of SMS can begin.

There are several general steps that are involved when creating the SMS System. The steps need not be taken in any particular order, with the exception of the first step—installing the central site server.

The following is a listing of the other tasks involved when setting up an SMS system: Create primary SMS sites, Establish a hierarchy between the sites, Create secondary sites, Create and configure the appropriate senders and addresses for site-to-site communication, Add additional domains to sites, Add clients to the system.

Our site server installation starts with the installation of Windows NT Server 4.0.

Several methods exist for the installation of NT Server. The most common is direct installation from a CD-ROM; another method is an over-the-network installation. Either is relatively simple. In both cases a boot disk is created with the appropriate drivers for either the C-ROM or network interface card. You then boot from this disk and access the installation files from the CD-ROM or over the network. ■

Installation Steps for Microsoft NT Server 4.x

To install NT 4.x from a CD-ROM, or from a network share point, follow these steps:

TIP Before you begin to install any software on the computer, make sure you set and record the configuration settings (IO address, IRQ, Transceiver Type, and so on) for the network adapter card(s) in the machine.

1. Create a DOS (version 5 or higher) bootable floppy disk using format a:/s command.
2. Use this disk to create a bootable startup disk containing the appropriate network card driver to allow you to connect to a source file distribution point. See Chapter 19, "Installation Overview," for step-by-step instructions on creating a network installation disk.

NOTE Disks can easily be created for automatically loading Windows For Workgroups from a network server using the Network Administration utilities that come with NT. Once created, they are easily modified to connect to an NT server installation point. ■

   or Use the newly created boot disk to create a startup disk containing the appropriate CD-ROM drivers that will allow the use of a CD-ROM for the NT Server installation.
3. After creating a bootable startup disk, copy the fdisk and format utility programs to it. The utility versions must match the version of DOS the disk was formatted under.
4. Boot the target server using the startup disk that you've just created.
5. From the DOS command prompt, run the fdisk utility to partition the computer's hard disk, and then reboot the computer.

NOTE A partition must be created that is large enough to contain the NT Server OS files, the system paging file, and a temporary copy of the NT source files. A partition of at least 120MB is recommended. ■

6. After the system reboots, use the format utility on the startup disk to format the hard drive partition you created in step 5. The use of the /s switch with the format command is not needed when running the utility.
7. Once the formatting is complete, reboot the system if needed. Then connect to the installation point containing the NT Server source files by changing to the appropriate CD-ROM or network drive.
8. Move into the setup directory appropriate for the platform you're installing NT Server on, and run the following command from the DOS prompt:

   ```
   drive:\i386>winnt /b
   ```

   This will start the text-based portion of the NT Setup program. The /b command instructs the Setup program not to make the three NT Setup disks that are normally made during the Setup process.

9. You will next be prompted to verify the path to the installation point. Confirm that the drive and directory are correct, and press the Enter key to continue. Temporary installation files are then copied to your local hard drive. Process time can vary from two to thirty minutes, depending on method of transfer. During this period, you'll see a yellow progress bar, and the percentage of files copied will be displayed.
10. The file copy process will stop with a message instructing you to remove any floppy disk that may be in the diskette drive. Remove the startup floppy disk and press the Enter key. This will restart your computer.
11. After rebooting, the computer will display a message indicating that its hardware configuration is being inspected. It will then load the appropriate startup drivers, load the NT Kernel, and boot to the operating system. Next, the Welcome to Setup screen appears, as shown in figure 5.1.

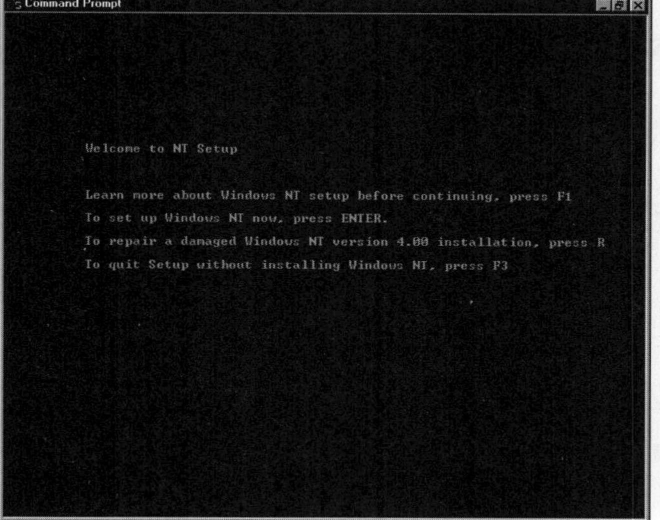

FIG. 5.1
The Welcome to Setup message.

12. The Windows NT server Setup will then display a list of the mass storage devices it has found in your computer, along with the messages shown in figure 5.2.

    Follow the on-screen instructions to add any devices that were not detected. When you've finished adding devices, press the Enter key to continue.
13. The next screen to appear will display a message similar to the one shown in figure 5.3.

    Follow the instructions to change any of the options listed. When you're finished, highlight the option for No Further Changes and press the Enter key to continue.
14. The next message to appear (shown in figure 5.4) will instruct you on choosing the destination partition on which to install the NT operating system files.

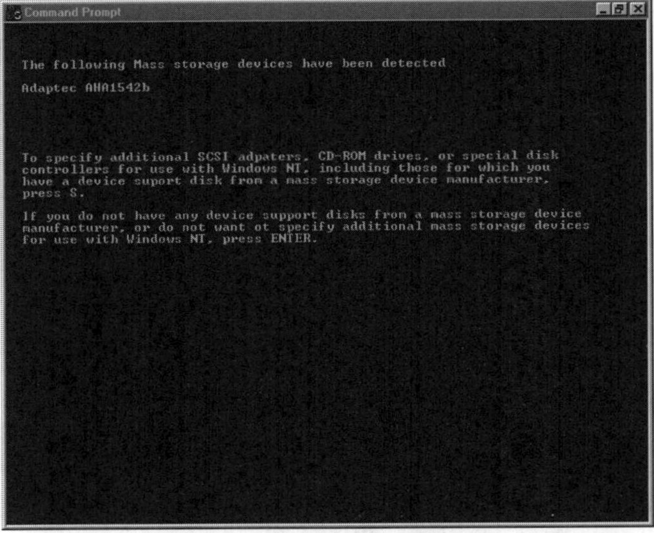

Command Prompt
The following Mass storage devices have been detected
Adaptec AHA1542b
To specify additional SCSI adpaters, CD-ROM drives, or special disk controllers for use with Windows NT, including those for which you have a device suport disk from a mass storage device manufacturer, press S.
If you do not have any device support disks from a mass storage device manufacturer, or do not want ot specify additional mass storage devices for use with Windows NT, press ENTER.

FIG. 5.2
Specify additional hardware devices.

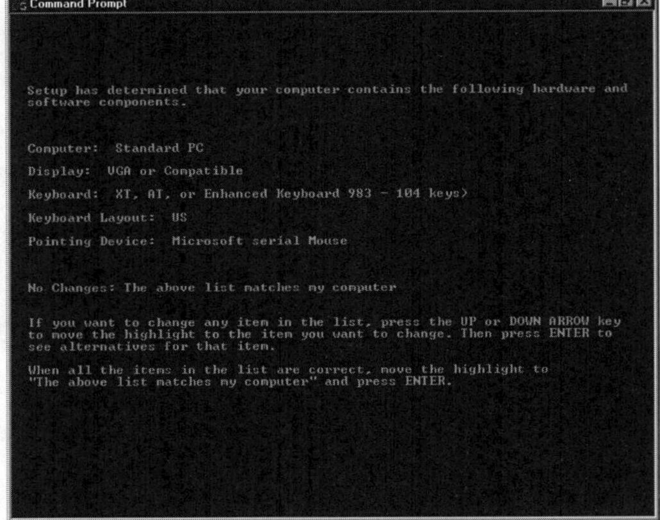

Command Prompt
Setup has determined that your computer contains the following hardware and software components.
Computer: Standard PC
Display: VGA or Compatible
Keyboard: XT, AT, or Enhanced Keyboard 983 - 104 keys)
Keyboard Layout: US
Pointing Device: Microsoft serial Mouse
No Changes: The above list matches my computer
If you want to change any item in the list, press the UP or DOWN ARROW key to move the highlight to the item you want to change. Then press ENTER to see alternatives for that item.
When all the items in the list are correct, move the highlight to "The above list matches my computer" and press ENTER.

FIG. 5.3
Verify that the detected components are correct.

The bottom of the screen contains a box that shows the available disk devices, the drive space of the device, the remaining space on the device, and how they are currently partitioned. Use the arrow key to highlight the desired destination partition, and press Enter.

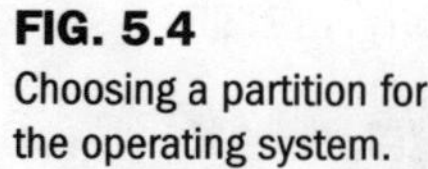

FIG. 5.4
Choosing a partition for the operating system.

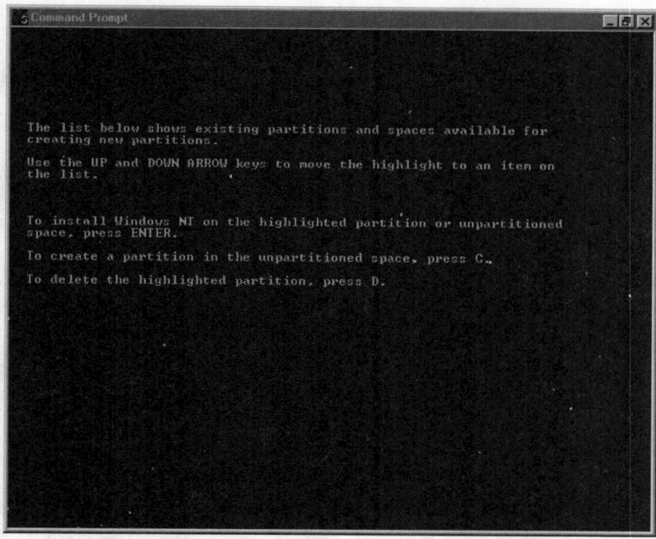

Command Prompt
The list below shows existing partitions and spaces available for creating new partitions.
Use the UP and DOWN ARROW keys to move the highlight to an item on the list.
To install Windows NT on the highlighted partition or unpartitioned space, press ENTER.
To create a partition in the unpartitioned space, press C.
To delete the highlighted partition, press D.

15. If the drive was formatted as a FAT drive, you will be given the opportunity to have Windows automatically convert the drive to NTFS during installation. The screen will display the chosen partition format type, size, remaining space, and device information, as shown in figure 5.5. Highlight the Convert the Partition to NTFS option, and press the Enter key to continue.

FIG. 5.5
Convert the FAT partition to NTFS.

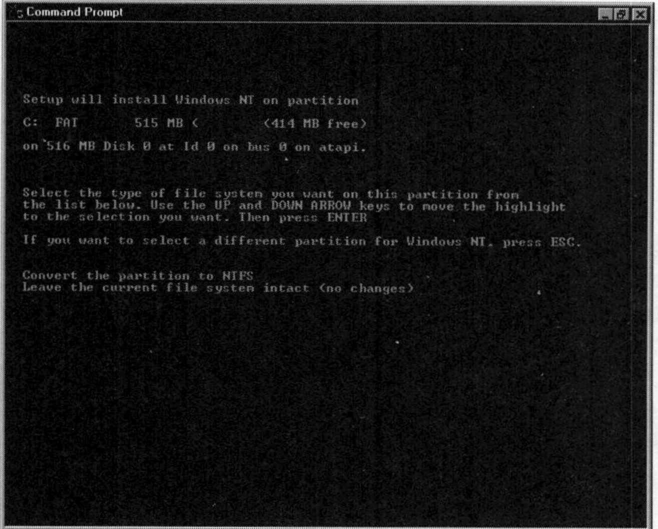

Command Prompt
Setup will install Windows NT on partition
C: FAT 515 MB ((414 MB free)
on 516 MB Disk 0 at Id 0 on bus 0 on atapi.
Select the type of file system you want on this partition from the list below. Use the UP and DOWN ARROW keys to move the highlight to the selection you want. Then press ENTER
If you want to select a different partition for Windows NT, press ESC.
Convert the partition to NTFS
Leave the current file system intact (no changes)

16. You will see the message shown in figure 5.6 if converting a FAT partition to NTFS.

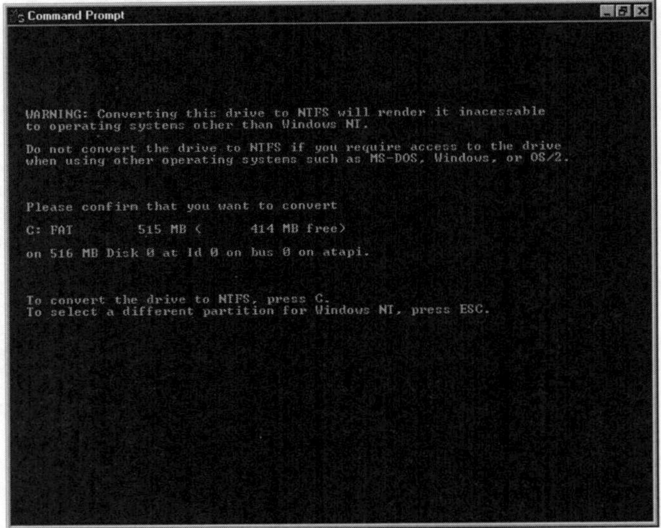

FIG. 5.6 Confirm the conversion of the FAT partition to NTFS.

Press C to convert the drive to an NTFS format.

17. Before Setup installs the Windows NT files onto your hard disk, you must choose the location where you want these files to be installed. The default is to place the operating system files in the \WINNT directory of the boot drive. To change the suggested location, press the BACKSPACE key to delete characters and then type the directory where you want Windows NT installed. When finished, press the Enter key to continue.
18. The next screen (shown in figure 5.7) prompts for the type of hard disk examination you would like to have performed on your destination drive.

    Your drive has just been formatted and is relatively clean. Go ahead and press the Enter key to perform the exhaustive examination. This process usually won't take very long for even the largest drive. If it does, you may have reason to suspect a problem with the drive or controller hardware. On our example 515MB drive, the inspection took less than 20 seconds.
19. After the drive has been examined, the file transfer process of moving and expanding the source files into the destination directory begins. A progress bar will be shown, along with the percentage of files that have been copied. When the copy process has completed, the message shown in figure 5.8 appears.

    Press the Enter key to conclude the text-based portion of the Setup and restart the computer.
20. At this point the computer will reboot and continue with the Windows-based portion of the Setup. At this phase of the Setup, some preliminary files are copied, followed by the

appearance of the first in a series of Windows NT Setup screens that are used in guiding you through the rest of the installation, as follows:

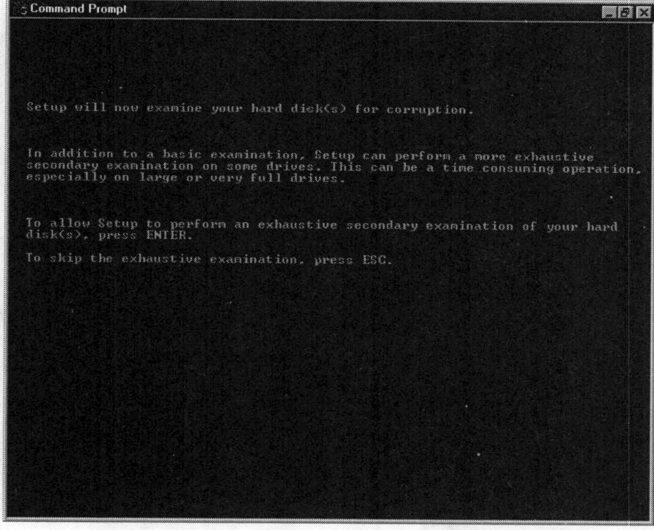

FIG. 5.7
Perform an exhaustive examination of the destination drive.

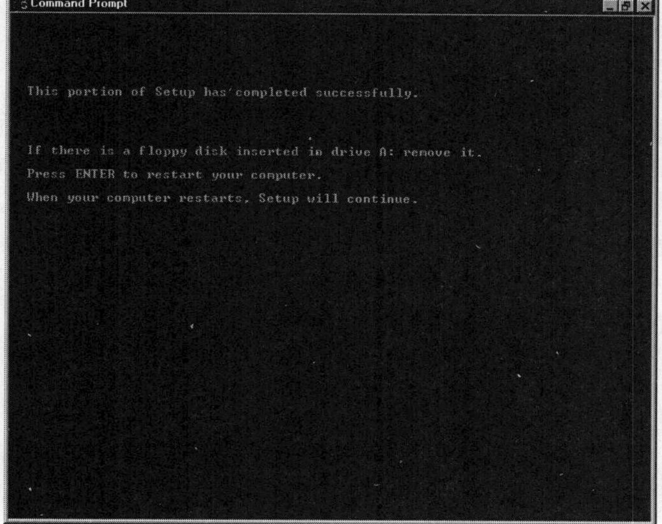

FIG. 5.8
Restart after the copy process.

Welcome to the Windows NT Setup Wizard, which will guide you through the rest of Setup. To continue, click Next.

The next three parts of Setup are:

1. Gathering information about your computer.
2. Installing Windows NT Networking.
3. Finishing Setup.

Click or press the Next button.

21. The message "Please wait while NT prepares the directory for installation" will briefly appear, followed by the dialog box prompting you for name and organizational information. This information is then used to personalize your installation of Windows NT. Complete the informational fields, and then click or press the Next button.

22. The licensing mode screen will appear next, prompting you to select the licensing mode you wish to use. Two modes are available, as follows:

    - Per Server—each concurrent connection to this server requires a separate CLIENT ACCESS LICENSE.
    - Per Seat—each computer that accesses Windows NT Server requires a separate CLIENT ACCESS LICENSE. Use License Manager (located in Network Administration program group) to record the number of CLIENT ACCESS LICENSES purchased and avoid violation of the license agreement.

    Choose the method of licensing that is appropriate for your installation by marking the button next to your choice.

23. The next screen will prompt you for a machine Name for the new server with the following message:

    "Windows NT needs a computer Name to identify your computer. Please enter a name of 15 characters or less.

    NOTE: You must ensure that the name you enter is unique on your network. Ask your network administrator if you are not sure what name you should enter."

    Enter the name of your choice, then click or press the Next button.

24. You will next be asked to select a server type with the following message:

    "Please select a type for this server."

    Your SMS server must be a Primary Domain Controller (PDC) or Backup Domain Controller (BDC). The SMS server cannot be a stand-alone server. You may choose BDC if you already have a domain in place with a PDC. If you are starting a new domain, you must choose PDC. In our example, we chose the PDC as our server, since it won't be performing heavy user validation (see the caution below regarding larger networks and choosing PDC).

CAUTION

Note that the PDC for an organization's logon domain (or account domain in a trust relationship) is usually kept very busy validating user logon requests, especially on larger networks. If you intend to load SQL Server on this same box and you designate the server as a PDC during this step, you could seriously impair the controller's ability to perform logon requests. In turn, the SQL Server (and SMS) services running on the server may be affected. PDCs being used as SQL Servers with the boost (Boost SQL Server Priority) option set (in the SQL Setup program) may be rendered inoperable by the use of such a configuration. This may even cause the PDC to crash.

25. Since we chose to configure the server as a PDC, the next screen will prompt us for the password for the default Administrator account.

    "Please enter a password of 14 characters or less to use for the Administrator account. Reenter the same password in the Confirm Password field.

    The Administrator account allows maximum access to your computer's resources. Therefore the administrator password is an important piece of information which you should guard carefully.

    Note: take special care to remember the password you supply. It is recommended that you write the password down and store it in a safe place."

    Enter the administrator password of your choice in both boxes and click or press the Next button to continue.

26. The next screen prompts you to make a repair disk for your system. You may wish to do this step now, or you may wait until later after your system has been completely configured with accounts and devices.

    "Setup can create an emergency repair disk, which is a floppy disk that can be used later to repair Windows NT should it become damaged. (In some cases Windows NT can be repaired without an emergency repair disk.)

    Note: you can create an emergency repair disk at any time by using the RDISK utility. Would you like to create a repair disk during setup?"

    Make your selection and click or press Next. In our example, we will choose to skip this step. The RDISK utility will be used later to construct a more up-to-date repair disk.

27. The Setup program will now allow you to select the components you wish to have installed.

    "To add or remove a component, click the check box. A shaded box means that only part of the component will be installed. To see what's included in a component, click Details."

    If you would like to use the SQL mail feature you should check the Exchange client box. This will enable you to later set up, and configure, a MS Exchange Client profile. When the SQL mail feature is enabled, you can then specify the profile name in the SQL Mail configuration. SQL is then able to send e-mail to users when a SQL event occurs. An event can be a SQL alert, a notification of a SQL performance monitor threshold that's been exceeded, or a notification of the success or failure of a scheduled task. You can also setup the MS Exchange Client from the installation CD at a later time, or you can install the Exchange client that ships with the site and enterprise versions of MS Exchange version 4.0. For our example we will not install the Exchange components at this time.

Check the components you wish to install and click or press Next to continue.

28. We now begin the Setup phase that deals with the network components and their configuration. The following message will be displayed:

    "Setup is now ready to guide you through the installation of Windows NT Networking. If you want to review or change any settings before continuing, click Back.

    To begin installing Windows NT Networking, click Next

    1. Gathering information about your computer
    2. Installing Windows NT Networking
    3. Finishing Setup

    Click or press Next to continue."

29. The message "Setup is preparing to initialize the NT network installation" will appear briefly, followed by:

    "Windows NT needs to know how this computer should participate on a network.

    Wired to the network: Your computer is connected to the network by a ISDN Adapter or Network Adapter.

    Remote access to the network: Your computer uses a Modem to remotely connect to the network."

    Assuming that your computer is wired to a LAN (as we are in our example) check the box for Wired to the Network, and click or press Next to continue.

30. Setup will then display the message:

    "To have setup start searching for a Network Adapter, click Start Search button."

    Go ahead and click on the Start Search button to have Setup automatically detect your network interface card. If you have additional cards, you may have Setup scan for them also. If your adapter is not detected, you can choose the Select from List... button to manually specify an adapter. You can choose from a list of supplied drivers or you can supply drivers using a disk containing the adapter board OEMSETUP.INF and other setup files for the card.

NOTE You may be asked for your network card configuration settings later during the installation, this will depend on the network interface card (NIC) you're using. Cards such as PCI NICs do not usually require any manual setup and are configured automatically. ■

CAUTION

Always verify the type and settings of the NIC before starting the NT Server installation, especially if this machine is joining a domain as a Backup Domain Controller (BDC). If you do not insure that the configuration parameters are correct for the NIC, the network services may fail to start later in the installation due to hardware failure.

> If the network services fail to start, the server will not be able to connect to the Primary Domain Controller (PDC) and will be unable to join the domain and receive its security identification (SID). This will usually result in a failed installation.

Any network adapters that are found will be displayed. After all the network adapter drivers have been installed, choose the Next button to continue.

31. The next screen will allow you to choose the network protocol(s) you want to use by displaying the message:

    "Select the networking protocols that are used on your network. If you are unsure, contact your system administrator."

    The following protocol choices are then given:

    - TCP/IP Protocol
    - NWLink IPX/SPX Compatible Transport
    - NetBEUI Protocol

    By default both NWLink and NetBEUI are marked. Modify the choices if needed to reflect the protocol appropriate to your network environment. When finished, click Next to continue.

32. Now we are shown the services that will be installed on the system, and given a chance to add or change the choices. The screen displays:

    "Listed below are the services that will be installed by the system. You may add to this list by clicking the Select from list button."

    The Network Services shown by default are as follows:

    - Remote Access Service
    - RPC Configuration
    - NetBIOS Interface
    - Workstation
    - Server

    All but Remote Access Service (RAS) are actually installed by default. Add additional services if desired, and click Next to continue.

33. Setup gives us the opportunity to go back and make changes before installing the network components by displaying the message:

    "Windows NT is now ready to copy and install networking components that you selected and others required by the system.

    This process will allow individual components to install themselves and raise dialogs so that they may install correctly.

    Click Next to continue.

    Click Back to make changes to your selections."

Go back and make changes if needed; otherwise choose the Next button to continue with the installation.

34. Your adapters will now be installed. Depending on the adapter, a dialog box will usually appear asking you to set or confirm the adapters configuration settings (IO address, IRQ, Transceiver Type, and so on). Choose the proper settings for your adapter and click the OK button.

    Setup will install the protocols and services at this point. You may be asked to provide additional information depending on the protocols and services you have selected. For example, if you chose TCP/IP as one of your protocols, you'd be asked for IP address information. If you had selected to install the Remote Access Service, you'd be asked to choose a COM port and modem to use.

    After the configuration of the protocols and services is completed the next screen that appears is as follows:

    "Windows NT is now ready to start the network so that you can complete the installation of networking.

    Click Next to continue.

    Click Back to stop the network if it is running and make changes to your selections."

    This is another chance to go back and reconfigure anything you may have missed. If you've finished, click on the Next button to continue.

35. Since we have chosen to configure the server in our installation example to be a primary domain controller, the next screen will appear, as follows:

    "You have requested that Windows NT create a Primary Domain Controller.

    You must supply the name of the domain that this Primary Domain Controller will manage."

    Supply the name for the new domain, and click the Next button to continue.

36. The final phase of the NT Server will begin with the following message:

    "Setup is almost finished. After you answer a few more questions, Setup will complete installation. If you want to review or change any settings before continuing, click Back.

    To continue, click Finish.

    1. Gathering information about your computer
    2. Installing Windows NT Networking
    3. Finishing Setup

    Click on the Finish button to start the last phase of the Setup."

37. The brief message "Setup is configuring your computer to run Windows NT" is then followed by the screen that allows you to set the properties for the date, time, and time zone. It is important to set this information accurately, particularly if your SMS sites are spread across different time zones.

First choose the correct time zone for your area from the drop-down scroll box. After that, move to the Date & Time tab, and verify that the settings are accurate. If they aren't, adjust them as needed so they reflect an accurate time.

Click OK when you've finished.

38. Next you will be able to choose the display properties of your screen, based on the video adapter detected by the Setup program. The system will display the adapter type it has detected. You may then set and test the screen resolution, color palette, font, and refresh frequency appropriate for your video adapter. Once you've tested the screen properties, press the OK button to continue the installation process.
39. The final Setup screens will start by displaying the message, "Setup is configuring your computer to run Windows NT." Setup then saves the configuration information to the registry and removes the temporary installation files. When it's finished, the Setup program will display the restart message:

    "Windows NT 4.0 has been installed successfully.

    Remove disks from floppy drives and choose Restart Computer."

    Click on the Restart Computer button to reboot your machine.

Congratulations—you have completed the installation of the NT Server software. The following events take place after the restart of the computer:

- The FAT file system will be detected. This will be followed by the check disk utility (Chkdsk) being automatically run on the FAT partition prior to NTFS conversion.
- The FAT partition is converted to NTFS. This is followed by an automatic reboot of the computer.

After rebooting, the system will set the security on the file system and then display the Windows NT logon screen. Use the administrative password you set in step 25 to logon to the server under the account named Administrator. Once you have logged on as the administrator, you can add additional user accounts to the system as needed.

Creating the Service Accounts

Before you continue with the installation of SQL Server and the SMS components, you need to create some service accounts. Three service accounts are needed, as follows:

- The Replicator Service Account—this account is required if you're going to be using the Directory Replication Service. It will maintain logon scripts uniformly across all domain controllers available for validating user logon requests. This account is not required if there are no other logon servers.
- The SQL Service Account—this account is used for the MS SQL Server Executive service.
- The SMS Service Account—this is a required account needed to run the SMS services.

All of these service accounts must be members of the following user groups:

Administrators Group

Domain Administrators Group

In addition to these accounts, the Replicator Service Account must also belong to both the Replicator Group and the Backup Operators Group.

Once the service accounts have been created they must be given "logon as a service" rights so they can start up automatically when NT starts. Let's go through the process of installing the accounts.

For our example we'll add the Replicator Service Account into the user database. We have chosen to use this account because it must be a member of all the aforementioned groups. Use the following procedure as a template for creating the other service accounts:

1. Click Start, Programs, Administrative Tools, User Manager for Domains. This brings up the User Manager for Domains administrative utility.
2. From the User menu, click on New User. This brings up the new users screen, as shown in figure 5.9.

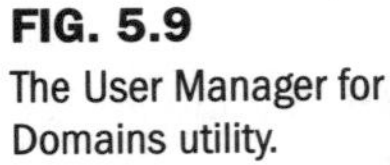

FIG. 5.9
The User Manager for Domains utility.

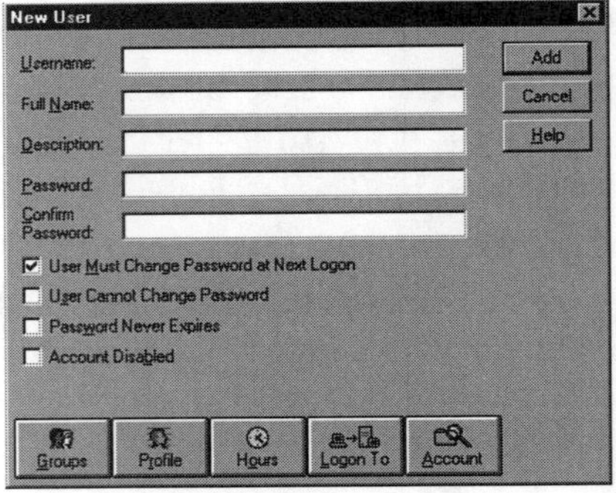

3. Enter a Username that's descriptive of the service: REPSvc.
4. Enter a Full Name for the service, such as: Replicator Service.
5. Enter a description for the service account, such as: Service Account for Dir Replication.
6. Next, enter a password for the service. This is important, because these accounts have administrative access in the NT domain. You'll need to remember the passwords you assign to these accounts later in the Setup process.
7. Uncheck the box User Must Change Password at Next Logon.
8. Check the box User Cannot Change Password.
9. Check the box Password Never Expires. After you've entered these values, you should have a New User screen that looks like figure 5.10.

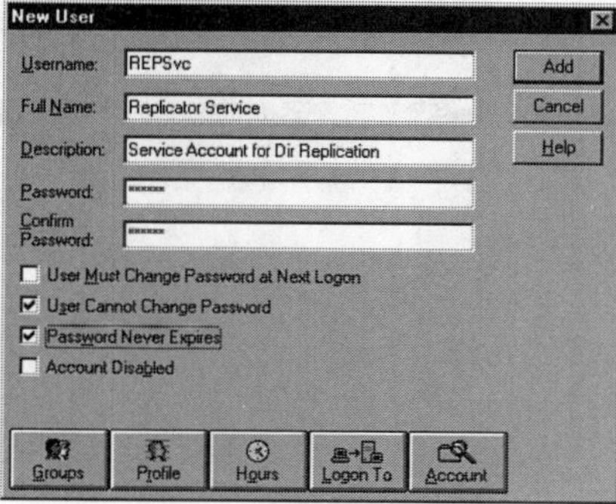

FIG. 5.10
The completed New User property page.

10. Click the Groups button to open up the Group Memberships window.
11. From the Not Member Of: box, highlight the Local Administrators group and click on the Add button. Repeat this step with the Global Domain Admins group, the Local Backup Operators group, and the Local Replicator group. The Group Memberships screen should look like figure 5.11. When you've finished, click OK. This will take you back to the New User window.

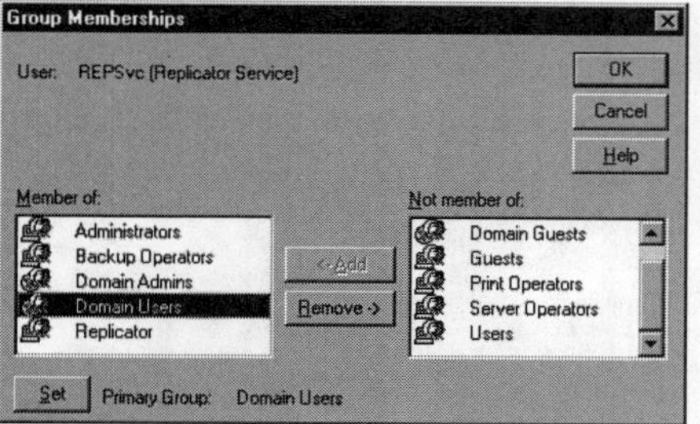

FIG. 5.11
Add the Service Account to the appropriate User Groups.

12. Click on the Add button to enter the service account into the user database.
13. Repeat steps 3 through 11 to add the SQL and SMS service accounts. Change step 11 to include only the Local Administrators group and the Global Domain Admin group in the services group membership. Do not add the service account to the Local Backup Operators or the Local Replicator groups. When you've finished, the User Manager windows will show the service accounts, as shown in figure 5.12.
14. Next you need to set "Log on as a service" privileges for the accounts. Choose User Rights... from the Policies drop-down menu.
15. Check the Show Advanced User Rights box, and then use the Right: pull-down menu to scroll down to the option "Log on as a service," and click on it.
16. Click on the Add button to bring up the Add Users and Groups window. Click on the Show Users button to display the service accounts in the Names window.

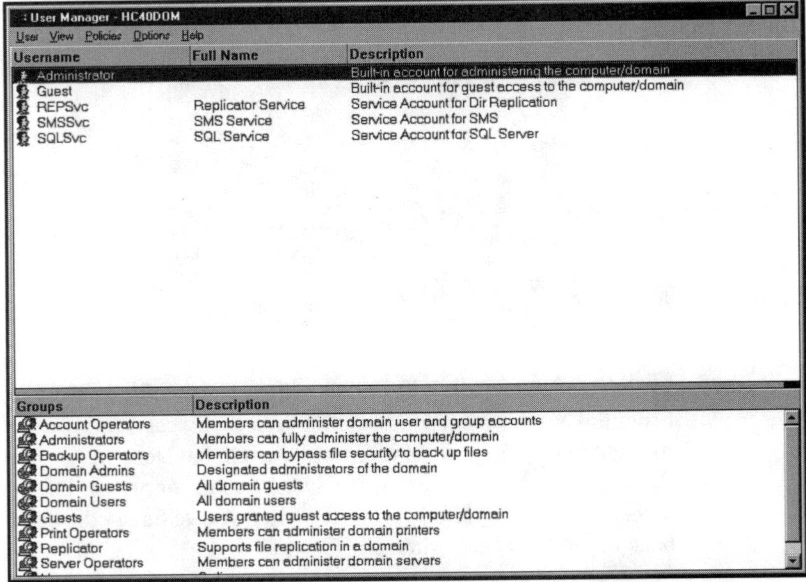

FIG. 5.12 The User Manager displays the new Service Accounts.

17. Scroll down the list of names and add each of the new service accounts to the A<u>d</u>d Names: box, as shown in figure 5.13, and then click the OK button.

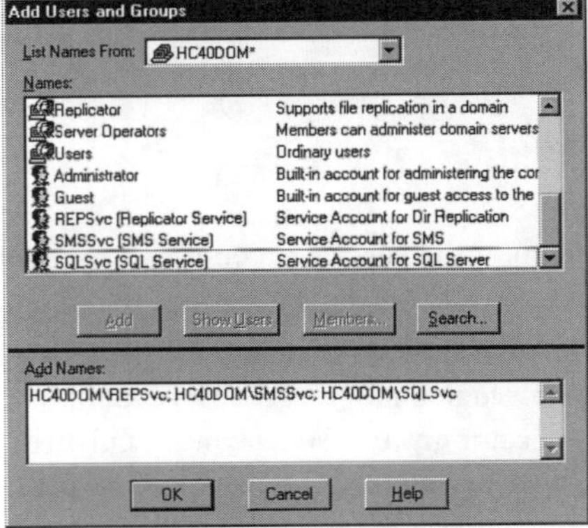

FIG. 5.13 Add the service account names from the account listing.

The User Rights Policy will now show the service accounts listed under the <u>G</u>rant To: pane, as shown in figure 5.14.

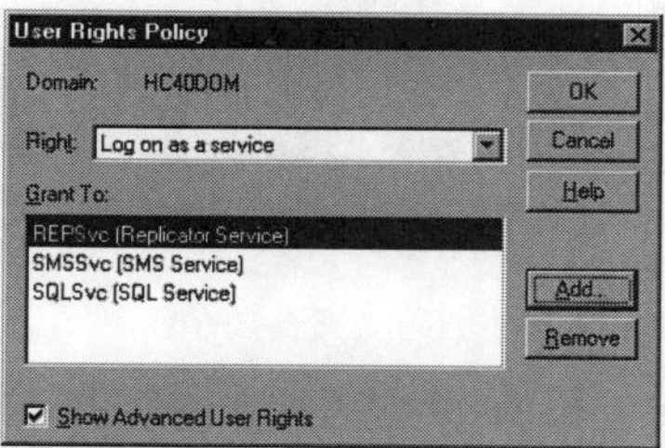

FIG. 5.14
Grant "Log on as a service" privilege to the service accounts.

The next steps (18 to 21) in the installation process apply only if you have multiple logon servers (backup domain controllers). You can also skip these steps if you use only Novell NetWare as the NOS.

18. Open the Server Manager administrative utility by choosing Administrative Tools from the Programs option in the Start menu. The Server Manager will display the machines located in your domain. The Server Manager screen for our example is shown in figure 5.15.

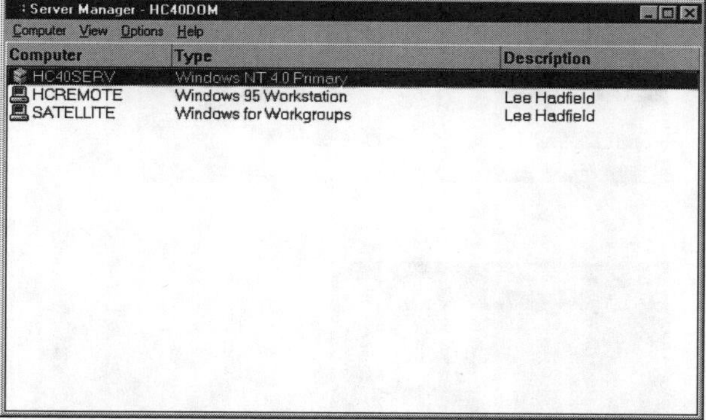

FIG. 5.15
The Server Manager window.

19. Highlight the computer listed as the "Windows NT 4.0 Primary" under the Type heading. Choose Services under the Computer drop-down menu, as shown in figure 5.16.
20. From the Services page, highlight the Service named "Directory Replicator," as shown in figure 5.17, and click the Startup button.
21. Configure the Directory Replicator service for Automatic Startup Type. Then configure the service to Log On As the Replication Service account we created earlier. Do this by marking the This Account button and supplying the service account name and password, as shown in figure 5.18. When you've finished, click the OK button, then the Close button.

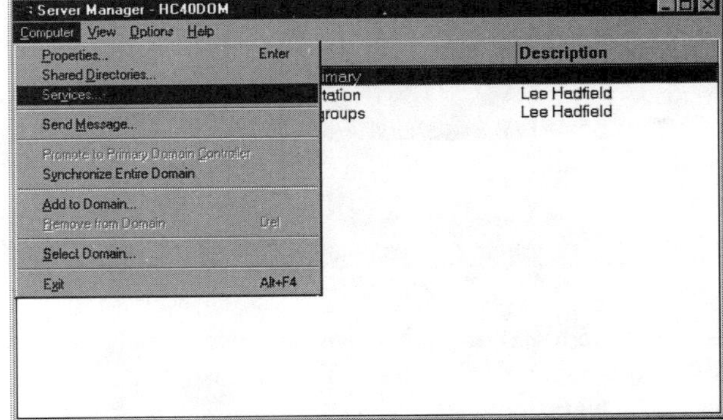

FIG. 5.16
Choose the Services... option from the menu.

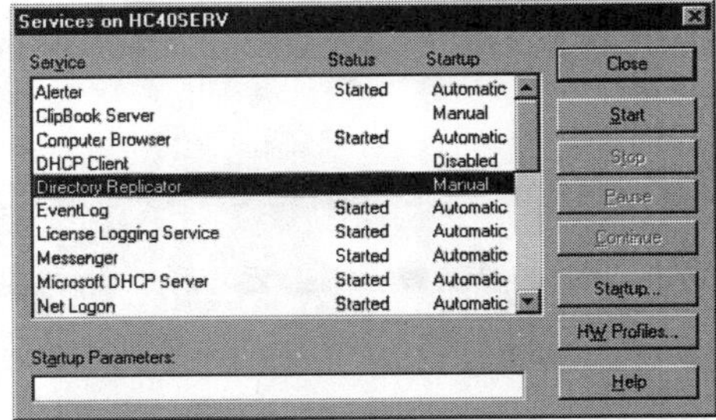

FIG. 5.17
Configure the Directory Replicator service.

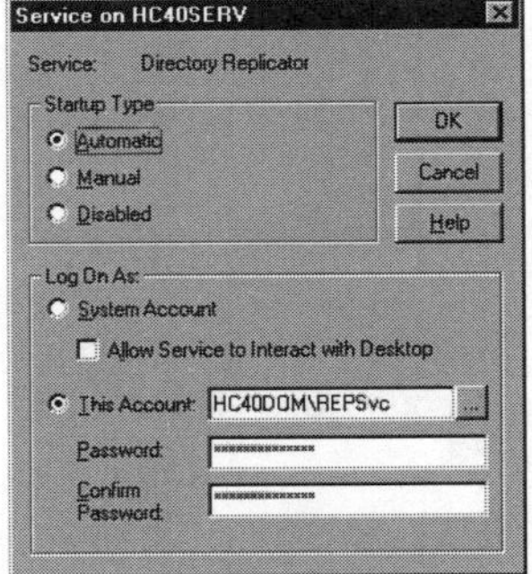

FIG. 5.18
Configure the Directory Replicator for Automatic Startup.

22. Back in the Server Manager window, double-click the computer listed as the "Windows NT 4.0 Primary" under the Type heading. The Properties page will appear. On the Properties page, click the Replication button.
23. Click the Export Directories and the Import Directories buttons, as shown in figure 5.19.

24. Click the OK button to start the Replicator Service. NT will then attempt to start the Directory Replication service.

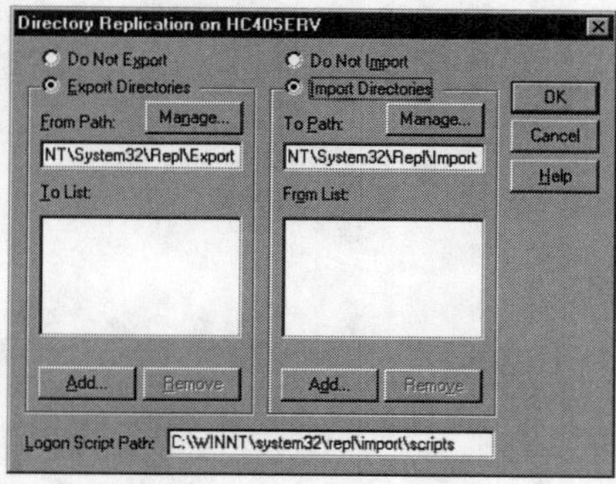

FIG. 5.19
Configure the Directory Replication properties.

We can now begin the SQL Server portion of the SMS Server installation.

Installation Steps for Microsoft SQL Server 6.5x

The next step to perform is the SQL Server installation. You may choose to skip this step if utilizing an existing SQL Server. For our example, we have chosen to install SQL on the same server that will be acting as the SMS primary site server.

Follow these steps to install Microsoft SQL 6.x:

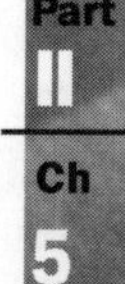

1. Connect to the CD-ROM drive or the network installation point for SQL 6.x. Change to the proper directory (I386, Alpha, or MIPs) according to the hardware platform you're installing on. Run the Setup program located in this directory.
2. The SQL Server Setup Welcome screen appears. Click the Continue button to proceed with the installation.
3. The next screen (see fig. 5.20) prompts you for your Name, Company, and Product ID. Enter the appropriate values and click the Continue button. The Product Identification number can be found on the back of the SQL CD-ROM jewel case.
4. Verify that the correct values were entered and click the Continue button.
5. On the next Setup screen verify that the button for Install SQL Server and Utilities is marked as shown in figure 5.21, and click Continue.
6. The next screen will prompt you for the licensing mode you wish to use. Fill in the appropriate values and click the Continue button.
7. The next screen (see fig. 5.22) prompts you for the installation destination path. Choose an appropriate drive that has sufficient space for the installation, and click Continue.

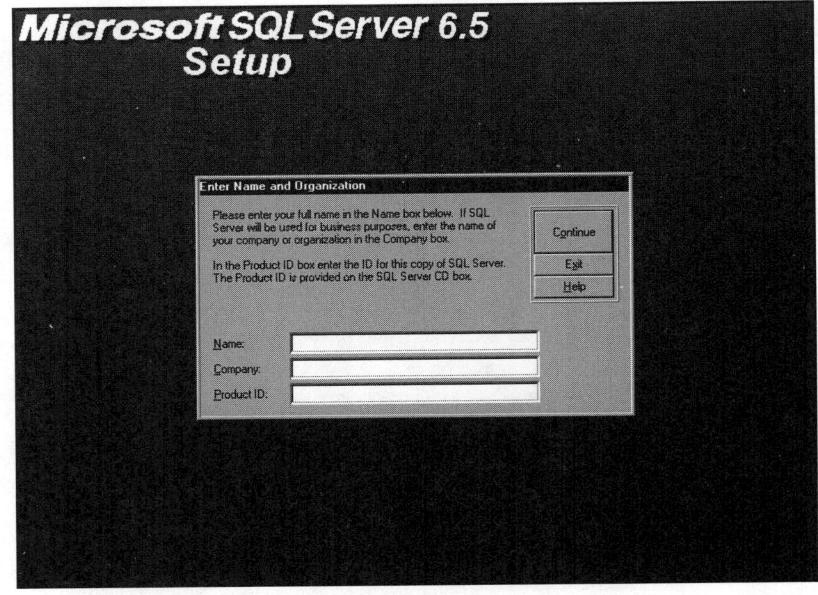

FIG. 5.20
Start by filling in the Name, Company and Product ID.

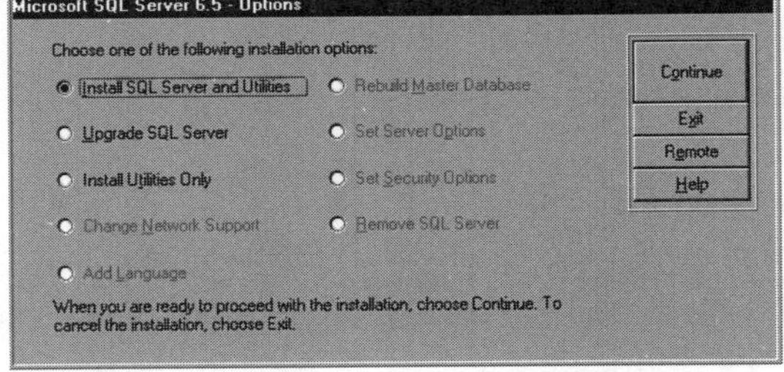

FIG. 5.21
Choose Install SQL Server and Utilities.

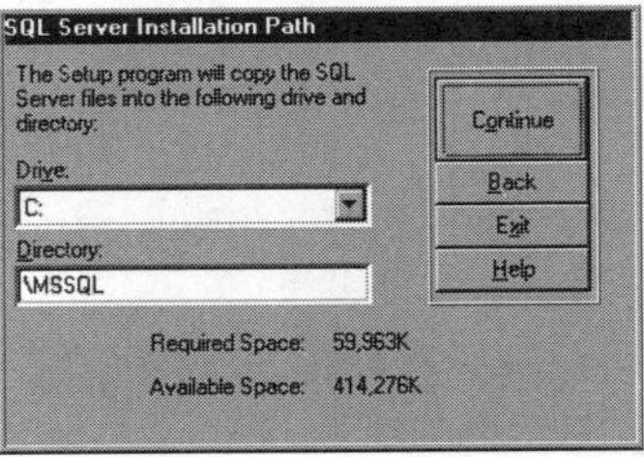

FIG. 5.22
Enter the destination drive and directory for the SQL files.

8. The MASTER Device Creation screen (see fig. 5.23) will appear. Verify the target drive and directory for the SQL database MASTER device. Also specify the size of the database. In most cases the default of 25MB will work if the SQL Server is to be used only for SMS. Click Continue to proceed.

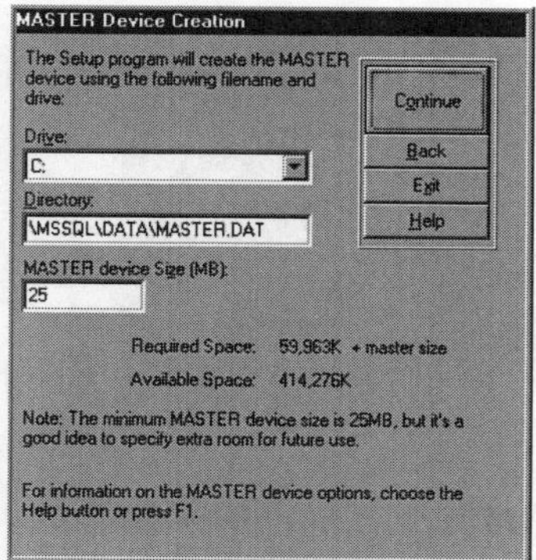

FIG. 5.23
Create the SQL MASTER Device.

You can save steps later if you create a MASTER device with a size of 45MB. This extra space will be used when we expand the SQL temporary database (TempDB) from its default size of 2MB to the minimum 20MB size required by SMS.

9. You are then prompted for the SQL Server Books Online installation options. The files may be installed to the local hard disk (15MB of disk space are needed) or run from the CD-ROM (1MB of disk space is needed), or you may choose to skip the online book installation entirely. Choose an option and click Continue.
10. Next you'll be presented with the Installation Options dialog box, as shown in figure 5.24. From here you can set the Character Set, Sort Order, Additional Network Support, and SQL Startup options. Begin by clicking the Sets button to choose the Character Set.

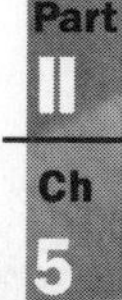

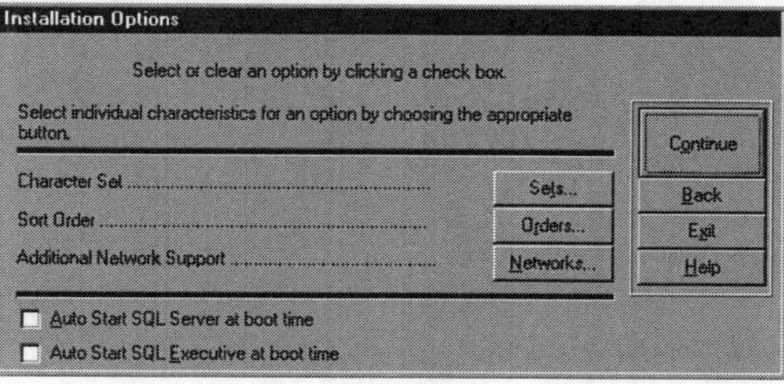

FIG. 5.24
Configure the installation options.

11. In the Select Character Set dialog box (see fig. 5.25), choose the appropriate character set for the language you're working with. The default is ISO (International Standards Organization) Character Set, which is appropriate for most installations. When the correct character set is highlighted, click the OK button.
12. Click the Orders button to view the sort order options (see fig. 5.26). The most important thing to remember is that if you have multiple SQL Servers in your organization, they should all be consistent in the Sort Order that they use. In our example we have chosen "Dictionary order, case-insensitive, uppercase preference." Highlight the desired sort order and click the OK button.

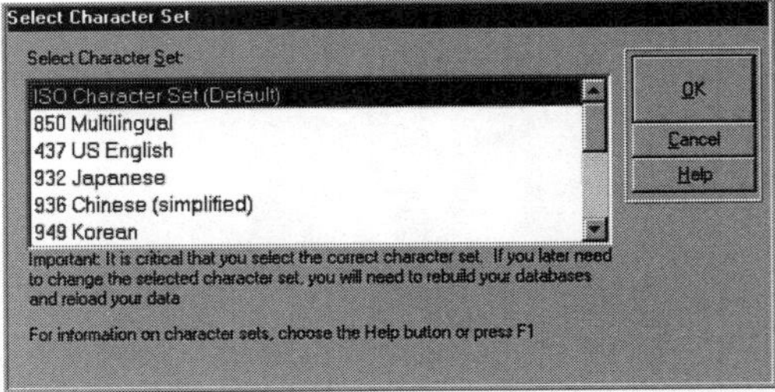

FIG. 5.25
Select the character set.

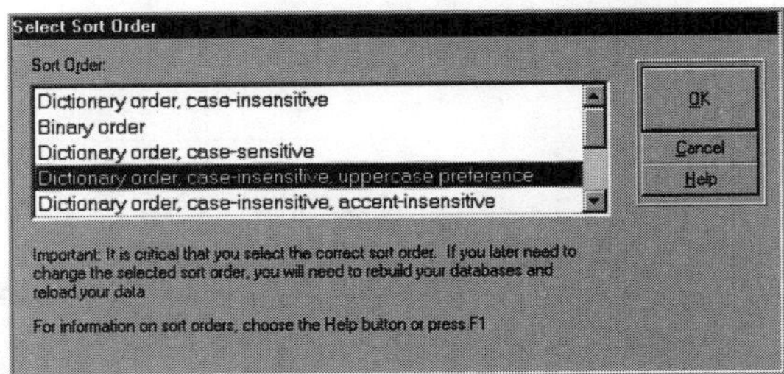

FIG. 5.26
Select the sort order.

13. To view the network options, click the Networks button. This screen will allow you to select which Net-Libraries will be installed. By default, Named Pipes is selected as the communications mechanism.

CAUTION

You may choose additional mechanisms, but DO NOT deselect Named Pipes at this time. Setup uses Named Pipes during the installation process. If you desire to remove Named Pipes as a communications mechanism, run the Setup program after the initial setup and remove the Named Pipes support.

For our example we have chosen to include the Multi-Protocol Net-Libraries, as shown in figure 5.27. When you have made your choice(s), click the OK button to continue.

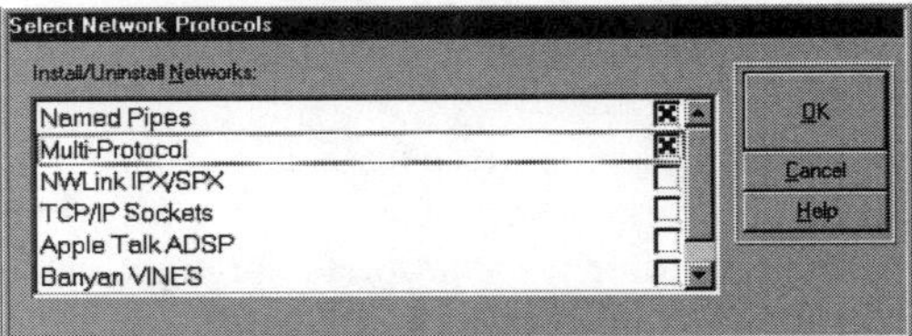

FIG. 5.27
Select the desired network protocols.

An Explanation of Net-Libraries and IPCs

In order for clients to talk to the SQL server, a mechanism must be in place that allows the appropriate programs, processes, and devices to communicate with each other over the network. This mechanism is called Interprocess Communication (IPC). It is a set of techniques used by multitasking operating systems and networked computers that allow programs and processes to communicate. There are two types of IPCs, as follows:

- Local Procedure Calls (LPC)—multitasking operating systems use LPCs to allow concurrently running programs or processes to communicate with each other. Using LPCs, the tasks can share memory spaces, synchronize tasks, and send messages to each other.
- Remote Procedure Call (RPC)—RPCs (sometimes referred to as coupling mechanisms) are the communications mechanism used in Client-Server model. Similar to LPCs, they allow communication of programs and processes over a network.

SQL uses RPCs in the form of Network libraries (called Net-Libraries) to provide the communications mechanism that allows client applications (the front-end) to send requests for service to the SQL Server (the back-end).

Several different types of Net-Libraries exist. The one(s) you use will depend on the network operating system and the protocols in place on your network. SQL will allow you to run several libraries at once to provide simultaneous connections from clients running different IPCs.

Following is a look at the different Net-Libraries available for installation:

- Multi-Protocol Net-Library—uses the RPC facility that is built into Windows NT to provide communication over TCP/IP Windows Sockets, NWLink IPX/SPX, and Named Pipes.
- NWLink IPX/SPX Net-Library—use this library if your network is running the Novell IPX/SPX protocol.
- TCP/IP Net-Library—uses standard Windows Sockets as the Interprocess Communications method over TCP/IP.
- AppleTalk ADSP Net-Library—permits Apple Macintosh-based clients to connect to SQL Server using their native AppleTalk protocol instead of TCP/IP.
- Banyan Vines Net-Library—allows communications using Banyan VINES IP network protocol by supporting the Banyan VINES Sequenced Packet Protocol (SPP). This will allow communication between Windows NT-based clients and an SQL Server, but only if the SQL Server resides on an Intel platform. MIPs and Alpha AXP platform are not supported at this printing.
- DECnet Sockets Net-Library—allows clients running VMS to use DECnet Sockets as the IPC to communicate with the SQL Server over a Pathworks network. This server-side library is supported on Intel, MIPS, and Alpha AXP platforms.

14. Make sure the boxes for both Auto Start SQL Server at boot time and Auto Start SQL Executive at boot time are checked, as shown in figure 5.28. When you've finished, click the Continue button.

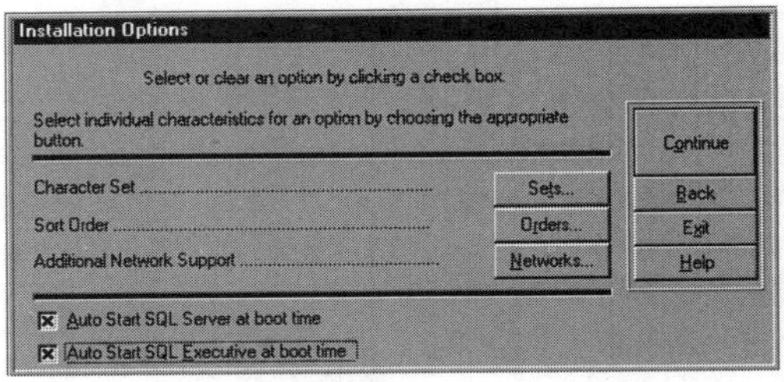

FIG. 5.28
Make sure the Auto Start options are selected.

15. The dialog box for the SQL Executive Log On Account information will be presented next. Be sure the button for Install The SQL Executive service to log on to Windows NT as: is marked. In the Account box, provide the name of the SQL Service account that you set up earlier (see fig. 5.29). Click the Continue button to proceed.

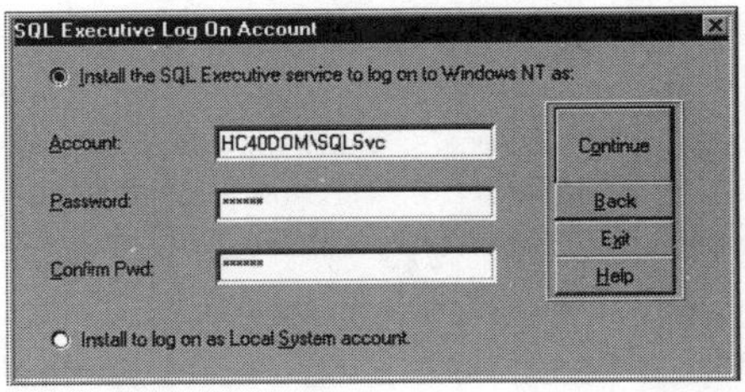

FIG. 5.29
Provide the SQL Executive Log On Account information.

16. In our example, the Multi-Protocol Net-Libraries were selected earlier, so we are now presented with a dialog box (see fig. 5.30) that will allow you to enable Multi-Protocol Encryption on Multi-Protocol connections. The default of no encryption was chosen.

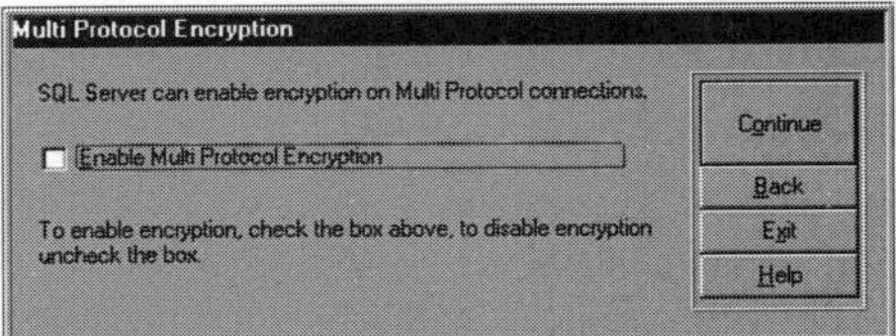

FIG. 5.30
Enable Multi-Protocol Encryption if desired.

At this point the File Copy In Progress screen appears, and the copy phase of the installation begins. This is followed by several messages indicating the following activities:

- The creation of the MASTER Database Device
- Update of the Service Control Manager
- Reindexing of the SQL Server system tables
- Installation of the initial SQL Server configuration

Expect a long setup period to take place at this time. The only indication that install is proceeding is the animated hourglass with sand pouring in the letter Q. There is one other indication that install is proceeding: disk drive activity, and plenty of it.

The Setup program then displays a message saying that you can continue with another task. I would refrain from starting any other process. The server is quite busy performing installation tasks at this time; any other processes would only slow the installation down.

The last informational screen tells you that the installation has been successfully completed. You can then exit back to NT by clicking the Exit to Windows NT button. You will notice that the Microsoft SQL Server 6.5 program group has been added to the desktop. It contains the program icons for all the SQL Server components (see fig. 5.31).

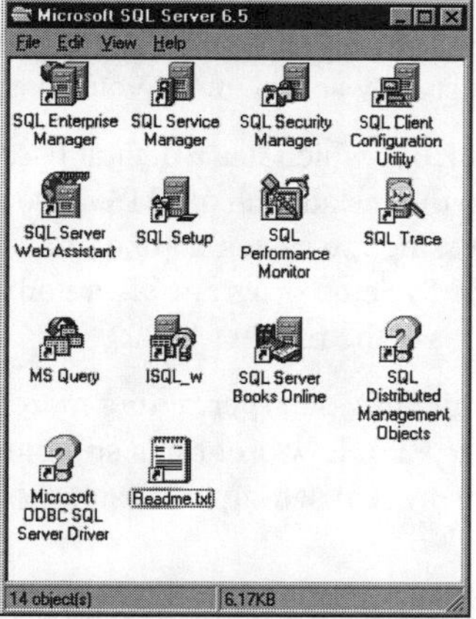

FIG. 5.31 The SQL Program Group is created on the desktop.

At this point, SQL is not yet running. To ensure that the SQL server components are installed correctly and that the services start automatically on system startup, take the time to reboot the server. After the reboot, you'll be able to tell if the SQL services have been started properly by the following:

- Examining the NT System and application event log
- Checking to see if the SQL services have started in Control Panel's Services window
- Watching for startup messages indicating that one or more services has failed to start

Before we install SMS, we need to make some minor configuration changes in SQL Server. The size of the temporary database (TempDB) must be expanded from its default size of 2MB to a size of 20MB. In addition, the setting that configures the number of simultaneous user connections may also need to be increased. We'll begin by first checking the current value of the user connection setting, using the ISQL/w program. Then we'll use the program to increase the number of user connections from the default of 15 to the required number of 20.

Configuring the SQL User Connection Setting

You must ensure that the maximum user connections setting is appropriate for the number of simultaneous SMS administrators that may be on the system. The suggested setting is 20, with five user connections per administrator. This would allow four SMS administrators to be active on the system at once. If you think you will have more administrators using the system during the same period, increase the number of user connections appropriately. For each additional administrator, add five user connections.

The default number of user connections set during the SQL 6.5 installation is 15. The default number of user connections will vary depending on the version of SQL you are using. For SQL 4.21a, the default is five; for SQL 6.0, the number is 20.

If you're not sure what the current setting is, you can easily find out by running the ISQL/w program's sp_configure command without any parameters. Use this method to determine if the number of default user connections is currently sufficient for your installation.

In our example we have just installed SQL 6.5, which has a default user connection setting of 15. This is below the required setting for the installation of SMS. If we don't intend to have any more than four SMS administrators accessing the system at one time, we can skip manually bumping up the user connections. The SMS Setup program will automatically detect the current setting of 15 and prompt you to increase the number to 20.

If you would like to set the number to a higher value (permitting more administrative connections), you can do so manually by using the ISQL/w programs sp_configure command. To illustrate this, we'll manually confirm the present setting is 15, and then reset the user connections to 20, as follows:

1. Start by opening the ISQL/w program located in the Microsoft SQL Server program group.
2. The Connect Server screen will appear, as shown in figure 5.32. Click the List Servers button to display a list of servers to choose from, or type the name of your server in the Server box. The Login Id should already be set to "sa" (system administrator); if it's not, type "sa" in the box. No password will be needed, since members of the NT administrators' group are granted SQL administrative rights by default (see the sidebar "The SQL Security Modes" later in this chapter for more information on SQL security).

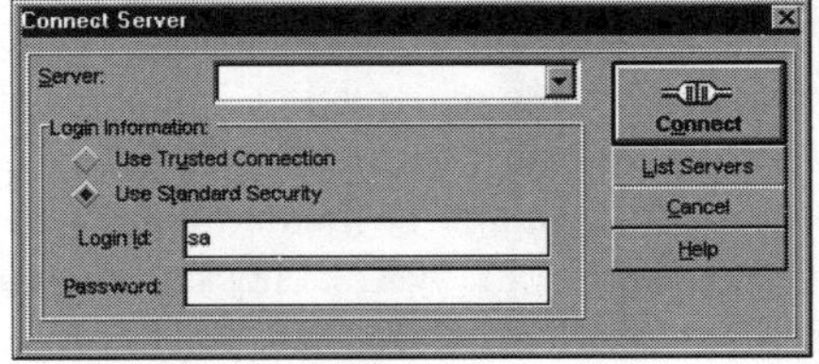

FIG. 5.32
Connect to the SQL Server.

3. When the Server name and Login Id have been entered, click the Connect button. The main ISQL/w screen will appear. First we'll take a look at the current SQL configuration values by typing in the command sp_configure with no arguments under the Query tab (see fig. 5.33).

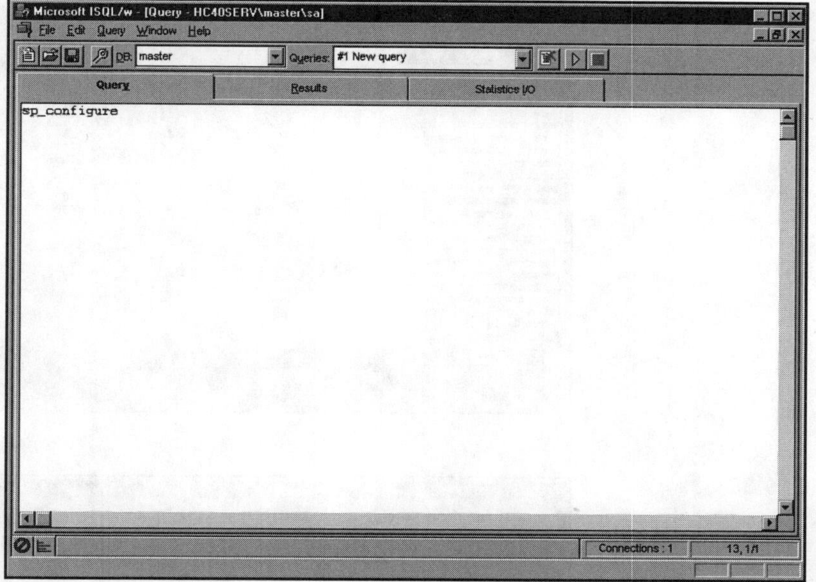

FIG. 5.33
Use the sp_configure command to view configuration information.

4. Execute the query by using the Execute option in the Query menu. You can also execute the query by pressing the Ctrl+E keys or by simply clicking the green right arrow located in the toolbar. After the query has executed, the Results tab will come to the foreground and display a listing of the configuration parameters and their current settings (see fig. 5.34). As we can see, the current value of 15 user connections is shown under the config_value column.
5. To set this number to 20, click the Query tab and then click the New Query button located on the toolbar (first button on the left). This will clear the current query from the screen. Next, type in the command line `sp_configure user_connections, 20`, as shown in figure 5.35, and execute the query.
6. The Results screen will display the message shown in figure 5.36. This informs us that in order to install the new value the RECONFIGURE command must be run. And because the user connections setting is not a dynamic setting, the SQL Server must be stopped and restarted before the new setting takes effect. Switch to the Query screen and clear the current query, then type in the RECONFIGURE command and execute it.

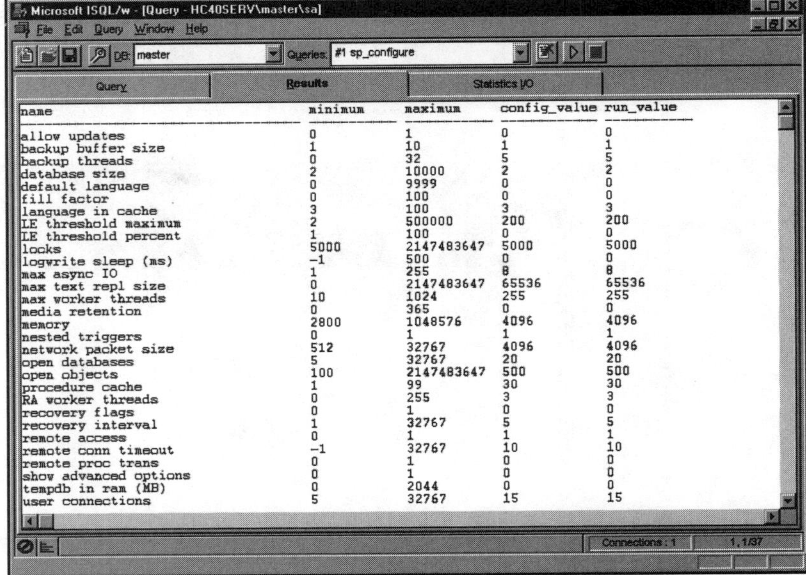

name	minimum	maximum	config_value	run_value
allow updates	0	1	0	0
backup buffer size	1	10	1	1
backup threads	0	32	5	5
database size	2	10000	2	2
default language	0	9999	0	0
fill factor	0	100	0	0
language in cache	3	100	3	3
LE threshold maximum	2	500000	200	200
LE threshold percent	1	100	0	0
locks	5000	2147483647	5000	5000
logwrite sleep (ms)	-1	500	0	0
max async IO	1	255	8	8
max text repl size	0	2147483647	65536	65536
max worker threads	10	1024	255	255
media retention	0	365	0	0
memory	2800	1048576	4096	4096
nested triggers	0	1	1	1
network packet size	512	32767	4096	4096
open databases	5	32767	20	20
open objects	100	2147483647	500	500
procedure cache	1	99	30	30
RA worker threads	0	255	3	3
recovery flags	0	1	0	0
recovery interval	1	32767	5	5
remote access	0	1	1	1
remote conn timeout	-1	32767	10	10
remote proc trans	0	1	0	0
show advanced options	0	1	0	0
tempdb in ram (MB)	0	2044	0	0
user connections	5	32767	15	15

FIG. 5.34
The results of the query are displayed.

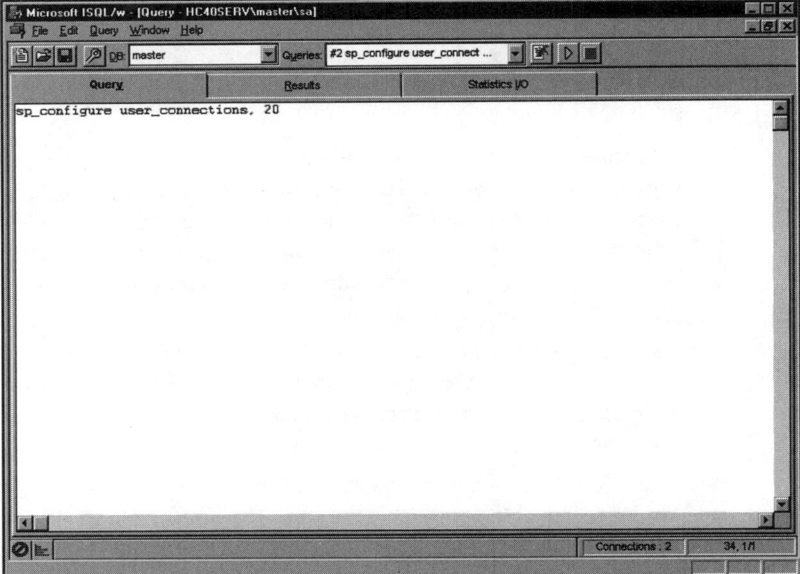

FIG. 5.35
Set the number of user connections to at least 20.

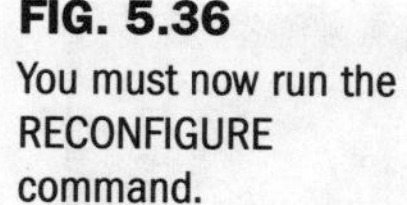

FIG. 5.36
You must now run the RECONFIGURE command.

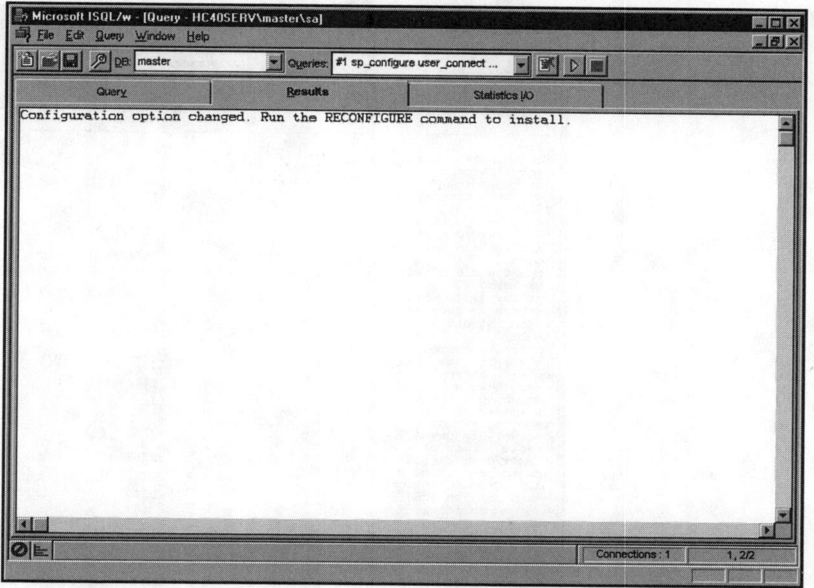

7. The Results screen will inform you that the query returned no data or rows. This is normal for the RECONFIGURE command. Exit from the ISQL/w program. Answer Yes to the dialog box informing you that query results are still open.
8. The next step is to stop and start the SQL server. The easiest way to accomplish this is to run the SQL Service Manager, located in the Microsoft SQL Server program group. After you start the program, you should see an SQL Service Manager window, similar to figure 5.37, that indicates that SQL Server is running. Double-click Stop, and SQL Server will stop, as indicated by the traffic light turning red (see fig. 5.37).

FIG. 5.37
Use the SQL Service Manager to stop and restart the SQL services.

9. Restart SQL by double-clicking Start/Continue. The traffic indicator will turn green again when SQL is once again running. Exit the SQL Server Manager and restart the ISQL/w program.
10. Run the sp_configure command to verify the settings have taken place (see fig. 5.38).

FIG. 5.38
Verify the settings have been changed.

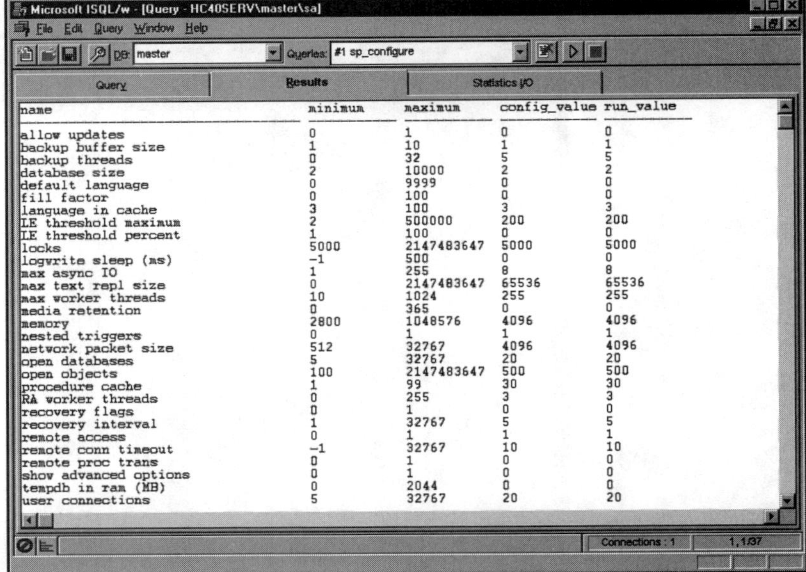

name	minimum	maximum	config_value	run_value
allow updates	0	1	0	0
backup buffer size	1	10	1	1
backup threads	0	32	5	5
database size	2	10000	2	2
default language	0	9999	0	0
fill factor	0	100	0	0
language in cache	3	100	3	3
LE threshold maximum	2	500000	200	200
LE threshold percent	1	100	0	0
locks	5000	2147483647	5000	5000
logwrite sleep (ms)	-1	500	0	0
max async IO	1	255	8	8
max text repl size	0	2147483647	65536	65536
max worker threads	10	1024	255	255
media retention	0	365	0	0
memory	2800	1048576	4096	4096
nested triggers	0	1	1	1
network packet size	512	32767	4096	4096
open databases	5	32767	20	20
open objects	100	2147483647	500	500
procedure cache	1	99	30	30
RA worker threads	0	255	3	3
recovery flags	0	1	0	0
recovery interval	1	32767	5	5
remote access	0	1	1	1
remote conn timeout	-1	32767	10	10
remote proc trans	0	1	0	0
show advanced options	0	1	0	0
tempdb in ram (MB)	0	2044	0	0
user connections	5	32767	20	20

Increasing the Size of the Temporary Database (TempDB)

The TempDB is a database created during SQL Setup and placed on the MASTER database device. It provides the storage area for temporary tables and data. To run SMS you need to make sure that the TempDB is at least 20MB in size. The default size is 2MB. By default the MASTER size was set in our example to 25MB. This is insufficient space to contain a 20MB Temporary Database as required by SMS. So, in order to have room to increase the size of the TempDB file, you must create additional space on the MASTER device.

Two methods are available to expand the MASTER device, as follows:

- Use the SQL Enterprise Manager.
- Use the DISK RESIZE statement.

For our example we'll use the SQL Enterprise Manager to expand the size of the MASTER device, as follows:

1. Begin by starting the SQL Enterprise Manager located in the Microsoft SQL Server program group. If this is the first time you've run the Enterprise Manager, you'll get a registration screen (see fig. 5.39). This will allow you to register your server with the Enterprise Manager. You will not be able to administer your server using the Enterprise Manager until you perform this step.

FIG. 5.39
Register the SQL Server with Enterprise Manager.

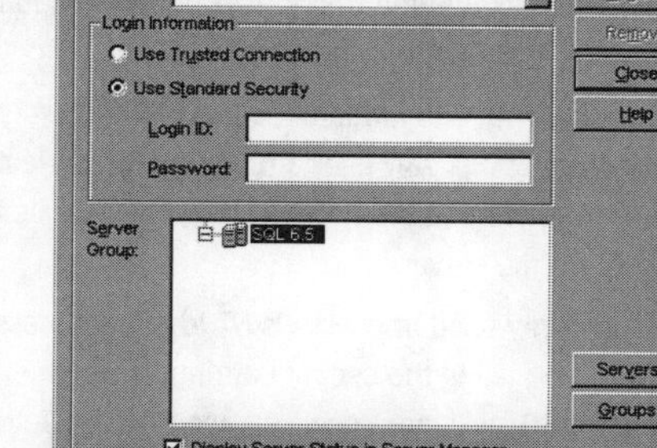

2. Click the Servers button to list the current SQL Servers. If you happen to have more than one SQL Server, you will see multiple server names appear in the Server Group box. Highlight your server, if it's not already highlighted, and click OK. Your server's name will then be placed in the Server list box on the Register Server page.
3. Mark the Use Standard Security option (see the sidebar "The SQL Security Modes" for more information on Standard security) and type in the Login ID "sa," as shown in figure 5.40.

NOTE Our SQL server has been set up to use Standard security when validating access to its database. This is the default mode of security set during installation process.

In order to administer the SQL Server, you must have system administration privileges (SA Privileges) on the server. By default, all members of the NT Server Administrators group have "sa" privileges under Standard security. This means you can connect to the SQL server using the Login ID of "sa" with no password as long as you are currently logged on under an NT administrators group account.

If you are not currently logged on as a member of the NT administrators group, you must enter a valid SQL Server account ID and password before you will be allowed to connect. If you have created your SMS devices on an external or preexisting SQL server that is using another mode of security, enter an appropriate system administrator account name and password valid on that SQL server. ■

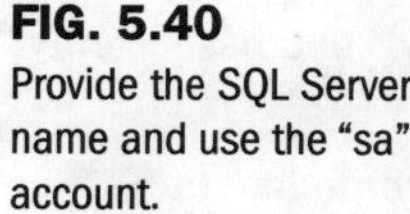

FIG. 5.40
Provide the SQL Server name and use the "sa" account.

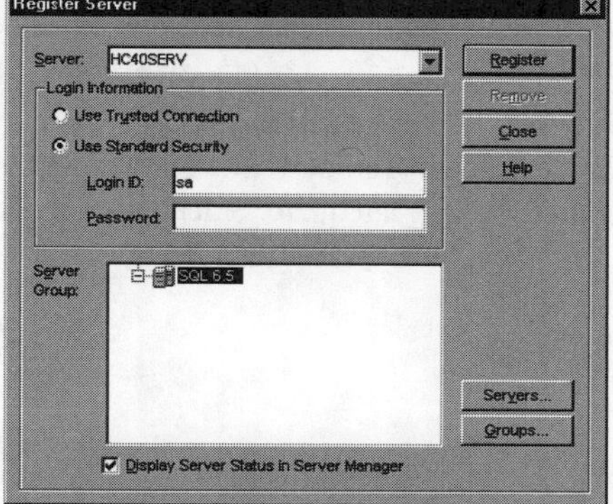

The SQL Security Modes

SQL server allows you to set up the type of security method that it uses when validating access to its database. Three types of security modes exist, as follows:

- Standard Security–is the default mode. With this mode of security, SQL uses its own validation process to authenticate connections. Any user attempting to connect must supply a valid user ID and password. SQL will verify the name and password against its own syslogins table before allowing any connection to the server.
- Integrated Security–integrates the security used in Windows NT to allow access to the SQL Server. Verification of a user is performed using the security attributes assigned to the user during the Windows NT logon process. SQL will grant access based on the authenticated NT user name alone, without requiring a separate SQL logon ID and password.
- Mixed Security–allows SQL to use each of the previous methods when validating user connections. If a blank name and password are given during SQL logon (or if the SQL logon name matches the NT logon name), the SQL server uses the Windows NT integrated logon rules (Integrated Security mode) to grant access. If validation cannot be performed based on an NT account name, the user must supply a valid SQL logon name and password. This name and password are the verified using the Standard security method before any connection is permitted.

Setting the security mode can be accomplished by using the SQL Setup program or the SQL Enterprise Manager.

4. Click on the Register button and then on the Close button. You'll be presented with a Tip of the Day. Mark the Show Tips at Startup box if you want to continue getting informational tips during startup of Enterprise Manager. Then click OK.
5. The Server Manager window will now appear, displaying the name of the our SQL server (see fig. 5.41).

   Expanding the tree under the newly registered server will show several other items. The one we're looking for will be contained under the Database Devices folder. Expand the folder to reveal the MASTER device icon, as shown in figure 5.42.
6. Double-click the MASTER device icon to bring up the Edit Database Device—*Servername* dialog box, as shown in figure 5.43. This dialog box lists the usage of the device by the various databases it contains. As you can see, the TempDB database is only 2MB in size.
7. In the Size (MB) box, increase the size of the MASTER device to accommodate the increase in size that's planned for the TempDB file. For our installation, the 20MB minimum size of the TempDB will be adequate. Since the current size of TempDB is 2MB, the size will need to be increase by 18MB. This means we also have to expand our

MASTER device by at least that amount. In our example, we'll increase the size of the MASTER device by 20MB (to a total size of 45MB) using the Size (MB) box (see fig. 5.44).

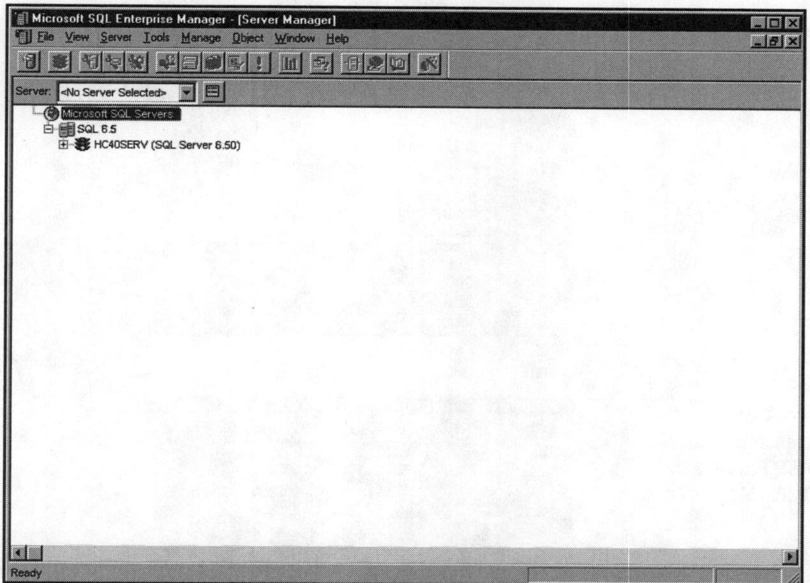

FIG. 5.41 The Server Manager after registering the SQL Server.

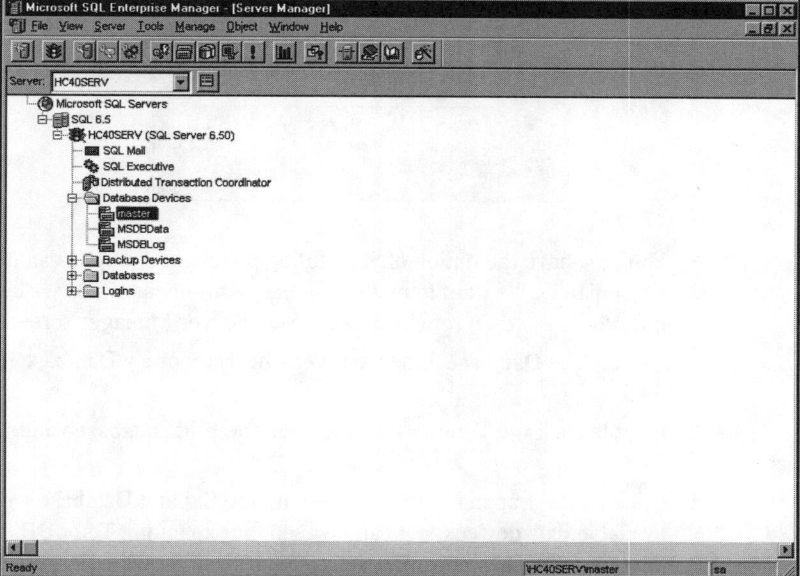

FIG. 5.42 Expand the tree to reveal the MASTER device icon.

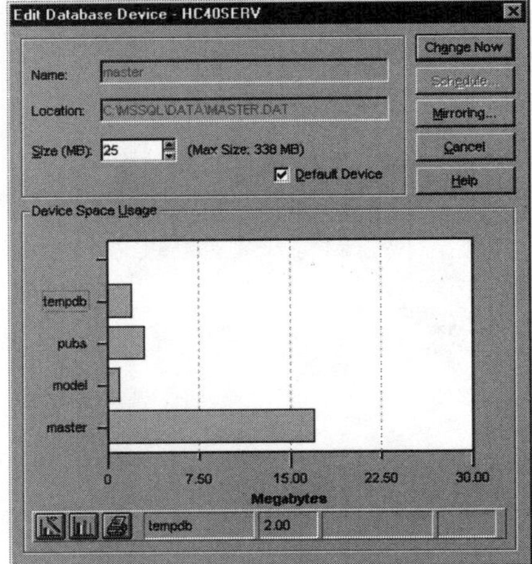

FIG. 5.43
Edit the properties of the MASTER device by double-clicking its icon.

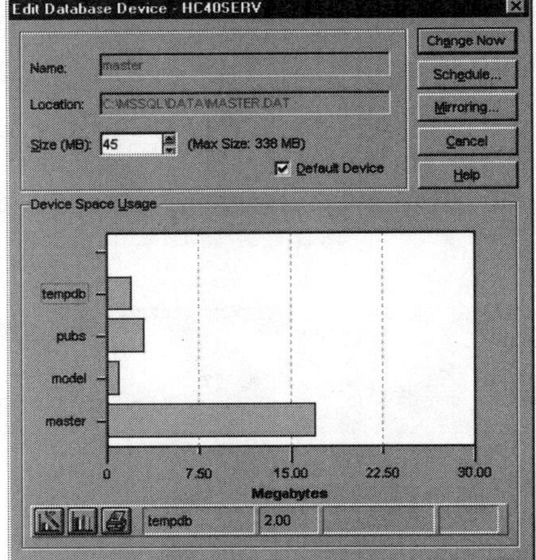

FIG. 5.44
Increase the size of the MASTER device by 20MB.

8. You now have the option of Scheduling the change, or you can force the change to occur immediately. We want to make the change immediately, so we'll click the Change Now button. You're then returned to the SQL Server Manager screen.
9. Expand the Database folder to reveal the Temporary Database icon, as shown in figure 5.45.
10. Double-click the TempDB icon to open the Edit Database window, as shown in figure 5.46.
11. Click on the Expand button to bring up the Expand Database window. This shows us the available data devices that can be used for expanding TempDB. Figure 5.47 shows us that the MASTER has available space (indicated by the darker region of the MASTER database bar on the chart).

FIG. 5.45
Find the TempDB icon.

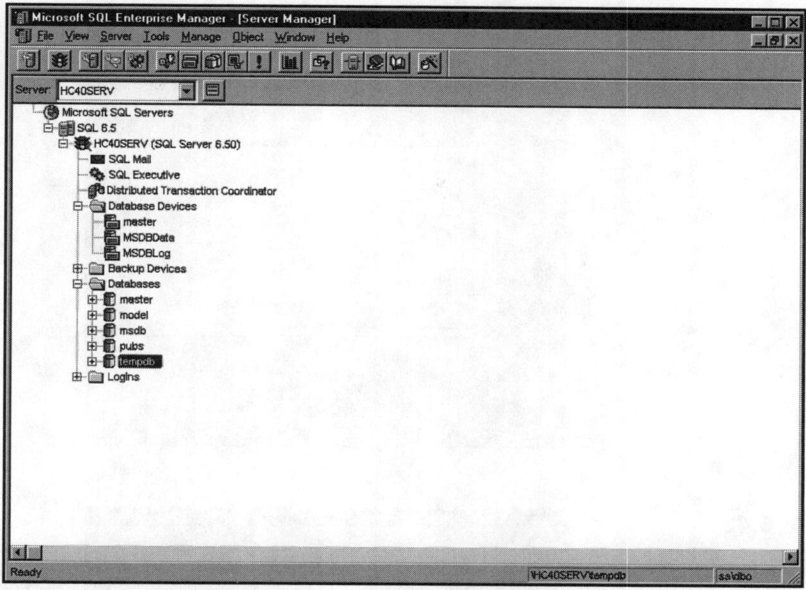

FIG. 5.46
Edit the properties of the TempDB to increase its size.

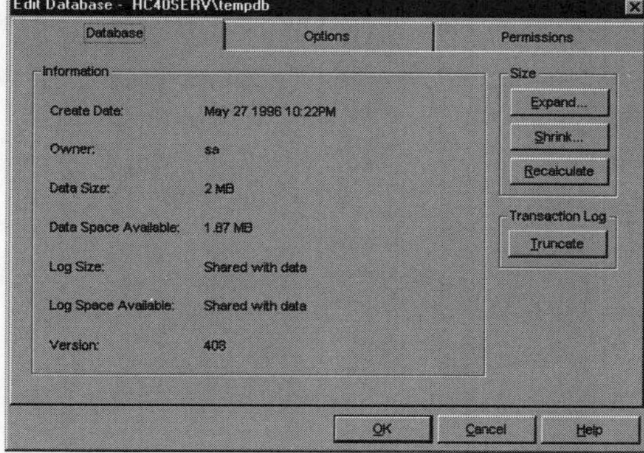

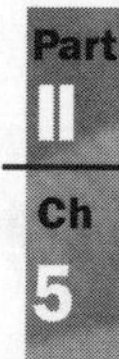

12. Choose MASTER from the Data Device drop-down box. The Size (MB) box shows the available space on the MASTER device (21MB in our example, see fig. 5.48). Since we want to expand our TempDB only to 20MB, we replace the 21 in the Size (MB) box with 18. This will leave 3MB of free space remaining on the MASTER device (shown by the bar on the graph).
13. You may either use the Expand Now button to immediately expand the database, or you can Schedule the expansion for a later time. For our example, we'll click the Expand Now button. After a few seconds, the Edit Database window will reappear, indicating the new size of the Temporary Database (see fig. 5.49). Click OK when done.

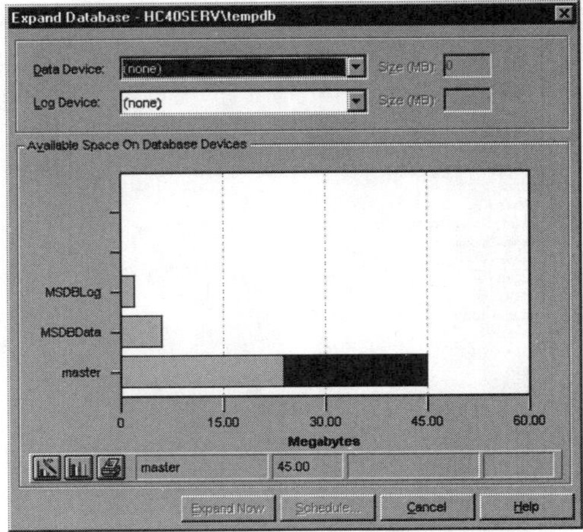

FIG. 5.47
Expand the TempDB on the MASTER device.

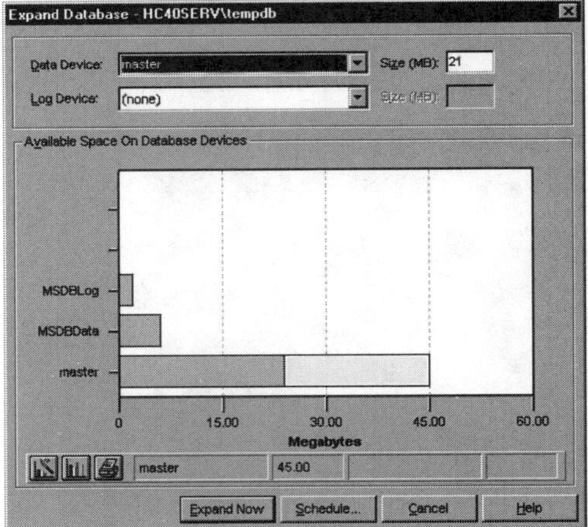

FIG. 5.48
Free space on the MASTER device is shown in yellow.

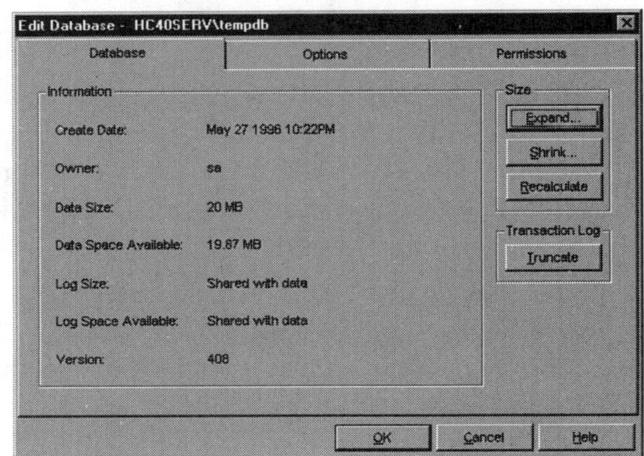

FIG. 5.49
The Data Size is now set to 20MB.

14. Verify the new size of the TempDB database by double-clicking the MASTER device icon under the Database Devices folder. Figure 5.50 shows that the Device Space Usage portion of the Edit Database Device window now reflects a 20MB TempDB on the MASTER device.

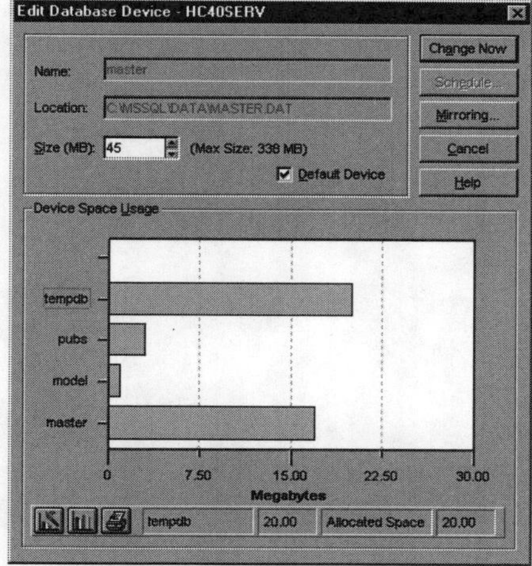

FIG. 5.50 Verify that the size of the TempDB has changed to 20MB.

15. Exit the SQL Enterprise Manager.

You've completed the SQL Setup and configured the user connections and TempDB size. Now it's time to start installing SMS!

From Here...

The actual installation of SMS and its components begins with:

- Chapter 6, "Server Installation, Part II," covers the installation of SMS on the primary site server. We follow this with the installation and configuration of a secondary site. Later in the chapter we examine the procedures required when integrating a NetWare or Macintosh environment with SMS.
- Chapter 7, "Installing Client Sites," covers the installation and configuration of the SMS client components.

CHAPTER 6

Server Installation, Part II

There are actually two kinds of SMS installations that can be done. The one you perform will depend on the type of site you are installing.

As you recall from Chapter 3, "Understanding Domains, Sites, and the SMS Hierarchy," SMS sites are classified as either primary or secondary sites. A primary site has an SQL database which stores the information from that site (and any site below it). The secondary site has no database, and must report all its information to the primary site.

This chapter will review both types of installations, starting with the installation of the primary site. Let's start by taking a quick look at the topics you'll learn about in this chapter. ■

Installation of the SMS Server components on the primary server is shown

We'll start the chapter with the installation of the SMS primary site server, followed by a detailed explanation of the SMS setup events that take place during the installation.

The section of the SMS Administrator program that is used to configure the SMS site properties is examined

We'll look at the SMS Administrator program which will be used later in the chapter to create a secondary site. You'll see the tools and functions used within the program to specify various SMS site properties, including the functions related to establishing site to site connectivity, and the installation of a secondary site.

The installation of a secondary site is illustrated

We'll use what we've learned about the SMS Administrator program to perform a secondary site installation. We then follow up with a discussion of the process used by SMS to add the secondary site to the system.

Installation Steps for Microsoft SMS 1.x

Here are a few things to remember before we continue with the setup. If your server does not already have an NTFS partition with at least 100MB of free space, you will need to provide one before continuing. This figure represents the minimum amount of space needed for the installation of the SMS site server. In practice, you should provide much more disk space than 100MB. If you plan to deploy any large software packages, such as Windows 95 or Office 95, via SMS you will want to consider providing 1GB or more of drive space.

If you have installed SQL Server on the same computer on which you intend to install SMS, the SMS Setup program will create the SMSLog and SMSData devices on the server for you. If you are installing SMS on a separate computer that's not running SQL Server, it is necessary manually to create the SMSLog and SMSData devices on your SQL Server.

Begin the installation by running the Setup program located in the directory appropriate for the platform you're installing. In our examples, our hardware platform is based on the Intel x86 architecture. Setup directories also exist for Alpha and MIPS platforms.

NOTE If you're starting an installation of SMS on a Windows NT server that has previously had SMS (or any of its components) installed on it, you must do the following:

1. Remove the hidden file named SMS.INI from the server. This file will be located in the C:\ directory of the server.
2. Remove any references to SMS that are located in the registry running the Windows NT registry editor (REGEDIT.32). Remove any references to SMS found in the registry key named \HKEY_LOCAL_MACHINE by using the Find Key option in the View menu. Search for all occurrences of the string SMS with the Match Whole Word Only box cleared. When a key is found containing the string SMS, delete it (along with any of its subkeys). ■

In our example, we'll install the x86 version of SMS on the same server on which we installed SQL Server. We begin the installation from the BackOffice or SMS CD-ROM as follows:

1. Log on to the server under an administrative account (this account must belong to the NT local Administrators' group and the Global Domain Administrators group). Find the proper installation directory on the CD-ROM for your server platform type (Alpha, MIPS or X86), and run the Setup program it contains. Note that you can use the following optional switches with the setup command:

   /TRACING:on—this switch will cause tracing to be started on all Windows NT computers running SMS services in the site.

   /noacctcheck—this switch is used to bypass the verification of the SMS Service Account. Use this switch when: The SMS Service Account will be a user account from a trusted domain; and the SMS Service Account does not have an account in the site server domain; and the user account you used to log on to the site server does not have access to the domain containing the SMS Service Account.

If this switch is not used, the Setup program will by default verify that the SMS Service Account and SMS SQL logon ID both exist, and that they both have the required account permissions.

NOTE If you're using a user account from a trusted domain as the SMS Service Account and that user account does not exist on the current site server domain, you will need to log on to the site server domain, using an administrative account (an account belonging to both the local Administrators and the Global Domain Administrators' groups).

In addition, that administrative account must have access to the trusted domain containing the SMS Service Account. If the trusted domain containing the SMS Service Account is inaccessible, use the /noacctcheck switch with the setup command. ■

2. Click the Continue button when the Welcome screen appears. SMS build and setup version information is then displayed, followed by the registration screen. Figure 6.1 shows the registration screen. Type in the following information:
   - User Name—name of the registered owner of the software
   - Organization—name of your company or organization
   - Product ID—number used when working with Microsoft technical support

   Click the Continue button once to bring up the verification screen. Verify that the information is correct and click the Continue button again. If the information is incorrect, go back and make any necessary changes before you proceed (see fig. 6.1).

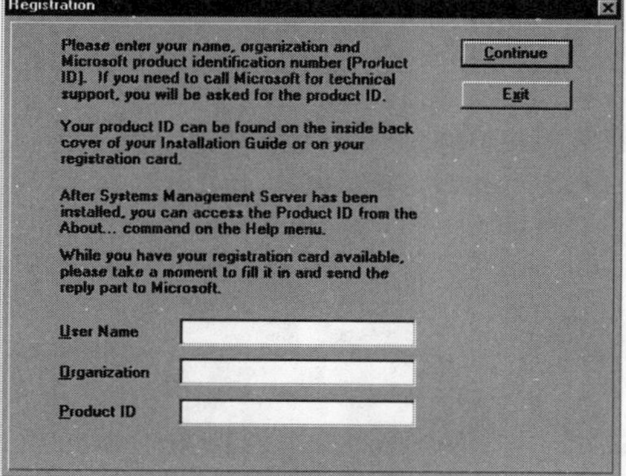

FIG. 6.1 Supply the registration information.

3. The next screen (see fig. 6.2) will present the installation options available. Click the Install Primary Site button.
4. Read the software licensing information, check the I agree that: box and then click the OK button. The next dialog box contains information on the prerequisites that must be completed prior to installing SMS. If you've been following our installation example, then

these requirements have been met, and you can click the Continue button. If the prerequisites have not been met, you must cancel the setup and complete them before attempting to install SMS again.

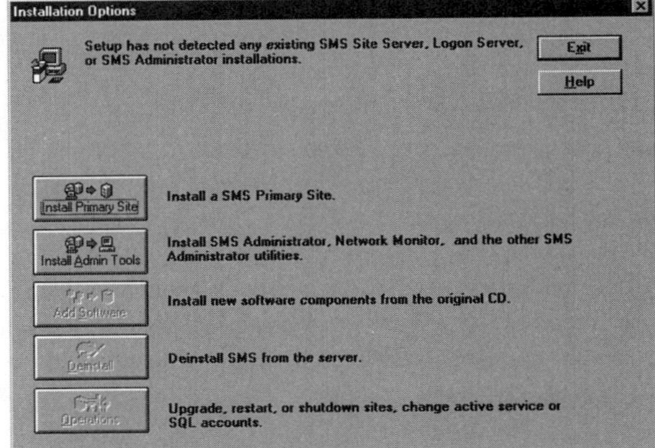

FIG. 6.2
Choose Install Primary Site.

5. The next dialog box (see fig. 6.3) will prompt you for the installation directory. Accept the default (*drive*:\SMS) or enter the location of your choice. Make absolutely sure your target destination has a minimum of 100MB of available space and is located on an NTFS partition before proceeding. You must specify both the drive and the target directory. By default, SMS uses the root of the NTFS drive containing the most available drive space to install the \SMS directory. We'll accept the default destination in this example and click the Continue button.

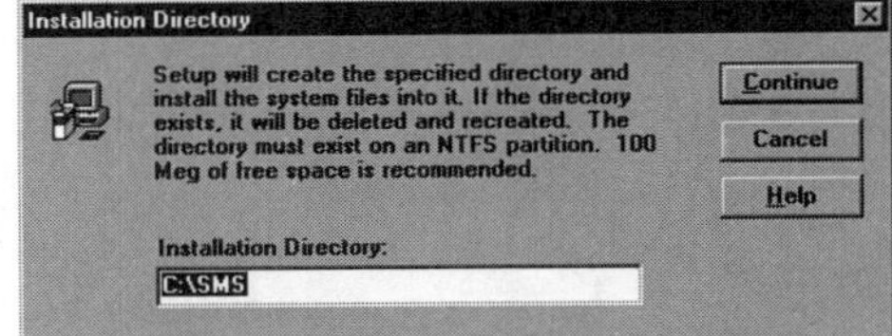

FIG. 6.3
Specify an NTFS destination drive containing at least 100MB of free space.

NOTE The directory name you specify will be the name used when creating the root SMS directory on all the site's logon servers. Since LAN Manager and NetWare servers use the 8.3 naming convention, you must specify an SMS directory name that conforms to the 8.3 naming convention if you are using (or will be using) LAN Manager or NetWare servers as logon servers. ■

6. The Setup Install Options dialog box, shown in figure 6.4, will then display the default components that will be included in the installation.

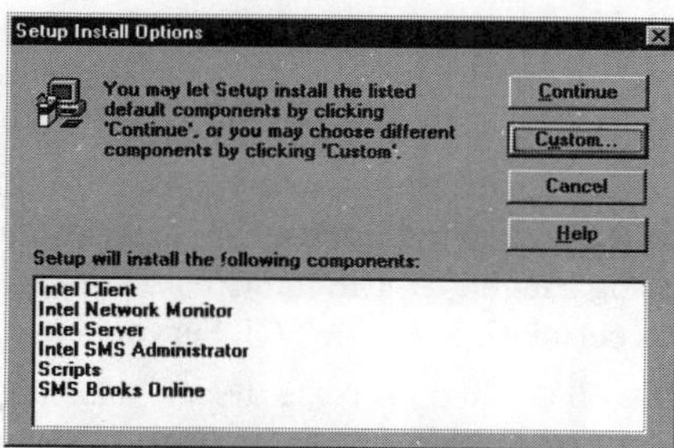

FIG. 6.4 The installation defaults are displayed.

You may add or remove components by clicking the Custom button to display the Software Installation Options dialog box (shown in fig. 6.5). We'll accept the default for our example and click the Continue button.

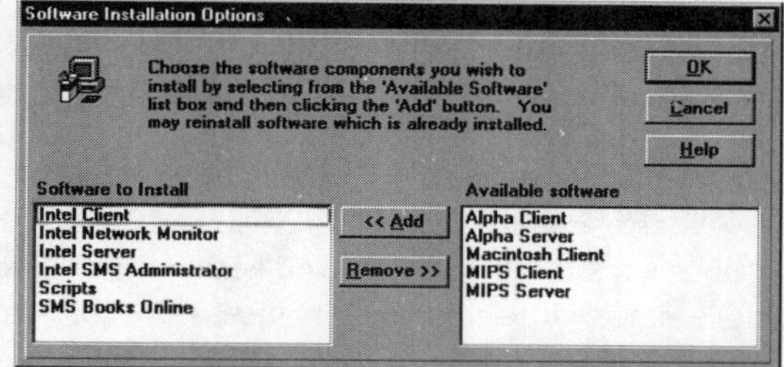

FIG. 6.5 You may add or remove components at this time.

NOTE If you want to support hardware platforms at your site (or in secondary sites) with processors different from the processor in the server you are currently installing (Intel versus MIPS), choose the Custom button to add support for other platform type(s).

For example, to add an Alpha logon server to a site using an Intel site server, you must add the Alpha components using the Custom button. This additional support can also be added any time later by running the Setup program.

7. The dialog box shown in figure 6.6 will prompt you for the following information on the SQL Server to be used with SMS:

SQL Database Configuration

SQL Server Name	HC40SERV
SQL Login	sa
Password	
Confirm Password	
Database name	SMS
Database device	SMSData
Log device	SMSLog

Continue
Exit
Help
Device creation...

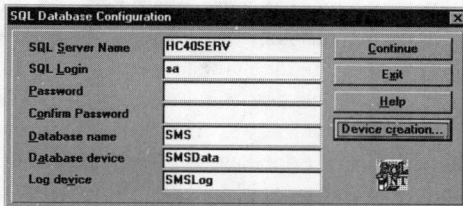

FIG. 6.6 Provide the information on the SQL Server to be used with SMS.

- SQL Server Name—provide the name of the SQL Server that will contain the site database. This can be any SQL Server that the SMS site server has access to. If this is an SQL Server that is not physically located on the SMS site server, the SMS database devices (data and log devices) must be created at the SQL server before continuing the Setup program. After the devices are created, you can create the site database using a logon ID with the Create Database, Dump Database, and Dump Transactions permissions on the SQL Server's master database.
- SQL Login—this ID will be used to create the site database on the target SQL server during the setup procedure. The SQL Logon ID specified in this box will be used by SMS services (such as the SMS Executive and Site Hierarchy Manager) when accessing the site database. The account must have database owner (dbo) privileges to the site database.
- Password—provide the password for the SQL logon ID.
- Confirm Password—retype the password.
- Database Name—specify a name for the SMS site database. The name must follow the SQL Server rules for identifiers (a name from 1 to 30 characters long, with a first character consisting of a letter or the symbols @ or _). The default name is SMS. You may also use the name of an existing database that is accessible by the site server. When using the name of an existing database, insure the database is free from any useful information that you wish to keep. The database name is not case-sensitive, since we selected a "case-insensitive sort order" during the SQL installation.
- Database Device—specify a name for the device that will store the site database. The name must follow the SQL Server rules for identifiers (a name from 1 to 30 characters long, with a first character consisting of a letter or the symbols @ or _). The default name is SMSData. The only database allowed on the device is the SMS database. You can specify the name of an existing device (that is accessible by the site server) as long as this device is free of any other databases. The Setup program will attempt automatically to create the SMS database on the device during installation. If another database is found, you will be prompted to delete it, or you will be forced to go back and specify (or create) another device.
- Log Device—specify a name for the device that will store the site database's transaction log. The name must follow the SQL Server rules for identifiers (a name from 1 to 30 characters long, with a first character consisting of a letter or the symbols @ or _). The default name is SMSLog. The transaction log will use the entire device. You can specify the name of an existing device (that is accessible by the site server) as long as this device is free of any other databases. The Setup program will attempt automatically to create the transaction log on the device during installation. If another database is found, you will be prompted to delete it, or you will be forced to go back and specify (or create) another device.

Fill in the information for each of the fields.

If you set up SQL Server on a separate computer, you must supply the name of that server. This SQL Server must have had the SMS database and log devices created on it in advance. Since we're installing SMS on the same server on which we've installed SQL, the SQL Database Configuration dialog box will allow us to create the SMS-related database devices at this time.

8. Click the Device Creation button to bring up the SQL Device Creation dialog box. This dialog box allows you to configure the size and location of the site database and transaction log. You'll be asked to complete the following information:
   - Database Device—displays the name of the device used to store the site database. This item was specified in step 7 and is shown here for informational purposes only.
   - Path—(Database Device) this entry specifies the path (and name) of the actual database device file. The default name and path of the file is *drive*:\SMSDATA\SMS.db. The default drive is where the SMS site server components were installed. If you specify a directory path that does not exist, the Setup program will prompt you to create it.
   - Size—(Database Device Size) allows you to specify the size of the database device in megabytes. The size will default to 45MB. This device cannot be used for any purpose other than holding the site database.
   - Log Device—displays the name of the device used to store the site transaction log. This item was specified in step 7 and is shown here for informational purposes only.
   - Path—(Log Device) this entry specifies the path (and name) of the actual log device file. The default name and path of the file is *drive*:\SMSDATA\SMS.log. The default drive is where the SMS site server components were installed. If you specify a directory path that does not exist, the Setup program will prompt you to create it.
   - Size—(Log Device Size) allows you to specify the size of the log device in megabytes. The size will default to 8MB. This device cannot be used for any purpose other than holding the site transaction log.

The defaults shown here (see fig. 6.7) will provide adequate space for storing the inventory information for approximately 2,200 PCs.

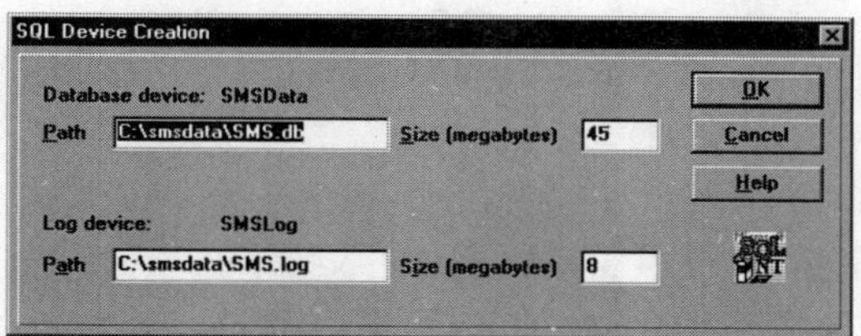

FIG. 6.7 Create the SMS database and log devices.

Table 6.1 can be used for determining the size of your SMSData and SMSLog devices.

Table 6.1

Determining the Size of the Data and Log Devices

# of PCs	SMS Data Device Size	SMS Log Device Size	TempDB Size
250	5MB	5MB	20MB
500	10MB	5MB	20MB
1000	20MB	5MB	20MB
2000	40MB	8MB	20MB
5000	100MB	20MB	20MB
10000	200MB	40MB	40MB
20000	400MB	80MB	80MB
50000	1GB	200MB	200MB

The general rule for estimating the size of the different devices is as follows:

- SMSData device—allow at least 20K for every PC that will be on the SMS system.
- SMSLog device—20 percentof the SMSData device size, with a 5MB minimum size.
- TempDB device—20 percent of the SMSData device size, with a 20MB minimum size.

This dialog box also allows you to choose the location of the devices. Accept the defaults or modify them to suite your installation, then click the OK button to return to the SQL Database Configuration dialog box.

9. Confirm that the SQL Login box contains the name "sa" and that the password boxes are blank (see fig. 6.6) and click the Continue button.
10. The Primary Site Configuration Information dialog box appears, prompting you for the Site and Service Account information, as follows:
    - Site Name—this is a three-letter site designation that is unique across the SMS system. No two sites within the SMS system may have the same three-letter designation.
    - Site Server—the name of the SMS site server that you are setting up. This will be the computer name you assigned to the machine during the NT Server portion of the installation.
    - Site Server Domain—the name of the domain that the site server belongs to.

    Begin by entering the Site Code, which can be any three-letter combination of alphanumeric characters. Special characters are not allowed.
11. Enter an appropriate name for your SMS site in the Site Name box. This can be any descriptive name you like.

12. Insure the name of your server appears in the Site Server box.
13. Insure the correct domain name is present in the Site Server Domain box.
14. Check the Automatically Detect All Logon Servers box.

    When this box is checked, all of the site server domain's logon servers will automatically be enumerated and added to the SMS site. This includes Windows NT Servers acting as primary domain controllers (PDCs), backup domain controllers (including LAN Manager version 2.x BDCs), and servers in the domain. LAN Manager PDCs and BDCs will be enumerated, but LAN Manager member and stand-alone servers will not. All NetWare versions 3.x and 4.x (running bindery emulation) servers will be detected and enumerated. Detection of Novell servers can take place over as many as 16 router hops. Checking this box will also cause the Site Configuration Manager to monitor continuously for any new logon servers being added to the network. If any are detected, the new logon server is automatically configured and added to the SMS site.

    If this box is cleared, the only server added to the site is the site server itself. All other servers will have to be manually added to the site using the Site Properties dialog box.

CAUTION

Do not check this box if you're using several SMS sites that have servers belonging to the same domain. In other words, clear this box if the NT (or LAN Manager) domain spans several sites.

15. In the Server Account portion of the dialog box, you are prompted for the user name and password of the SMS Service Account. This is one of three service accounts we set up immediately after the NT Server installation. (For more information, see the section "Creating the Service Accounts" in Chapter 3, "Understanding Domains, Sites, and the SMS Hierarchy.") The name you specify may be a local user account, or it may be a user account from a trusted domain.

    - Local Domain Account—a local domain account is specified by simply typing the local user account ID (the local ID designated as the SMS Service Account) in the Username box.
    - Trusted Domain Account—precede the user name with the name of the trusted domain in which the SMS Service Account resides. For example, if the SMS Service Account we wanted to use was an account from a trusted domain named "CORPHQ," we would type in the name as CORPHQ*username*. Keep in mind that this trusted user account must have the appropriate privileges that will allow the SMS Site Configuration and Maintenance Managers to access and maintain the local domain's logon servers. It must also have the appropriate rights to any subsequent domains that are added to the site. Also bear in mind that the trusted account will be used for any further domain additions to that site, even if a duplicate account with exactly the same name and password exists on the local domain. This implies that if you're using a trusted SMS Service Account, the trusted account must have the proper privileges in all subsequent domains that are added to the site.

NOTE The user account you specify will be the user account that SMS uses in any subsequent domains that are added to the site. This account must have the proper permissions in each domain that will allow the Site Configuration Manager and Maintenance Manager to access any logon server in the added domain(s). In addition, both the Package Command Manager and the SMS Inventory Agent are installed on any added domain using this account. ■

Enter the name and password of the SMS Service Account in the appropriate boxes, as shown in figure 6.8. Reconfirm the password and click the Continue button.

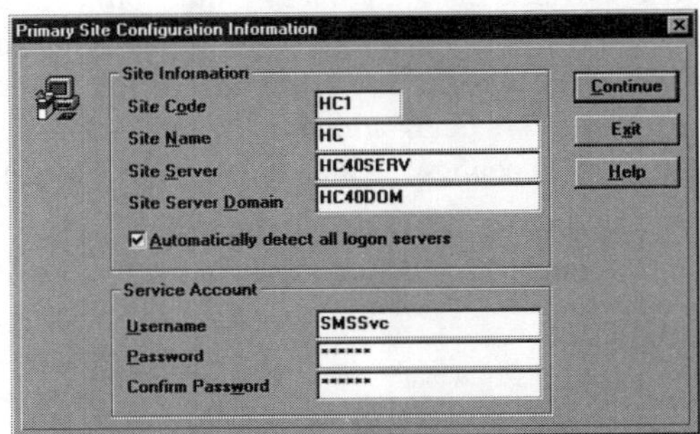

FIG. 6.8
Enter the SMS Service Account information.

At this time the Service Account and password will be validated, the file installation will take place, and the database devices will be created. The Setup Progress screen is as shown in figure 6.9.

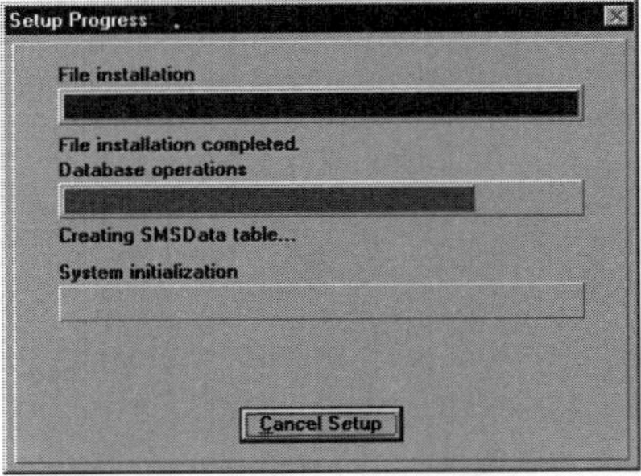

FIG. 6.9
The Progress screen.

16. If you chose to install the Network Monitor, the screen shown in figure 6.10 will appear.

    This dialog box gives you the option of installing the Network Monitor components now or at a later time. For our installation example, we'll install the Network Monitor now. Read the screen and click the OK button to include the setup of the Network Monitor in the installation process. The SMS Setup program will continue to run in the background while you set up the Network Monitor. When the setup completes, the message shown in figure 6.11 will appear, to indicate that the setup was successful.

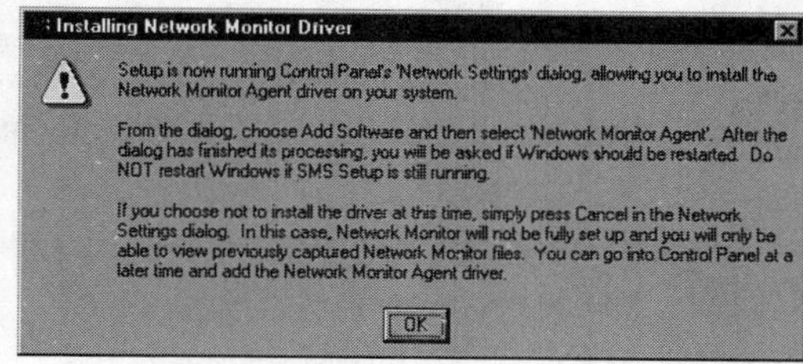

FIG. 6.10 Follow the instructions in the dialog box to install the Network Monitor.

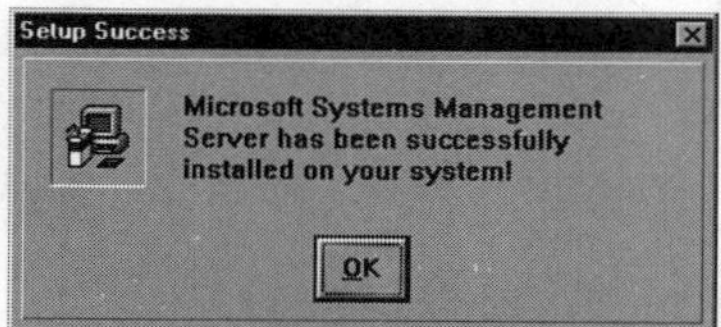

FIG. 6.11 SMS has been set up successfully.

17. To add the Network Monitor, choose Add from the Services tab, then select "Network Monitor Agent and Tools" from the Network Service option list (see fig. 6.12) and click the OK button. Then click the Close button.

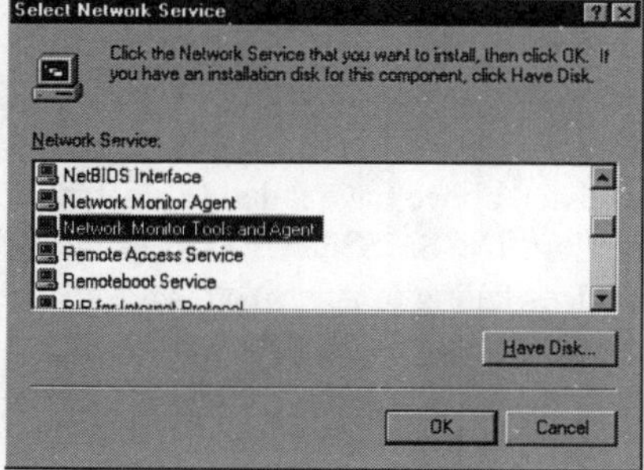

FIG. 6.12 The Network Service options list.

The service installation will take place, followed by the Restart message, as shown in figure 6.13. DO NOT restart Windows if the SMS Setup program is still running in the background. Note that the Setup program will continue to run in the background while you set up the Network Monitor. If the SMS Setup program completes by the time you get the Restart message, you may go ahead and click Yes to restart Windows without any problems. If the Setup program is still running, click No and restart the server after the SMS Setup program completes.

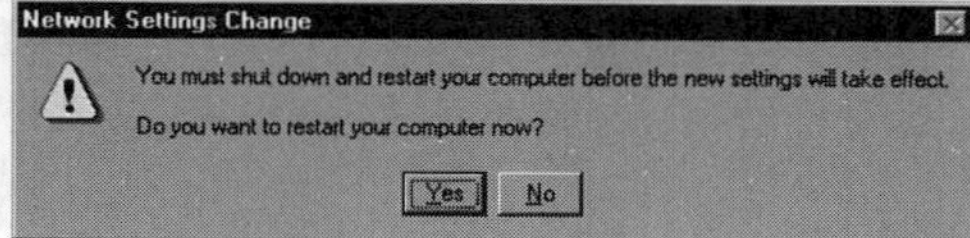

FIG. 6.13 Restart the computer when the installation is complete.

After restarting the server, log back on under the same administrative account you used previously. Check to see if the SMS services have been started properly by opening the Services icon in Control Panel (see fig. 6.14). Make sure the following services have started:

- SMS_CLIENT_CONFIG_MANAGER (the SMS Client Configuration Manager)
- SMS_EXECUTIVE (the SMS Executive)
- SMS_HIERARCHY_MANAGER (the SMS Site Hierarchy Manager)
- SMS_INVENTORY_AGENT_NT (the SMS Inventory Agent for Windows NT)
- SMS_PACKAGE_COMMAND_MANAGER (the SMS Package Command Manager for Windows NT)
- SMS_SITE_CONFIG_MANAGER (the SMS Site Configuration Manager)

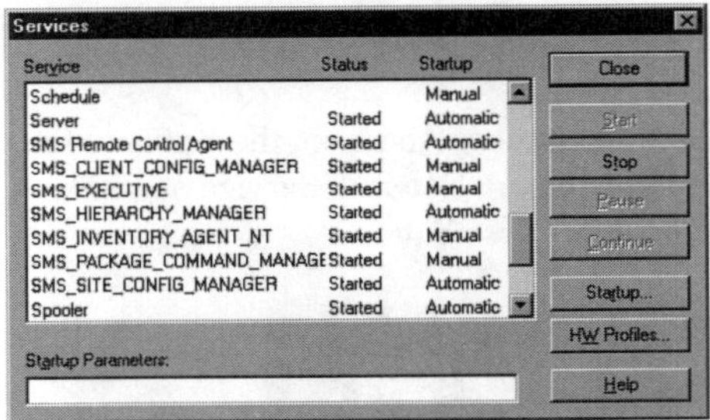

FIG. 6.14 Verify that the SMS services have started.

If you find that any of the services listed above have failed to start, check for error messages in the Windows NT Application event log. The SMSSETUP.LOG is another source of information when resolving problems with services failing to start. You can also use the SMS Service Manager to take a look at the ten secondary services (not shown in Control Panel) to see if they're running. The SMS Service Manager allows you to turn on Tracing logs for each of the SMS services. These logs can be used later when troubleshooting problems with the system.

What Happens During the SMS Setup?

After the configuration information has been entered, the Setup program attempts to verify that the SMS Service Account you specified is a valid user account in the site server's domain. Next, the two SQL database devices (named SMS.DB and SMS.LOG) are created in the target directory you specified (in step 8 of the SMS 1.x setup). If either the Service Account validation or the device creation fails, you will be returned to the appropriate screen to re-enter the missing or invalid configuration settings.

Next, the minimum user connection setting in SQL Server is checked. If this value is not set to 20 or higher, the Setup program will prompt you to increase the number. If you have other databases running on the same SQL Server, you should add at least 20 user connections to the present number. See the Chapter 5 section titled "Configuring the SQL User Connection Setting" for instructions on increasing the value.

The next event is the actual file installation of the SMS components. The files will be installed into the location we designated (in step 5 of the SMS 1.x setup). After the file installation, approximately 80MB of disk space will be consumed on the target drive by the SMS directory structure and its files.

After the files have been installed, the SQL SMS database is set up. Following this, two of the SMS services are started. The first service is the Site Hierarchy Manager, and the second is the Site Configuration Manager. In turn, the Site Configuration Manager starts the SMS Executive, Package Command Manager for Windows NT, and the Inventory Agent for Windows NT services.

The SMS Setup program will then modify the NT registry to include the key named:

HKEY_LOCAL_MACHINE\SOFTWARE\Microsoft\SMS

The Site Hierarchy Manager creates a temporary site control image (*.CT1) file named:

drive:\SMS\SITE.SRV\SITECFG.BOX_INIT.CT1

The Site Configuration Manager then reads the site control image (*.CT1) file and uses the data contained in it to configure and modify the newly created NT registry key (including its subkeys). Based on this NT registry information, the Site Configuration Manager performs several actions related to creating and maintaining the site configuration. These actions include enumerating servers, adding SMS components to new logon servers, and adding domains and their associated components.

When the Site Configuration Manager is finished, it reports any actions that were performed back to the Site Hierarchy Manager in the form of a another file called a site control (*.CT2) file. The Site Hierarchy Manager uses the information contained in the *.CT2 file to update the SQL SMS database.

During the setup routine, a new program group named Systems Management Server is created. The icon for the SMS Service Manager can be found in this newly created program (shown in fig. 6.15). It will contain icons for all the SMS components you install.

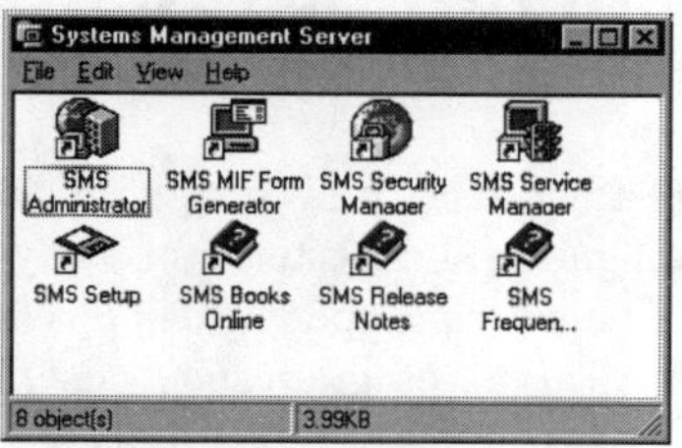

FIG. 6.15
The System Management Server program group is added to the desktop.

Before we go any further, let's take a brief look at the utilities contained in the Systems Management Server program group.

What's in the SMS Program Group?

You'll notice the new SMS program group contains icons for the following utility programs:

- SMS Administrator—the tool used to do most of the administrative tasks within SMS. This is the tool we'll use later in the chapter when installing secondary site servers, logon servers, helper servers, and distribution servers. We'll also use it to configure the different Senders that are needed for site-to-site communications.
- SMS MIF Form Generator—allows you to create custom information forms that can be distributed to the users on your network. Users fill in these forms, which the SMS system then retains in its database for administrative use.
- SMS Security Manager—use this tool to grant users access to the SMS administrative functions.
- SMS Service Manager—can be used to start or stop SMS services or Tracing (service logging) on any site, helper, or NT Server-based logon server.
- SMS Setup—used when upgrading, installing, or deinstalling SMS components.
- SMS Network Monitor (optional)—gives you a tool for examining real-time and statistical information on your network's activity.

In addition, the online Help File icon will be displayed. You will also find the latest release notes and frequently asked questions in the form of Help File icons in this program group.

Each of the utility programs will be covered in more detail later in the book. But before we continue with the rest of our examples, we need to become more familiar with the functions of the SMS Administrator program. We'll use this utility to configure logon servers, helper servers, distribution servers, and site connections later in the chapter. It will also be used when configuring client computers for automatic inclusion in the SMS inventory system.

▶ For a complete look at the SMS Administrator program and all its functions, see Chapter 8, "Using the SMS Administrator Program."

Accessing the SMS Administrator Program's Installation Functions

Logon, helper, and distribution servers are installed and configured using the SMS Administrator program. It's also utilized when configuring site-to-site connectivity and when using the Automatically Configure Workstation Logon Scripts option to set up client inventory. For this reason, we need to take a look the Administrator program and its user interface.

The SMS Administrator must establish a connection to the SQL Server that contains the SMS database before you can manage the site. Starting the utility will bring up the Microsoft SMS Administrator Logon box. The server name, database, user ID, and password fields will be blank if this is the first time you've run the SMS Administrator. Subsequent starts of the Administrator program will have the name, database, and user ID fields filled with the values used in the previous startup.

NOTE Access to the SMS database is controlled using one of the three SQL Server Security modes. The Standard, Integrated, and Mixed modes of security are discussed in the Chapter 5 sidebar, "The SQL Security Modes." Our example installation uses the SQL Setup's default Standard mode, which requires that a valid SQL account and password be provided before a connection is established to the SQL Server. ■

You'll need to supply the appropriate values for the fields listed below:

- SQL Server Name—the name of the SQL Server the SMS database resides on.
- Database—the name of the SQL database that SMS uses to store information. By default, the name of the database is SMS.
- Logon ID—ID of an SQL account that has system administrator privileges on the database.
- Password—the password used with the Logon ID.

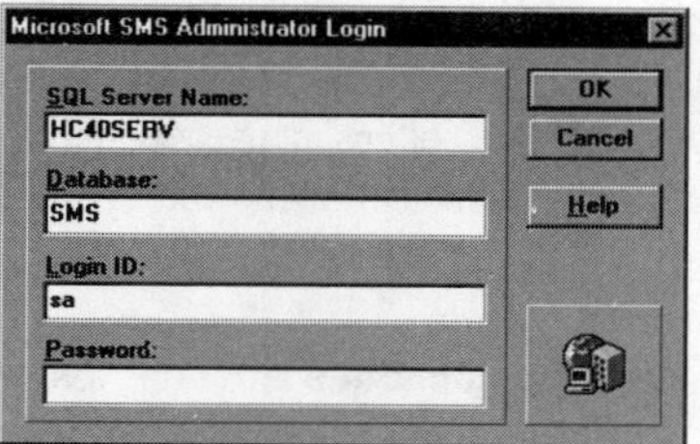

FIG. 6.16 Enter the logon information when starting the SMS Administrator.

Follow the steps below to log on to the SMS Database (fig. 6.16 shows the completed logon screen for our example):

1. Type the name of the SQL Server where the SMS database is located in the SQL Server Name box. In our example, the server name is HC40SERV.
2. Type the name of the SMS database in the Database box. The name of the database in our example installation is SMS. This is also the default database name used by the SMS Setup program.
3. Type in the name "sa" for the Logon ID. This SQL user ID can be used if you are logged on as a member of either the NT administrators or the domain administrators groups. If you are not logging on as a member of one of these groups, you must log on to the SQL Server using an account with dbo (database owner) privileges on the SMS database.
4. Supply the password for the logon ID. In our example, we can leave the Password field blank, since we're using an account with "sa" privileges.
5. Click the OK button.

Next, the Open SMS Window dialog box will appear (see fig. 6.17) and display a list of window types that are available. Each different window type represents a different view or management function available in the Administrator program. A description is given for each window type as it is highlighted.

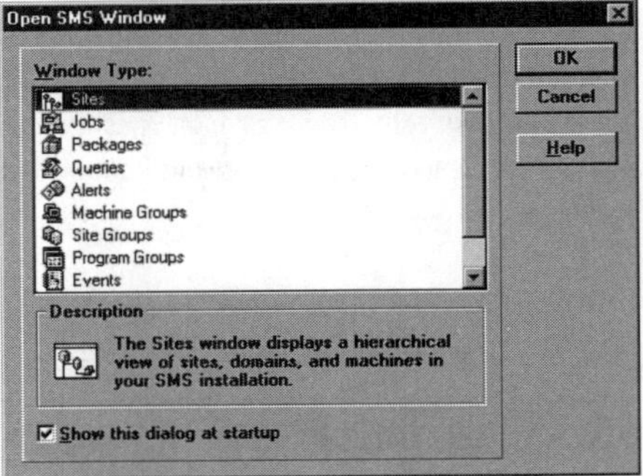

FIG. 6.17
The Open SMS Window.

NOTE This dialog box will appear by default each time you start the Administration program unless you clear the Show This Box At Startup box located at the bottom of the window. Since the Administrator program will recall and reopen any windows that were open when the Administration program was last shut down, it is not necessary to choose a window type every time the Administration program starts. If needed, the Open SMS Window dialog box can be accessed at any time by choosing Open from the File menu. In addition, buttons for each window type (with the exception of SQL Server Messages) are located on the toolbar (the toolbar is shown above the Sites windows in fig. 6.18). ■

At this time all the windows, with the exception of Sites and Queries, will be empty. The Sites windows will contain an icon representing the SMS site that was just created when we installed SMS. The Queries window contains some predefined queries that can be run against the database.

Choose Sites from the Window Type box and click the OK button. The Sites window shown in figure 6.18 appears, giving us a hierarchical view of our SMS system. The window is divided up into right and left viewing panes. The left pane displays the site hierarchy, using the DMTF (Database Management Task Force) standard tree structure, with icons representing site and domain objects. The right pane displays any SMS objects (sites, domains, or servers) that are contained within the object being highlighted in the left pane. The tree in the left pane can be expanded or collapsed by using the options located in the Tree menu at the top of the screen, or by double-clicking the appropriate icon.

Figure 6.18 shows us a view of the site we have just installed, with the tree expanded. Highlighting the domain name shows us the SMS object(s) within the domain. At this point, the only object in the domain is our SMS server named HC40SERV.

To complete the rest of the installation tasks, we'll use the Site Properties dialog box. This dialog box (see fig. 6.19) is opened by highlighting the site icon in the left pane and choosing the Properties option from the File drop-down menu.

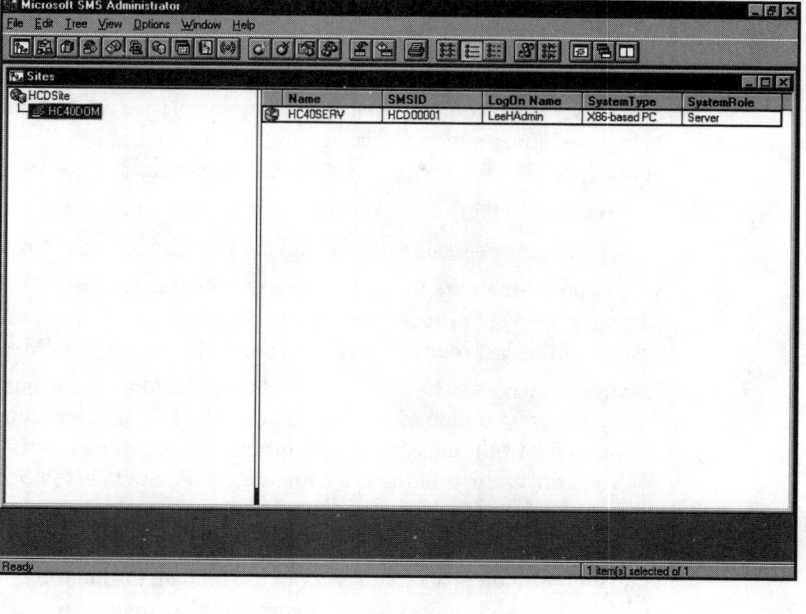

FIG. 6.19
Continue the installation using the Site Properties dialog box.

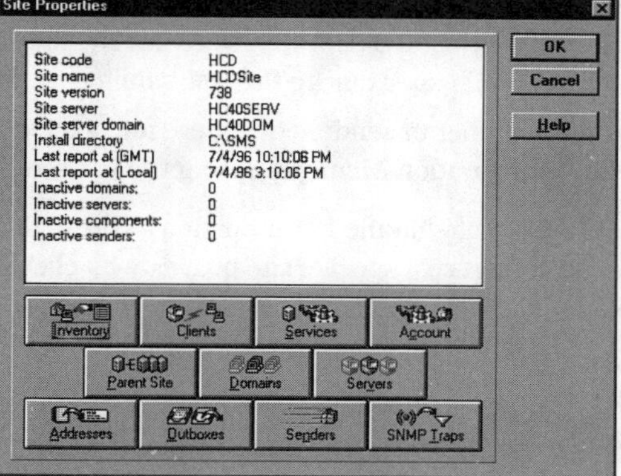

We will continue installing the other components using the site property buttons found in this dialog box. Let's begin by taking a closer look at the information displayed in the Site Properties dialog box, as follows:

- Site Code—the unique three-character code used to identify the site. This code is used in site-to-site communications.
- Site Name—a text label used to identify the site within the Inventory window of SMS.
- Site Version—the version number of the SMS components installed at the site.
- Parent Site—the name of the SMS site that is directly above the current site in the SMS hierarchy. The parent site will receive all inventory information from the current site;

in turn, the inventory of the current site will appear in any site above it in the SMS hierarchy. If no parent site is displayed, the current site is considered a central site at the top of the SMS hierarchy.

- Site Server—the computer name given to the NT server running the SMS components being used to monitor and manage the site. For a primary site, the computer must be running NT Server; secondary site servers can run NT Workstation.
- Site Server Domain—the name of the domain in which the site server resides.
- Install Directory—designates the full path of the SMS root directory on the site server.
- Last Report—the time the last site control file was processed by the Site Configuration Manager. Current property settings in a site are based on the last report that occurred at this time. The last report is given in both GMT (Greenwich Mean Time) and local time.
- Inactive Domains—when the Site Configuration Manager is unable to verify the existence and configuration of a domain during the last monitoring interval, the Inactive Domains field will reflect a number other than zero. Refer to the Events window of the SMS Administrator and the NT Event logs to find detailed information on any inactive domains or their components.
- Inactive Servers—when the Site Configuration Manager is unable to verify the existence and configuration of a logon server in the domain during the last monitoring interval, the Inactive Servers field will reflect a number other than zero.
- Inactive Components—the number of SMS services or components (located on the site server and any logon servers in the site) that were not started (and could not be started) by the Site Configuration Manager during the last monitoring interval.
- Inactive Senders—the number of senders that were not started (and could not be started) by the Site Configuration Manager during the last monitoring interval.

The Site Property buttons are located in the lower portion of the dialog box. Each of the buttons allows you to view and configure a specific site property by clicking it. Let's look at each of the buttons in more detail.

Inventory

Choosing this button allows you to set the frequency at which the Inventory Agent scans computers in the site for software and hardware inventory. It also allows you to configure how the inventory is collected over slow links (such as RAS links). The frequency is defined as follows:

> The amount of time between the last hardware or software scan and when the next hardware or software scan is invoked.

Scans may be run automatically during the execution of the user logon script or they can be invoked directly from the command line by running the SMS client batch file. Both hardware and software inventories can be set for different frequencies if desired. Any changes made to the frequency of the software or hardware inventory collection settings will apply to all clients within a site.

Figure 6.20 shows the Inventory dialog box. When the radio button next to the Current Properties option is marked, the properties will all be grayed out (except for the Current and Proposed property options) and cannot be changed. This reflects the current property settings in effect at the site.

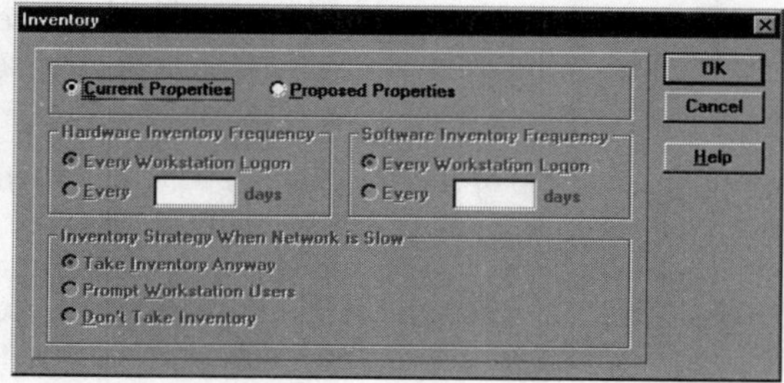

FIG. 6.20
The current settings for inventory collection are shown in the Inventory dialog box.

The Inventory Properties The Inventory dialog box allow us to change two properties related to the site's inventory collection frequency, and one property that lets us establish how logons over a slow network link are handled. We'll start with the two properties related to the inventory collection frequency.

Collection Frequencies You can specify separate settings for each of the properties listed below:

- Hardware Inventory Frequency—determines the frequency at which the hardware inventory data is collected from the client machines.
- Software Inventory Frequency—determines the frequency at which the software inventory data is collected from the client machines.

Each of these two frequency settings has the same options available, as follows:

- Every Workstation Logon—specifies that the scan should take place every time Inventory Agent is invoked. The Inventory Agent is invoked either by running an SMS-enabled logon script, or by manually running the SMS batch file.
- Every (*x* days)—specifies that the scan should take place only if the set number of days have passed since the completion of the last scan. This means that when a user logs on a consecutive number of times within a short period, a scan will not be taken each time. If the designated number of days has not passed, the scan will not be taken.

Scans can take 30 seconds or longer, and some users will find it annoying to have SMS scan their workstation every time they log on. This is especially true if your users are working in a software development or test environment. Make sure you consider those users when setting up the hardware and software scanning frequency on your SMS sites.

Setting the Inventory Strategy The other property that we can modify in the Inventory dialog box is the Inventory Strategy When Network Is Slow option. This setting becomes important if you have users who are automatically running the SMS script file during logon *and* the user is making a connection via a slow link, such as Remote Access Service (RAS), using an asynchronous modem.

Login Servers serve as inventory collection points, and they can be configured to collect inventory automatically when a user logs on. For this reason, a remote user logging on who runs the SMS logon script may experience a considerable delay while the Inventory Agent runs over the slow link. The typical logon period over an RAS connection using a 28.8 VFC modem can be from five to ten minutes. This is unacceptable in most situations.

Fortunately, this property provides an option for handling slow links without disabling the SMS logon script for the user. This is done using the SMS logon script's Netspeed program. This program will detect the speed of the network link and automatically set an error level code. This error level code then determines how the rest of the script file executes, by causing the script file to branch in a manner consistent with the desired inventory strategy.

▶ For a closer look at the SMS script file (SMSLS) and the SMS batch file (RUNSMS), see the Appendix B section titled "SMSLS/RUNSMS."

The execution of the logon script will continue in one of three ways, based on the Inventory Strategy When Network Is Slow setting you make. The available options are as follows:

- Take Inventory Anyway—causes the Inventory Agent to collect inventory data even if a slow network connection to the logon server is detected.
- Prompt Workstation Users—allows the user to skip the inventory scan when a slow network connection to the logon server is detected.
- Don't Take Inventory—automatically skips the inventory scan when a slow network connection to the logon server is detected.

Changes to the site configuration using the Inventory dialog box (or any other site configuration dialog box) are permitted only when the button next to the Proposed Properties option is marked. And then once the modifications are made, they won't take effect until the changes have been processed by the SMS system.

Let's go over this process in more detail and see what happens when you make a site configuration change.

Making a Change to the Site Properties In order to make changes to the frequency settings (or the inventory strategy over a slow network link), you must first mark the radio button next to the Proposed Properties option. Then the other configuration options in the dialog box will be available for editing, as shown in figure 6.21.

At this time you can make changes to any of the available settings contained in the dialog box by marking the appropriate buttons and typing in any additional information that may be needed. Then click the OK button to initiate the change.

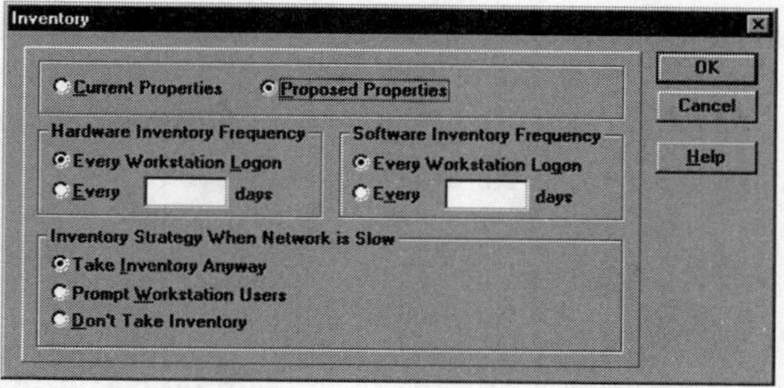

FIG. 6.21 Marking the Proposed Properties button allows you to modify the site inventory properties.

Changes made to the configuration will not take effect immediately. The time it takes to complete the changes will depend on the type of changes that are being made and the location of the site in which they are being made. A modification to the current site will be implemented before that of a child site.

The following list describes what takes place after a change is made to the site's configuration properties:

NOTE The following uses the Inventory dialog box properties as an example, but it actually outlines the steps taken by SMS whenever a change is made to *any* site. This includes the rest of the configuration properties found in the other site configuration dialog boxes, and not just the properties contained in the Inventory dialog box. ■

1. Database information related to the site's inventory configuration is modified when changes are made to the frequency or slow link properties in the Inventory dialog box.
2. The Site Hierarchy Manager service will detect the change(s) to the site database and either create a site control image (*.CT1) file (if the modification is to the current site), or create a System Job (if the modification is to a child site).
3. The site control image (*.CT1) file is used by the Site Configuration Manager at the target site to make the modifications to the site.
4. Once the modification(s) have been made, the Site Configuration Manager reports completion of the change(s) back to the Site Hierarchy Manager in the form a site control file (*.CT2) file. If the change was made at a child site, the Site Configuration Manager at the child site will also create a System Job to report the changes to the parent site.

NOTE Any site configuration changes implemented on a site will be reported to all sites that are above the current site in the SMS hierarchy. This means that a change made by an administrator at a child site will be seen by the administrator of the parent site and, in turn, by the administrators of any sites above the parent site in the SMS hierarchy. ■

5. The Site Hierarchy Manager then uses the information contained in the site control file (*.CT2) to update the site database.
6. After the site's database has been updated by the Site Hierarchy Manager, the Inventory dialog box will reflect the new configuration parameters, with the Current Properties option marked.

Clients

Clicking the Clients button in the Site Properties window brings up the Clients dialog box. This box enables you to view and set the properties associated with the SMS client configurations at your site. As you can see in figure 6.22, the Clients dialog box is divided into two areas; each allows changes to different aspects of the client configuration.

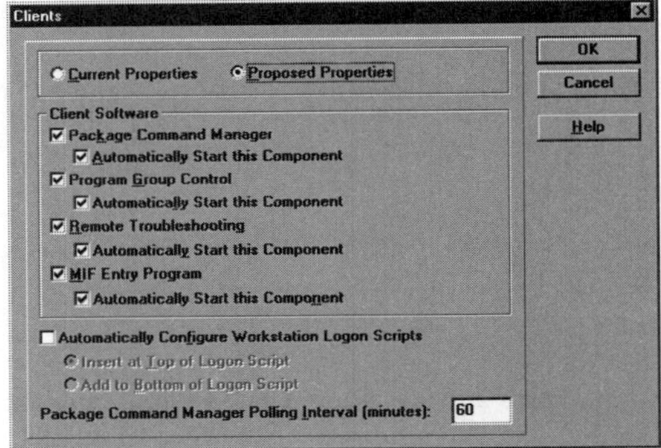

FIG. 6.22
Use the Clients dialog box to specify which client components are installed at your site.

Client Software This portion of the Clients dialog box lets you specify which of the client components will be installed at the user's machine when the SMS client Setup program is run. It also allows you to specify if the installed components will be started automatically during logon. Here's a closer look at each of the client components.

Package Command Manager (Clients) Check this box to install the client Package Command Manager (PCM). This is a program used by SMS to run package commands on the SMS clients. Package commands are commands placed in an SMS object called a package, which is created by the SMS Administrator to distribute and install software programs on the client machines within the site or its subsites. The package contains all the information needed to identify and install a specific software application on a client platform.

When a package is distributed to a client workstation for installation, the Package Command Manager allows the user to view the package and its description. Two types of packages are distributed to the client workstations.

With Optional Packages, users can choose to skip the installation if they wish. If a user decides to accept the package, the installation can be performed at his or her convenience. If the package is a Mandatory Package, it must be executed before the user will be allowed to continue working on the computer.

Clearing the box next to the Package Command Manager option will prevent the PCM from being installed on the client workstations during the SMS client installation. If the PCM components were already installed on the clients, clearing the box will cause the SMS system to remove the components from any client workstation in the site they are currently installed on.

Checking the Automatically Start This Component option will cause the PCM to start automatically when the workstation is started. The PCM for Windows 3.1, Windows for Workgroups, Windows 95, and Windows NT will start when the Windows environment is initialized. On MS-DOS workstations, the PCM is started as a program in the AUTOEXEC.BAT file.

Program Group Control (Clients) Check this box to install the Program Group Control (PGC) components (APPCTL and APPSTART) on the user workstations. This feature can be installed only on Windows 3.1, Windows for Workgroups, Windows 95, and Windows NT clients. PGC enables network applications so that they can be run over the network from distribution servers.

Clearing this box will prevent the PGC from being installed on the client workstations during the SMS client setup. It will also deinstall any PGC components currently installed on any client workstations in the site.

When the PGC components are installed, checking the Automatically Start This Component option will cause the PGC to start automatically when the Windows environment is started.

Remote Troubleshooting When this box is checked, the remote troubleshooting support components are installed on the client workstations. Remote troubleshooting support is required to be running on the client when using the remote help desk and remote diagnostic features of the SMS Administrator. Remote troubleshooting support can be installed on computers running MS-DOS, Windows 3.1, Windows for Workgroups, Windows 95, and Windows NT 3.51 and later.

Deselecting this box will instruct the SMS system to remove the remote troubleshooting support from the computers the next time the client Setup program is run.

Selecting the Automatically Start This Component option will cause the remote troubleshooting support to start automatically when the workstation is started. MS-DOS, Windows 3.1, Windows for Workgroups, and Windows 95 workstations run the Remote Troubleshooting agent (USERTSR.EXE) from the computer's AUTOEXEC.BAT file. Remote support is then available when the Windows environment is initialized and started. Windows NT machines run the Remote Troubleshooting agent as a service that is configured with the Auto Start option enabled.

MIF Entry Program (Clients) SMS installs the MIF Entry Program on all client computers in the site when this box is checked. MIF is an acronym for Management Information Format, a standard for accessing desktop information across different hardware and software platforms using an ASCII file that complies to a set of standard formatting rules. This program allows clients to enter information on forms that can then be kept in the SMS database for future reference. The forms can be generated using the MIF generator that's included with SMS software. The forms can be distributed automatically to be filled out by the users of the network's workstations. Forms can be created for a wide variety of purposes. Anything from user information to computer serial numbers can be stored in the database, using these forms.

Clearing the MIF Entry Program check box will cause SMS to deinstall the MIF Entry Program from all workstations at the site.

The Automatically Start This Component option will start the MIF Entry Program when the workstation is started. On clients running Windows 3.1, Windows for Workgroups, Windows 95, and Windows NT, the program will start when the Windows environment is started. MS-DOS machines start the program from the AUTOEXEC.BAT file during startup.

The Automatically Configure Workstation Logon Scripts (Clients) Option Checking this box allows you to have SMS automatically set up and maintain user workstations in the site. It does this by configuring the user logon scripts in LAN Manager and Windows NT domains to run the SMSLS script file as the user's logon script. In NetWare domains, the system logon script is modified on all servers in each domain. If the user already has a logon script, a call to the SMSLS batch file will be placed in the user's existing logon script. You can designate the location of the call statement in the user logon script by marking the Insert at Top of Logon Script button or the Add to Bottom of Logon Script button.

CAUTION

Before enabling this option, consider the number of users who potentially may be loading the SMS client components at the same time over your network. This can cause a strain both on network bandwidth and on network support personnel. Consider using a phased approach by adding clients to the system in smaller groups, which are more manageable and will cause less impact on both network and support resources.

Setting the Package Command Manager Polling Interval This property allows you to set the default polling interval that the client Package Command Manager uses when polling the logon server for new packages. The default polling interval is 60 minutes. This means that every 60 minutes the PCM will check with the logon server to see if any new packages are available for installation.

Services

Choosing the Services button from the Site Properties window (see fig. 6.23) will enable you to view and configure the properties for the SMS services at the site.

You can change both the location of services, and the frequency at which the services are set to monitor the site.

Specifying a Service Location You can move four of the SMS services off the site server on to helper servers. This can reduce the load placed on an overworked site server. The four services that may be moved off on helper servers are as follows:

- The Scheduler service
- The Inventory Data Loader service

- The Inventory Processor service
- The Despooler service

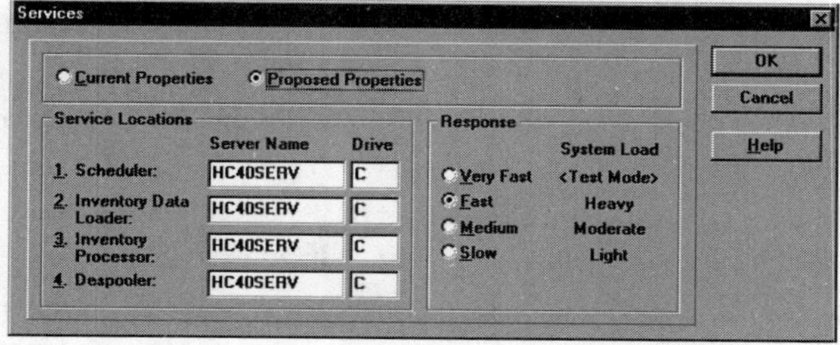

FIG. 6.23
Use the Services dialog box to change the location of a service.

The helper server must be a Windows NT Server running version 3.5 or higher. It must also have an NTFS partition on one of its drives. Specify a new location for a service by typing in the name of a Windows NT Server designated to be the helper server. Then designate one of the helper server's drives that has an NTFS partition.

Setting the Response Option This portion of the Services dialog box allows you to set the response time used by the services when monitoring the site. SMS services monitor the site database, SMS directories, and the system files on both the site server and logon servers. The faster the response time, the more frequently the services monitor the site. The more a service monitors a site, the more the service uses server resources, thus placing a heavier load on the server.

The Response setting controls the polling period that is used for each of the services. Table 6.2 shows the services that are effected by the Response property, along with the polling period (in minutes) used for each response rate setting.

Table 6.2

The Polling Time (in Minutes) for Each Response Rate Setting Will Vary Depending on the Service

Service Name	Slow	Medium	Fast	Very Fast
Site Hierarchy Manager	30	15	5	1
SMS Alerter				
SMS Scheduler				
Applications Manager				
Maintenance Manager	360	180	60	12
Site Configuration Manager	720	360	120	24
Despooler				

Each of the services will perform certain actions at each polling period that contributes to the operation of the SMS system. Following is a brief description of the actions taken by each service:

- Maintenance Manager—verifies that the correct and most current files are installed on all the sites' logon servers.
- Site Configuration Manager—checks active logon servers to ensure all SMS services are running.
- Site Hierarchy Manager, SMS Alerter, SMS Scheduler, and Applications Manager—these services check the site database for any changes.
- Despooler—setting the Response rate for the Despooler controls the retry rate at which the Despooler will attempt to process failed Despooler instructions.

CAUTION

Setting the Response rate at Very Fast will place a very heavy load on the server, especially in a large site. This setting is usually reserved for testing purposes only.

Accounts

The Accounts dialog box (see fig. 6.24) appears when you click the Accounts button, allowing you to change the SMS Service Account (and SQL Logon ID) used by SMS services.

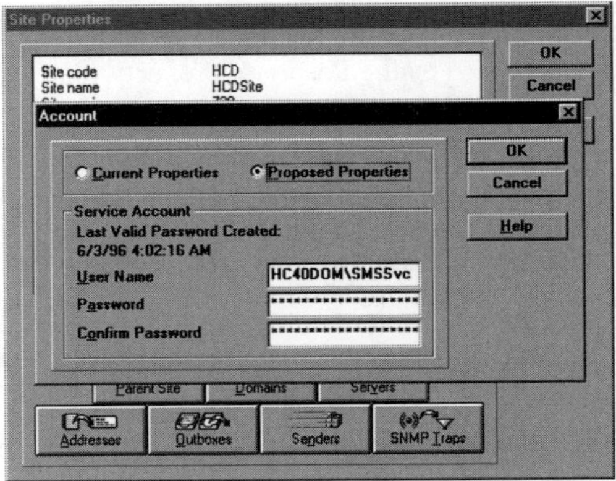

FIG. 6.24
The Accounts dialog box allows you to change the SMS Services Account.

Changing this dialog box affects only SMS services and not the actual user account. It does not actually configure the logon domain user account or password. This dialog box only specifies a user account name and password for the SMS services to use.

The Accounts dialog box prompts you for the following information:

- Username—the ID of the user account that will be used for running SMS services. This account must be a member of both the local Administrators' group and the Global Domain Administrator group.
- Password—for the user account designated for running SMS services.
- Confirm Password—confirmation for the SMS service account password.

CAUTION

It is suggested that when changing the Account properties you do not change just the password, but change both Username and Password.

Assigning the SMS Services to a new user account will prevent problems if the site server happens to get restarted during the configuration changes. By changing only the password, you risk the chance that the Site Configuration Manager will not be able to restart. This can happen because the new password may not have been processed by the time the server gets restarted. Since the Site Configuration Manager will try to use the old password to log on, the service logon will fail, which in turn will prevent the service from starting.

When a new account is created, the Site Configuration Manager service is still able to log on using the old account (and password) in the event the new account information has not been processed. Once logged on under the old Service Account, the Site Configuration Manager can continue to process the transition to a new account and password.

Parent Site

Choosing this button will display the Parent Site dialog box, as shown in figure 6.25. This dialog box allows you to view or set a parent site for the currently selected site.

FIG. 6.25
Use the Parent Site dialog box to create the SMS hierarchy.

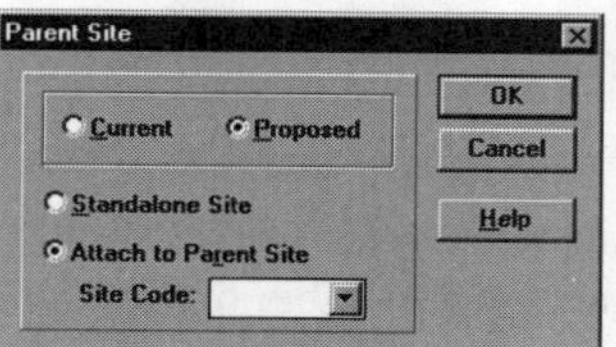

By designating parent sites, you are able to create the hierarchical site structure within the SMS system. The Parent Site dialog box contains the following properties:

- Stand-alone Site—the default setting when installing a site server, it designates the site as a central site. If the server already reports to a parent site, deselecting this option will cause the site to detach from the parent site.
- Attach To Parent Site—choose this option to attach the selected site to a parent site.
- Site Code—the three-letter code that describes the parent site. This code will be available in the drop-down box if an address to the parent has been defined.

When attaching to a parent site, you must set up an address for the parent site. You must also determine which sender will be used to access the parent site. By default, the LAN Sender is installed during setup. If the parent site is on the same LAN, you do not have to install another sender. If accessing the parent over Remote Access Service (RAS) or SNA LU 6.2 links, the proper sender must be installed.

In addition to the configuration needed at the current site (now the child site), you must configure the parent site with a sender that can communicate with the child site. An address for the child site must also be provided to the parent site.

Domains

This button opens the Domains dialog box, as shown in figure 6.26. It allows you to view, add, delete, and modify the properties for logon server participation for specific domains within the selected site. As you recall, a domain is a collection of servers and clients that are grouped together in an administrative unit. Using the Domains dialog box, you can selectively add and delete domains from the SMS site. You can also specify the way in which a domain's logon servers are added to the system.

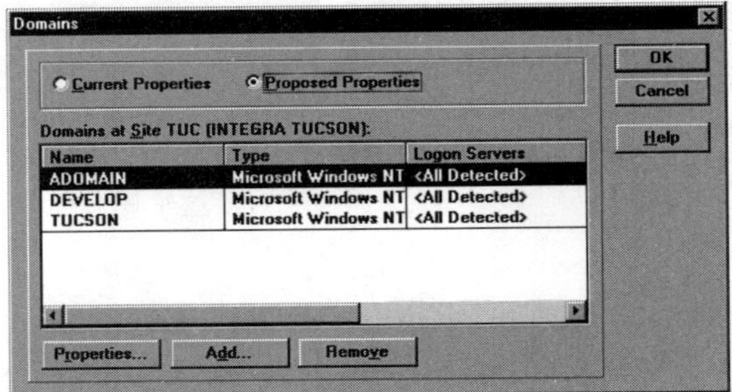

FIG. 6.26 Add or remove domains using the Domains dialog box.

The Domains at Site *sitecode* (*sitename*) dialog box will show you the domains that are currently members of the site. The following information is displayed:

- Name—designates the names of any domains that are currently members of the site. By default, the site server's domain is always a member of the site.
- Type—specifies the type of operating system being used on the (*name*) domain. The domain types will be either Microsoft Windows NT/LAN Manager or Novell NetWare version 3.x or later.
- Logon Servers—displays the names of the (*name*) domain's logon servers that are running SMS components. If the Use All Detected Servers option is used, the text <All Detected> will be displayed, indicating that all of the (*name*) domain's logon servers are participating in the SMS system.

Properties To view the current properties of a domain, highlight the domain name in the domains list and click the Properties button (or just double-click the highlighted name). All of the information shown is grayed out and cannot be changed unless the Proposed Properties button in the Domain dialog box is marked. With the Proposed Properties button marked (as shown in fig. 6.27), we can specify how the logon servers in the currently displayed domains are added to the SMS system.

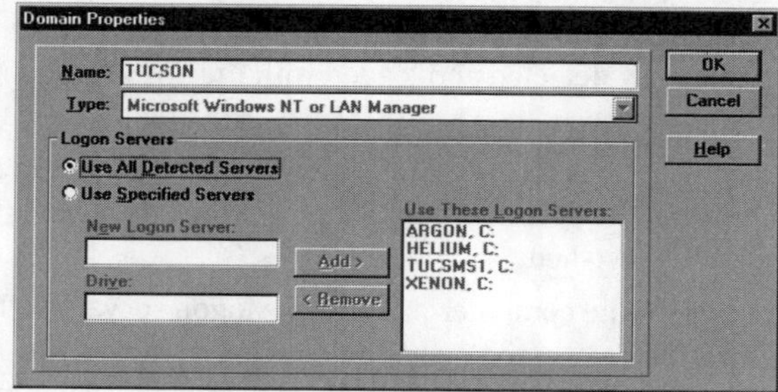

FIG. 6.27 Designate how logon servers are detected, using the Domains dialog box.

The first option is to have all logon servers in the domain automatically be detected. SMS will find all logon servers in the target domain and install the proper SMS components on each, allowing them to act as logon servers.

The second option is to specify logon servers in the target domain which will receive the SMS components and participate as SMS logon servers.

Note that the Name and Type properties are still grayed out and cannot be changed. These can be entered only when adding a new domain. In order to change either of these, you must create a new domain entry.

Add Domain The Add button is used when adding a domain to the current site. It can be used only when the radio button next to the Proposed Properties option is marked. Choosing this button brings up the Domain Properties dialog box, as shown in figure 6.28.

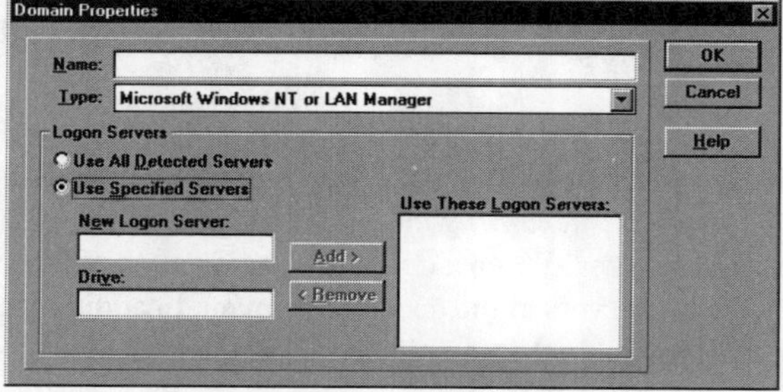

FIG. 6.28 Specify the Name, Network Operating System type, and detection method when adding domains.

Provide the following properties with the appropriate values:

- Name—designates the name of the domain that will become a member of the site. We will call this the target domain.
- Type—specifies the type of operating system being used on the target domain. The domain types will be either Microsoft Windows NT/LAN Manager or Novell NetWare.

- Logon Servers—allows you to choose the method of logon server detection used.
- Use All Detected Servers—if the Use All Detected Servers button is marked, all logon servers in the target domain will be detected, and the SMS components will be installed on them automatically. Also, when new logon servers are added to the target domain, they are automatically detected and loaded with the SMS components.
- Use Specified Servers—if you mark the Use Specified Servers button, each logon server in the target domain must be specifically identified and added. In addition, you must designate a drive on the specified logon server, which designates where the SMS components will be installed.
- New Logon Server—the computer name of the logon server (in the target domain) that you want to load the SMS components on. The logon server you specify here can be added to the list of SMS logon servers for that domain by using the Add button.
- Drive—designates the drive on the New Logon Server box where the SMS components will be installed.
- Add—adds the server specified in the New Logon Server box to the domain list. This button is available only when the Use Specified Servers option is marked.
- Remove—removes the server highlighted in the Use These Logon Servers list from the domain. This button is available only when the Use Specified Servers option is marked.

CAUTION

If you select the Automatically Configure Workstation Logon Scripts option as a method of adding users to your site, you must choose the Use All Detected Servers option when adding a domain to the site. Specifying the Use Specific Servers option will stop the Site Configuration Manager from setting up the logon scripts for users in the target domain.

NetWare domains can be set up with either box marked when the Automatically Configure Workstation Logon Scripts option is being used. This is because the Site Configuration Manager will always set up the system logon scripts on the NetWare file servers.

Remove Domain The Remove button is used to remove a domain that is currently listed in the Domains at Site *sitecode* (*sitename*) window. It can be used only when the button next to Proposed Properties is marked. When a domain is removed, the SMS components are removed from all the logon servers in the specified domain. In addition, any references to the SMSLS batch file that may be in the domain users' profiles will also be removed.

▶ For further information on the actions taken by SMS when adding or removing a domain from the site, see Chapter 12, "Changing Your Site Configuration."

Servers

Use this button to open the Servers dialog box, as shown in figure 6.29. This dialog box allows you to specify the names of servers in the site that will be members of the Default Servers machine group. This is a special machine group used by SMS to process jobs at target sites. Each site creates a default users machine group with the site server as its only member.

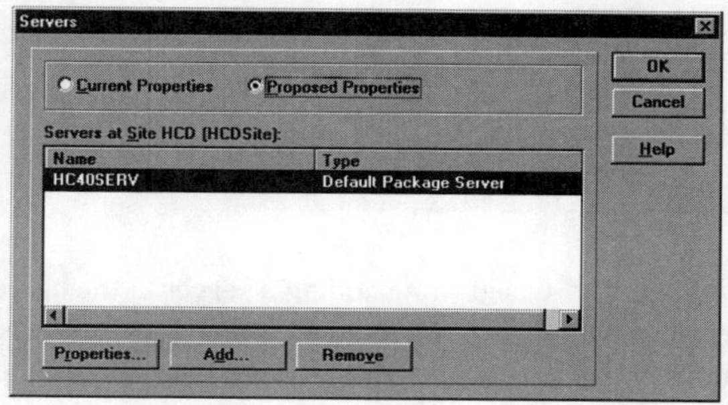

FIG. 6.29
The Servers dialog box specifies servers that are members of the default machine group.

Before we go any further, let's look at the meaning of the terms "machine group" and "jobs," as follows:

- Machine Group—a number of computers that are grouped together for administrative purposes. This allows the administrator of the SMS system to use the machine groups as targets for jobs. This provides an easy method of delivering jobs to a specific set of computers, without having to identify each one individually as the target of the job. Machine groups are also used to specify distribution servers for Run Command On Workstation and Share Package On Server jobs.
- Job—an object that stores instructions. SMS uses job instructions when delivering a software package or maintaining the system. The SMS administrator can create three types of jobs. The first allows the delivery of software packages to clients, the second lets the administrator share a software package over the network, and the third permits the removal of a package source directory from a distribution server. SMS also creates its own jobs for system maintenance.

The default servers machine group designates the servers where the source directories for software packages will be installed. But in order to do this, Default Servers must be selected as the target distribution servers for the package, and the target site cannot contain any servers specified by Put On New Distribution Servers.

The Servers at Site *sitecode* (*sitename*) box displays the following information:

- Name—displays the name of any servers that are in the default servers machine group.
- Type—displays the current role the server has in the SMS system.

Properties To view the current properties of a server that's listed, highlight the server name and click the Properties button (or just double-click the highlighted name). All of the information shown is grayed out and cannot be changed unless the Proposed Properties button in the Servers dialog box is marked. With the Proposed Properties button marked, you can edit the properties of the highlighted server, as shown in figure 6.30.

- Server Name—allows you to edit the current name of the server in the default servers machine group.
- Server Type—used to specify the role of the server in the SMS system. The role of a server in the default servers machine group is always a Default Package Server. You cannot change this option.

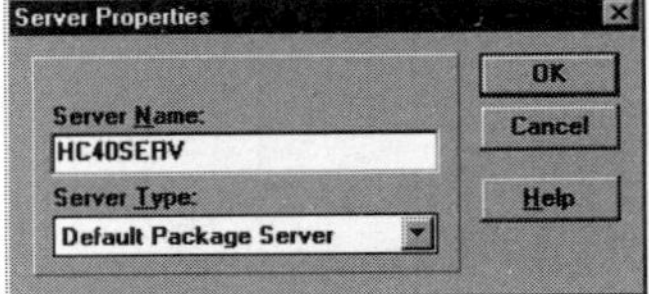

FIG. 6.30
Edit the Server Name using the Server Properties dialog box.

Add Server The Add button is used when adding a server to the current default server machine group. It can be used only when the radio button next to Proposed Properties is marked. Choosing this button brings up the Server Properties dialog box, as shown in figure 6.31.

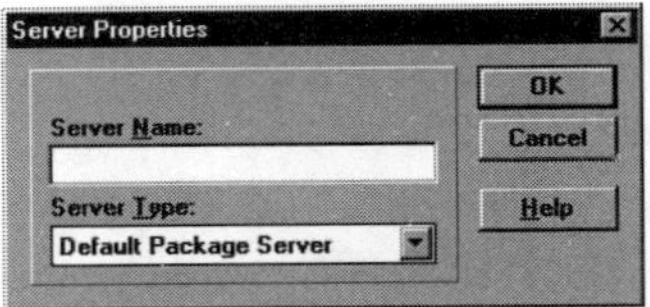

FIG. 6.31
Adding a new server to the default servers machine group.

The only property you can set in the Server Properties dialog box is the server name. By default, the Server Type is set to Default Package Server and cannot be changed.

Remove Server The Remove button is only available when the Proposed Properties button is marked in the Servers dialog box. It allows the removal of a server from the default servers machine group.

Addresses

Clicking the Addresses button will allow you to edit the properties in the Addresses dialog box, as shown in figure 6.32. An address contains information used when connecting to other SMS sites. The Addresses dialog box lets you edit that information. It is one of the two configuration properties that must be configured when building an SMS hierarchy of parent and child sites (using the Parent Site dialog box described earlier). The other property that must be configured is the Sender, which will be discussed later in the chapter.

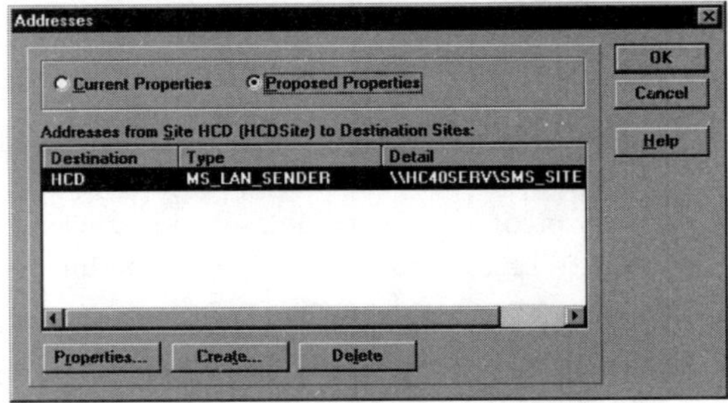

FIG. 6.32
View and modify connection information in the Addresses dialog box.

The Addresses from Site *sitecode* (*sitename*) to Destination Sites window lists the addresses currently set up for site-to-site communication. The site that the currently selected server resides in will (by default) have an address and appear on the list.

Here's a look at the information fields shown in the Addresses dialog box:

- Destination—the site code for the currently displayed destination site entry.
- Type—the type of Sender being used with the corresponding destination site entry. Senders may be specified for use over LANs, Remote Access Service (RAS) connections using ASYNC or ISDN, and SNA LU 6.2 links in both batch and interactive mode.
- Detail—gives us a look at the specific address being used for the Sender entry Type. This may reflect a UNC path to a server if using a LAN Sender, or it can be a phone book entry when using a RAS Sender over an asynchronous modem. By default, the Detail will show the UNC path to the site server.

Properties To view the current properties of a specific address, highlight the destination site's entry in the Addresses from Site *sitecode* (*sitename*) to Destination Sites listing, and click the Properties button (or just double-click the highlighted entry). All of the information shown is grayed out and cannot be changed unless the Proposed Properties button in the Addresses dialog box is marked. With the Proposed Properties button marked, modifications can be made to the currently highlighted entry.

Create Address The Create button allows you to set up the destination, type, and detail information needed for communication with another site. This button is active only when the Proposed Properties button is marked. Clicking the Create button displays the Address Properties dialog box, as shown in figure 6.33.

FIG. 6.33 Create a new Address when setting up site-to-site communication.

From this dialog box you must specify the following properties:

- Destination Site Code—the three-letter site code of the destination site.
- Type—the type of Sender that will be used for communications to the destination site.
- Details—you supply the connection details by clicking this button. The addressing details that you supply will vary according to the type of Sender you have chosen to use.

Each of the connection types have different configuration requirements which are based on the physical method of transport they use. To accommodate the different connection methods, SMS uses a Sender (an SMS component controlled by the SMS Executive service) to send instructions and data from on site to another. Each physical method of connection between sites has a specific Sender that must be used with it. For example, on a Local Area Network where site servers are connected directly via high-speed network lines, the LAN Sender would be used. On sites being connected over dial-up phone lines, the Async RAS Sender would be used. Here's a look at the different Sender types and the detailed properties information you must supply for each one of them.

LAN Sender The LAN Sender (MS_LAN_SENDER) is used when the destination site can be accessed over an established LAN (or a WAN with high-speed links). Choosing the Detail button reveals the dialog box shown in figure 6.34, which will require you to provide the following connection information:

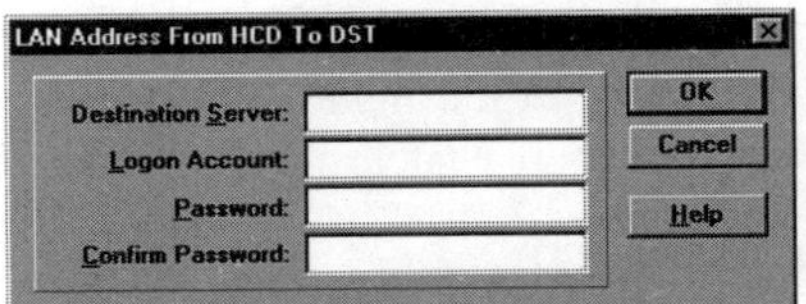

FIG. 6.34
You must provide the server name and logon information when creating a LAN Address.

- Destination Server—supply the server name of the destination server in this box. This is the NetBIOS name used to identify the server on the network or domain.
- Logon Account—the account that will be used when accessing the destination site. It must have the appropriate privileges to its directory structure and files. Change or Full Control permissions are required on the destination site's SMS_SITE share, in addition to Read and Write permissions on its SITE.SRV\DESPOOLR.BOX\RECEIVE directory. You can specify the name of a local domain account or one from a trusted domain. To specify an account from a trusted domain, precede the user name with the name of the trusted domain (*domain\username*). When a trusted domain account is specified, it must also have the necessary permissions required for accessing the destination server's directories and files. Since this trusted account will be used even if an identical account exists in the local domain, the destination site domain must trust the domain that the specified trusted user account resides in.
- Password and Confirm Password—you must supply and confirm the logon password for the Logon Account.

RAS Senders Three types of Remote Access Service (RAS) Senders are available for connecting sites. The ASYNC RAS Sender (MS_ASYNC_RAS-SENDER) is utilized when asynchronous modems and dial-up phone lines are used for connecting sites. The ISDN RAS Sender (MS_ISDN_RAS_SENDER) is used when ISDN connectivity exists, and the X.25 RAS Sender (MS_X25_RAS_SENDER) is used when X.25 connections exist between sites. Clicking the Details button with any of the three brings up the common dialog box that they share (shown in fig. 6.35). Both the RAS Access and Destination Access information must be provided. RAS Access fields require information needed to dial up or connect to the destination site's RAS Server. Destination Access fields contain information needed when accessing a specific destination site server's directories and files.

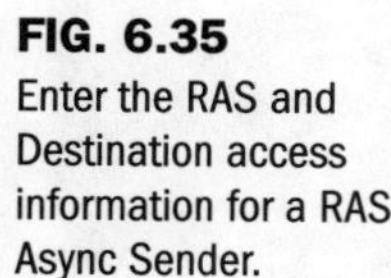

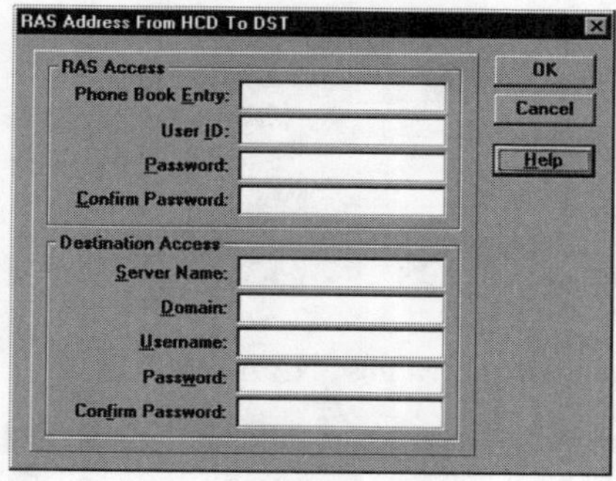

FIG. 6.35
Enter the RAS and Destination access information for a RAS Async Sender.

You must furnish the appropriate information for each of the following properties:

- Phone Book Entry—the name of an entry defined in the local site's RAS phone book. This entry will be used when making a connection to the destination site. Each phone book entry contains the information needed to dial up or connect to the RAS Server at the destination site. When specifying a phone book entry, make sure that you use the proper phone book for the Sender Type you are using. For example, if using an ISDN RAS Sender, you must choose a phone book entry from the ISDN phone book.
- RAS User ID—the RAS user account specified here is used when making the connection to the destination site's RAS Server. You must make sure that this account has RAS dial-up permissions on the destination site's RAS Server.
- Password/Verify Password—provide and verify the password for the RAS User ID account.
- Server Name—identifies the name of the site server in the destination site.
- Domain—specifies the name of the domain that the destination server resides in.
- Username—the account name that will be used when accessing the destination site. It must have the appropriate privileges to the site server's directory structure and files. Change or Full Control permissions are required on the destination site's SMS_SITE share. In addition, Read and Write permissions are required on its SITE.SRV\DESPOOLR.BOX\RECEIVE directory.
- Password/Confirm Password—provide and confirm the password for the Username user account.

SNA Senders If you're running Microsoft SNA Server (Version 2.1 or higher) using LU 6.2 links on a domain in each one of the SMS sites, there are two types of SNA Senders available for your use. The BATCH mode SNA Sender (MS_BATCH_SNA_SENDER) is used when the SNA communication uses LU pairing set to #BATCH, and the INTER mode SNA Sender (MS INTER_SNA_SENDER) is used when the SNA communication uses LU pairing set to #INTER. You may install one or both Senders on a server, but you cannot install more than one Sender of each type. The same dialog box (shown in fig. 6.36) is used for configuring both of the SNA Sender types.

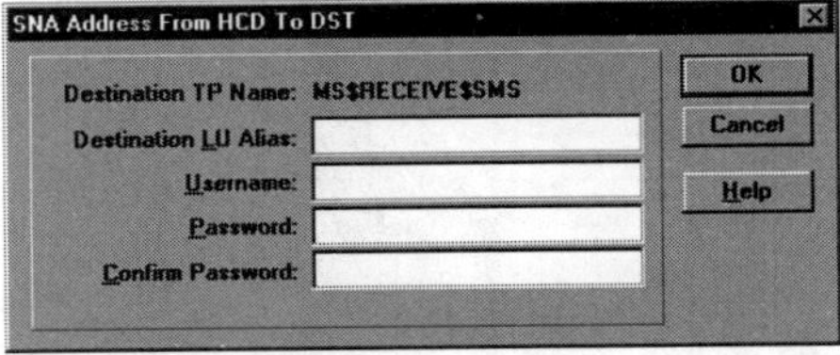

FIG. 6.36
Supply the LU Alias and username information when creating an SNA Address.

Provide the following information when creating SNA Addresses:

- Destination LU Alias—the name of the target site's LU alias. Each target site must have an SNA server running the SMS SNA Receiver with an LU alias defined. In addition, the current site must have an SNA Sender LU alias defined that is paired with that target site's LU alias.
- Username—the account name that will be used when accessing the destination site. It must have the appropriate privileges to the site server's directory structure and files. Change or Full Control permissions are required on the destination site's SMS_SITE share. In addition, Read and Write permissions are required on its SITE.SRV\DESPOOLR.BOX\RECEIVE directory.
- Password/Confirm Password—provide and confirm the password for the Username user account.

The other information shown in the dialog box is the Destination TP Name. It refers to the transaction program (TP) SMS uses at the target server to receive and process the data sent from the current site's SNA Sender. The data and instructions are placed in the target server's SITE.SRV\DESPOOLR.BOX\RECEIVE directory by the TP. From there, the data and instructions are processed by the Despooler service on the target site.

Delete Address The Delete button is available only when the Proposed Properties radio button is marked in the Addresses dialog box. It allows the removal of any address from the address listing.

Outboxes

Clicking the Outboxes button lets you view or set the properties in the Outboxes dialog box, as shown in figure 6.37. Outboxes are nothing more than a set of directories where send request files are placed. These files contain instructions for transferring data and instructions to the other sites linked by the various senders. In turn, each type of sender has its own separate Outbox (or directory) used to store the send request files specific to that sender.

Each of the six senders has an Outbox created by default during the installation of the site server. The properties for each one of the six resulting Outboxes are displayed in the Outboxes At Site *sitecode* (*sitename*) box, as follows:

- Name—text used to label the Outbox.
- Type—describes the type of sender that will use this Outbox. Each sender monitors its Outbox for send request files and processes them when detected.

- Server—name of the Server where the Outbox (directory) had been created.
- Drive—drive letter on the specified Server where the Outbox (directory) has been created.

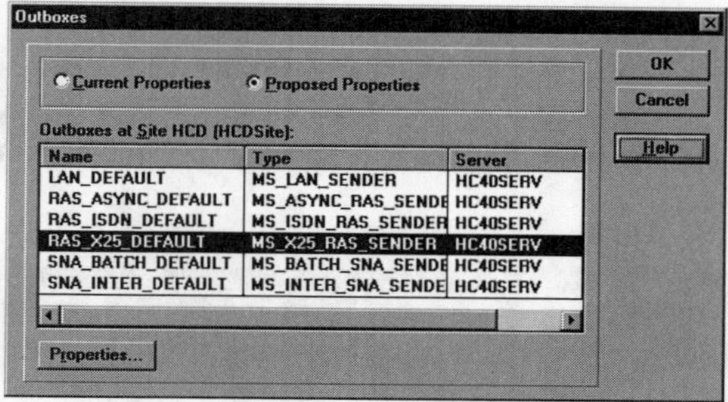

FIG. 6.37 The Outboxes dialog box allows you to specify directory and scheduling properties.

You may need to move the horizontal scroll bar at the bottom of the window to the right in order to see the Drive properties for each Outbox. Clicking on the Properties button while the Current Properties radio button is marked will allow you to view the properties associated with each Outbox. Clicking on the Properties button with the Proposed Properties radio button marked will allow you to edit the Name and Schedule properties on each of the Outboxes (see fig. 6.38).

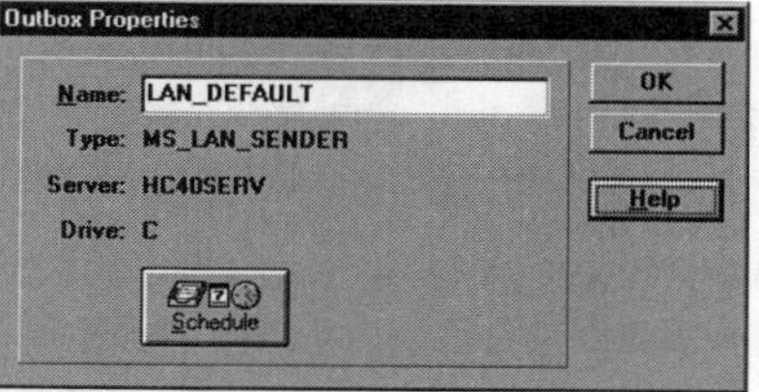

FIG. 6.38 You can edit the Name and Schedule properties from the Outbox Properties dialog box.

Clicking the Schedule button causes the Outbox Schedule dialog box to appear, as shown in figure 6.39. Each Outbox has its own schedule that its associated sender uses in determining when a job will be processed.

The schedule is divided up by the days of the week, and each day is then broken down into 24 one-hour increments in which job priority-level filters can be set. This allows the administrator to restrict the processing of jobs during a specific period of time, based on the priority level of the job. The different priority levels are as follows:

- Low & Up—used to allow the sender assigned to the Outbox to process all send requests for jobs. It includes any jobs with Low-, Medium-, or High-priority levels.
- Medium & Up—allows only Medium- and High-priority jobs to be processed by the Outbox's assigned sender. Low-priority jobs are not processed during periods designated with this priority level.

- High—only High-priority jobs are processed by the Outbox's assigned sender when this priority level has been designated. Low- and Medium-priority jobs will not be processed during any period designated as High priority.
- Closed—restricts the assigned sender for the Outbox from processing any send requests. No jobs are processed if this option is designated.
- Disable Backup—when a job cannot be sent for over 72 hours because the Outbox is unavailable to process it, the priority on the Outbox will be overridden to allow the job to be sent. This feature can be disabled for a specific period(s) of time using the Disable Backup option.

FIG. 6.39 Schedule the processing of jobs by priority using the Outbox Schedule dialog box.

For example, you can use the schedule to restrict all but high-priority jobs from being processed by the LAN sender during periods of high network traffic. Designating the different priority levels on the schedule can be done in several ways, as follows:

- You can choose an individual one-hour increment of time with the cursor, and then use the desired priority button (High, Medium & Up, or Low & Up) to mark it.
- The numbers across the top of the schedule can be used to mark the same one-hour time period on each day of the week with the priority level of your choice.
- Choosing a weekday from the left side of the schedule allows you mark an entire day.
- In addition, you can click a section of the schedule and drag the cursor across to combine several one-hour increments into a whole block of time. This entire block can then be marked with the priority level you want.
- Selecting the ALL button will allow you to mark the entire schedule with a single priority level.

By default the schedule is set to allow the assigned sender to process any job with a priority of Low and above. For example, the schedule in figure 6.40 shows modifications made to the LAN Default Outbox's schedule to prevent the network's bandwidth from being exceeded during weekday business hours (when network usage is at its peak).

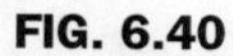

FIG. 6.40
Modify the schedule to reduce network traffic generated by SMS during business hours.

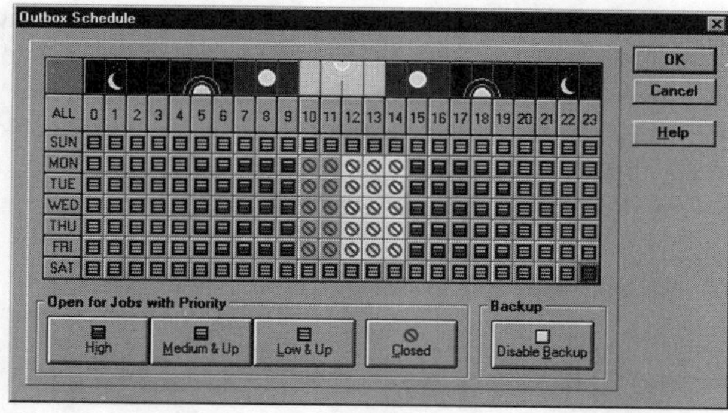

The example illustrates the ability to configure the Outbox Senders to process all send requests during evening hours and weekends. During business hours, the priority required varies from Low in the morning and late afternoon to a totally restricted schedule in the midday.

Senders

Choosing the Senders button allows you to view, modify, install, and remove senders in the selected SMS site. As we saw earlier in the chapter, SMS uses a sender (an SMS component controlled by the SMS Executive service) to send instructions and data from one site to another. There are six different types of Senders that can be installed on a site server, as follows:

- MS_LAN_SENDER—the LAN Sender is used when the destination site can be accessed over an established LAN (or WAN with high-speed links).
- MS_ASYNC_RAS-SENDER—utilized when asynchronous modems and dial-up phone lines are being used for connecting sites.
- MS_ISDN_RAS_SENDER—used when ISDN connectivity exists.
- MS_X25_RAS_SENDER—used when X.25 connections exist between sites.
- MS_BATCH_SNA_SENDER—used when the SNA communication configuration uses LU pairing set to #BATCH mode.
- MS_INTER_SNA_SENDER—used when the SNA communication configuration uses LU pairing set to #INTER mode.

The one you use will depend on the method of connectivity being used to connect the sites together. Each physical method of connection between sites has a specific sender that must be used with it. For example, on a Local Area Network where site servers are directly connected via high-speed network lines, the LAN Sender would be used. On sites being connected over dial-up phone lines, the ASYNC RAS Sender would be used. Each of the Senders and its properties are described earlier in the section covering creating addresses in Chapter 4, "Installing the SMS Site."

The Senders dialog box (shown in fig. 6.41) lets you view the name and location properties for any currently installed Sender. The Senders at Site *sitecode* (*sitename*) box displays the type of

Sender and the name of the Windows NT server the Sender component is installed on. Any Windows NT Server can run the Sender component, as long as it is in one of the site's domains. Clicking the Properties button with the Current Properties radio button marked will allow you to view the drive properties for the highlighted Sender (in addition to the Sender properties already displayed). The drive property specifies the drive letter on the NT Server where the SMS Sender components are installed.

FIG. 6.41
The Senders dialog box is used to view, modify, install, and remove Sender properties.

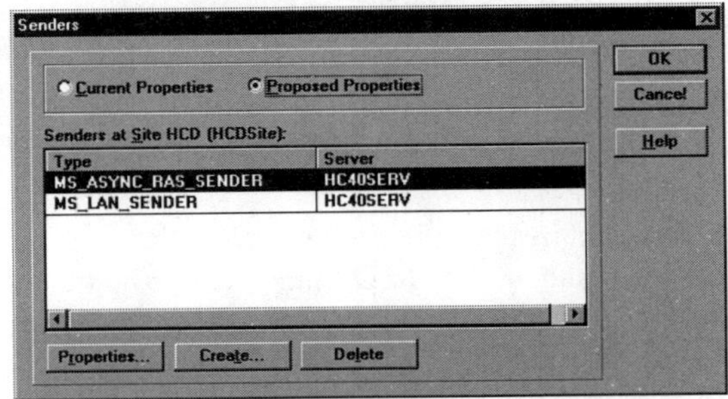

Marking the Proposed Properties button enables you to modify any current Sender properties, and also lets you install and remove Sender components.

Properties To view the current properties of a specific Sender, highlight the Sender's entry in the Sender at Site *sitecode* (*sitename*) listing, and click the Properties button (or just double-click the highlighted entry). All of the information shown is grayed out and cannot be changed unless the Proposed Properties button in the Senders dialog box is marked. With the Proposed Properties button marked, modifications can be made to the currently highlighted entry.

Create Sender The Create button allows you to set up the components for any of the six Sender types on any Windows NT Server in the site (or on any NT server belonging to one of the site's domains). This button is active only when the Proposed Properties button is marked. Clicking the Create button displays the Senders Properties dialog box, as shown in figure 6.42.

FIG. 6.42
Configure the Sender component(s) location using the Senders dialog box.

The Sender properties that need to be specified are the following:

- Ty—you must specify one of the six default Senders from the drop-down list.
- Server—specifies the name of the Windows NT Server where the Sender components will be installed. This must be an NT Server currently in the site or one of its domains.

- Drive—specifies the drive letter of the disk drive that will be used to hold the Sender components directory structure and its associated files. The disk drive letter must point to a valid drive on the NT Server specified earlier in the Server property entry.
- Details—this button is used only when creating (or modifying) SNA Senders. It allows you to add the additional configuration information that specifies what Sender LU Alias name will be used by the SNA Sender.

After a location has been specified, the SMS system will create an SMS root directory on the designated server and drive (if one does not already exist). It will then create the SITE.SRV\HELPER.SRV\X86.BIN directory on Intel-based servers, the SITE.SRV\HELPER.SRV\ALPHA.BIN on ALPHA-based servers, and the SITE.SRV\HELPER.SRV\MIPS.BIN on MIPS-based servers. In addition, the SMS system makes modifications to the server's registry to include configuration information for the Sender.

Delete Sender The Delete button is available only when the Proposed Properties radio button is marked in the Senders dialog box. It allows the removal of any Sender from the listing of site senders. Choosing this button will cause SMS to remove any Sender components from the NT Sever they were installed on. This includes removing from the server any directories, files, and registry references that are associated with the deleted Sender.

SNMP Traps

SNMP stands for Simple Network Management Protocol. It is a mechanism used for sending event information to network management applications when monitoring the network devices in a site. The SNMP Traps button, with its associated dialog box (see fig. 6.43), is a new site configuration property introduced with SMS version 1.2. It lets you modify, create, and delete filters that specify how SNMP traps are reported by SMS. SMS can both translate Windows NT Server events into traps, and also receive traps using the SMS Administrator.

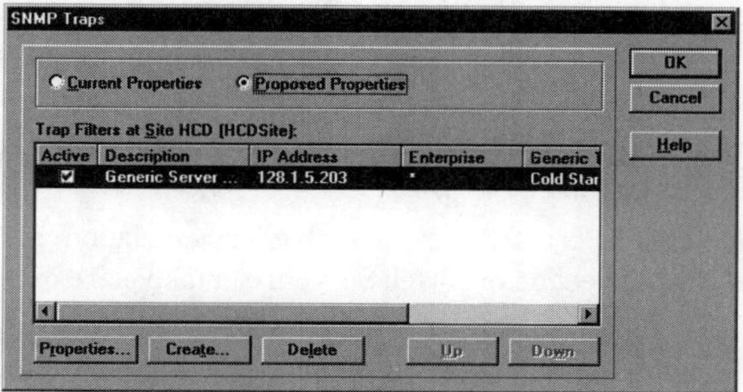

FIG. 6.43
SNMP Traps can now be configured with SMS version 1.2.

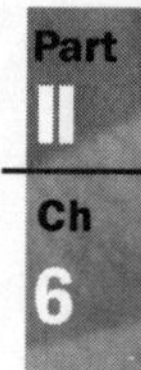

Since SNMP traps are used when monitoring a site, a complete discussion on SNMP Trap configuration will be found in the section entitled "Monitoring the SMS Site" in Chapter 15, "Changing Your Site Configuration."

We have now been introduced to the administrative interface's Site Properties dialog box and its different configuration options. Now we can begin to install additional Logon, Helper, and Distribution servers using the appropriate property dialog box.

Installing Logon Servers

Logon Servers are used by SMS to support the configuration, inventory, software distribution, and shared applications of the SMS clients in the logon (or account) domain the server resides in. The site server is configured as an SMS Logon Server by default during installation. Other logon servers will be included only if you chose the Automatically Detect All Logon Servers option during the setup of the SMS site server. SMS will allow you to change the detection method from automatic to manual, or manual to automatic. It also will let you control which servers are used as SMS Logon Servers when the manual configuration method is selected.

Modification of a site's Logon Server configuration is accomplished using the Domain Property dialog box, accessed using the Domains button in the Site Properties dialog box. Two options are available when configuring the site for SMS logon servers, as follows:

- Use All Detected Servers will cause all logon servers in the domain to be detected automatically. This is the default configuration. Any new logon servers that are added to the domain will automatically be configured with the SMS Logon server components.
- Use Specified Servers will require you to specify specific logon servers (including their destination drive letters) in the selected domain that will receive the SMS components and participate as SMS logon servers.

When the Use All Detected Servers radio button is checked, SMS will find all logon servers in the selected domain and will install the proper SMS components that allow them to act as SMS Logon servers. In addition, the following will happen:

- All of the site server domain's logon servers will automatically be enumerated and added to the SMS site. This includes Windows NT Servers acting as primary domain controllers (PDCs), backup domain controllers (including LAN Manager version 2.x BDCs), and servers in the domain.
- LAN Manager PDCs and BDCs will be enumerated, but LAN Manager member and stand-alone servers will not.
- All NetWare version 3.x and 4.x (running bindery emulation) servers will be detected and enumerated. Detection of Novell Servers can take place over as many as 16 router hops.
- The Site Configuration Manager will continuously monitor for any new logon servers being added to the domain. If any are detected, the new logon server is automatically configured and added to the SMS site. When a logon server in removed from the network, and/or has been inactive on the site domain for seven days, it will be removed from the site configuration by the SMS system.

NOTE Once a server has been removed from the site domain configuration, you must remove any logon server components from the server before it can be added back into the site domain. For more information on which specific components need to be removed see Chapter 15, "Changing Your Site Configuration." ■

This method is good to use when the domain structure is simple and NetWare servers are not present. Using the Use All Detected Servers option when a multiple domain model is being used, or when NetWare Servers are present, is not recommended without careful study. Close examination of your network domain structure is necessary because it's possible (under some circumstances) for the SMS system to include the same logon server in more than one SMS site. This in turn creates serious problems with the SMS site reporting of configuration and inventory information.

CAUTION

Do not check the radio button next to Use All Detected Servers if you're using several SMS sites that have servers belonging to the same domain. In other words, clear this button if the NT (or LAN Manager) domain spans several sites. Not doing so will create severe configuration and inventory problems.

If you choose the Use Specified Servers option, only the server added to the site will be the site server itself. All other servers will have to be manually added to the site using the Domain Properties dialog box.

To select the method that SMS uses to add logon servers to a site, perform the following steps:

1. Log on to the SMS site server using an administrative account, and start the SMS Administrator program.
2. Open the Sites window in the Administrator program. On the left side of the Sites window, highlight the name of the site you wish to configure.
3. Click Properties from the File menu (or press Alt+Enter). The Site Properties dialog box appears.
4. Click the Domains button in the Site Properties dialog box to bring up the Domains dialog box.
5. Find the name of the domain you wish to configure in the Domains at Site window, and highlight it.
6. Mark the Proposed Properties radio button at the top of the Domains dialog box.
7. Click the Properties button at the bottom of the Domains dialog box to reveal the Domain Properties dialog box.(shown in fig. 6.44).
8. Specify that the SMS System automatically detect and configure all logon servers within the selected domain by marking the radio button next to Use All Detected Servers. SMS will detect all current logon servers in the selected domain and will install the SMS components on each of them. The drive containing the most amount of available space on each server will be designated as the target for the SMS logon component directories

and files. Any logon servers added to the domain in the future will automatically be configured with the SMS logon server components.

or

Configure the site to use specific domain logon servers by marking the radio button next to Use Specified Servers. You must then supply the domain logon server name and its associated target drive for the SMS logon components. Each domain logon server that will be running the SMS logon components must be individually specified when this option is selected.

9. Click the OK button to close the Domain Properties dialog box, then click the OK button to close the Domains dialog box. Click the OK button a third time to close the Site Properties dialog box.
10. The Microsoft SMS Administrator dialog box will appear, asking you to confirm the update of the site. Click the Yes button to confirm the proposed changes.

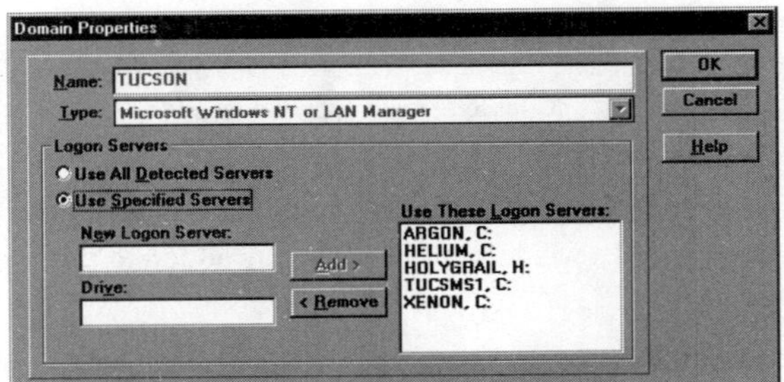

FIG. 6.44
Use the Domains dialog box to configure logon servers.

CAUTION

If you select the Automatically Configure Workstation Logon Scripts option as a method of adding users to you site, you must choose the Use All Detected Servers option when adding a domain to the site. Specifying the Use Specific Servers option will stop the Site Configuration Manager from setting up the logon scripts for users in the target domain.

NetWare domains may be set up with either box marked when the Automatically Configure Workstation Logon Scripts option is being used. This is because the Site Configuration Manager will always set up the system logon scripts on the NetWare file servers.

Once a domain logon server has been configured as an SMS logon server, it will be polled frequently for updates, availability, and inventory information. In addition, each SMS logon server will be replicating large amounts of data with the site server. As a result, any domain logon servers which are already heavily used for user validation will be loaded down even more when the SMS components are installed and running on them.

On larger networks, NT servers acting as primary or backup domain controllers should be used only for account validation. The servers should not have any other shared resources or services running on them (besides those installed by SMS). Other shared resources or services would include (but not be limited to) shared drives, print queues, and RAS services.

In addition, it's strongly suggested that you do not run SQL Server on a PDC (Primary Domain Controller) that validates user logons for a large network. This could seriously impair the controller's ability to perform logon requests and replicate account information to any BDCs (Backup Domain Controllers). In turn, the additional SQL services running on such a server may be affected. PDCs being used as SQL Servers with the boost (Boost SQL Server Priority) option set (in the SQL Setup program) may be rendered inoperable by the use of such a configuration. This could even cause the PDC to crash.

When planning your NT domain, it's also a good idea to reserve at least two or more NT servers for use as the domain controllers. More servers may be needed in larger account domains, but even in small domains, two controllers are required to maintain the integrity of the account's database should one of the domain controller servers fail. In the instance of a failed PDC, the BDC (Backup Domain Controller) would still be able to authenticate users on the network. It would also possible to promote the BDC to PDC if modification of the user database was required, or if the original PDC could not be salvaged.

You can distribute (and decrease) the load on any current domain logon servers by adding additional logon servers to the domain. Splitting up the user validation tasks between several servers can significantly reduce the impact of the validation process on an individual logon server.

CAUTION

Although splitting up user validation tasks distributes the load over more logon servers, it also places a heavier load on the site server. This is because services running on the site server that are used to monitor and control the SMS logon servers now have more logon servers to deal with.

The SMS Site Configuration Manager is the service that configures any new logon servers with the SMS components and services. During the setup of a new logon server, the Site Configuration Manager performs the following duties:

- Creates the SMS root directory on the NTFS drive with the most available space, and then shares the directory with the name of SMS_SHR*x* (*x* specifies the drive letter the directory was created on). If an NTFS drive is not available, the share is created on the largest non-NTFS drive. On NetWare servers, the files are placed on the NetWare volume with the most available space.
- Creates the LOGON.SRV directory under the SMS root directory. This directory is then shared as SMS_SHR.
- Logon server components are then copied to the LOGON.SRV directory.
- When the new logon server is a Windows NT machine, the SMS Inventory Agent for

Windows NT is installed and started. This service is then used to collect inventory from the logon server.

- When the new logon server is a LAN Manager version 2.x server, the SMS Inventory Agent for OS/2 is installed and started. This service is then used to collect inventory from the logon server.
- When the Automatically Configure Workstation Logon Scripts option is used at the site, the SMSLS batch file is added to the NETLOGON and REPL$ shares. In addition, the SMSLS batch file will be added to all user profiles. The SMSLS batch file will inserted into the user's existing logon script if one exists, or it alone will serve as the user's logon script file if the user has no current logon script file assigned to him or her.
- When the Automatically Configure Workstation Logon Scripts option is used at a site containing NetWare servers, the system logon script for each of the NetWare servers is modified to run the SMS Client Setup and SMS Inventory Agent for MS-DOS during NetWare user logon.

Installing Helper Servers

If you find that your site server is being heavily loaded and its resources are becoming strained, you can relieve some of the load by moving one or more of the SMS services off the site server and on to one or more helper servers. This can greatly reduce the load placed on an overworked site server. The four services that may be moved off onto helper servers are the following:

- The Scheduler service
- The Inventory Data Loader service
- The Inventory Processor service
- The Despooler service

In addition to these services, the various sender components can be installed on helper servers.

The helper server must be a Windows NT Server (running version 3.5 or higher), and it must currently be acting as a logon server in the SMS site. If you're using the Use Specified Servers method of choosing logon servers, the helper server must be one of the servers specified in the Use These Logon Servers list for that domain. It must also have an NTFS partition on one of its drives.

Designate a new location for a service by performing the following steps:

1. Log on to the SMS site server using an administrative account and start the SMS Administrator program.
2. Open the Sites window in the Administrator program. On the left side of the Sites window, highlight the name of the site you wish to configure.
3. Click Properties from the File menu (or press Alt+Enter). The Site Properties dialog box appears.

4. Click the Services button in the Site Properties dialog box to bring up the Services dialog box.
5. The four services available for relocation are listed in the Service Locations portion of the dialog box. Move a service by designating the name of another NT 3.5 (or later) server in the Server Name box.
6. Designate the drive letter of an NTFS drive on the specified server to act as the recipient of the service component's associated directories and files.
7. When you've finished making any modifications, click the OK button to close the Domain Properties dialog box, then click the OK button to close the Domains dialog box. Click the OK button a third time to close the Site Properties dialog box.
8. The Microsoft SMS Administrator dialog box will appear, asking you to confirm the update of the site. Click the Yes button to confirm the proposed changes.

On the server designated as the helper server, the directory SMS\HELPER.SRV*platform*.BIN will be created, and the root of this directory will be shared as SMS_SHR*x* (where *x* equals the NTFS drive letter). This share may or may not already exist, depending on which drive the logon server components were installed, as follows:

- If the helper server components are being installed on the same drive as the logon server components, a new share will not be created. However, a new directory named SMS\HELPER.SRV*platform*.BIN will be created within the existing shared SMS root directory.
- If the helper server components are being installed on a different drive, a new share will be created from the root of that drive's new SMS directory structure.

Distribution Server Considerations

Distribution servers are designated by specifying a machine group as the target of a Share Package On Server or Run Command On Workstation job. Since we'll cover the actual sharing and distribution of software applications in Chapter 11, "Software Distribution," here we'll focus on things to consider before designating any server as member of a target machine group for a job.

Choosing a machine group as the target of one of these jobs will cause SMS to perform certain tasks on each server in the specified group. Exactly which tasks are performed, and what the resulting impact is on the network, depend on the type of job being issued. The purpose of a job will fall under one of the following categories:

- Sharing applications over the network from designated servers using Share Package On Server jobs.
- Distributing applications over the network from designated servers using Run Command On Workstation jobs.

When a Share Package On Server job is created, the Despooler is responsible for creating and sharing the appropriate package directories. Exactly where the package is installed will depend on the type of distribution server that is targeted, as follows:

- LAN Manager and Windows NT Servers acting as SMS Logon Servers—the Despooler will attempt to install the software package on the root of the drive containing the most space. The share name you specify for the package will be used for the directory name.
- Window NT Workstations—the Despooler will attempt to install the software package on the root of the drive containing the most space. The share name you specify for the package will be used for the directory name. Note that the package will be installed only if the SMS Service Account is a member of the workstation's Administrative Group.
- NetWare Server acting as SMS Logon Servers—the Despooler will attempt to install the package on the volume you specify. If for some reason the volume is not available, the Despooler will attempt to install the package on the volume that contains the SMS components. The volume name you specify for the package will be used for the directory name.

When a Run Command On Workstation job is initiated, it is again the job of the Despooler to create the necessary directories. The target location for the package once again depends on the type of server (or workstation) being used, as follows:

- LAN Manager and Windows NT Servers acting as SMS Logon Servers—the existing SMS root directory will have a \LOGON.SRV\PCMPKG.SRC*packageID* directory created under it. In this case the *packageID* part of the directory name is the actual Package ID. The exception is when the SMS root directory is installed on a FAT drive and the application package requires an NTFS drive for long filename use. When this happens, the Despooler attempts to find an available NTFS drive on the server. If an NTFS drive is located, the Despooler will create a directory and share named SMSPKG*x* (where *x* equals the target drive's letter) in the root directory of the NTFS target drive. Under the SMSPKG*x* directory, the Despooler will then create a directory with the same name as the Package ID and will install the package into it.
- Window NT Workstations—the Despooler will check to see if a share named SMS_PKG exists on the workstation. If it does not exist, the Despooler creates the SMS_PKG directory on the workstation drive containing the most free space, and shares it under the same name (SMS_PKG). A directory is then created under the SMS_PKG directory with the Package ID as its name. The package is then installed into this directory. Note that the package will be installed only if the SMS Service Account is a member of the workstation's Administrative Group.
- NetWare Servers acting as SMS Logon Servers—the Despooler will attempt to install the package on the volume that contains the SMS components. A subdirectory named \LOGON.SRV\PCMPKG.SRC*packageID* directory will be created under the SMS root, and the package will be installed into it. The *packageID* part of the directory name is the actual Package ID name.

NOTE The Package ID is an eight-character identifier that SMS assigns to a package. The first three characters of the ID are the site code letters of the site where the package was created. These are followed by the sequential package number which indicates the number of packages created on this site to date. An example of a Package ID would be HCD00012. ■

Whether it's sharing applications or distributing software, it's clear that these activities can place a significant load on a server. That's why it is very important to choose a machine(s) that can handle the extra load without becoming a bottleneck. The sharing of software applications will place the greatest load on the distribution server, due to a continual exchange of data between the workstation and the server. While the distribution of a software package may be a one-time event, it can still create a significant load on a server if several package distributions are taking place at the same time over the network.

Another consideration when choosing distribution servers is the amount of free disk space available on the servers you have specified. Typically you'll need disk space available equal to two-and-a-half times the size of the software package you're distributing when executing a Run Command On Workstation job.

Also consider the location of any potential distribution servers that may be on network segments connected by slower WAN links. As you'll see in Chapter 11, "Software Distribution," users are given access to an application by creating a program group that grants access to global groups. When a user runs the Program Group Control (PGC) application, it (or the client proxy agent) will retrieve a list of available servers containing the application package share from the logon server. From the list, a server will randomly be chosen to provide the application share. A temporary connection is then made to the share on the selected server, and the application is executed. If the server that was picked is busy or does not respond, another server will be selected from the list. The intention here is to provide a means of load-balancing server use on busy networks. It works well, but the random selection can create problems if you're not careful about the placement of the distribution servers.

Because of the random selection, the situation can arise where a user is trying to connect and run an application over a slow link. This can happen when a software application has been distributed across an SMS hierarchy that spans sites with slow network links, and the user belongs to a global group (one granted access to the program group) that spans the entire user base of the network. The distribution server that is randomly chosen as the application source may not necessarily be on the same network segment as the user. At the same time, a distribution server that was on the list and is located on the same LAN segment may not be used just because it didn't happen to be the server that was randomly picked.

Avoid problems and carefully consider the environment you're working in before grouping severs into machine groups that will be designated as distribution server groups. This includes the setup of the domain structure, global user group assignments, and the physical layout of the network.

Installing Secondary Site Servers

As you will recall, secondary sites are created under primary sites in the SMS hierarchy. A secondary site is created when you install a secondary site server. The secondary site server contains no online books, user interface, SQL server database, or administrative utilities. In addition, it will have no subsites beneath it. All information gathered by the secondary site server is forwarded on to the primary site server for processing and storage.

The secondary site is both installed and managed from a primary site within the SMS system. Several prerequisites must be satisfied before designating a computer as a secondary site server, as follows:

- Confirm that the computer you've designated to be the secondary site server meets the minimum system requirements for a site server. The prerequisites were given earlier in the chapter, in the Chapter 4 section titled "Site Server Requirements."
- Common SMS Senders must be configured to allow communication between the primary site and the secondary site server. If the Sender types are dependent on another service (such as RAS or SNA Links) you must make sure that the appropriate communications service software/hardware has been installed, configured, and is operating properly.
- Insure that the primary site server for the secondary server has at least 40MB to 60MB of free hard disk space available.
- Create an SMS Service Account on the computer that's been designated to be the secondary site server. For more information on creating an SMS Service Account, see the Chapter 5 section titled "Creating the Service Accounts" found earlier in this chapter. Note that this account does not have to be the same SMS Service Account that's used in the primary site.
- You may also want to configure the NT Server's event log to overwrite events as needed in the server's Application Log. This will prevent the log from filling up and issuing notices.

Before you go any further, insure that you have sufficient drive space available on the primary site server to perform the secondary installation. The disk space required on the primary site server will vary, depending on the number of different hardware platforms types (Intel, Alpha, and MIPS) installed within the primary site.

The SMS System creates a compressed package file that contains all the binaries and data needed for a secondary site server installation. This package is sent to the secondary site server (using one of the Sender services discussed earlier), where it is decompressed and stored. The contents and size of the package when only a single platform type is installed at the primary site is approximately 17MB. However, if your primary site contains Intel, Alpha, and MIPS platforms, the size of the compressed package file would increase to over 48MB. Why? Because by default it would contain the binaries for each of the other platform types installed at the primary site, not just the Intel platform. This is an important point to remember. The binaries for each of the other platforms types installed at the primary site will be included in the compressed package file that is sent to the secondary site server, even if the secondary site contains only one platform type.

For example, if your current site runs only Intel-based machines, then the resulting package file would contain binaries for only the Intel platforms. The package file sent to your Intel-based secondary site server would deliver, decompress, and store only the Intel binaries. If your current site runs all three platforms, a package file containing the binaries for all three platform would be created and sent to the secondary site. The package would be decompressed at the secondary site server, and the binaries for all three platforms would be stored, even if the secondary site contains only Intel platforms.

Install SMS software only for those platforms at the primary site which are present within the primary site. That is, if you run only Intel platforms at the primary site, do not install the Alpha or MIPS software. Doing so will only waste disk space at both the primary site server and the secondary site server. Also plan your sites so that your secondary sites are running the same platform type that the primary sites are running.

Steps for Installing a Secondary Site Server

The actual installation of a secondary site server is done using the SMS Administration program from the primary site server immediately above the server designated to be the secondary site server. Perform the following steps to configure a secondary site server:

1. Log on to the SMS site server using an administrative account and start the SMS Administrator program.
2. Open the Sites window in the Administrator program. On the left side of the Sites window, highlight the name of the site current site (indicated by the globe).
3. From the File menu choose New. The New Secondary Site dialog box will appear, as shown in figure 6.45.

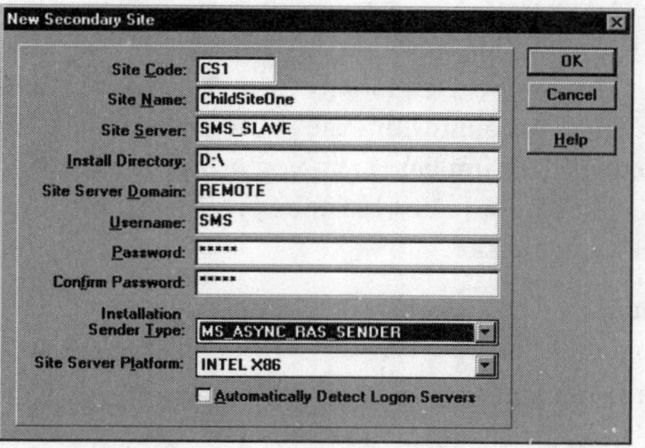

FIG. 6.45
Install secondary site servers using the SMS Administration program from the primary site server.

4. Enter the Site Code for the new site. This is the unique three-character code used to identify the site. This code is used in site-to-site communications. It can be any three-letter combination of alphanumeric characters; special characters are not allowed. This code must be unique within the SMS System.
5. Next type a name for the new site in the Site Name box. This name can be any text you wish, up to a maximum length of 255 characters (including spaces). Short but descriptive site names usually work the best.

6. In the Site Server box, enter the computer name of the Windows NT Server designated to be the secondary site server. This server must be available using the SMS Sender type you designate in step 12.
7. Enter the target drive letter and directory path on the secondary server that will receive the SMS components and shared directories in the Install Directory box. The drive you designate must be running an NTFS partition.
8. Supply the name of the domain that the target server belongs to in the Site Server Domain box.
9. Next, in the Username box, supply the name of the user account that will be used as the SMS Service Account at the new site. This user name may be one of the following:
   - Local Domain Account—specified simply by typing the local user account ID (the local ID designated as the SMS Service Account) in the Username box. The user account must have the appropriate privileges that will allow the SMS Site Configuration and Maintenance Managers to access and maintain the local domain's logon servers.
   - Trusted Domain Account—precede the user name with the name of the trusted domain in which the SMS Service Account resides. For example, if the SMS Service Account we wanted to use was an account from a trusted domain named "CORPHQ," we would type the name in as CORPHQ*username*. Keep in mind that this trusted user account must have the appropriate privileges that will allow the SMS Site Configuration and Maintenance Managers to access and maintain the local domain's logon servers. It must also have the appropriate rights to any subsequent domains that are added to the site. Also bear in mind that the trusted account will be used for any further domain additions to that site, even if a duplicate account with exactly the same name and password exists on the local domain. This implies that if you're using a trusted SMS Service Account, the trusted account must have the proper privileges in all subsequent domains that are added to the site.
10. Supply and confirm the password for the designated SMS Service Account in the Password and Confirm Password boxes.
11. Choose the type of Sender that will be used to link the primary and secondary servers together from the Installation Sender Type drop-down box. You may choose from the following Sender types:
   - MS_LAN_SENDER—the LAN Sender is used when the destination site can be accessed over a established LAN (or WAN with high-speed links).
   - MS_ASYNC_RAS-SENDER—utilized when asynchronous modems and dial-up phone lines are being used for connecting sites.
   - MS_ISDN_RAS_SENDER—used when ISDN connectivity exists between site locations.
   - MS_X25_RAS_SENDER—used when X.25 connections exist between sites.

- MS_BATCH_SNA_SENDER—used when the SNA communication configuration uses LU pairing set to #BATCH mode.
- MS_INTER_SNA_SENDER—used when the SNA communication configuration uses LU pairing set to #INTER mode.

The one you choose will depend on the type of connectivity currently in place between your site locations. In our example we have picked the ASYNC RAS Sender.

CAUTION

The use of the ASYNC RAS Sender for installing a secondary site server is not recommended. Even at high asynchronous baud rates, the installation done over dial-up phone lines can take many hours to complete. It is used here for example purposes only.

12. Specify the target server's platform type in the Site Server Platform box. The default, which is set to INTEL X86, specifies that SMS components for Intel-based platforms should be installed on the target server.
13. Check the Automatically Detect Logon Servers box if you wish the secondary server to detect logon servers in its domain.

    When this box is checked, all of the site server domain's logon servers will automatically be enumerated and added to the SMS site. This includes Windows NT Servers acting as primary domain controllers (PDCs), backup domain controllers (including LAN Manager version 2.x BDCs), and servers in the domain. LAN Manager PDCs and BDCs will be enumerated, but LAN Manager members and stand-alone servers will not. All NetWare version 3.x and 4.x (running bindery emulation) servers will be detected and enumerated. Detection of Novell Servers can take place over as many as 16 router hops. Checking this box will also cause the Site Configuration Manager to monitor continuously for any new logon servers being added to the network. If any are detected, the new logon server is automatically configured and added to the SMS site.

    If this box is cleared, only the server added to the site will be the site server itself. All other servers will have to be manually added to the site using the Site Properties dialog box.

CAUTION

Do not check the Automatically Detect Logon Servers box if you're using several SMS sites that have servers belonging to the same domain. In other words, clear this box if the NT (or LAN Manager) domain spans several sites.

14. When you're finished supplying the properties for the secondary site server, click the OK button.
15. No further configuration is need if the default LAN Sender was used as the Sender type. If a RAS or SNA Sender was picked, additional dialog boxes will appear. They require that you supply the addressing information for the RAS or SNA Sender to use.

NOTE You must supply the connection information for each server, not just the current server. This means that the RAS or SNA address information dialog box will appear twice. The first time you will specify the Secondary Site To Primary Site connection information. In the subsequent address dialog you specify the Primary Site To Secondary Site connection information.

16. For the ASYNC RAS Sender used in our example, we must first provide the Secondary Site To Primary Site addressing information in the RAS Address From *secondary sitecode* To *primary sitecode* dialog box, as shown in figure 6.46. This means that we will be designating the values used by the secondary site server to connect to the primary.

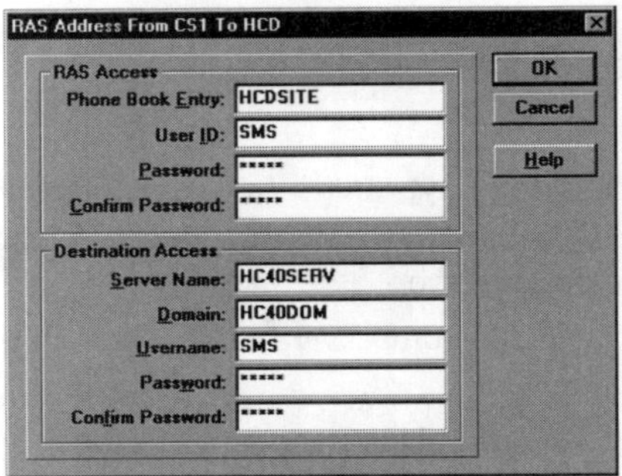

FIG. 6.46
First supply the secondary to primary connection information.

You'll need to supply information for the following fields when configuring the RAS addressing component:

- Phone Book Entry—the name of an entry defined in the secondary site server's RAS phone book. This entry will be used when making a connection to the primary site. Each phone book entry contains the information needed to dial up or connect to the RAS Server at the primary site. When specifying a phone book entry, make sure that you use the proper phone book for the Sender Type you are using. For example, if using an ISDN RAS Sender, you must choose a phone book entry from the ISDN phone book.
- RAS User ID—the RAS user account specified here is used when making the connection to the primary site's RAS Server. You must make sure that this account has RAS dial in permissions on the destination site's RAS Server.
- Password/Verify Password—provide and verify the password for the RAS User ID account.
- Server Name—identifies the name of the site server in the destination site.
- Domain—specifies the name of the domain in which the primary server resides.
- Username—the account name that will be used when accessing the primary site. It must have the appropriate privileges to the primary site server's directory structure and files. Change or Full Control permissions are required on the primary site server's SMS_SITE share. In addition, Read and Write permissions are required on its SITE.SRV\DESPOOLR.BOX\RECEIVE directory.

- Password/Confirm Password—provide and confirm the password for the Username user account.

After completing the addressing information for the secondary site server, click the OK button to be presented with the next addressing dialog box (see fig. 6.47). This dialog box will allow you to specify the Primary Site To Secondary Site connection information. You supply the same values, but this time they are appropriate to the primary site server, as follows:

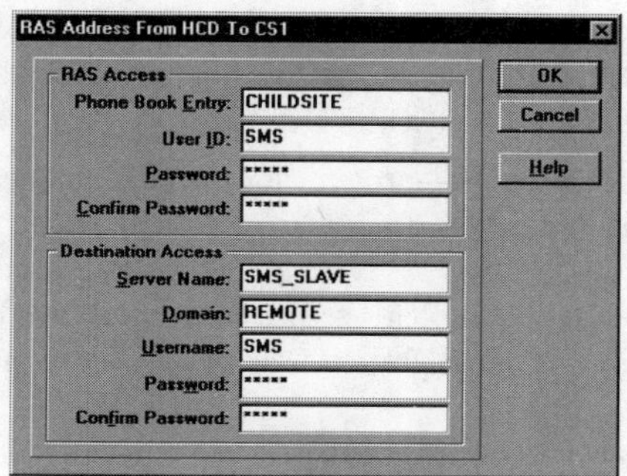

FIG. 6.47
Supply the primary to secondary connection information next.

- Phone Book Entry—the name of an entry defined in the primary site server's RAS phone book. This entry will be used when making a connection to the secondary site server. Each phone book entry contains the information needed to dial up or connect to the RAS Server at the secondary site. When specifying a phone book entry, make sure that you use the proper phone book for the Sender Type you are using. For example, if using an ISDN RAS Sender, you must choose a phone book entry from the ISDN phone book.
- RAS User ID—the RAS user account specified here is used when making the connection to the secondary site RAS Server. You must make sure that this account has RAS dial in permissions on the secondary site RAS Server.
- Password/Verify Password—provide and verify the password for the RAS User ID account.
- Server Name—identifies the name of the secondary site server.
- Domain—specifies the name of the domain in which the secondary site server resides.
- Username—the account name that will be used when accessing the secondary site server. It must have the appropriate privileges to the site server's directory structure and files. Change or Full Control permissions are required on the secondary site server's SMS_SITE share. In addition, Read and Write permissions are required on its SITE.SRV\DESPOOLR.BOX\RECEIVE directory.
- Password/Confirm Password—provide and confirm the password for the Username user account.

Part II Ch 6

Had we picked the SNA Sender, you would have been required to supply the following address information for each server:

- Destination LU Alias—the name of the target site's LU alias. Each target site must have an SNA server running the SMS SNA Receiver with an LU alias defined. In addition, the current site must have an SNA Sender LU alias defined that is paired with that target site's LU alias.
- Username—the account name that will be used when accessing the destination site. It must have the appropriate privileges to the site server's directory structure and files. Change or Full Control permissions are required on the destination site's SMS_SITE share. In addition, Read and Write permissions are required on its SITE.SRV\DESPOOLR.BOX\RECEIVE directory.
- Password/Confirm Password—provide and confirm the password for the Username user account.

NOTE When SNA Sender is used, the SNA Receiver service must be installed and started on the SNA Server used at the secondary site. This installation will be covered later in the chapter.

17. When you've finished supplying any supplemental addressing information, click the OK button. The message shown in figure 6.48 is displayed. Click the Yes button to begin the secondary site server installation process.

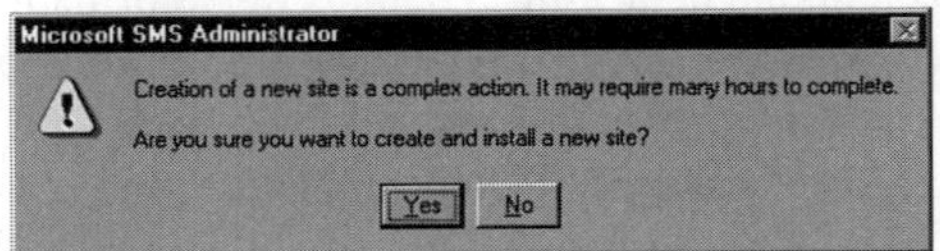

FIG. 6.48 Confirm the creation of the new site.

18. A dialog box will then appear, verifying the successful initiation of the secondary site installation. This is not indicating a successful completion of the installation, only the initiation. During the initialization phase, the new secondary site will be indicated by an Under Construction icon with the new secondary site's name next to it in the Sites window (see fig. 6.49).

Monitoring the Installation Progress

You can monitor the progress of the installation by highlighting the new secondary site's Under Construction icon and looking at its properties using the File menu. The Site Properties dialog box will look similar to the one shown in figure 6.50.

Progress can also be monitored by viewing the specific System Job from the Jobs window in the SMS Administrator. When you install a secondary site server, the SMS System creates and schedules a System Job to carry out the installation. SMS automatically assigns a Job ID for the System Job. If you open the Jobs window (see fig. 6.51), you can look at the specific job properties for this System Job ID (and any other job for that matter) by highlighting it and either double-clicking, or choosing Properties from the File menu.

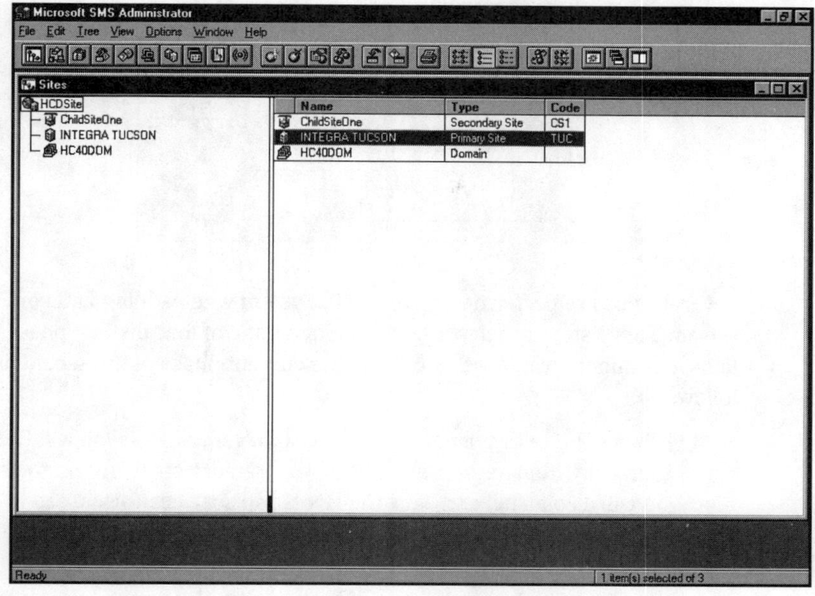

FIG. 6.49
SMS will indicate that the site creation has been initiated with an Under Construction icon in the Sites window.

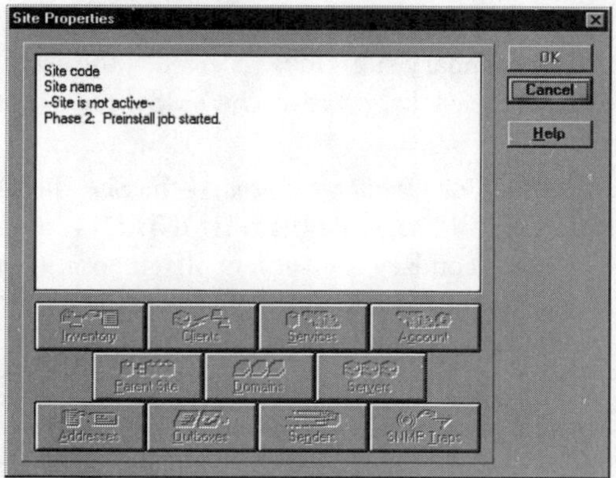

FIG. 6.50
Progress can be monitored by viewing the new site's properties.

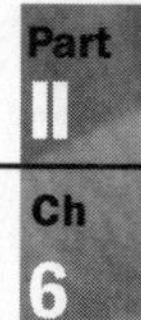

Jobs

ID	Type	Status	Time	Priority	Repeat	Comment
HCD0000E	System Job	Complete	7/10/96 11:03:00 AM	Medium	Never	System job to resync client.
HCD0000F	System Job	Complete	7/10/96 2:31:00 PM	Medium	Never	System job to resync client.
HCD00010	System Job	Complete	7/10/96 2:32:00 PM	Medium	Never	System job to resync client.
HCD00011	System Job	Complete	7/10/96 4:07:00 PM	Medium	Never	System job to resync client.
HCD00012	System Job	Complete	7/11/96 10:00:00 AM	Medium	Never	System job to resync client.
HCD00013	System Job	Complete	7/16/96 6:01:00 PM	Medium	Never	System job to resync client.
HCD00014	System Job	Active	7/22/96 12:45:00 AM	High	Never	Site Preinstall Job For <CS1>

FIG. 6.51
The Jobs Window will list the new System Job.

This will display the Job Properties dialog box, as shown in figure 6.52.

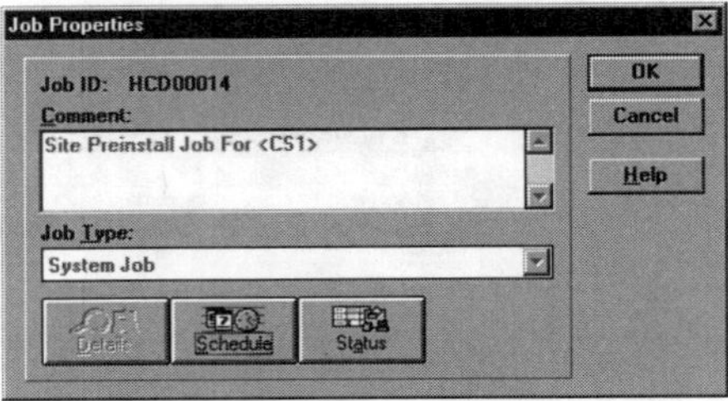

FIG. 6.52
View the System Job properties from the Job Properties dialog box.

Several steps are performed by the SMS System when adding and configuring a secondary site server. These steps are described as being in one of four distinct phases. The dialog box contains a Comment window that reflects the current phase of the secondary site installation, as follows:

- [Phase 1] Site Preinstall Job For *secondary sitecode*—a job will be initiated by the Site Hierarchy Manger to create the SMS directory structure on the secondary server. This job will also install and start the Bootstrap services (discussed later) at the secondary server. The Scheduler service passes the job to the Sender at the primary site for delivery to the secondary site.
- [Phase 2] Site Install Job For *secondary sitecode*—in this stage of the installation a job is initiated by the Site Hierarchy Manager to send a package containing site components to the secondary site. The Scheduler service passes the job to the Sender at the primary site for delivery to the secondary site. Once received at the secondary site, the Bootstrap service will decompress the package, create the SMS directory structure, and install the components into it.
- [Phase 3] Site Control Job For *secondary sitecode*—the Site Hierarchy Manager creates a job to deliver the Site Control Image file (named _INIT.CT1) to the secondary site. The Bootstrap service on the secondary site server will temporarily store the file on hard disk for later decompression and use. In this phase the Site Configuration Manager is started on the secondary site and finishes installation.
- [Phase 4]—the Site Hierarchy Manager waits for a Site Control file (*.CT2) file containing the current secondary site configuration information to arrive from the secondary site. After receiving the file, the Site Hierarchy Manager uses the data it contains to update the parent site's database with configuration data from the new secondary site. After this update has been performed, the new site will be available for viewing and modification using the Administrator facility at the parent site server (or any other primary server above it in the site hierarchy).

The System Job that's created is given a high priority and is automatically scheduled for immediate execution as a job that never repeats. This can be seen by clicking the Schedule button, which will then display the specific scheduling information for the System Job (see fig. 6.53).

In addition to scheduling information, the current status of the System Job can be viewed by clicking the Status button located in the lower portion of the Job Properties dialog box. This will display the Job Status dialog box (see fig. 6.54) that allows you to view specific status information for each stage of the job's progress.

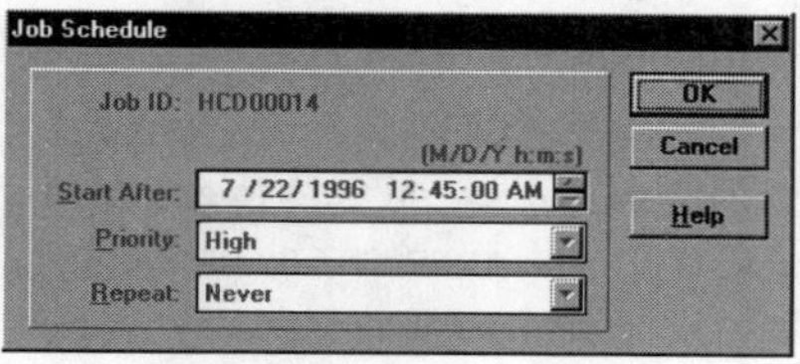

FIG. 6.53 View the scheduling information for the System Job using the Schedule button.

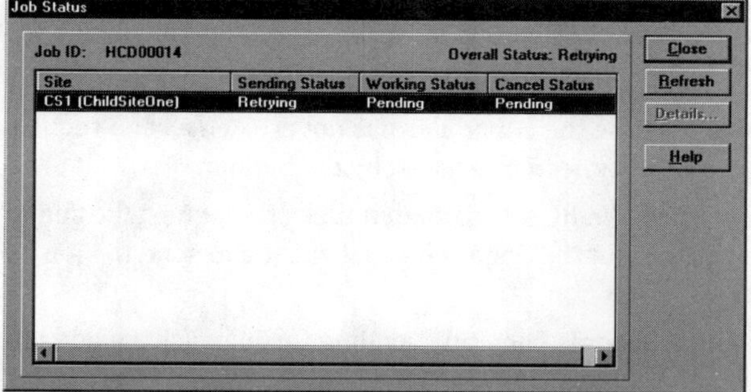

FIG. 6.54 The Job Status dialog box shows detailed status information on the System Job.

Let's look at the Job Status dialog box in greater detail by examining the information fields that it displays. A brief explanation for each of the fields shown in the dialog box is given below:

- Overall Status—shows the job as being in one of six jobs states. Each of these states indicates the specific progress of the job across all the target sites.
- Sending Status—indicates the progress of a job in terms of its sending and delivery status while en route to a remote target site.
- Working Status—gives an indication of the job's progress while at the remote target site.
- Cancel Status—you can cancel jobs that have been initiated as long as they are not System Jobs. When canceling a job, the Cancel Status will display the progress information relative to the job being canceled.

For each of the status indicator types, there are several different job states that can be indicated.

Job States Indicated by Overall Status Six job states can be specified by the Overall Status indicator located in the upper right portion of the Job Status window. They are as follows:

- Pending—the job has not yet been activated by the Scheduler. Since the job has not started, it can be deleted or modified.
- Active—the job has been started by the Scheduler and is progressing without error. The job may be active or completed at target sites and computers.

- Retrying—for some reason the job has failed at one or more of the target locations, and SMS is attempting to retry the job at the target.
- Complete—the job has been completed successfully on all target computers.
- Canceling—the job is currently being canceled.
- Failed—for some reason the job has failed at one or more of the target locations after several retry attempts and SMS has stopped trying to complete the job. A status of Failed will be indicated even if the job ran with success on some of the target sites or computers.

What the Sending Status Indicators Mean In the Job Status window (see fig. 6.54) we are given Sending Status information for each job listed in the window. The indicators listed below tell us about the progress of a job in terms of its sending and delivery status while en route to a remote target site.

- None—at this time the Scheduler has not created a send request (*.SRQ) file for the job and thus it has not been processed by the Sender.
- Pending—the Scheduler has created the send request file and has placed the file in the Sender outbox, but the Sender has not started to send the job package and instructions to the target site.
- Active—the Sender is currently sending the job package and instruction information to the target site.
- Retrying—for some reason the Sender has failed to send the job package and instructions to the target site(s) and is now attempting to retry the operation.
- Complete—the job package and instructions have successfully been sent to the target sites.
- Canceled—the job was canceled successfully before the job package and instructions were sent to the target sites.
- Failed—for some reason the Sender has failed to send the job package and instructions to the target site(s) and has now stopped any attempts to retry the operation.

What the Working Status Indicators Mean The informational dialog that indicates the Working Status will show you the current status of the job at the target site. The Working Status may be indicated as any one of the following states:

- Pending—the job package and instructions have not yet been received by the target site.
- Active—the target site has received the job package and instructions, and is now processing the job.
- Retrying—for some reason the job has failed to complete on one or more of the computers at the target site, and attempts are currently being made to retry the job.
- Completed—the job has successfully completed on all of the designated computers at the target site.
- Canceled—the job was successfully canceled before it was processed by the computers in the target site.

- Failed—for some reason the job has failed to complete on one or more of the designated computers at the target site, and all attempts to retry the operation have been stopped.

Status Indicators for a Canceled Job Since the job used to install the secondary site server was created by the SMS system (called a System Job) it cannot be canceled using the SMS Administrator. However, other jobs that you create can be canceled at your discretion. When this is done, the status of the job cancellation is indicated as being one of the following:

- None—the job has not been designated for cancellation at this time.
- Pending—the job has been designated to be canceled, but the target site has not yet received the instructions for cancellation.
- Active—the site has received the cancellation instructions and is in the process of canceling the job.
- Retrying—for some reason the job cancellation has failed on one or more of the designated computers at the target site. Attempts are currently being made to retry the job cancellation.
- Complete—the job has been successfully canceled on all the designated computers at the target site.
- Failed—for some reason the job cancellation has failed on one or more of the designated computers at the target site. No further attempts are being made to retry the cancellation of the job.

How SMS Completes the Installation

The actual steps taken by the SMS System when installing a secondary site are outlined below. These steps will be followed unless the SNA-link services will be used for communication between the sites. The installation of the SNA Receiver on the secondary site and the associated setup steps performed by the SMS System when the SNA Receiver is used will be covered later in this chapter. For now let's take a look at what SMS does when setting up a secondary site server using LAN or RAS Senders, as follows:

1. The administrator of the SMS System uses the Administrator program to supply the information needed to install and configure the secondary site. This information is then placed in the parent site's SMS database.
2. The Site Hierarchy Manager detects the new site information contained within the SMS database. Using this information, the SMS System will update the registry information pertaining to the site addressing information for the new site. This registry information will be used by the current site's Sender service to establish a connection with the new site.
3. The Site Hierarchy Manager then requests information for a secondary site files list. The information used for this file list is derived from the SYSTEM.MAP file. The SYSTEM.MAP file contains a listing of all the components and files that are needed for each specific type of hardware platform, language, and operating system that runs SMS. It is located in the SMS root directory on the parent site server. Based on the current

platform types installed at the parent site, and the information you provided during the site configuration, a secondary site files list is created using the SYSTEM.MAP file data. This secondary file list will be used to designate which files, directories, and components the SMS site package contains. The components contained in the SMS site package are in turn installed at the secondary site server.

4. A special job is created by the Site Hierarchy Manager and sent to the Scheduler. The Scheduler in turn creates a send request file and passes it to the Sender. This instructs the Sender service to connect to the target server and create an installation directory, into which it then installs and starts the SMS Bootstrap service.
5. The SMS System then verifies that the Bootstrap service in the secondary site server is running before it creates the second job of the installation process. This second job delivers the SMS site package. The contents of the SMS site package include all the files, directories, and components specified by the secondary file list that was created earlier. The job is given a high priority, and a send request is created for it by the Scheduler and passed to the Sender service. The Sender will process the request and deliver the package to the secondary site.
6. The Bootstrap service running on the secondary site server will receive the SMS site package and place it in the SMS root directory as BOOTSTRP.PK1.
7. The Site Hierarchy Manager creates a third job to deliver a package containing the Site Control Image file (_INIT.CT1) to the secondary site server. This file contains information pertaining to the configuration of the secondary site. The Bootstrap service at the secondary site receives the package and places it in the SMS root directory as BOOTSTRP.PK2.
8. The Bootstrap service at the secondary site server then verifies the integrity of both packages. If either of the package files is found to be corrupted, an event will be written to the NT Event log and the trace log, and the installation will be halted.
9. The Bootstrap service then checks to see if adequate space is available for the installation of the site components. If space is not available, an event will be written to the NT Event log and the trace log, and the installation will be halted.
10. The Bootstrap service decompresses both packages, creates the SMS directory structure on the server, and places the components into the appropriate directory within that structure.
11. Once the components have been installed into the directory structure, the Site Configuration Manager is started on the new secondary site server and the Bootstrap service is stopped.
12. The site control file delivered earlier is now used by the secondary site server's Site Configuration Manager to complete the installation and configuration tasks.
13. SMS services at the secondary site are then started by the Site Configuration Manager.
14. Once the SMS services have started, the Site Configuration Manager will create a Site Control (*.CT2) file that contains the current configuration for the new site. A fourth job is created to send the Site Control file back to the parent site. Since all of the SMS

services are running at this point, the normal Scheduler/Sender process is used to deliver the Site Control file back to the parent site.

15. The Despooler at the parent site places the Site Control file into the SITE.SRV\SITECFG.BOX directory of the SMS_SHR*x* on the site server.
16. The parent site's Site Hierarchy Manager then uses the data contained within the Site Control file to update the SMS database with the actual site configuration information from the secondary site. Once this is completed, the SMS Administrator program's Sites window will reflect the new site in the site hierarchy. You can then modify the site properties for the secondary site in the same manner that the site properties for the parent site are modified.

Installing the SNA Receiver

The SNA Receiver and SMS Bootstrap services must be installed on the secondary site server manually when using the SNA Sender/Receiver services as the means of communication between sites. This installation is performed at the SNA Server at the secondary site, using the SMS or BackOffice CD-ROM. First we'll look at the installation steps that are performed at the remote SNA Server; then we'll look at how SMS completes an installation when using SNA Receiver.

Our SNA Receiver installation begins after completing the secondary site setup procedure at the parent site server. The properties we specified in the New Secondary Site dialog box during setup at the parent site are shown in figure 6.55. We will use the property values specified here when configuring the SNA Receiver and Bootstrap Setup program at the server targeted to be a secondary site server.

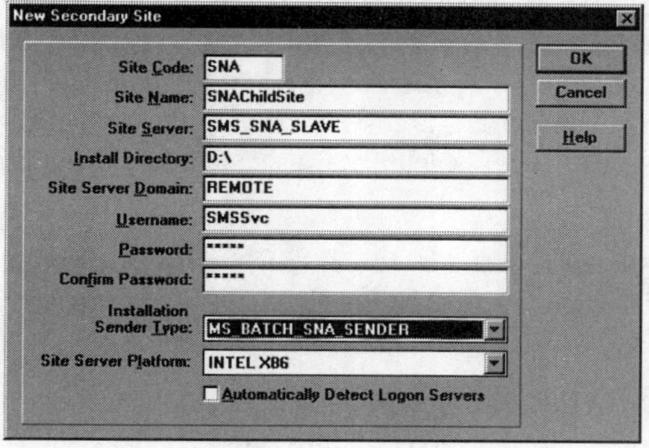

FIG. 6.55
The values specified during the secondary site server setup are used when installing the SNA Receiver.

Follow the steps listed below to install the SNA Receiver component.

1. Log on to the SNA server as an administrator and access the SMS or BackOffice CD-ROM. Run the SNASETUP.EXE application appropriate for your hardware platform. You'll find the version specific to your hardware in the X86, MIPS, or ALPHA directory. The Setup program will display the SNA Setup dialog box.

2. In the Install Directory box type the same path you specified for the Install Directory property for the New Secondary Site dialog box on the parent site server. Our earlier setup of the secondary site (see fig. 6.55) specified D:\ as the installation directory, so that's the value used here.
3. Next, in the Site Code box, enter the same three-letter site code that was specified in the New Secondary Site dialog box. We specified "SNA" as the site code during the earlier setup on the parent site server (see fig. 6.55), so that's the value we'll use here.
4. In the Domain box, enter the same domain name that you specified earlier in the New Secondary Site dialog box. This should be the name of the domain in which the secondary site server resides. The domain that our secondary resides in was specified earlier in the New Secondary Site dialog box as "REMOTE," so that's the value entered her.
5. Enter the username for the SMS Service account in the Username box. This must also match the value specified earlier when configuring the New Secondary Site dialog box at the parent site server (see fig. 6.55). The name of the SMS Service account we specified earlier was "SMSSvc," so that's the account name we'll enter here.
6. Type the SMS Service account password in the Password box, then verify it in the Confirm Password box. This must be the correct password for the SMS Service account and must be the same password specified earlier in the New Secondary Site dialog box.
7. When you've completed entering the information for each of the properties, click the OK button.

At this point, the Setup program installs and starts the SNA Receiver and SMS Bootstrap services. The rest of the process is completed by the SMS System.

How SMS Completes an Installation with SNA Connectivity

The series of events that SMS performs when installing a secondary site using SNA-links is similar to the steps taken when using LAN or RAS Senders. A major difference is that the Site Hierarchy Manager no longer creates and sends a job to the secondary site to start the Bootstrap service. It is has already been started at the secondary site server by the SNASETUP.EXE program.

Listed below are the steps performed by the SMS System when adding a secondary site server using SNA-links. In this scenario the SNA Receiver and Bootstrap services are started on the secondary site server and await instructions from the parent site, as follows:

1. The administrator of the SMS System uses the Administrator program to supply the information needed to install and configure the secondary site. This information is then placed in the parent site's SMS database.
2. The Site Hierarchy Manager detects the new site information contained within the SMS database. Using this information, the SMS System will update the registry information pertaining to the site addressing information for the new site. This registry information will be used by the current site's Sender service to establish a connection with the new site.

3. The Site Hierarchy Manager then requests information for a secondary site files list. The information used for this file list is derived from the SYSTEM.MAP file. The SYSTEM.MAP file contains a listing of all the components and files that are needed for each specific type of hardware platform, language, and operating system that runs SMS. It is located in the SMS root directory on the parent site server. Based on the current platform types installed at the parent site, and the information you provided during the site configuration, a secondary site files list is created using the SYSTEM.MAP file data. This secondary file list will be used to designate which files, directories, and components the SMS site package contains. The components contained in the SMS site package are in turn installed at the secondary site server.
4. The SNA Receiver at the secondary site sends confirmation to the parent site's Scheduler indicating the Bootstrap services at the secondary site have started. The parent site's Site Hierarchy Manager, having verified that the Bootstrap service in the secondary site server is running, will schedule the first job of the installation process. This first job delivers the SMS site package. The contents of the SMS site package includes all the files, directories, and components specified by the secondary file list that was created earlier. The job is given a high priority, and a send request is created for it by the Scheduler and passed to the SNA Sender service. The SNA Sender will process the request and deliver the package to the secondary site.
5. The Bootstrap service running on the secondary site server will receive the SMS site package and place it in the SMS root directory as BOOTSTRP.PK1.
6. The Site Hierarchy Manager creates a second job to deliver a package containing the Site Control Image file (_INIT.CT1) to the secondary site server. This file contains information pertaining to the configuration of the secondary site. The Bootstrap service at the secondary site receives the package and places it in the SMS root directory as BOOTSTRP.PK2.
7. The Bootstrap service at the secondary site server then verifies the integrity of both packages. If either of the package files is found to be corrupted, an event will be written to the NT Event log and the trace log, and the installation will be halted.
8. The Bootstrap service then checks to see if adequate space is available for the installation of the site components. If space is not available, an event will be written to the NT Event log and the trace log, and the installation will be halted.
9. The Bootstrap service decompresses both packages, creates the SMS directory structure on the server, and places the components into the appropriate directory within that structure.
10. Once the components have been installed into the directory structure, the Site Configuration Manager is started on the new secondary site server, and the Bootstrap service is stopped.
11. The site control file delivered earlier is now used by the secondary site server's Site Configuration Manager to complete the installation and configuration tasks.
12. SMS services at the secondary site are then started by the Site Configuration Manager.

13. Once the SMS services have started, the Site Configuration Manager will create a Site Control (*.CT2) file that contains the current configuration for the new site. A third job is created to send the Site Control file back to the parent site. Since all of the SMS services are running at this point, the normal Scheduler/Sender process is used to deliver the Site Control file back to the parent site via its SNA Receiver.
14. The Despooler at the parent site places the Site Control file into the SITE.SRV\SITECFG.BOX directory of the SMS_SHR*x* on the site server.
15. The parent site's Site Hierarchy Manager then uses the data contained within the Site Control file to update the SMS database with the actual site configuration information from the secondary site. Once this is completed, the SMS Administrator program's Sites window will reflect the new site in the site hierarchy. You can then modify the site properties for the secondary site in the same manner that the site properties for the parent site are modified.

Integration with Other Network Operating Systems

The SMS system will support the following types of operating systems on both servers and clients:

- Windows NT Server 3.5 or later
- Windows NT Workstation 3.5 or later
- Microsoft LAN Manager version 2.2c or later
- Microsoft Network Client for MS-DOS
- NetWare 3.12
- NetWare 4.1 (NetWare 3.x Bindery Emulation Mode is required)
- IBM LAN Server 3.0, 3.1, or 4.0
- Apple Macintosh System 7.*x* (client only)

You can reference tables in Chapter 4, "Planning, Design, and System Requirements," for a full list of compatible servers and clients. The tables list any limitation of SMS with the other system environments, and if any perquisites are needed for integration with SMS. Two environments that require additional setup to support are Novell NetWare and Macintosh.

When integrating SMS with a NetWare environment, you must first install the Gateway Service for NetWare on the site server. When using SMS to support Macintosh clients, you must first install the NT Services for Macintosh on all logon servers that will be supporting Macintosh clients. We'll cover both of these environments and the additional steps needed to integrate them into SMS starting with NetWare.

Integration with Novell NetWare

SMS can be easily integrated into a NetWare environment provided you keep in mind the following points:

- SMS will only support NetWare version 4.*x* file servers in bindery-emulation mode.
- SMS will only support NetWare 3.1*x* and 4.*x* (versions 4.02 or later).
- NetWare 4.*x* clients must log on in bindery mode using the logon command's /b switch.
- NetWare 4.*x* system logon script requires additional modification.
- Each NetWare client must have a free drive letter available. The same drive letter should be available on all client workstations.
- The SMS Service account must have a valid user account with supervisor privileges on each NetWare server that will be integrated into the SMS System. Make sure that the connection limit feature is not enabled for the NetWare SMS Service Account, since SMS will initiate multiple connections during its operation.
- You must create the group named NTGATEWAY on the NetWare server and place the NetWare SMS Service account into the group.
- You must create the group named EVERYONE on 4.*x* servers. SMS uses this group when granting access permissions to its directories. This group is automatically created on NetWare 3.1*x* servers.
- The Window NT Gateway Service for NetWare must be installed on the SMS site server.

We must first prepare the NetWare Server by creating the NetWare SMS Service account and the NTGATEWAY group. If we are preparing a 4.*x* server, the group EVERYONE must be created with all users in the bindery context added to it.

On NetWare 4.*x* servers you can use the NWADMIN or NETADMIN program to create the groups named NTGATEWAY and EVERYONE in the NDS container that you have SET as the bindery context root on the NetWare Server. Then create the NetWare SMS Service account and add it to the group. Both of the groups and the user account must be in the same bindery context. You may, however, find it difficult to grant Supervisor equivalency to the NetWare SMS Service account (a required step) using the NDS administrative utilities. This is because the Supervisor object does not exist in NDS, but only in bindery mode. So in order to grant Supervisor rights to the NetWare SMS Service account, you must be able to run the Syscon program on the NetWare 4.*x* server.

The only catch is that when NetWare 4.*x* is installed NDS (NetWare Directory Service), services are used instead of the bindery that was used in earlier versions of NetWare. Running the Syscon program with NetWare version 4.*x* will simply run a batch file that displays a message which states Syscon is not used with NetWare 4.*x*. In order to run Syscon, you must find and copy a NetWare 3.*x* version of the SYSCON.EXE program (along with the supporting files SYS$MSG.DAT and IBM$RUN.OVL) to the NetWare 4.*x* server's SYS volume \Public directory. Once installed, the Syscon utility can be run on the 4.*x* NetWare server just as if it were a 3.*x* server.

Adding the NTGATEWAY Group Before installing the Gateway Services for NetWare, you'll need to create a user group named NTGATEWAY on the NetWare file server. If this is a NetWare 4.*x* Server, you will need to create NTGATEWAY group object in the context designated as the bindery context using the NWADMIN or NETADMIN utilities. You can also use the older 3.*x* Syscon utility to make the modification to a 4.*x* server. Do this by copying the utility and its associated files from an existing 3.*x* server into the \Public directory of the SYS volume on the NetWare Server. Use the NetWare Server console utility SERVMAN to set the bindery context to the location containing the server, user, and group objects.

To create the NTGATEWAY group on each NetWare Server using the Syscon utility, perform the following steps:

1. Log on to the NetWare server as a supervisor or equivalent, and run the Syscon Utility (found in the SYS:Public directory). Highlight the Group Information in the Available Topics menu, and press Enter.
2. The Group Names box will appear. If this is a NetWare 3.*x* Server, the group EVERYONE will already be listed. Press the insert key to add a new group.
3. The New Group Name box will appear. Type in NTGATEWAY and press Enter. The group name NTGATEWAY will now appear in the Group Names list (see fig. 6.56).

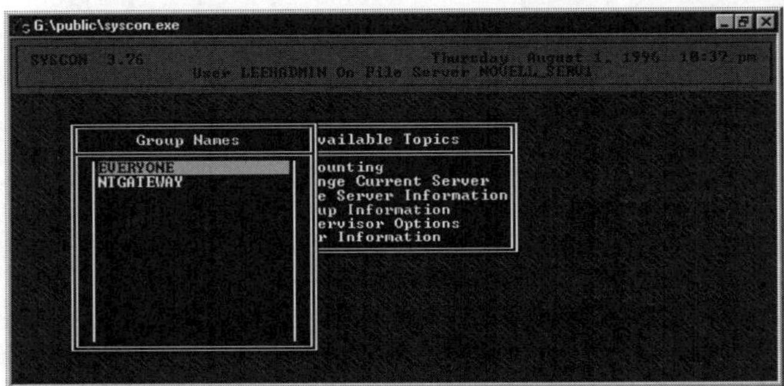

FIG. 6.56
Use Syscon to add the NTGATEWAY group.

4. Press Escape to return to the Available Topics menu.

The next step in the preparation of the NetWare Server is the creation of the NetWare SMS Service account.

Adding the NetWare SMS Service Account This account must have the same name and password as the SMS Service account that is currently being used on your SMS system. The account must also have supervisor rights, so that SMS is able to install the directory structure, files, and components on the server.

Follow the steps listed below to add the SMS Service Account the NetWare server:

1. Log on to the NetWare server as a supervisor or equivalent, and run the Syscon Utility (found in the SYS:Public directory). Highlight the Group Information in the Available Topics menu, and press Enter.
2. Highlight User Information, and press Enter. A window containing current users will be displayed.

3. Press the Insert key to bring up the User Name dialog box, as shown in figure 6.57. Type the SMS Service account name in the box, and press Enter.
4. Press the Escape key when asked for a home directory path. The SMS Service Account is now added to the User Names dialog box.

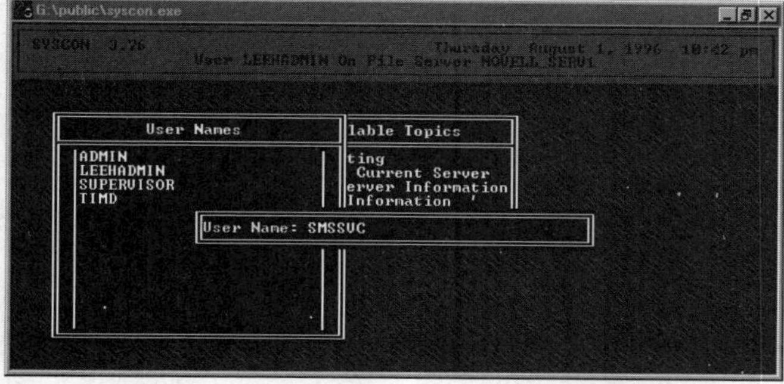

FIG. 6.57 Add the SMS Service account as a NetWare user.

Next, you must set the password for the Service Account.

Setting the NetWare SMS Service Account Password Set the password for the new Service Account to the same password currently being used for the SMS Service on the primary SMS site. Perform the following steps to modify the Service Account password:

1. Log on to the NetWare server as a supervisor or equivalent, and run the Syscon Utility (found in the SYS:Public directory). Highlight the Group Information in the Available Topics menu, and press Enter.
2. Highlight User Information, and press Enter. A window containing current users will be displayed.
3. Highlight the name of the SMS Service account, and press Enter.
4. The User Information dialog box will appear (see fig. 6.58). Highlight the Change Password option, and press Enter. The Enter New Password dialog box appears.

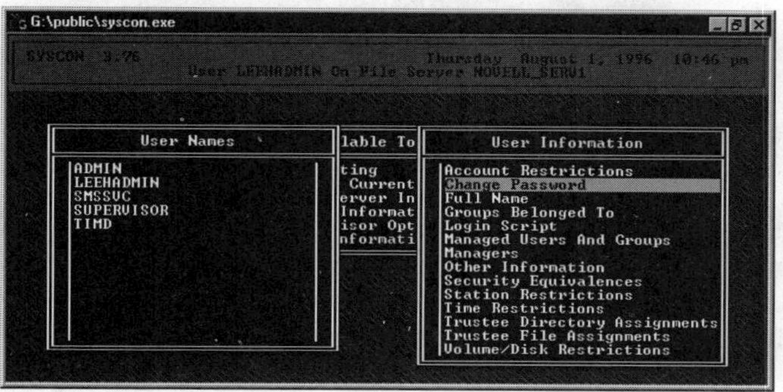

FIG. 6.58 Highlight Change Password in the User Information dialog box and press Enter.

5. Type in the same password used for the Service Account on the SMS primary site server, and press Enter.
6. Verify the password by reentering it and pressing Enter.
7. Press Escape twice to return to the Available Topics menu.

The NetWare SMS Service account must now be added to the NTGATEWAY group.

Adding the Service Account to the NTGATEWAY Group Perform the following steps to add the NetWare SMS Service account to the NTGATEWAY group we created earlier, which allows SMS to use the Gateway Service for NetWare:

1. Log on to the NetWare server as a supervisor or equivalent, and run the Syscon Utility (found in the SYS:Public directory). Highlight the Group Information in the Available Topics menu, and press Enter.
2. Highlight User Information, and press Enter. A window containing current users will be displayed.
3. Highlight the name of the SMS Service account, and press Enter.
4. In the User Information menu, highlight Groups Belonged To, and press Enter.
5. The Groups Belonged To dialog box appears. Press the Insert key to display the Groups Not Belonged To dialog box.
6. Highlight the NTGATEWAY group, and press Enter (see fig. 6.59). NTGATEWAY will now be listed in the Groups Belonged To dialog box. Press Escape to return to the User Information dialog box.

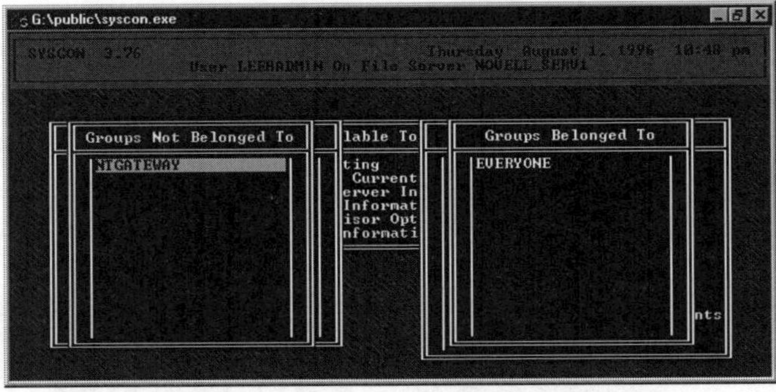

FIG. 6.59
Add the SMS Service account to the NTGATEWAY group.

The next step is to grant supervisor privileges to the NetWare SMS Service account.

Granting Supervisor Rights to the Service Account You must give the NetWare SMS Service account supervisor equivalence, or it will not be able to create the needed directory structures and copy components on the NetWare Server. Perform the following steps to grant supervisor rights to the Service Account:

1. Log on to the NetWare server as a supervisor or equivalent, and run the Syscon Utility (found in the SYS:Public directory). Highlight the Group Information in the Available Topics menu, and press Enter.
2. Highlight User Information, and press Enter. A window containing current users will be displayed.
3. Highlight the name of the SMS Service account, and press Enter.
4. In the User Information menu, highlight Security Equivalences, and press Enter.
5. The Security Equivalences dialog box will appear. Press Insert to display the Other Users and Groups dialog box.
6. Highlight SUPERVISOR, as shown in figure 6.60, and press Enter. The SUPERVISOR will now be listed in the Security Equivalences dialog box.

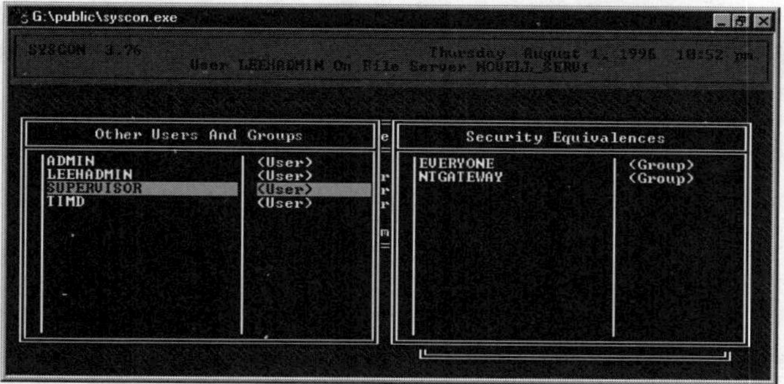

FIG. 6.60
Give the SMS Service Account Supervisor equivalence.

Installing the Gateway Services for NetWare Before SMS can talk to any of the Novell Servers on your LAN, the Gateway Services for NetWare must be installed on the site server. Installing the Gateway Services will also load the NWLink IPX/SPX Compatible Transport and the NWLink NetBIOS interface on the site server. Perform the following steps to load the Windows NT Gateway (and client) for NetWare; you will need to have the Windows NT Server CD-ROM available for installation access:

1. Log on to the site server as the administrator or equivalent, and open the NT Server Control Panel. Double-click the Network icon to display the Network dialog box.
2. Click the Services tab to reveal the Network Services list. Click the Add button to display the Select Network Service dialog box.
3. In the Network Service list, highlight the Gateway (and Client) Services for NetWare option and click the OK button.
4. The Windows NT Setup dialog box will appear, prompting you for the path to the Windows NT Server installation files. Provide the correct path to the distribution files, and click the Continue button.

5. At this time the IPX Protocol and related services will be installed on the server. When the files copying has completed, you will be returned back to the Network dialog box. Click the Close button to start the protocol binding process.
6. After the binding has completed, the Network Settings Change dialog box will appear, prompting you to restart your computer in order for the new changes to take effect. Click the Yes button to proceed with the reboot of the system.

The first time you log on after restarting the server, you will be prompted to choose the name of a preferred NetWare Server. Choose the name of the Server where the NetWare SMS Service account and NTGATEWAY group are installed, and click the OK button.

Resharing a NetWare Volume to Check the Account Setup You can insure that the Gateway Service for NetWare is working by resharing one of the NetWare server's volumes through the NT Server. If you are allowed to share the volume, you have the correct access set up between the servers. This step is not required when adding a NetWare Server domain to the site. It is used only to verify that the SMS Service account has been set up with the correct permissions at the NetWare Server.

To share a NetWare volume or directory, perform the following steps:

1. Log on to the site server as the administrator or equivalent and open the NT Server Control Panel.
2. In the Control Panel you will see a new icon named GSNW (Gateway Service for NetWare). Double-click the icon to open the Gateway Service for NetWare dialog box, as shown in figure 6.61.

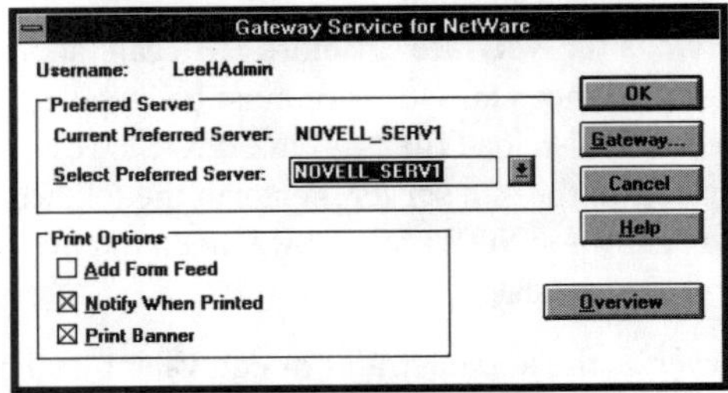

FIG. 6.61
Select the NetWare Server that's set up with the SMS Service and group accounts.

3. Verify that the name of the NetWare server with the NTGATEWAY group and SMS Service account is displayed in the Select Preferred Server box, and click the Gateway button.
4. Mark the Enable Gateway box, and then type the NetWare SMS Service account name in the Gateway Account box (see fig. 6.62). This must be the same account name that was set up on the NetWare Server.
5. Type and verify the password for the account in the Password and Confirm Password boxes. Make sure the password you enter is the same password used for the account at the NetWare Server.

FIG. 6.62
Enable the Gateway and supply the SMS Service Account information.

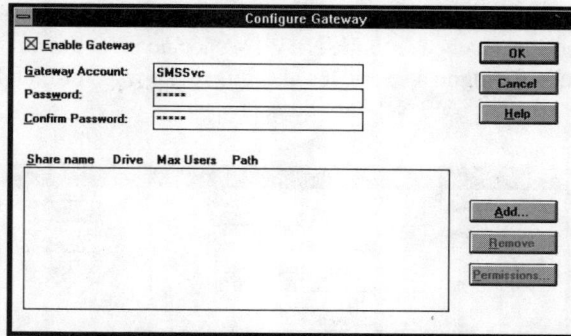

6. Click the Add button to display the New Share dialog box. In the box you will enter the properties that will be used to identify and share the NetWare server's volume or directory. In the Share Name box, type a name for the share. Keep the name to eight character or less if MS-DOS users will be accessing the share. Otherwise the share name may be up to 12 characters in length.
7. Next type in the UNC (Universal Naming Convention) path to the volume or directory on the NetWare Server that you wish to share. This is done by preceding the server name with two backslashes and then typing out the full path to the target. In the example shown in figure 6.63, we have shared the documentation directory on the SYS volume on the NetWare Server named Novell_serv1. Click OK when you've finished entering the information.

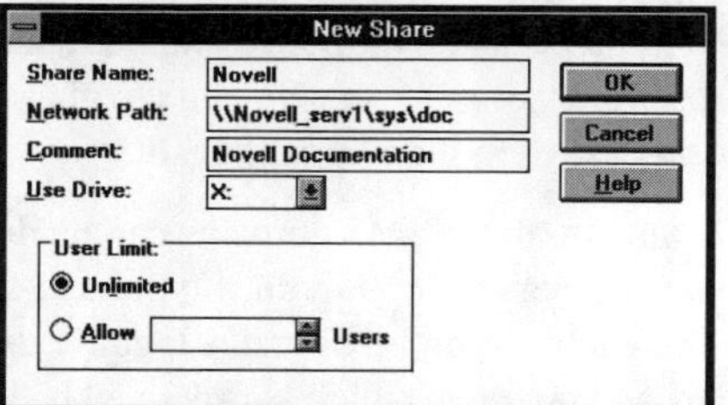

FIG. 6.63
Sharing a NetWare Server volume or drive share.

8. If you have set up the accounts correctly, the Configure Gateway dialog box will now list the new share you've just created (see fig. 6.64). Click OK to return to the Gateway Service for NetWare dialog box, then click OK a second time to exit back to the Control Panel.

Adding a NetWare Domain to the SMS Site After you have verified that the Service Accounts have been set up correctly, you can add the NetWare Servers to the system using the site properties dialog box in the SMS Administration program.

Integration of NetWare servers and clients is accomplished by creating NetWare-based SMS domains using the SMS Administration program. Each of these SMS NetWare domains contains only NetWare servers and clients. This separation of NetWare servers and clients into their own domain is partially due to the NetWare-specific SMS components that must be installed on the NetWare logon servers. It's also due to the way in which NetWare servers are detected and added to an SMS NetWare domain.

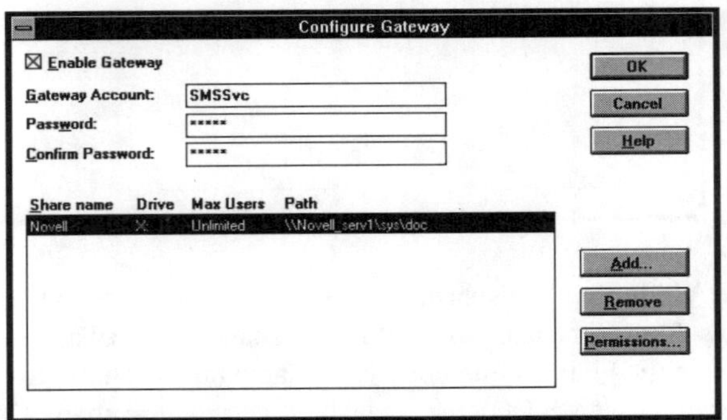

FIG. 6.64
The shared NetWare directory is now listed.

You'll recall that users in an NT (or LAN Manager) environment log on to a domain. Each domain contains a group of servers that use a common user account database to authenticate users. Users then log on to the domain (or group of servers) rather than a single server. Users are granted rights to all the domains' (and trusting domains') resources based on the common accounts database. This eases the administrative burden of managing multiple user databases on separate servers.

SMS takes advantage of this domain concept by using the preestablished NT domains to group NT (or LAN Manager) servers and their clients into SMS Site domains. The SMS Administrator program's Site window represents a group of servers and clients as being members of these NT domains. One or more domains are then members of a Site.

The grouping of servers and clients into these SMS domains can be done manually, but is most often done using the Use All Detected Servers option during domain setup. This instructs SMS to install the logon components on each one of the domains logon servers. You know what servers belong to the NT domain, so you know which servers will be included in the SMS domain. When choosing the Detect All Logon Servers option, you still maintain control over which logon servers will participate in the SMS domain.

Since NetWare 3.*x* environments do not use the domain concept, NetWare 3.*x* servers are not already neatly grouped like servers in an NT (or LAN Manager) environment. Because no domains for the NetWare servers exist, we must group NetWare servers into pseudo-domains for use by SMS. We have two options available when grouping NetWare servers into an SMS domain, as follows:

1. Automatically have every NetWare server within 16 router hops detected and added to a single SMS NetWare server/client domain. This is done when the Use All Detected Servers option is selected in the Domain Properties Dialog box. This is not recommended for any but the simplest network environments.

2. Manually specify each NetWare server to be included within a specific SMS NetWare server/client domain by selecting the Use Specified Servers option in the Domain Properties dialog box. This is the default and preferred method to use with most NetWare environments.

By allowing all NetWare servers to be detected automatically, you lose any control you have over the grouping of NetWare servers and their clients within the SMS System. In larger and more complex networks, you also risk the possibility of having a NetWare logon server reporting its inventory to more than one SMS site. This causes serious Site configuration and reporting problems.

NetWare 4.*x* does utilize the domain concept with the introduction of NetWare Directory Services (NDS) in NetWare 4.*x*. This allows for a method similar to the NT domain for managing a centralized user database of NetWare clients. But unlike NT domains, NDS used with NetWare 4.*x* does not work with SMS. In order to use NetWare 4.*x* servers as SMS logon servers, the NetWare clients that normally would log on to a NetWare 4.*x* environment using NDS now have to log on using the old NetWare 3.*x* method, called bindery mode.

Remember that NetWare 3.*x* servers do not participate in a domain structure like NT servers, and thus do not use a common user database to authenticate users. Instead 3.*x* servers use the bindery or flat database to store user account information at each server. When a user wants to use the resources on a 3.*x* server, he or she must first log on to that specific NetWare 3.*x* server. The NetWare server's bindery is then used to authenticate the user and allow access to the server's resources. Logging on under bindery mode on a NetWare 4.*x* server allows the client to access resources just like a NetWare 3.*x* server client, but only the resources on that individual server (specifically in the bindery context). The result is the major downside of NetWare 4.*x* server integration with SMS. SMS clients in a NetWare environment can no longer use NDS resources available under 4.*x*.

The steps that follow will take you through the installation procedure for adding a NetWare domain to your current SMS site:

1. Log on to the SMS site server using an administrative account, and start the SMS Administrator program.
2. Open the Sites window and highlight the Site icon in the left pane. Choose Properties from the File menu to display the Site Properties dialog box.
3. Click the Domains button to display the Domains dialog box.
4. Mark the Proposed Properties button and then click the Add button to display the Domain Properties dialog box.
5. In the Name box type the display name for the NetWare domain. For our example, we'll use the name NOVELL41.
6. In the Type box, use the drop-down list to choose Novell NetWare.
7. Now look at the Logon Servers area of the Domain Properties dialog box. You'll notice that when you pick Novell NetWare in the Type box, the Use All Detected Servers button becomes unmarked, and the Use Specified Servers option becomes the default

choice. Leave the option with the new default setting. Please take note of the caution statement if you decide to select the Use All Detected Servers option.

CAUTION

Using the Use All Detected Servers option when NetWare Servers are present is not recommended without careful study. All NetWare version 3.x and 4.x (running bindery emulation) servers will be detected and enumerated. Detection of Novell Servers can take place over as many as 16 router hops. It's possible under some circumstances for the SMS system to include the same logon server in more than one SMS site. This in turn creates serious problems with the SMS site reporting of configuration and inventory information.

8. In the New Logon Server box, type the name of the NetWare server you've configured.
9. In the Volume box, type the name of the disk volume for the NetWare Server.
10. Click the Add button to add the server (and volume name) to the Use These Logon Servers list. (see fig. 6.65). Note that if no volume is specified, the SMS System will install its components on the volume with the most available space.

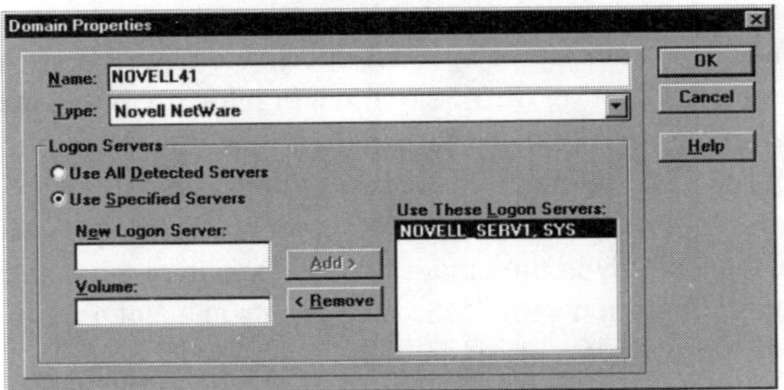

FIG. 6.65
The values specified here determine which NetWare Serves are included in the new domain.

11. When you've completed entering the names of servers to be included in the NetWare domain, click the OK button. Remember that any other NetWare servers that are specified here must also be set up with the NetWare SMS Service account, NTGATEWAY, and EVERYONE groups.
12. The Domains dialog box will now display the NetWare domain in the Domains at Site dialog box. Click the OK button to return to the Site Properties box, then click OK again to bring up the Microsoft SMS Administrator dialog box, asking you to confirm the update of the site. Click Yes to initiate the changes.

The time it takes before the process is initiated will depend on the Watch-dogging Interval specified at the primary site. This is the frequency in minutes between the initiation of a new watchdog cycle. The specifics of both the Watch-dogging Interval and the watchdog cycle are detailed in Appendix B, "SMS System Files and Utilities." For now it's sufficient to say that checks are performed at the beginning of each watchdog cycle to see whether changes in the site configuration have been detected. If changes are detected (such as adding a new domain to the site), the SMS Site Configuration and Maintenance Managers begin their job of installing the SMS components on the NetWare Servers we've specified. The default Watch-dogging Interval is set to 120 minutes, so it may take that long before changes to the site begin.

For smaller or less complex sites, you can force the initiation of the watchdog cycle by using the SENDCODE utility found on the SMS CD-ROM's \PSTOOLS directory to perform a site reset. The command line syntax to use is the following:

```
sendcode sms_site_config_manager 196
```

Executing this command from the command prompt of the primary site server will cause the immediate initiation of the watchdog cycle and modification of the logon scripts. The utility will initiate the reset and indicate its completion with the message "—Success—" at the Command Prompt.

You can also perform a site reset by running the local copy of the SMS Setup program. You'll find its icon in the Systems Management Server program group. Start the Setup program, continue past the welcome screen to the Installations Options dialog box. Click the Operations button to display the Site Operations dialog box. Click the Reset Site button to initiate a new watchdog cycle.

When the process starts, the SMS root directory will be added to the NetWare server's volume with the most free space (unless a specific volume was designated during the domain setup). After setting up the root directory, the Site Configuration Manager will create the subdirectory LOGON.SRV within the SMS root. It will then copy the appropriate SMS files to this subdirectory. The same files and directories that are copied to an NT logon server during its setup are copied to the NetWare server(s). Once the files have been copied, they will initially occupy approximately 20MB of disk space on the NetWare server.

SMS also performs the following tasks:

- Sets the appropriate trustee rights for each of the SMS directories installed on the NetWare Server.
- Modifies the System Login Script by inserting the statements needed run the Client Setup and Inventory Agent for MS-DOS programs when a user logs on to the NetWare Server.
- Scans the NetWare Server(s) for hardware and software inventory.

NOTE Note that the SMS command lines placed in the System Login Script all have a REM statement in front of them. The System Login Script *must* be manually modified before the SMS components of the Login Script will actually become active.

The SMS system (using the NetWare SMS Service account) will set the permissions on each of the SMS subdirectories using the EVERYONE group. The permissions will vary depending on the subdirectory. You can use the Filer utility to view the permissions given to a specific SMS subdirectory. We can see in figure 6.66 that the EVERYONE group has been given read and file scan rights to the LOGON.SRV directory.

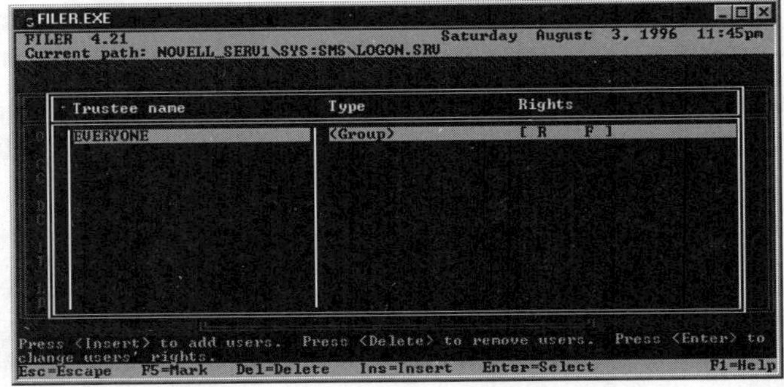

FIG. 6.66 The LOGON.SRV directory is read-only with file scan rights for the EVERYONE group.

Figure 6.67 shows the EVERYONE group having read, write, create, modify, erase, and file scan rights to the LOGON.SRV\CCR.BOX directory.

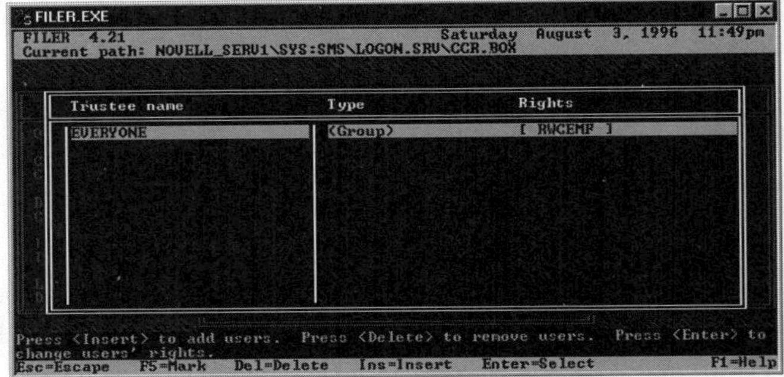

FIG. 6.67 Full rights are given to the EVERYONE group for some directories.

After setting permissions on the SMS-related directories, the SMS system will modify the System Login Script on the NetWare server to include a call to the SMS Script file (SMSLS.SCR). SMS places REM statements at the beginning of the command lines used to call the SMS script, as shown in figure 6.68.

```
Syscon
SYSCON 3.76                                   Friday August 2, 1996 2:11 pm
              User LEEADMIN On File Server NOVELL_SERV1

                        System Login Script
REM SMS Build 738

write "Administrator modifications necessary to activate SMS automatic logon
scripts"
REM  To activate automatic logon scripts, the following section should be
REM  un-commented out and the question mark "?:" replaced with an
REM  unused drive letter. The drive letter must be entered in uppercase.
  REM set SMS_DRIVE="?:"
  REM map %<SMS_DRIVE>=SYS:
  REM set SMS_LOGON="%<SMS_DRIVE>\SMS\logon.srv"
  REM INCLUDE %<SMS_LOGON>\SMSLS.SCR
  REM set SMS_LOGON=
  REM map DEL %<SMS_DRIVE>
  REM set SMS_DRIVE=

REM Microsoft Systems Management Server (end)
```

FIG. 6.68 The System Login Script must be modified before the SMSLS script will run.

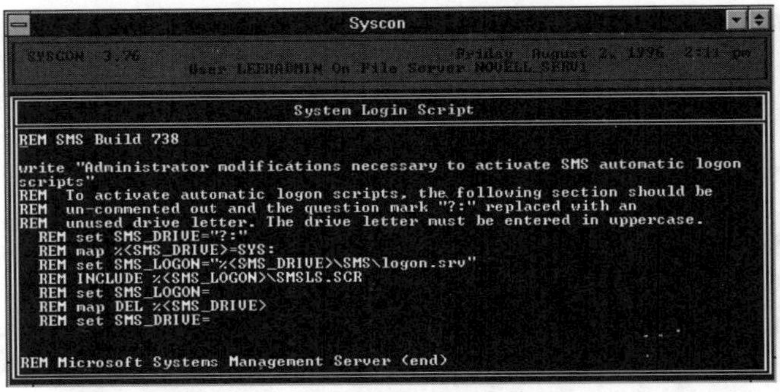

The REM statements must be removed before the SMS script file will run. In addition, a drive letter designating an available drive common to all NetWare clients must be specified. Although the drive is released after running the SMS script, it must be available at the time a client logs in. In our example, shown in figure 6.69, we have removed the REM statements and supplied the drive letter of S for the commonly available drive letter.

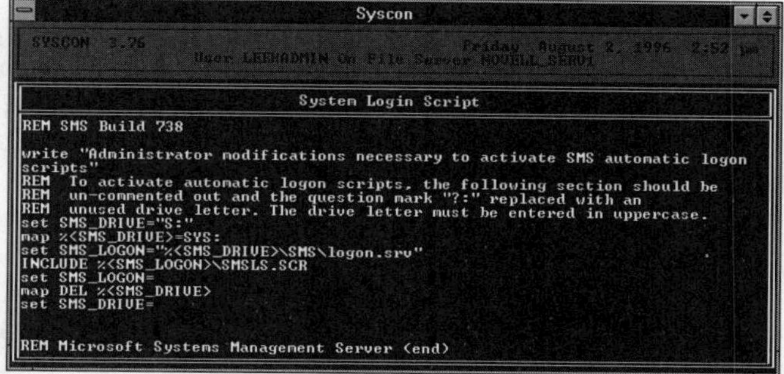

FIG. 6.69
The modified System Login Script file.

A new Domain icon will appear in the Sites window representing the new NetWare domain. This icon will appear even if the detection and installation of the NetWare servers in that domain fail. If none of the NetWare servers start appearing under the NetWare domain within a reasonable amount of time, you'll need to monitor the primary site server's event log for errors. The NetWare server(s) appearance in the Sites window should be fairly quick if you've used the SENDCODE utility. If you find errors in the event log, or if the servers just don't appear, you'll need to recheck that the NetWare groups and NetWare SMS Service account have been set up properly. Most of the time these problems are cured with a double-check of the NetWare server setup.

Once the NetWare server(s) start to appear in the Sites window, you can view the properties for each server(s) by clicking the server's icon to open the Personal Computer Properties—[*servername*] dialog box. Limited information is gathered on the actual NetWare server (see fig. 6.70) besides some network and volume information.

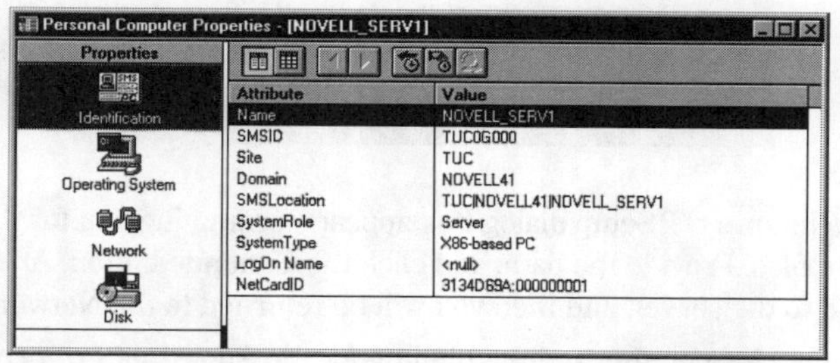

FIG. 6.70
Inventory Information is limited for NetWare server.

In Chapter 7, we'll look at the NetWare client. For now we'll move on to the support of Macintosh clients using the SMS System, specifically the prerequisite steps that need to be taken at the primary site server in order to support a Macintosh environment.

Integration with Macintosh

Inventory of Macintosh clients can be supported by the SMS system by performing some additional configuration on the SMS logon and primary site servers, as follows:

- Install the Windows NT Services for Macintosh on all NT/SMS logon servers in the site that will be used for Macintosh client logon.
- Install the Macintosh Client components on the SMS site server.

You can use any Windows NT Server in the site that's currently acting as an SMS logon server, as long as it's running the Services for Macintosh (SFM) NT version 3.1 or later. Note that neither LAN Manager services for Macintosh nor NetWare for Macintosh are supported for Macintosh Clients and simply will not work with SMS.

Let's go through the process of installing the Services for Macintosh first, then we'll look at the installation of the additional Macintosh Client components.

Installing the Windows NT Services for Macintosh Follow these steps to install Services for Macintosh on your Windows NT 4.0 SMS logon server(s):

1. Log on to the site server as the administrator or equivalent, and open the NT Server Control Panel.
2. Double-click the Network icon to display the Network dialog box.
3. Click the Services tab to show the list of currently installed network services. Click the Add button to display the Select Network Service dialog box.
4. Scroll down and highlight the Service for Macintosh option, as shown in figure 6.71, then click the OK button.

FIG. 6.71
Install the Windows NT Services for Macintosh.

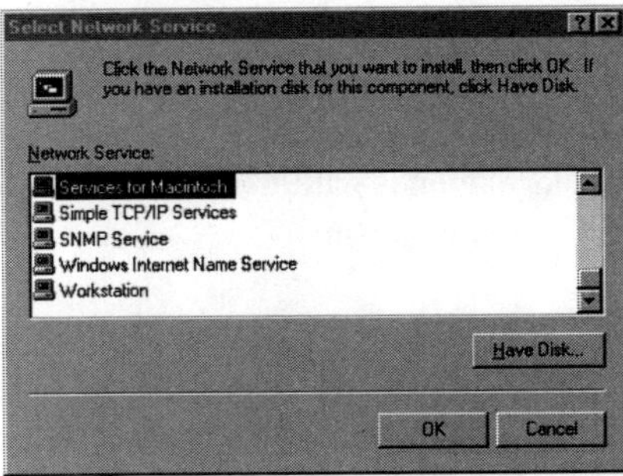

5. The Windows NT Setup dialog box appears, prompting you for the path to the NT Server source files. Provide the path, and click the Continue button. At this point the files will be copied to the server, and then you will be returned to the Network dialog box.
6. Click the close button, and the binding for the AppleTalk Protocol will take place. This will be followed by the Microsoft AppleTalk Protocol Properties dialog box.

7. Under the General tab, choose the LAN adapter that you wish to configure for AppleTalk by choosing it in the Default Adapter drop-down box.
8. Next, choose the zone from the Default Zone drop-down box. This is the zone in the Macintosh Chooser in which the Windows NT File and Print services will appear.
9. Click the OK button to finish the binding configuration for the AppleTalk Protocol. This will be followed by the Network Settings Change dialog box, prompting you to restart the computer. Click Yes to restart the server.

After the server has rebooted, you'll notice the addition of the MacFile menu option in the Server Manager. The subdirectory named \Microsoft UAM Volume will also be created on the server's disk drive.

Next, we'll install the Macintosh Client components for SMS on the site server.

Installing the Macintosh Client Components To install the Macintosh Client components, you must run the SMS Setup program from the SMS source CD-ROM. Running the local copy of the SMS Setup program from the icon found in the Systems Management Server program group will not allow you to add additional software components to the SMS System.

Follow the instructions listed below to install the Macintosh Client components:

1. Log on to the site server as the administrator or equivalent, and open the NT Server Control Panel.
2. Locate the SMS CD-ROM or other distribution point, move into the directory appropriate to the site server's hardware platform, and run the Setup program.
3. Click the Continue button twice to proceed past the Welcome screen and the Existing Installation dialog box. The Installation Options dialog box will appear.
4. Click the Add Software button to display the Software Installation Options dialog box. Highlight the Macintosh Client option in the Available software list, and click the Add button to place the option in the Software to Install list (see fig. 6.72). Click the OK button.

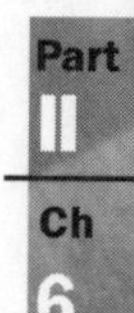

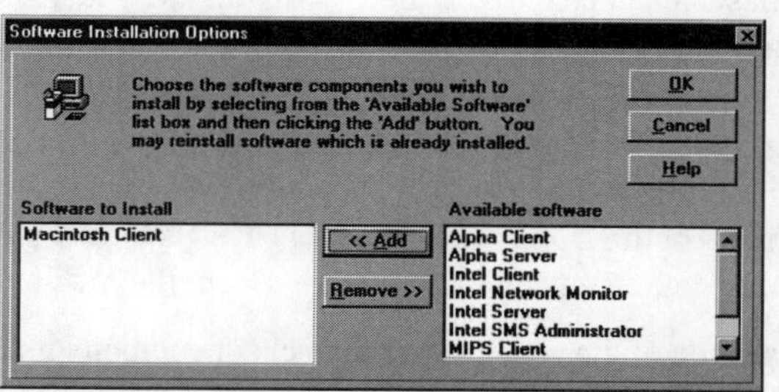

FIG. 6.72 You must add the Macintosh Client components using Setup from the original CD-ROM.

5. The Secondary Site Upgrade Option dialog box will appear. This enables you to specify if the Macintosh Client components should be sent to secondary sites. If you choose Yes,

any logon server located at a secondary site that's running SFM will receive the Macintosh Client components automatically. For our example, we'll restrict installation of the Macintosh Client components to the current site by clicking No.

6. Click OK in the Release Note dialog box, which notifies you that the Apple Installer version 3.4 or greater is needed to complete the installation. We'll cover the installation of the Installer software shortly. The file installation will then begin.
7. When the installation of the Macintosh components is complete, a Success dialog box will appear. Click OK to return to the Installation Options dialog box, then click the Exit button to end the installation.

Copying the Apple Installer to the Site Server The next steps involve copying the Apple Installer to the Site server's SMS directory. SMS cannot automatically configure logon scripts for Macintosh clients as it does for other clients. Instead, the Macintosh client must manually connect to a Macintosh volume created on the SMS site server to run the Apple Installer software. Since this software doesn't come with SMS (and is not even distributed by Microsoft), it must be copied from off the Macintosh System 7.1 or 7.5 operating system diskettes onto the SMS site server.

A new Macintosh volume that will receive a copy of the Apple Installer program has been created by the SMS system using the site server's \SMS\LOGON.SRV directory. If you open up the NT Service Manager, you can look at the new volume's properties by choosing Volumes from the MacFile menu. You'll see the Microsoft UAM Volume created by the SFM installation and the new SMS_SHR volume created by SMS. Highlight the SMS_SHR volume and click the Properties button to view and edit permission, security, and path properties for the volume.

Perform the following steps to copy the Apple Installer software to the site server:

1. Insert the Macintosh System 7.1 or 7.5 installation disk containing the Apple Installer version 3.4 or later into the Macintosh computer.
2. On the Macintosh computer, mount the SMS_SHR volume and then copy the Apple Installer file from the diskette to it.
3. After the file has been copied to the SMS_SHR volume, you'll need to copy it manually into the site server's SITE.SRV\MAINCFG.BOX\CLIENT.SRC\MAC.BIN directory. From here the file will automatically be copied to all logon servers and secondary sites.
4. Create users accounts in the NT domain containing the SFM SMS site server for any Macintosh clients that will be SMS clients on the system. The user accounts you create must be members of the Domain Users group. This is the account that will be used to access the SMS components on the site server from the Macintosh client.

We'll cover the installation of the actual Macintosh client components to the Macintosh computer in Chapter 7 "Installing Client Sites."

From Here...

Now that we've covered the SMS server installation and integration with other operating systems, it's time to turn our attention to the installation of the client workstation components. You may also want to check out the other chapters listed here for more information on related topics.

- Chapter 7, "Installing Client Sites," looks at the methods available for adding clients and inventory to the SMS System.
- Chapter 8, "Using the SMS Administrator Program"—we've taken a look at some of the properties in the SMS Administrator's program. Chapter 8 covers the details of its use.
- Chapter 15, "Changing Your Site Configuration" examines the procedures involved with site maintenance, such as the deleting or moving of a site from the system.
- Appendix B, "SMS System File and Utilities," takes a close look at the files that make up the SMS system, along with some of the utilities used to maintain SMS.

CHAPTER 7

Installing Client Sites

First, we'll look at using the Automatically Configure Workstation Logon Scripts option

You'll see how it works, and what prerequisites must be completed before using it.

Then we cover the manual setup of login scripts

The manual installation of SMS Login scripts in a LAN Manager or Windows NT environment, and the manual setup of login scripts in a NetWare environment are both covered in the course of this chapter.

Adding clients manually

Finally in the last section of the chapter we'll see how to add clients manually to the SMS inventory.

The last piece of the SMS System that must be put in place is the installation of the client software on the various users' operating systems and platforms. In this chapter, the client component installation methods for SMS-compatible operating systems are outlined.

Fortunately the task of loading the SMS components at the client has been automated and requires a minimal amount of administrative intervention. The actual process can be carried out automatically by SMS if you choose the Automatically Configure Workstation Logon Scripts option in the Site Properties Client setup. Although automatic installation works for LAN Manager and NT domain clients, Novell and Macintosh clients will still require some additional manual configuration. We'll begin the section by looking at the steps required to enable the Automatically Configure Workstation Logon Scripts Option for use in an NT or LAN Manager environment. Then we'll go on to see how to add a client manually to the SMS System. In the last part of this chapter, the configuration of Novell and Macintosh clients will examined. ■

Using the Automatically Configure Workstation Logon Scripts Option

This is the simplest way to add users into the SMS System. It requires that the Directory Replicator service be running on all SMS logon servers at the site. Setting up the Directory Replication service and its associated service account were covered earlier in Chapter 5. If you have a small or very simple site, you may have already enabled this feature during the installation procedure for SMS. If not, you can implement it at any time, as long as you are aware of the ramifications it may cause (especially in the larger site installations). This topic was also discussed earlier in Chapter 5 and may merit your quick review before you actually activate the Automatically Configure Workstation Logon Scripts option.

> **CAUTION**
>
> On a Windows NT or LAN Manager domain, the Use All Detected Servers option in the Domain Properties dialog box must be used if you've specified the Automatically Configure Workstation Logon Scripts option, because otherwise the process to configure the site for SMS logon scripts will fail. If you have specified logon servers, or have domains that span sites (and can't use the Use All Detected Servers option), you will have to set up logon scripts manually.

To add all the DOS, Windows 3.1, WFW, Windows 95, Windows NT Workstation, and NT Server machines residing in an NT or LAN Manager domain system to the SMS site, follow these steps:

1. Log on to the SMS site server using an administrative account and start the SMS Administrator program.
2. Open the Sites window and highlight the SMS site you wish to configure. From the File menu, choose Properties to display the Site Properties dialog box.
3. Click the Clients button to display the Clients dialog box.
4. Mark the Proposed Properties button at the top of the dialog box.
5. Mark all the features of the client software you wish installed during the automatic installation under the Client Software section of the dialog box.
6. Mark the box next to the Automatically Configure Workstation Logon Scripts option.
7. Next, decide where you would like the call to the SMS logon script to be placed in any preexisting domain logon script. If no logon script exists, the SMSLS batch file will become the logon script. If a script does exist, the Insert at Top of Logon Script and Add to Bottom of Logon Script options allow you to place the SMSLS batch file call where you want.

Often an existing logon script will be used to synchronize the workstation's time with that of a server. If this is the case, the set time call should be left at the beginning of any logon script that is presently being used. The SMSLS batch file call should follow it. If a logon script is not currently being used for synchronizing time between servers and workstations, it's a wise idea to create one, since SMS relies heavily on time synchronization for the distribution of software. Use the command line:

net time *servername* /DOMAIN:*domain name* /s /y

at the beginning of the logon script, and choose Add to Bottom of Logon Script option to place the SMSLS batch file call after it.

8. When you've finished making your selections, click the OK button twice and then verify the update by clicking the Yes button in the Microsoft SMS Administrator dialog box.

In the next monitoring cycle, the Site Configuration Manager will detect the configuration change and start to transfer SMS directories and files to the SCRIPTS directory of the REPL$ share on the Directory Replicator export server (the primary domain controller). The files that get transferred into this directory are then exported by the Directory Replication service to all the other servers that have been configured for directory replication import. The process time will vary for this operation, depending on the number of servers, position of the Site Configuration Manager in the monitoring cycle, and length of the monitoring cycle (120 minutes is the default). The following lists the major files that are replicated to the NETLOGON shares—all of these files perform a specific function to support the SMS logon and inventory process:

- CLRLEVEL.COM—restores the path and removes any environment variables that may have been set during execution of the logon script. CLRLEVEL.COM is called to reset the DOS error level flags.
- DOSVER.COM—used to detect the version of DOS running at the client.
- NETSPEED.COM—called from the SMSLS batch file to detect slow network links. If a slow link is detected, certain parameters are set to determine if client inventory should be taken.
- SETLS—used to call, execute, and pass parameters to the Client Setup and Inventory Agent programs. A specific version of SETLS is required for each operating system and processor architecture. The SMSLS batch file determines the operating system and processor architecture, and calls the proper version of SETLS.
- SMSLS.CMD and SMSLS.BAT—these are the SMS batch files is used to run CLRLEVEL.COM, DOSVER, NETSPEED and the SETLS program. While DOS, Windows, and NT users would execute the SMSLS.BAT file, OS/2 users would execute the SMSLS.CMD file instead.
- SMSLS.INI—the initialization file used by the SETLS program which is called by the SMSLS batch file.

When the files are replicated, they are placed on each logon server's NETLOGON share for access by the user during logon. The SMS system will assign a logon script to each user account in the domain. If the user already has a logon script, a call to the SMSLS script file is placed either at the beginning or at the end of the current script file. The placement was determined by choosing the appropriate option in the Client Properties dialog box in step 7 of our example.

▶ **See** Detailed information on each of the files mentioned above, as well as the file installation process, can be found in Appendix B, "SMS System Files and Utilities." **p. 551**

The next time a user logs on, the SMSLS script file is executed. This in turn runs the SMS Client Setup program on the computer. This setup process will detect the platform type and install the appropriate files (approximately 3MB) to the local machine. It will modify files and registry settings to configure the computer as an SMS Client. The setup process will also create the SMS Client program group.

After that, Setup will launch the MIF Entry program and then prompt the user to complete the standard MIF form (included with SMS) as shown in figure 7.1.

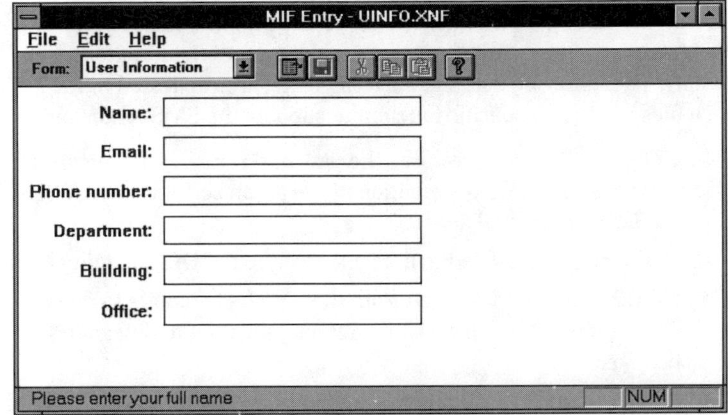

FIG. 7.1
Users can fill out the default MIF form at setup time.

The user may fill the MIF form out now or at a later time. The user will also see the Welcome to Package Manager dialog box, which explains the features of the Package Manager application. This dialog box will not appear again if you mark the box beside the text that says: Don't display this message at startup.

The full functionality of the SMS client components is not available until the client's computer is restarted and the memory-resident portions of the client software are activated. The exception to this is when the SMS client components are loaded on NT-based computers. Since NT-based machines don't rely on TSR programs loaded from a DOS AUTOEXEC.BAT file, they do not need to be restarted after the client Setup program initially executes.

Setting Up Logon Scripts Manually in a Windows NT or LAN Manager Environment

To configure user logon scripts manually, you must copy files from the site server into the NETLOGON share (*drive*:\winnt\system32\RepNImport\Scripts directory) of each logon server in the domain. The files you need to copy will all be located in the SMS_SHR share (*drive*:\sms\logon.srv directory) on the site server, with one exception. The SMSLS.INI file is located in the *drive*:\sms\site.srv\maincfg.box subdirectory on the site server.

The version of SETLS will depend on the hardware platforms in place at your site. Different versions of SETLS exist for different NT hardware platforms. You'll find the version of SETLS you need under the processor-specific subdirectory (X86.BIN, ALPHA.BIN, or MIPS.BIN) of the SMS_SHR share. You need to copy the file SETLS32.EXE from this directory to the NETLOGON share.

Follow the steps listed below to set up user logon scripts manually:

- Intel processors—copy SETLS32.EXE from the SMS_SHR share's X86.BIN directory to X86.BIN\SETLS32.EXE on the NETLOGON share of the logon server.
- Alpha processors—copy SETLS32.EXE from the SMS_SHR share's ALPHA.BIN directory to ALPHA.BIN\SETLS32.EXE on the NETLOGON share of the logon server.
- MIPS processors—copy SETLS32.EXE from the SMS_SHR share's MIPS.BIN directory to MIPS.BIN\SETLS32.EXE on the NETLOGON share of the logon server.

The other files that need to be copied to the logon server are as follows:

- CLRLEVEL.COM
- DOSVER.COM
- NETSPEED.COM
- NETSPEED.DAT
- SMSLS.BAT and SMSLS.CMD
- SMSLS.INI

You'll also need to copy the SETLS16.EXE and SETLSOS2.EXE to the bin directory, along with the following files:

- NLSMSG16.EXE
- NLSMSG32.EXE
- NLSMSGO2.EXE
- NLSRES.INI

Part II Ch 7

Setting Up Scripts Manually in a NetWare domain

You can manually set up the logon scripts on NetWare servers by modifying the system or user login script. Insert the following lines into the login script:

```
set SMS_DRIVE="?:"
map %<SMS_DRIVE>=SYS:
set SMS_LOGON="%<SMS_DRIVE>\SMS\logon.srv"
INCLUDE %<SMS_LOGON>\SMSLS.SCR
set SMS_LOGON=
map DEL %<SMS_DRIVE>
set SMS_DRIVE=
```

Replace the question mark "?:" with the name of a free drive letter that can be used during login. This drive will be released after the script has run.

Manually Adding Client Inventory

If you don't want to configure logon scripts to take inventory automatically when a user signs on, you can manually run the client setup and inventory agent from the site server's SMS_SHR share (*logonserver\volume*\sms\logon.srv on NetWare servers). Then the file name RUNSMS is executed instead of the SMSLS batch file. The RUNSMS batch file does not contain the NETSPEED.COM program to detect slow network links. Otherwise its content is the same as the SMSLS batch file that's normally run in logon scripts.

To manually take inventory on a client machine, connect to the logon server's SMS_SHR share (or NetWare volume and drive) and type RUNSMS at the command prompt.

Adding Macintosh Clients to the System

As we learned earlier, Services For Macintosh must be running on the site logon server that will be used by the Macintosh clients. Once SFM is running, you can use the following steps to add a Macintosh client to the SMS system:

1. At the Macintosh machine, connect to the SMS_SHR volume that SMS created when SFM was installed.
2. Open the MAC.BIN folder in the SMS_SHR volume.
3. Find the Installer program and start it.
4. When the SMS Script dialog box appears, click Install.
5. You will be prompted to close any open applications. If you agree, the Setup program will close any open programs and proceed to install the SMS client components on the computer. A message will appear when the installation is complete.
6. Click Restart.

After the restart, the Inventory Agent will scan the computer and report the inventory information to the logon server. When it's finished, it will start the Package Command Manager

(PCMMac) on the Macintosh. The Inventory Agent program (INVMac) is placed in the Startup Items folder, and will run automatically each time the system is started.

INVMac creates a local SMS.INI file and two other files, as follows:

- InvHWScanResult—used for storing hardware inventory history information at the local machine.
- InvSWScanResult—used for storing software inventory history information at the local machine.

Inventory results are placed in the logon server's LOGON.SRV\ISVMIF.BOX directory in the form of a *.MIF file (ASCII text). The file is then moved by the Maintenance Manager from the logon server to the site server's SITE.SRV\ISVMIF.BOX where it is processed by the Inventory Processor.

From Here ...

This finishes the chapter on installing your site servers and clients. By now you should have a good understanding of the installation steps needed to put the basic SMS components in place. From here we'll look at the administrative interface used to control SMS.

- Chapter 8, "Using the SMS Administrator Program," takes a close look at the Administration program's user interface and features.
- Chapter 12, "Queries and Reports," shows you how to query the SMS database for information on client inventory. It also shows you how to install and use Crystal Reports, an optional program that's packaged with SMS, to create informative reports in a format appropriate for management review.
- Chapter 13, "Using Help Desk and Diagnostics on a Remote PC," will explain how to use the Help Desk and Diagnostics functions within SMS to assist any user that has the SMS client components installed and has enabled the remote control options.

PART III

Managing Your System with SMS

CHAPTER 8

Using the SMS Administrator Program

Learn about the SMS Administrator Program

Become familiar with how the program works, and what it can do.

Install the SMS Administrator Program

SMS Setup makes installation fast and easy.

Use Diagnostic tools

There are a variety of different tools you can use to diagnose and troubleshoot problems.

SMS Administrator will be your "command central" in SMS. From it you can do virtually anything in SMS: run your packages and jobs for hardware and software inventory, collect files, run queries, distribute software, share software, and more.

It is important for you to understand the SMS Administrator interface, as well as understand what is happening "under the hood" with the SMS Administrator program. There are many SQL user connections being utilized, RAM being used, and background tasks running that you need to be aware of to allocate resources properly.

There are also some changes you will almost surely want to make; for instance, automatically configuring workstations for SMS inventory. ■

Using the SMS Administrator

SMS Administrator is an important part of the System Management Server. After SMS has been installed, use the SMS Administrator utility to configure the SMS site. You will also use the SMS Administrator to configure the client properties and set the Domain and Server properties, as in figure 8.1.

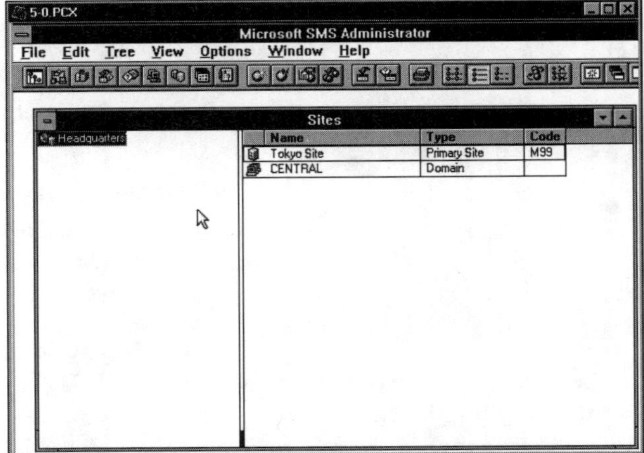

FIG. 8.1 Use SMS Administrator utility to configure your client properties.

The following are considerations when installing the SMS Administrator:

- Requires 37MB of disk space
- Uses at least 5 SQL user connections
- Requires a minimum of 2MB of RAM

Opening the SMS Administrator consumes about 2 MB of RAM, but what if you want to crunch some data inside the Administrator tool with query processing or inventory reporting? Running hardware queries uses 726 bytes per machine queried. What if you have a site with 5,000 clients? That is an additional 3.6MB of RAM.

The SMS Administrator may cause a lot of data traffic between the SQL Server and the SMS Administrator, especially when opening a Sites window with a lot of machines. This will be a consideration when running SQL on a separate server on the network. You will want to maximize network bandwidth in your plan. Running a query, or a frequently repeating alert, can also have a large impact on net traffic and system performance.

You can set the estimated bandwidth to a high value in the Sender dialog box to increase performance.

By default, opening the Sites window runs a background query against all machines in the site hierarchy. If the Sites window is opened in a site with 10,000 machines in the hierarchy, the SMS Administrator requires about 8 MB. If an ad hoc query is initiated while the background

Sites window query is still running, the SMS Administrator requires double—16 MB. You can decrease the impact of opening the SMS Administrator by clearing the Background Query in Sites checkbox under Options, Preferences.

It goes without saying that you want to run the SMS Administrator on a fast computer with ample memory and a high-speed link to the SQL Server database. However, SMS Administrator can be installed to any Windows NT Workstation; it does not have to run on the site server.

Installing SMS Administrator

In the SMS Setup, one of your installation options will be Install Admin Tools. This will install the SMS Administrator. You can do this on any machine from which you will be monitoring the SMS site, and you can also install SMS tools on an NT Workstation.

To install SMS:

1. From the SMSETUP directory, run SETUP.BAT. This batch file examines your system to determine which platform to install: X86, Alpha, or MIPS.
2. From the Installation Options dialog box, choose Install Primary Site. This starts the primary site installation.
3. From the Setup Install Options dialog box, choose Continue to install the default SMS components. If you plan to use different computers, select the Custom dialog box and choose the computers that you plan to use.

   If you are installing SMS on the same server as the SQL Server, the SQL Database Configuration dialog box appears with the SQL Server configuration information. Fill in the SQL Login (SMSAdmin) and the password you assigned to that account, as shown in the following illustration.
4. Enter the primary site configuration information for your installation, using the following illustration as a model. Note that the check box for Automatically detecting all login servers has been selected; it is cleared by default.

The fields in this dialog should be filled in as follows:

- Code: Any unique combination of three alphanumeric characters (no special characters)
- Name: A descriptive name
- Server: Leave as default
- Domain: Leave as default
- Automatically Detect Logon Servers: Select
- Username: The SMSAdmin account that you created. If trust relationships are used between domains, include the domain prefix with the user name.
- Password: The SMSAdmin password (must be different from SMSAdmin account name)

The Setup program copies files, completes the database configuration, automatically installs the Network Monitor Agent if it is not already installed, and starts the SMS Services.

Setting Properties

Once SMS has been installed, use SMS Administrator to configure the SMS site. You can configure automatic client inventory, among other things. To use SMS Administrator, you must first log on using the SMS Administrator account that you created during your initial primary site installation of SMS.

Changing Proposed Versus Current Properties

SMS works on a schedule, so if you want to initiate a change to the Site, Domain, Server or properties, you always go into Proposed Properties in each of the respective dialog boxes to initiate your change. Later in this chapter we discuss adding a Novell Server under Domain Properties.

Behind the scenes, after you make a proposed change, the following will happen:

- The Hierarchy Manager monitors the database for proposed changes and create a site control file with the proposed change.
- The Site Configuration Manager creates a site control response file for each site.
- The site control response file is passed up to the Hierarchy Manager at the primary site.
- The Hierarchy Manager updates the SMS database and the change is implemented.

Setting Site Properties

All properties changes, including Domain and Server properties, Client properties, Sender properties, and so on, are made from the Site Properties dialog box.

The necessary settings are made from the Site Properties dialog box, which you reach by choosing Sites from the SMS Administrator Window. From the SMS Administrator toolbar, click Sites.

Open the Site Properties dialog box by choosing the Site button from the SMS Administrator Window toolbar.

Setting the Client Properties

SMS can automatically modify the logon scripts for all users in all Windows NT and LAN Manager domains and modify the system login script for all users in Netware domains so that the SMSLS batch file is run every time a user logs on to one of the site's domains. In this way you can collect inventory from each workstation and automatically install SMS client software on each machine (see fig. 8.2).

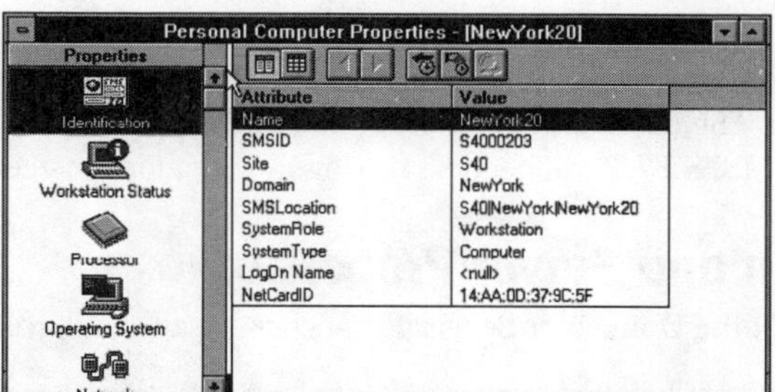

FIG. 8.2
Use the Client Properties dialog box to configure information about your client.

To set up SMS to modify logon scripts, choose Clients from the Sites Properties dialog box and make the following adjustments:

To automatically configure Workstation Logon Scripts:

1. Under Clients, choose the Automatically Configure Workstation Logon Scripts option.
2. Click the Proposed Properties radio button.
3. Choose the Detect All Servers option if your network includes Windows NT or LAN Manager domains.
4. In most cases, choose the Add to Bottom of Logon Script option so that the modifications that SMS makes to the logon script are added to the end of the script. This could depend on what else is done by the script.

Figure 8.3 shows a completed Clients dialog box.

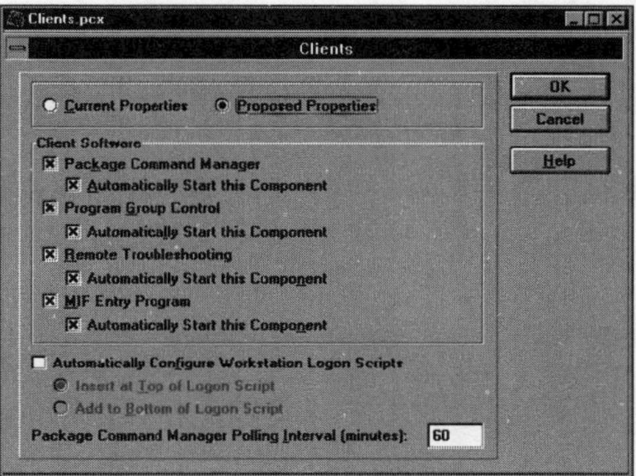

FIG. 8.3
The completed Clients dialog box.

NOTE The Use All Detected Servers option in the Clients dialog box should be checked for Automatic Configuration of NT or Lan Manager Network clients. SMS will not add SMSLS.BAT to users' logon scripts otherwise, because it might affect non-SMS users in a site. ■

SMS will copy the SMSLS batch file and SMS client executables to the Primary Domain Controller in NT, the Netware Servers in Netware, and the LAN Manager Servers in LAN Manager that are appropriate. The users' logon scripts are all modified for SMS. If there is no logon script at the time, SMSLS.BAT will become the logon script for the user.

Setting the Domain and Server Properties

You may want to edit the Domain or Server Properties if, say, you have a Novell site.

After SMS has been installed, and during SMS site configuration, you need to take special steps so that SMS uses the NetWare server as a logon and distribution server. Begin by choosing the Sites button from the SMS Administrator toolbar.

To set the domain properties:

1. From the Sites Properties dialog box, click Domains.
2. Choose Proposed Properties, and then click Add. The Domains Properties dialog box appears.
3. Enter the domain name in the Name text box. Do not choose a name that is the same as the name of any Windows NT or LAN Manager domain in your organization.
4. Select Novell NetWare from the Type list box.
5. Type name of your NetWare server in the New Logon Server text box, and click Add. Repeat for each NetWare logon server in your domain, until they all appear in the Use These Logon Servers list box.

To set the Server Properties:

1. From the Sites Properties dialog box, click Servers. The Servers dialog box appears.
2. Choose Proposed properties, and then click Add. The Server Properties dialog box appears.
3. Enter the name of the NetWare server in the Server Name text box.
4. Select Default Package Server from the Server Type list box.

In the Site Properties dialog box, click Domains. If you click Proposed Properties, you can add a new domain. You can choose the name and type of the domain. With Netware, you would choose a Netware domain and enter the name of the Novell Server and volume you want to use for SMS operations.

If your servers are all running Windows NT Server or LAN Manager, you probably will not need to make changes to the Domain and Server properties.

Viewing the Site Inventory

As each computer in the site logs on to the network, SMS detects it, installs the appropriate SMS client software, and adds the computer to the inventory.

To explore your inventory, start SMS Administrator, logging on with the SMS Admin login ID.

When you choose Expand All from the tree menu, the computers in the inventory for the site appear in the right pane of the Sites window.

You can view the properties of any computer in the inventory by selecting it and then choosing Properties from the File menu.

Defining Distribution Servers

Under Site Properties is a Server button. This is the key to changing the server configuration under a site.

Any server in the Servers list becomes part of the default package servers group, and these will be distribution points for software packages. These will also be points for applications to be shared from for Application Sharing.

You may want to add distribution servers to make application distribution and sharing more local to your users.

Another administrative task might be to remove the site server from the list of Default Package Servers. This is because the site server has other duties, and you may want to off-load the application distribution and sharing function to the remote site level. Also, you save hard disk space, because there is always a separate copy of every package kept on the site server as on the distribution server.

To stop a site server from being a distribution server, choose the Servers button from Site Properties to get the Servers dialog box.

Any server on this list is part of the Default Package Servers group. Select your site server from the list, then click the Remove button. It will let you remove your site server from the list of default package servers.

Creating a Helper Server

Under the Services button under Site Properties, you may elect to configure a helper server. This way you can off-load key SMS processes to other servers. If your primary server has a CPU bottleneck, it may be time to create a helper server.

All you have to do is specify a different server name for one of the four key services listed: Scheduler, Inventory Data Loader, Inventory Processor, or Despooler.

You can also set response options on this screen: Very Fast, Fast Medium, and Slow. Very Fast is considered best for test mode or rollout mode. However, once your SMS site stabilizes, it is common to choose medium.

Sender Properties

Under the Sender dialog under Site Properties, the default sender is an MS_ LAN_SENDER. You can create an MS_BATCH_SNA_SENDER, an MS_ASYNC_RAS_ SENDER, or an MS_INTER_SNA_SENDER.

Say you want to configure for MS_ASYNCH_RAS_SENDER. This is useful for data transport over dial-up RAS connections. You do this by clicking the Sender button inside the Site Properties dialog. Click Proposed Properties as you would for any change you initiate. You need to enter an alias name for internal SMS addressing, and also a server name to be the sender.

Diagnostic Tools

SMS provides a wealth of diagnostic tools utilities and for the most part they don't require a strategy to be used effectively. The bad news is that the tools cover a wide range of skills required to be used effectively. The low end helpdesk tools are easy to use and understand—remote execute, remote file transfer, remote boot and remote control. The mid-range helpdesk tools are easy to use but require windows knowledge to comprehend—Windows memory, Windows classes, Global Heap, GDI Heap and others. Finally the high end that requires high skill levels to operate and understand—Network Monitor. We will discuss some of these diagnostic tools in the next pages.

File Manager/Explorer

File Manager/Explorer will probably be the tool used most often to troubleshoot SMS. You can actually watch the files flow through their respective directories in real time. It can be helpful to open multiple windows for file monitoring.

Using Windows NT Remote Control

The remote control process allows the administrator to take control of an SMS client's keyboard and mouse. As shown in figure 8.4, this is done using SMS Administrator and a corresponding client TSR program. These two applications communicate over a NetBIOS or IPX session.

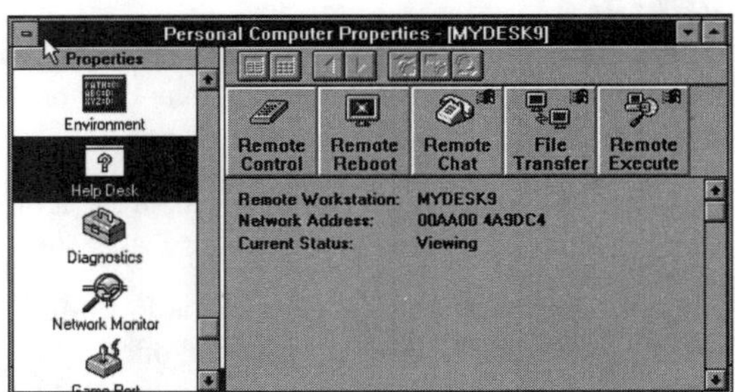

FIG. 8.4
The Windows NT Remote Control function allows you to manipulate a remote client system.

Working with Trace Logs

SMSTRACE.EXE is the graphical tool to view trace log files. It will allow you to watch the trace logs update in real time.

Usually, the job event details provide you with all the information you need to resolve any problems with failed jobs. If you need more information, you can use the SMSTRACE utility to examine trace logs for the services and components in the SMS Executive service. The SMS Executive and its components are described in the *Systems Management Server Administrator's Guide*, Appendix A, "SMS System Reference."

SMS maintains a log for each component of the SMS Executive. These log files can be examined if the job failed or produced unexpected results to help you pinpoint the source of the problem.

To determine which log file to examine, first use the flow charts in the *Systems Management Server Administrator's Guide*, Appendix C, "SMS System Flow," to determine which component was active when the failure occurred. These flow charts, and the accompanying text, describe the actions of each component and the files involved. Using File Manager, you can check for the existence of files created by the various components. You know the process failed at the point where an expected file is not found.

For example, the flow of Run Command On Workstation jobs includes a step in which the Sender transfers the instruction file to the target SMS site as a .TMP file and then renames it as a valid instruction file (*.INS). If the .TMP file appears on the target computer but is not renamed to *.INS, then the error affected the Sender component. To learn the nature of the error, examine the log file for the Sender component.

SMSTRACE.EXE, which you copied to your SMS server while setting up the lab, is used to view these log files. When you start this program, the SMS Tracer window appears. You can open a log file by clicking Open from the File menu to view the contents of the log file.

For more information on trace logs, see the *Systems Management Server Administrator's Guide*, Appendix J, "Tracing SMS Services."

Several new features add creature comforts inside SMS. There's an Add-In menu that will launch the Security Manager, Service Manager, DBCLEAN, and the other utilities. There is no indication as to how one might add other applications but this is probably possible. They have made allowances for the SNMP feature. That seems to be the most notable change to the Admin Tool. Otherwise, the Tool remains pretty much the same. It has not been rewritten to the new Windows 95 User Interface Guidelines.

Using Network Monitor

Some SMS version 1.2 features allow you to find routers and DNS entries.

- Frame—all frames captured during one capture session are numbered in order of capture time. The frame number appears in this column. If you have set a display filter, this column displays only those frames matching the filter.
- Time—this column displays the frame's capture time relative to the beginning of the capture process. Depending on display settings (see the Display Options menu item), the time could indicate time of day when the frame was captured, or time elapsed since the previous frame was captured.

A list of all the diagnostic tools Microsoft provides is on the SMS CD-ROM, located under the \PSSTOOLS subdirectory. Check out the file TOOLS.DOC which comprehensively describes tools provided with the SMS application.

SMS Administrator Tips and Tricks

The following are not tools but rather miscellaneous hints that were not covered in any of the above sections.

- Enter correct database name—make sure that the correct database name is entered when logging into the SMS site. It is case sensitive. Also make sure that the user account (not the database login ID) is defined or has permissions on the machine that houses the SMS database.
- Allow five times the disk space for Application Packages—when creating the compressed package file at the sending site for Run Command on Workstation or Share Package on Server jobs, the worst case for disk space is about four to five times the size of the source files, assuming compression is enabled.

NOTE If SMS runs out of disk space during processing, it will just stop until more space is made available. ■

- SMS does not support dual boot machines—in order to use dual boot, multiple SMS.INI files would have to be used, renaming them depending on which operating system is being loaded. For example, with Windows NT and DOS dual boot, the machine would be scanned in initially while running Windows NT. This creates an SMS.INI file. Note: you could have a dual boot machine show in inventory if you manually renamed your SMS.INI from Windows NT every time you booted DOS and renamed your DOS SMS.INI every time you booted NT.
- The SMS Administrator's windows do not dynamically refresh—you must choose F5 or Options, Refresh to repaint the window.
- Use SMSVIEW.EXE to create views for SMS database tables—these views will present the data in the SMS database in a more usable format. An ODBC-based front-end tool such as Access 2.0 or Excel 5.0 can be used to attach to the SMS database views. Information can then be processed to create detailed reports or can be incorporated into another application.
- Use the SMS Security Manager tool to give people different SMS admin rights at that site—you may want to give varying degrees of control to people for Network Monitor, Remote Control, and so on.

From Here...

Now that we've discussed the SMS Administrator Program, you'll want to learn more about common SMS management tasks.

- Refer to Chapter 25, "SMS Management Tasks," for a further look at SMS Management tasks including use of SMSView, DBClean utilities.

CHAPTER 9

Collecting Hardware Inventory

Setting up SMS for Hardware Inventory Collection

You can configure SMS to suit your administrative needs.

Adding a Computer to the Hardware Inventory

You can manually add computers to the inventory or let SMS do it automatically.

Managing Your Hardware Inventory

You can modify the SMS inventory database and you can customize the items that SMS collects from computers

How SMS Performs the Hardware Inventory

Understanding the flow of data between SMS servers and the client computers aids in troubleshooting problems.

Perhaps the most labor-intensive part of a system administrator's job is maintaining a hardware inventory of all the machines (and their associated peripherals and add-ons) in the organization. In fact, in a large enough organization, this task alone could consume most of your time or that of your staff. The problem is compounded by users who like to tinker with their machines without necessarily informing anyone. Lacking any automated assistance, you've got no alternative to the practice of periodically visiting each PC to verify its configuration.

SMS addresses this task very well and supports a variety of the more popular PC operating systems. SMS provides a centralized hardware inventory collection and queries over a large and geographically split organization by virtue of its hierarchical and distributed architecture. And most important, SMS makes it all incredibly painless. ■

Configuring SMS for Hardware Inventory Collection

Before you start collecting inventory, you must ensure that SMS is configured correctly. Certain files are required, and you must decide on the frequency of inventory collection and other settings.

Required Files

For hardware inventory to function correctly, the files and directories listed in table 9.1 must be present on your site servers and all logon servers.

Table 9.1 Files Required on Site Servers and Logon Servers for Hardware Inventory

File or Directory	Location	Description
SMSLS.BAT	NETLOGON share	A script file that is run by SMS client computers, typically at network logon. It invokes programs to install or verify the SMS client files and to scan the client computer for hardware and software inventory.
SMSLS.CMD (for OS/2 clients)	NETLOGON share	
SMSLS.SCR (for Netware clients)	\SMS\LOGON.SRV	
\SMS\LOGON.SRV (and all files and subdirectories)	Normally the C drive of a server	This directory contains the executables for the inventory agents for various clients.

It's usually not necessary to verify client configurations, because SMS will verify (and reinstall, if necessary) the required files on a client computer when that client runs SMSLS.BAT. Table 9.2 lists the required client computer files.

Table 9.2 Files Required on Client Computers for Hardware Inventory

File or Directory	Location	Description
SMS.INI	The root of the C drive	A hidden file that contains configuration information critical to the functioning of SMS, including the client's SMS ID.
\MS\SMS (and all files and subdirectories)	Normally the C drive. SMS chooses the drive location at initial installation based on the drive with the most free space.	This directory contains the executables for the package command manager and the user agent for remote control and diagnostics.

Frequency of Inventory

For each site in the SMS hierarchy, you can decide how frequently the hardware inventory scan is performed. Your choices are Every Workstation Logon or Every *N* days (where *N* is any number of days you choose). Your choice will apply to every computer in the site you are configuring. When choosing the frequency, balance your need for an up-to-date inventory with the impact on the overall system and your users. For example, setting an SMS hardware scan for every workstation logon could be quite annoying to a group of testers who need to reboot their machines frequently.

To set the hardware inventory frequency, perform the following steps:

1. Start the SMS Administrator program and log on to the site you wish to configure or any primary site above it in the hierarchy. For a secondary site, you must log on to a primary site above it.
2. Open the Sites window by choosing it from the list that SMS Administrator presents when it starts, or by clicking the toolbar icon for the Sites window if the program is already running.
3. Click the desired site once to select it.
4. Choose File, Properties. This brings up the Site Properties dialog box, as shown in figure 9.1.

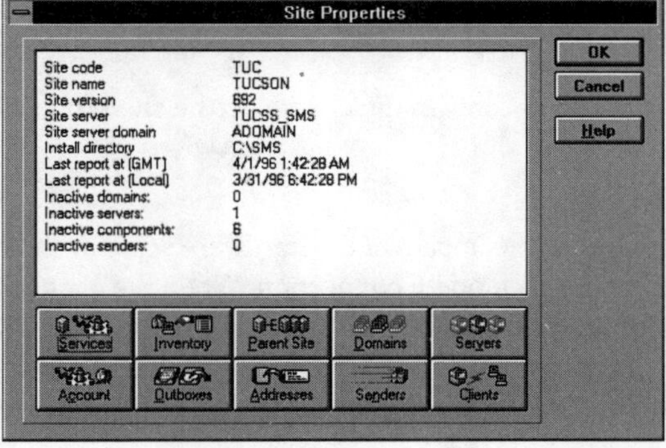

FIG. 9.1
Use the Site properties dialog box to configure the SMS components.

5. Choose the Inventory button. This brings up the Inventory dialog box, as shown in figure 9.2.
6. Click the Proposed Properties button.
7. Click the Every *N* Days button and type in the desired number of days to allow between hardware scans. The inventory agent stores the date and time of its last scan in the file SMS.INI and compares that date with the current date every time it is invoked. The inventory agent will not perform the scan as long as the number of days set with this option has not passed since its last scan.

Alternatively, click the Every Workstation Logon button to perform a hardware scan every time the client computer logs on to the network. This option effectively sets the interval between scans to zero days, thus forcing the inventory agent to perform a scan anytime it is invoked, whether by logon script or manually from the client computer.

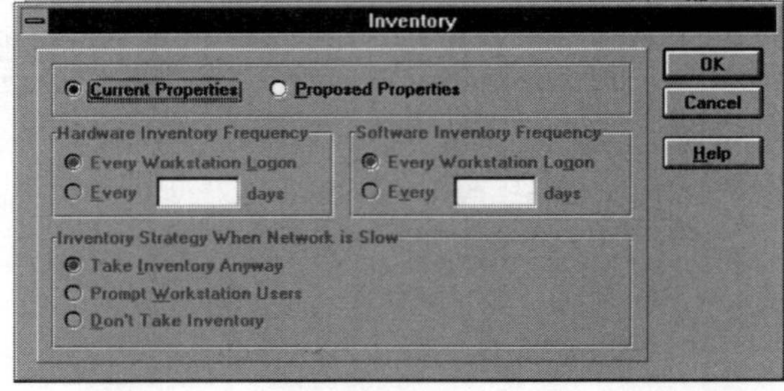

FIG. 9.2 Inventory properties are set using the Inventory dialog box.

8. Choose the OK button to close the dialog box. The confirmation dialog box shown in fig. 9.3 will appear.

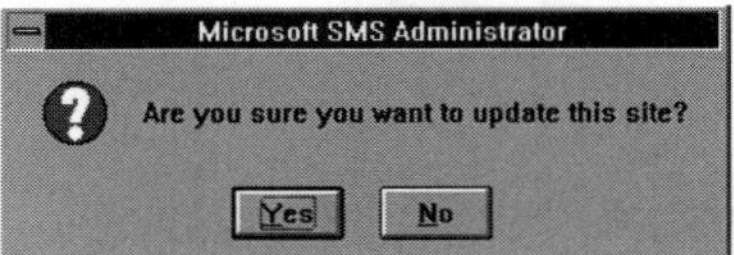

FIG. 9.3 Confirm the site property changes.

9. Choose the Yes button to confirm the change to the site properties.

Working with Slow Links

SMS enables you to minimize the impact of the hardware scan for those users who are connected via a slow link, such as a modem connection. When the client computer runs SMSLS.BAT, the first program that is invoked is NETSPEED.COM. This program calculates the speed of the link and compares it to a threshold value in the logon server's NT registry. Based on this comparison, SMS decides if the link qualifies as slow, and uses the strategy that you have specified.

To set the inventory strategy when network is slow, perform the following steps:

1. Perform steps 1 through 5 as described in the previous section.
2. Click on one of the following choices, as shown previously in figure 9.2.
    - Take Inventory Anyway

      SMS will take the inventory regardless of the network speed.

- Prompt Workstation Users

  SMS will offer a message box to the user asking for permission to take the inventory.

- Don't Take Inventory

  SMS will not take the inventory if the network is slow.

NOTE The threshold value used to determine a slow link is the amount of time required to send 1 KB of data (the default is 500 milliseconds). This can be changed for a site by opening the registry editor on the site server and changing the value of the key:

```
HKEY_LOCAL_MACHINE\SOFTWARE\Microsoft\SMS\Components\SMS_MAINTENANCE_MANAGER\
Slow Net Threshold Speed
```

SMS will then update the file NETSPEED.DAT on all logon servers in that site with the new value. ■

False Logon Count

SMS uses a parameter known as the False Logon Count (the InvAgtFalseLogonCount entry in the client computer's SMS.INI file) to determine that a computer in its inventory has moved from one domain to another. Each time a computer logs on from a domain different from the one SMS has assigned to it, SMS increments a counter in the SMS.INI file on that computer. When that counter reaches the False Logon Count Setting, SMS automatically reassigns the computer to the new domain. If the computer logs on to its assigned domain before the False Logon Count is reached, the counter is reset to zero. The client computer retains its original SMS ID when it is moved to the new domain.

NOTE The False Logon Count can be changed for a site by opening the registry editor on the site server and changing the value of the key:

```
HKEY_LOCAL_MACHINE\SOFTWARE\Microsoft\SMS\Components\SMS_MAINTENANCE_MANAGER\
Inventory False Logon Limit
```

SMS will then update the file DOMAIN.INI on all logon servers in that site with the new value and this value will eventually be propagated to the SMS.INI file on each client computer. ■

Client Drives Scanned

By default, SMS scans every drive on a computer, including removable media. A user may have an *NTFS* drive (see the sidebar on NTFS drives) that is unreadable under Windows 95 or a removable hard drive that often has no cartridge in it. You can prevent the scan for a particular drive by adding the following line to the SMS.INI file on the client computer:

In the [WorkstationStatus] section add

```
FailedHardwareChecks=DriveN (where N is the drive letter in uppercase)
```

What is NTFS?

NTFS (New Technology File System) is one of the file systems used with Windows NT. The other file systems that NT will support are the familiar MS-DOS FAT (File Allocation Table) file system, and the HPFS (High Performance File System) file system used with OS/2. Although Windows NT will support the other file types, NTFS is intended to be the primary file system used with Windows NT. It is designed to speed up Windows NT file access while maintaining compatibility with the older FAT file system's 8.3 naming convention. NTFS adds transaction tracking as a method of fault tolerance, and is the only file system that can be made secure according the government's C2 level security specifications. Windows NT can use NTFS partitions to create striped disk sets or RAID (Redundant Array of Inexpensive Disks) drives without the use of special array hardware. This feature of the Windows NT Operating System allows you to combine from 3 to 32 NTFS partitions together into a single array. In addition, NTFS partitions will support a Macintosh-accessible directory format (using the Services For Macintosh) so Macintosh users can share store, retrieve and share files on a Windows NT Server.

Adding Computers for Inventory Collection

SMS adds a computer to its inventory whenever that computer logs onto a domain that is part of an SMS site and runs SMSLS.BAT. SMS can be configured to configure each computer's NT logon script automatically to run SMSLS.BAT, or you can configure computers to connect manually. Depending on your domain configuration and other factors, you may not have a choice. This section will identify your options.

Adding Computers Automatically

In order for SMS automatically to configure logon scripts for all computers in a site, the following steps must be performed:

- Select the Use All Detected Servers option in the Domain properties dialog box for each domain in the site.

CAUTION

You can't select the Use All Detected Servers option if one of your domains spans multiple sites. For a detailed discussion of domain considerations in site planning, see Chapter 4, "Planning, Design, and System Requirements."

- You must set up the Windows NT or the LAN Manager Replicator Service for each domain in the site.
- Select the Automatically Configure Workstation Logon Scripts option in the Clients properties dialog box.

CAUTION

SMS can automatically configure workstation logon scripts only for Windows, LAN Manager, and Netware clients. You must manually add Macintosh clients as described in the next section.

To configure SMS to detect all servers, perform the following steps:

1. From the Sites properties dialog box, choose the Domains button to bring up the Domains dialog box, as shown in fig. 9.4.

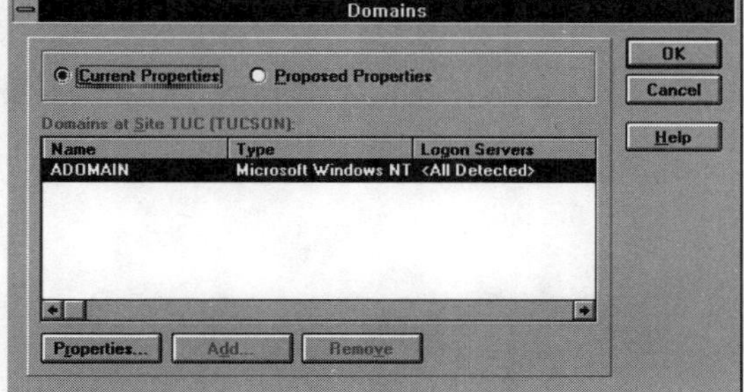

FIG. 9.4
The Domains dialog box is used for adding, removing or modifying domains

2. Click the Proposed Properties button and select the Domain you want to configure.
3. Choose the Properties button to bring up the Domain Properties window, as shown in fig. 9.5.

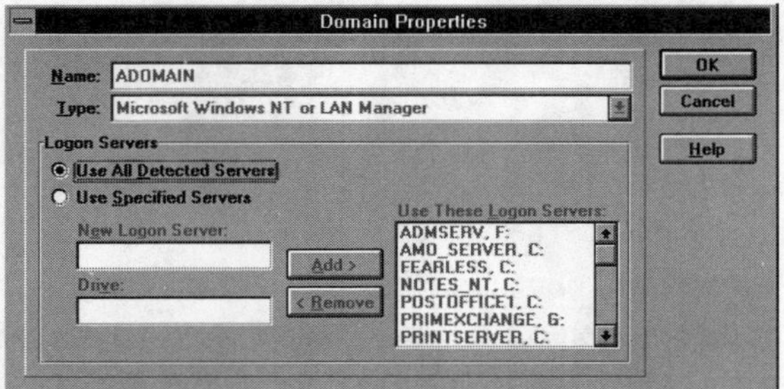

FIG. 9.5
Use the Domain Properties dialog box to modify the properties of a domain.

4. Click the Use All Detected Servers option to cause SMS to install the logon server files on every server that is a member of the domain.

NOTE For Netware domains, this setting has no effect on the ability to configure workstation logon scripts automatically. When using the Automatically Configure Workstation Logon Scripts option in a Windows NT or Lan Manager domain environment, you must select the Use All Detected Servers option or the user login scripts will not be set up by SMS.

This is not true with a NetWare domain set up in SMS. You do not have to use the Use All Detected Servers if you're using the Automatically Configure Workstation Logon Scripts in a NetWare domain. Why? Because a NetWare user always logs into a known server in a NetWare 3.*x* (or 4.*x* in 3.*x* compatibility mode) environment. This is unlike the NT or LAN Manager user that logs on to a domain containing several servers capable of authenticating the user's account. Since we don't know which specific server in the NT (or LAN Manager) domain will authenticate the user, we must ensure the logon components are included on all of the domain's logon servers. The Use All Detected Servers option accomplishes this by enumerating all logon servers found in the domain.

5. Choose the OK button three times to close the Domain dialog boxes and the Site Properties dialog box, and then choose Yes to confirm the changes.

To configure SMS to configure workstation logon scripts automatically, perform the following steps:

1. From the Sites properties dialog box, choose the Clients button to bring up the Clients dialog box, as shown in fig. 9.6.

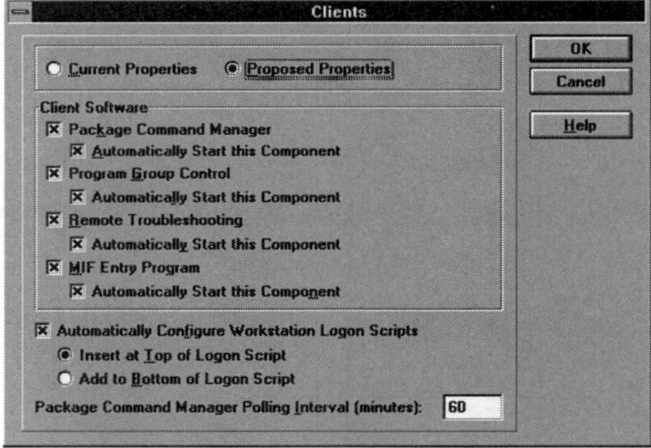

FIG. 9.6
Use the Clients dialog box to modify client properties.

2. Click the Proposed Properties button.
3. Click the Automatically Configure Workstation Logon Scripts option.
4. The next option allows you to determine the location of the call statement to the SMSLS batch file in any existing user logon script files. Some users may already be running logon scripts to execute various commands automatically when they log on to the domain. Since the users still need to use their current logon scripts, the SMS system adds a call statement, out to the SMSLS batch file, in the existing script. SMS will place the call to the batch file at the beginning or at the end of a user's current script file according the option you select here. You can choose the Insert at Top of Logon Script option, or the Add to Bottom of Logon Script option to specify the placement of the call. If the user(s) is not currently using a logon script, the SMSLS batch file will become the logon script file for the user and this setting will not apply.

5. Choose OK twice to close this dialog and the Site Properties dialog, and then choose Yes to confirm the changes.

To set up the Replicator Service, please refer to your Windows NT or LAN Manager documentation. The following conditions must be met to ensure correct SMS operation:

- The primary domain controller must be the export server for replication.
- The share REPL$ must exist on the primary domain controller, since the SMS Site Configuration Manager looks for this share.
- The correct SETLS programs must be in the SCRIPTS subdirectory.
- The logon scripts must be in the SCRIPTS subdirectory of the REPL$ share.
- The NETLOGON share and its associated NTFS directory must have Read permissions for the group Everyone.

NOTE The amount of time it takes for SMS to complete the process of configuring the logon scripts for all the users in a domain will depend polling cycle intervals being used by SMS. The SMS Site Manager has a two-hour cycle for verifying and installing the SETLS programs and a 24-hour cycle for modifying logon scripts. More information on the different polling cycles can be found in Chapter 6 "Server Installation Part II."

Adding Computers Manually

You will need to add computers manually to SMS for any of the following situations:

- You have a domain that spans multiple sites, as mentioned in the previous section, or you have some other consideration that prevents you from selecting the Use All Detected Servers option.
- You need to have the SMSLS script at a specific place in the logon scripts of your computers other than at the beginning or at the end.
- You need to add a Macintosh computer to the inventory.

To add a Windows computer manually to SMS, perform the following steps:

1. At a command prompt, type the appropriate NET USE command to connect to the NETLOGON share on a logon server.

   An example would be NET USE N: \\TUCSS_SMS\NETLOGON, where N: can be any available drive letter.
2. Change to the drive you just connected, and type SMSLS.
3. You can automate this procedure by adding these commands to the computer's AUTOEXEC.BAT file.

NOTE The same SMSLS script that collects inventory is also used for installing SMS files on a computer and for adding that computer to the SMS database.

CAUTION

If you attempt the above procedure on a slow link, it may fail because SMSLS checks for slow links. There is an alternate script, RUNSMS.BAT, in the SMS_SHR share that does the same thing as SMSLS but omits the check for slow links.

To add a Netware computer manually to SMS, perform the following steps:

1. At a command prompt, type the appropriate MAP command to connect to the Netware server and volume that contains the logon server files.

   An example would be MAP N: TUCSS_NW\SMSVOL, where N: can be any available drive letter.

2. Change to the drive you just connected, and switch to the LOGON.SRV subdirectory of the SMS root directory.

   An example would be CD \SMS\LOGON.SRV.

3. Type SMSLS.BAT.
4. You can automate this procedure by adding these commands to the computer's AUTOEXEC.BAT file.

CAUTION

You can't run SMSLS.BAT from a Netware logon script. If you wish to use logon scripts, you must use the file SMSLS.SCR located in the LOGON.SRV directory on the Netware logon server.

To add a Macintosh computer manually to SMS, perform the following steps:

1. Connect to the SMS_SHR volume on a Windows NT Server running Services for Macintosh.
2. Open the MAC.BIN folder in SMS_SHR.
3. Run the Installer program.

The Installer program installs SMS files, takes inventory, and adds the Macintosh to the SMS database. It also places the inventory agent in the Mac's startup folder.

Managing Your Inventory

As a business changes, so does its computer network. People move, departments grow, and equipment gets replaced. Because of this, computers will need to be removed from SMS inventory or moved to new locations within the SMS site hierarchy. First we'll look at what's involved when you want to remove a computer from your SMS database. Then we'll take a look at what happens when a computer gets moved from one site or domain to another. And finally, we'll explore some ways to customize the way your database inventory is collected.

Removing Computers from the System

Completely removing a computer from the SMS database, cleaning up the software components on the client workstation, and preventing the workstation from being reinventoried involves the following four steps:

1. Delete the computer from the SMS inventory.
2. Use the SMS Database Maintenance Utility to remove the unneeded database records.
3. Remove the SMS client components from the client machine.
4. Remove any logon script references to the SMSLS batch file that the user of the machine may have.

We'll look at each step, starting with the removal of the workstation from the SMS inventory.

Deleting a Computer from the SMS Inventory The first task in this process is to remove the computer from the SMS inventory. This is done using the SMS Administrator program, as follows:

1. Log on to the SMS Administration program and open the Sites window. See fig. 9.7.
2. In the left window pane, expand the site tree structure by double-clicking the site icon. If you have multiple site icons, expand the site icon that holds the domain in which resides the computer you wish to remove.
3. A list of domains will appear. Choose the domain containing the computer to be removed by clicking it. The computers with inventory records in that domain will be listed in the right window pane.
4. Highlight the name of the computer you wish to remove.

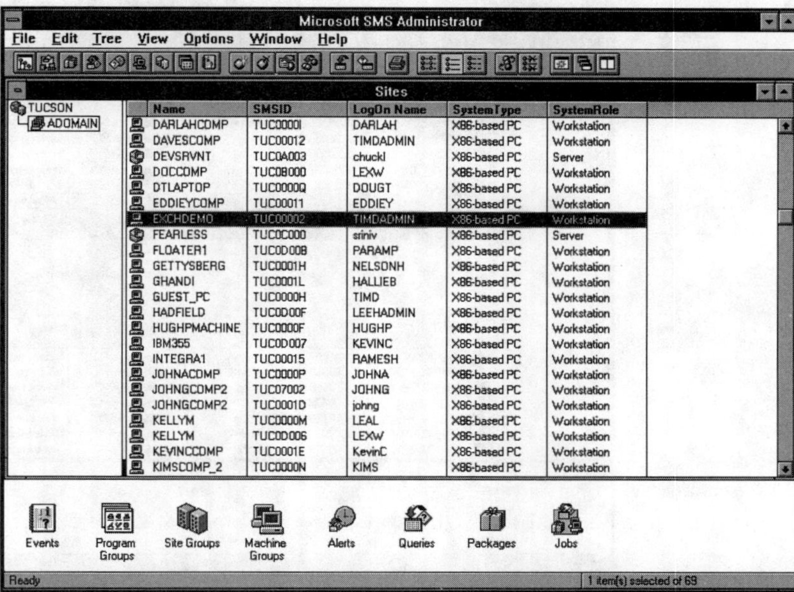

FIG. 9.7
The SMS Sites window displays site, domain, and machine information.

5. From the Edit menu choose Delete. See fig. 9.8.

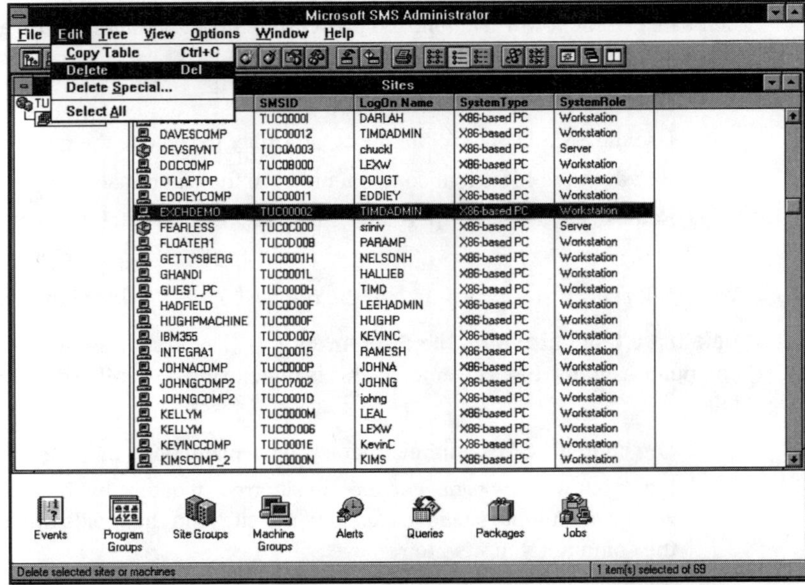

FIG. 9.8
From the Edit Menu, choose Delete.

6. Confirm your choice to delete the computer by answering Yes to the dialog box. See fig. 9.9.

FIG. 9.9
Confirm that you want to delete the computer from inventory.

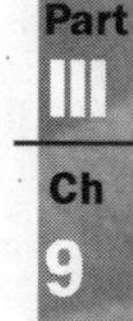

The computer is then deleted from the domains inventory. You will notice that the computer is no longer listed in the Sites window, as shown in fig. 9.10.

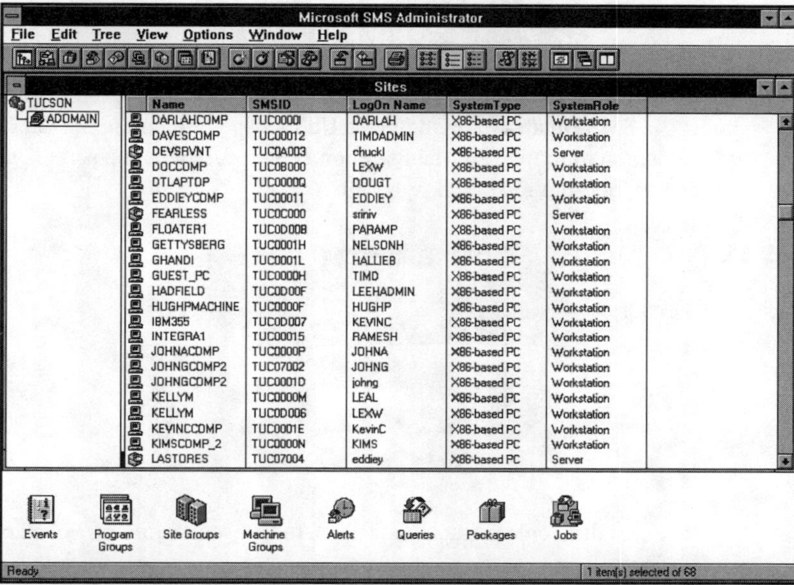

FIG. 9.10
The Sites window after the computer has been removed.

Even though the Sites window no longer lists the computer as part of inventory, history records for the computer still remain in the site database. Since the computer has been deleted from the current inventory, these records no longer reference themselves to any current member of the database inventory. Records of this nature can be removed from the SMS database using the SMS Database Maintenance Utility, also known as the SMS Database Manager.

Using the SMS Database Maintenance Utility to Remove Unneeded Database Records Now use the SMS Database Maintenance Utility to delete any old or unused records from the SMS database. In this step we are removing records that no longer reference any computer listed in inventory. If you have several computers to remove, you need perform this step only once, after you have finished deleting the last computer from the inventory.

The file name of the SMS Database Maintenance Utility is DBCLEAN.EXE. It is located in the SITE.SRV*platform*.BIN directory on all computers that have the SMS Administrator installed.

CAUTION

Before you use the SMS Database Maintenance Utility, please note that this utility is a very powerful tool and should be used only by experienced SMS systems administrators. It contains no help files and can be confusing to the novice administrator. In addition, it is always wise to have a current backup of the database before performing any maintenance tasks on it.

The SMS Database Maintenance Utility allows you to perform several maintenance tasks on the SMS database. You can use the utility to delete or merge duplicate machine records, delete unused database records, delete Group Classes, and remove collected files that are no longer referenced to the SMS database.

▶ A complete explanation of SMS Database Maintenance Utility (DBCLEAN.EXE) and its functions can be found in Appendix B, "SMS System Files and Utilities."

Start the SMS Database Maintenance Utility by logging on to the database in the same way you would log on to the SMS Administration Program. The logon screen, shown in fig. 9.11, looks similar to the Administration programs.

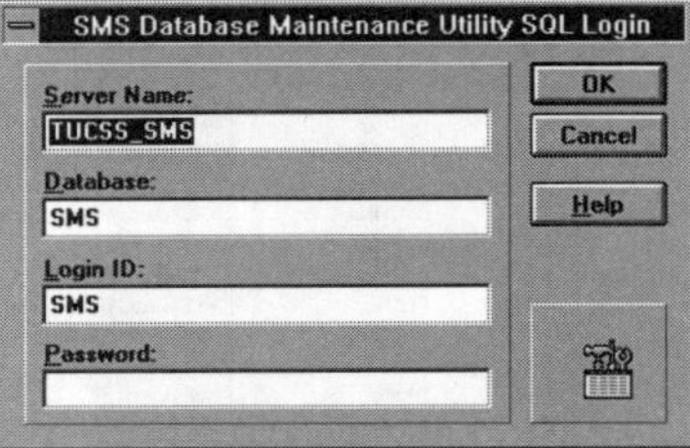

FIG. 9.11 SMS Database Maintenance Utility SQL Logon screen.

1. From the Tools menu, choose Delete Unused Common/Specific Records, as shown in fig. 9.12.

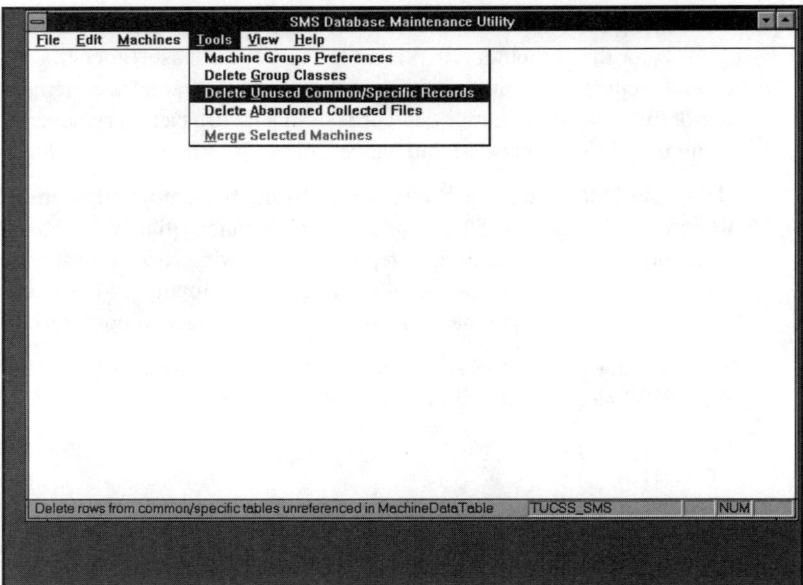

FIG. 9.12 The SMS Database Maintenance Utility.

CAUTION

Before you remove records, remember that database problems can result if the SMS Database Maintenance Utility is used to remove or alter objects in the database while that database is currently opened by another administrator using the SMS Administration program.

2. Click Yes in the confirmation box to begin removing nonreferenced records from the database, as shown in fig. 9.13.

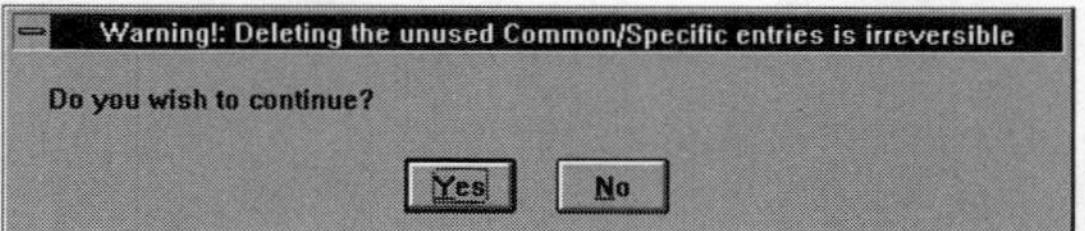

FIG. 9.13 The SMS utility warns that the actions are irreversible.

This process may take several minutes or longer, depending on the size of the database. During this time, the only indication you have that the process is running is the rotating hour glass on the screen. Upon successful completion the utility will display the message shown in fig. 9.14.

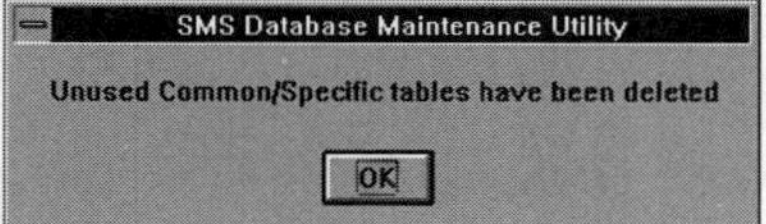

FIG. 9.14 Message indicating the successful deletion of unused records.

Since the release of SMS version 1.1, much of the functionality of the SMS Database Maintenance Utility has been incorporated into the Administration program's Edit, Delete Special menu option.

Our attention thus far has been centered on the SMS database-related steps, first with the deletion of the computer from the inventory, and then with the cleanup of the database. Now our focus turns to removing the SMS components from the client machine, and then to the elimination of any references to the SMSLS batch file in the user logon script.

Removing the SMS Client Components from the Workstation This next step cleans up any SMS statements that are in the system files on the client workstation, and it will remove the SMS components that are installed on the local drives of the workstation. This step must be completed at the client machine, and is started by invoking the client setup program in Removal mode. There are two ways to do this. You can run the DEINSTAL.BAT batch file, or you can manually run the client setup program with the /r switch. Both methods are started by connecting to the SMS_SHR on one of your logon servers.

Using DEINSTAL.BAT Using the DEINSTAL.BAT file has the advantage of detecting the platform and automatically choosing the correct client setup program to run. This saves you the trouble of having to locate the correct setup program yourself. In the first example, we'll remove the SMS components from a DOS workstation on a LAN Manager/NT network using the DEINSTAL.BAT file, as follows:

1. Log on to the network and make a connection to your logon server's SMS_SHR share using any free drive letter.

   An example would be C:\>net use Z: *logonserver*\sms_shr.

2. Move to the Z: drive.
3. Run the DEINSTAL.BAT file, for example, Z:\>DEINSTAL.

This second example lists the steps to run DEINSTAL.BAT from the WFW File Manager, as follows:

1. Make sure you are logged on to the network.
2. From the Windows File Manager Disk menu, choose Connect Network drive.
3. Pick any free drive letter that is available. In our example we will use Z:.
4. In the Connect Network Drive window, type the UNC path name to the SMS_SHR share.

   An example would be *logonserver*\SMS_SHR.
   Alternatively, browse for the SMS_SHR share in the lower window. Click the OK button when you're done.

5. Find the DEINSTAL.BAT file in the directory windows and double-click it.
6. Exit Windows and reboot the machine to start phase two of the removal process.

The deinstallation procedure will vary slightly, depending on the operating system from which you're removing the components.

On DOS workstations, the removal process is completed in a single pass. For NT, Windows 3.1, WFW, and Windows 95, two passes are required. The first pass modifies the SMS.INI file by placing the statement DEINSTALL in the SetupPhase entry of the SMS.INI [Local] section. This instructs the client to deinstall the next time it is run.

After this modification, the NT user must log off and then back on to start the second phase of the removal process. Windows 3.1, WFW, and Windows 95 systems require a reboot and logon to initiate the second phase.

You may experience problems when removing SMS Version 1.1 components from a Windows 95 client unless a cold boot of the workstation is done between phase one and phase two.

Running the Client Setup Program Manually If you find the DEINSTAL.BAT file fails to run, or if it fails to properly detect the platform you're trying to remove the components from, it may be necessary to start the client setup program manually in removal mode. Begin this procedure from the client machine by connecting to the SMS_SHR on the logon server. In order to remove the components, you must run the appropriate client setup application for the processor type you're running. The three current processor types supported are ALPHA, MIPS, and Intel. These correspond to the three subdirectories that contain the client setup applications: ALPHA.BIN, MIPS.BIN, and X86.BIN. A logon server share showing the directory structure for an Intel platform is illustrated in fig. 9.15.

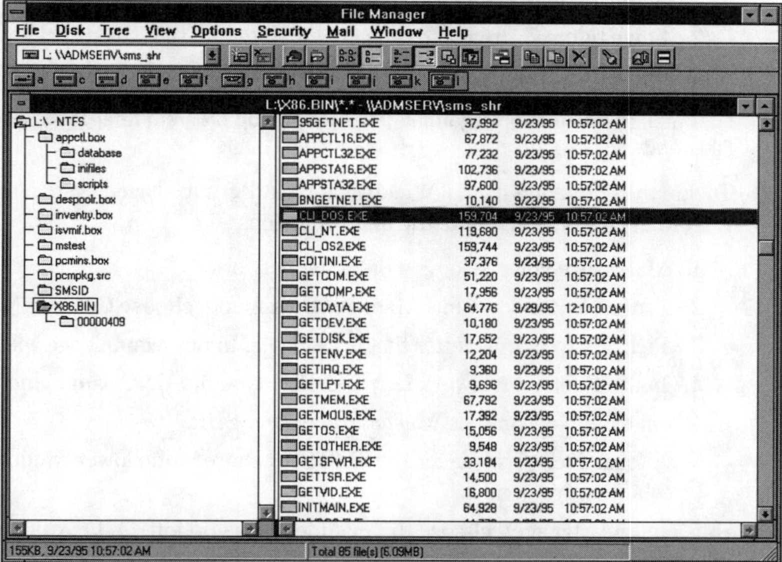

FIG. 9.15
Client files located on SMS_SHR share.

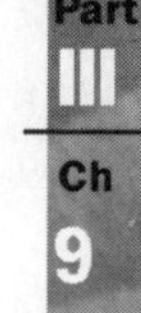

Table 9.3 lists the file names used for the client setup application based on the platform and operating system type.

Table 9.3 Client Setup Program File Name Cross-Referenced to Platform and Operating System

Operating g System	INTEL	MIPS	ALPHA
NT	X86.BIN\CLI_NT.EXE	MIPS.BIN\CLI_NT.EXE	ALPHA.BIN\CLI_NT.EXE
Win95	X86.BIN\CLI_DOS.EXE	N/A	N/A
WFW	X86.BIN\CLI_DOS.EXE	N/A	N/A
Win 3.1	X86.BIN\CLI_DOS.EXE	N/A	N/A
DOS	X86.BIN\CLI_DOS.EXE	N/A	N/A
OS/2	X86.BIN\CLI_OS2.EXE	N/A	N/A

To run the command on a DOS-based system using the LAN Manager network client software, follow the steps below:

1. Log on to the network and make a connection to your logon server's SMS_SHR share using any free drive letter.

   An example would be C:\>net use Z: *logonserver*\sms_shr.
2. Move to the Z: drive and then change into the X86.BIN directory.
3. Run the client setup program with the /r option, for example, Z:\X86.BIN>CLI_DOS /r.

For detailed information regarding the Client setup program refer to Appendix B, "SMS System Files and Utilities."

To run the command from a Windows for Workgroups-based system connected to an NT or LAN Manager network, take the following steps:

1. Make sure you are logged on to the network.
2. From the Windows File Manager Disk menu, choose Connect Network drive.
3. Pick any free drive letter that is available. In our example we will use Z:.
4. In the Connect Network Drive window type the UNC path name to the SMS_SHR share.

   An example would be *logonserver*\SMS_SHR.

   Alternatively, browse for the SMS_SHR share in the lower window. Click the OK button when you're done.
5. In File Manager, choose the File menu Run option. In the Run box, type the command line Z:\X86.BIN\CLI_DOS /r, and click OK.
6. Exit Windows and reboot the machine to start phase two of the removal process.

During the second phase of client removal, the SMSRUN file scans the SMS.INI file and detects the DEINSTALL phrase. SMSRUN continues the process by starting the SMSSRV program with the /c switch. SMSRUN then exits, leaving SMSSRV to call the client setup program to complete the removal process. Once the user has logged back on, SMSSRV invokes the client setup program with the /k switch. The client setup program then removes any SMS-related files and directories.

Any SMS-related statements in the systems configuration files are then removed, and the client component deinstallation is completed.

Before the user of that machine logs back on to the system, you must remove any logon script commands the user may have that reference the SMSLS batch file. If this is not done, SMS will reinstall the client components on the computer and record the computer's newly scanned information back into the SMS database. If you want to reinstall the SMS components on the client machine and place the computer back into the SMS inventory, just skip the next step.

Removing User Logon Script References to the SMSLS Batch File In order to prevent the reinstallation of the SMS components back on the workstation, it's necessary to insure the SMSLS or RUNSMS batch file is not executed during the next system startup or user logon.

The RUNSMS command is typically placed in the AUTOEXEC.BAT file on the user's system. This is most often done on networks that want to run the SMS client at startup but do not employ the use of logon scripts. Use your text editor to look at the AUTOEXEC.BAT file and make sure the RUNSMS command does not appear anywhere in it or in any batch file it may call.

On networks that use logon scripts, or on SMS installations where the Automatically Configure Workstation Logon Scripts option has been chosen, it is necessary to remove one of the following:

1. The logon script named SMSLS for that user's profile.
2. Any calls to the SMSLS batch file from a user logic script of a different name.

Find out if the user has a logon script by using the NT User Manager administrative utility to view the account profile information. If the user has a logon script and the name is SMSLS, you'll need to clear the name from the Logon Script Name box. If the logon script name is another file, note its name and use a text editor to open it. Remove any statements in the logon script file that call the SMSLS batch file or any of its components.

Use the following steps to check for the presence of the SMSLS logon script:

1. Open the NT Server User Manager for Domains utility located in the Administrative Tools program group.
2. Find the account for the user of the deleted computer and double-click the user name.
3. In the User Properties window, click the Profile button to open the User Profile window, as shown in fig. 9.16.
4. Note the name of the file (if any) in the Logon Script Name field. If the file name is SMSLS, clear the name from the field and click the OK button twice. If a different file name is in the field, note its name, and click the Cancel button, then the Close button.
5. Exit the User Manager for Domains utility.
6. If a different script name was noted, use a text editor to view the script file and remove any references to the SMSLS batch file or its components.

This completes the section on removing computers from the SMS inventory. During this section we found that the removal of a computer from the SMS system is actually a four-step process. In our examples we started with the deletion of a computer from the database, then illustrated the cleanup associated with the database records. After that, we removed the client components and finished up by making changes to the user's logon script.

Next, we'll look at what happens when you need to move a computer from one place to another within the SMS hierarchy.

FIG. 9.16
The User Profile window.

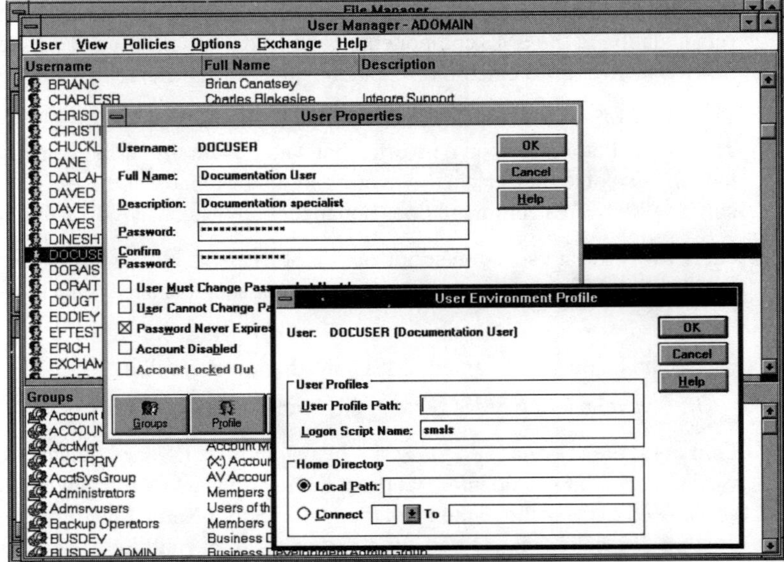

What Happens when you Move a Computer?

Often computers will need to be moved within the SMS site hierarchy. This can be caused by organization changes, user moves, network reconfiguration, or a host of other reasons. For this reason, SMS allows for the easy movement of computers within the SMS hierarchical structure.

Most of the associated tasks are automatically taken care of by the SMS system. This is especially true if the target domain has the Automatically Configure Workstation Logon Scripts option enabled.

How SMS Tracks Workstation Movement SMS is able to track and move client computers by using entries in the SMS.INI file and the DOMAIN.INI file. The SMS.INI file is a hidden file located in the root of the workstation's local boot drive, and the DOMAIN.INI is found in the root of the SMS_SHR share on the logon server.

SMS.INI contains the SMS client configuration settings for that workstation. During the execution of the SMSLS logon script (or the RUNSMS.BAT file) the Inventory Agent checks two of the SMS.INI file entries. It compares these entries with corresponding entries in the logon servers DOMAIN.INI file. It does this to determine if the user of the computer is logging on to a different domain.

If differences are found between SMS.INI and DOMAIN.INI files' Domain and SiteCode entries, the Inventory Agent will proceed to check a counter entry in the SMS.INI file. It checks this counter entry against another SMS.INI file entry called the False Logon Setting. This comparison is done to determine if the user has logged on to the current domain enough times in a row for the workstation's inventory to be moved. If the user has logged on often enough, the workstation's inventory will be moved to the current SMS domain. If the user hasn't, the counter entry gets incremented by one, and nothing is moved. In subsequent sections we'll look at the False Logon Setting and why you might want to change it from its default setting. You'll see how to use the setting to designate exactly when a machine's inventory gets transferred from one SMS domain to another.

Comparing the INI files Let's go over what takes place in more detail by first looking at the SMS.INI and DOMAIN.INI entries that the Inventory Agent uses. The entries the Inventory Agent uses are shown in table 9.4.

Table 9.4 SMS.INI and DOMAIN.INI Entries Checked by the Inventory Agent

SMS.INI	DOMAIN.INI	Description
[Server] Domain=	[Server] Domain=	Name of the current SMS logon domain.
[SMS] SiteCode=	[SMS] SiteCode=	SiteCode for the current SMS logon domain.
[SMS] InvAgtFalseLogonCount=	[SMS] InvAgtFalseLogonCount=	Number of consecutive domain logons before the workstation's inventory is transferred to the new domain.
[LogonHistory] Entry=		Site code and domain where the user has logged on.
[LogonHistory] Counter=		Number of consecutive domain logons into the new domain.

Moving a Workstation to a New Domain Let's look at an example.

John, our user, normally logs on to the SALES domain at the company's BIG site. Currently John's SMS.INI file and the SALES domain DOMAIN.INI file have matching values for Domain and SiteCode entries, as shown in table 9.5.

Table 9.5 John's Current SMS.INI Entries Compared to the SALES Domain's DOMAIN.INI File

John's SMS.INI file	SALES DOMAIN.INI file
[Server] Domain=SALES	[Server] Domain=SALES
[SMS] SiteCode=BIG	[SMS] SiteCode=BIG
InvAgtFalseLogonCount=3	InvAgtFalseLogonCount=3

The Domain and SiteCode entries that are present in John's SMS.INI file match their corresponding entries in the SALES domain logon server's DOMAIN.INI file. As long as they match, John's workstation inventory will continue to be reported to the SALES domain by the Inventory Agent.

John was moved to a new job in the Research Department. His account was removed from the SALES domain and he was given a new account in the RESEARCH domain. John then started logging on to the RESEARCH domain logon servers.

These logon servers have their own DOMAIN.INI file. A comparison of the pertinent entries from John's SMS.INI and those in the new DOMAIN.INI file from the RESEARCH domain are shown in table 9.6.

Table 9.6 Comparison of the .INI file Entries

John's SMS.INI file	RESEARCH DOMAIN.INI file
[Server] Domain=SALES	[Server] Domain=RESEARCH
[SMS] SiteCode=BIG	[SMS] SiteCode=BIG
InvAgtFalseLogonCount=3	InvAgtFalseLogonCount=3

As illustrated in Table 9.6, the Domain entry in John's SMS.INI file no longer matches the one in the DOMAIN.INI file for the RESEARCH domain. When the SMSLS batch file is run, the Inventory Agent scans the two files and notices the difference.

At this time the Inventory Agent creates a new section in John's SMS.INI file named [LogonHistory]. This section contains two entries. The first is Entry; it lists the current site and domain John has logged on to. The second is Counter; it counts the number of times that John has logged on to the RESEARCH domain.

By default, John must log on to his new domain three times before his workstation will be scanned for inventory and added to the RESEARCH domain. The number of times a user has to log on before the workstation is scanned is determined by the value in a configurable parameter named InvAgtFalseLogonCount. This is referred to as the False Logon Count entry.

This entry exists in both the SMS.INI file and the DOMAIN.INI file. You can control the number of logons it takes before a workstation is added to a domain by changing the value of this parameter. Changing the value in the DOMAIN.INI file on the logon server will cause the same value to be placed in the InvAgtFalseLogonCount entry in all client SMS.INI files across the domain.

Changing the InvAgtFalseLogonCount entry in the DOMAIN.INI

Because the DOMAIN.INI file can be located on several logon servers in a single domain, you cannot edit any one DOMAIN.INI file to make changes across all the logon servers. You must change the value of the InvAgtFalseLogonCount by modifying the Windows NT registry key:

HKEY_LOCAL_MACHINE\SOFTWARE\Microsoft\SMS\Components\SMS_MAINENANCE_MANAGER\Inventory False Logon Limit

Changing the setting (the default is 3) to another value will cause the InvAgtFalseLogonCount parameter in the DOMAIN.INI files of all the domains' logon servers to be changed. In turn, this will cause all client SMS.INI files to be updated with the new value.

A user will occasionally need to log on to a domain other than his or her own. The False Logon Count parameter prevents the SMS system from automatically adding the workstation inventory to another domain if the user logs on to that other domain only occasionally. The default value of 3 means that the user must log on to the new domain three times before the workstation inventory is removed from the old domain and moved to the new domain. The move process is initiated on the fourth logon to the new domain. The logic behind this is that if a user logs on to a new domain three times in a row, he or she must have moved to the new domain permanently. You may wish to increase this value in environments where users must log on to different domains frequently.

Let's look at the first three logons by John into his new domain.

The First Logon

- When John first logs on to his new domain, the Inventory Agent notices the difference in the Domain statement entries between the local workstation's SMS.INI file and the DOMAIN.INI file for the Research domain. The workstation's SMS.INI file has the statement Domain=SALES, while the DOMAIN.INI file has the statement Domain=RESEARCH.
- The Inventory Agent then creates the [LogonHistory] section in the workstation's SMS.INI file. In this section it places the Entry and Counter parameters.
- The Entry value is set to the current site and domain name, in this example Entry=BIG:RESEARCH.
- The Counter entries value is set to one (1) and checked against the value of the InvAgtFalseLogonCount entry.
- The Inventory Agent finds the Counter value one (1) to be less than the value of InvAgtFalseLogonCount three (3).
- The Inventory Agent does not scan the workstation.

At this point, if John were to log back on to his old domain, the Inventory Agent would remove the [LogonHistory] section and its entries from John's SMS.INI file. Then it would scan John's workstation as usual and report his workstation's inventory to the SALES domain.

The Second Logon

- The second time John logs on to his new domain, the Counter entry is again incremented by one (1) because the Domain statement values between the SMS.INI and DOMAIN.INI still don't match.
- The Inventory Agent again checks the Counter value, now two (2), against the value of the InvAgtFalseLogonCount entry.
- The Inventory Agent finds the Counter value of two (2) to be less that the value of InvAgtFalseLogonCount three (3), so it does not scan the workstation.

John can still log back on to his old domain before his inventory is moved. The Inventory Agent would still remove the [LogonHistory] section of his SMS.INI, and then scan his workstation's inventory into the SALES domain as usual.

The Third Logon

- The third time John logs on to his new domain, the Counter entry is checked by the Inventory Agent. Again, because the Domain values between the SMS.INI and DOMAIN.INI don't match, the Inventory Agent increments the Counter value by one (1).
- The Inventory Agent checks the Counter value, now three (3), against the value of the InvAgtFalseLogonCount entry.

This time when the Counter value of three (3) is compared to the InvAgtFalseLogonCount value of three (3), the two values are equal. This triggers the following events which, in turn, will cause the workstation's inventory to be moved on the fourth logon:

1. The Inventory Agent changes the Domain and/or the SiteCode entries in the workstation SMS.INI file to that of the new domain and/or site name. In this example the Domain entry is changed to RESEARCH.
2. The [LogonHistory] section of the SMS.INI file is removed.
3. The Inventory Agent then exits without scanning the drive into inventory.

The Fourth Logon

On the fourth logon to the new domain, the Inventory Agent will scan the workstation as usual, but now the Domain and SiteCode entries in the SMS.INI file match those located in the logon server's DOMAIN.INI file. This will cause the Inventory Agent to scan the workstation's inventory and report it to the RESEARCH domain. The following actions are taken by SMS:

1. The workstation inventory is added to the new domain with the workstation's inventory history records included. John's workstation now appears under the RESEARCH domain inventory.
2. All affected SMS sites are updated with the workstation's inventory information.
3. The workstation is removed from the previous domain's inventory. In our example, all the inventory information for John's workstation is removed from the SALES domain and placed into the RESEARCH domain.

An important point to note is that during this entire process the workstation's SMS ID did not change. The workstation will report its inventory to the RESEARCH domain using the same unique ID that it used when it reported to the SALES domain. This ID is stored in the workstation SMS.INI file under the [SMS] section's SMS Unique ID entry.

▶ The complete listing of the SMS.INI file and its entries can be found in Appendix B, "SMS System Files and Utilities."

Keeping the Process Automated From now on, John's workstation inventory will be listed as part of the RESEARCH domain. Since the administrators of John's network have enabled the Automatically Configure Workstation Logon Scripts option on all of the domains, they don't need to update the SMS database manually when a user moves from one domain or site to another.

▶ Further information on setting up the Automatically Configure Workstation Logon Scripts option can be found in Chapter 6, "Server Installation Part II."

The process is automated by having all users run the SMSLS batch file from their network logon script. The Inventory Agent is invoked and compares the workstation and domain initialization files, and then either modifies the SMS.INI files' entries or scans the workstation's inventory into the current domain. If the SMSLS logon script is not utilized, users will need to have the RUNSMS batch file executed from their AUTOEXEC.BAT file (or other startup file) to keep the process automated.

If users do not have an SMSLS logon script or a startup file with the RUNSMS batch file in it, the RUNSMS batch file must be manually run four times before the workstation's inventory is scanned in to the domain.

Customizing Inventory Collection

In this section, you'll see how you can customize the way your workstations report their inventory. You will see how this allows you to organize the site tree by specifying which domain will collect a specific workstation's inventory, even if the user at the workstation logs on to a different domain.

Controlling How Inventory Is Gathered As we saw in the preceding sections, the initialization files control much of the inventory process. These files are looked at and compared to one another. This happens during the execution of the current domain server's Inventory Agent program on the workstation. If certain entries between the two initialization files (SMS.INI and DOMAIN.INI) don't match, it could indicate the workstation has been moved to a new domain, as we saw in our last section. Differences in the entries will set certain processes in motion. The first process will monitor the workstation logon activity. If the user's logon count to the new domain equals the False Logon Count, the second process will move the workstation's inventory to the current domain.

We can use a file created by SMS to control how workstations are reported within the SMS domain structure. The file used to manipulate the collection process is the SMSLS.INI file. It is located in the root of the Netlogon share on all enumerated logon servers.

By editing certain parameters in the SMSLS.INI file located in the user's regular logon domain, you can designate a new target domain within the SMS tree for a workstation's inventory. Changing the settings will automatically start the move process without a workstation's user actually logging on to a new domain. A modification to the Windows 3.x and Windows NT WIN.INI file can also be used to designate a new target domain.

Before we get into the detail, let's take a quick look at the process for determining the workstation's domain.

Mapping to a Domain The general steps that SMS takes when determining how a workstation will mapped to a domain are as follows:

- A user logon script activates the SMSLS batch file, or RUNSMS is called from the workstation's startup file (or run manually by the user).
- The proper SETLS file for the workstation's operating system is determined and called. This will be SETLS16.EXE, SETLS32.EXE, or SETLSOS2.EXE on Intel-based platforms. All three are located in the X86.BIN directory of the Netlogon share on any enumerated logon server. The other platform directories, MIPS.BIN and ALPHA.BIN, also contain processor-specific versions of the SETLS file.
- The SETLS program scans the SMSLS.INI file. Entries in the SMSLS.INI file can be set to designate what domain the workstation reports in. The details of the SMSLS.INI are discussed below.
- If the SMSLS.INI has designated a new domain, the new domain will be mapped as the workstation's domain. SETLS will then randomly connect to one of the new domain's logon servers, and then it will run the Client Setup and Inventory Agent from that server.
- At this time the Inventory Agent will compare the workstation's SMS.INI file Domain and SiteCode values with those of the current domain's DOMAIN.INI file.

NOTE Note that the workstation's SMS.INI file Domain and SiteCode values do not change when SETLS connects with a new domain server. ■

- If the values do not match, the process for moving a computer from one domain to another is initiated.

NOTE The number of logons required before the workstation is listed in the new domain is still controlled by the InvAgtFalseLogonCount parameter in the DOMAIN.INI file. Refer to the preceding section, "What Happens when you Move a Computer?" for further information. ■

How to Control Domain Mapping To control domain mapping, we need to edit the SMSLS.INI file.

CAUTION

The SMSLS.INI file is located in the Netlogon share of the user's regular logon domain, but this *is not* the location from which you edit the file. You must edit the master copy of the file, which is located in the site server's SITE.SRV\MAINCFG.BOX directory. From here SMS will distribute the file to all LAN Manager and Windows NT logon servers' REPL$ share, but only if the Automatically Configure Workstation Logon Scripts option has been enabled. If it hasn't been enabled, you will need to copy the file manually from the SITE.SRV\MAINCFG.BOX to the Netlogon shares.

If you take a look at the SMSLS.INI file, you will see that the file is divided up into several sections that are reasonably well documented. The file's header includes information about the SMSLS.INI file and how it works. I think you'll find the comments in the file to be clear, so we won't go over them in great detail here. We'll take a quick look at each section just to review its purpose.

A file listing of SMSLS.INI can be found in Appendix B, "SMS System Files and Utilities."

The [WIN.INI] Section This part of the SMSLS.INI file contains instructions on creating the [SMS] section in the WIN.INI file of a Windows 3.x or Windows NT machine. This method can be used instead of modifying the SMSLS.INI file.

The [Other Domains] Section This section of the file contains instructions on how to use the Lan Manager 2.x enhanced workstation's LANMAN.INI file, [Workstation] section, "OTHDOMAINS" statement, to designate which domain SMS will map the workstation to.

The [Workgroup] Section This section lets you know how you can map workgroups to SMS domains. You should take into consideration the following rules concerning Windows NT and LAN Server clients:

- If you have a Windows NT machine that belongs to a domain, you can specify the current domain name as the workgroup parameter. Since this section appears before the [domain] and [machine] sections, a domain match here will be the name used for mapping the workstation to the SMS domain.
- When running a LAN Server client, the SMSLS batch file or the SETLSOS2.EXE program may be unable to detect the current logon server. If this happens, you must define the LAN Server domains in both the [workgroup] and [domain] sections of the SMSLS.INI.

The [Domain] Section This section maps the user's logon domain to the SMS domain of your choice. This is handy if you have users logging on to several domains and would like the workstation inventory to be listed in a single SMS domain.

The [Machine] Section If you want to map an individual workstation to a specific SMS domain, this is the section where you can do it. In the other section statements, you were designating groups of machines to be mapped to a specific SMS domain. In this section, you can target a specific workstation for mapping. If you use a Master Domain Model, this makes it easy to split up workstations among the resource domains they most often use. Modifying this section would then allow you to construct a site tree which is more representative of the workstations' logical use of network resources.

This completes the section on how to manage your computer inventory. In it we've gone over the steps necessary to remove a computer from the SMS System, seen what happens when a computer is moved from one domain to another, and taken a look at how we can control workstation-to-domain mapping.

Next, we will follow the flow of the workstation inventory data through the SMS System.

Understanding the Hardware Inventory Data Flow

At times it may be necessary to troubleshoot problems with the SMS inventory collection process. A good understanding of the files associated with the collection process and their respective data flow paths can be a big help when trying to locate the source of a problem. In this section we'll take a general look at the data files and how they move through the system. A detailed look at the data flow process for all system components is given in Appendix D, " A Detailed Look at the Data Flow."

The Files Associated with Workstation Inventory

The Inventory Agent is responsible for much of the collection process. Four versions of the Inventory Agent are used. Which one is used will depend on the client's operating system. The SMSLS batch file will determine the correct version of the Inventory Agent that needs to be run on the workstation. The different versions of the Inventory Agent and the types of clients they are used with are listed in table 9.7.

Table 9.7 The Inventory Agent Used for Each Type of Client

Inventory Agent File Name	Type of Client
logonserver\sms_shr\INVDOS.EXE	LAN Manager NT Workstation Netware Clients
logonserver\sms_shr\INVWIN32.EXE	LAN Manager NT Server NT Workstation (See the sidebar "How to Install the Inventory Agent as a Service on NT Workstations" for more information)
logonserver\sms_shr\INVOS2.EXE	OS/2 Client
System Folder:Startup Item INVMac	Macintosh Client

There are three methods of starting the Inventory Agent. Which method is used also depends on the type of client platform being used.

1. The Inventory Agent is called from the SMSLS or RUNSMS batch file. This is the method used for LAN Manager, NT Workstation, and Netware clients.
2. The Inventory Agent is run as a service on LAN Manager and NT Servers. This method can also be used on NT Workstations, but is not supported by Microsoft. See the sidebar "How to Install the Inventory Agent as a Service on NT Workstations" for more information.
3. The Inventory Agent is run from the Macintosh as a Startup Folder startup item.

How to Install the Inventory Agent as a Service on NT Workstations

The SMS distribution CD-ROM contains a tool by the name of INSTSRV.EXE that can be used to install the INVWIN32.EXE file as a service on a NT Workstation. To install the Inventory Agent as a service, follow the steps listed below:

1. Create a directory on the NT Workstation that will hold the INVWIN32.EXE file.
2. Copy the INVWIN32.EXE file from the *logonserver*\sms_shr*platform* directory to the directory you just created.
3. Run the INSTSRV utility from the SMS distribution CD-ROM and supply the following information:
   - The Service Name—the name you want to call the service you are creating. The service will use this name in the NT Control Panel, Services window.
   - A User Account Name—the name of the user account that will be used to start the service.
   - The Password—the password for the user startup account you just specified.
   - The Workstation Machine Name—the workstation's name as it is listed in the NT Server Manager for the domain.
   - Path—the path to the INVWIN32.EXE file that you copied in step 2.
   - Start the Service—when starting the service, you must specify the logon server that the service will report its inventory to. You do this as a command line argument that lists the path to the logon server's sms_shr share.

Besides the executable files, data files in the form of .RAW and .MIF files are created by the Inventory Agents. These are the files that carry the inventory information which is eventually stored in the SMS database. The type of data file that's generated and the process for moving it are again determined by the type of client being inventoried.

The Data Flow Process

The data flow process is the same for all clients with two exceptions: the Macintosh and the OS/2 client. First we'll look at the normal flow process, and then the Macintosh and OS/2 processes.

Lan Manager, NT, and Netware Clients It doesn't matter if you're running the INVDOS.EXE file from the SMSLS batch file or you're using the INVWIN32.EXE agent as a service. They will both collect and process inventory in the same way. The only difference is that the agent running as a service will automatically wake up every 24 hours and determine if a scan is needed based upon properties set in the SMS administrator. The INVDOS program must be called from either the SMSLS batch file or the RUNSMS batch file. An outline describing the data flow process for these clients follows:

- The Inventory Agent scans the workstation and creates a RAW Inventory Agent file (*.RAW). This file is placed in the \\logonserver\sms_shr\INVENTORY.BOX directory on Windows NT and LAN Manager logon servers. On Netware logon servers the file is placed in the logon.srv\INVENTORY.BOX directory of the SMS root share.
- The site server Maintenance Manager monitors all Windows NT and LAN Manager logon servers' SMS_SHR\INVENTORY.BOX directories for new files. It collects any *.RAW files it finds in these directories and puts them in the site server's SITE.SRV\INVENTORY.BOX directory. On Netware servers the INVENTORY.BOX directory is polled by the Maintenance Manager for new *.RAW files.
- From here, the site server's Inventory Processor takes over. It processes the *.RAW files, converts them into *.MIF files (Delta-MIFs), and places them in the site server's SITE.SRV\DATALOAD.BOX\DELTAMIF.COL directory.
- Next, the Inventory Data Loader processes the files, now called Delta-MIFs, and updates the site database with the new inventory information.

OS/2 Clients The OS/2 Inventory Agent (INVOS2.EXE) reports inventory a little differently. Instead of creating *.RAW files, it creates *.MIF text files. The process is as follows:

- The OS/2 Inventory Agent scans the workstation or server and creates text-based *.MIF files. The *.MIF files are placed in the LOGON.SRV\ISVMIF.BOX directory (not the INVENTORY.BOX directory).
- From here, the Inventory Processor converts the text-based *.MIF files to Delta-MIFs and places them in the SITE.SRV\DATALOAD.BOX\DELTAMIF.COL directory.
- The Inventory Data Loader processes the files and updates the site database with the new inventory information.

Macintosh Clients Macintosh Clients must manually connect to an NT server running Services For Macintosh, and then run the Installer program. This copies the Inventory Agent for Macintosh (INVMac) to the Macintosh workstation, where it is run from the Startup Folder. The inventory process is as follows:

- INVMac is run when the Macintosh is started up and collects the inventory.
- The inventory is placed in the NT logon server's LOGON.SRV\ISVMIF.BOX directory in the form of an *.MIF file by the INVMac program.
- The Maintenance Manager moves the *.MIF files from the NT logon server running the Services For Macintosh to the site server's SITE.SRV\ISVMIF.BOX directory.

- From here, the *.MIF files are processed into Delta-MIFs by the Inventory Processor and put into the SITE.SRV\DATALOAD.BOX\DELTAMIF.COL directory.
- The Inventory Data Loader then uses the Delta-MIFs to update the site database.

From Here...

In this chapter, we found out what it takes to configure SMS for hardware inventory collection. We saw how to add computers to site, remove them from a site, and how to move them around within the site. Methods to customize the way inventory is reported were discussed, and we ended by examining how data flows through the system. You may want to refer to the following sections for more information on related subjects.

- Appendix B, "SMS System Files and Utilities," the section titled "SMS Files" will give you a detailed look at the initialization files used in the various SMS processes.
- Appendix B, "SMS System Files and Utilities," the section titled "DBCLEAN.EXE" gives a completed description of the capabilities of the SMS Database Maintenance Utility.
- Appendix D, "A Detailed Look at the Data Flow," gets into the specifics of the SMS data flow process.

CHAPTER 10

Software Inventory and Audit

In this chapter, you'll learn how to:

Perform a software inventory

You can specify which software packages SMS should look for and how often the inventory should be performed. You can even have SMS collect specific files from each machine during the inventory process.

Perform a software audit

SMS includes a database of several thousand software packages that it will search for during a software audit. You can specify exactly when to perform the audit and which machines to audit.

Customize audit and inventory to suit your administrative needs

SMS enables you to add your own software packages to the set that it knows about.

Tracking software on people's machines is one of the more time-consuming and disagreeable aspects of the System Administrator's job. But it's vital for at least two important reasons: software licensing and software updates. You got to be able to show that you are not using more copies of a software package than you've bought licenses for, and you've got to be able to identify all the machines running particular versions of a software package in order to be able to bring everyone up to the latest revision. SMS addresses these issues with two similar but separate functions: software inventory and software audit. Because of their similarity, we'll cover them in the same chapter and show you why you would use one versus the other. ■

Collecting Software Inventory

Before we get involved in the details of configuring the software inventory process, let's understand what it does for you and how it works.

Software inventory, as its name implies, searches the hard drives attached to each client computer for specific software applications and reports any that it finds back to SMS. You specify to SMS which software applications you want to inventory (by default, none are inventoried) and how frequently you want to perform the inventory. For each software application you want to inventory, you must create an SMS inventory package that specifies the files and those file properties that uniquely specify that particular application. Then, SMS will perform the inventory according to the frequency you've set. For any package you've defined, you can also specify that those files be collected from the client computer. This means that those files will actually be copied from the client computer to the logon server and eventually end up at the site server. As you'll see, this is all configured in the SMS Administrator program.

The inventory process is actually driven by the client computer. In other words, the client computer starts the software inventory by connecting to an SMS logon server. When the client computer runs the logon script, the Inventory Agent is started. This agent performs the software (and hardware) inventory scan on the client computer. If it identifies any of the packages you've configured, it uploads the information to the logon server and, from there, it eventually gets to the site server (for details, see the "Understanding Software Inventory Data Flow" section in this chapter). The key points about SMS software inventory are as follows:

- You must configure SMS inventory packages with the SMS Administrator program before software inventory will start. You don't have to configure an SMS job to perform the inventory.
- Software inventory applies to every computer in the site. You can't selectively perform a software inventory and you can't schedule it.
- You can specify how often the software inventory will run on each client computer (the default is every seven days).
- The client computer, not SMS, initiates the software inventory process. That is, the software inventory process is triggered only when the client computer connects to an SMS logon server and runs the logon script.
- You can specify that particular files be collected from each client computer during the software inventory process. The recommended use for this feature is to collect important configuration files that will help you diagnose problems or enable you to copy these back to the client computer if one of them gets lost or becomes corrupted.

Configuring SMS for Software Inventory Collection

You use the SMS Administrator program to configure software inventory collection. The main things you'll want to specify are the frequency of inventory and the packages to be inventoried. But there are other ways that the inventory can be tailored to better accommodate various machines.

Frequency of Inventory For each site in the SMS hierarchy, you can decide how frequently the software inventory scan is performed. Your choices are "Every Workstation Logon" or "Every *N* days" (where *N* is any number of days you choose). The frequency of inventory is set in the SMS Administrator program, and can be changed at any time. To see how this works, open the SMS Administrator, highlight the site you want to inventory, select File, Properties..., and choose the Inventory button from the Site Properties dialog box.

You can view both current properties and proposed properties. You can make changes only to the proposed properties. When SMS has finished making the proposed changes to the site, the current properties will change to match the proposed properties. To change the software inventory frequency to "every 5 days," for example, you just click the Proposed properties button and type "5" in the Every *N* days input box and choose OK twice. SMS will ask you to confirm that you want to update the site. Choose the Yes button, and the changes will be carried out.

Slow Links The other part of this dialog box, "Inventory Strategy When Network is Slow," applies to both the software and the hardware inventory. For each client computer logon, SMS measures the speed of the connection and decides, based on a set threshold, whether the link is slow or not. This is primarily for the benefit of laptop users who are dialing into the network, because taking inventory can be very time-consuming over a typical modem connection. This section gives you three options for taking the inventory over a slow link. You can have SMS take the inventory regardless of link speed, skip the inventory if the link is slow, or let the user decide whether or not the inventory will be taken.

CAUTION

In spite of Microsoft's best efforts, SMS is not very good at judging the speed of a link. Although there is a setting in the NT registry that you can use to change the threshold that SMS uses to make the decision, you may still have problems with SMS trying to inventory laptops regardless of the settings you've made in the SMS Administrator. The following workaround ensures that SMS won't inflict itself on your dial-up users:

In your NT logon script, prior to the part that SMS added, insert the line:

IF "%SMS%" == "1" GOTO ENDSMS

After the part that SMS added, insert the line:

:ENDSMS

Finally, on each dial-up machine, insert the following line in AUTOEXEC.BAT before SMS is called:

SET SMS=1

Creating the Software Inventory Package

You need to create a software inventory package for each software application you want to inventory. This package gives SMS enough information about key files in the application to enable unique identification of that application. A single SMS file contains all the inventory packages, and this file is automatically distributed to all logon servers in the site. To create a software inventory package, start by opening the Packages window in the SMS Administrator program. Microsoft's documentation confusingly applies the term "package" to both the SMS package and the software application represented by the package. In this book, when we refer to "package," we mean the SMS package.

> **CAUTION**
>
> The use of software inventory should be limited to a relatively small number of packages. Microsoft recommends that you create no more than 200 packages. If you want a more comprehensive list of software from client computers, you should use the software audit function described later in this chapter.

1. In the SMS Administrator program, select File, Open... and choose Packages from the Open SMS Window dialog box. You'll see the Packages window, as shown in figure 10.1.

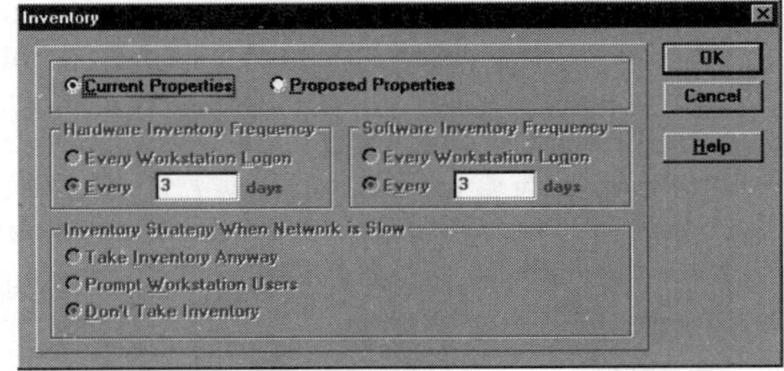

FIG. 10.1 Creating a Software Inventory Package.

2. With the Packages window active, select File, New... to bring up the Package Properties dialog box, in figure 10.2.

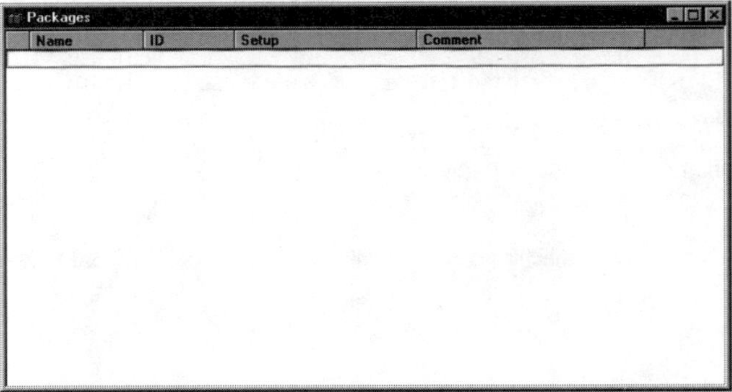

FIG. 10.2 Configuring package properties.

NOTE SMS has three different sets of package properties: Workstation, Sharing, and Inventory. You can apply any or all of these to the same package, depending on what you want to do with a particular software application. ■

3. You must supply a name and, optionally, a comment for the package. Both of these fields will appear in the Package Command Manager running on client workstations for a Run Command on Workstation job and in the SMS Administrator. After you've created the package, SMS will assign a unique package ID.

Importing the Inventory Rule The simplest way to create the inventory package is to import from a package description (.PDF) file. To do this, choose the Import... button shown in figure 10.3. This brings up the file dialog box shown in figure 10.4. For this example, we'll select WWD60C.PDF, which is the description for Word for Windows 6.0c.

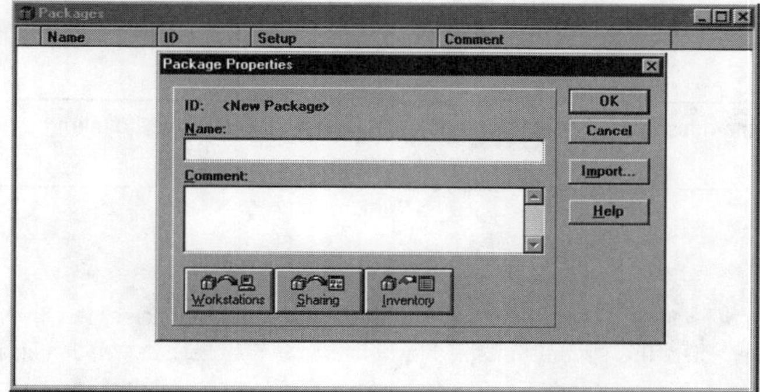

FIG. 10.3 Selecting a PDF file to import.

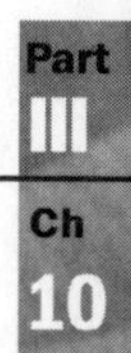

This returns you to the Package Properties window, as shown in figure 10.4. Note that the Name and Comment fields have been filled in for you. Now choose the Inventory button to see what the rule looks like (see fig. 10.5).

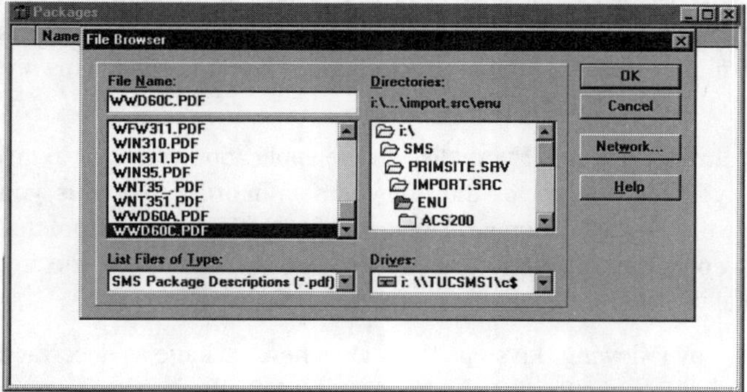

FIG. 10.4 A predefined package for Word 6.0c.

You can see that a rule doesn't have to be very complex. Word 6.0c can be identified simply by finding the file WINWORD.EXE with file size 3490816 bytes and date 06/16/94. Other software applications may require more complex rules, but the simpler the better.

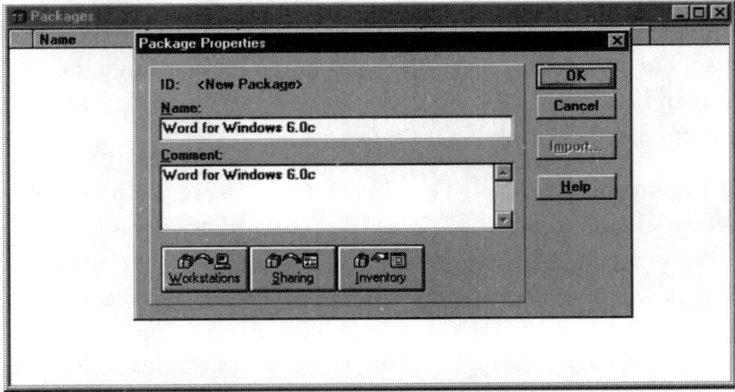

FIG. 10.5
The rule for Word 6.0c.

Examining the rules in the package description files is an excellent way to learn how to create your own rules.

CAUTION

SMS will not inventory the software application you have specified unless the "Inventory this package" option is enabled. This option is enabled by default in the package description files, but you must enable it manually if you create your own rules. You may not want to enable it right away if you are creating a package that installs an application on a workstation and inventories the application. Instead, you may want first to ensure that the application was successfully installed and then enable the "Inventory this package" option.

Choose OK to complete the package. SMS will inform you that it will update the inventory rules for this package at all sites. Choose OK to clear the information dialog and OK again to close the Package Properties dialog, and you're done. SMS will now distribute this package, after a 15-minute delay to let you make changes if you need to. This prevents unnecessary updates to the PACKAGE.RUL file.

Creating Inventory Rules Manually If the application you want to inventory doesn't have a .PDF file, you'll have to create the rule yourself. In order to do this, you should have access to a machine with the application already installed. SMS provides a tool that will examine existing files and report the characteristics you want. To see how this works, let's create a rule for Word 6.0 manually.

1. Start by following the steps to create a new package as described in the previous section, but, instead of choosing the Import... button, choose the Inventory button. You'll get the Setup Package for Inventory dialog box, as shown in figure 10.6.
2. To add a file property for WINWORD.EXE, choose the Add AND... button. This brings up the File Properties dialog box, as shown in figure 10.7.

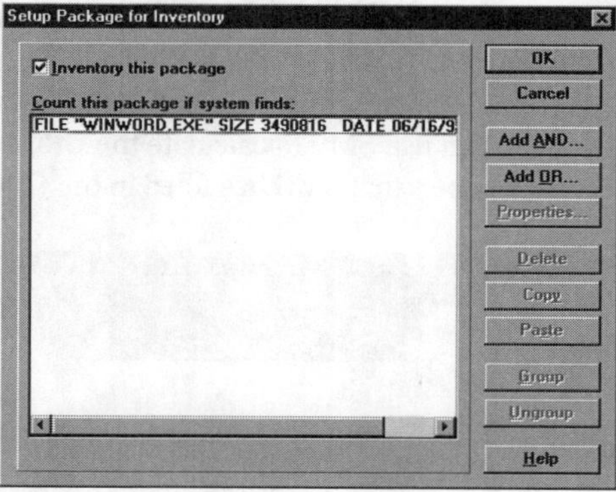

FIG. 10.6
Creating a rule manually for Word 6.0.

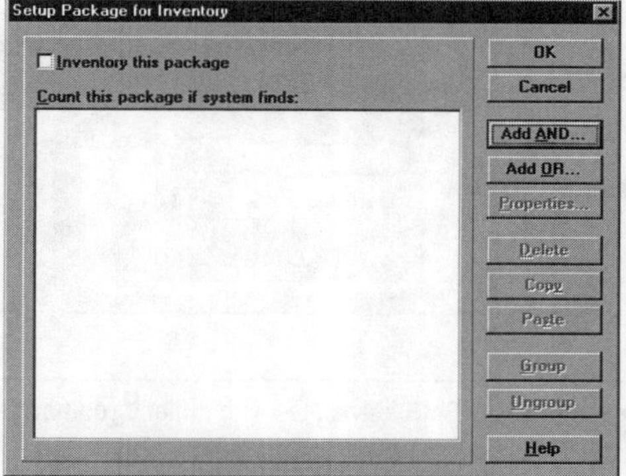

FIG. 10.7
Adding file properties to the rule.

3. In the File Name input box, type the full path to the file WINWORD.EXE or click the Browse button to find the file that way. Now you're ready to add properties for this file. The choices are:
   - BYTE—the value of the single byte at a specified byte location in the file.
   - CHECKSUM—the checksum calculated from a specified sequence of bytes.
   - CRC—the Cyclical Redundancy Check (CRC) calculated from a specified sequence of bytes (SMS uses the CCITT-CRC algorithm).
   - DATE—the date of the file.
   - LONG—the value of the long integer (4 bytes) at a specified byte location in the file.
   - SIZE—the size of the file in bytes.
   - STRING—the ASCII string at a specified byte location in the file.
   - TIME—the time of the file.
   - WORD—the value of the word (2 bytes) at a specified byte location in the file.

4. To add a CRC value, in the Properties Available selection box, double-click the CRC selection. This brings up the CRC-16 dialog box, as shown in figure 10.8. For this example, we'll start at byte 100 and specify a length of 500. After filling in the appropriate boxes with these values, you can use SMS to calculate the CRC for you by choosing the Retrieve button. Figure 10.9 shows that SMS has filled in the CRC-16 field for us.

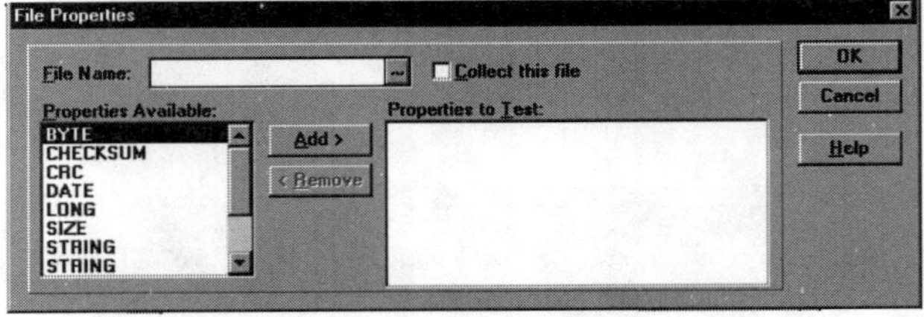

FIG. 10.8
Adding a CRC property to the file WINWORD.EXE.

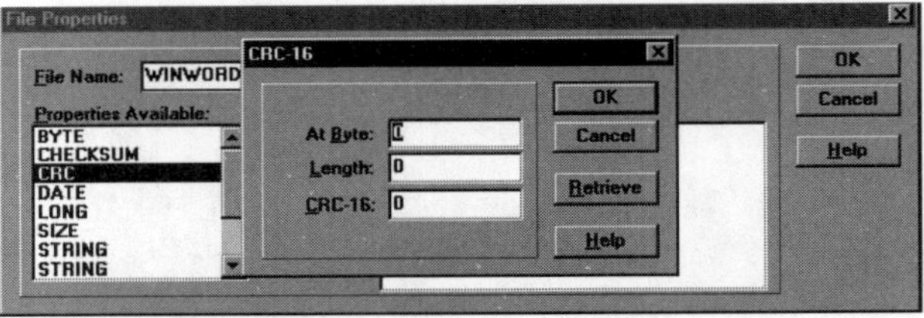

FIG. 10.9
SMS has calculated the CRC for us.

There is a Retrieve button for each property SMS associates with a file. If you have access to the files that make up the application, this makes it easy to create the rule.

5. Choose OK twice to accept this property and return to the Setup Package for Inventory dialog box. You'll now see a single line for the file WINWORD.EXE. To show off some of the features, we'll continue the example, making it a little more complex.
6. Let's say you want to check for the above property of WINWORD.EXE and the existence of the file WINWORD.HLP. Choose the Add AND button and fill in the File Name box with WINWORD.HLP. Then choose OK. Now the dialog box looks like figure 10.10.

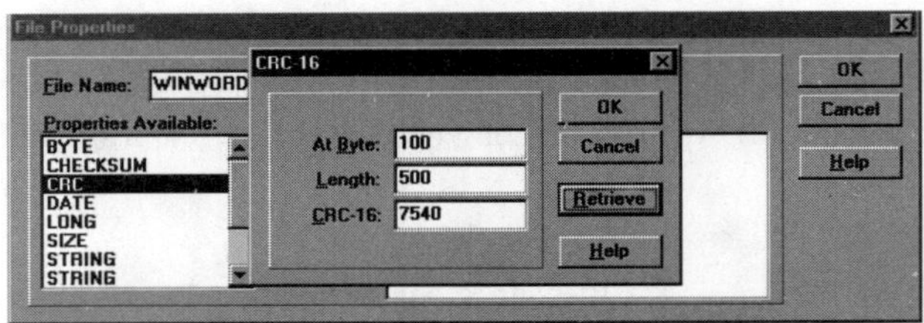

FIG. 10.10
Using a logical operator in the rule.

7. Now, suppose we goofed and we really meant this test to be an OR instead of an AND. Just select the AND line and choose the Toggle button to change it to OR.
8. Finally, let's add the file WORDCBT.DLL and its file size and AND it to the previous expression. The result is shown in figure 10.11.

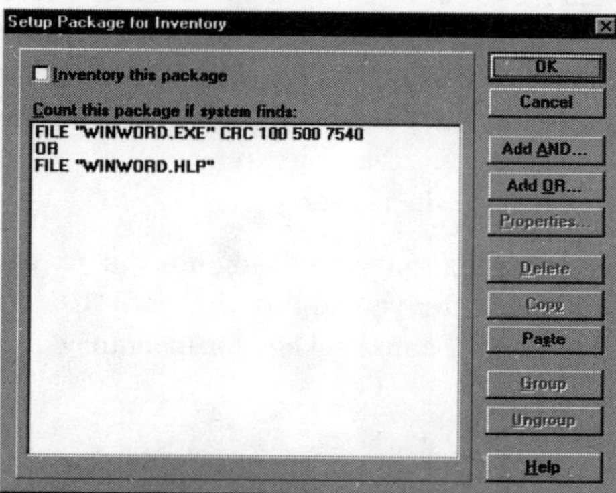

FIG. 10.11
A complete rule.

9. To make sure we get what we really want and make the expression more readable, we can group the expression. To see how this works, highlight the first three lines in the dialog box and choose the Group button. The resulting parentheses, as shown in figure 10.12, ensure that the OR expression is performed first. The Ungroup button reverses this operation.

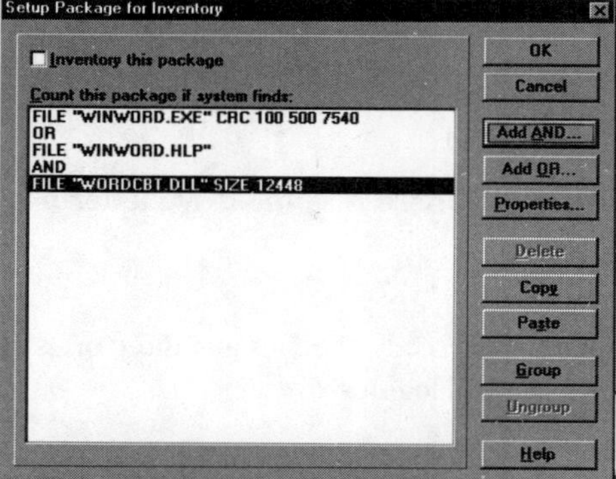

FIG. 10.12
Grouping an expression.

The other buttons in this dialog box are fairly straightforward. Properties... lets you modify the file properties of the currently selected file. Delete lets you delete a file, but you must have the file line plus the adjacent logical operator line selected. Copy lets you copy one or more selected lines to the clipboard and Paste inserts those lines after the line currently selected, but always pastes the selection as an "AND." If you wanted an "OR," you must use the Toggle button after pasting.

To complete this package, enable the Inventory this package option and choose OK. At the Package Properties dialog box, you can fill in a name for the package and choose OK. The package is now complete and ready to be distributed.

Collecting Files SMS can collect files for you while it is performing the software inventory. The intended use of this feature is to collect fairly small files that would be of use in troubleshooting machine problems or restoring a damaged configuration. Files like AUTOEXEC.BAT, CONFIG.SYS, WIN.INI, and SYSTEM.INI are all good candidates. When SMS collects a file from a client computer, it sends that file to the computer's logon server, and from there, it eventually goes to the site server. If you have a hierarchy of site servers, the file will continue up the chain until it gets to the central site server.

You activate this feature from the File Properties dialog box that we saw in Figure 10.7 by enabling the Collect this file option. After you do this, the word "COLLECT" will appear at the end of that file's properties line in the Setup Package for Inventory dialog box.

CAUTION

Use the Collect feature sparingly! Keep in mind that it will collect the files you specify from every client computer and store them on the site server for the current site and every site above it in the hierarchy. You can quickly fill your server's disks if you're not careful.

Client Drives Scanned

By default, SMS scans every drive on a computer, including removable media. A user may have an NTFS drive that is unreadable under Windows 95 or a removable hard drive that often has no cartridge in it. You can prevent the scan for a particular drive by adding the following line to the SMS.INI file on the client computer:

In the [WorkstationStatus] section add

FailedHardwareChecks=DriveN (where N is the drive letter in uppercase)

Required Files

For software inventory to function correctly, the files and directories listed in Table 10.1 must be present on your site servers and all logon servers.

Table 10.1 Files Required on Site Servers and Logon Servers for Hardware Inventory

File or Directory	Location	Description
SMSLS.BAT	NETLOGON share	A script file that is run by SMS client computers, typically at

File or Directory	Location	Description
SMSLS.CMD (for OS/2 clients)	NETLOGON share	network logon. It invokes programs to install or verify the SMS client files and to scan the client computer for hardware and software inventory.
SMSLS.SCR (for NetWare clients)	\SMS\LOGON.SRV	
\SMS\LOGON.SRV (and all files and subdirectories)	Normally the C drive of a server	This directory contains the executables for the inventory agents for various clients.

It's usually not necessary to verify client configurations, because SMS will verify (and reinstall, if necessary) the required files on a client computer when that client runs SMSLS.BAT. Table 10.2 lists the required client computer files.

Table 10.2 Files Required on Client Computers for Hardware Inventory

File or Directory	Location	Description
SMS.INI	The root of the C drive	A hidden file that contains configuration information critical to the functioning of SMS, including the client's SMS ID.
\MS\SMS (and all files and subdirectories)	Normally the C drive. SMS chooses the drive location at initial installation based on the drive with the most free space.	This directory contains the executables for the package command manager and the user agent for remote control and diagnostics.

Understanding the Software Inventory Data Flow

Understanding the flow of data throughout the software inventory process will help you to analyze and correct problems. This section presents a high-level view of the data flow. Appendix D, "A Detailed Look at the Data Flow," provides a more detailed description.

The process starts with the client computer. The client computer runs the SMS Inventory Agent program in one of four different ways depending on what type of machine it is:

1. On Windows 3.x or Windows 95 clients, the logon script invokes Inventory Agent. The inventory files are copied to an SMS logon server.
2. On SMS servers, the Inventory Agent (INVWIN32.EXE) is run as a service, allowing it to run when no one is logged on. The inventory files are copied to an SMS logon server.

3. On non-SMS servers running Windows NT, the Inventory Agent (INV32CLI.EXE) is run as a service and it stores the inventory files locally. A separate service, the Client Monitor service (CLIMONNT.EXE) copies the inventory files to an SMS logon server.
4. On NetWare servers, SMS does not run any inventory agent. SMS actually goes out to NetWare servers and takes inventory.

From Client Computer to Logon Server The Inventory Agent first verifies the SMS software configuration on the client computer. Then it checks the speed of the network, comparing the value it computes with a value stored in the NT registry. If the network is determined to be "slow," the Inventory Agent takes action based on the Slow Network strategy defined in the SMS Administrator program for that site. If the action is to perform the inventory, Inventory Agent examines the time of the last inventory scan for that client computer, determines the time elapsed since that scan, and compares it to the software scan interval set up in the SMS Administrator program. If that interval has passed, the Inventory Agent performs the software scan. The collected data is sent to that client computer's logon server as either an .MIF file (ASCII text) or a .RAW file (binary). Most client computers generate .MIF files, but NetWare servers, Macintosh, and OS/2 computers report .RAW files.

From Logon Server to Site Server The Maintenance Manager service collects inventory files from logon servers and moves them to the site server for further processing.

The Inventory Processor then takes over and makes a number of decisions. If a client computer has reported its inventory for the first time, the Inventory Processor writes a history file for that computer and sends the full .MIF file to the Inventory Data Loader. On subsequent inventories for that computer, the Inventory Processor compares the current inventory with previous data and generates a partial .MIF file (or Delta-MIF file) that includes only the changes since the last inventory. If the Inventory Processor determines that the inventory hasn't changed since the last report, it looks at how much time has elapsed since the previous report. If this duration is greater than the "heartbeat" interval (default is four days), the Inventory Processor sends a "heartbeat" .MIF. This is a small file (about 2 KB) that simply indicates the client computer is still active. Otherwise, the Inventory Processor sends nothing. All .MIF files are forwarded to the Inventory Data Loader.

From Site Server to Central Site The Inventory Data Loader has the task of loading .MIF files into the SMS database. If the .MIF files were generated at a secondary site, they are forwarded to the primary site and then loaded into the database. After the local site database is loaded, the inventory data is forwarded up the hierarchy until it reaches the central site.

Performing a Software Audit

Software audit performs an intensive search on client computers for over 5,000 software applications and reports any that it finds back to SMS. You can use the list of applications that Microsoft has predefined or you can create your own list. You can schedule the audit and you can specify which computers to audit. By default, software auditing is not enabled. To enable software auditing, you must create a single workstation package and then schedule it using a Run Command on Workstation job. This is all done in the SMS Administrator program.

Software audit sounds a lot like software inventory, and, in fact, they are similar, but there are important differences, as follows:

- Software audit requires a single workstation package, whereas software inventory requires a separate inventory package for each application.
- You must configure a Run Command on Workstation job to initiate and schedule the software audit. Software inventory does not use an SMS job, so you can't schedule software inventory to run at a specific time.
- Software audit allows you to specify the computers that get audited.
- Software audit does not allow you to collect files from the client computers.

Installing Software Auditing

Software auditing is part of the Scripts component. If you can't find the files mentioned in this chapter, you need to rerun SMS setup and install the Scripts component. Additionally, if any of your client computers are other than Intel machines (such as DEC Alpha), you'll need to install the client components for those architectures.

The Software Audit Rule File

The key to the software audit process is the audit rule file, AUDIT.RUL. This is a text file that contains a list of inventory package descriptions using the same format that the SMS Administrator program uses to describe file properties. The following is a sample entry from this file:

```
package 4670 "Visual Basic 3.0 English (International Win16, Microsoft)"
file "CRW.EXE" size 1789440 date 04/28/93 crc 763648 262145 23673
file "CRPE.DLL" size 910848 date 04/28/93 crc 324352 262145 64639
file "DEMO.EXE" size 301659 date 04/28/93 crc 60331 180997 9689
```

There is an implicit AND operator between each file line. You can also specify operators as you did when creating the software inventory package. You can use the Retrieve function that was discussed in the section "Creating the Software Inventory Package" earlier in this chapter to get the properties for each file.

The AUDIT.RUL file that comes with SMS contains descriptions for over 5,000 applications. You'll find it in the directory \SMS_SHRC\PRIMSITE.SRV\AUDIT on your site server. You can use the file as is or edit it to add your own descriptions. This is done outside the SMS Administrator using your favorite text editor. Be sure to do your editing on a copy of the file. Once you're satisfied with the file, you must convert it to a .CFG file before you can run the audit. To do this, on your site server, change directories to \SMS_SHRC\PRIMSITE\AUDIT and execute the following command:

```
RUL2CFG.BAT AUDIT.RUL
```

This will generate the file AUDIT.CFG, which is the file SMS actually uses during the audit process. You must run this command every time you change your package rule file.

If you create your own customized rule file, name it something besides AUDIT.RUL. This prevents it from getting overwritten when you upgrade SMS.

Creating the Software Audit Package

Software Audit requires one workstation package. You create this in the SMS Administrator by using the Import command to import the package definition from the file AUDIT.PDF, supplied with SMS and located in the directory \SMS_SHR\PRIMSITE.SRV\IMPORT.SRC\ENU. After importing this file, you can examine the workstation properties. The only thing you need to fill in to complete the package is the Source Directory field, as shown in figure 10.13. This will be the directory \SMS_SHR\PRIMSITE.SRV\AUDIT\PACKAGE on your site server.

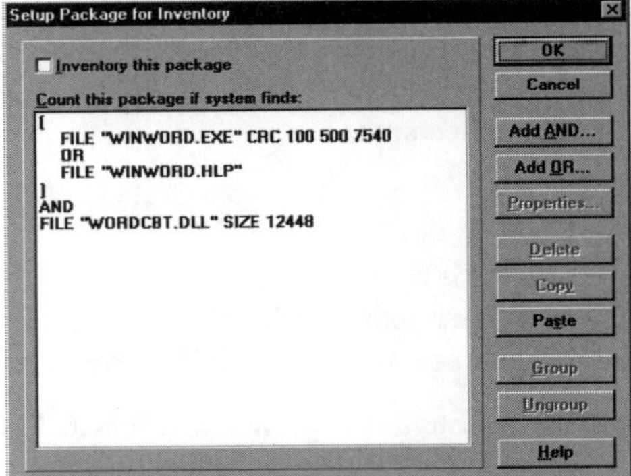

FIG. 10.13
Examining the properties of the software audit package.

Creating and Running a Job for Software Audit

After you've created the AUDIT.CFG file and the package for software audit, you must create a Run Command on Workstation job to actually schedule and run the software audit process. The software audit package is treated like any other command that you schedule to run on a client computer. For a detailed description of the Run Command on Workstation job and how to use it, see Chapter 11, "Software Distribution."

Software audit is a computationally intensive process, so it's best to schedule it to run at a time that will not interfere with work.

Understanding the Software Audit Data Flow

Software audit is initiated using a standard SMS Run Command on Workstation job. When this command executes on the client computer, it first identifies the operating system and processor type, and then runs the appropriate software auditing program from the site server.

The software auditing program scans all local drives on the client computer for all packages defined in the AUDIT.CFG file. Upon completion, it creates an .MIF file and places it on the current SMS logon server. This .MIF file contains an Audited Software group for each detected package. From the logon server, the flow is the same as for .MIF files generated by the Inventory Agent.

Software Inventory versus Software Audit

The SMS software inventory and software audit functions do seem very similar, so how do you decide which one to use? The following are some guidelines:

1. If you need to collect files from client computers, you must use software inventory.
2. If you need the ability to schedule the inventory or target specific machines, you must use software audit.
3. If there is a small set of important applications that you must maintain and track on client computers, then software inventory is the appropriate choice.
4. If you need periodically to search out all applications on client computers, then software audit is the appropriate choice.
5. Software audit scans for thousands of applications and requires you to create only one SMS package, but it's a burden on the client computer. Software inventory looks for a relatively small number of applications (Microsoft recommends no more than 200) and requires you to create a package for each one, but it doesn't tie up the client computer for very long.

From Here...

- Chapter 8, "Using the SMS Administrator Program," and Chapter 12, "Queries and Reports," both show you how to view and query the information that is collected by the software inventory and audit processes.
- Chapter 9, "Collecting Hardware Inventory," is relevant to the topic of software inventory because the same SMS Administrator dialog control settings are used for both and they are both kicked off by the client computer when it logs on and runs the Inventory Agent.
- Chapter 11, "Software Distribution," provides greater detail on the creation of packages and jobs, both of which are required for software inventory and software audit.
- Chapter 20, "Taking the Hardware and Software Inventory," presents some examples of both software inventory and audit.

CHAPTER 11

Software Distribution

- Create workstation command packages
- Create jobs to send workstation command packages
- Use Package Command Manager to run jobs received by the client
- List the configuration and status files used in SMS Software Distribution
- Troubleshoot a failed software distribution

The most ambitious feature of SMS is software distribution. Not only can you install and remove client software with SMS, you can copy system or data files to clients, and you can run utilities locally at their workstation, such as virus scan software or network card "auto-config" utilities.

The software distribution feature consists of two main processes: sending packages and sending jobs. Packages and Jobs are the "Bonnie and Clyde" of software distribution. In SMS, an administrator distributes applications or single files as packages. These packages get routed to distribution servers in a Systems Management Server site. After a package has been distributed, the administrator can send a job to run any application or install an application, provided the client has access. ■

Understanding Software Distribution Flow

To use SMS for software distribution, you must have an understanding of the distribution flow and the components and processes involved.

Why would we want to create a software distribution “package?” In short, you can create an SMS package to do anything that you would do at the local client’s command line. What might an administrator or technician do at a client command line? Tasks could be checking for a virus, updating a config.sys for a WFW client or dosstart.bat for a Win95 client. You might also install an off-the-shelf or custom application.

When we speak of software distribution, we are talking about “packages” of .exe commands, .bat files, or single files that an administrator would want to implement to the SMS site and subsites, in lieu of walking up physically to a client computer to do a task.

On the target computers, The Package Command Manager (PCM) application runs commands. The PCM is part of the SMS client software. It uses a “workstation command package,” which is a combination of the application’s files and the actual command to run the application, like “Setup.”

The main steps of distributing software or command packages to client computers are as follows:

At the Site Server:

1. The administrator creates a software package.
2. The administrator creates a job—that is, Run Command on Workstation.
3. The administrator determines which servers will be distribution points for the application.
4. The Scheduler and Senders send the job to each distribution server containing the target client computers.
5. Packages are placed on the distribution servers within that site.
6. Instruction files are created for Package Command Manager and placed on the logon servers.

At the Client:

1. The user selects available applications from the Package Command Manager (see fig. 11.1 below).
2. The Package Command Manager connects to a distribution server and runs the application.

First, let’s take a look at the creation of packages and jobs.

FIG. 11.1
Creating a client package.

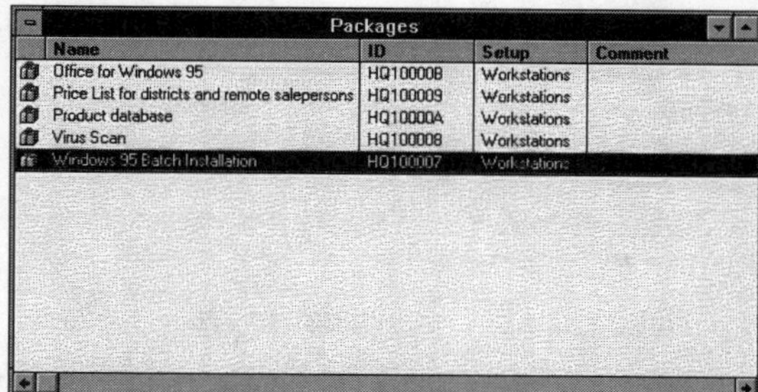

Working with Packages

An SMS package consists of application files and the command line commands that can be used to run the application. Multiple command lines can be used if an application can be started using different switches or if there are several different executables in the package. You can copy the application to the SMS site server's local hard disk or place it on the network share which SMS processes can then access.

FIG. 11.2
Setting a Package Setup Package for Workstations.

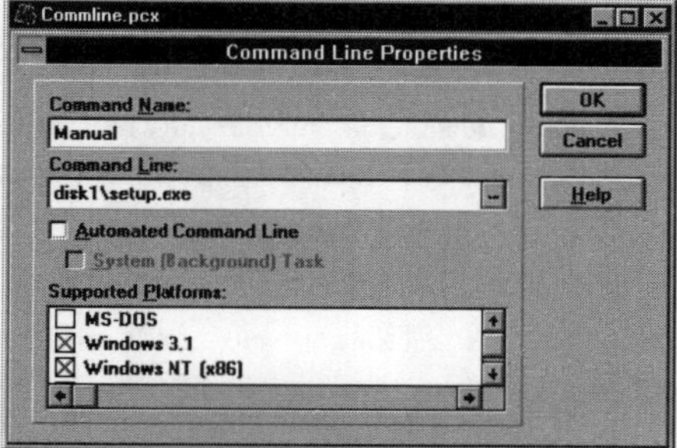

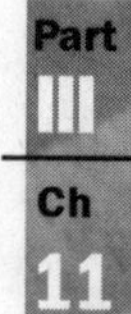

The following steps are used to create a package:

- Use File, Open to the Packages window and then from the File menu, choose New.
- In the Package Properties window, enter a name for the package and a comment, such as "Refresh system files for WFW Workstations, Ver 2.0."
- Choose Workstations.
- Enter the Source Directory for the application files. (For an SMS predefined package, look in SMS\Primsite.srv\import.src for *.PDF files, or package definition files, discussed further in Chapter 21, "Sharing Applications.") Use a UNC pathname to refer to the server and share directory.
- Choose New to configure the command line properties.

FIG. 11.3
Use the Command Line Properties dialog box to set options.

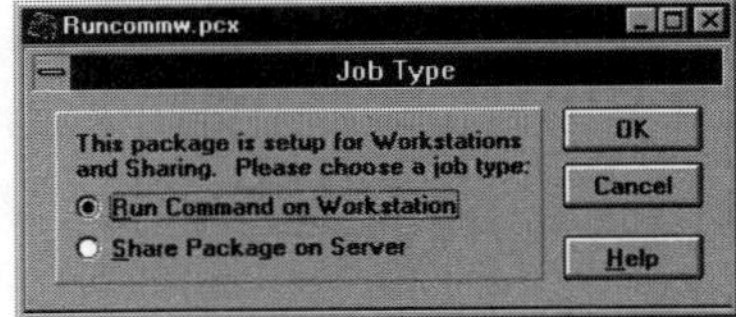

Here are explanations about options in Command Line Properties:

Command Name—the name used when creating a job to distribute the command and package files. Also the name of the command that will appear on the target computer.

Command Line—the actual command line and parameters necessary to run the application, for example, SETUP.EXE.

Automated Command Line—use this option to run a job unattended. For example, run a virus check overnight.

System (Background) Task—this allows the command to be run by the Package Command Manager as a background service on a Windows NT computer. If run as a system task, an application cannot display anything on the screen.

Support Platforms—select the client platform(s) that will run the command line. Uncheck boxes if they don't apply (for example, MIPS, Alpha).

NOTE Create your own package directory outside the SMS directory tree for new packages. When upgrading SMS to future releases, the SMS setup will wipe out any directories it doesn't recognize. ■

NOTE If you are installing a package on a Novell Network, you have to copy the source directory to the Novell Server so that the clients can find the package. ■

After a package is created, it appears in the main Packages window with a status comment.

Installing a Package on a Novell Server

The steps for creating a package on a Novell Server are as follows:

1. Setup a subdirectory on the Novell Server for SMS packages.
2. Setup a package in SMS Administrator, referring to the Novell Source Directory.

SMS will convert the directory to the UNC convention "\\Server_Name\Share."

Understanding Jobs

Once you have a package, you can install software with SMS by running a job. A job consists of a set of instructions that initiates the communication between SMS processes to carry out a variety of tasks. The following three types of jobs can be initiated by an administrator:

- Run Command on Workstation
- Share Package on Server
- Remove Package from Server

With software distribution, we will be concerned primarily with Run Command on Workstation jobs.

You might ask, "Why do you need a job when you've already configured a package?" Jobs actually put the package into implementation mode. A package can reside on a site server for months, waiting to be used and reused. A job actually schedules the package to be distributed to the destinations you specify.

After the job is created, it is assigned a job ID. This ID is used to track job events. You can later see a job in a list of jobs, along with the status of the job, such as Active, Pending, or Completed.

When configuring a job, you define a set of distribution servers to act as distribution points for packages. Once the package is present on the distribution servers, the job is sent as a control file (.CT*) to the target machines where it is executed by a component of the Systems Management Server client code called the Package Command Manager or PCM. Jobs can be automatically executed or manually executed by launching the PCM application.

NOTE Once the package is copied to each distribution server, the client must be able to access components of the package from a distribution server. In a Microsoft Network client, files are accessed from a share point on the distribution servers. From a NetWare client, a NetWare server that's accessible must be included in the list of distribution servers for the job. If the target machines for a package include Macintosh machines, then a Windows NT-based machine with the Services for Macintosh that is connected to the target machine must be included in the list of distribution servers. Distribution servers do not have to include all the logon servers in a domain. ■

Configuring a Job: Job Setup

The details of distributing software are defined in the Run Command on Workstation dialog box, as shown in figure 11.4. This is where you create a Run Command on Workstation Job to distribute packages. In the following sections we'll learn the salient points about the Job Setup screen:

Job Details The Job Details screen includes information about the package being sent, target computers, and instructions regarding how and where to send the package. To display the Job Details dialog box, choose the Details button (see fig. 11.4).

Another way to bring up the Job Details dialog box is to drag a package to the Sites window and drop it on target computers. If the package has only the Workstations property defined, SMS Administrator opens up the Run Command on Workstation Job Details dialog box and fills in the correct package and job target information.

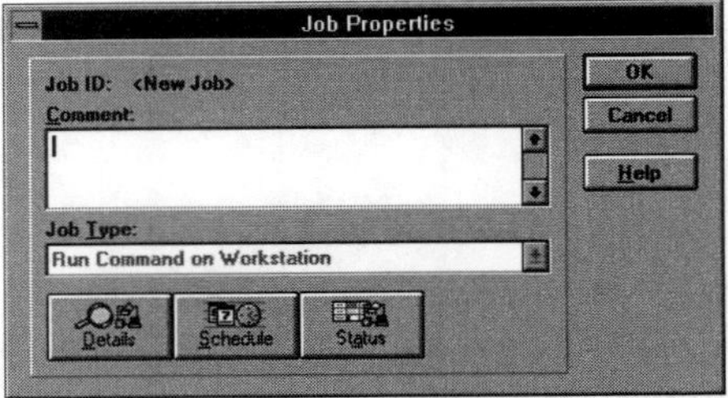

FIG. 11.4
Job Properties screen—where jobs get created.

Package This refers to the package to be distributed. Only one package is used by a Run Command on Workstation job. Only packages configured with Workstations properties defined are available in the drop-down list.

Job Target This is a list of the target computers that will run the application. The list of computers can be one of the following:

- The results of a query
- A predefined machine group

NOTE You can target machines that are the results of a query when the job target is Query Results. Here the Query Results are resolved right when the job executes, whereas other options determine which workstations should be included when the job is created. If your job is scheduled for several days from now, it could make a difference. Your query may tell you which workstations meet the standards for a Windows 95 upgrade. The Query Results feature guarantees a more up-to-date view for your job. However, you may choose Machine Group as a job target if your groups are static and well defined. ■

After selecting the target computers, the job target can be narrowed down to specific sites containing the target computers by using the Limit to Sites and Include Subsites options.

NOTE When a job is destined for a subsite, it sends the package and instructions directly to the subsite, not through the site hierarchy. Therefore, subsites need only the address of their immediate parent, not of every site above it. ■

Machine Path Identify the machine path of site, domain, and machine name, and separate with a pipe symbol, "|". The asterisk character is available as a wild card to represent "all" for any of these three fields. For example, to send a job to all the computers of a specific domain, the machine path would be SiteName|DomainName|*.

NOTE You can also type the name of a specific machine in a Microsoft Network, or a Network Card ID in a Novell Network. ■

Send Phase The Send Phase portion of the screen specifies whether SMS should overwrite existing packages.

The Only If Not Previously Sent option can help you avoid recompressing and resending a package if all you want to do is send to a new distribution server.

NOTE If you are running a job because you have updated a package, choose the Even if Previously Sent option, or else the old package will be used. ■

The other option, Even If Previously Sent, is important when you need to modify the package on the source directory. Creating a job with this option will recompress and redistribute the package so that all sites will be updated with the new modules. This avoids the need to create a new package and job to distribute when changes are needed only at the source directory on the server.

After a Run Command on Workstation job is created, the Scheduler detects the job in the Jobs table in the SMS database and begins to process it.

The Scheduler creates a list of sites containing the job's target computers, and determines whether to schedule the package to be sent to the site. If the package does not exist at the destination site, it is always sent. If the package exists, the Scheduler checks the Send Phase configuration to see whether it should overwrite the current package or not send it at all.

The Scheduler knows which packages exist at a site or subsite by looking at the PackageLocations table in the SMS database. The administrator can create a query choosing PackageLocations in the Architecture Field under AdHoc query, Queries window in SMS Administrator to see which packages are installed and where they are located in a site.

Distribute Phase The Distribute Phase options control the next step of the distribution process—the decompression of the package to the distribution servers. The Put On Specified Distribution Servers option is used to tell SMS which distribution servers to decompress the package to. The best approach is to create machine groups containing the distribution servers you are targeting, based on your purposes. That way you will have other groups to rely on besides the <Default Servers> machine group.

The Distribute Phase specifies which servers at a site will receive the package.

The Distribute Phase options are as follows:

- Refresh Existing Distribution Servers—if this option is checked, the package will be overwritten on any distribution servers where it already exists.
- Put On Specified Distribution Servers—this option specifies on which servers a new copy of this package will be placed. If the package already exists on the server, it will not be modified.

When a package is received at a site, it is placed on distribution servers by the Despooler. The Distribute Phase can be configured to overwrite the package at existing distribution servers or place it on a group called <Default Servers>.

If the Despooler cannot find the specified distribution servers to place a package, it will go to the <Default Servers> group. The <Default Servers> group, which initially contains only the site server, can be modified in the Site Properties dialog box by choosing the Servers button.

CAUTION

If any target computers are Novell NetWare clients, be sure to place a NetWare server in the <Default Servers> group. Likewise, if any of the target computers are Macintosh clients, be sure to include an NT Services for Macintosh server.

If the target computer cannot access the distribution server, the user still sees the command on the target computer, but running the command will always fail. This might be due to incorrect account permissions or server type. For example, a NetWare client cannot access a Windows NT server.

Run Phase The Run Phase section specifies how the Package Command Manager on the target computer processes the command.

- Run Workstation Command—each job specifies one command to run at the target computer. The list of available commands is from the commands defined in the package.
- Offer After This Time and Date—the command will be made available on the target computer.
- Mandatory After This Time and Date—the command will be forced to run on the target computer.
- Not Mandatory Over Slow Link—the command is not forced to run over a slow link if this box is selected.
- Expires After This Date and Time—the command will no longer be available on the target computer. The package is removed only from the Package Command Manager window, not from the site and distribution servers.

NOTE If a Run Command on Workstation job is created that specifies the Run Phase information but not the Distribute Phase information, SMS ensures that the package is available to the target computers. It will automatically send and distribute the package to the default server as part of the job.

It is helpful to understand how running just one job phase might be advantageous, as follows:

Send Phase Only–use to allow local administrators to run jobs manually.

Distribute Phase Only–use to add a new distribution server to a job or to a site.

Run Phase Only–use after Send and Distribute phases are completed. Also used for repeated jobs or multiple commands.

Implementing Jobs

After configuring a job, you actually schedule a job to run. You will also interact with the Schedule screen to see what a job's status is, like "pending" or "active." The Job Properties screen is where you would implement a job.

Job Properties Job Properties is the first screen you get when you go to run a job, and the last screen you see before you press OK and submit the job. Job Properties are specified in the Job Properties dialog box. To display this dialog box, open the Jobs window. Highlight and double-click the job you want to view.

The following are the options in the Job Properties box:

- Comment—a description of the job that shows in SMS Administrator, for example, "Copy System Files Ver. 2.0." It is a good idea to describe each change you make to a job in the comments, for example rather than having the job "Copy System Files 2.0," then 2.1, 2.2, and so on, include something in the comments like "Copy System Files 2.1, ver. includes win : in AUTOEXEC.BAT"—then you'll know exactly what version of a job you have in the queue.
- Job Type—specifies the types of jobs that can be initiated by an administrator.
- Details—specifies the exact instructions the job will carry out. The job details also specify any data (such as a software package) that will be used in the job (see fig. 11.5).

FIG. 11.5
Specifying Job Details.

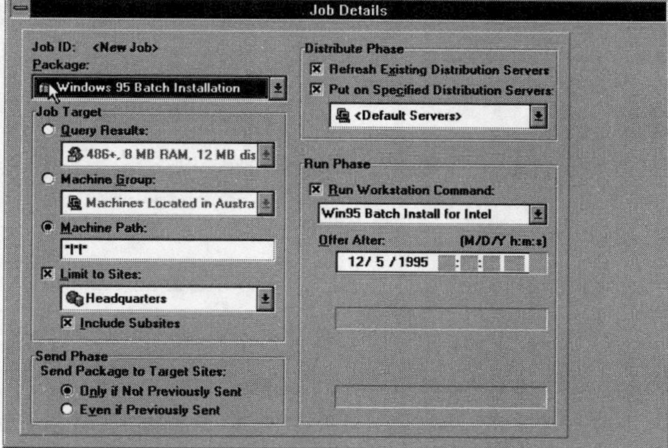

- Schedule—designates when the job will start, what priority it has compared to other jobs, and whether it will repeat.
- Status—you will use this to track job status once the job is created.

Job Schedule It is possible to control a job's schedule through the Job Schedule button in the Job Properties dialog box (see fig. 11.6). The options you may control include the following:

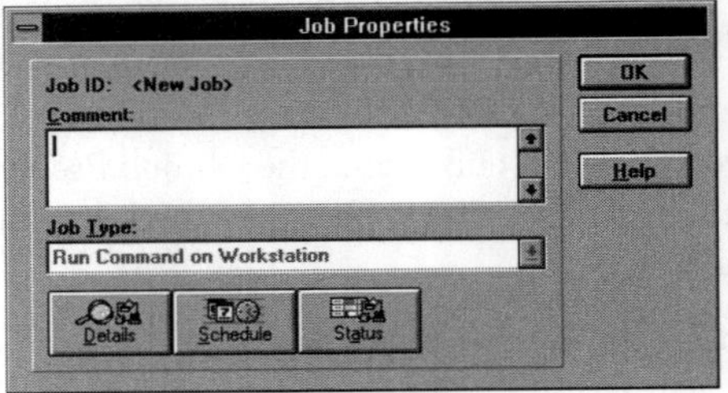

FIG. 11.6
Setting up the Job Schedule.

- Start After—Informs the Scheduler when to activate the job. The specified time is compared to the SQL Server time. The default is the current time, which means that the Scheduler begins processing the job as soon as it is created.
- Job Priorities— A job can be assigned one of three priorities: Low, Medium, or High. The Scheduler uses this priority to schedule the job ahead or behind other jobs.
- Repeating Jobs—A job can be configured to occur on a repeating basis. The repeat interval can be set to Never, Daily, Weekly, Biweekly, or Monthly. When the Scheduler starts a repeating job, it automatically creates an identical job and schedules it to start at the current time plus the repeat interval. For example, if it is a daily job, the Scheduler automatically creates an identical job to starts the next day, the Scheduler will create another job, and so on. The default is Never.

Completing the Job

Once the job is set up and scheduled, you have submitted the job. To see your job you can use File, Open to open the Job Window. There is also a Job icon near the top left part of the SMS Administrator screen (see fig. 11.7).

SMS now is submitting the job to the NT Scheduler, and is preparing to distribute the job to all your sites.

NOTE Do not delete an active job. Cancel an active job first, otherwise you may leave portions of the job on the server. You will later have to delete them manually to save space on the server. You may also get "ghost" records on the SQL Server database.

NOTE You cannot modify a job once it is active, so make doubly sure that your job settings are correct. Otherwise, you will have to cancel and delete the job.

FIG. 11.7
Submitting a Job.

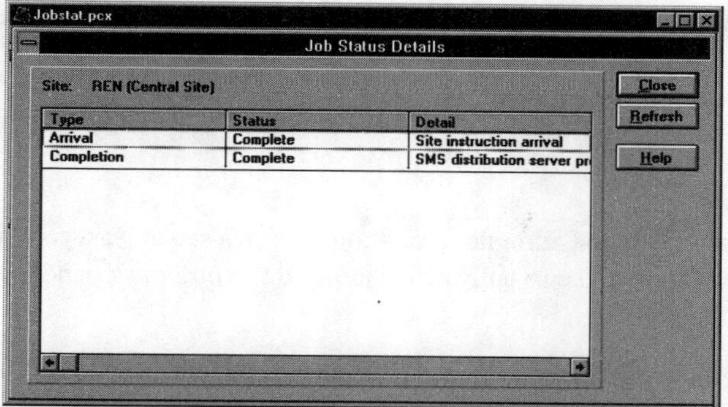

Jobs Behind the Scenes

After a Run Command on Workstation job is configured, there are three main SMS elements that do the work: the Scheduler, the Sender, and the Despooler. The actual distribution follows these steps:

- The Run Command on Workstation job is stored in the SMS database.
- The Scheduler monitors the SMS database for jobs that need to be activated. It compresses the package for sending and places it in a sender outbox.
- Senders pass the package to the target site servers.
- The Despooler at each target site decompresses and stores a master copy of the package.
- The decompressed package files are placed on the distribution servers you specified.
- The target computers use the instructions to run the command.

Monitoring Jobs

Once the job is created and submitted, the Job Status screen will help you to keep track of status.

The Workstation entry will be key to understanding what has occurred at the workstation. There will be a separate entry for every workstation that gets the software. The point to remember is that the workstations entry status will reflect the current state of the job at the workstation.

If the job has not been set to expire, the workstation will be able to rerun the job over and over. The Status field in the Job Status Details screen will be updated appropriately. When the workstation first runs the job and it is successful, the Status field will show success, but if the workstation re-executes the job and it fails, that status will then be reflected in the job status details.

NOTE Once you create a job and it appears as active in the Jobs window, don't delete the underlying package. Always cancel the job first to insure there will be no "phantom" jobs on user's screens that are no longer valid.

Repeating Jobs

With a repeating job, the administrator should always see at least two entries for the job in the Jobs window. One is the currently active job, and the other is a pending job scheduled to start at the next interval.

If a repeat job becomes active before the original job completes, the original job is canceled and the repeat job stays active. This prevents a flood of jobs from building up if they are not fully completing. For example, if a virus scan job is configured to repeat and the current job has not completed before it is time for the pending job to become active, the current job is canceled.

If a repeating job uses static files and data, you might want to create two jobs. The initial job can distribute the package. The repeating job runs the command.

Working with the Scheduler and the Sender

The Scheduler manages sending the job's data to the job's destination sites. The Scheduler selects a sender to move the data to the destination site, creates the data and instructions for that sender, and then monitors and handles any errors reported by the sender.

If there are multiple jobs that have to send data, the Scheduler will prioritize the jobs for servicing. The order is determined first by job priority (low, medium, high) and then by job start time.

Selecting a Sender for the Job

When scheduling a job's data to be sent, the Scheduler creates a list of the addresses assigned to the job's destination site. From the list of available addresses and their associated senders, the Scheduler then decides which sender to use. For instance, you could have a LAN Sender, a dial-up RAS Sender, and so on. The Scheduler always uses the sender that will move the data to the destination site in the shortest time.

Creating the Send Request

The Scheduler will detect a Pending job and start it by preparing a package file, an instruction file, and a send request file for each target site, as follows:

1. A compressed package file (.WOO) contains the files being transferred to the destination site. This could be all the files of a software package source directory or a single executable. The .WOO file is placed in the \SITE.SRV\SENDER.BOX\TOSEND directory.
2. A compressed instruction file (.IOO) instructs the destination Despooler service how to process the sent package. This file is also in the SITE.SRV\SENDER.BOX\TOSEND directory.

3. Send request files (.SRQ) have the instructions for the sender to connect to a destination site and to transfer the data onto the site. Each file is placed in the outbox for the sender. For example, SENDER.BOX\REQUESTS\LAN_DEFA.OOO is the outbox for the LAN sender. The file is renamed *.SRS as soon as it is processed by the sender.

Monitoring the Job's Sender

The Scheduler checks the current status of each send request to check that it has started and that the status is Running. If the status is something else (Finishing, Failing, Being Suspended, or Canceled), the Scheduler will try scheduling the send request for another available outbox. If a job has failed to be sent for over seven days, the job is canceled, the Send Request files are deleted, and the job status is set to Failed.

The Scheduler can preempt any lower-priority jobs that are in the process of being sent, in favor of higher-priority jobs. The sender can suspend sending at any point and later resume sending the lower-priority job where it left off. The only kind of job that cannot be preempted is a job that creates a secondary site.

When the send is successful and the job is completed, the Send Request is deleted along with any job files (.IOO,.WOO,.SRS).

When a site is first installed, a LAN sender is installed by default. This sender is used by every job that is addressed to the local site.

Understanding the Despooler

When Application Packages travel across a WAN, they are in compressed form. The Despooler is the SMS process responsible for decompressing the packages. In addition to receiving and decompressing packages, the Despooler does the following:

- copies packages to distribution servers,
- updates instruction files for the client PCM,
- and deletes temporary decompressed files.

The Despooler receives, decompresses, and distributes the package. The Despooler monitors its inbox (SITE.SRV\DESPOOLER.BOX\RECEIVE) for compressed instruction files (.I*).

The Despooler completes the following tasks:

1. Copies the compressed package file to the \DESPOOLER\STORE directory. In doing so, it follows the instructions regarding whether or not to overwrite an existing package.

NOTE It is important to remember to synchronize the time on all SQL Server computers and site servers in an SMS hierarchy. For example, if an instruction file has a time stamp ahead of the Despooler computer (Target Site), it will not be processed. SMS can work with computers in different time zones, but their times need to be synchronized with the central SQL server that holds the central SMS database. ■

2. Decompresses the package on the drive with the most available free space, and creates a temporary directory (S_xxxxx.TMP). This might reside on the site server or a helper server. A master copy of the package is kept on the site server.
3. Creates a list of servers to copy the decompressed package. The Despooler decides whether to overwrite copies of the package on the distribution servers, and keeps a list of package locations in the Windows NT Registry, in HKEY_LOCAL_MACHINE under \Software\Microsoft\SMS\Components\SMS_Despooler.
4. Creates the distribution server share for the package directory and copies the files to the distribution servers. The share name is SMS_PKGx, where x is the NTFS partition with the most free space. If no NTFS partition exists, the drive with the most free space is chosen. The directory name is SMS_PKGSx, with subdirectories named after the SMS Package IDs.
5. Deletes the temporary directory and all its files.
6. Adds a record to each target client's Package Command Manager instruction file (*smsid*.INS) in the SMS\SITE.SRV\MAINCFG.BOX\PCMDOM.BOX directory. The record includes the run command instructions, package information such as path and server type (Windows NT, LAN Manager, or NetWare servers), and zone information if the server is running Services for Macintosh. The Maintenance Manager moves the .INS files to the SMS\LOGON.SRV\PCMINS.BOX directory on the logon servers for the target client computers.

Hard Disk Space Considerations

A Run Command on Workstation job can use disk space equal to as much as five times the size of the package. This occurs because package files are copied to the five locations, all of which can reside on the site server. Table 11.1, below, describes each of those locations.

Table 11.1

Package File Locations

Original source directory files	The source directory stores the original software application files.
Sender box	The \SENDER.BOX\TOSEND directory on the site server receives the compressed package. This copy is not deleted by SMS.
Despooler master copy	The \DESPOOLR.BOX\STORE directory has the master copy for the site. The master copy is used to place files on the distribution server. It can be used later to put the package on new distribution servers without having to send the package to the site again. The packages stored in this directory are stored both in the

Package File Locations	
	SMS database and in the registry of the site server under HKEY-LOCAL-MACHINE in \Software\Microsoft\SMS\Components\SMS\Despooler\Master Packages (located on destination site server).
Temporary directory	The temporary directory is used to decompress a package before the files are copied to the distribution servers. The temporary directory is removed when the job is completed.
Final distribution copy	The shared directory on the distribution server stores the final distribution copy for the target computers to use. In many cases the site server is also a distribution server and will therefore receive these files.

There are several ways to reduce the use of disk space on the site server, as follows:

- Delete original files on any server other than the site server.
- Delete the package in the \SENDER.BOX\TOSEND directory, after the package has been sent successfully to the distribution servers.
- Use a Remove Packages job to remove the master copy for the site in \DESPOOLR.BOX\STORE. This also removes the distributed copy.
- Exclude the site server from being a distribution server.

Compression Levels

SMS supports seven levels of compression. Level 1 provides the least amount of compression and therefore the fastest compression/decompression time. Level 7 provides the highest amount of compression and the slowest compression/decompression time. The default compression level is 1.

To set the compression level, change the value of Compression Level in the Windows NT Registry under the HKEY-LOCAL-MACHINE\SOFTWARE\Microsoft\SMS\Compression Key.

To disable compression completely, set the Enable Compression value to NO.

NOTE The Compression key is not created until a package is sent from the site server. You can create the key and its values or send a test package to have it automatically created.

Package Command Manager

Commands are run on the target computer by the Package Command Manager (PCM) application. It uses a workstation command package, which is a combination of the application's files and the actual command to run the application.

Once the package has been delivered to the distribution servers that were specified in the job, a control file is delivered to the target clients and is processed by the Package Command Manager (PCM) on the client. PCM is the Systems Management Server client component that is responsible for receiving the package on the client, controlling the installation, and reporting the status of the installation back to the Systems Management Server.

When PCM receives a control file for the installation of the package, it reads the file to determine the attributes of the job. If the job requires that a package directory be available for the job to execute, then PCM connects to the appropriate share point on the specified distribution server and starts to process the job.

Processing of the job begins with PCM changing the active directory to the package share point and executing the command line specified in the job. When this command is finished, PCM reports status back to Systems Management Server and dismounts the package share.

At the Client Workstation

When a package arrives at a workstation, the Package Command Manager pop-up box will appear at the workstation. It has a simple interface with just three buttons on the button bar: Execute, Archive, and Details. There are three yellow file folders that appear on the left—Pending Commands, Archived Commands, and Executed Commands, as follows:

- Execute—clicking the Execute button will execute a job manually from the Package Command Manager. You just locate a job in the pending commands list, then PCM will automatically move the job to the Executed Commands file.
- Archive—you can archive a pending job, and it will be put in a queue and will not run until the job becomes mandatory.
- Details—the Details button brings up a pop-up box showing the job, the expiration date, the job ID, the site sent from, and Package Comments.

Eventually, jobs will become mandatory and run on their own on the client workstation. A pop-up box will appear on the client, counting down: "in 5 more minutes the package will start executing."

Creating Installation Programs

The command line that is specified in the installation job is the setup or installation program for the application contained in the package. This command line can be anything that is appropriate to the actions required to install the software and the platform where the installation is to take place. The installation program should take any actions that are required to install the application and should also take account of the fact that it is running in the Systems Management Server environment by supporting the requirements of the installation process in Systems Management Server.

Systems Management Server Requirements for Software Products

Some software out there will behave more favorably in an SMS job than others. A software setup or installation program that is used in the Systems Management Server environment should support that environment in the following ways:

- Operates in Unattended Mode—programs have a setup option that does not require input from the user during the installation, deinstallation, or maintenance of the application. Any information or options that are required by the setup program should be supplied by command line switches to the program, or should be provided in a configuration file that is read by the program at run time.
- Does Not Force a Reboot of the Machine—since multiple packages could be installed by Systems Management Server, and the installation may be forced on the user for mandatory packages, no individual package installation should force a reboot of the machine as part of its installation program. Instead, PCM has the capability to intercept these restart requests, queuing them up until all packages have been installed, and offering the user the chance to clean up any work in progress before the restart.
- Passes Restart Instructions to PCM—to copy system files that may be in use, setup programs restart the Microsoft Windows operating system and run a program for the MS-DOS operating system using ExitWindowsExec. In order to set up multiple programs before a restart, PCM prevents a reboot, and then itself performs an ExitWindowsExec when a user elects to do so. Setup programs generally construct a batch file that contains the operations that must be performed during a restart. To coordinate multiple unattended setups, the following procedure must be followed. Concatenate the setup's batch file to the file _MSSETUP.BAT, or, if _MSSETUP.BAT doesn't yet exist, rename the setup's batch file. If it doesn't already exist, create an _MSRSTRT.EXE program to be executed by PCM when it calls ExitWindowsExec. This MS-DOS-based program must execute the batch file _MSSETUP.BAT and then delete the batch file and itself. If PCM detects both of the files _MSSETUP.BAT and _MSRSTRT.EXE in the Windows directory, then it decides that a restart must be performed and it displays a restart dialog box. This dialog box does not interfere with subsequent installations.

Report Status Back to Systems Management Server Using a Status MIF

To report either success or failure of a PCM application installation, a .MIF file must be created in the Windows directory. The .MIF file should be named *appname*.MIF where *appname* is the name of the application. In fact PCM will pick up any file in the Windows directory that has an extension of .MIF and that was created after PCM began the installation, and will send this back to Systems Management Server.

Package Directory

The package directory is simply a directory structure that contains all of the files required to support the installation or deinstallation options that are in the Package Definition File. When a job is created that uses a package, the contents of the package directory, including any subdirectory structure, are compressed and sent to all of the site servers of the target clients of the job. Once the compressed package is received at the site server, it is copied to the distribution servers specified in the job, and decompressed. The package contents are then sent from the distribution server with the appropriate permissions.

All of the files required to support the operation of the job should be included in the package directory. This includes any dynamic-link libraries (.DLLs) or configuration files that might be required to support the operation of the setup program.

SMS Installation Scripts

When distributing software to a large client base, an administrator might want to install software without the usual user intervention. SMS provides scripts to install various Microsoft Products in unattended mode. Here are some of the following products for which a script is provided in SMS:

- Microsoft Access
- Microsoft Excel
- Microsoft Foxpro
- Microsoft Office
- Microsoft Powerpoint
- Microsoft Project
- Microsoft Access

You can find a complete list of scripts in the \SMS\PRIMSITE.SRV\IMPORT.SRC directory of the SMS_SHR_d share on your primary site servers.

Microsoft Test

Microsoft Test is an application to tests scripts. Although it does not come with SMS, some companies may have it as a stand-alone installation.

SMS provides scripts to distribute most Microsoft products. Scripting can take on several forms, as follows:

```
Batch files
Custom setup programs
Microsoft Test scripts
Other 3rd party scripting products
```

Creating a Status MIF File

A status .MIF is a custom file that you create for testing installations. Variables from an .INI file are read at the time the script executes. The success or failure status information is determined through the script execution.

The status .MIF file following is a .MIF file used in a Microsoft Test script:

Listing 11.1 A Sample MIF Status File

```
SUB CreateMIFile(sMIFMessage as String)
'*************************************************************'
A Sample Status MIF File
Will report job status
'************************************************************
DIM iReturn as Integer
DIM hMIFile as Integer
'
' Open the MIF file.
'
 hMIFile = FREEFILE
 OPEN GetWindowsDir+"SMSMIF.TXT" FOR OUTPUT AS #hMIFile
'
' Create the contents of the MIF file.
'
 PRINT #hMIFile, "START COMPONENT"
 PRINT #hMIFile, , "NAME = " ; CHR$(34) ; "WORKSTATION" ; CHR$(34)
 PRINT #hMIFile, , "START GROUP"
 PRINT #hMIFile, , , "NAME = " ; CHR$(34) ; "ComponentID" ; CHR$(34)
 PRINT #hMIFile, , , "ID = 1"
 PRINT #hMIFile, , , "CLASS= " ; CHR$(34) ; "DMTF¦ComponentID¦1.0" ; CHR$(34)
 PRINT #hMIFile, , , "START ATTRIBUTE"
 PRINT #hMIFile, , , , "NAME = " ; CHR$(34) ; "Manufacturer" ; CHR$(34)
 PRINT #hMIFile, , , , "ID = 1"
 PRINT #hMIFile, , , , "ACCESS = READ-ONLY"
 PRINT #hMIFile, , , , "STORAGE= SPECIFIC"
 PRINT #hMIFile, , , , "TYPE = STRING(64)"
 PRINT #hMIFile, , , , "VALUE = " ; CHR$(34) ; sManufacturer ; CHR$(34)
 PRINT #hMIFile, , , "END ATTRIBUTE"
 PRINT #hMIFile, , , "START ATTRIBUTE"
 PRINT #hMIFile, , , , "NAME = " ; CHR$(34) ; "Product" ; CHR$(34)
 PRINT #hMIFile, , , , "ID = 2"
 PRINT #hMIFile, , , , "ACCESS = READ-ONLY"
 PRINT #hMIFile, , , , "STORAGE= SPECIFIC"
 PRINT #hMIFile, , , , "TYPE = STRING(64)"
 PRINT #hMIFile, , , , "VALUE = " ; CHR$(34) ; sProductName ; CHR$(34)
 PRINT #hMIFile, , , "END ATTRIBUTE"
 PRINT #hMIFile, , , "START ATTRIBUTE"
 PRINT #hMIFile, , , , "NAME = " ; CHR$(34) ; "Version" ; CHR$(34)
 PRINT #hMIFile, , , , "ID = 3"
 PRINT #hMIFile, , , , "ACCESS = READ-ONLY"
 PRINT #hMIFile, , , , "STORAGE= SPECIFIC"
```

continues

Part III Ch 11

Listing 11.1 Continued

```
PRINT #hMIFile, , , , "TYPE = STRING(64)"
PRINT #hMIFile, , , , "VALUE = " ; CHR$(34) ; sVersion ; CHR$(34)
PRINT #hMIFile, , , "END ATTRIBUTE"
PRINT #hMIFile, , , "START ATTRIBUTE"
PRINT #hMIFile, , , , "NAME = " ; CHR$(34) ; "Serial Number" ; CHR$(34)
PRINT #hMIFile, , , , "ID = 4"
PRINT #hMIFile, , , , "ACCESS = READ-ONLY"
PRINT #hMIFile, , , , "STORAGE= SPECIFIC"
PRINT #hMIFile, , , , "TYPE = STRING(64)"
PRINT #hMIFile, , , , "VALUE = " ; CHR$(34) ; sUserName ; " at " ; sCompanyName
; CHR$(34)
PRINT #hMIFile, , , "END ATTRIBUTE"
PRINT #hMIFile, , , "START ATTRIBUTE"
PRINT #hMIFile, , , , "NAME = " ; CHR$(34) ; "Installation" ; CHR$(34)
PRINT #hMIFile, , , , "ID = 5" PRINT #hMIFile, , , , "ACCESS = READ-ONLY"
PRINT #hMIFile, , , , "STORAGE = SPECIFIC"
PRINT #hMIFile, , , , "TYPE = STRING(64)"
PRINT #hMIFile, , , , "VALUE = " ; CHR$(34) ; DATETIME$ ; CHR$(34)
PRINT #hMIFile, , , "END ATTRIBUTE"
PRINT #hMIFile, , "END GROUP"
PRINT #hMIFile, , "START GROUP"
PRINT #hMIFile, , , "NAME = " ; CHR$(34) ; "InstallStatus" ; CHR$(34)
PRINT #hMIFile, , , "ID = 2"
PRINT #hMIFile, , , "CLASS = " ; CHR$(34) ; "MICROSOFT¦JOBSTATUS¦1.0" ;
CHR$(34)
PRINT #hMIFile, , , "START ATTRIBUTE"
PRINT #hMIFile, , , , "NAME = " ; CHR$(34) ; "Status" ; CHR$(34)
PRINT #hMIFile, , , , "ID = 1"
PRINT #hMIFile, , , , "ACCESS = READ-ONLY"
PRINT #hMIFile, , , , "STORAGE = SPECIFIC"
PRINT #hMIFile, , , , "TYPE = STRING(32)"
If ( sMIFMessage = "Success" ) Then
PRINT #hMIFile, , , , "VALUE = " ; CHR$(34) ; "Success" ; CHR$(34)
Else
PRINT #hMIFile, , , , "VALUE = " ; CHR$(34) ; "Failed" ; CHR$(34)
End if
PRINT #hMIFile, , , "END ATTRIBUTE"
PRINT #hMIFile, , , "START ATTRIBUTE"
PRINT #hMIFile, , , , "NAME = " ; CHR$(34) ; "Description" ; CHR$(34)
PRINT #hMIFile, , , , "ID = 2"
PRINT #hMIFile, , , , "ACCESS = READ-ONLY"
PRINT #hMIFile, , , , "STORAGE = SPECIFIC"
PRINT #hMIFile, , , , "TYPE = STRING(120)"
PRINT #hMIFile, , , , "VALUE = " ; CHR$(34) ; sMIFMessage ; CHR$(34)
PRINT #hMIFile, , , "END ATTRIBUTE"
PRINT #hMIFile, , "END GROUP"
PRINT #hMIFile, "END COMPONENT"
CLOSE hMIFile
Copy GetWindowsDir+"SMSMIF.TXT" TO GetWindowsDir+sMIFile
ENDSUB
```

Software Distribution Strategies

Standard software is usually installed initially with the packages included with SMS, with slight variations depending on unique business needs. The following are cases where SMS is needed to distribute standard software:

- A new machine is installed without software.
- The machine has a technical problem that requires reinstallation.
- The standard software is upgraded by the manufacturer.

Standard software should be distributed to each SMS Site server. This provides backup, and can be particularly useful in disaster recovery. Whenever a user requires a standard software download, the SMS administrator can schedule an immediate SMS job to run the installation from the user's local SMS site server, which already has the standard software in uncompressed form. If the user's site server is down, the SMS administrator can redirect the installation to be run from the nearest working site server.

The following are some recommendations for staging standard software or distributing a new version to many users:

- Distribute the SMS package to site servers in phases to minimize (or at least stagger) network bandwidth utilization across the WAN.
- Decentralized software distribution, distributing packages from remote sites rather than centrally. This approach uses more disk space on site-level servers, but can save bandwidth by not transmitting standard software across the WAN to satisfy user requests. From the time the SMS administrator creates a new SMS package to the time it arrives and is decompressed on the distribution server, users can install standard software within 15 minutes of requesting it.
- Schedule software installation in staggered phases. Since the standard software packages exist on each site server, you can schedule just a portion of the client installations each day, to minimize use of network bandwidth and site server CPU time during working hours. You can apportion how much software to distribute, depending on whether you have to share a crowded WAN link during the day or not.
- Schedule package distribution for weekend nights to avoid interfering with normal workday network traffic and/or weekday evening backup and maintenance routines.
- Query the SMS database. For example, query on the machines running Word 6, then target that group for Word 7 installation.
- Use a Share Package on Server job to target groups of users based on their group function (telephony users, accounting, sales, and so on).

Troubleshooting at the Server

Assuming that the administrator has successfully created a package and job in SMS Administrator, the following steps should track down problems with getting the command to appear and run on the target computer(s). When the problem is isolated, the specific processes involved can be examined further.

NOTE Always look first at the error log for the job. This is done by querying the SMSEvent "architecture" and specifying the correct job ID . Several specific job errors are logged as events, which can quickly reveal the reason for failure. For example, when the distribution servers do not have enough disk space to hold the job's package, an event is logged. ■

Symptom	Check for:
The Despooler has not processed the package.	Check that the destination site's master copy of the package exists in its site server's DESPOOLR.BOX\STORE directory. If it is not there, check the job request's sending status and troubleshoot the sending process.
The Run Command on Workstation job is not configured for the correct target computer(s).	When the job is activated by the Scheduler, the Scheduler creates job requests for each site containing target computers. It also creates a job details record for each target computer at that site. Both the request and the target computers can be viewed in the Job Status and Job Status Details dialog boxes. If the target computer(s) and target distribution server(s) are not listed here, the job should be recreated. The current job should be either canceled or deleted. This prevents the same command from showing up multiple times on the target computer if the job completes later.
The Scheduler is not functioning correctly or creating the send request.	Check that a send request has been scheduled by looking in the appropriate outbox under SENDER.BOX\REQUESTS. A send request should be in the outbox associated with the destination site address, unless the job has finished or has been canceled or deleted.
The package didn't arrive at the destination site.	Check that the package exists in the SITE.SRV\DESPOOLR.BOX\RECEIVE directory on the destination site server.
The job's data (package and instructions) is not being correctly placed on distribution servers at target sites.	Check the target distribution servers. The job was sent to a specific group of servers such as <Default Servers> or to existing distribution servers. Check that the list of distribution servers that received the package is correct by viewing the Job Status Details window. It displays which servers SMS is trying to place the package on at a specific site

Symptom	Check for:
	(these are the entries of type Servers). If the list of distribution servers is not correct, the job will have to be recreated with the correct job target and distribution phase information. Check that the package exists at each distribution server and is not corrupt. Check that the package was decompressed correctly at the distribution server. The files in \\distribution_server\SMS-PKGd\Package_ID should be exactly the same as the source directory for the package. If they are not, the package might have an incorrect source directory, the compressed package at the destination site could be corrupt (this is unlikely because a CRC check is done on the file), or the files on the distribution server might have become corrupted during copying of the decom pressed package from the site server. Creating a job that simply distributes the package to that site and distribution servers should correct this problem. Check that the PCM instruction files exist at each logon server in the SMS\LOGON.SRV\PCMINS.BOX directory.

From Here...

In conclusion, with the Software Distribution feature of SMS you can install and remove client software with SMS, copy system or data files to clients, or run utilities locally at their workstation, such as virus scan software or network card "auto-config" utilities.

This is done by sending packages and sending jobs. The administrator distributes applications or single files as packages. These packages get routed to distribution servers in a Systems Management Server site. After a package has been distributed, the administrator can send a job to install an application from a package, provided the client has access.

For further information, check out Chapter 21, "Sharing Applications."

CHAPTER 12

Queries and Reports

The Query function allows you to search for objects in the Systems Management Server (SMS) inventory database by creating a set of instructions, or criteria, that can be run, saved, and used anytime later. These queries can be used to find both hardware and software objects stored in the SMS database. You can also use the query function to find targets for Run Command On Workstation jobs and to trigger alerts when a specific condition occurs. Besides allowing you to custom-create queries, SMS comes with a set of predefined queries that you can use immediately to do searches. They can easily be modified to your needs and saved for future use. The results of the queries can be formatted for output and printed with relative ease.

The ability to create inventory reports quickly makes SMS a valuable tool when tracking the assets of a company's network system. This feature is enhanced by using Crystal Reports to create tailored reports from the information contained in the SMS database. These reports can be used to provide management with a detailed look at the resources of the network. In this chapter, we'll look at the query features built into SMS and how to use them. Then we'll take a look at the added functionality that Crystal Reports gives us. ■

The fundamentals of the SMS Query function

You'll see what the basic components of a query consist of, and how to work with Expressions and Logical operators.

How to create a Query

This will include Ad Hoc queries that can be executed without leaving a query object saved in the database.

Running a Query and viewing the information it returns

You'll see how to customize the result format of our query so that it gives us only the information you are interested in.

Modifying and deleting existing Queries in the database

You'll see how to take an existing query and modify it to your needs. In addition, several sample queries are included in SMS that can be modified or used as templates for your own queries. You'll also show you how to delete any unneeded queries from the database.

Querying the SMS Database

You can search the site database by creating a query object. This is a database object that stores the criteria used to identify the targets for a search. These targets of the database search are objects stored under different classifications, called architectures. Examples of an architecture would be Personal Computer or JobDetails. Each architecture in the site database consists of objects that are further subdivided into groups. Each of the groups contains specific attributes, and each attribute for the group has its individual values. It is these values that are used when matching the search criteria specified in the query. The search criteria specified in the query will be compared to the attribute values for the architecture we are querying. When a match is made it is displayed in the Query Results window.

As we mentioned, we base our searches on a specific architecture. An architecture is a structure, or format, used when recording the inventory for a specific type of object. Currently SMS supports queries for the following architectures:

- UserGroups—the UserGroups architecture allows you to specify the objects of a search based on a single group consisting of the Domain, UserGroup, and SiteCode attributes.
- PackageLocation—allows you to specify the object of a search based on attributes related to the delivery of an SMS package. Examples of the attributes that can be used in the search criteria are Package ID, SiteCode, ServerName, ShareName, PackageType, and MasterCopy.
- JobDetails—this architecture allows you to specify the object of a search based on attributes related to execution of an SMS job. Attributes in this architecture are JobID, RequestID, Type, Status, Time, and DetailData.
- SMSEvent—enables you to specify search criteria based on events logged to the site database. For example, you can search for all events logged to the database that are related to a specific machine by searching against the MachineName attribute. This architecture has numerous attributes that can be used to search against, including Identification, MachineName, Component, and JobID.
- SNMP Traps—allows you to specify the attributes of an SNMP Trap as the subject of a search. Search attributes include IP Address, Nt Event Source, Time Ticks, and Specific Trap ID, to name a few.
- Personal Computer—this is the only architecture that contains multiple groups of attributes. All of the other architectures mentioned to this point contain only one Group (the Identification Group), in which all the attributes of that architecture reside. In contrast, the Personal Computer architecture has numerous groups, including Disk, Environment, Game Port IRQ Table, Identification, Mouse, Netcard, Network, Operating System, PC Bios, PC Memory, Parallel Port, Processor, Serial Port, Services, User Information, Video, and Workstation status. Each of these groups contains attributes specific to it. For example the attributes for the group named Processor include Processor Name, Processor Type, and Quantity, while the attributes for the group named Netcard include Manufacturer, IRQ, and Port Address. Search criteria used in your query can be based on any of the attributes found in these groups.

In addition, you can query any custom architectures that you've created.

Before we go any further let's take a look at the Queries window in the SMS Administration program by following these steps:

1. Start the SMS Administrator program.
2. From the menu bar choose File, Open to display the Open SMS Window dialog box. Highlight Queries in the Window Type list and click OK.

   or

   Click the Queries button on the icon bar.

The Queries window shown in figure 12.1 will appear showing the predefined queries that come with SMS. This window will also show our custom queries after they have been defined. The window shows the following information for each query object in the list:

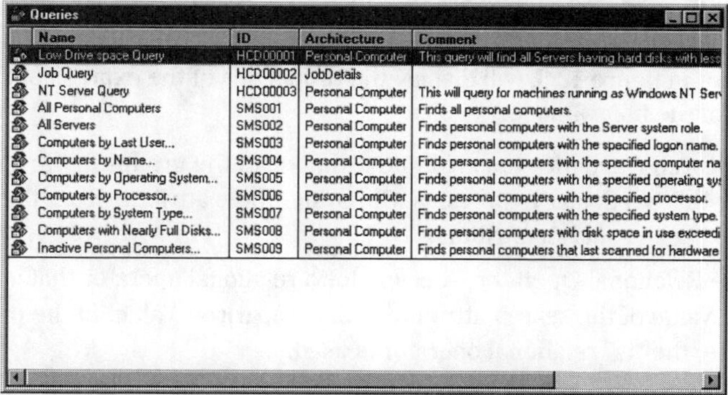

Queries
Name | ID | Architecture | Comment
Low Drive space Query | HCD00001 | Personal Computer | This query will find all Servers having hard disks with less
Job Query | HCD00002 | JobDetails
NT Server Query | HCD00003 | Personal Computer | This will query for machines running as Windows NT Ser
All Personal Computers | SMS001 | Personal Computer | Finds all personal computers.
All Servers | SMS002 | Personal Computer | Finds personal computers with the Server system role.
Computers by Last User... | SMS003 | Personal Computer | Finds personal computers with the specified logon name.
Computers by Name... | SMS004 | Personal Computer | Finds personal computers with the specified computer na
Computers by Operating System... | SMS005 | Personal Computer | Finds personal computers with the specified operating sy
Computers by Processor... | SMS006 | Personal Computer | Finds personal computers with the specified processor.
Computers by System Type... | SMS007 | Personal Computer | Finds personal computers with the specified system type.
Computers with Nearly Full Disks... | SMS008 | Personal Computer | Finds personal computers with disk space in use exceedi
Inactive Personal Computers... | SMS009 | Personal Computer | Finds personal computers that last scanned for hardware

FIG. 12.1
The Queries window lists all currently defined query objects in the database.

- Name—the unique name used to identify the query.
- ID—SMS assigns a unique ID to each query that you define.
- Architecture—identifies the architecture the query will run against.
- Comment—a field provided to the administrator that allows comments to be entered regarding the function of the query.

Let's begin by examining the properties for one of the queries that come predefined with SMS. Double-click the All Servers entry in the Queries window to display the Query Properties dialog box, as shown in figure 12.2.

The Find All '*Architecture*' Items Where box actually lists the search criteria used for this particular query. This search criteria can contain two components: the Expression, and the Logical Operator. Our predefined query contains only one component, the expression. A little later you'll see how logical operators can be used to combine one or more expressions into a complex query. But we'll begin by looking at the parts that make up an expression.

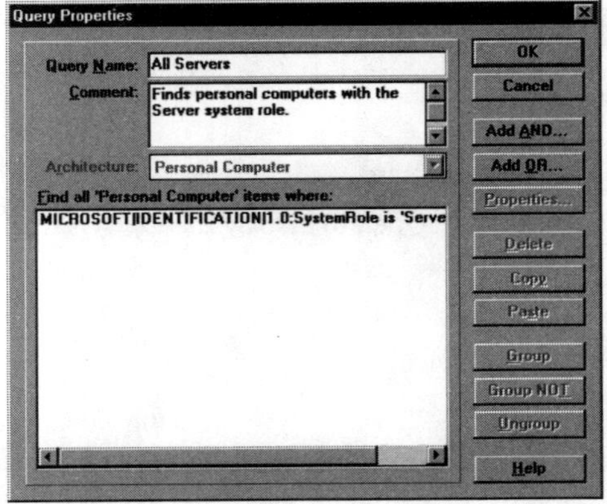

FIG. 12.2
The Queries Property dialog box for the predefined query named All Servers.

To look at the properties for the expression in the predefined query, either double-click it, or highlight the expression and click the OK button. The Query Expression Properties dialog box, shown in figure 12.3, will display the properties of the expression. Each expression is made up of the following:

- A Search Attribute—an attribute from one of the groups in the specified architecture. For this particular expression, the SystemRole attribute from the Identification Group is used as the search attribute.
- The Relational Operator—designates a relational operator that is used when comparing the value of the search attribute with comparison Value. In the predefined expression here, the "is" relational operator is used.
- A Comparison Value—the value we want to compare with the actual value of the search attribute using the relational operator. For the "this" expression, the Value has been set to Server.

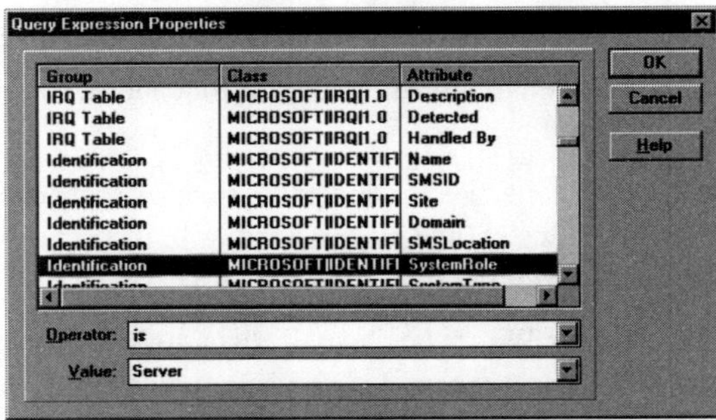

FIG. 12.3
The specific properties for each expression are shown in the Query Expression Properties dialog box.

The expression in the predefined query is as follows:

MICROSOFT|IDENTIFICATION|1.0:SystemRole is 'Server'

This specific query will search for all Personal Computers (architecture type) with a System Role (search attribute) that "is" (relational operator) the same as Server (comparison value). The logical operator was not used in this predefined query to combine and group multiple expressions, since this query has only one expression.

Using logical operators to define relationships between multiple expressions is an easy way to refine searches. The logical operators AND and OR are used to define a relationship between two adjacent expressions. Logical operators are also used to group several expressions together into what is called a subclause. Each subclause may in turn be used with logical operators to define relationships with other expressions and other subclauses. All this results in the ability to create very specific searches in a short amount of time. Let's take a closer look at each of the logical operators and how each one can be used when combining or creating relationships between multiple expressions.

Three logical operators exist: AND, OR, and NOT, as follows:

- AND—when two adjacent expressions (or subclauses) are joined with the AND logical operator, the query is directed to search for those objects that satisfy both the expressions.
- OR—when two adjacent expressions (or subclauses) are joined with the OR logical operator, the query is directed to search for objects that satisfy one or both of the expressions.
- NOT—the NOT logical operator is used to find all objects that do not satisfy the expression that is listed after it.

Here are some examples showing the usage of the logical operators in some simple searches. We'll start by looking at an example of the AND logical operator, as follows:

```
MICROSOFT¦OPERATING_SYS¦1.0:Operating System Name is 'Microsoft Windows NT'
AND
MICROSOFT¦IDENTIFICATION¦1.0:SystemRole is 'Server'
AND
MICROSOFT¦X86_PC_MEMORY¦1.0:Total Physical Memory (Kbyte) is greater than '24000'
```

The search criteria shown here look for all objects in the database that meet all the expressions—in this case, all Windows NT Servers with more than 24MB of physical memory. If we substituted the OR logical operator in place of the AND logical operator, our search criteria would look like the following:

```
MICROSOFT¦OPERATING_SYS¦1.0:Operating System Name is 'Microsoft Windows NT'
OR
MICROSOFT¦IDENTIFICATION¦1.0:SystemRole is 'Server'
OR
MICROSOFT¦X86_PC_MEMORY¦1.0:Total Physical Memory (Kbyte) is greater than '24000'
```

This specifies that any of the expressions listed above can be used alone or in combination to satisfy the search. In other words, this query's results would list any machine running Windows NT, any machine that has a system role of Server, and any machine that has more than

24MB of physical memory. Whereas the previous query required that the object of the search meet the criteria of all three expressions, this query only requires that the conditions for one of the expressions be met.

The third logical operator that we can use to narrow searches is the NOT operator. This can be used to find all the objects that do not satisfy a particular search expression. This operator is placed before the search expression, as follows:

```
MICROSOFT¦OPERATING_SYS¦1.0:Operating System Name is 'Microsoft Windows NT'
AND
MICROSOFT¦IDENTIFICATION¦1.0:SystemRole is 'Server'
NOT
MICROSOFT¦X86_PC_MEMORY¦1.0:Total Physical Memory (Kbyte) is greater than '24000'
```

The objects that satisfy the criteria for this query will be Windows NT Servers that do NOT have more than 24MB of physical memory installed. As with our first example (the AND operator), the criteria for each expression must be met before any results from the query are returned.

Expressions are combined with logical operators to form complex search patterns, so a set of rules has been put in place to set the precedence of each logical operator. The search criteria listed are evaluated starting from the top down. During this evaluation, the AND operator will take precedence over the OR operator. This is to say that two expressions joined by the AND logical operator are evaluated together. In this same way, the parentheses take precedence over both the AND and the OR logical operator.

We'll show more examples of expressions and logical operators, along with how to use a sub-clause, in the next section of the chapter.

How to Create a Query

SMS queries can be created, stored in the site database, and used anytime after that to search the site database. This comes in very handy when you need to use the same search criteria over and over again. Another method of creating and executing queries is done using an Ad Hoc query. This is a one-time query that isn't stored in the site database. It executes automatically after it's created and will supply the results of the query right away. The Ad Hoc query has the advantage of conserving database space, but the criteria for that particular search are lost and must be reconstructed in order to do the search again. Since it's not important to save queries to the database when experimenting with the query functions, you can create queries using the Ad Hoc function until you get to the point where you'd like to start actually saving queries to the database.

For our first example, we'll create a simple Ad Hoc query that looks for all the machines with disk drives that have more than 80 percent of their disk space used. Take the following steps:

1. Start the SMS Administrator program.
2. From the menu bar choose File, Execute Query to display the Execute Query dialog box, as shown in figure 12.4. This dialog box can be used to run any query defined in the

database, not just Ad Hoc queries. It also allows you to choose the target site for the query and the result format the query well be returned in.

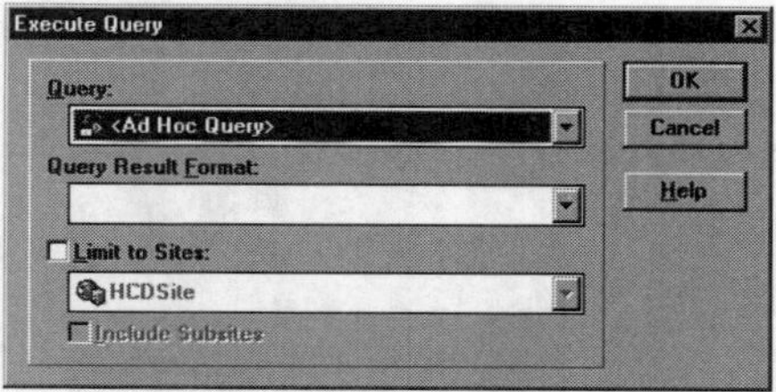

FIG. 12.4 Perform an Ad Hoc query or quickly run an existing query.

3. Leave the Query box with the default entry of <Ad Hoc Query>. Leave the Query Result Format box blank and the Limit to Sites box unmarked. Later we can define alternate result formats that we'll be able to choose from. Until then the box will remain empty. Click the OK button to display the Query Properties dialog box, as shown in figure 12.5.

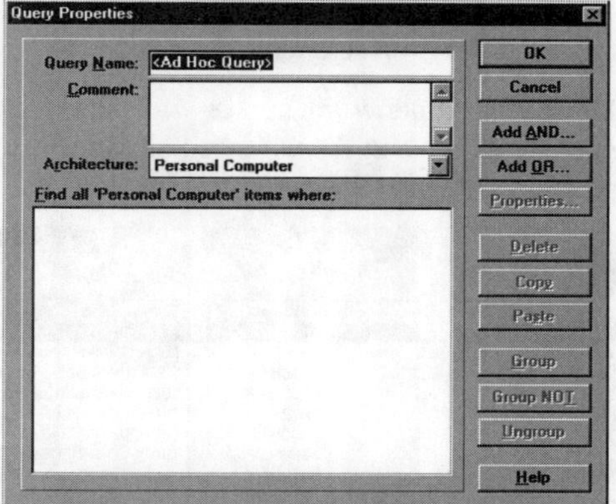

FIG. 12.5 Specify the search criteria in the Query Properties dialog box.

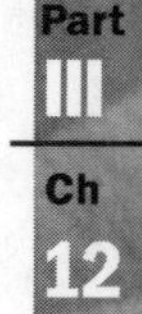

4. Leave the Comment box blank and make sure that Personal Computer is shown in the Architecture box. Click the Add AND… button to open the Query Expression Properties dialog box.
5. This dialog box lists each group and its associated attributes that belong to the Personal Computer architecture. Scroll down the list until you find the group Disk. Find the line in the Disk group that contains the attribute named % Disk Full (see fig. 12.6) and highlight it.
6. In the Operator box, use the drop-down list to find the relational operator "is greater than."
7. In the Value box, type 80. When you've done that, the dialog box should look like figure 12.6. Click OK to return to the Query Properties dialog box. You'll notice that the following expression:

MICROSOFT|DISK1.0:% Disk Full is greater than '80'

has been added to the Find All *'Architecture'* Items Where box. From here, we could add other expressions, using the Add AND or Add OR buttons. Doing this would add both a logical operator and the next expression to the search criteria. But for this example we'll just use the single expression we've already created for our Ad Hoc search the database.

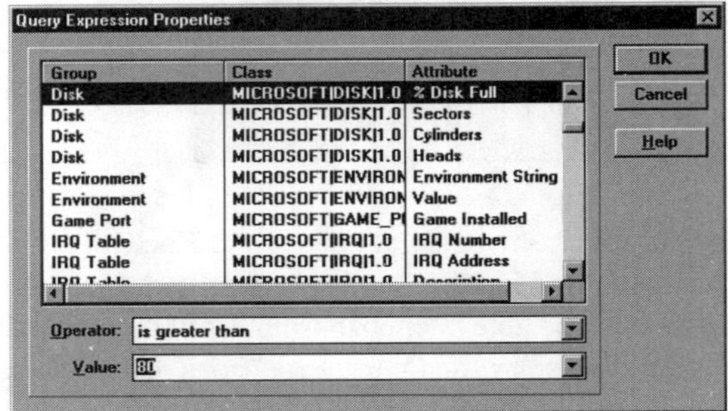

FIG. 12.6
A simple Ad Hoc search query.

8. Click the OK button to start the Ad Hoc query.

The Query Results <Ad Hoc Query> window will appear while the query is being performed. Any matches are displayed using the default result format, as shown in figure 12.7.

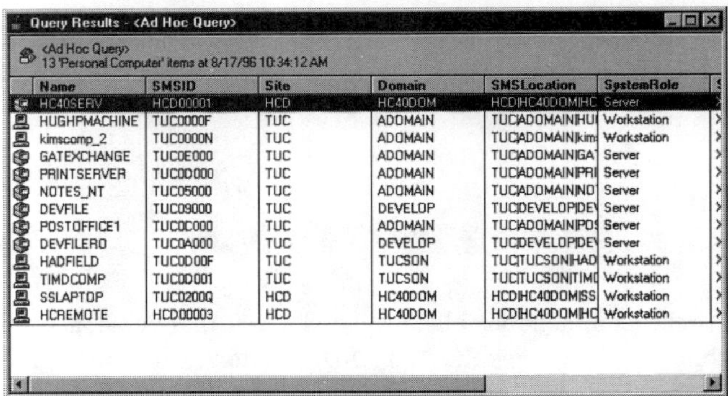

FIG. 12.7
The results of an Ad Hoc query are shown immediately.

You can look at the detailed drive space information or other attribute information for any machine listed in the results box by double-clicking on it. In addition, we can print out the result list by choosing Print from the File menu or by pressing Ctrl+P.

The next step in working with queries is to start creating more complex searches by using the logical operator and subclause options available to us in the Queries Properties dialog box. Figure 12.5 shows us the Query Properties dialog box with most of the option boxes grayed out. In the next few examples we'll start to use these options, so let's review the purpose or function for each of the operational buttons in the Query Properties dialog box, as follows:

- Add AND—used to open the Query Expressions Properties dialog box. This dialog box allows you to define an expression. If an expression is already present in the Find All '*Architecture*' Items Where box, the AND operator and the new expression will be placed before the existing expression. If no expressions currently exist, the Add AND button will allow you to define the first expression of the search criteria.
- Add OR—also used to open the Query Expressions Properties dialog box. This dialog box allows you to define an expression. If an expression is already present in the Find All '*Architecture*' Items Where box, the OR operator and the new expression will be placed before the existing expression. If no expressions currently exist, the Add OR button will allow you to define the first expression of the search criteria.
- Properties—enabled when you highlight an expression in the Find All '*Architecture*' Items Where box. It will open the Query Expression Properties dialog box, allowing you to modify the contents of the highlighted expression.
- Delete—allows you to delete a clause. A clause consists of both the expression and one of its adjacent logical operators. An expression cannot be deleted without including an adjacent logical operator unless it is the only expression present in the Find All '*Architecture*' Item Where box.
- Copy—allows you to copy an expression or subclause to the clipboard. It does not allow you to copy a clause to the clipboard.
- Paste—pastes the contents of the clipboard copy to the Find All '*architecture*' Items Where box directly under the currently highlighted expression. The AND logical operator is always used to join the pasted expression or subclause with the preceding expression or subclause.
- Group—allows you to group expressions together. Grouping expressions (along with the logical operators that separate them) together gives you the ability to have them treated as a single entity. When expressions are placed in a group, they are also given precedence over the standard AND, OR, and NOT logical operators. This can be a very useful tool when constructing complicated search criteria. Parentheses are used to designate expressions that have been grouped together. Each group will consist of at least two expressions and one logical operator.
- Group NOT—groups a set of expressions together as a single entity and precedes the group expression with the NOT logical operator.
- Ungroup—allows you to remove the grouping of expressions. Highlight the group expression and click the Ungroup button to remove the parentheses.

For our next example, we'll search for any server that has a drive with less than 20 percent of its space left, or any workstation that has a drive with less than 5 percent of its space left, as follows:

1. Start the SMS Administrator program.
2. From the menu bar, choose File, Execute Query to display the Execute Query dialog box.

3. Leave the Query box with the default entry of <Ad Hoc Query>. Leave the Query Result Format box blank, and the Limit to Sites box unmarked. Click the OK button to display the Query Properties dialog box.
4. Leave the Comment box blank, and make sure that Personal Computer is shown in the Architecture box. Click the Add AND button to open the Query Expression Properties dialog box.
5. In this box, scroll down the list until you find the group Disk. Find the line in the Disk group that contains the attribute named % Disk Full (see fig. 12.6) and highlight it.
6. In the Operator box, use the drop-down list to find the relational operator "is greater than."
7. In the Value box, type 80. When you've done that, click OK to return to the Query Properties dialog box.
8. Click the Add AND button to open the Query Expression Properties dialog box.
9. Scroll down the Group list until you find the group Identification. Find the line in the Identification group that contains the attribute named SystemRole and highlight it.
10. In the Operator box, use the drop-down list to find the relational operator "is."
11. In the Value box, use the drop-down list to find the name Server and click it. Then click OK to return to the Query Properties dialog box.
12. Click the Add AND button to open the Query Expression Properties dialog box.
13. In this box, scroll down the Group list until you find the group Disk. Find the line in the Disk group that contains the attribute named % Disk Full (see fig. 12.6) and highlight it.
14. In the Operator box, use the drop-down list to find the relational operator "is greater than."
15. In the Value box, type 125. When you've done that, click OK to return to the Query Properties dialog box.
16. Click the Add AND button to open the Query Expression Properties dialog box.
17. Scroll down the list until you find the group Identification. Find the line in the Identification group that contains the attribute named SystemRole and highlight it.
18. In the Operator box, use the drop-down list to find the relational operator "is."
19. In the Value box, use the drop-down list to find the name Workstation and click it. Then click OK to return to the Query Properties dialog box. You should have a list of expressions in the Find All '*architecture*' Item Where box that looks like those listed in figure 12.8.
20. Highlight the first set of expressions, as shown in figure 12.9, and click the Group button.
21. Next, highlight the second set of expressions, as shown in figure 12.10, and click the Group button.

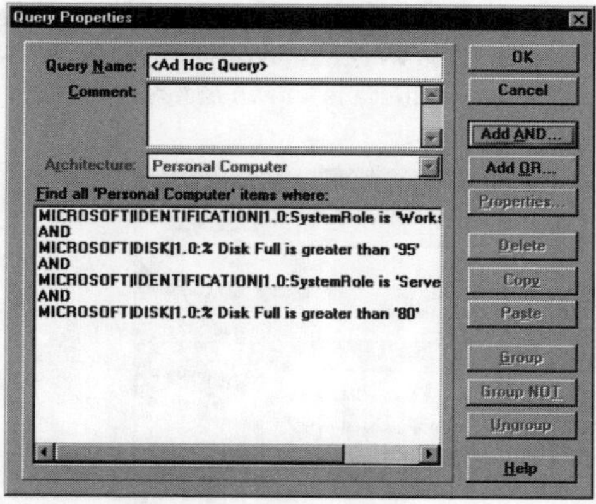

FIG. 12.8
The list of expressions must be grouped before executing the query.

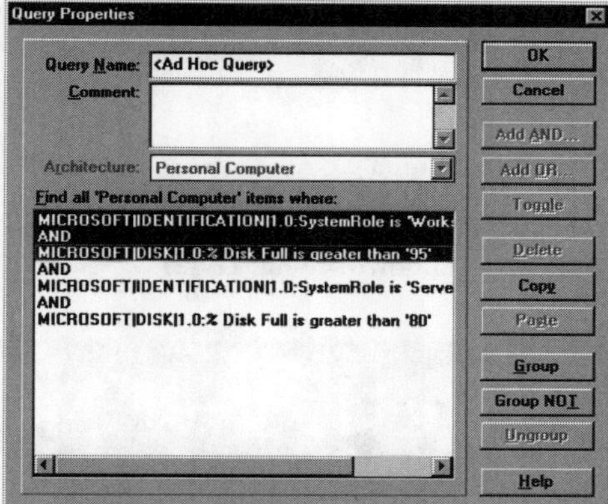

FIG. 12.9
Group the first set of expressions.

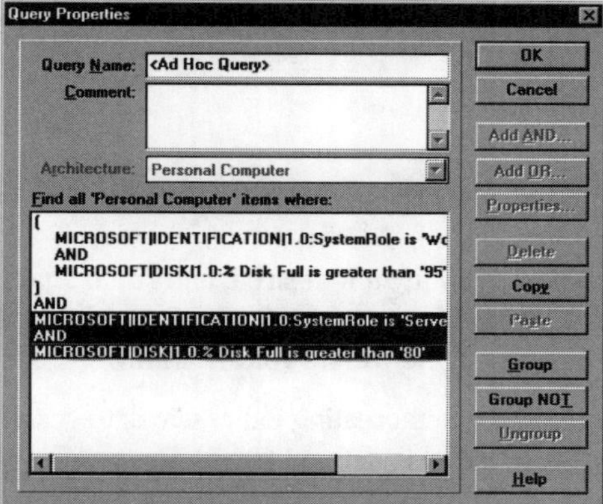

FIG. 12.10
Now group the second set of expressions.

22. Highlight the AND logical operator located between the two subclauses we just created, and click the Toggle button. This will change the AND logical operator to the OR logical operator. The resulting search criteria is shown in figure 12.11.

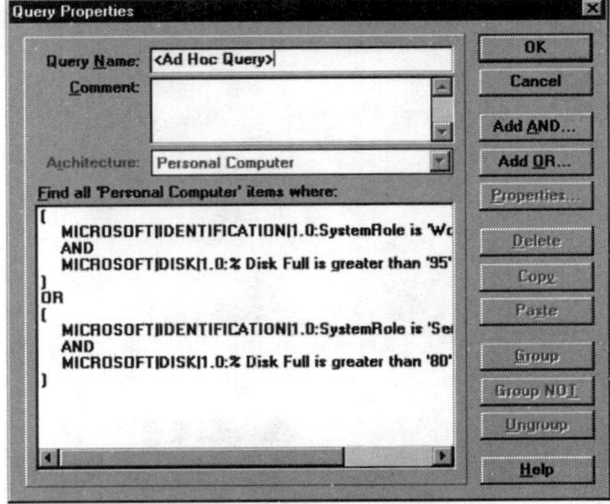

FIG. 12.11 The completed search criteria.

23. Click the OK button to begin the query.

The query will then return the names of any servers and workstations that meet the criteria in the Query Results <Ad Hoc Query> window (see fig. 12.12).

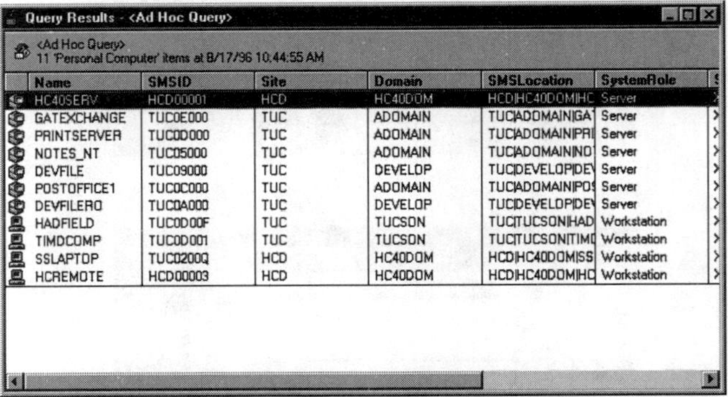

FIG. 12.12 The results of the example query.

You can reopen the Ad Hoc query, modify it if desired, and run it again by double-clicking the Query Results window panel. This will reopen the Query Properties dialog box, where you can make any modifications needed to further refine your search.

There are two points to remember when creating expressions to search for software packages and job details. The package group that is defined for the Personal Computer architecture will appear under the group name Software in the Query Expression Properties dialog box. Also, when doing a search on the JobDetails architecture, keep in mind that the Job Type and Status attributes are reported as numeric values instead of text. Table 12.1 lists each numeric value that has a corresponding Job Type or Status meaning.

Table 12.1 Job Type and Status Attributes Are Returned as Numeric Values

Numeric Indicator Value	Job Type Attribute Value	Status Attribute Value
1	Arrival	Pending
2	Workstation	Active
3	Server	Canceled
4	Completed	Complete
5		Failed
6		Retrying

If you want to use a query that is already defined in the database as the basis for an Ad Hoc query, follow the steps below. In this example we'll use one of the predefined queries that come with SMS, as follows:

1. Start the SMS Administrator program.
2. From the menu bar choose File, Execute Query to display the Execute Query dialog box.
3. Instead of Leaving the Query box with the default entry of <Ad Hoc Query>, use the drop-down list button to show the queries that already exist in the database. Find the name of the query you wish to modify, and highlight it. The Query Result Format will default to the identification format. Leave the Limit to Sites box unmarked and click the OK button to execute the query. If any additional input is needed for the query, a dialog box will appear and prompt you for any values it needs.
4. When the query is complete the results will be shown in the Query Results window. Double-click the Query Results window panel to open the Query Properties dialog box. From here you can modify the search criteria from the original query to fit your specific search needs.
5. After you've finished making your modifications, click the OK button to start the query.

Any modifications made in this manner do not alter the original query; it will remain unchanged in the database. This remains true regardless of whether the query is an Ad Hoc or defined query.

If you want to save the search criteria from an Ad Hoc query to the site database, create the Ad Hoc query as you normally would. Then, before executing the query, highlight the search criteria in the Find All '*architecture*' Items Where box and copy it to the clipboard using the Copy button.

At this point, you'll need to perform the actions required when adding a query to the site database. When this new query is created, the clipboard information from the Ad Hoc query is pasted into the Query Properties dialog box, and the query is saved. For example, we'll save the Ad Hoc query we created earlier (the one that finds low disk space) to the site database using this procedure as follows:

1. Follow the procedure listed earlier to create the low disk space search on Server and Workstations. Perform steps 1 through 22. Do not perform step 23.
2. Highlight all the information contained in the Find All '*architecture*' Items Where box (see fig. 12.13) and click the Copy button.

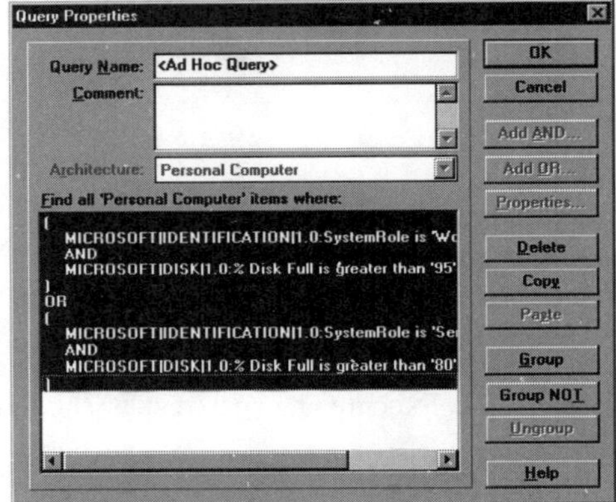

FIG. 12.13
Copy the search criteria information to the clipboard.

3. Click the OK button to execute the query, then close the results window. You can also click Cancel if you don't want to run the query at this time. Either way, the search criteria information we copied to the clipboard will still remain in the clipboard.
4. Select Open from the File menu to display the Open SMS Window. Highlight Queries and click the OK button to open the Queries window. You can also open this window by clicking the Open Queries icon from the button menu.
5. Select New from the File menu to display the Query Properties dialog box. This is the same dialog box used when creating Ad Hoc queries and is used in the same way.
6. Specify a unique name with which to identify the query in the database.
7. Enter a comment to further identify the query.
8. Make sure that Personal Computer appears in the Architecture box.
9. Click the Paste button to insert the contents of the clipboard into the Find All '*architecture*' Items Where box, as shown in figure 12.14.
10. Click the OK button to save the query to the site database.

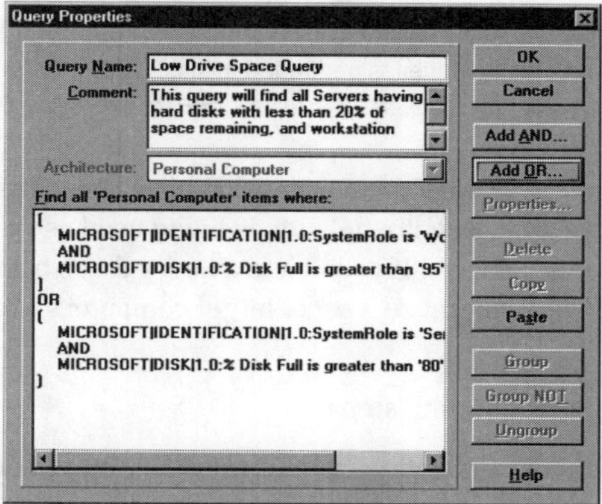

FIG. 12.14
Paste the contents of the clipboard into the properties box.

The Queries window will now list the query that was just created. The query is now available for execution at any time. To run the query, follow these steps:

1. Select Open from the File menu to display the Open SMS Window. Highlight Queries and click the OK button to open the Queries window. You can also open this window by clicking the Open Queries icon from the button menu.
2. Highlight the query you want to run and choose Execute Query from the File menu. You can also run the query by clicking the Execute Query icon from the button menu.
3. The Execute Query dialog box will appear. The query you have selected in the Queries window will appear as the default selection in the Query box. Click the OK button to execute the query.

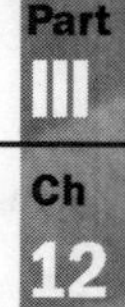

You can also use the drag-and-drop shortcut for running queries on specific sites. To do this, perform the following steps:

1. Open the Sites window and make sure the Site icon for the site you want to run the query against appears.
2. Open the Queries window.
3. Choose Tile Horizontally from the Window menu. This allows you to view both windows on the screen at the same time.
4. In the Queries window, highlight the query you want to run and drag it to the target site's icon in the Sites window. The query will be run against the machines in that site only. The execution of the query will be initiated immediately without further prompting.

Another way to target a specific site is to mark the Limit to Sites box in the Execute Query dialog box, then use the drop-down list to designate which site to run the query against. You can also designate if the query should be run against any of target site's subsites by marking the Include Subsites box.

NOTE The Limit to Sites setting applies only to queries performed against the Personal Computer architecture. It has no effect on queries performed against other architectures. The query is run against all objects of the architecture. ■

Eventually you'll want to delete some of the queries that have been created. This will not present a problem unless the query you're deleting is being used as the Job Target for a pending Run Command On Workstation job. If you delete a query that's been designated as the Job Target, the associated job will fail because a list of target computers won't be generated by the query.

To delete a query, perform the following steps:

1. Open the Queries window and highlight the query you want to delete.
2. From the Edit menu, choose Delete.
3. An administrative caution message will appear, informing you that pending jobs or alerts that use this query will fail. Click the OK button.
4. A confirmation box is presented to confirm the deletion of the query. Click the Yes button to complete the deletion.

How to Create a Custom Result Format

By default, each of the six architectures have a result format named Identification that is normally used to display the results of a query. But many times the default format does not display the specific attribute information you're looking for in the Query Results window.

Customizing the result format for a query allows you to determine which of a returned object's attributes will be shown in the Query Results window. You can define a default result format for each of the six architectures. When you perform a query using the drag-and-drop shortcut, the results are returned in the default format for that architecture. Designating one of the modified result formats as the default for a specific architecture will enable you to see results of a drag-and-drop query in the format you desire.

To give you an example, we'll start by making up a simple query that will find all the Windows NT Servers in the site hierarchy. We're interested in finding out what versions of NT server are running at the site. We'd also like to know what service packs have been applied, what type of processor is running, and how much memory is in each. Executing the query using the default Identification format would force us to look manually at the properties of each returned object in order to find the attribute information we want. Instead we'll define a custom result format to show information we're looking for in the Query Results window.

Let's begin by creating a simple query to search for all the NT Servers in the site hierarchy, as follows:

1. Open the Queries window. From the File menu, choose New to display the Query Properties dialog box.
2. In the Query Name box, type a name for the query.

3. Add a comment to the Comment box if you desire.
4. Click the Add AND button to open the Query Expression Properties dialog box.
5. Scroll down to the Identification Group and highlight the line that contains the Attribute named SystemRole.
6. Leave the "is" relational operator in the Operator box.
7. In the Value box, use the drop-down list and choose Server by clicking it.
8. Click the OK button to return to the Query Properties dialog box.
9. Click the Add AND button to open the Query Expression Properties dialog box.
10. Scroll down to the Operating System Group and highlight the line that contains the Attribute named Operating System Name.
11. Leave the "is" relational operator in the Operator box.
12. In the Value box, use the drop-down list and choose Microsoft Windows NT by clicking it.
13. Click the OK button to return to the Query Properties dialog box. You should have a Query Properties dialog box similar to the one shown in figure 12.15. Click OK to return to the Queries window.

FIG. 12.15
Create a simple query to search for NT Servers.

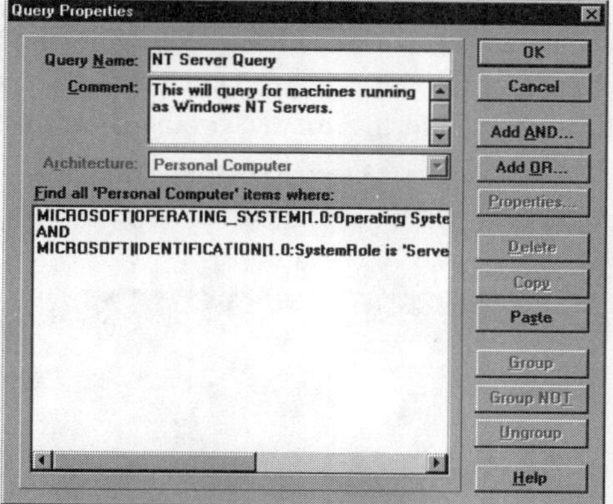

The new query will now be listed in the Queries window.

To run the query using the default Identification result format, perform the following steps:

1. Highlight the new query in the Queries windows.
2. From the File menu, choose Execute Query to open the Execute Query window.
3. Make sure that the name of the query you've just created is in the Query box and that the text "Inventory" is in the Query Result Format box, then click the OK button.

The "Query Results—All Personal Computers" window (similar to the one shown in figure 12.16) will appear listing all the objects returned for the search. As you can see, none of the information we're looking for is listed in the Results window. In order to get the information we desire for any of the objects, we have to look manually at the object's properties by double-clicking it. It would be much easier if the information we wanted was listed in the results windows in the first place. Fortunately, SMS gives us a simple way of defining the Results window to do just that.

Query Results - NT Server Query

NT Server Query
15 'Personal Computer' items at 8/17/96 10:53:49 AM

Name	SMSID	Site	Domain	SMSLocation	SystemRole
HC40SERV	HCD00001	HCD	HC40DOM	HCD|HC40DOM|HC	Server
ADMSERV	TUC0B000	TUC	ADOMAIN	TUC|ADOMAIN|ADI	Server
TUCSMS1	TUC02000	TUC	TUCSON	TUC|TUCSON|TUC	Server
XENON	TUC03000	TUC	TUCSON	TUC|TUCSON|XEN	Server
BRIDGEXCH	TUC0F000	TUC	ADOMAIN	TUC|ADOMAIN|BRI	Server
ARGON	TUC00001	TUC	TUCSON	TUC|TUCSON|ARG	Server
HELIUM	TUC01000	TUC	TUCSON	TUC|TUCSON|HEL	Server
GATEXCHANGE	TUC0E000	TUC	ADOMAIN	TUC|ADOMAIN|GAT	Server
PRINTSERVER	TUC0D000	TUC	ADOMAIN	TUC|ADOMAIN|PRI	Server
PRIMEXCHANGE	TUC07000	TUC	ADOMAIN	TUC|ADOMAIN|PRI	Server
NOTES_NT	TUC05000	TUC	ADOMAIN	TUC|ADOMAIN|NOT	Server
DEVFILE	TUC09000	TUC	DEVELOP	TUC|DEVELOP|DEV	Server
POSTOFFICE1	TUC0C000	TUC	ADOMAIN	TUC|ADOMAIN|POS	Server
DEVFILERD	TUC0A000	TUC	DEVELOP	TUC|DEVELOP|DEV	Server
LASTORES	TUC07004	TUC	ADOMAIN	TUC|ADOMAIN|LAS	Server

FIG. 12.16 The results displayed using the default identification format.

To create a custom query Results windows, follow these steps:

1. From the File menu, choose Define Query Result Formats. The Define Query Result Formats dialog box appears, allowing you to edit or create different formats. It also allows you to set a default result format for each of the six architectures.
2. Click the New button to display the Query Result Format Properties dialog box, as shown in figure 12.17.

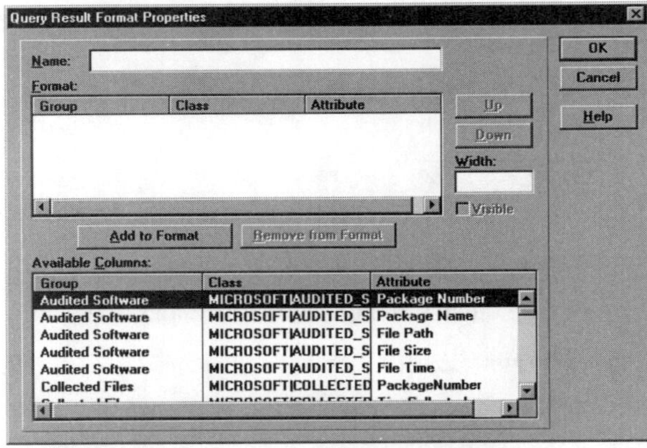

FIG. 12.17 Use the Query Result Format Properties dialog box to specify the result format.

We'll use this dialog box to designate the attributes that will appear in our custom Query Results window.

3. Assign a name to the result format by typing a unique name in the Name box.
4. Scroll down the Available Columns listing until you find the Identification Group. Highlight the line in the Identification Group that has the Name Attribute on it.
5. Click the Add to Format button to place the attribute choice in the Format window.
6. Repeat steps 4 and 5 to complete the result format. One by one, highlight the following attribute lines in the Available Columns window and add each of them to the Format window by clicking the Add to Format button.

Table 12.2 Add the Following Attribute Lines to the Format Window

Group	Class	Attribute
Identification	MICROSOFT|IDENTIFICATION|1.0	Name
Identification	MICROSOFT|IDENTIFICATION|1.0	Site
Operating System	MICROSOFT|OPERATING—SYSTEM|1.0	Operating System Name
Operating System	MICROSOFT|OPERATING—SYSTEM|1.0	Version
Operating System	MICROSOFT|OPERATING—SYSTEM|1.0	CSD Version
Processor	MICROSOFT|PROCESSOR|1.0	Processor Name
PC Memory	MICROSOFT|X86_PC_MEMORY|1.0	Total Physical Memory (Kbyte)

7. When you've finished adding in the attributes to the Format window, the Query Result Format Properties dialog box will look similar to figure 12.18. Click the OK button to return to the Define Query Result Formats dialog box. You'll notice the name for the result format we've just created is shown in the Formats listing.
8. Click the OK button to exit the Define Query Result Formats dialog box.

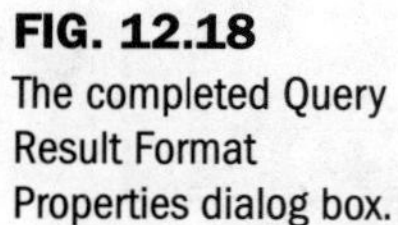

FIG. 12.18
The completed Query Result Format Properties dialog box.

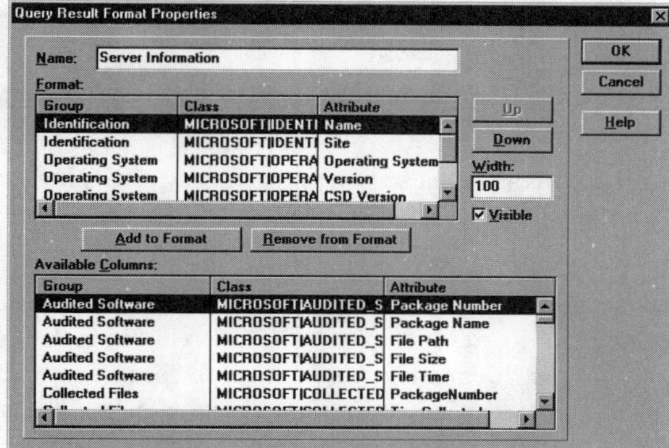

Now we can run the query using this custom format we have created, as follows:

1. Highlight the new query in the Queries windows.
2. From the File menu, choose Execute Query to open the Execute Query window.
3. Make sure that the name of the query you've just created is in the Query box.
4. From the Query Result Format drop-down list, choose the name of the result format we have just created (see fig. 12.19), then click the OK button to start the query.

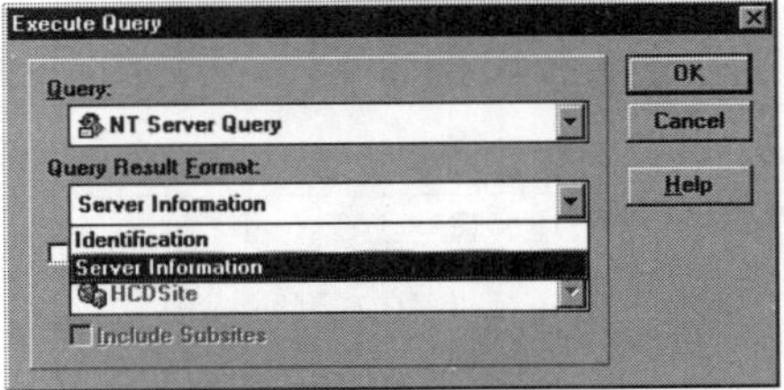

FIG. 12.19
Choose the new result format from the Query Result Format drop-down list.

You'll notice that the information we're seeking is now displayed in the results window (as shown in fig. 12.20). You can edit the column width for each attribute to match your screen size and resolution by reopening the Define Query Result Formats dialog box, highlighting the name of the result format you wish to edit in the Formats list, and clicking the Properties button.

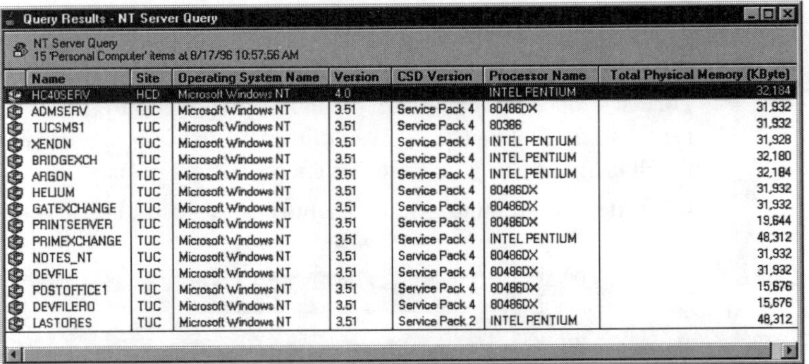

Name	Site	Operating System Name	Version	CSD Version	Processor Name	Total Physical Memory (KByte)
HC40SERV	HCD	Microsoft Windows NT	4.0		INTEL PENTIUM	32,184
ADMSERV	TUC	Microsoft Windows NT	3.51	Service Pack 4	80486DX	31,932
TUCSMS1	TUC	Microsoft Windows NT	3.51	Service Pack 4	80386	31,932
XENON	TUC	Microsoft Windows NT	3.51	Service Pack 4	INTEL PENTIUM	31,928
BRIDGEXCH	TUC	Microsoft Windows NT	3.51	Service Pack 4	INTEL PENTIUM	32,180
ARGON	TUC	Microsoft Windows NT	3.51	Service Pack 4	INTEL PENTIUM	32,184
HELIUM	TUC	Microsoft Windows NT	3.51	Service Pack 4	80486DX	31,932
GATEXCHANGE	TUC	Microsoft Windows NT	3.51	Service Pack 4	80486DX	31,932
PRINTSERVER	TUC	Microsoft Windows NT	3.51	Service Pack 4	80486DX	19,644
PRIMEXCHANGE	TUC	Microsoft Windows NT	3.51	Service Pack 4	INTEL PENTIUM	48,312
NOTES_NT	TUC	Microsoft Windows NT	3.51	Service Pack 4	80486DX	31,932
DEVFILE	TUC	Microsoft Windows NT	3.51	Service Pack 4	80486DX	31,932
POSTOFFICE1	TUC	Microsoft Windows NT	3.51	Service Pack 4	80486DX	15,676
DEVFILERO	TUC	Microsoft Windows NT	3.51	Service Pack 4	80486DX	15,676
LASTORES	TUC	Microsoft Windows NT	3.51	Service Pack 2	INTEL PENTIUM	48,312

FIG. 12.20
The custom result format now gives us the information we need at a glance.

In fact, you can edit any of the result screen properties by reopening the Define Query Result Formats dialog box. This includes adding and removing attribute fields from the results window.

You can also designate the order in which the attributes are displayed in the Query Results windows. Changing the order in which the attributes are listed in the Format list section of the Query Result Format Properties dialog box will alter the order in which the attributes are displayed in the Query Results window. Entries at the top of the Format list will appear as the first attributes (going from left to right) in the results window. Entries at the bottom of the

Format list will appear as the last attributes in the results window. You can easily move the position of any attribute in the Format list by highlighting the attribute you want to move and clicking the Up or Down button.

Once you have decided on a result format that you like for a particular architecture, you can designate it as the default query result format for that architecture. You can create and assign a different custom query result format for each of the six architectures. We can create a custom result format name inventory and assign it to the Personal Computer architecture as follows:

1. From the File menu, choose Define Query Result Formats. The Define Query Result Formats dialog box appears, allowing you to edit or create different formats. It also allows you to set a default result format for each of the six architectures.
2. In the Architecture drop-down list, choose the architecture that you want to set up a default for. In this example we're changing the default for the Personal Computer architecture.
3. In the Formats list, highlight the name of the result format that you want to use as the default and then click the Set as Default Format button. The custom format will now be listed as the Default Format in the Define Query Result Formats dialog box (see fig. 12.21).

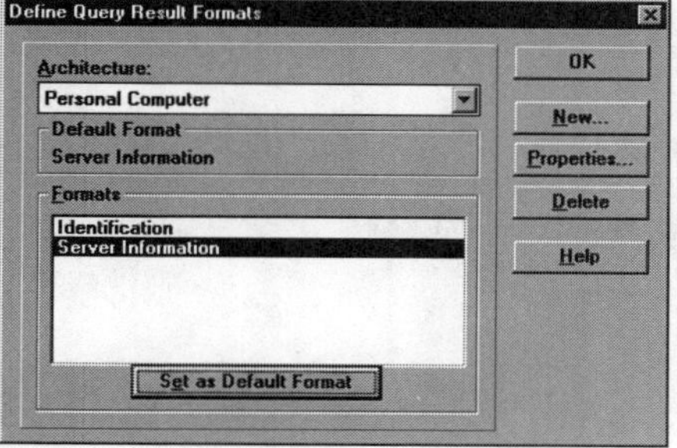

FIG. 12.21
Inventory is now listed as the default result format for the Personal Computer architecture.

4. Click the OK button to exit from the Define Query result Formats dialog box.

Now that we've seen how to work with queries, it's time to take the information reporting capabilities of SMS one step further, using Crystal Reports. Although the query function of SMS is adequate for most support staff needs, it does not usually produce the types of reports that are preferred by management. To provide that capability, Crystal Reports has been included on the SMS CD-ROM. This requires a little extra setup, but is well worth it if you need to produce quality reports for your company's management.

Using Crystal Reports

Crystal Reports is a third-party application that allows you to create reports using information stored in the SMS database. Its use is not a direct function of SMS, so it does require some extra setup. We'll need to set up two other components in addition to Crystal Reports. The first is the database view.

The database view allows programs other than SMS to read information contained in the SQL database. A view is created using a program called SMSVIEW.EXE.

The other component that must be installed is Microsoft's Open Database Connectivity (ODBC) tool. This is needed in order for Crystal Reports to be able to access the database view. We'll go through each of the setup steps involved, starting with the setup of the database view.

Using SMSVIEW to Set Up the Database View

Before installing Crystal Reports, we need to set up a view of the SMS database. This is done using the program named SMSVIEW. This program is automatically installed on the primary site's site server during installation. It is placed in the SMS\SITE.SRV*platform* directory of the site server.

Follow these steps to create the database view:

1. Log on to the SMS site server with administrator privileges, locate the executable file name SMSVIEW.EXE, and start it.
2. The Create Views dialog box appears, as shown in figure 12.22. In the ServerName box, supply the name of the computer that is running the site's SQL Server. If SQL is installed on the site server, this will be the name of the site server.

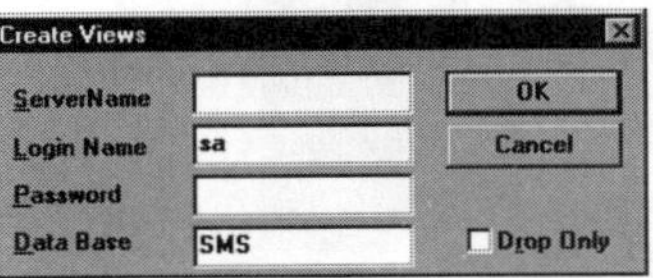

FIG. 12.22 Supply the login information for the site's SQL server.

3. In the Login Name box, supply the name of an account with database owner (dbo) privileges.
4. In the Password box, supply the password for the Login Name account you've entered.
5. Type the name of the SMS database in the Data Base box. This is SMS by default.
6. Click the OK button to create the database view. When the view has been created, the success message is displayed, as shown in figure 12.23.

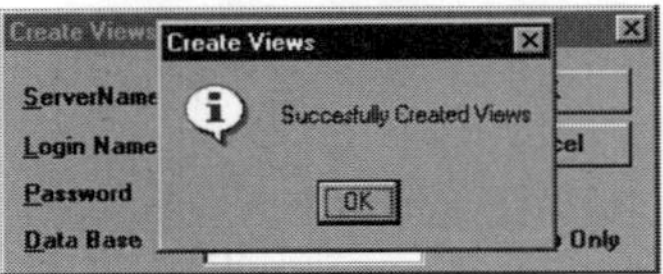

FIG. 12.23 The database view has been created successfully.

7. Click the OK button to close the Success Message window.

Now that we've successfully created the database view, Crystal Reports can be installed. If you're running NT 4.0, you can install Crystal Report directly from the SMS Task screen that appears when you insert the SMS CD-ROM. If you're using an earlier version of NT, run the setup program located in the \SMS12\REPORTS directory on the SMS CD-ROM.

Follow these steps to install Crystal Reports:

1. Insert the SMS CD-ROM. The SMS Task screen appears, as shown in figure 12.24. Click on the Set up Crystal Reports icon.

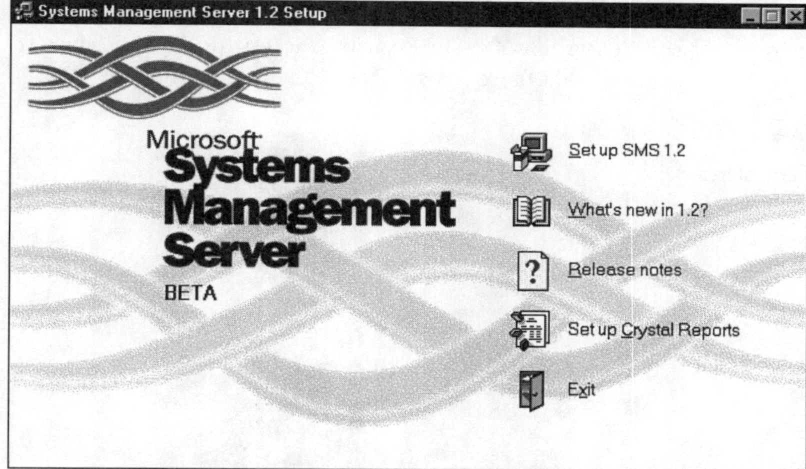

FIG. 12.24
Start the Crystal Reports installation from the SMS Task screen.

2. The Installation Options dialog box will appear, as shown in figure 12.25. Make any changes that are needed to the installation path and click the Continue button.

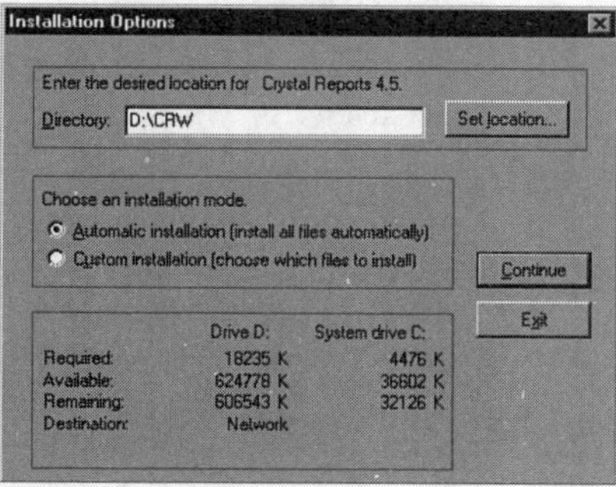

FIG. 12.25
Modify the installation options if needed.

3. The Workstations Options dialog box will appear. This allows you to create a setup point if other workstations on your network will be using Crystal Reports. This step is not needed to install Crystal Reports. Continue by clicking either Yes or No.

4. The file copy and installation process will start. A notification will be given when the setup has completed. Click OK to continue.
5. Another setup dialog box will appear, asking if you would like to create the Crystal Reports program group. Click the Yes button to create the program group.
6. The next dialog box indicates that ODBC has been installed on the system and that further setup is required to complete its installation. Click the OK button to continue.
7. If you'd like to view the README file, click Yes in the last dialog box.

The setup program will create a new program group (see fig. 12.26) with icons for both Crystal Reports and ODBC. In the next step, we'll use the ODBC setup icon to start the install of the components that allow Crystal Reports to access the database view. To configure the ODBC components, follow these steps:

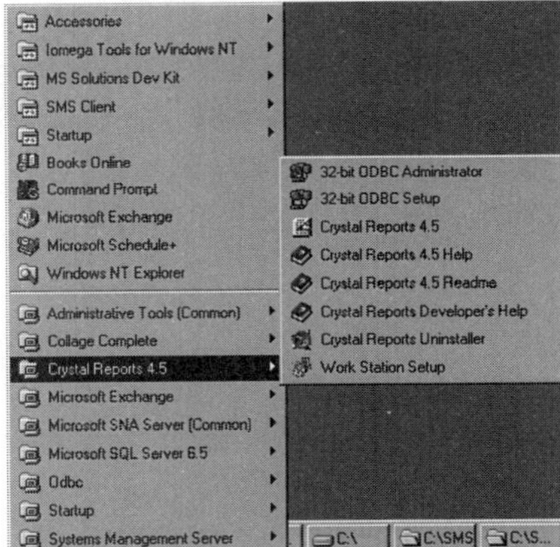

FIG. 12.26
The Crystal Reports program group.

1. Double-click the 32-bit ODBC Setup icon located in the newly created program group.
2. The ODBC setup Welcome screen will appear. Click the Continue button to continue.
3. The Install Drivers dialog box will appear (see fig. 12.27). Highlight SQL Server in the Available ODBC Drivers box, and click the OK button.
4. The Data Sources dialog box appears. You must supply information that specifies the data and data source. Click the Add button to display the Add Data Source dialog box (see fig. 12.28).
5. Highlight SQL Server in the Installed ODBC Drivers list and click the OK button. The ODBC SQL Server Setup dialog box will appear.
6. In the Data Source Name box, type the name of the SMS database data log. If you left this at its default during installation, the name will be SMSData.
7. In the Description box, type a short description.

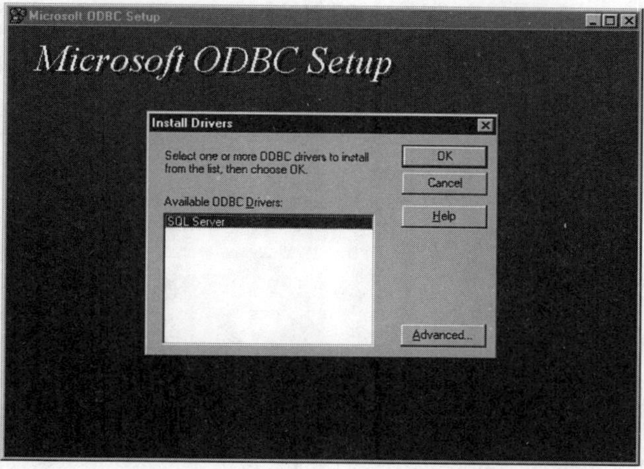

FIG. 12.27
Configure the SQL Data connection.

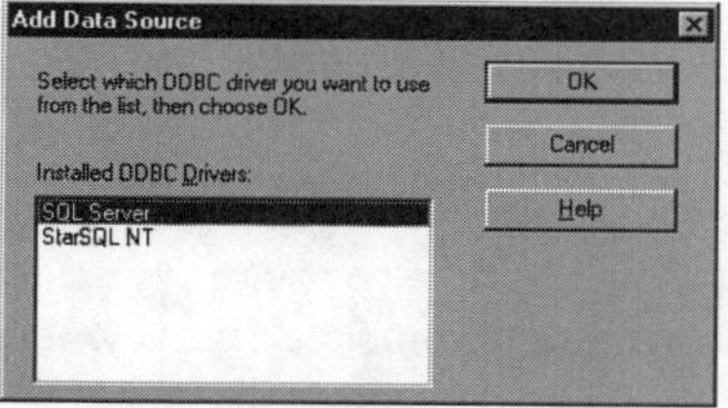

FIG. 12.28
Configure the Data Source information.

8. In the Server box, type the name of the site's SQL Server. Use the drop-down list to select (local) if SQL is on the site server (see fig. 12.29). If the server is not local, supply the address of the computer in the Network Address box. This box can usually be left at the default when using SQL Server.

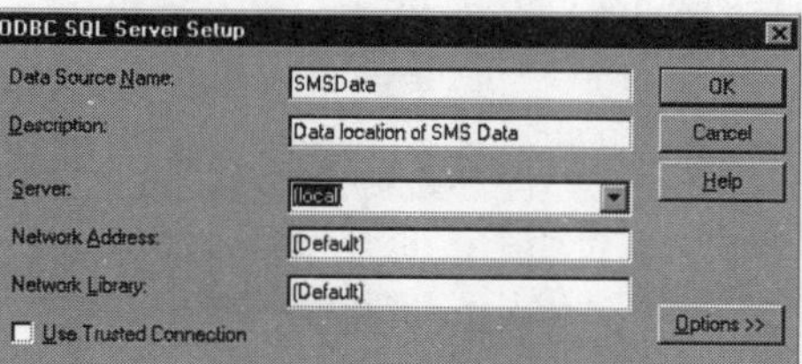

FIG. 12.29
Designate the SQL Server.

9. Click the Options button to display the Login area of the ODBC SQL Server Setup dialog box (see fig. 12.30).

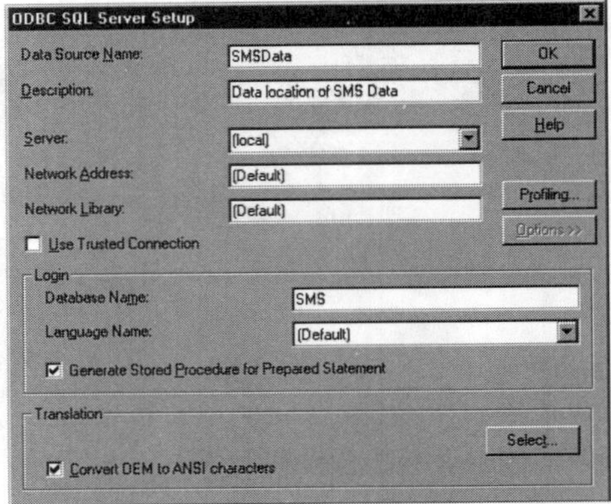

FIG. 12.30
Supply the SQL Login information.

10. In the Database Name box, type the name of the SMS database. If you installed SMS with the default database name, the name is SMS.
11. Click OK to return to the Data Sources dialog box, and then Close to complete the setup. A screen indicating the successful installation of ODBC will be displayed. Click the OK button to continue.

This completes the setup for Crystal Reports. The program can now be started by clicking on the icon labeled Crystal Reports 4.5. The first time you start Crystal Reports, you'll be prompted to enter registration information and complete a survey. You can then register your copy of Crystal via modem or print it out and register via fax. You will be supplied a serial number which will prevent the registration screen from appearing each time you start the program.

The easiest way to start using Crystal Reports is to use some of the predefined reports that come packaged with it. These reports have been customized for use with SMS and can be used without any prior modification. Let's take a look at one of the predefined reports that gives the details on the disk usage of your computers. This is a very handy report that points out one of the advantages of using Crystal Reports over the built-in query functionality of SMS.

You may have tried to create a query result format that contains attribute information from an object that has more than one instance. For example, if you tried to create a query result format that showed the percentage of free disk space, you may have noticed that you could designate the attribute % Free Disk in the result format. But when you run the query using the format, only information on drive A: (the first instance of the attribute) is displayed. And since drive A: information is very limited, nothing will show up in the Query Results windows for the % Disk Free attribute for any objects returned.

Crystal Reports gets around this by allowing you to designate both the attribute and the instance for reporting purposes. This is illustrated in our next example, where we'll use a predefined report to show the available disk space information as follows:

1. Start Crystal Reports and choose Open from the File menu to display the File Open dialog box.
2. Scroll down the list of files, highlight the file named SPACE.RPT, and click the OK button.
3. The report will appear (see fig. 12.31) with default data in it. From the Report menu choose Refresh Report Data.

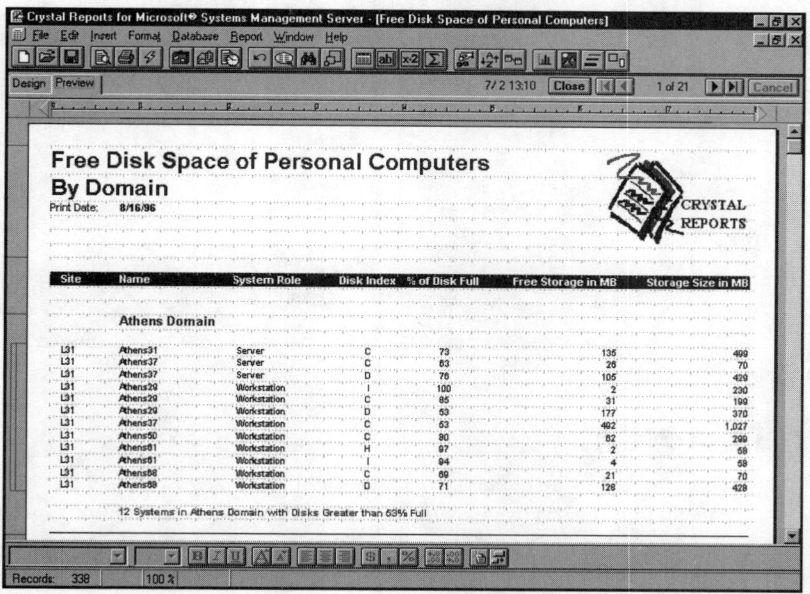

FIG. 12.31
The Disk Space Report with the default data.

4. Click Yes in the Refresh Report data confirmation box.
5. The SQL Data Sources dialog box appears. Highlight the database data log file name in the Select Data Sources list (SMSData is the default) and click the OK button.
6. The SQL Server Login box will appear. Enter the account name of a dbo (sa) in the Login ID box along with the account password in the Password box. Then click the OK button.

The default data that was in the report is now replaced with the data from the SMS SQL database, as shown in figure 12.32. These reports can be easily reformatted and tailored to suit your needs.

Crystal Reports is a very powerful tool that can yield some impressive results with a little practice. The actual construction of queries is well documented within the Crystal Reports help files and will not be discussed here. The purpose of this section is to help you get Crystal Reports up and running. Now that's done, you'll have little trouble creating meaningful reports in a short amount of time.

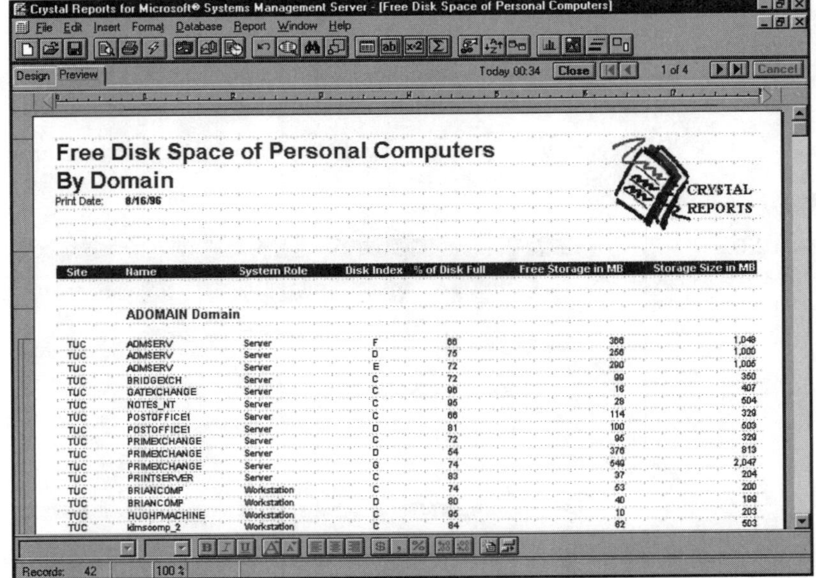

FIG. 12.32
The report after its update with site database information.

From Here...

This concludes the chapter on queries and reports. You should be able to create both queries and custom result formats after reading this chapter. In addition, you should be able to perform the installation of Crystal Reports with its associated components and use Crystal Reports to gather information on your system using the predefined reports that come packaged with it.

The next section of the book deals with remote troubleshooting and diagnostics. Here's what's in store.

- Chapter 13, "Using Help Desk and Diagnostics on a Remote PC," examines the use of the Help Desk and the remote Diagnostics features of SMS. You'll discover how to save time and energy by using this set of tools to support remote PCs and their users.
- Chapter 14, "Using the Network Monitor," shows you how to use the Network Monitor to capture packet and frame information from your network. You'll be able to look at the traffic patterns of your network and identify problems before they become serious.

PART IV

Remote Diagnostics and Troubleshooting

CHAPTER 13

Using Help Desk and Diagnostics on a Remote PC

Help Desk and Remote Diagnostics are real-time tools that complement the SMS batch-oriented tools very nicely. These tools give you instant access to any PC that you can connect to on your network. How many times have you had to walk across the building to sit in front of someone's PC because the fix would be too difficult for them to attempt or because they simply weren't able to describe the problem well enough for you to handle it over the phone. And how many of those times does it turn out to be something pretty simple? This situation is bad enough if you're all in the same building, but what if you and your users are in different cities? Help Desk enables you to take control of the remote PC and manipulate it as though you were sitting in front of it. Remote Diagnostics lets you gather very detailed information about a PC's configuration. Although these tools don't completely replace other types of remote access software you may have or have heard about, they have the advantage of being integrated with SMS and they work quite well across all of the Windows platforms. ■

Connect to and Manipulate a Remote PC with the Help Desk

Help Desk includes remote control, remote reboot, remote execute, remote chat, and file transfer. You'll see how to connect to a client computer and use each of these functions.

Connect to and Collect Configuration Information from a Remote PC with Remote Diagnostics

Remote Diagnostics includes five diagnostics for DOS, six diagnostics for Windows, and a ping test that checks the speed of the network connection to the client computer. You'll see how to connect to a client computer and perform each of these diagnostics.

Configure a Client Computer for Remote Access with Help Desk and Remote Diagnostics

A client computer must be configured with several pieces of software and must have at least one network protocol in common with the SMS Administrator workstation in order to support remote access. In addition, the user has a variety of options that can be configured to allow or disallow access by the administrator.

Using Help Desk on a Remote PC

In this section, we'll explore the SMS Help Desk and see how it enables an administrator to fix PC problems remotely.

What is Help Desk?

Help Desk is a remote control program that enables you to connect to a particular PC in your SMS database and use the keyboard and mouse as if you were physically there. You can start and stop programs, open and close windows, transfer files, chat with the user, and even reboot the machine, and you see everything that appears on the screen of the remote PC. Help Desk is actually part of the SMS Administrator, so you must have that program running in order to use it.

Connecting to a Remote PC

In order to connect to a remote PC, you must have a continuous network connection to that PC. Although this sounds obvious, it's easy to overlook when you're on a far-flung network. Your WAN connections may be dial-up RAS connections, which allow SMS to populate the SMS database but doesn't allow you to make a real-time connection to a PC across the WAN. Additionally, your SMS workstation and the client computer must have at least one network protocol in common—again, a detail that's easy to overlook. Finally, the client computer must be configured to permit remote control and the remote control agent must be running. If all of these requirements are satisfied, then making the connection should be easy. The following tells you how to do it:

1. In the SMS Administrator, open the Sites window and select the client computer you want to connect to, as shown in figure 13.1.

NOTE You can't connect to a client computer unless it appears in the Sites window. ■

2. Double-click the selected client computer to bring up its Properties window. Then select the Help Desk icon in the Properties list box. This causes SMS to attempt to connect to the selected client computer. You'll see the message "Attempting to locate ___" and possibly the subsequent message "Trying additional protocols," and then the grayed icons will become available as an indication that you have successfully connected, as shown in figure 13.2.

From here, you have five different remote access functions you can use. We'll examine each of them.

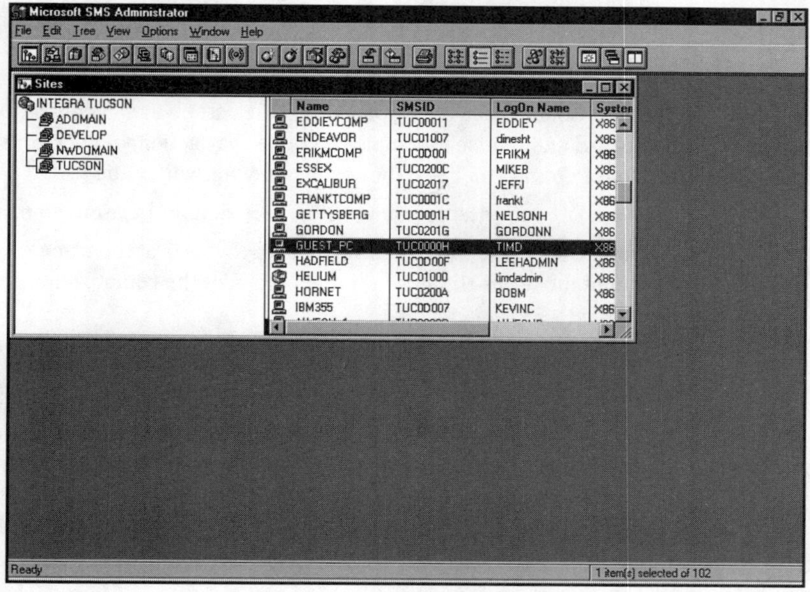

FIG. 13.1
Selecting a client computer for remote control.

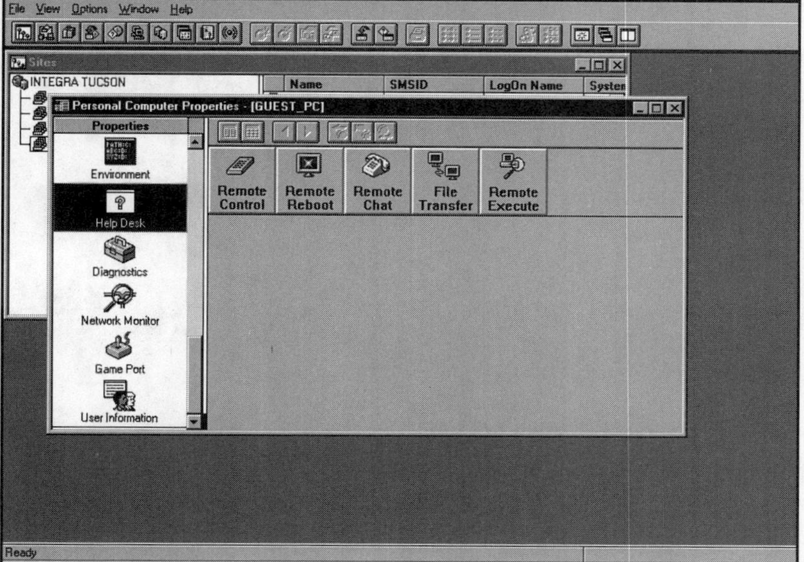

FIG. 13.2
A successful remote connection to TIMDCOMP.

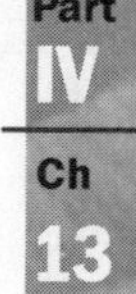

The Help Desk Tool Set

The Help Desk provides five different remote access tools, as follows:

- Remote Control—enables you to view the screen of a client computer and manipulate all keyboard and mouse functions remotely. Any action you perform will occur on the remote PC, and you'll see the results on your workstation.
- Remote Reboot—allows you to reboot the remote PC from your workstation.
- Remote Chat—starts a chat session with the user at the remote PC. This is especially useful in those situations where the person at the remote site doesn't have access to a telephone.
- File Transfer—enables you to send and receive files to and from the remote PC.
- Remote Execute—lets you execute a program on the remote PC.

Remote Control You choose the Remote Control icon to start a remote control session with the client computer. A window will appear that displays the screen of the remote PC. You can then interact with this screen just as you would if you were sitting at the remote PC. From where we were at the screen shown in figure 13.2, choose the Remote Control icon and you'll see a window that represents the screen of the remote PC, as shown in figure 13.3.

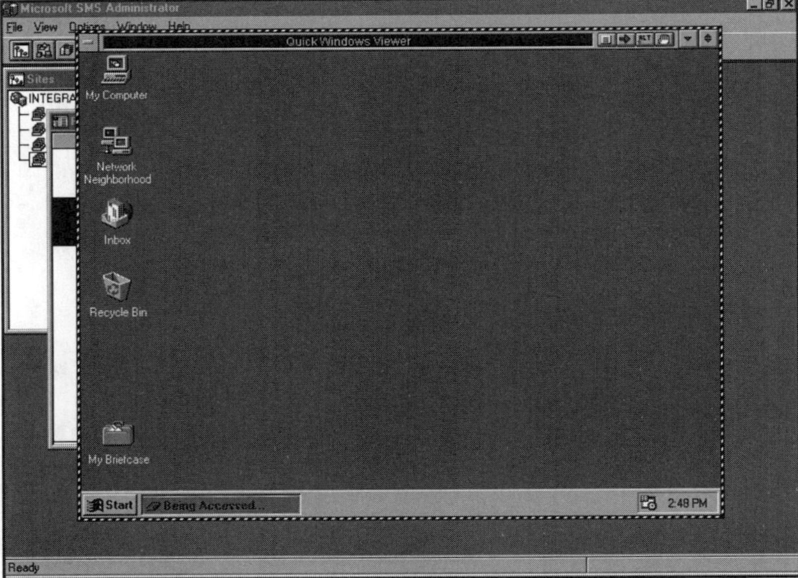

FIG. 13.3
You're now in control of the remote PC.

You can now interact with any application on the remote PC. Figure 13.4 shows the Start menu being accessed, and figure 13.5 shows Microsoft Excel running on the remote PC.

FIG. 13.4
Using the remote PC's desktop.

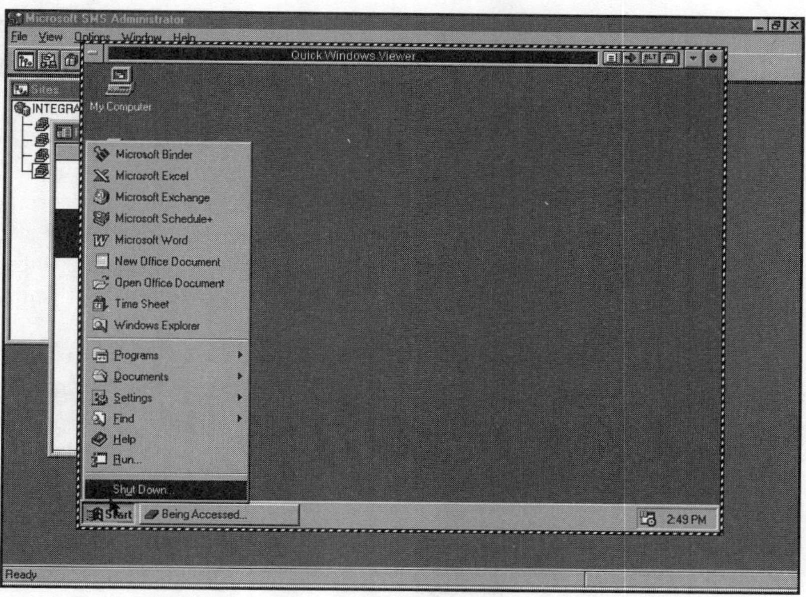

FIG. 13.5
Calling up Microsoft Excel remotely.

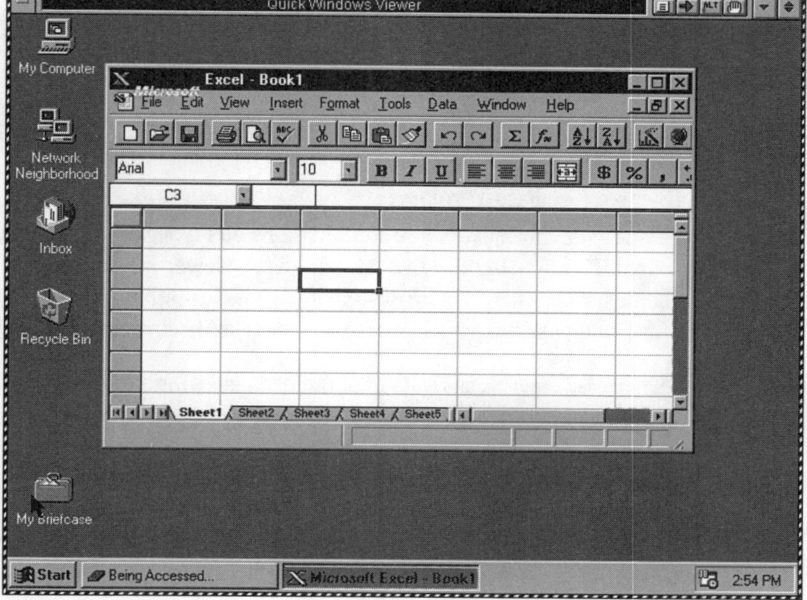

Remote Control Session Features The viewer window has the following features accessible from the top window border that enhance your remote control session:

- Scrollable Viewing Area

  If the remote PC has a higher display resolution than your SMS workstation, or your viewer window is sized large enough to view the entire remote screen, then you can use the scroll bars on the viewer window to move around on the remote screen or you can choose the Hand button on the viewer window, and you'll get a miniature window representation of the remote screen with a rectangle representing your viewing area. You can then grab the rectangle and drag it around to shift your view, as shown in figure 13.6.

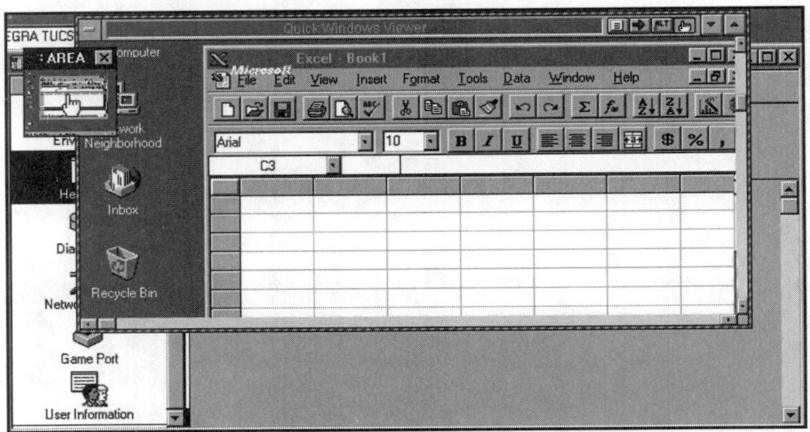

FIG. 13.6
Dragging your viewer around on the remote desktop.

- System Key Pass-Through

  By default, any system key combinations you type will not go through to the remote client. By choosing the ALT button on the viewer window border, you can toggle this behavior on and off. With system key pass-through on, for example, the key combination Alt-F will pass through to Microsoft Excel and activate the File menu.

NOTE The key combinations Alt-Tab, Ctrl-Esc, and Ctrl-Alt-Del are never sent to the client computer. If you need to reboot a client computer, use the Remote Reboot function described later in this section.

- Remote Window Switching

  Because the key combination Alt-Tab is never passed through to the client, the Arrow button is provided to accomplish the same function. When you click the Arrow button, you are presented with an application icon representing one of the applications running on the client. Clicking the Arrow button again switches to that application. You must repeat the above steps until you get the application you want to switch to.

Remote Control Configuration Settings There are a number of configuration settings that control the behavior of the remote control program. To access these, from the Control menu of the viewer window, select Configure. This brings up the Control Parameters dialog box shown in figure 13.7.

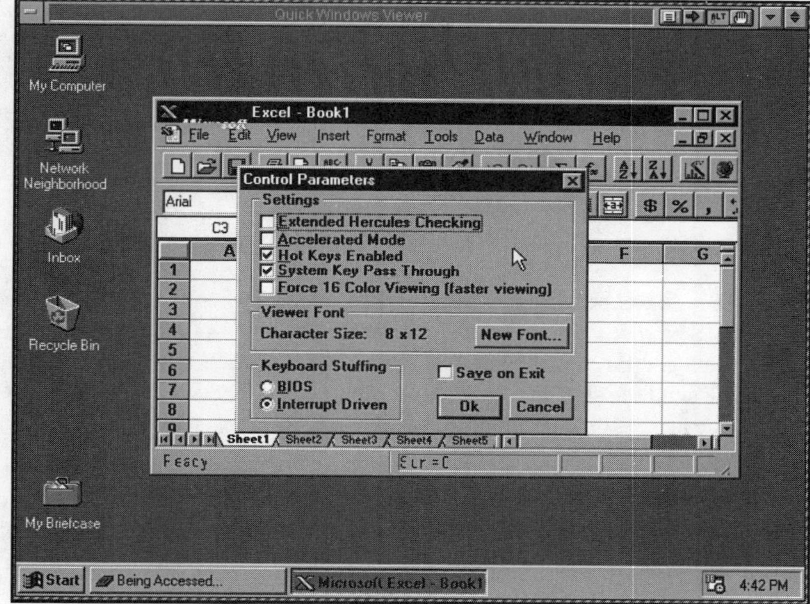

FIG. 13.7
Configuring Remote Control.

You can configure the following parameters:

- Extended Hercules Checking (MS-DOS only)—required if your client has a Hercules graphics card. It monitors the display mode of the client computer (text mode or graphics mode).
- Accelerated Mode (MS-DOS only)—causes the client computer to send screen updates to your SMS workstation as fast as the network will allow.
- Hot Keys Enabled—enables the hot keys that are defined in a separate dialog box.
- System Key Pass-Through—controls whether or not system key sequences are passed through to the client computer. To pass system key sequences through, clear the check box.
- Force 16-Color Viewing (faster viewing) (Windows Only)—forces the client computer to use a 16-color display in order to get faster updates on your SMS workstation.
- Viewer Font—you can change the default display font size.
- Keyboard Stuffing—gives you two different ways of sending keystrokes to the client computer: BIOS or Interrupt Driven. Choose Interrupt Driven for Windows.

The hot keys that you enable in the configuration parameters dialog box are defined in a separate dialog box. From the Control menu of the viewer window, select Hot Keys. This brings up the Hot Keys dialog box, as shown in figure 13.8. These definitions can be edited, if necessary.

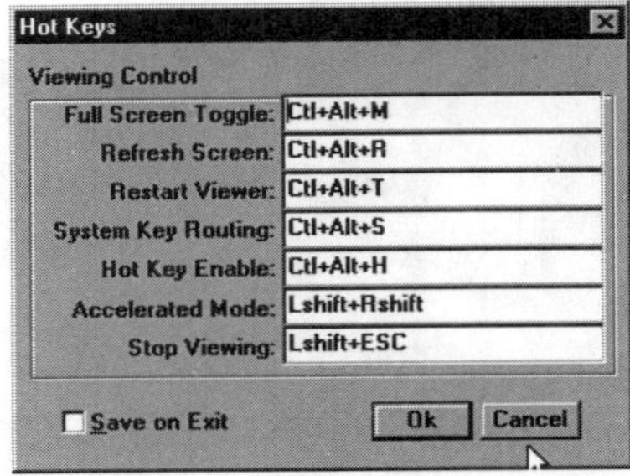

FIG. 13.8
Configuring hot keys.

Remote Reboot You can't send the Ctrl-Alt-Del command to a client computer to reboot it, so SMS provides a remote reboot function. You simply choose the Remote Reboot button, and you'll get the confirmation box shown in figure 13.9. When you choose the Yes button, SMS will send the signal to the client computer, and that computer will acknowledge the request (see fig. 13.10) and immediately reboot. Of course, you'll have to reconnect to it when it comes back.

Remote Chat Choosing the Remote Chat button opens up a two-way chat window on your SMS workstation and a similar window on the client computer. Everything you type in the local user window appears in the remote user window on the client computer, and vice versa. Figure 13.11 shows an example chat session.

File Transfer SM File Transfer enables you to copy files to and from a client computer. Suppose we wanted to send a particular .DLL file to a client computer. First, choose the File Transfer button, and you'll see a screen similar to figure 13.12.

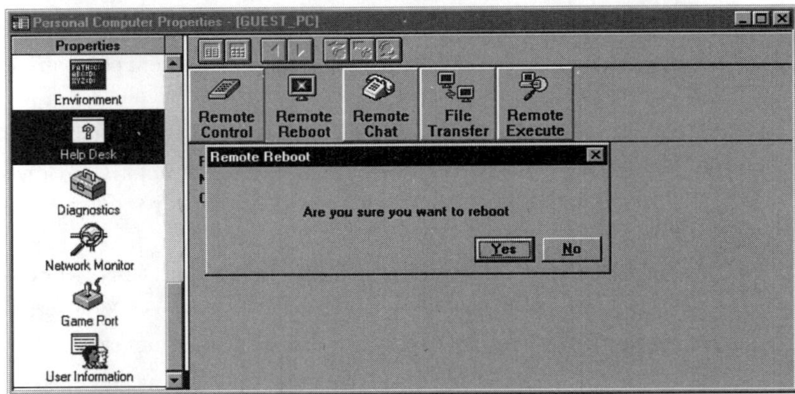

FIG. 13.9
Performing a remote reboot on a client computer.

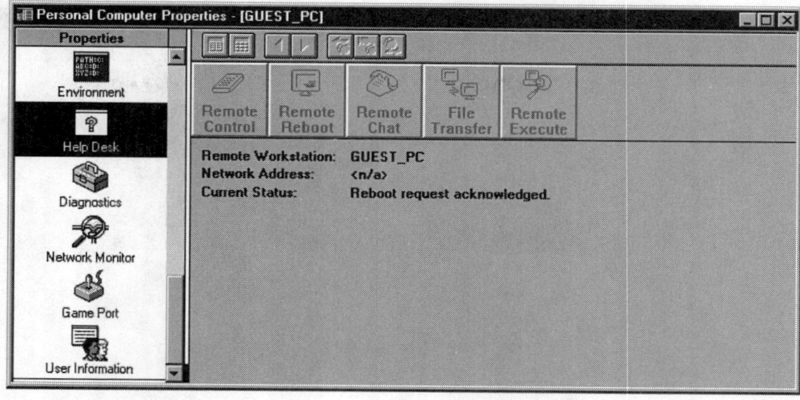

FIG. 13.10
A successful remote reboot.

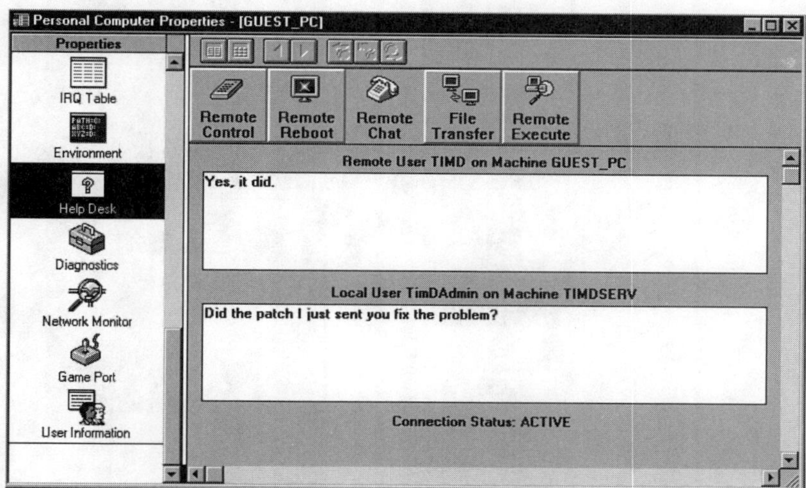

FIG. 13.11
A chat session.

Now we'll change the file mask to make it easier to zoom in on the file we want. Choose the File Masks button, and you'll get the dialog box shown in figure 13.13. Select the line *.*, choose the Modify button, and then type *.DLL in the input box (see fig. 13.13). Choose OK twice to change the file mask.

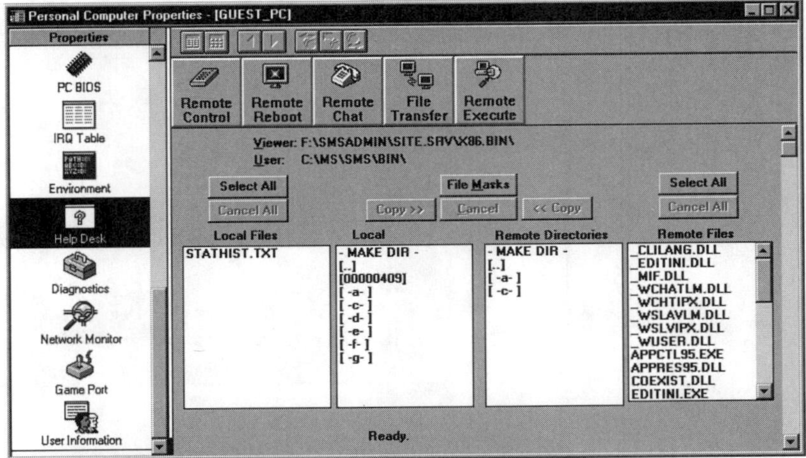

FIG. 13.12
Transferring a file from the SMS Administrator workstation to a client computer.

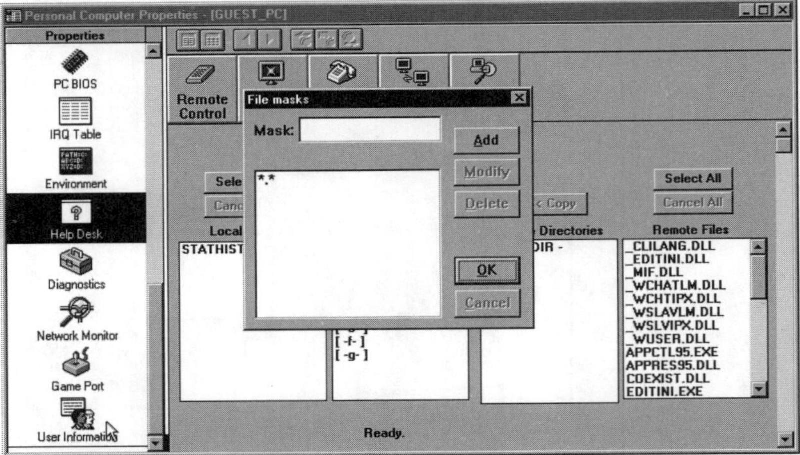

FIG. 13.13
Changing the file mask.

Using the Local drive and directory selection box, we'll change the local path to F:\COLLWIN and select the file we want to copy, as shown in figure 13.14. Using the Remote drive and directory selection box, we'll change the remote path to C:\ and double-click the MAKE DIR selection. This brings up an input box that we've filled in with the name of the directory we want to create (see fig. 13.15).

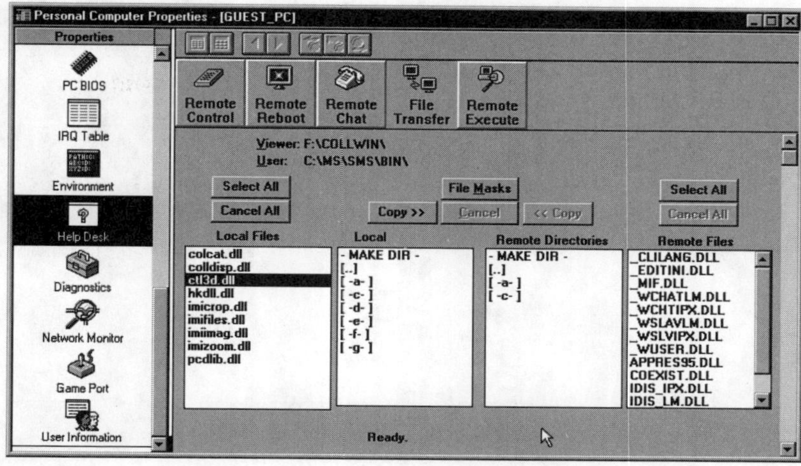

FIG. 13.14
Selecting the local file CTL3D.DLL.

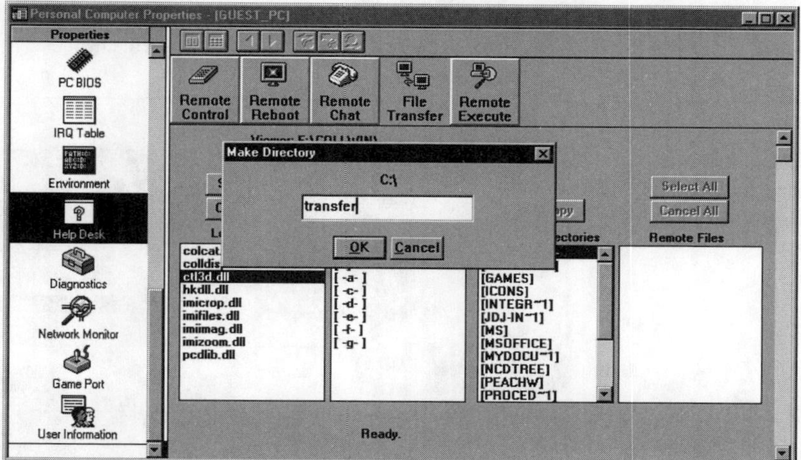

FIG. 13.15
Creating the directory C:\TRANSFER on the remote PC.

Finally, we change the remote path to C:\TRANSFER and choose the COPY >> button. Figure 13.16 shows that the file has been copied.

Remote Execute You can execute a program on a client computer. When you do this, you won't see the results unless you open a remote control session. SMS will let you know if there was a problem running the program. To see how this works, choose the Remote Execute button. This brings up the Run Program at User's Workstation dialog box. Figure 13.17 shows this dialog box filled in with the program we want to run.

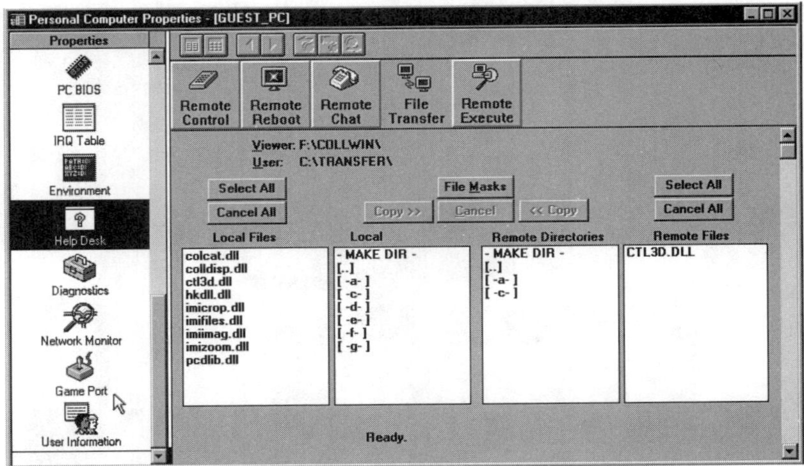

FIG. 13.16
Completing the file copy.

Remote Execute uses the PATH environment variable on the client computer to find the program. It's a good idea to fill in the full path to the executable to be sure you get the right one. Also, Remote Execute doesn't recognize long file names.

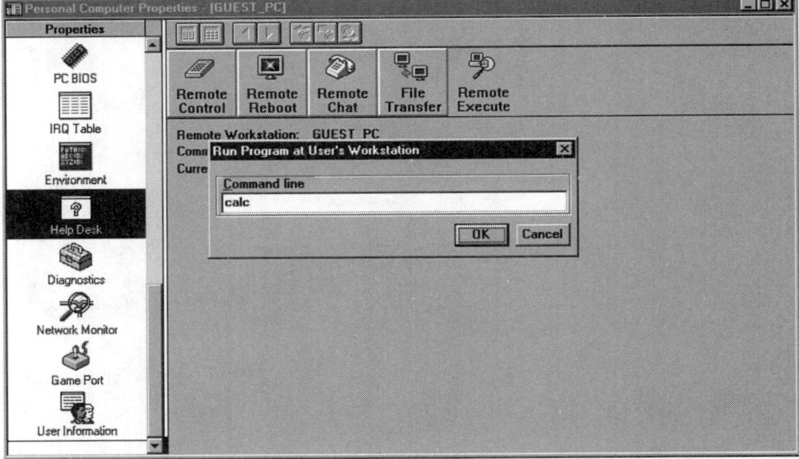

FIG. 13.17
Running the Windows Calculator program on a remote PC.

Choose OK to run the program. Figure 13.18 shows the response from SMS for a program that executed correctly.

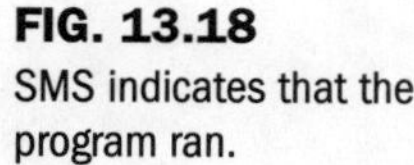

FIG. 13.18
SMS indicates that the program ran.

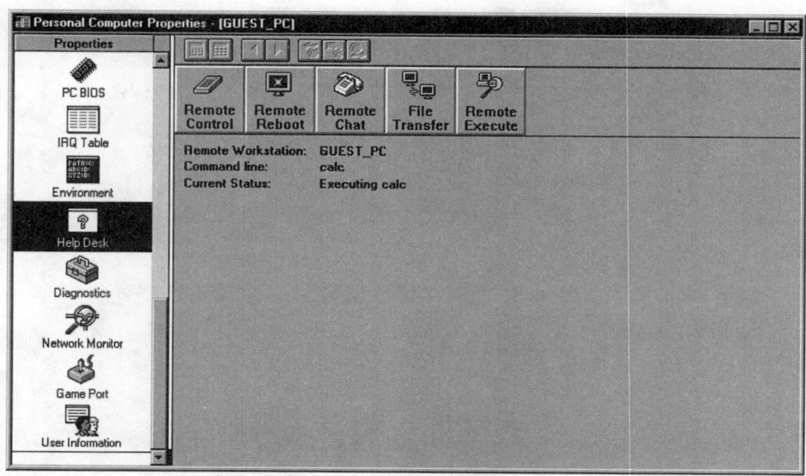

Supported Clients Help Desk and Remote Diagnostic functions are supported on DOS and all Windows clients, including Windows 95 and Windows NT. They are not supported on Macintosh clients.

Supported Protocols Help Desk and Remote Diagnostic functions are supported on the protocols NetBEUI, TCP/IP, and IPX only. The SMS workstation and the client computer must have at least one of these protocols in common.

Client Setup and Options The client software required to execute both Help Desk and Remote Diagnostic tools is automatically installed during the client setup process that occurs when the client computer first logs on to an SMS logon server. The following client components are required:

- Remote Support TSR—either USERTSR.EXE (for NetBEUI or TCP/IP support) or USERIPX.EXE (for IPX support). It is usually started automatically on a client computer.
- Remote Control Agent (Windows Clients)—the program that sends display updates to the SMS workstation and enables control of the keyboard and mouse on the client computer. This program (WUSER.EXE) must be run manually by the user to enable Help Desk or Remote Diagnostic functions. It is included in the SMS Client program group. Figure 13.19 shows the window that indicates that the Remote Control Agent is running.
- Help Desk Options—gives the user ultimate control over which functions the administrator is allowed to perform on the user's computer. This program is included in the SMS Client program group. Figure 13.20 shows the dialog box that you use to view and modify the Help Desk Options.

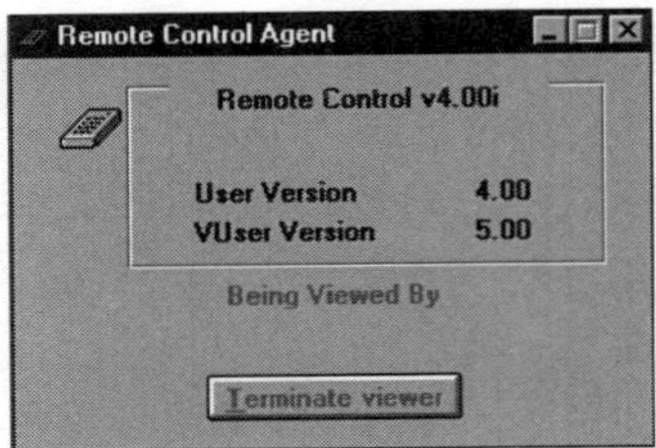

FIG. 13.19
Running the Remote Control Agent.

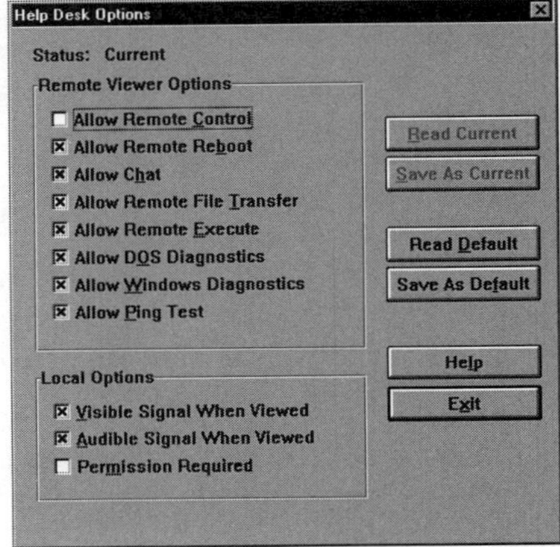

FIG. 13.20
Viewing the Help Desk Options.

Note that the Help Desk Options dialog box controls both Help Desk and Remote Diagnostic functions. The following options are available:

- Allow Remote Control—enables the administrator to view the client computer's display and manipulate the keyboard and mouse.
- Allow Remote Reboot—enables the administrator to reboot the client computer.
- Allow Chat—enables the administrator to initiate a chat session.
- Allow Remote File Transfer—enables the administrator to transfer files between the client computer and the SMS workstation.
- Allow Remote Execute—enables the administrator to execute a program on the client computer.
- Allow DOS Diagnostics—enables the administrator to perform DOS diagnostics (CMOS Info, Device Drivers, ROM Info, Interrupt Vectors, and DOS Memory).
- Allow Windows Diagnostics—enables the administrator to perform Windows diagnostics (Windows Memory, Windows Modules, Windows Tasks, Windows Classes, Global Heap, and GDI Heap).
- Allow Ping Test—enables the administrator to perform the ping test.
- Visible Signal When Viewed—provides a visual signal to the user when the administrator attempts to access the client computer.

- Audible Signal When Viewed—provides an audible signal to the user when the administrator attempts to access the client computer.
- Permission Required—provides an additional level of control. If activated, a confirmation dialog box pops up on the user's screen whenever the administrator attempts to access the client computer. The user can then decide whether or not to allow access.

Running Diagnostics on a Remote PC

The Diagnostics tool can give you an amazing amount of very detailed information about a client computer. It's all real-time information that can be very useful for solving computer problems: everything from CMOS settings to Windows Heaps. Both DOS and Windows diagnostics are available, and you also get a network connection test (the ping test).

Connecting to the Remote PC

Connecting to the remote PC for remote diagnostics is very similar to connecting to run Help Desk. As with the Help Desk connection, you must have a continuous network connection to the remote PC, your SMS workstation and the client computer must have at least one network protocol in common, the client computer must be configured to permit remote diagnostics, and the remote control agent must be running. If all of these requirements are satisfied, then making the connection should be easy. The following tells you how to do it:

1. In the SMS Administrator, open the Sites window and select the client computer you want to connect to, as shown in figure 13.1.
2. Double-click the selected client computer to bring up its Properties window. Then select the Diagnostics icon in the Properties list box. This causes SMS to attempt to connect to the selected client computer. You'll see the message "Attempting to locate ___" and possibly the subsequent message "Trying additional protocols," and then the grayed icons will become available as an indication that you have successfully connected, as shown in figure 13.21.

From here, you have 12 different remote diagnostic functions you can use. We'll examine each of them.

Viewing the Diagnostic Information

Each diagnostic is represented by a button in the Personal Computer Properties window. To access a particular diagnostic, choose its button and wait for the screen of data to appear. There are five DOS diagnostics (CMOS Info, Device Drivers, ROM Info, Interrupt Vectors, and DOS Memory), six Windows diagnostics (Windows Memory, Windows Modules, Windows Tasks, Windows Classes, Global Heap, and GDI Heap), and the ping test.

CMOS Info CMOS is a small amount of battery-powered RAM in each PC that contains disk, memory, ports, and other configuration information. If this information is incorrect, the PC may not start or may have other problems. Figure 13.22 shows a typical CMOS information screen.

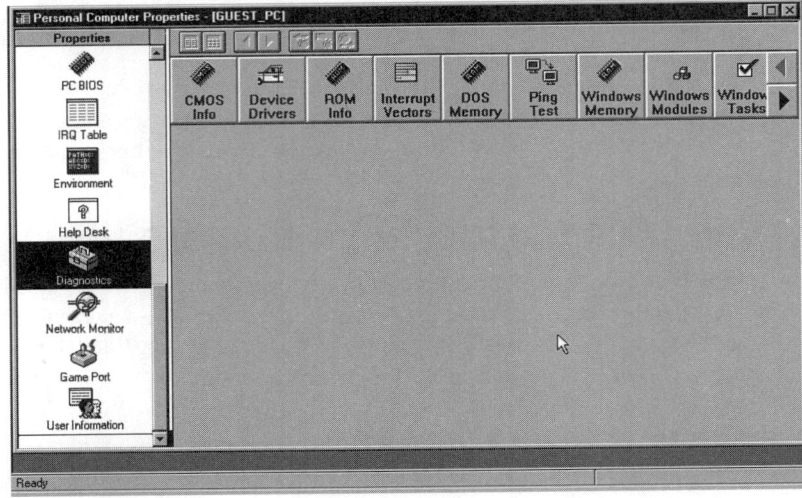

FIG. 13.21 A successful remote diagnostics connection.

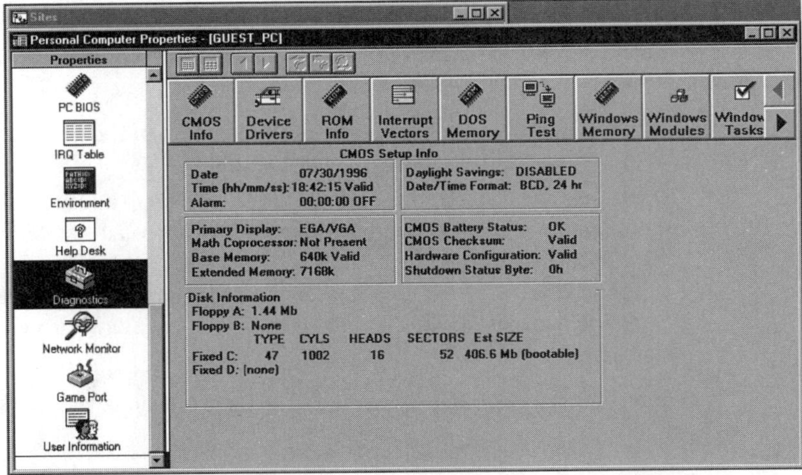

FIG. 13.22 Viewing CMOS info.

NOTE Only IBM PC/AT compatibles or later models contain CMOS. Also, the fields that SMS recognizes are not necessarily supported on every PC.

The fields that SMS looks for are:

- Date—current date in the PC's internal clock;
- Time—current time in the PC's internal clock;
- Alarm;
- Daylight Savings—enabled or disabled;

- Date/Time Format—12 or 24 hour;
- Primary Display—the type of video card (set to EGA/VGA for all modern video cards);
- Math Coprocessor—indicates whether one is present;
- Base Memory—amount of conventional memory (most machines will show 640 KB);
- Extended Memory—amount of extended memory installed;
- CMOS Battery Status—indicates the condition of the CMOS battery;
- CMOS Checksum—results of the CMOS checksum test;
- Hardware Configuration—indicates the status of CMOS memory;
- Shutdown Status Byte—affects the way 80286-based PCs switch from protected mode to real mode;
- Floppy Disk Information—installed floppy drives and their drive letters;
- Fixed Disk Information—reports the type code, number of cylinders, number of heads, number of sectors per track, and estimated size (in megabytes) for each installed hard drive.

NOTE Hard drive information for Micro Channel PCs or PCs with SCSI drives is not stored in CMOS. ■

Device Drivers Device drivers are relatively small programs that reside in memory and control the various hardware components within the PC. The Device Driver diagnostic lists the device drivers running on the client computer, along with some detailed information about each one, as shown in figure 13.23.

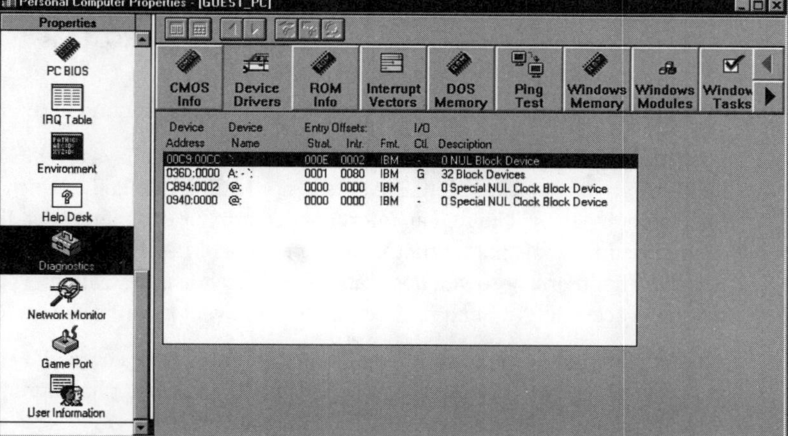

FIG. 13.23
Viewing Device Driver info.

The Device Driver diagnostic reports the following items for each device driver:

- Device Address—starting address in memory
- Device Name—name of the driver
- Entry Offset of Strategy Routine—the (offset) starting address of the driver's strategy routine
- Entry Offset of Interrupt—the (offset) starting address of the driver's interrupt routine
- Format-indicates support for IBM-compatible disk media. "IBM" in this field indicates support. A dash indicates no support
- I/O Ctl—indicates support for generic I/O Ctl functions. The four possible values are:

Value	Meaning
-	No support for generic I/O Ctl functions
G	Generic I/O Ctl functions supported
Y	Nongeneric I/O Ctl functions supported
B	Generic and nongeneric I/O Ctl functions supported

- Description—identifies a device driver as a block or character device, and may contain other information from the device driver header.

ROM Info The ROM Info diagnostic identifies and provides details on each ROM chip in a client computer. This typically includes the Video ROM and the System BIOS ROM, as shown in figure 13.24. In the list box, you'll typically see the ROM name, the memory address, and the size (in kilobytes). When you select a particular ROM, you'll get the following additional information:

- Hooked Interrupt Vectors—the interrupts that the ROM has "hooked" (it supplies its own interrupt handling routines for these);
- ROM Strings—lists all printable ASCII text strings found in the ROM chip.

Interrupt Vectors The Interrupt Vectors diagnostic displays the MS-DOS table that contains all hardware and software interrupts (see fig. 13.25). This is the table that is consulted during execution of an application if an interrupt occurs. For each interrupt, the table provides the memory address of an interrupt handling routine. MS-DOS actually provides many of the interrupt handlers; however, applications can provide their own interrupt handlers and modify this table accordingly. Such redirected interrupt vectors are referred to as "hooked."

The first column in each row identifies the four interrupts covered by that row, and the next four columns identify the memory locations of the interrupt handlers for those four interrupts.

DOS Memory The DOS Memory diagnostic lists all programs currently loaded in the first 1 MB of memory on the client computer. In the list box, there is a single line for each program, and each line contains three items: the starting address in memory, the size of the program (in bytes), and the name of the program, if available (some programs don't make their names available). Figure 13.26 shows a typical DOS Memory diagnostic screen.

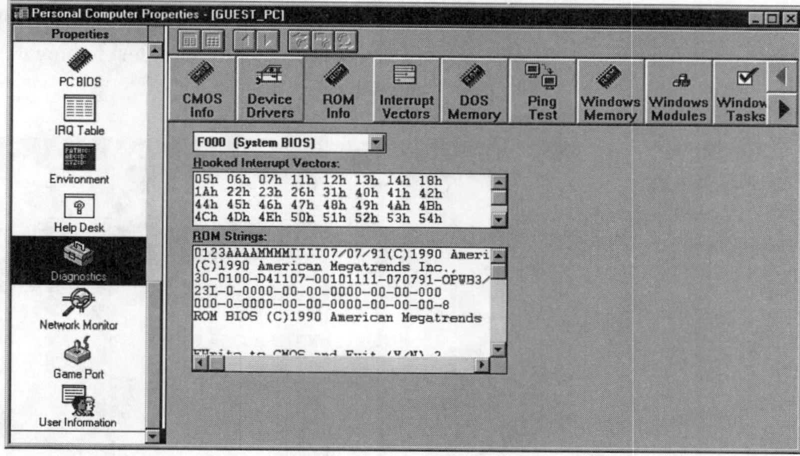

FIG. 13.24
Viewing System BIOS ROM details.

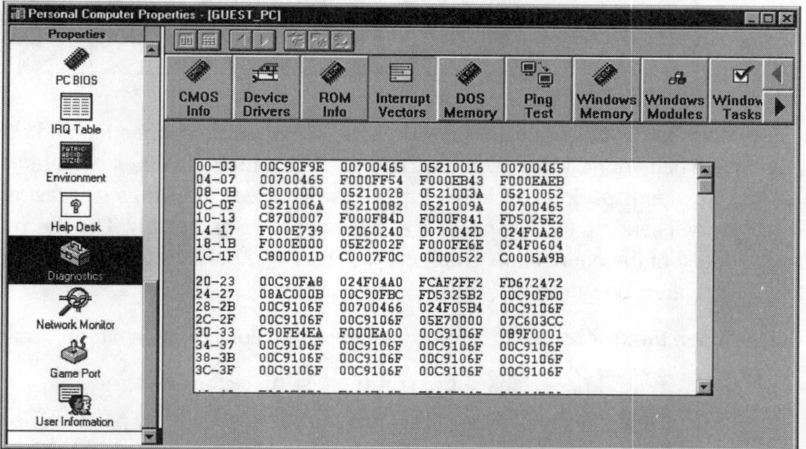

FIG. 13.25
Viewing Interrupt Vector details.

When you make a selection in the list box, you get the following detailed information about the program:

- Hooked Interrupt Vectors—a list of interrupt vectors that point to the program (the program has hooked these interrupts)
- Parent Process ID—if the program was executed by another program, that program is its parent, and this field identifies the process ID of the parent
- Environment Segment—the segment address for the program's environment memory block
- File Handle Count—the maximum number of file handles (open files) that program can have simultaneously

- File Handles At—the (offset) starting address of the program's file handle table
- File Handles Box—a list of the program's files handles. Each value represents an offset into the MS-DOS master file table.

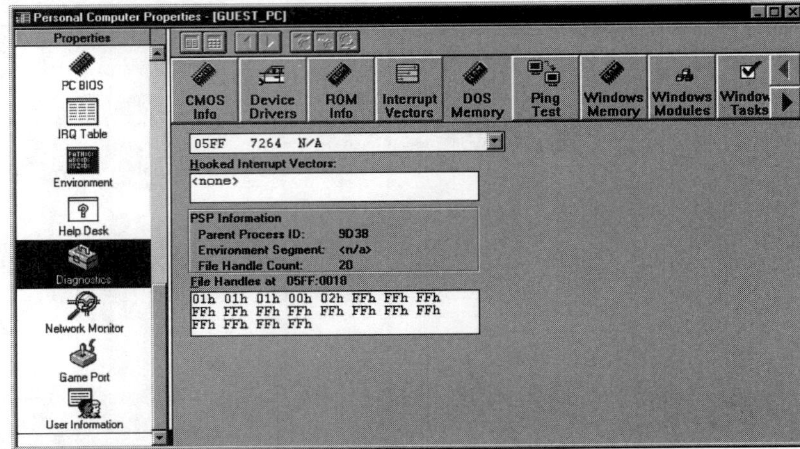

FIG. 13.26
Viewing DOS Memory details

Ping Test The ping test measures the speed of the connection and quality of the connection between your SMS workstation and a client computer. When you choose the Ping Test button, SMS sends packets back and forth between the two machines as fast as possible. The diagnostic will send up to 1000 packets and then stop automatically. The thermometer displays the speed of the connection graphically. Figure 13.27 shows the results of a ping test between two machines on the same Ethernet segment.

When the test has completed, you'll get the following information:

- Test Time—elapsed time for the test (in seconds)
- Total Packets—total number of round trips made by packets. Sending a packet from the SMS workstation to the client computer and getting a packet in response counts as one round trip
- Packets/Second (Current)—number of packets per second measured over the last time period
- Packets/Second (Average)—average number of packets per second measured since the start of the test
- Total Errors—total number of packet errors observed during the test

Windows Memory The Windows Memory diagnostic shows the utilization of memory under Windows on the client computer. As figure 13.28 shows, the diagnostic breaks down memory usage into a number of useful categories. You get details on the following:

- Largest Free Block—the largest block of contiguous linear memory (in bytes), composed of both free RAM and unused swap file space;

- Windows Memory (Locked)—amount of memory in use by processes
- Windows Memory (Unlocked)—amount of memory that can be swapped to disk
- Windows Memory (Free)—amount of memory that is not currently allocated
- Swap File—size of the swap file (temporary or permanent) and the amount that is currently in use
- System Heaps—percentage of heap space used by GDI.EXE (for graphics and printing) and USER.EXE (keyboard, mouse, and windows management).

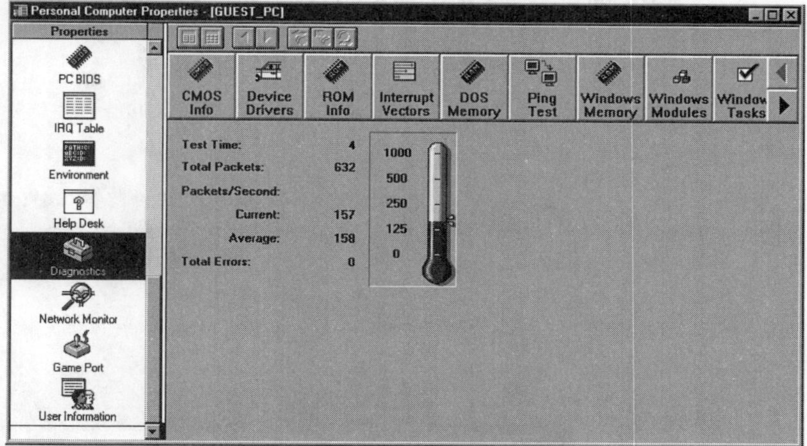

FIG. 13.27 Viewing the results of the Ping test

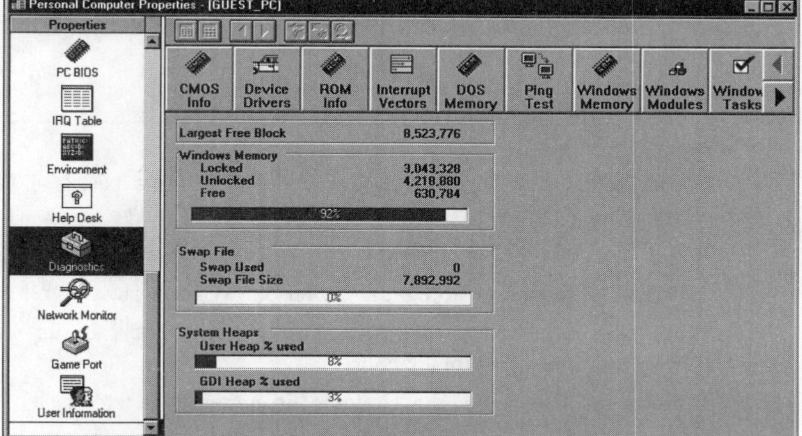

FIG. 13.28 Viewing Windows Memory details.

Windows Modules The Windows Modules diagnostic presents a list of .DLLs, drivers, and active applications running on the client computer. Figure 13.29 shows a typical display for this diagnostic. When you select a particular module in the list box, you get the following information for that module:

- Handle—a unique identifier that Windows uses to reference objects. The handle is typically an index into an internal table. Applications use handles to reference objects they want to manipulate instead of manipulating the object directly.
- Use Count—in Windows, a module can be in use by more than one process at once. The use count indicates how many processes are using the module.
- Path—the full directory path to the module.
- Memory Objects—a list of memory segments that are reserved for the module. The columns identify for each segment the starting memory address, the size (in bytes), and the type (code or data).

FIG. 13.29
Viewing the GDI Module details.

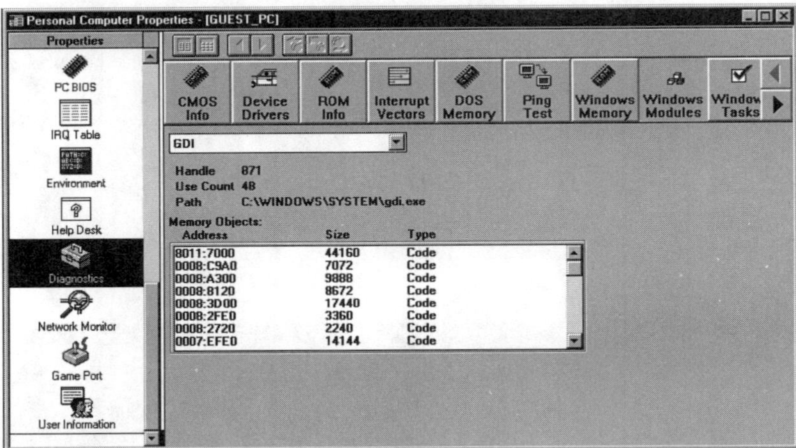

Windows Tasks The Windows Tasks diagnostic presents a list of all Windows programs running on the client computer (see fig. 13.30). When you select a particular task in the list box, you'll get the following details on it:

- Handle—the unique integer identifier that Windows uses to reference the task
- Instance—the address of this copy of the selected task. Under Windows, multiple copies of a task may run simultaneously.
- Module—the module that contains the currently selected task
- Queue Location—the starting memory address for the task's message queue. This is where all keyboard, mouse, and timer events that were directed at that task wait to be processed.
- Queue Size—the number of messages waiting for the task

- Events Waiting—the number of system events in the queue for the task.
- Current Dir—the directory containing the executable associated with the task.
- Command Line—the command line options specified when the program was run.

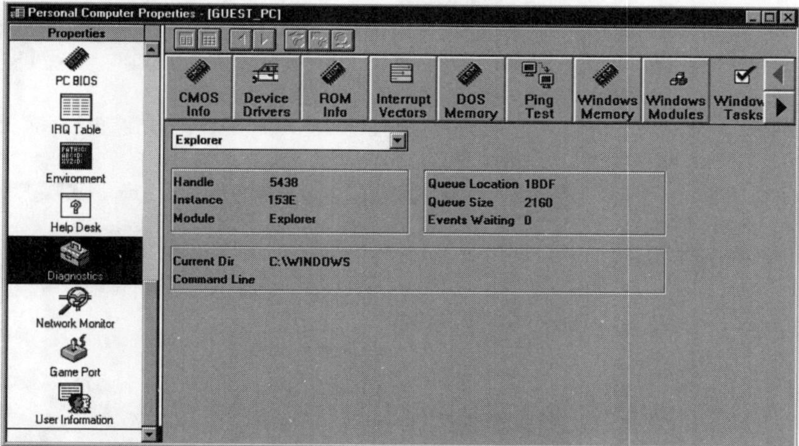

FIG. 13.30
Viewing the Explorer Task details.

Window Classes The Window Classes diagnostic lists all the active classes on the client computer. Examples of classes are scrollbar, button, and list box. Figure 13.31 shows a typical screen for this diagnostic. When you select a particular class in the list box, the diagnostic reports the following information:

- Style—the characteristics defined for the selected class
- Window Proc Address—the memory address of the process used for the selected class
- Extra Class Bytes—the number of extra bytes allocated at the end of the WNDCLASS structure created for the selected class
- Extra Window Bytes—the number of extra bytes allocated in the data structure that Windows maintains internally for a window created by a user's application
- Instance—the memory address of this instance (copy) of the selected class

Global Heap The global heap is a pool of memory that is managed by Windows and available to all applications. Each application can allocate blocks of memory from the global heap for its exclusive use. The Global Heap diagnostic lists all the allocated blocks and provides detailed information about each block (see fig. 13.32). In the list box, each entry includes the memory address of the allocated block and the program module that owns that block. When you select a memory block in the list box, you get the following additional information:

- Handle—the unique integer identifier that Windows uses to reference the memory block
- Address—the memory address of the first instance of the selected program module
- Size—the size of the memory block (in bytes)
- Lock Count—the number of processes that have a lock on the memory object

- Page Lock Count—the number of 64KB page frames locked within the memory block
- PDB Is Owner—this is Yes if the process data block (PDB) for the selected task is the owner of the selected memory object
- Has Local Heap—this is Yes if the memory block contains a local heap area
- Owner—the memory address of the module that the memory block is allocated to
- Object Type—the type of information stored in the memory block—types include code, data, unknown, and resource
- Contents—if the object type is resource, this identifies the type of resource

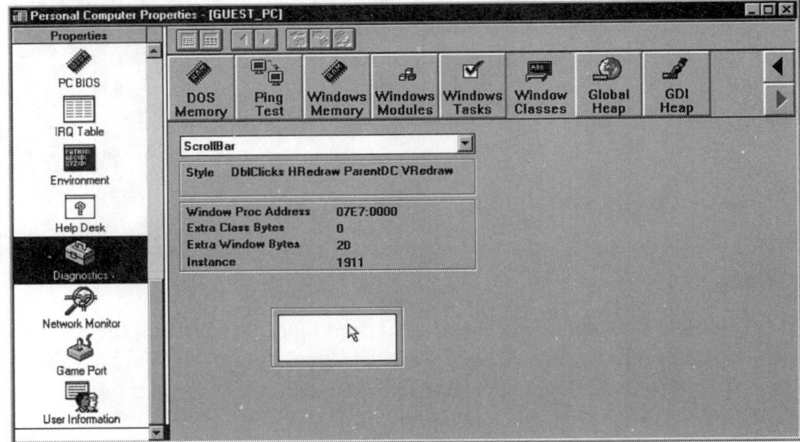

FIG. 13.31 Viewing details of the scrollbar class.

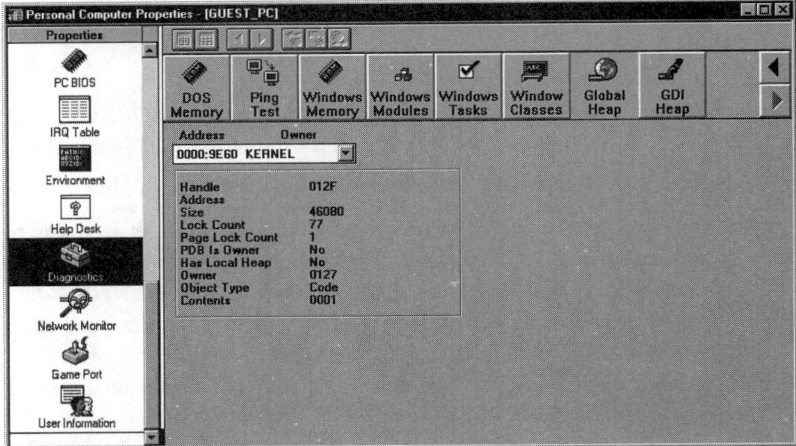

FIG. 13.32 Viewing details of the Global Heap.

GDI Heap The Graphical Device Interface (GDI) heap is a local heap reserved for the GDI. Every window created in Windows must be allocated some memory from the GDI heap. The GDI Heap diagnostic presents a list memory objects and details about each object's memory allocation (see fig 13.33). You can use either the Type or the Address list to select a memory object, and the size (in bytes) of each memory object is displayed in the list box. When you can select a memory object, you'll receive the following additional information:

- Handle—the unique integer identifier that Windows uses to reference the memory block
- Size—the size (in bytes) of the local memory object
- Flags—indicates that the memory object is fixed (resides in a fixed location), free (part of the free memory pool), or moveable (can be moved if necessary to compact memory)
- Lock Count—the number of processes that have a lock on the memory object
- Object Type—the type of information stored in the memory object (for example, BITMAP)

FIG. 13.33
Viewing details of the GDI Heap.

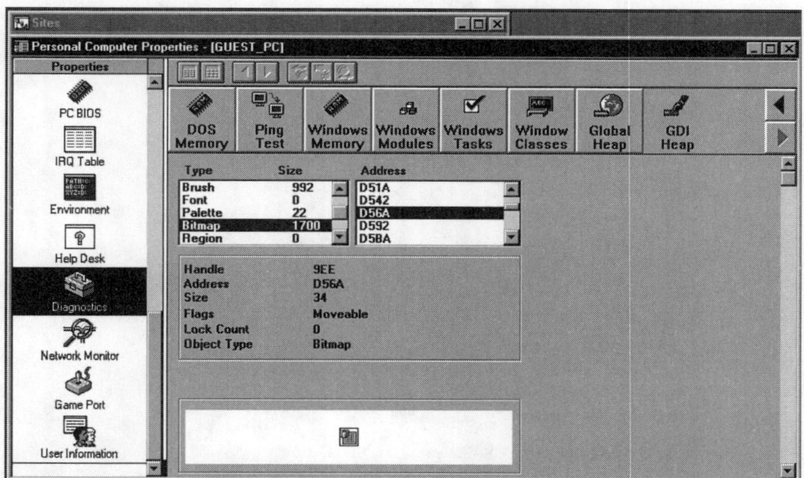

From Here...

- Chapter 23, "Investigating Remote PC Problems," presents examples of solving real problems on remote client computers using Help Desk and Remote Diagnostics tools.
- Chapter 8, "Using the SMS Administrator Program," covers all parts of the Administrator program.

CHAPTER 14

Using the Network Monitor

Network Monitor is one of the excellent real-time analysis tools that SMS provides. In many cases you can solve network problems by good intuition and deduction, but there are those times when there is simply no substitute for seeing the actual bytes that you're sending and receiving on the wire. You could go out and buy a Sniffer™ to do this (you may already have one, or a device like it), but you get one "free" with SMS! The Network Monitor does many of the same things a Sniffer™-like device does, and gives you the added convenience of being able to run it from your SMS administrator workstation. Do you want to view the individual packets that are flowing from workstation A to server B? And the responses from the server? And you only care about the one protocol that's causing problems? But what if this traffic is occurring on a network segment that your administrator workstation is not directly attached to? Network Monitor can handle all of these tasks and more. ■

Install and Configure Network Monitor

Network Monitor is one of the installation options in SMS setup. It's a stand-alone program that can be installed on any Windows NT machine.

Capture and View Packets on Your Workstation's LAN Segment(s)

Network Monitor's primary function is to receive and store in your workstation's memory a copy of every frame that passes over the network segment it is monitoring. After you've completed a capture you can view a list of the frames in time sequence, and Network Monitor will even decode the contents of the frames so you can easily view the protocol layers.

Capture and View Packets on Remote Network Segment(s)

By running Network Monitor Agents on remote machines, you can use your workstation to monitor network traffic on network segments that your workstation isn't directly attached to. We'll show you how to install the Network Monitor Agent and make the connection.

Setting up the Network Monitor

Network Monitor is one of the installation options in the SMS setup program. You can install it on the same machine on which you installed the SMS Administrator program, or you can install it on a different machine. It can be run as a stand-alone tool, or you can use it in conjunction with SMS Administrator, as you'll see later. Assuming you didn't select this option when you installed SMS, the following are the steps for installing Network Monitor:

1. From the BackOffice CD-ROM, run the SMS setup program which brings up the Installation Options dialog box shown in figure 14.1.

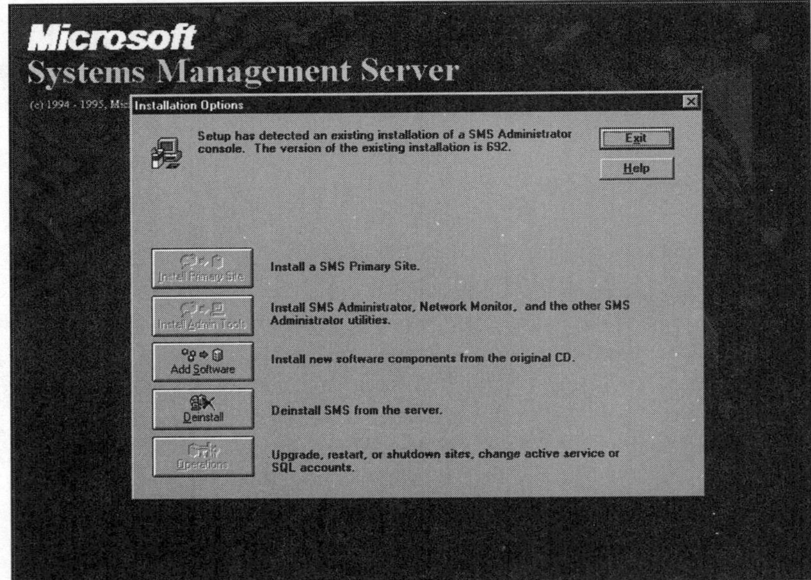

FIG. 14.1 Installing the Network Monitor.

2. Choose the Add Software button. This brings up the Software Installation Options dialog box shown in figure 14.2.

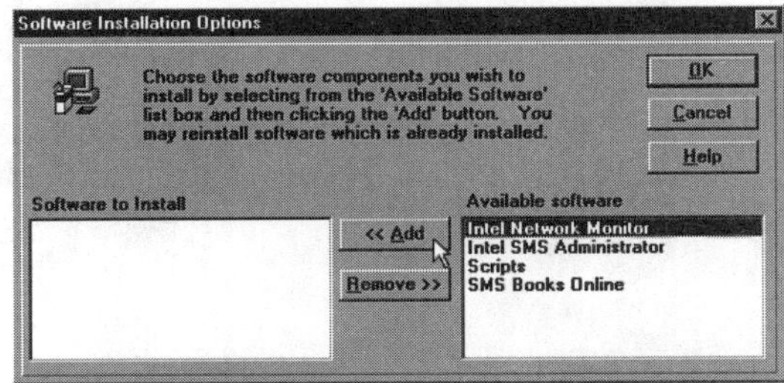

FIG. 14.2 Choose Intel Network Monitor from the listed options.

3. In the Available software column, select Intel Network Monitor, choose the Add button, and choose the OK button.
4. Setup will copy files and then present the informational dialog box shown in figure 14.3, if Network Monitor Agent needs to be installed. When you choose OK to continue, the Network dialog box will appear, as shown in figure 14.4.

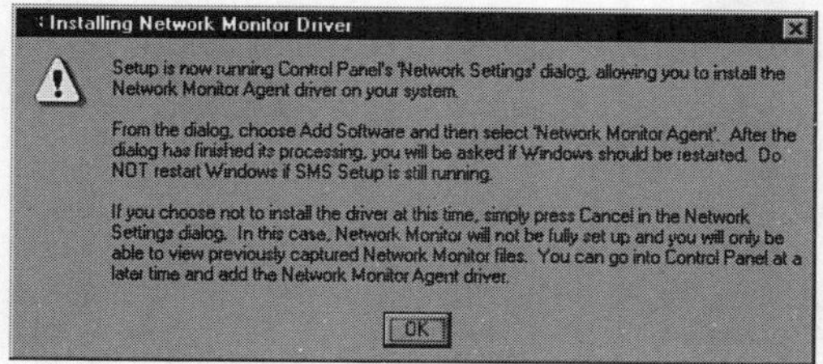

FIG. 14.3
This appears if you don't have the Network Monitor Agent installed.

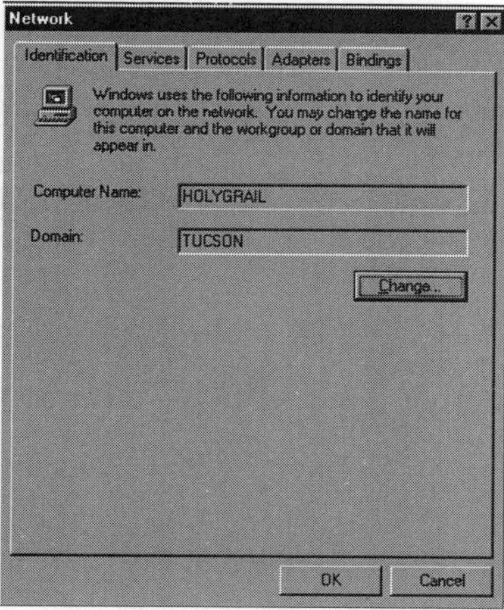

FIG. 14.4
Installing the Network Monitor Agent.

5. Click the Services tab, then the Add button. Select Network Monitor Agent or Network Monitor Tools and Agent, and choose the OK button, as shown in figure 14.5.
6. NT will return to the Network dialog box. Note that Network Monitor Agent will be listed in the Protocols section, not the Services section. Choose the Close button to allow NT to reconfigure bindings. A dialog box will appear asking if you want to restart your computer now. Choose the No button.
7. Switch back to SMS setup and close the program. Then manually shut down and restart Windows NT.
8. This completes the Network Monitor installation. Upon restarting, you should have SMS Network Monitor in your Systems Management Server program group and you should have a Monitoring Agent icon in the Control Panel.

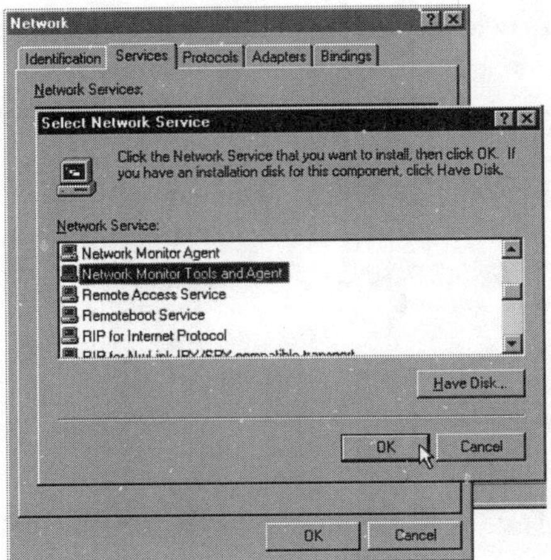

FIG. 14.5
Selecting Network Monitor Agent from the list of services.

Starting the Network Monitor

Network Monitor can be started from its icon in the Systems Management Server group or from the command line. Starting Network Monitor from the command line allows you to specify parameters that affect how it starts up. Start Network Monitor by double-clicking its icon, and you'll see the screen shown in figure 14.6.

NOTE By default, all four panes are displayed. You can toggle any of them to display or not, and you can zoom a pane to full size and back to its current size. ■

You can start Network Monitor from the command prompt as follows:

1. Change directory to the Network Monitor subdirectory. On an Intel machine, the path will be something like \SMSADMIN\NETMON\X86.
2. Issue the command "start netmon [options]." The options are:

   /REMOTE *computername*—Network Monitor connects to a computer you specify that is running Network Monitor Agent.

   /NET *number*—Network Monitor connects to the network number you specify. These numbers refer to the networks your Network Monitor workstation is attached to. They can be obtained from the dialog box that comes up when you select Capture... from the menu bar and then Networks.

   /CAPTUREFILTER *path*—Network Monitor loads the specified capture filter.

   /DISPLAYFILTER *path*--Network Monitor loads the specified display filter.

   /BUFFERSIZE *number*—Network Monitor starts with this capture buffer size.

   /AUTOSTART—Network Monitor starts with capturing turned on.

/QUICKFILTER *type, address*—Network Monitor starts with a capture filter set to the specified address. Sample types are ETHERNET, TOKENRING, and FDDI, and the address is a hexadecimal string.

/AUTOSTOP—Network Monitor automatically stops when its capture buffer is full.

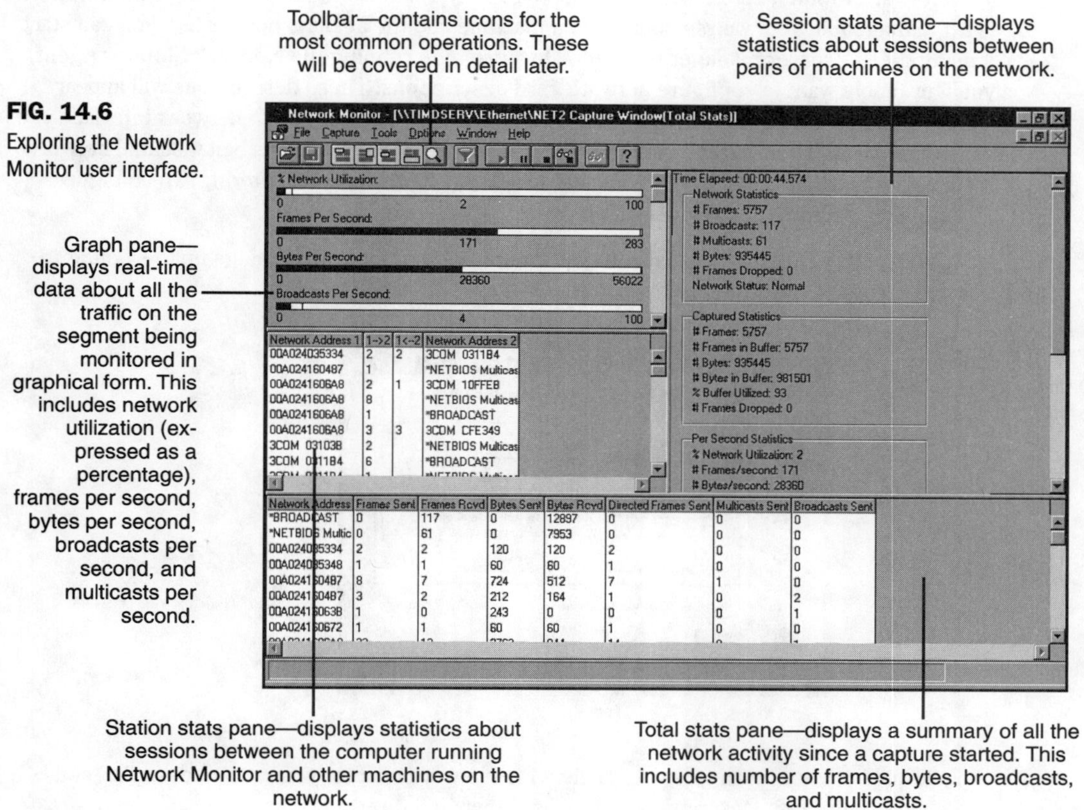
Toolbar—contains icons for the most common operations. These will be covered in detail later.
Session stats pane—displays statistics about sessions between pairs of machines on the network.
Network Monitor - [\\TIMDSERV\Ethernet\NET2 Capture Window(Total Stats)]
Graph pane—displays real-time data about all the traffic on the segment being monitored in graphical form. This includes network utilization (expressed as a percentage), frames per second, bytes per second, broadcasts per second, and multicasts per second.
Station stats pane—displays statistics about sessions between the computer running Network Monitor and other machines on the network.
Total stats pane—displays a summary of all the network activity since a capture started. This includes number of frames, bytes, broadcasts, and multicasts.

FIG. 14.6 Exploring the Network Monitor user interface.

Network Monitor Agent

The Network Monitor Agent is a service that is included with both Windows NT and Windows 95. You can install it completely separately from SMS and Network Monitor. The Network Monitor Agent enables you to monitor traffic on any network segment, but its main purpose is to monitor LAN segments that your workstation is not directly attached to.

NOTE Network Monitor Agent does not have to be started on your workstation in order to capture packets on local LAN segments using that workstation's net card(s). ■

You simply set up a machine running the Network Monitor Agent on the remote segment of interest and connect to it using the copy of Network Monitor on your workstation. Network Monitor Agent performs the packet capture and sends the results back to your workstation (the capture frame stays in the buffer of the remote machine). Of course, your workstation must have network connectivity to the machine running Network Monitor Agent, but the point is that now your workstation will see traffic that normally wouldn't appear on your LAN segment, because the segments are separated by a router, for example.

The Network Monitor Agent service is not started by default, and its NT startup configuration is set to manual. If you want to connect to a machine and the agent is not started, you can start it using the NT server manager program. On a machine running the Network Monitor Agent, you'll probably want to configure network card descriptions. These descriptions will appear when you try to connect to that machine, and will help you decide which network interface you want to monitor. If you haven't configured descriptions, all you'll see is a hexadecimal network address for each card, and it won't be clear which segment you're monitoring. To configure descriptions, perform the following steps:

1. In Control Panel, double-click the Monitoring Agent icon. This brings up the Configure Network Monitoring Agent dialog box shown in figure 14.7.

FIG. 14.7
Describing your network cards.

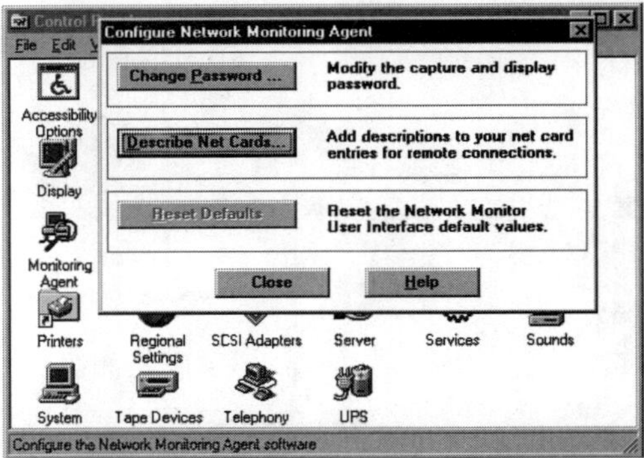

2. Choose Describe Net Cards ..., select the Network adapter you want to describe, and choose the Edit Description button, as shown in figure 14.8.

FIG. 14.8
Choosing the card you want to describe.

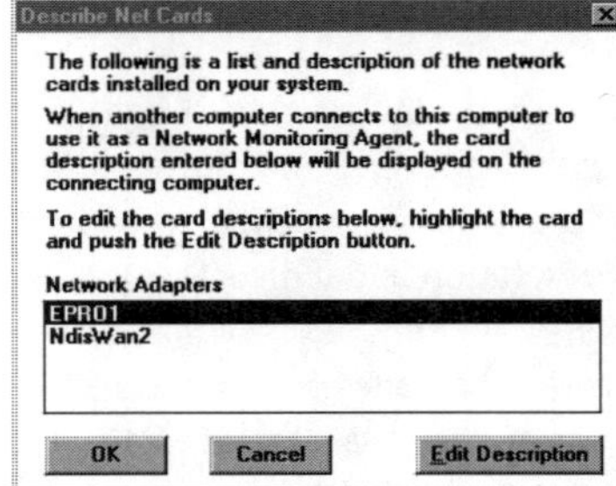

3. Enter a description for the card ("Development LAN," for example) and choose the OK button. Figure 14.9 shows that the net card has been tagged with that description. Now, when you connect to the agent on this machine, you can be sure that you are monitoring the network traffic you want.

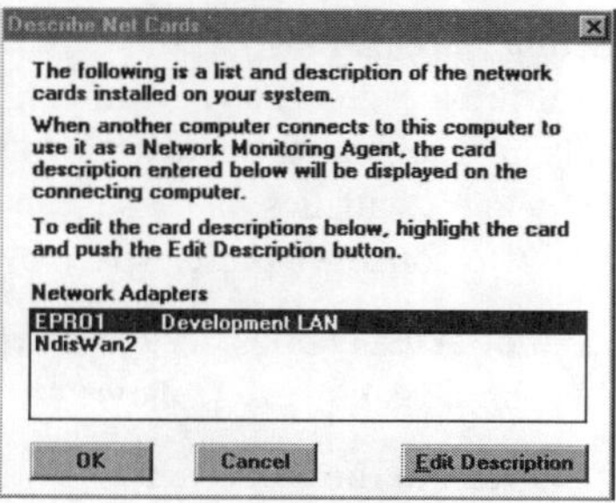

FIG. 14.9
Verifying your descriptions.

Capturing Network Traffic

The most common use for Network Monitor is capturing and viewing frames, so we'll start with that. For those unfamiliar with the basic concept, we'll present a brief tutorial and then refer you to some good books on networking concepts. It's generally assumed that you're pretty knowledgeable about networking before you pick up a tool like Network Monitor, but it's also true that Network Monitor can be a terrific learning tool, and it can tell you in no uncertain terms what is going on in your network.

The Basics

The typical corporate network has a wide variety of network protocols competing for the same wires. These protocols differ in the problems they solve and the data they handle, but they all have one thing in common—frames. Every modern protocol has provisions for taking the data that you are sending, be it an Excel spreadsheet or a mail message, and splitting it into a number of smaller pieces (or frames) prior to sending it out over the wire. It is these frames that Network Monitor is designed to capture and display for you. Of course, if it simply captured and displayed every single frame and did nothing else, you'd be left with the tedious job of sifting through the bytes trying to decode addresses and protocol frame types, and you'd soon give up. That's why Network Monitor is designed to understand a wide variety of the most popular network protocols. Once the data is captured, Network Monitor does all the hard decoding work for you. And to help you out even more, Network Monitor has capture filters that prevent certain packets from being captured in the first place, and display filters to weed out all but the most interesting frames from the ones that were captured.

Network Monitor relies on a feature of Network Driver Interface Specification (NDIS) 4.0 to enable it to capture every frame that is detected by your workstation's network card(s). Normally, a network card passes on only those frames that have your workstation as the destination address.

NOTE The Network Monitor drivers included in versions of Windows NT prior to 4.0 relied on a feature of certain network cards that allowed them to be placed in "promiscuous" mode. This mode enabled those network cards to pass on all detected frames to your workstation. The Windows NT 4.0 Network Monitor drivers will work with any network card. ■

Network Monitor sets aside its own memory area, known as the capture buffer, to store frames that it captures. This can't be changed during a capture, so it's important to size it properly beforehand. Once the capture buffer fills up, the default behavior is to start overwriting the earliest frames. Network Monitor will still keep statistics on these frames; it just won't store them for later viewing. Later, we'll see how to conserve buffer space by using capture filters.

To give you a feel for what Network Monitor actually does, let's jump right in and start capturing network traffic. We'll walk through a simple capture, as follows:

1. Start Network Monitor by selecting it from the Start menu.
2. From the toolbar choose the Start Capture button, or select this function from the Capture menu.
3. Network Monitor starts displaying counts of frames that it has detected, along with the source and destination addresses, as shown in figure 14.10. Your view will be slightly different depending on what type of network you're monitoring. The example in figure 14.10 shows statistics for an Ethernet segment.

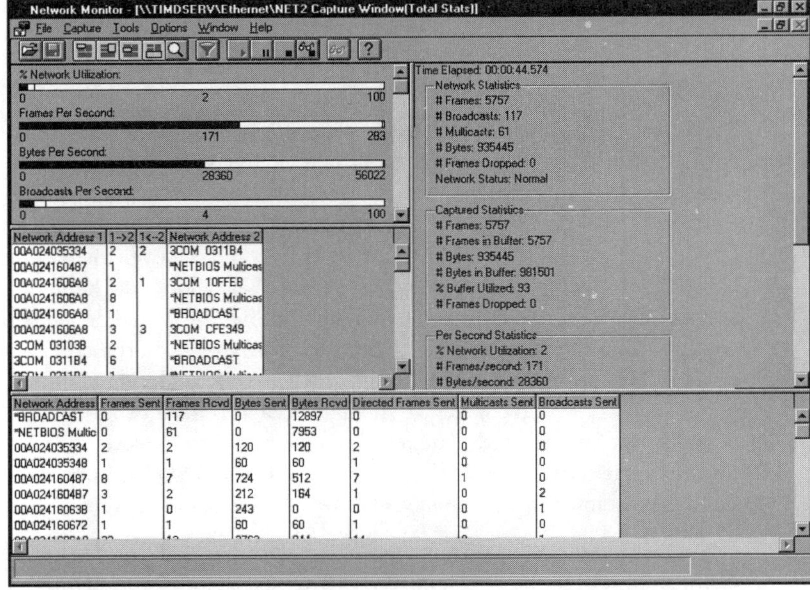

FIG. 14.10 Viewing a typical capture session.

Now that we're capturing, what can we do with all this data? When you are capturing, you can pause, stop, or stop and view. Let's pause by choosing the Pause button on the toolbar and look at what we've got so far. Figure 14.11 shows what the window looks like, and we can point out a few features here.

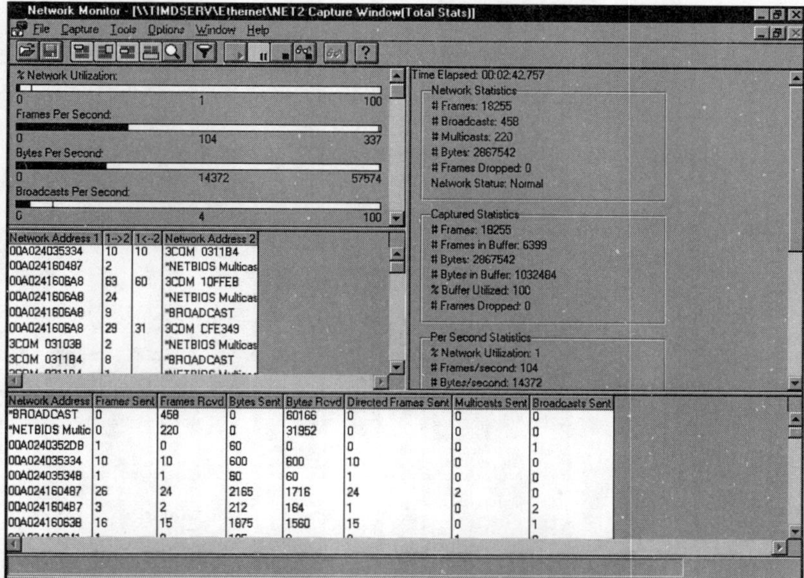

FIG. 14.11
Looking at a paused capture window.

In the Graph pane, each graph displays the current value for each statistic as a colored bar and as a numeric value in the center of the graph line. Note the thin vertical line on the % Network Utilization bar. Network Monitor displays these markers to indicate the peak value that has been measured for each statistic.

In the Session Stats and Station Stats panes, you can see that they've filled up quickly with Ethernet addresses. By default, these windows sort based on the first column, in ascending order. You can sort the window based on a different column by double-clicking that column's heading. The sort order is predefined as ascending for network addresses and descending for all other columns.

In the Total Stats pane, you'll see a variety of accumulated and real-time statistics. In particular, the Per Second Statistics section merely mimics the information in the Graph Pane. In the Network Statistics section, the Network Status applies only to Token Ring networks (for Ethernet, it's always Normal). In the Captured Statistics section, note that the % Buffer Utilized is 100 percent. This indicates that the capture buffer has filled. In the Network Card (MAC) Error Statistics section and the Network Card (MAC) Statistics section, you may see "Unsupported" next to some of the entries. This means that those particular statistics are not supported by your network card.

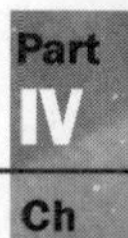

There are a number of things you can do while a capture window is paused. For example, you can change the capture filter if you see that you're not getting the traffic you'd like. You can also change the capture trigger. Unfortunately, you can't display the individual frames you've collected. You must always stop a capture in order to display frames. Now we're ready to look at some of the captured data.

Displaying Captured Data

Network Monitor requires you to stop a capture if you want to view specific frames. You can stop the capture by choosing the Stop Capture button on the toolbar or the Stop and View Capture button (which saves you a step if you want to immediately view the frames). To display the captured data, choose the Stop and View button. This brings up the Capture window with the Summary pane maximized, as shown in figure 14.12.

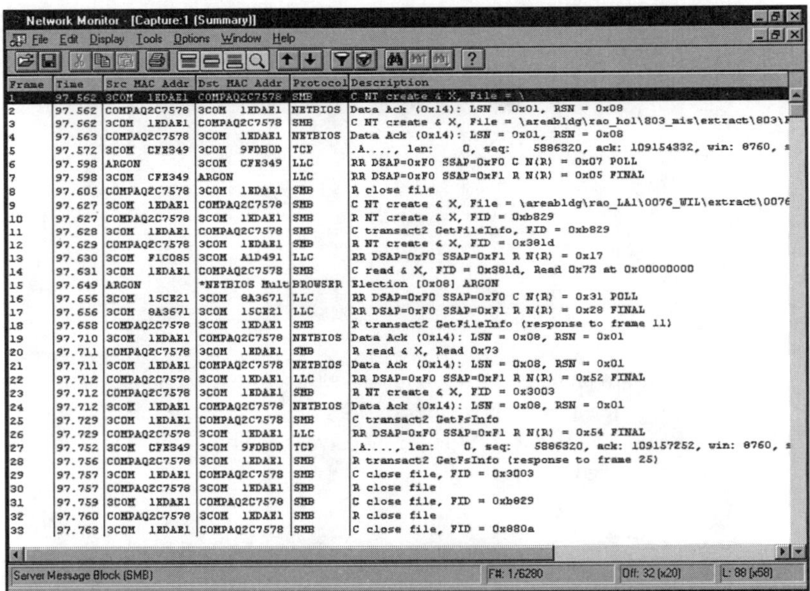

FIG. 14.12
Displaying the captured frames.

The Summary pane displays a list of all frames currently in the capture buffer in the order they were captured. This pane contains the following columns:

Column	Description
Frame	Sequence number for each frame.
Time	Time of capture for each frame (in Display Options, you can specify three different time references—Time of Day, Seconds from beginning of capture, and Seconds from previous frame).

Column	Description
Src MAC Addr	The MAC address of the machine that sent the frame. MAC address refers to the unique network address for each network card that is set by the manufacturer. For Ethernet, this is a 6-byte (or 12 hexadecimal digit) string.
Dst MAC Addr	The MAC address of the machine identified as the destination for the packet.
Protocol	The network protocol that generated the frame.
Description	A summary of the contents of each frame. This information varies depending on the protocol and type of frame.
Src Other Addr	The IP or IPX\XNS address of the source machine.
Dst Other Addr	The IP or IPX\XNS address of the destination machine.
Type Other Addr	The address type for Src Other Addr and Dst Other Addr (IP or IPX\XNS).

Besides the Summary pane, this window also contains the Detail pane and the Hex pane. If you "unzoom" the Summary pane by choosing the Zoom Pane button on the tool bar (or from the menu bar, Window, Zoom Pane), you'll see the other two windows, as shown in figure 14.13.

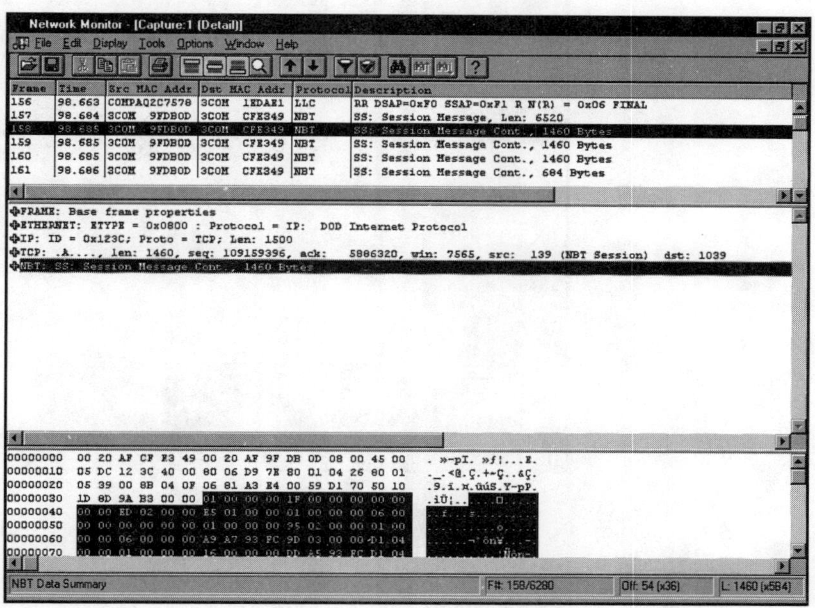

FIG. 14.13
Viewing the Summary, Detail, and Hex panes in the Capture window.

Notice in the Detail pane for frame 158 that a separate line is included for each network protocol layer, and that the protocol column in the Summary pane lists, by default, the highest level protocol (NBT for frame 158) that is contained in each packet. Network Monitor has decoded the 1,514 bytes that comprise frame 158 into its component protocols. And for each protocol, the Hex pane presents the byte level detail. In figure 14.13, you can see that, with the NBT line highlighted in the Detail pane, the bytes corresponding to that protocol layer are highlighted in the Hex pane. In the status line at the bottom of the window, Off: 54 (x36) indicates that the currently highlighted protocol (NBT) is offset from the beginning of the frame by 54 bytes and L: 1460 (x584) tells us that the length of the NBT portion of the frame is 1,460 bytes. Try clicking the different protocol layers in the Detail pane and see how the Hex pane changes. You can learn a lot about network packets this way.

If you click on the plus sign just to the left of each protocol in the Detail Pane, you'll see a list of detailed parameters that make up the protocol header. Again, you can highlight each one of these and see the byte(s) that govern that parameter. Additionally, a short description of the parameter will appear on the status bar at the bottom of the window.

One thing you'll want to do is assign names to all those cryptic MAC addresses. Network Monitor provides a single command to do this. From the menu bar, select Display, Find All Names. Figure 14.14 shows the result of the search.

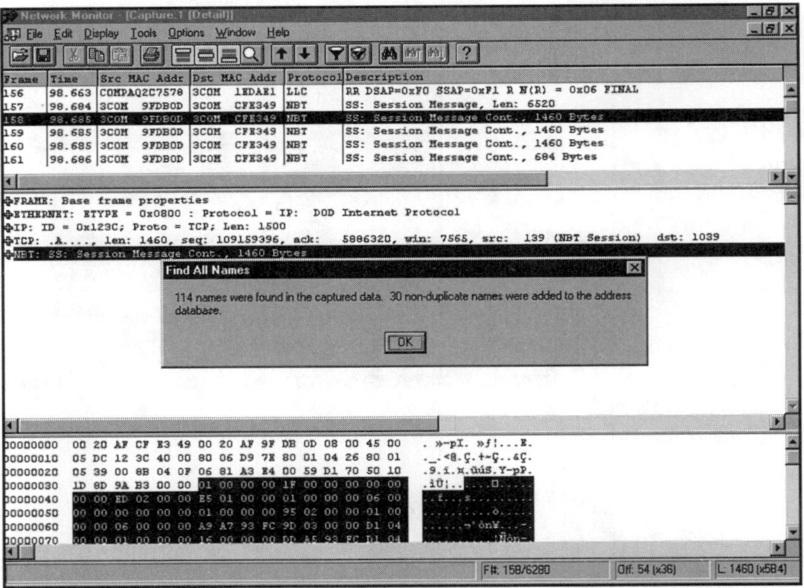

FIG. 14.14 Network Monitor tells you how many names it discovered.

After clicking OK, you can view the address database by selecting Display, Addresses. Figure 14.15 shows the list of addresses that have been found so far.

As you can see, for each address that it detects, Network Monitor identifies the machine name and the address type. There is also a comment field, which you can edit, and a type field, which gives the manufacturer of that particular network card. While we have the Address Database window open, let's explore some of its features.

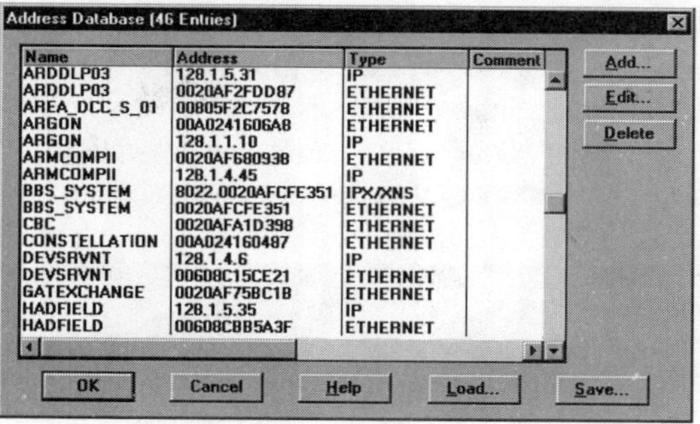

FIG. 14.15 You can view the database of addresses that Network Monitor has detected.

The Address Database Network Monitor creates an address database for each capture session. This database allows Network Monitor to display machine names in windows where a network address would normally be displayed. The database is updated whenever Network Monitor is able to associate a machine name with a network address. You can also manually add addresses that you know about to the database, and you can edit entries that Network Monitor has added. Finally, you can save the current database to a file for later use. Referring to figure 14.15 again, the Save... button brings up a dialog box that allows you to save the database as a file (with extension .ADR) to the directory you specify, along with an optional comment describing the file. The Load button allows you to open a previously saved address database file for the current session. The Edit button allows you to edit the information for the currently highlighted address. This is handy for entering a comment about a particular machine. Figure 14.16 shows an example of entering a comment for the machine Argon.

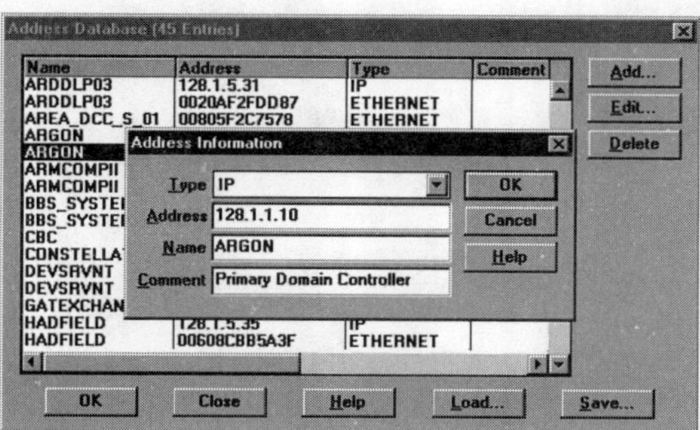

FIG. 14.16 This comment identifies Argon as the Primary Domain Controller.

The Add button lets you add your own addresses to the database using the dialog box shown in figure 14.16. Network Monitor checks to ensure that the address format you enter is appropriate for the address type you specify.

The rows in the Address Database window can be sorted by double-clicking the column heading of the column you want to sort. All columns are programmed to sort in ascending order.

Figure 14.17 shows the summary pane again, with machine names identified. If you want to view just the hexadecimal addresses, you can toggle the view using the Options menu. From the menu bar, uncheck Options, Show Address Names (to view hexadecimal addresses) and uncheck Options, Show Vendor Names (causes the vendor portion of the network address to display in hexadecimal). The summary pane now looks like figure 14.18.

FIG. 14.17
Now you can readily identify machines in the capture window.

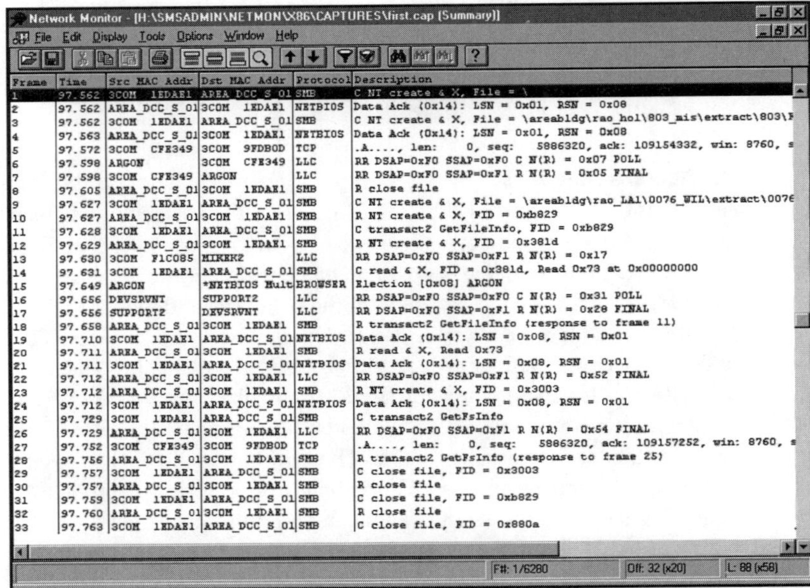

Navigating the Summary Pane Network Monitor provides a number of ways to move to a particular frame.

- To move to the previous frame, click the Up arrow button on the toolbar (or press Ctrl+Up, or select Display, Previous Frame).
- To move to the next frame, click the Down arrow button on the toolbar (or press Ctrl+Down, or select Display, Previous Frame).
- You can go to a particular frame if you know its sequence number by pressing F5 (or selecting Display, Goto Frame...). A dialog box will appear prompting you for the frame number.

These methods are fine for browsing, but usually you're looking for something specific. The Find command can perform a very detailed search that identifies the first packet that matches the criteria you specify. To execute a Find, perform the following steps:

1. In the summary pane, select a frame that you want to use as the starting point for the search.

2. Click the Edit Find Frame button on the toolbar (or press Alt+F3, or select Display, Find Next Frame...). This brings up the Find Frame Expression dialog box shown in figure 14.19.

3. Notice that the dialog box displays the protocol that was listed in the summary pane for the frame you selected in step 1. The Expression dialog box allows you to specify a filter criteria based on Address (both source and destination), Protocol, and Property (a byte-level criteria for searching frames). This same dialog box is also used to construct display filters. Let's examine it in more detail.

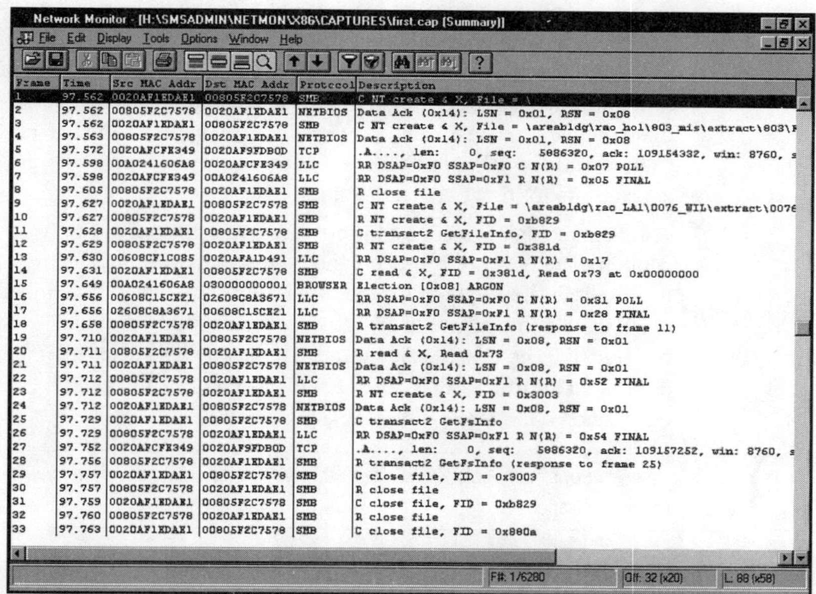

FIG. 14.18
You can toggle the way addresses are displayed.

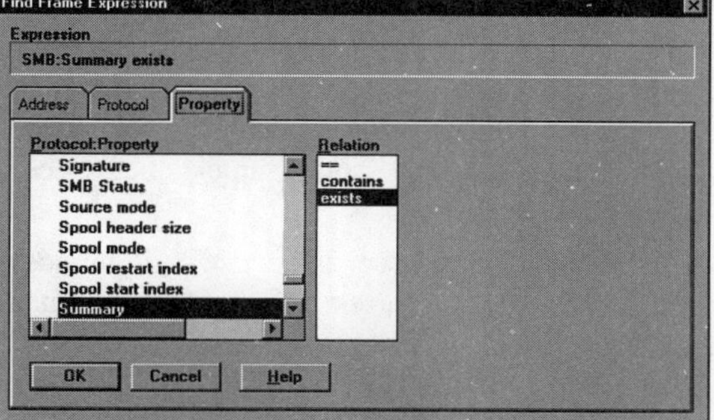

FIG. 14.19
Starting the Find Frame operation.

The Property tab enables you to base a search expression on a specific property of a particular protocol. The Protocol:Property column lists all the protocols that Network Monitor supports. By clicking on the plus sign to the left of a protocol, you can expand its listing to show all the individual properties making up that protocol. As we saw earlier, each one of these corresponds to a particular byte or sequence of bytes in a network frame containing that protocol. You construct a search expression by selecting the property you want, then the comparison operator from the Relation column, and finally the value to be used for comparison in the Value text box. As you scroll down through the different protocol properties, you'll see that the choices in the Relation column change, depending on what makes sense for the property you select. Also, the Value column will sometimes offer a discrete set of choices for you to select from or, in some cases, you'll have to enter a value and choose from a list of attributes. There are two radio buttons at the bottom of the Expression dialog box that let you specify the format that you want to use for entering comparison values. One is Hex (for hexadecimal values) and the other is either ASCII or Decimal (depending on whether or not ASCII is appropriate for that particular value).

The Protocol tab provides a higher-level search, based simply on whether or not a frame contains one or more protocols that you specify. You include a protocol in the search by moving it to the Enabled Protocols column. The dialog box defaults to all protocols enabled, which makes the search expression read "Protocol == Any." Usually you'll start by choosing the Disable All button. Then you can select the individual protocol(s) you're interested in from the Disabled Protocols column and click the Enable button. The expression changes as you enable protocols.

You can use Windows multi-select features in this window to select the protocols you want and then enable them all at once.

The Address tab allows you to search based on source and destination addresses in frames. You specify the source address in the Station 1 column and the destination address in the Station 2 column. Note that all addresses are listed in both columns, even though some are not appropriate selections. For example, the BROADCAST address should never be specified as a source address. You can also decide whether you want to see only traffic from the source to the destination or traffic in both directions by making the appropriate choice in the Direction column. The ANY address is useful for finding all traffic from or to a particular address. For example, the expression "ANY —> BROADCAST" would find all broadcast frames.

For this example, let's find the first occurrence of an IP broadcast frame from machine WCS. In the Expression dialog box, select the Address tab and make the selections, as shown in figure 14.20.

4. Choose the OK button to perform the search. Network Monitor finds a match at frame 145, as shown in figure 14.21. In this example we picked the IP address for WCS, and therefore the search will find only IP broadcast frames. If we had wanted all broadcasts from WCS, we would have picked the Ethernet address for WCS.

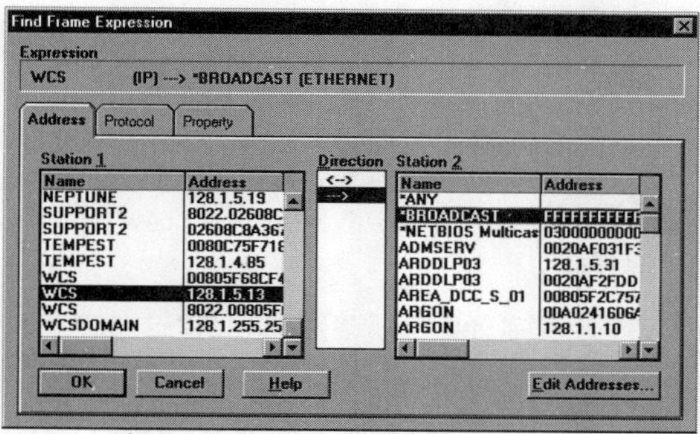

FIG. 14.20
Building an expression to look for IP broadcasts from WCS.

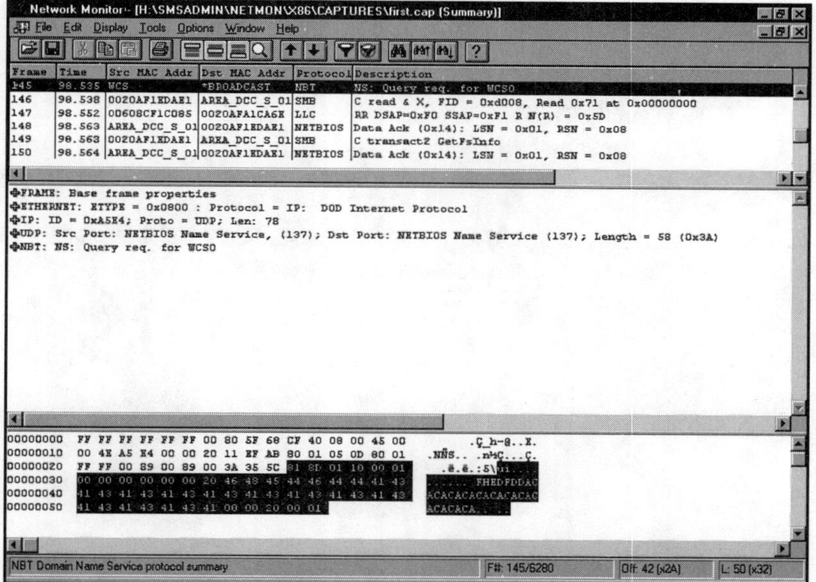

FIG. 14.21
The results of the Find Next Frame operation.

5. You can find the next matching frame by clicking the Find Next Frame icon on the toolbar (or pressing F3, or selecting Display, Repeat Find Next Frame). To go back to the previous matching frame, click the Find Previous Frame icon on the toolbar (or press Shift+F3, or select Display, Repeat Find Previous Frame). Note that Find Next Frame on the toolbar and Find Next Frame on the Display menu do completely different things!

Display Filters Referring again to figure 14.21, you can see that we've captured 6,280 frames! This is a lot of data to sift through, and it took less than three minutes to capture that many frames. Most of the time, you have a pretty good idea of the packets you're interested in and you'd like to look at only those packets. In this section, we'll show you how to filter the frames you've captured, based on network addresses, protocols, and even specific bytes within frames. Later, we'll show you how to set up capture filters that address the problem of capturing too many frames in the first place.

Display filters enable you to view only the subset of frames that you're really interested in. A display filter makes use of the expressions we used earlier to perform the Find Next Frame operation, but goes much further by allowing you to specify multiple expressions and join them using the familiar logical operators (AND, OR, and NOT). These logical operators and the expressions can be nested to many levels, allowing you to build very complex filters. The following example will show how this works. Suppose we want to look at broadcasts (a common concern on networks). Let's say we don't care about IP or SMB broadcasts and we want to exclude the machine WCS. Let's set up a display filter to handle this request.

1. Open the Display Filter dialog box by clicking the Edit Display Filter icon on the toolbar (or pressing F8, or selecting Display, Filter...). This brings up the dialog box shown in figure 14.22.

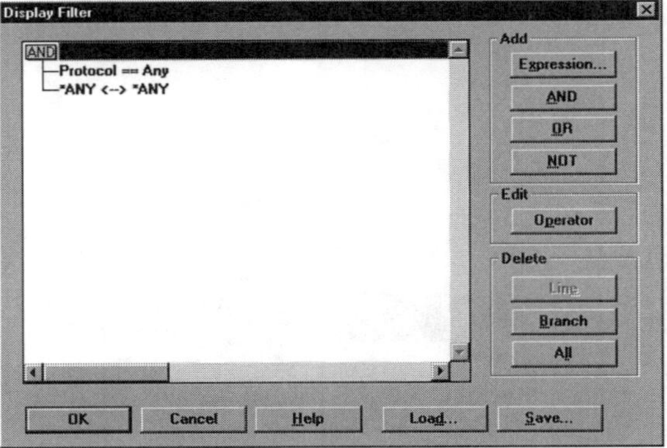

FIG. 14.22
Creating a display filter.

2. The main window displays the current filter. The default for the current filter is:

   "Protocol == Any" AND "*ANY <—> *ANY"

   This causes all frames to appear in the Summary pane. Before continuing, let's examine the window and explain some terminology. Each logical operator is referred to as a node. From each node, you can branch off to other nodes or to expressions. The Add section of the dialog box contains buttons that let you add AND, OR, or NOT nodes and expressions to the filter window. When you add a node, that node will be inserted just before the currently selected line, and that line item will become a child of the new node.

When you add an expression, it is inserted after the currently selected item. The Edit section contains a single button that is labeled either Operator or Expression... depending on the line that is currently selected. The Delete section is for deleting different parts of the filter. The Line button deletes a single expression or a single node, as long as that node has only one child. If a node has multiple children, and you want to delete all of them, select the node and choose the Branch button. Finally, if you want to delete the entire filter, choose the All button. The Save... button lets you save a filter (as a .DF file) for future use, and the Load... button lets you use your saved filters.

3. We'll edit the current filter to build the one we want. First, let's look at all broadcasts. Select the "*ANY <—> *ANY" line and choose the Edit Expression button. This brings up the Expression dialog box, like the one in figure 14.19. Change the expression to "*ANY <—> *BROADCAST (ETHERNET)" and choose OK.
4. Now we'll specify that WCS network traffic should be ignored. Choose the Add Expression button. Select the Address tab and change the expression to "WCS (ETHERNET) <—> *ANY" and choose OK. With this line selected in the filter window, choose the Add NOT button. Now our display filter looks like figure 14.23.

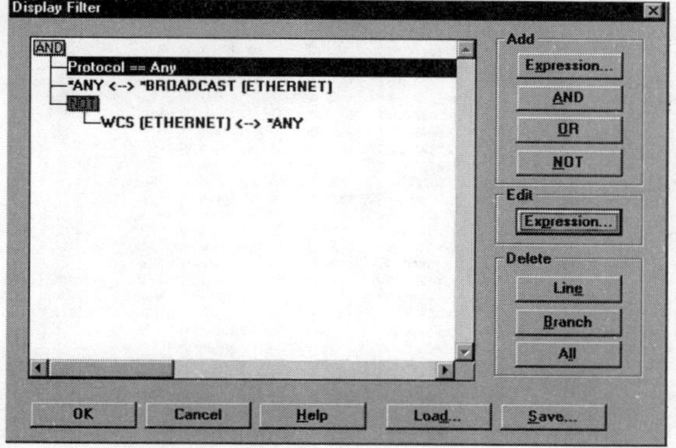

FIG. 14.23
This filter gives us broadcasts and no WCS traffic.

5. Select the "Protocol == Any" line and choose the Edit Expression button. Change the expression to "Protocol == IP."
6. In the filter window, with this line selected, choose the Add OR button.
7. Choose the Add Expression button. In the Expression dialog box, select the Protocol tab and change the expression to "Protocol == SMB."
8. In the filter window, select the "OR" line and choose the Add NOT button. Our completed filter looks like figure 14.24.
9. Now choose OK to apply the filter. The resulting filtered view in figure 14.25 shows that the machine MIKEK2 was generating a significant number of NETBIOS over IPX broadcasts during the capture period.

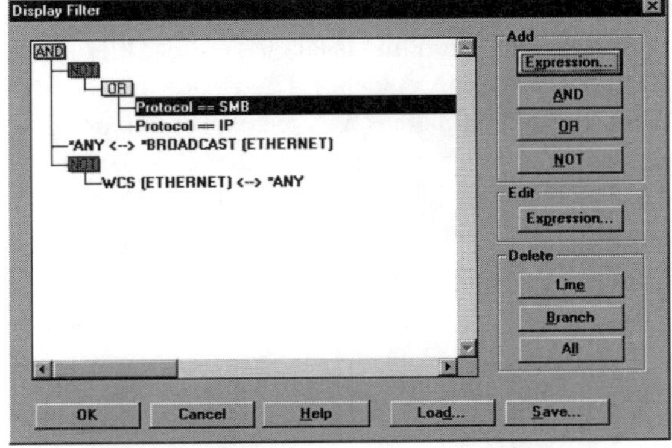

FIG. 14.24
This filter gives us broadcasts, no WCS traffic, and no IP or SMB traffic.

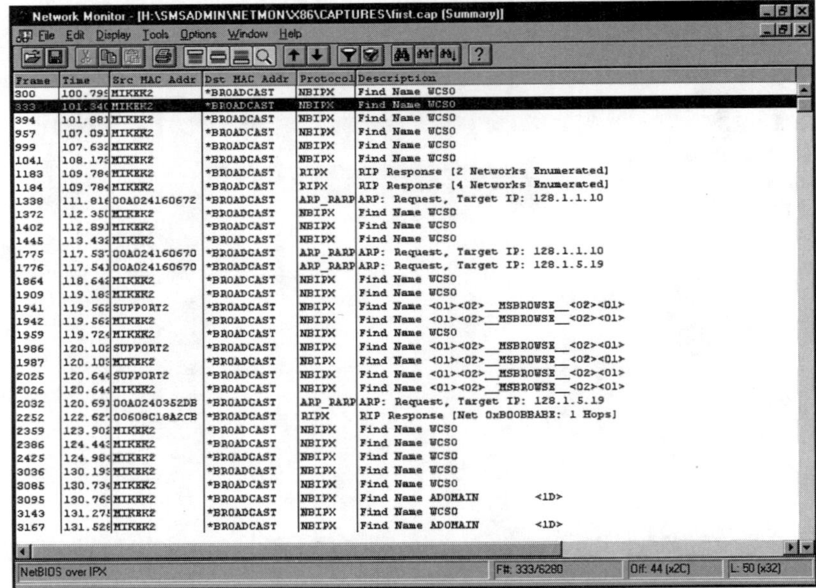

FIG. 14.25
The Summary pane looks like this with the filter applied.

You can temporarily turn off a filter to see all the frames again. To toggle the filter off, choose the Disable/Enable Filter button on the toolbar (or press F7, or select Display, Disable Filter).

Display Options Aside from filters, there are a number of display options that will make it easier to find the frames you're looking for. You can "colorize" your display by assigning both background and foreground colors to each protocol you're interested in. These protocols will then be highlighted in the summary, detail, and hex panes. To use the colors, perform the following steps:

1. From the menu bar, select Display, Colors. This brings up the dialog box shown in figure 14.26.

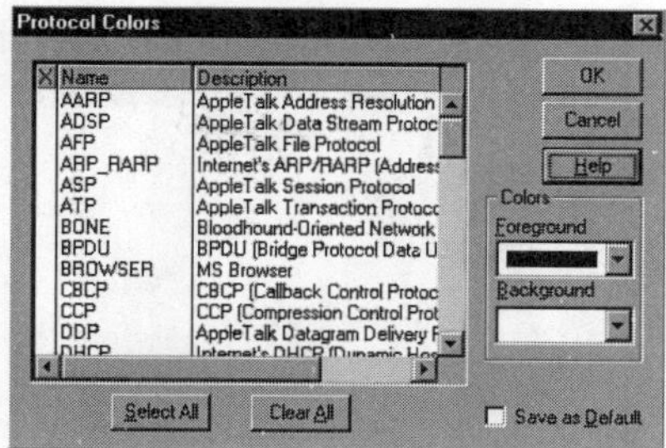

FIG. 14.26
Selecting colors that make interesting protocols stand out.

2. Click a protocol to select it (an X appears in the left-most column) and then apply colors to it. You can select more than one at a time and apply the same colors to each protocol in the selection. The Select All... and Clear All... buttons are self-explanatory. The Save as Default check box allows you to make these selections your default colors for new sessions. Figure 14.27 shows the window from figure 14.26 with the TCP protocol highlighted. Note that the frame will be highlighted only if the protocol displayed in the Protocol column of the Summary window is one that has been colored. If a frame simply contains a colored protocol, the frame will not be highlighted.

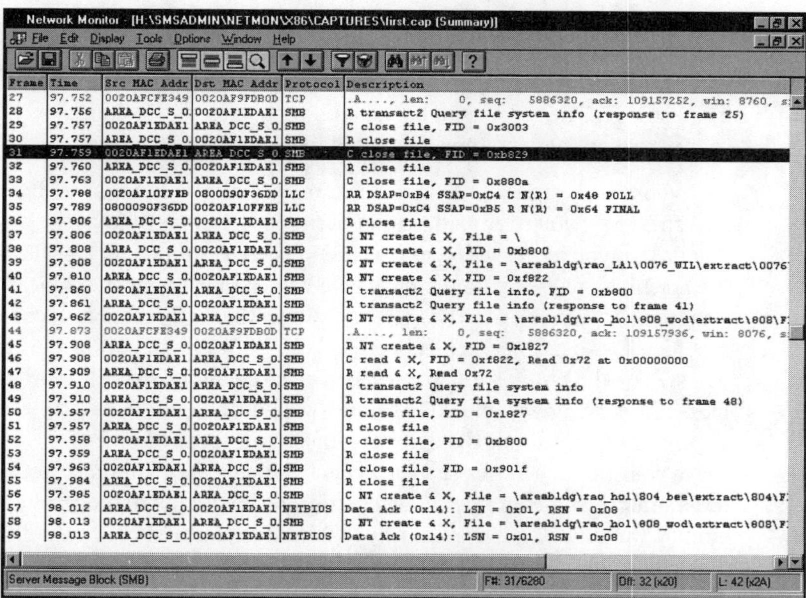

FIG. 14.27
The TCP protocol has been colored red.

You can specify how the Summary window chooses which of the protocols in a frame to display in the Protocol column. Select Display, Options... and you'll see that the default (under Summary Protocol) is Last protocol in frame (fig. 14.28). This really means the highest-level protocol in the frame. Your other option is Auto (based on protocols in the display filter). With this option, Network Monitor evaluates your display filter and chooses the protocol it thinks you'd like to see.

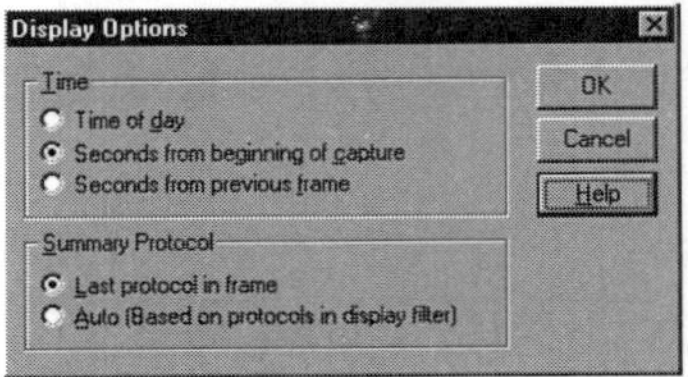

FIG. 14.28
Examining your display options.

In the Display Options dialog box, you can also configure the way the Time column is displayed. The default is Seconds from the beginning of capture, but you can also view the clock times (Time of day) or, for each frame, the time that elapsed after the preceding frame (Seconds from previous frame).

Setting up Capture Filters

You can see how quickly your capture buffer will fill up on even a moderately loaded network. When your buffer becomes full (the default buffer size is 1 MB), the default behavior for Network Monitor is to start dropping frames at the beginning of the buffer. There are a few ways you can slow the rate of capture to ensure that Network Monitor doesn't lose an event you're interested in. The most complex but also most effective technique is to simply avoid capturing frames that are not of interest, and this requires a capture filter.

But before we get going on capture filters, let's look at the easy techniques. The most obvious first strategy if you're running out of buffer is to increase the buffer size. Microsoft recommends that you increase the buffer size to equal the amount of available memory, but unless the machine you're running it on is a dedicated management workstation, you probably won't want to go this far, due to the memory paging that will probably occur (not to mention the resulting loss of frames). Selecting Capture, Buffer Settings... brings up a dialog box that lets you specify the buffer size. If you specify a large buffer size, Network Monitor may bring up a message warning you about excessive swapping and frame loss if you keep this setting. The Capture Buffer Settings dialog box also lets you specify frame size. This enables you to conserve your capture buffer space by capturing only partial frames. Your choices are Full (all of the frame) or some number of bytes from the beginning of the frame. Many network protocols employ variable-length frames, so you'll want to apply this setting with care to ensure that you don't cut off the part of the frame you really need.

Of course, capture filters not only help to keep your buffer from overflowing, they also limit the number of frames you have to wade through to get to what you're looking for. So let's see how to set one up.

1. Choose the Edit Capture Filter button on the toolbar (or select Capture, Filter..., or press F8). The Capture Filter dialog appears, as shown in figure 14.29.

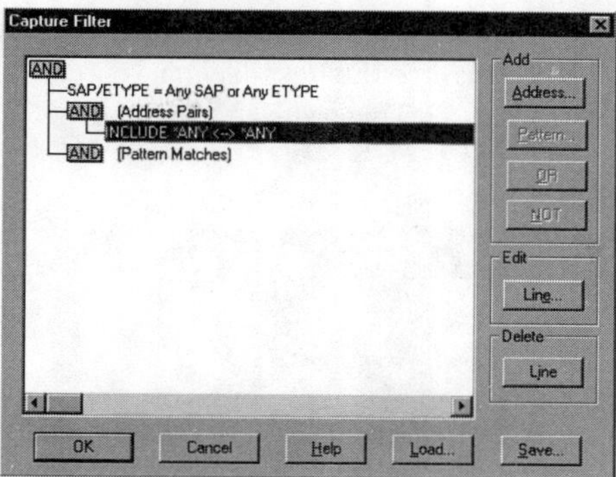

FIG. 14.29
Designing a capture filter

2. The default first line in the Capture Filter window is "SAP/ETYPE = Any SAP or Any ETYPE." SAP stands for Service Access Point and E-type is a 2-byte value in the Ethernet header that is used to indicate which protocol the frame is carrying. You can edit this line to specify which protocols you want Network Monitor to capture. The editing features work exactly the way they did for editing a display filter. You're allowed only one of these lines and you can edit the line but not delete it.

   The next line, AND (Address Pairs), and its default child, INCLUDE *ANY <—> *ANY, enable you to filter traffic based on the source and destination addresses. Again, you edit this just as you did for a display filter. Note that you can't add logical operators here, but you can add multiple lines under the AND operator.

   The final line, AND (Pattern Matches), is unique to the capture filter and the capture trigger. This section lets you set up highly specific capture criteria based on individual bytes and their offsets within frames. You can add multiple lines and you can make use of the OR and NOT operators to create an arbitrarily complex pattern of bytes to search for.

   Let's leave the first two lines at their defaults and set up a pattern-matching filter. We'll capture only IP traffic from the machine with address 128.1.4.38 the hard way. The best way, of course, would be to use the address pair line. First, we must know that the source IP address in an IP header starts 12 bytes from the beginning of the header. You can find this by consulting a book on TCP/IP or by looking at the details of captured IP packets in Network Monitor.

3. Select the AND (Pattern Matches) line and choose the Add Pattern... button. This brings up the Pattern Match dialog box. In the Offset (in hex) box, type "c" (which is 12 in hexadecimal).

4. You can then choose to apply this offset from the start of the frame or from the end of the topology header. The topology header is the very first header in a frame, and it varies depending on the type of network (Ethernet, Token Ring, FDDI, and so on) that you're running. Since we want to design a filter on a particular IP address (a higher-layer protocol) regardless of the underlying network, select From End of Topology Header.

5. Select the Hex radio button and type in the Pattern box the IP address. This must be entered as a series of 4 bytes that are the hexadecimal representations of the four parts of the dotted IP address 128.1.4.38. This translates to 80 01 04 26. Figure 14.30 shows the completed dialog box.

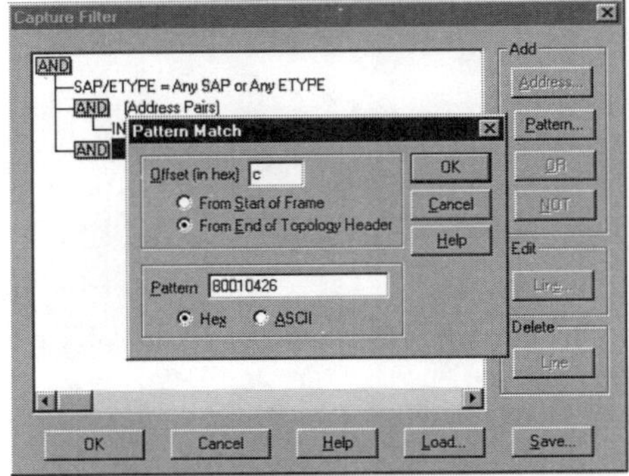

FIG. 14.30
This pattern will find packets with an IP source address of 128.1.4.38.

6. Choose OK twice to close the dialog box and complete the capture filter.
7. Press F10 to start the capture. The Network Statistics section shows there is traffic on the network, but no frames are showing up in the Session Stats pane because there hasn't been any IP traffic from the workstation we're monitoring. To remedy that situation, we'll force some traffic, using the TCP/IP "ping" command.
8. Open a Windows NT Command Prompt window and type the command `ping 128.1.4.38`. This causes four response packets to be sent from the workstation with that IP address.

The "ping" command is an incredibly useful utility that is included with every TCP/IP implementation. It's a quick and sure way to verify that a machine with TCP/IP is active on the network. Ping works by sending out a packet with some random data in it and waiting for that packet to be echoed back by the machine that's being pinged.

9. Press F11 to stop the capture and view the results, as shown in figure 14.31. As you can see from the Total Stats pane, there were 1,826 frames detected during the capture, but we captured only four of them.

CAUTION

It's important to define capture filters carefully and test them, because it's all too easy to filter out the traffic you really want.

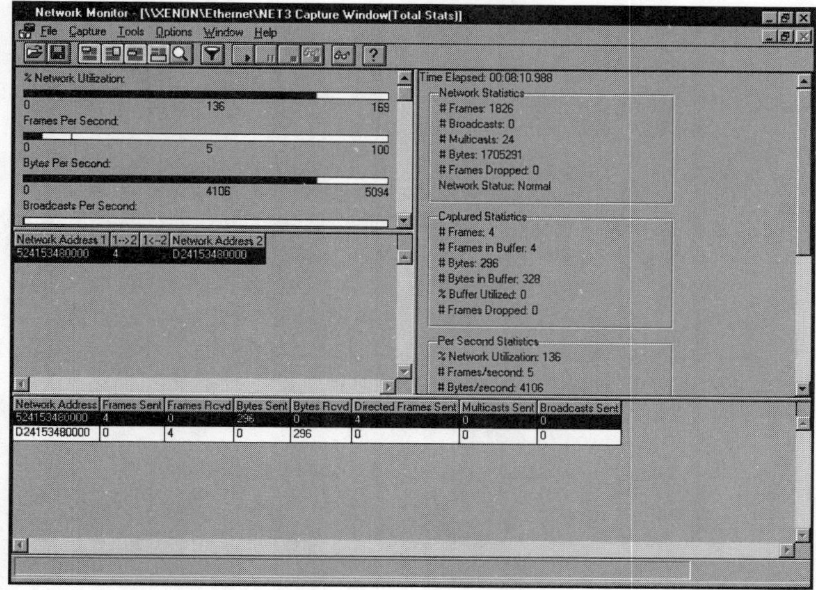

FIG. 14.31 The results of a capture session with capture filter applied.

10. Press F12 to view the captured frames. The Summary pane, as shown in figure 14.32, shows the four frames we just captured.

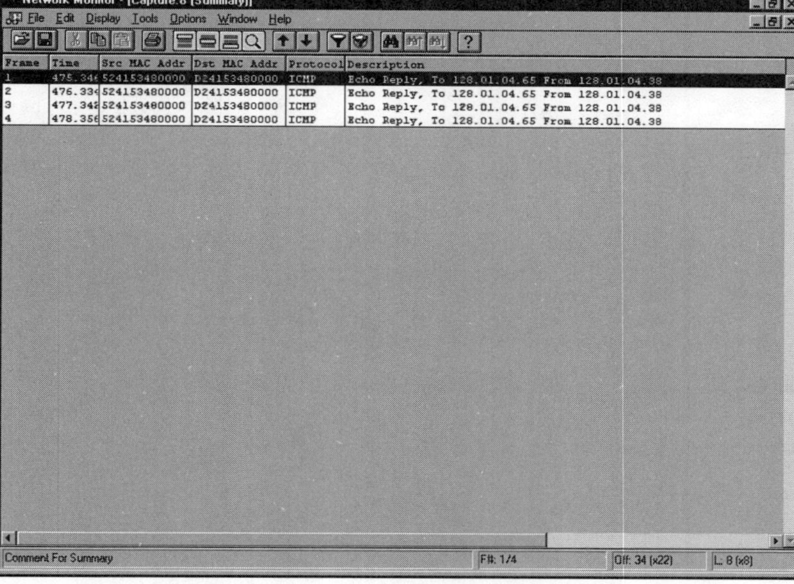

FIG. 14.32 Verifying that we captured frames from 128.1.4.38.

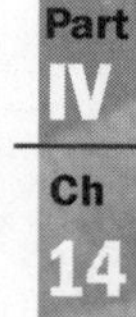

Setting up Capture Triggers

In the preceding section, we've seen how capture filters can be used to hone in on the frames you want while at the same time preventing your capture buffer from filling up too quickly. But what if you need to run the capture unattended? If the capture buffer fills up while you're away, Network Monitor starts overwriting the buffer with any new frames, and you might lose the frame(s) you really wanted. A capture trigger can handle this and provide other benefits. A capture trigger monitors your buffer space, or looks for a specific byte pattern in captured frames, or both, and performs an action based on conditions that you specify. The capture trigger can stop the capture and/or run a command. For example, you can set a capture trigger that will stop the capture when the buffer becomes full.

You can specify that Network Monitor stop capturing when its buffer fills via a command line startup option. The command is:

```
start netmon /autostop
```

This command simply creates the required capture trigger automatically.

We'll design a capture trigger that does the following: capture traffic until a specific frame is spotted, continue capturing until the buffer becomes full, and then stop capturing and send a message to the operator's console.

1. Select Capture, Trigger... from the menu bar and you'll see the dialog box shown in figure 14.33. Note that it defaults to Trigger on Nothing (the trigger is inactive). The Trigger on section lets you specify which things to monitor. The other choices are:
    - Pattern match—looks for a specific byte pattern at a specific byte offset within the frame.
    - Buffer space—monitors the amount of buffer space used.
    - Pattern match then buffer space—looks for a frame that matches your pattern first and then starts monitoring buffer space. Takes action when the buffer space criteria is met.
    - Buffer space then pattern match—monitors buffer space first until the buffer space criteria is met and then starts looking for a frame that matches your pattern. Takes action when the pattern match occurs.

    For this example, select Pattern match then buffer space.

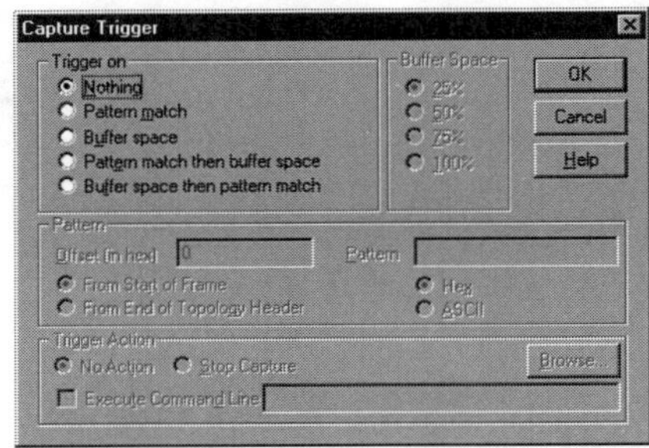

FIG. 14.33
Designing a capture trigger.

2. Now we can select Buffer Space 100% since we want to take action when the buffer fills up.
3. We're going to borrow from a previous example and look for IP traffic coming from the machine with address 128.1.4.38. In the Pattern section, select From End of Topology Header, select Hex, enter "c" in the Offset (in hex) field, and enter "80010426" in the Pattern field.
4. Finally, in the Trigger Action section, select Stop Capture and, in the Execute Command Line field, enter the command "net send timdcomp I'm Done!" This will send the message "I'm Done!" to workstation TIMDCOMP when the action is triggered. The filled-in dialog box is shown in figure 14.34. Choose OK to complete the capture trigger.

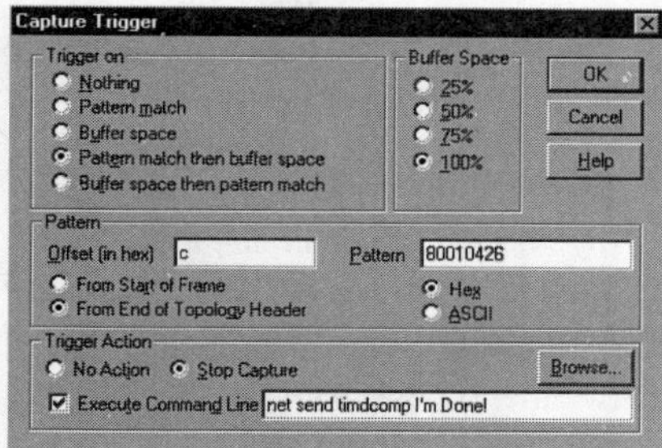

FIG. 14.34
A completed capture trigger.

NOTE When using the Pattern match then buffer space option, note that the buffer could fill up before the pattern is matched. As you would expect, the capture will continue (causing frames in the buffer to be dropped) until the pattern is matched. When that happens, the trigger will instantly activate, since the buffer test has already been satisfied.

Now that you've defined the capture trigger, you can start the capture, leave it running, and it will stop automatically and notify you when it's done. You can apply a capture filter and a capture trigger at the same time and you can, of course, apply a display filter on top of that.

Capturing on Local and Remote Network Segments

Up to this point, we've let Network Monitor decide which network to use when capturing frames. If your machine has multiple network connections (and RAS counts as a network connection), Network Monitor will pick one and connect to it when you start a capture. This may not be the network you wanted to monitor! You should always select the network first before you do a capture. Once you've selected a network, Network Monitor will stay with that choice for the duration of the session (or until you change it). Select Capture, Networks... to display the Select Capture Network dialog box, as shown in figure 14.35.

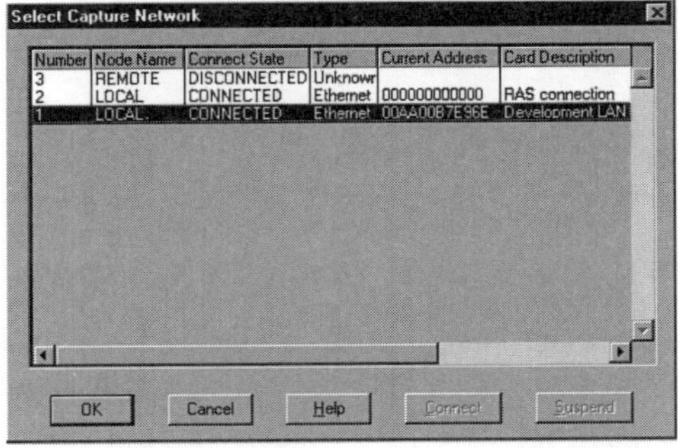

FIG. 14.35
You can choose which network you want to monitor.

Network Monitor will display one connection for each network card in your machine, one connection for RAS, and one remote connection. Unfortunately, the RAS connection is confusingly listed as an Ethernet connection. The remote connection is for connecting to a Network Monitor Agent running on a machine that is located on a remote (not directly attached) LAN segment. For the local connections, you can just select one to make it active. The remote connection requires a little more work. If you double-click the remote connection in the Select Capture Network dialog box, you'll get a dialog box like the one in figure 14.36. Notice that you can specify the agent status update frequency, and you can specify that you'll be connecting over a slow link (typically RAS).

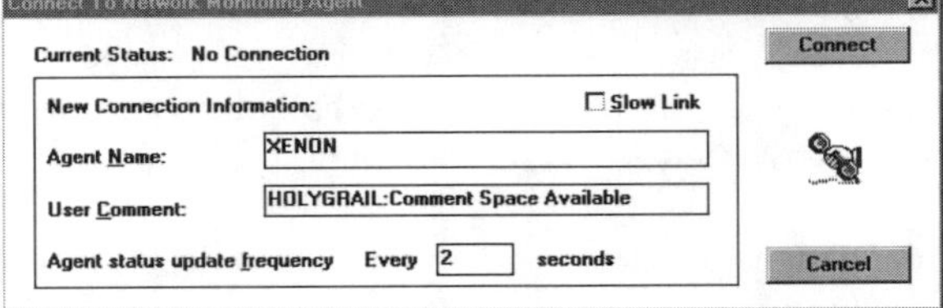

FIG. 14.36
Connecting to the Network Monitoring Agent on machine XENON.

When you choose Connect, you'll be presented with the dialog box shown in figure 14.37. This means that you have successfully connected to the remote machine's Network Monitor Agent, and you now have to decide which of the remote machine's network segments you want to monitor. After you double-click the appropriate network card, you're ready to start capturing.

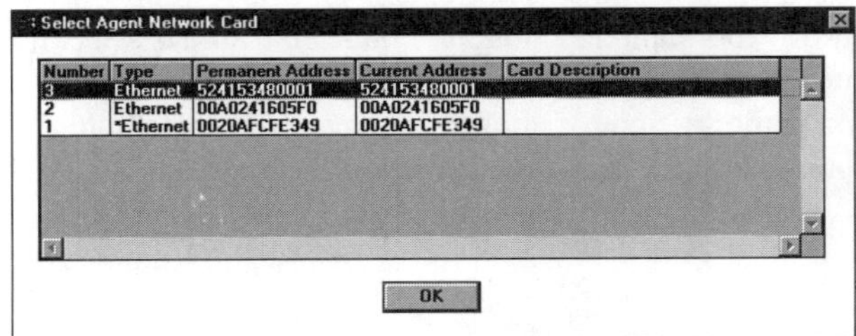

FIG. 14.37
You can select which network you want the remote machine to monitor.

Generating Network Traffic

Network Monitor can do more than just listen to network traffic—it can also generate network traffic. It does this in conjunction with the capture frame function. In other words, you capture a series of frames first and then you can play them back, in effect simulating that traffic on the network. Network Monitor lets you edit the details of the frames you want to transmit if, for example, you wanted to change the destination addresses. You can also use the ability to cut and paste whole frames to create a totally different sequence.

Why would you want to do this? Let's say that a particular machine seems to be giving inappropriate responses to a particular series of query packets. Think how helpful it would be to be able to "replay" those packets with variations until you isolate the exact problem. Or suppose that you need to see how the network handles various levels of loading. Network Monitor can act as your load generator.

CAUTION

This feature is meant for very knowledgeable network administrators and definitely not for the novice. Transmitting captured frames onto a network can cause major problems and even bring down the network, depending on the nature of the frames.

To see how this really works, let's send out a TCP/IP Address Resolution Protocol (ARP) request packet. ARP is a broadcast protocol that a TCP/IP machine uses to determine the hardware network address of a machine in the network, given that machine's IP address. In other words, if machine A (IP address 128.2.1.1) wants to send something to machine B (IP address 128.2.1.10), machine A has to eventually determine the hardware address corresponding to the IP address 128.2.1.10. The ARP protocol accomplishes this by broadcasting a packet containing machine A's hardware address and IP address and the IP address of machine B. Machine B will recognize its IP address in this broadcast and send a reply to machine A containing machine B's hardware address. Other machines on the network simply ignore the broadcast. Normally, ARP is invoked automatically on TCP/IP machines. For this example, we're going to do it manually.

First, we need to capture an ARP packet. We'll start by setting up a capture filter that captures only ARP packets. In the Network Monitor capture window, press F8 to build a capture filter. Double-click the SAP/ETYPE line and then, in the resulting dialog box, click the Disable All button to remove all the protocols. Then add back only the ARP protocol by double-clicking it. Finally, choose OK twice to complete the filter and press F10 to start the capture. It takes only about 12 seconds for some ARP packets to appear on our network. Click the Stop and View Capture button to see the results. Figure 14.38 shows what we got from our network.

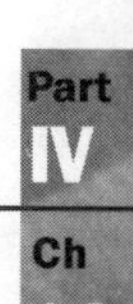

The figure shows both request and reply packets. For our example, we'll zoom in on a request packet (Frame 1). Double-click Frame 1 to bring up the detail and hex panes. Next, click the plus sign adjacent to the ARP-RARP detail line to expand it. This reveals the four items of interest in this packet: Sender's Hardware Address, Sender's Protocol Address, Target's Hardware Address, and Target's Protocol Address, as shown in figure 14.39.

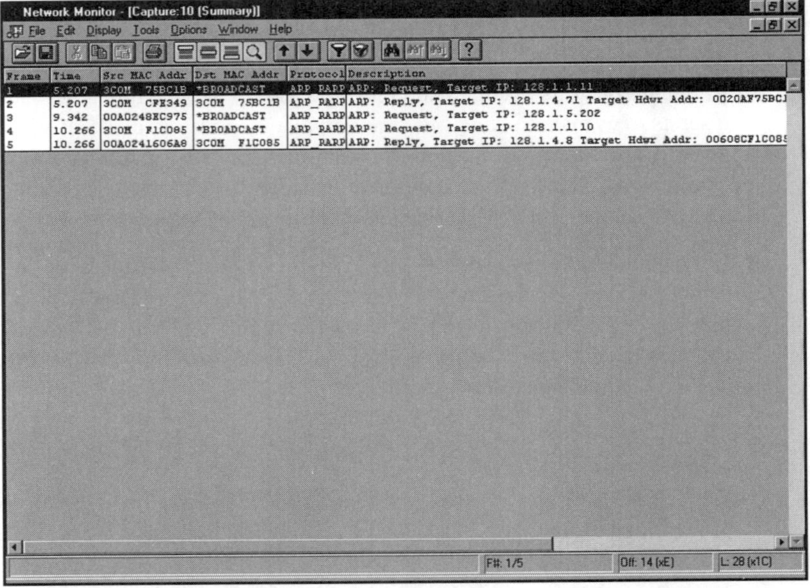

FIG. 14.38
Viewing some captured ARP packets.

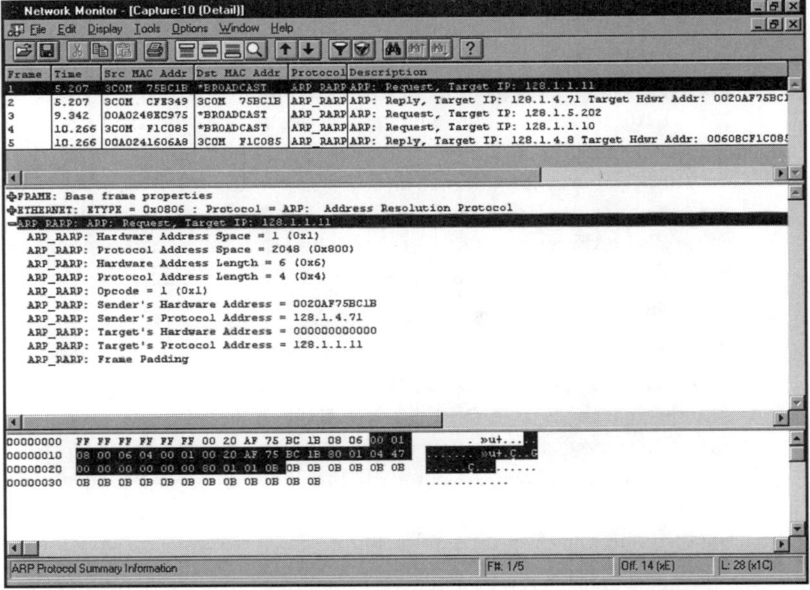

FIG. 14.39
Zooming in on the details of an ARP request packet.

What this tells us is that the sender (IP address 128.1.4.71) is trying to determine the hardware address of the target (IP address 128.1.1.11). For our example, we're going to edit this packet and transmit it on a different network. Our Network Monitor workstation has a network card with a connection to the IP network 128.2.0.0. We also know that the hardware address for that card is 00 AA 00 B7 E9 6E and the associated IP address is 128.2.1.1. The machine that we want to send the ARP request to has IP address 128.2.1.10. This is all we need to edit the packet. Up until now, we've been treating the display window as strictly a viewer window, and that is the default mode. You can also use this window to edit each frame at the byte level, but first you must change the mode of the window. Select Edit, Read Only to toggle the mode of the window. Now we can change the addresses within the frame as follows:

1. Select the detail line ARP-RARP: Sender's Hardware Address, and notice that the 6 bytes corresponding to this address are now highlighted in the hex pane.
2. Click the first digit in the first byte, and you'll see a solid blinking cursor to indicate that you can change that digit.
3. Type in 00 AA 00 B7 E9 6E. Note that the default behavior is to overwrite each digit as you type, and this is what you normally want. You can change this by pressing the Insert key. The solid cursor will change to a thin vertical line (this is the only indication that you are in insert mode, so be careful) and anything you type will be inserted and the rest of the frame will be preserved. Figure 14.40 shows what we've done so far.

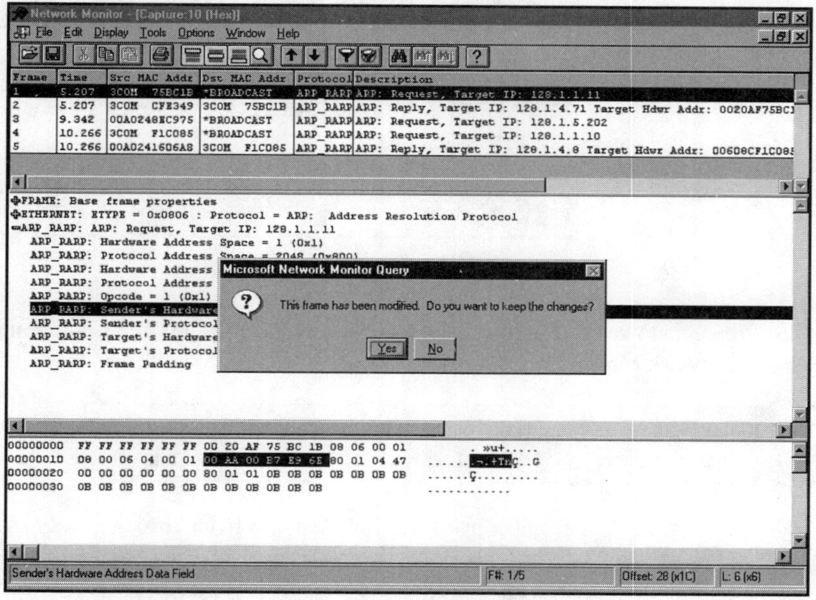

FIG. 14.40 Editing a hardware address in an ARP request packet.

4. Now select the detail line ARP-RARP: Sender's Protocol Address. When you change panes after editing, Network Monitor will ask if you want to keep the changes. Select the first byte of the four that are highlighted in the hex pane and type 80 02 01 01 (the hexadecimal representation of 128.2.1.1).
5. Finally, select the detail line ARP-RARP: Target's Protocol Address, and in the hex pane type 80 02 01 0A (IP address 128.2.1.10).

Once you get comfortable reading hexadecimal values and interpreting addresses, you won't need always to select the detail line to edit the corresponding bytes in the hex pane. You can simply cursor over to where they're located in the hex pane.

Figure 14.41 shows the finished frame.

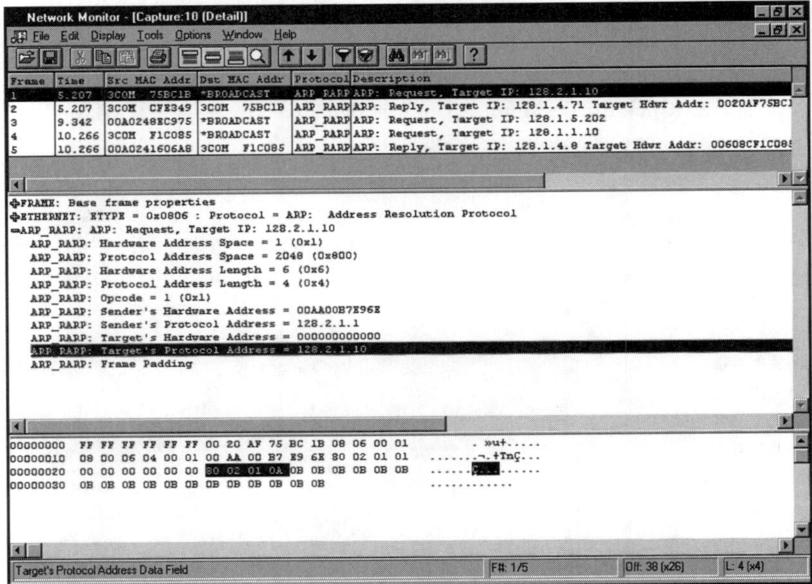

FIG. 14.41
A modified ARP packet ready to be sent.

Now the frame is ready to go, and all we have to do is send it. But before we do that, we want to be able to verify that it actually works as expected. The simple solution is to open another Network Monitor session and configure it to capture on the network we're going to use.

You can have as many copies of Network Monitor running as your workstation's memory will allow. This is useful for monitoring different segments of your network from one console.

Configure the second copy of Network Monitor to capture only ARP packets, as we did before. Now we need to tell Network Monitor to capture on the network that we intend to use. To choose the network for this example, we select Capture, Networks..., and the Select Capture Network dialog displays our choices, as shown in figure 14.42.

NOTE This dialog lets you choose both local LANs (those that your machine is directly connected to) and remote LANs (those that are reachable by connecting to a Network Monitor Agent). So far we've been connecting to local LANs, but later we'll cover connecting to Network Monitor Agents. ■

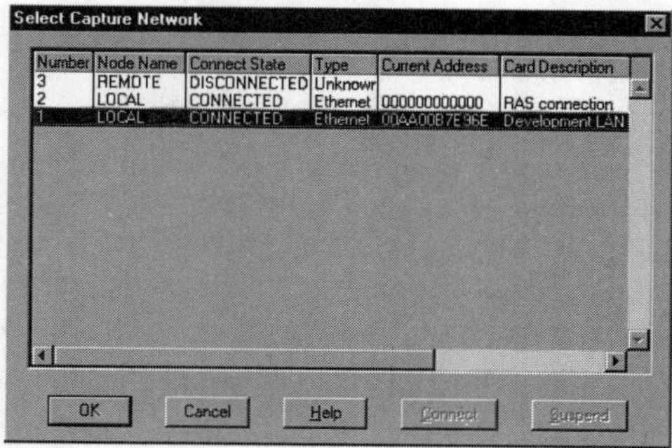

FIG. 14.42
Selecting the network to capture frames from.

The network we want for this example is Development LAN, so we double-click it and press F10 to start the capture. Now flip back to the first copy of Network Monitor to send the ARP packet. First, ensure that the modified packet is selected in the Summary pane, and then select Tools, Allow Transmit. This brings up the Select Transmit Network dialog box, similar to the Select Capture Network dialog box. The Allow Transmit command seems like an unnecessary intermediate step, but it's really a safety feature to prevent you from inadvertently transmitting frames onto the network. For this example, we'll again choose Development LAN. Note that after selecting Allow Transmit, additional menu choices become available. The Tools, Select Transmit Network... menu choice simply brings up the dialog box we just saw. The Tools, Transmit Frame menu choice transmits whichever frame is currently selected on the network we've already picked. The Tools, Transmit Capture... menu choice brings up the detailed dialog box shown in figure 14.43. You can now do the following:

- Transmit all captured frames or just a subset, and you can decide whether to apply the current display filter or not.
- Transmit the set of frames once or multiple times, and you can specify the time interval between transmissions.
- Transmit individual frames using the captured time intervals between frames, or specify a fixed time interval between each frame.

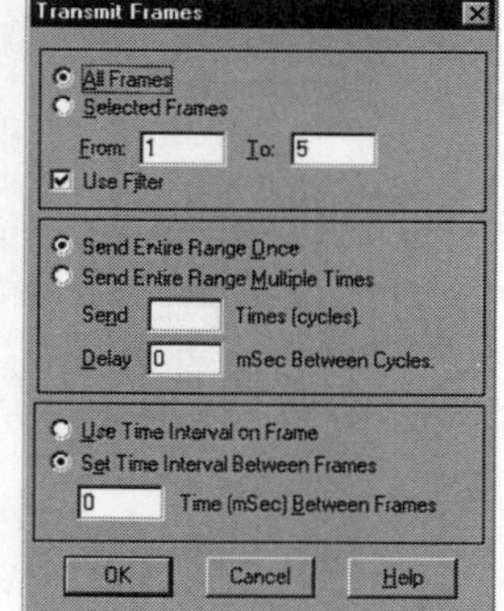

FIG. 14.43
You can specify a variety of options for transmitting one or more frames.

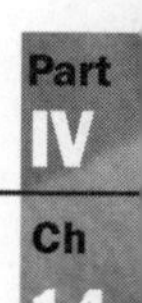

NOTE If you want to change the sequence of frames or use a frame from another display window, you can use the standard Windows cut, copy, and paste commands on entire frames. These commands act on frames in the Summary pane.

Now let's go ahead and transmit. Select Tools, Transmit Frame and then flip over to the copy of Network Monitor that's capturing. Click the Stop and View Capture button, and zoom in on the captured packets. Figure 14.44 shows the details of frame 1, our ARP request packet, and figure 14.45 shows the details of the ARP reply. Note that the Sender's Hardware Address (machine KELLY) has been filled in with the hexadecimal string 00 AA 00 B7 EB 21, which is just what ARP is supposed to do.

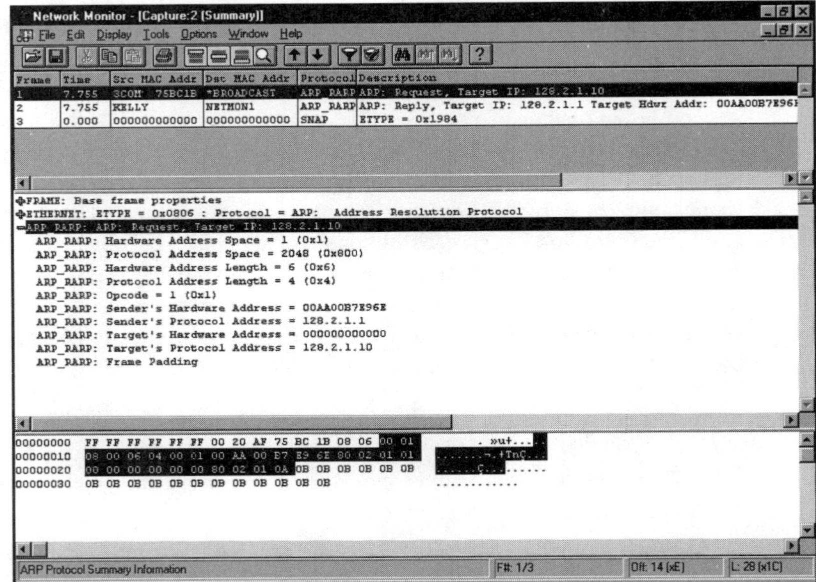

FIG. 14.44 This is the ARP request packet that was transmitted.

CAUTION

Most frame editing is much more difficult than the example presented here. Many protocols, IP in particular, include checksums to enable the receiver to verify the integrity of a packet. If you edit such frames in any way, you'll have to recalculate the checksum(s) in order for the frame to be acted on by the receiver. And we hope this goes without saying—don't play with this capability on your production network!

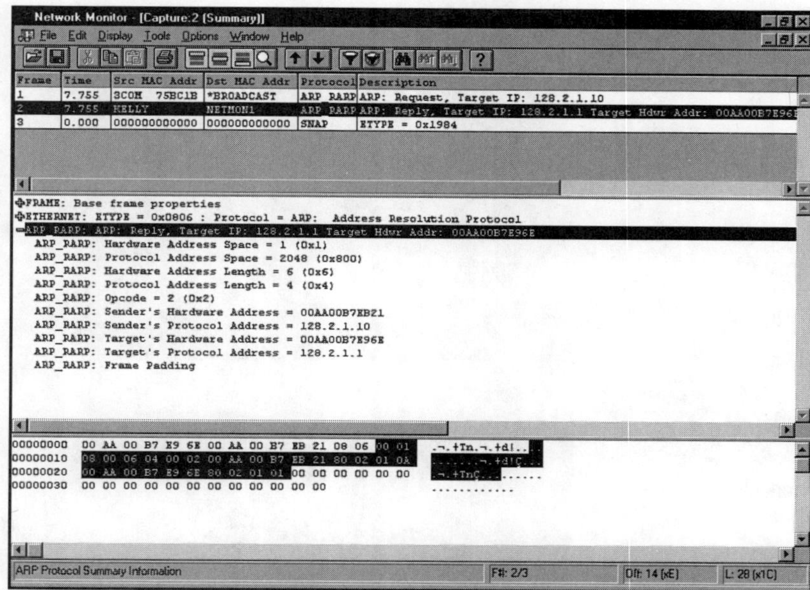

FIG. 14.45
The ARP reply from machine KELLY.

Additional Features

Network Monitor provides other features that are quite useful to a network administrator. This section will cover the most interesting ones.

Identifying Network Monitor Users

Network Monitor can identify other machines on the network that are running Network Monitor. This feature can be used for tracking down unlicensed copies, but primarily it lets you know if an unauthorized person is using Network Monitor to snoop on your network. Select Tools, Identify Network Monitor Users... and you'll get the dialog box shown in figure 14.46. In this case, two other machines, aside from the one we're using, are running Network Monitor.

Finding Routers

One very useful feature is the ability to identify which physical addresses represent routers. Network Monitor attempts to do this by performing a capture (if one is not already there) and analyzing the frames containing a specific set of protocols. The protocols it uses exhibit recognizable patterns when traversing a router, and Network Monitor is designed to detect them. First, from the Capture window, choose your capture network (Capture, Networks...) if you haven't already. Select Tools, Find Routers, and you'll get the dialog box shown in figure 14.47.

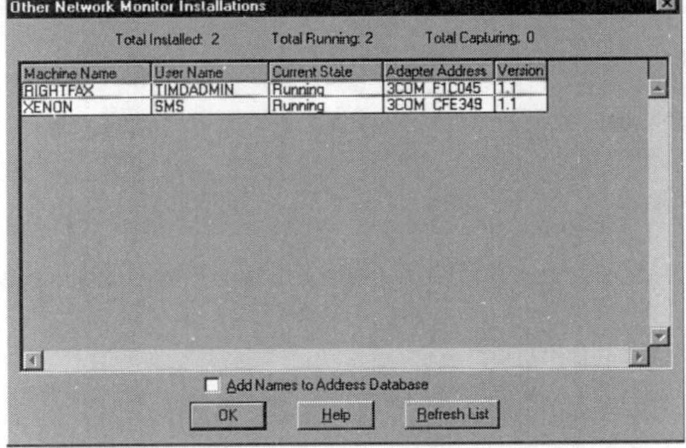

FIG. 14.46
Identifying other machines running Network Monitor.

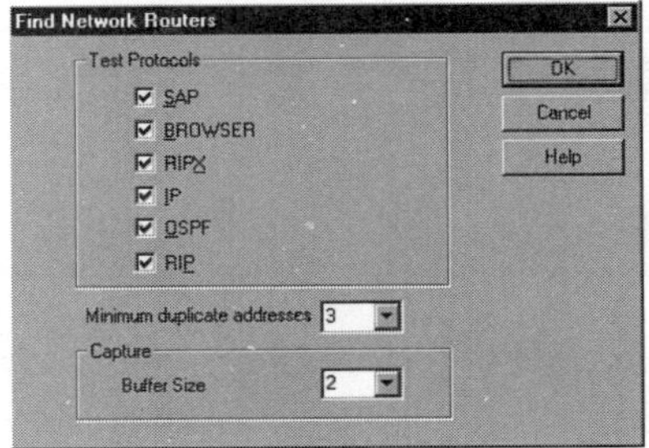

FIG. 14.47
You can change the way Network Monitor looks for routers.

The Find Network Routers dialog box identifies the protocols that Network Monitor uses to find routers and allows you to deselect some of them. This saves time if you know that the router(s) you're looking are configured to handle specific protocols. The Capture Buffer Size parameter allows you to specify the size of the capture buffer to be used for finding routers. You can change this setting if you initiated the Find Routers command from the Capture window, because Network Monitor will start a new capture. You can also initiate the Find Routers command from a display window, in which case Network Monitor will use the capture results that are displayed there. Finally, the Minimum duplicate addresses option is used by Network Monitor to avoid identifying multihomed Ethernet cards as routers. If you want to detect multihomed Ethernet cards, set this value to 2 (the default is 3). Figure 14.48 shows the results of the Find Routers command on our network.

Resolving Addresses from Names

You can obtain address information about machines on your network by selecting Tools, Resolve Addresses From Name. This brings up the dialog box shown in figure 14.49.

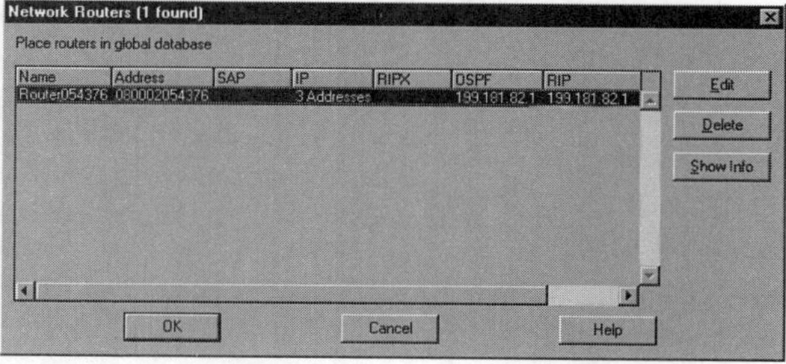

FIG. 14.48
Network Monitor correctly identified a router from a capture of 185 frames.

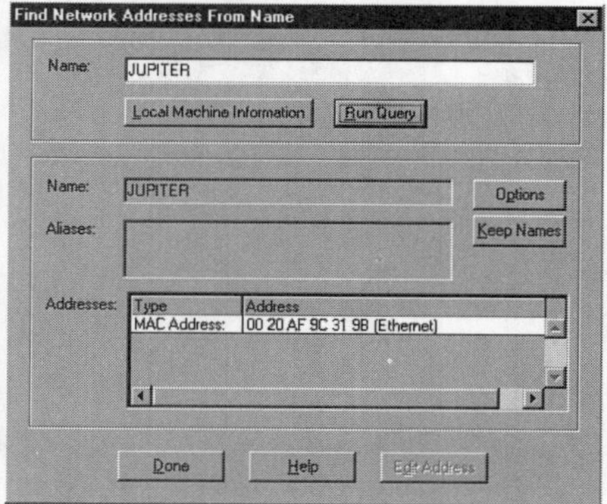

FIG. 14.49
A query for the name JUPITER correctly identified its MAC address.

The figure shows the results of a name query. To use this feature, you simply type in a machine name and choose the Run Query button. The Local Machine Information button gives you the name and addresses for the machine you are using. The Options button lets you specify which services you want Network Monitor to search for addresses and the search order. The choices are DNS, Local Address Database, NetBios, SAP, and SMS Remote Database.

Identifying the Heaviest Users of the Network

Wouldn't you like an easy way to determine who is hogging the network? Network Monitor provides a simple way to do this. First, you must perform a capture, and then stop and view it. Now select Tools, Find Top Users..., and you'll get the dialog box shown in figure 14.50.

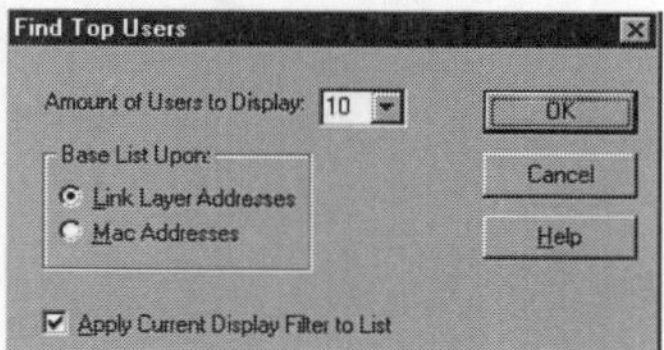

FIG. 14.50
Finding the largest network users.

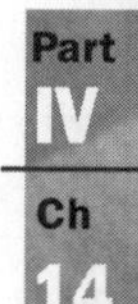

Here you can specify the number of users (both sending and receiving) to list in the output windows. The default is to list the top 10 senders and receivers. You also can choose whether to examine frames by link address or MAC address. You usually want to specify link address in order to ensure that Network Monitor identifies the actual machine that is generating the frames. The issue here is that routers retransmit packets using the router's MAC address versus the transmitting machine's MAC address, and therefore specifying MAC addresses may incorrectly identify a router as a heavy user of the network. This dialog box also lets you choose whether to apply the current display filter or not. Choosing OK brings up a window similar to the one in figure 14.51.

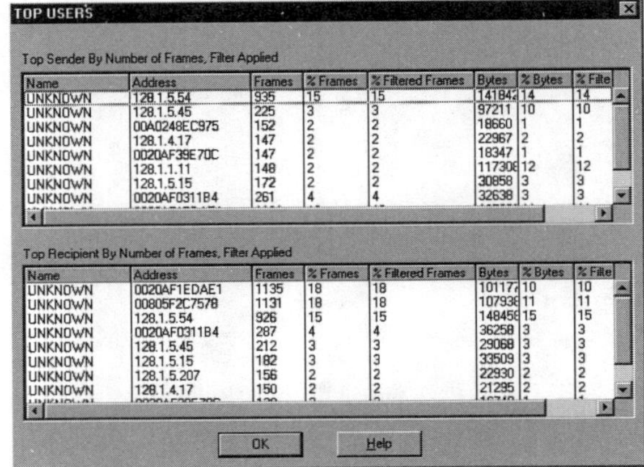

FIG. 14.51
The top 10 senders and receivers during our sample capture session.

You can sort the listings on any column by double-clicking the column heading. You can rearrange the columns by clicking and dragging the column heading. You can change the listings from By Frame to By Bytes by right-clicking either list.

Finding Protocols in Use on the Network

Network Monitor can analyze a group of frames, and produce a list of all the protocols identified within those frames and the percentage of frames or bytes that are used by each protocol. This command is available only from a display window, since you must have a set of captured frames first. Select Tools, Protocol Distribution... and you'll see the dialog box shown in figure 14.52.

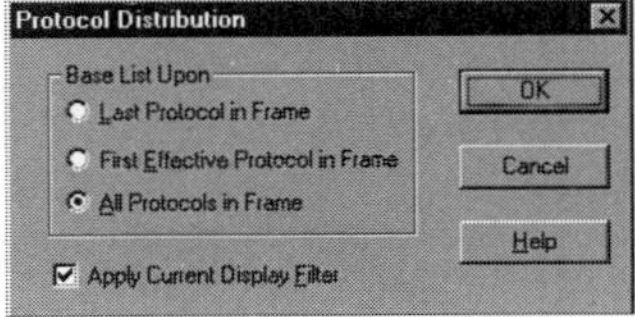

FIG. 14.52
You can specify options for analyzing the protocol distribution.

This dialog box gives you three ways of tailoring the resulting list. You can base the list upon one of the following:

1. Last Protocol in Frame—Network Monitor will look for the highest-level protocol in a frame and record all the bytes in that frame as belonging to that protocol. All other protocols in the frame are ignored. This mode is intended to give you a breakdown of high-level traffic (SMB and TCP are examples of these).
2. First Effective Protocol in Frame—Network Monitor will look for the first protocol in a frame that operates at the network layer, and record all the bytes in that frame as belonging to that protocol; in other words, the first protocol that is capable of moving a frame around on the network. This is great for determining what mix of network protocols you have on your network. Basically, this is the first protocol above SNAP or LLC (IP and IPX are examples of these). If there are no protocols matching this criteria, then the highest-level protocol in the frame is reported.
3. All Protocols in Frame—Network Monitor will report all the protocols in a frame and record the correct number of bytes that belong to each protocol. This mode is useful for seeing data on the lower-layer protocols that won't show up in the other two modes.

When you choose OK to close the dialog box, you'll get a Protocol Distribution Report similar to the one shown in figure 14.53.

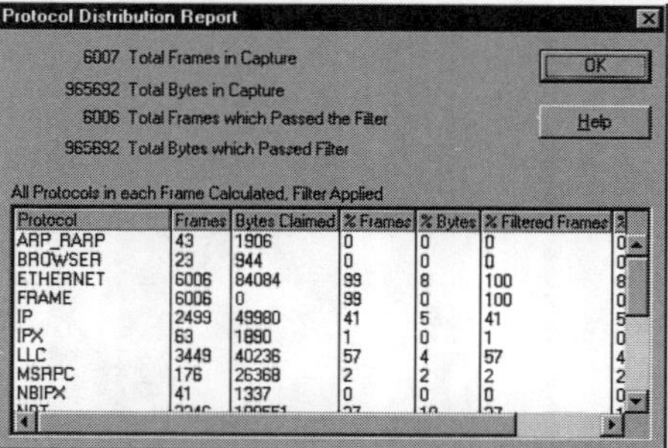

FIG. 14.53
Viewing the result of the protocol distribution analysis.

Performance Monitor

Network Monitor adds a number of counters to NT's Performance Monitor application. As a convenience, you can call up Performance Monitor from within Network Monitor by selecting Tools, Performance Monitor. When you click the Add Counter button on Performance Monitor's toolbar, you'll notice a new object, Network Segment, in the object list. There will be a separate instance of this object for each network card in your machine, and you'll have the following counters to select from:

- % Broadcast Frames
- % Multicast Frames
- % Network utilization

- Broadcast frames received/second
- Multicast frames received/second
- Total bytes received/second
- Total frames received/second

From Here...

- Chapter 24, "Investigating Network Problems," presents some examples of using Network Monitor to solve real network problems.
- The following reference books are recommended for a better understanding of computer networking:
  - *Computer Networks*. Tanenbaum, Andrew. Englewood Cliffs, NJ: Prentice Hall, 1996.
  - *LAN Protocol Handbook*. Miller, Mark. Redwood City, CA: M&T Publishing, 1990.
  - *LAN Troubleshooting Handbook*. Miller, Mark. San Mateo, CA: M&T Books, 1989.
  - *Troubleshooting TCP/IP*. Miller, Mark. San Mateo, CA: M&T Books, 1996.
  - *Internetworking with TCP/IP Vol I-III*. Comer, Douglas. Englewood Cliffs, NJ: Prentice Hall, 1994.

PART V

Managing SMS

CHAPTER 15

Changing Your Site Configuration

Here's a quick look at what you'll learn in this chapter:

- **Adding and deleting domains within a site**
- **Adding and removing primary sites within the SMS hierarchy**
- **Configuring and removing the SMS client components**
- **SMS services and their configuration options**
- **Changing service accoutns used with SMS and SQL**

Sooner or later, you'll be faced with modifying the configuration of your SMS site. A change to your site configuration could involve anything from moving a site to changing the SMS Service Account information. The changes will be caused by the addition of new network resources, the replacement of older servers, changes to the company or organizational structure, or any number of other reasons. Fortunately, SMS is very flexible with respect to changing the configuration of a site. The main sections in this chapter will examine how to add, delete, and move domains within the SMS site. You'll also see how to add, delete, and move sites. In addition, we'll look at how to configure and remove SMS Client software.

Our first section will look at the steps you need to take when working with domains. We'll start with a review of the domain preparation that's required before a domain can be added to the SMS site. ■

Adding, Deleting, and Moving Domains

After the primary site installation, the only domain shown within the SMS Sites window is the domain containing the primary site server. You must add any other domains to the site using the Domains dialog box. We'll cover the steps you need to take when adding a domain a little later in the chapter, but before we do that, we need to look at some domain preparation issues.

Preparing a Domain for SMS

You'll need to perform some simple preparation steps before adding a domain to a site. The type of domain will designate what specific steps must be taken. The different domain types are as follows:

- Windows NT Server
- Windows NT Server and LAN Manager 2.x
- LAN Manager
- NetWare

As you recall, a domain is a logical grouping of computers. Each domain contains a common security accounts database that is used when validating the access privileges of a user. Instead of logging on to each specific server to gain access to its resources, as is done with NetWare 3.x and earlier, a user in a domain environment logs on using a domain account. This method of logging on gives the user access to the resources contained on any of the servers within the domain. With Windows NT, this concept is taken a step further with the introduction of trust relationships. With trust relationships established between domains, users can log on to a single accounts domain and have automatic access to any domain containing network resources. Of course, the user must still have the proper access privileges to the resources contained on the resource domain's server (drive share, printer share, and so on). So why are we talking so much about domains? Because domains become important for two reasons when we're working with SMS.

First, computers are added to the SMS site by domain. The domain installed by default is the domain that the site server belongs to. By default, all logon servers in this domain are detected, enumerated, and loaded with the SMS logon server components. This domain may be the user accounts domain, it may be a resource domain, or it may be a domain with just the SMS site server and a Backup Domain Controller (BDC) in it. Whatever it is, most likely you'll have to add other domains to the SMS site in order to start collecting inventory over a majority of the computers in your network.

Second, the service account used by SMS must have certain privileges in the domain in order for the SMS system to function properly. The way you set up trust relationships between domains will impact the way you set up the SMS Service account in a domain. As you'll recall from Chapter 5, "Server Installation, Part I," the SMS Service account must have Log On As A Service right. It must also be a member of the domain's Administrators local group. With trust relationships in place, you can designate a user account from a trusted domain as the SMS Service account, just as long as it possesses the appropriate rights.

Domains Containing Only NT Logon Servers Let's begin by looking at the Service account setup for an NT domain that contains only NT servers. There are two possible setup conditions that can exist; each has its own requirements for the setup of the service account in a new domain, as follows:

- A trust relationship has been set up between the primary site domain and the domain we want to add to the SMS Site. The primary site domain, which contains the original SMS service account, is the trusted domain in this scenario. You should designate the SMS Service account located in the trusted domain as the new domain's service account. When you do this, you must ensure the trusted domain's SMS Service account is added as a member of the new domain's Administrators local group. You must also make sure the trusted account has Log On As A Service right on the new domain.
- The domain we want to add to the SMS Site has no trust relationship established between it and the SMS primary site domain. In this case, you must create a service account on the new domain that has the same name and password as the SMS Service account on the primary site domain. The new service account must also be a member of the Administrators local group and must have a Log On As A Service right in the new domain.

Domains with Both NT and LAN Manager 2.x Logon Servers In addition to the setup steps we just listed for NT-server-only domains, you must also place the SMS Service account in the Domain Admins global group in any domain that contains LAN Manager 2.x logon servers. This is because LAN Manager 2.x servers recognize only global groups in NT, and not local groups. Placing the SMS Service account only in the domain's Administrators local group prevents it from administering any of the LAN Manager 2.x logon servers due to insufficient rights. However, placing the service account in the Domain Admins global group permits the service account to function with adequate rights on the LAN Manager 2.x servers in the domain.

LAN Manager Domain Preparation Preparation for a LAN Manager domain is fairly simple. All you need to do is to create an account that has the same name and password that's used for the SMS Service account on the primary site domain. You must add the account to the Admins group for the LAN Manager domain. This will permit the SMS Services to administer the LAN Manager 2.x logon servers.

NetWare Domain Preparation So you may be saying to yourself that there's no such thing as a NetWare domain, and you're correct. At least, there wasn't anything similar in NetWare until the introduction of NetWare Directory Services (NDS) with version 4.x. However, even with NetWare 4.x, the concept of the "domain" doesn't really exist. Since NetWare domains don't exist, SMS groups together NetWare servers into pseudo-domains. These domains can then be managed by the SMS system as easily as any other domain in the site.

There are some things to remember about NetWare domains. NetWare 4.x servers can be used only if the clients will be allowed to log on under bindery mode. Unfortunately, this precludes the client's use of the NetWare NDS services. This alone can be a major drawback when considering the use of SMS in the NetWare 4.x environment.

Keep in mind that when you specify that the domain being added to the site is a NetWare domain, the Configuration Service Manager will attempt to locate and enumerate all NetWare servers within 16 router hops. This isn't always desirable if you want to exercise control over which servers are included within the NetWare pseudo-domain. Although each NetWare server is detected within 16 router hops, it doesn't mean that they will all be added to the NetWare domain. Each of the NetWare servers must first be configured with NTGATEWAY and EVERYONE groups. You must also create the SMS Service account on each NetWare server that will serve as a logon server for SMS, and give the account administrative permissions to the server. Another point to remember is that the Gateway Services for NetWare must be installed and configured on the site server that will support the NetWare domain.

For the complete installation and configuration instructions for adding a NetWare domain to an SMS site, see the section titled "Adding a NetWare Domain to the SMS Site" in Chapter 6, "Server Installation, Part II."

Preparing NT Stand-Alone Servers An NT server that is not running as a Primary Domain Controller (PDC) or a Backup Domain Controller (BDC) is called a stand-alone server. When the servers in an NT domain are detected by SMS, these servers are also detected and added to the system. However, they do not receive the SMS logon components, as the PDCs or BDCs do; instead, only the Inventory Agent and Package Command Manager components are installed. In order for these servers to be able to function within the SMS environment, you must perform some additional configuration tasks that are not required on a PDC or BDC, as follows:

1. Add the stand-alone NT server to a domain that is already or will be part of the SMS site. Use the Server Manager for Domains to add the machine name of the computer to the domain.
2. Make sure the SMS Service account has been created in the domain that the stand-alone server belongs to.
3. Add the SMS Service account to the stand-alone server's Administrators local group using the NT User Manager for Domains tool at the stand-alone server.
4. Give the SMS Service account Log On As A Service right on the stand-alone server using the NT User Manager for Domains tool at the stand-alone server.

Adding a Domain to a Site

The first configuration task we'll cover is the addition of a domain to the SMS Site. Adding a domain to an SMS Site allows you to start the inventory reporting process on all servers and clients that are part of the new domain. In addition, it allows you to start package distribution, use program group control, and utilize the SMS remote help desk and diagnostic functions on the new domain members.

We'll go over the configuration steps we need to take in the SMS Administrators program in order to add a domain to the site. Then we'll take a look at the underlying process and what happens to the new logon servers when SMS starts installing its components on them.

Perform the following steps to add a domain to the SMS Site:

1. Start the SMS Administrators program and open the Sites window.
2. In the left window pane, highlight the icon representing the site to which you want to add the new domain.
3. From the File menu, choose Properties to display the Site Properties dialog box.
4. Click the Domains button to display the Domains dialog box.
5. Mark the Proposed Properties button at the top of the dialog box.
6. Click the Add button in the lower portion of the dialog box to display the Domain Properties dialog box.
7. Type the name of the domain you wish to add to the site in the Name box at the top of the Domain Properties dialog box. When specifying a LAN Manager or NT domain, the name must be that of an existing domain or a domain that you intend on installing. When specifying a NetWare domain, you can specify any name you wish up to 15 characters in length. The name is not case-sensitive.

CAUTION

When creating a name for a NetWare domain, do not specify an NT or LAN Manager domain name that already exists within the site. Doing so can cause a duplicate domain name in the sites window, and may lead to serious inventory reporting problems.

8. In the Type box, choose the network operating system that is used on the domain you're adding to the site. The type of network you choose here will determine how SMS handles the installation of the Logon Server components. Pick Microsoft Windows NT or LAN Manager if the domain consists of NT or LAN Manager servers. Select Novell NetWare if the domain consists of NetWare 3.x servers (or NetWare 4.x servers running in 3.x compatibility mode).
9. In the Logon Server area of the Domain Properties dialog box, select the method of server detection that you want to use. A general rule is to pick Use All Detected Servers if the new domain is either a LAN Manager or Windows NT domain (see fig. 15.1).

   If the new domain is a NetWare domain, choose the Use Specified Server option and specify the names for each of the NetWare servers that will be included within the domain (see fig. 15.2) in the New Logon Server box.

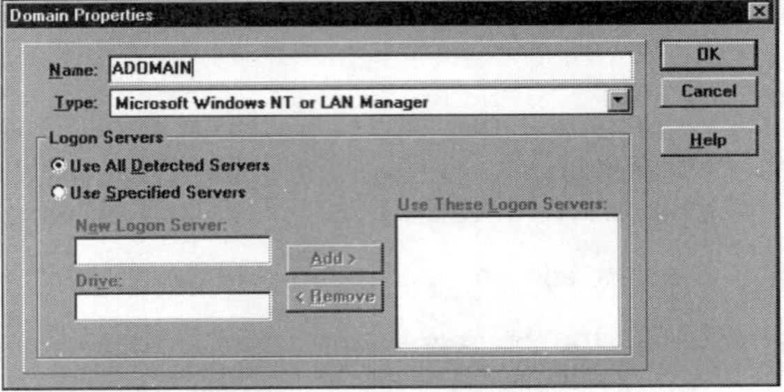

FIG. 15.1
Select the Use All Detected Servers with NT or LAN Manager domains.

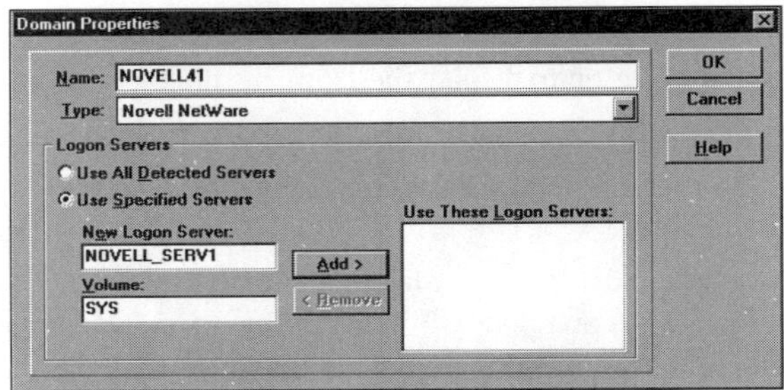

FIG. 15.2
Select Use Specified Servers with a NetWare domain.

You can also designate the target drive or volume of the server on which to install the SMS logon server components. Enter the drive letter (with colon, example: D:) or volume name (without colon, example: SYS) in the Volume box when designating a new logon server. Then click the Add button to place each of the server names (and target volume, if any) in the Use These Logon Server box.

CAUTION

When working with a new NT or LAN Manager domain, you must select the Use All Detected Servers option if the Automatically Configure Workstation Logon Scripts feature has been enabled. Failure to select the Use All Detected Servers option will prevent the user logon scripts from automatically being set up. Since the Automatically Configure Workstation Logon Scripts always inserts the SMS script in the NetWare server's System Logon Script, this setting makes no difference when setting up a NetWare domain.

10. When you've completed filling in the Domain Properties dialog box, click the OK button to return to the Domains dialog box. You will see the new domains listed in the Domain at Site box along with any current domains that are in the site. Click the OK button to return to the Site Properties dialog box.
11. Click the OK button in the Site Properties dialog box. A confirmation dialog box will prompt you to confirm the update of the site. Click Yes to initiate the changes.

After you've confirmed the update of the site, each of the target servers will have the SMS logon components installed on them. Which specific servers receive the components will depend on the method you used to specify the target servers.

How SMS Installs the Logon Server Components When using the Use All Detected Servers option on an NT domain, all Primary (PDC) and Backup (BDC) Domain Controllers are loaded with the SMS logon components. If any LAN Manager 2.x servers are in the domain acting as BDCs, they will also be detected and loaded with the SMS logon components. If a server happens to be offline during the initial configuration process, the Site Configuration Manager will detect it when it comes back online, and will configure it with the SMS logon components. In fact, the Site Configuration Manager will monitor the site for any new servers that get added to the domain; they'll be detected and automatically configured with the logon components.

CAUTION

Do not use the Use All Detected Servers option if you have logon servers that all belong to the same domain, but they are physically located at separate locations where individual SMS sites have been set up. Adding these servers to the local SMS sites using the Use All Detected Servers option will cause all servers to be detected, even the ones at the other remote locations. If the domain logon servers at the remote site have already been added to that remote SMS sites inventory, the possibility of a server being a member of several SMS sites at the same time can exist when it's detected by the current site.

For example, this can happen when a master domain model has been implemented with Backup Domain Controllers (used for local user logon) located at each of the remote locations. If each remote location has its own SMS site in place, and the master domain is added to each site using the Use All Detected Servers option, a serious configuration and inventory problem will result.

In a domain containing only LAN Manager servers, the Primary and Backup Domain Controllers are detected and loaded with the SMS logon components. Stand-alone or member servers are not loaded with the SMS logon components.

In a NetWare domain, the Site Configuration Manager will detect all NetWare (3.x or 4.x) servers within 16 router hops and will attempt to install the components on them. The setup will fail for any NetWare server that has not been properly prepared in advance.

Regardless of the domain type, the Site Configuration Manager will install the SMS logon components on the detected server's drive (or volume) that contains the most amount of free space. The only way to specify a particular target drive (or volume) on a server is to use the Use Specified Servers option in the Domain Properties dialog box.

Using the Use Specified Servers option will allow you to designate the specific target servers and drives for the SMS logon components. This is the recommended method of adding NetWare domain servers to the system, and is the default method of adding logon servers when the Novell NetWare domain type has been selected.

When using the Use Specified Servers option, the SMS logon components will be installed on the target server's drive (or volume) containing the most free space. The components will be installed to a specific drive only if the Volume box in the Logon Servers area of the Domain Properties dialog box was used to enter a drive or volume name.

The configuration process that SMS Site Configuration Manager initiates when adding a new domain server is as follows:

- Creates the SMS root directory on the NTFS drive with the most available space, and then shares the directory with the name of SMS_SHRx (x specifies the drive letter the directory was created on). If an NTFS drive is not available, the share is created on the largest non-NTFS drive. On NetWare servers, the files are placed on the NetWare volume with the most available space.
- Creates the LOGON.SRV directory under the SMS root directory. This directory is then shared as SMS_SHR.
- Logon server components are then copied to the LOGON.SRV directory.
- When the new logon server is a Windows NT machine, the SMS Inventory Agent for Windows NT is installed and started. This service is then used to collect inventory from the logon server. On a NetWare server, the Maintenance Manager collects and reports the machines hardware and software inventory.
- When the new logon server is a LAN Manager version 2.x server, the SMS Inventory Agent for OS/2 is installed and started. This service is then used to collect inventory from the logon server.
- When the Automatically Configure Workstation Logon Scripts option is used at the site, the SMSLS batch file is added to the NETLOGON and REPL$ shares. In addition, the SMSLS batch file will be added to all user profiles. The SMSLS batch file will be inserted into the user's existing logon script if one exists, or it alone will serve as the user's logon script file if the user has no current logon script file assigned.
- When the Automatically Configure Workstation Logon Scripts option is used at a site containing NetWare servers, the system logon script for each of the NetWare servers is modified to run the SMS Client Setup and SMS Inventory Agent for MS-DOS during NetWare user logon.
- The Site Configuration Manager sets the trustee rights on any SMS directories that were installed on a NetWare Server.

Manually Adding or Removing SMS Logon Servers You can manually add or remove SMS logon servers only if you selected the Use Specified Servers option in the Domain Properties dialog box.

If you picked the Use All Detected Servers option, any new logon servers meeting the domain controller requirements will automatically be detected by SMS. The server will then be loaded with the logon server components and added to the site. Any current SMS logon servers that are subsequently removed from the network will be reported as inactive by the SMS system for a period of seven days. After that, the server will be removed automatically from the site configuration. You'll have to manually remove the SMS components from the inactive server if you intend to use the server off the SMS system.

Keep the hidden file named SMS.INI that's located on the server if you ever plan to add the server back into the SMS system. This will retain its current SMSID in the system.

On the other hand, if you picked the Use Specified Servers option, you can both add and delete servers from the site at your convenience. To add a server to a domain, perform the following steps:

1. Start the SMS Administrators program and open the Sites window.
2. In the left window pane, highlight the icon representing the site you want to add the new domain logon server to.
3. From the File menu, choose Properties to display the Site Properties dialog box.
4. Click the Domains button to display the Domains dialog box.
5. Mark the Proposed Properties button at the top of the dialog box.
6. In the Domains at Site dialog box, highlight the name of the domain that you want to add a logon server to, and then click the Properties button.
7. The Domain Properties dialog box will appear. With the Use Specified Servers button marked, type in the name of the new server in the New Logon Server box.
8. You can optionally designate the target drive for the SMS components by entering a drive (or volume) name in the Volume box.
9. Click the Add button to add the server information to the Use These Logon Servers box.
10. Click the OK button to return to the Domains dialog box. The new server will now be listed under the Logon Servers column on the line for the target domain in the Domains at Site list. It is included with the servers that were previously listed.
11. Click the OK button to return to the Site Properties dialog box, then click OK again. Click the Yes button in the confirmation dialog box to initiate the changes.

Removing a logon server from a domain will remove the SMS logon components from the targeted server if it is still online. But it does not remove the server's computer inventory information from the site database. You must manually delete the server from the Sites window if the server is no longer an active member of the network.

To remove a server from a domain's logon server list, perform the following steps:

1. Start the SMS Administrators program and open the Sites window.
2. In the left window pane, highlight the icon representing the site from which you want to remove the domain logon server.
3. From the File menu, choose Properties to display the Site Properties dialog box.
4. Click the Domains button to display the Domains dialog box.
5. Mark the Proposed Properties button at the top of the dialog box.

6. In the Domains at Site dialog box, highlight the name of the domain from which you want to remove a logon server, and then click the Properties button.
7. The Domain Properties dialog box will appear. In the Use These Logon Servers list box, highlight the name of the server you want to remove, and click the Remove button. The server and volume entry will be removed from the list.
8. Click the OK button to return to the Domains dialog box. The server will now be removed from the Logon Servers column on the line for the target domain in the Domains at Site list.
9. Click the OK button to return to the Site Properties dialog box, then click OK again. Click the Yes button in the confirmation dialog box to initiate the changes.

Switching Methods of Server Detection You can change the method used to designate logon servers at any time. The implications of switching from the Use All Detected Servers option to the Use Specified Servers option, and vice versa, are as follows:

- Switching from the Use All Detected Servers option to the Use Specified Servers option will prevent the Site Configuration Manager from detecting new logon servers in the future. By default, any servers that were previously detected will be listed in the Use These Logon Servers list box in the Domain Properties dialog box. You can then add or remove servers from this list.
- Changing from the Use Specified Servers option to the Use All Detected Servers option will cause the SMS logon components to be installed on any eligible logon server in the target domain that does not currently have the components installed. In addition, it will cause the Site Configuration Manager to begin monitoring for any new logon servers that may be added to the network.

CAUTION

Changing the detection method on a NetWare domain from Use Specified Servers to Use All Detected Servers is not recommended for complex sites. Severe configuration and inventory problems can occur if the SMS site hierarchy already has NetWare domains defined within it, and the Use All Detected Servers option is used on one of the existing domains. The far-reaching detection method used by SMS will search for NetWare servers over 16 router hops. This has the potential of causing servers to be added to multiple SMS NetWare domains, possibly across multiple sites at the same time.

Removing a Domain from a Site

Any of the domains that you've added to a site can be removed. The original site server domain must remain in place and cannot be removed, for obvious reasons. Perform the following steps to remove a domain from an SMS site:

1. Start the SMS Administrators program and open the Sites window.
2. In the left window pane, highlight the icon representing the site from which you want to remove the domain.

3. From the File menu, choose Properties to display the Site Properties dialog box.
4. Click the Domains button to display the Domains dialog box.
5. Mark the Proposed Properties button at the top of the dialog box.
6. In the Domains at Site dialog box, highlight the name of the domain that you want to remove, and then click the Remove button.
7. Click Yes to confirm that you want to delete the domain.

After the process to delete the domain has been initiated, the Site Configuration Manager will begin to remove the SMS logon components from each server in the targeted domain, as follows:

- The SMS logon server components located in each server's LOGON.SRV directory are removed, along with the SMS shares on the each server (SMS_SHR and SMS_SHRx, where x designates the SMS root directory drive).
- The Inventory Agent and Package Command Manager for NT are removed from any NT logon servers, and the Inventory Agent service for OS/2 is stopped and removed from LAN Manager 2.x servers.
- The SMS root directory will be removed from each server.
- If the Automatically Configure Workstation Logon Scripts option is enabled at the site, the Site Configuration Manager will remove the SMSLS batch file components from the user profiles. If the SMS batch file call was placed in an existing user logon script, the call will be removed. If the server is a NetWare server, the modifications that were originally made to the server's System Logon Script are removed.

Moving a Domain to a Different Site

Moving a domain from one SMS site to another SMS site involves the following:

- Deleting the domain from the original site
- Adding the domain to the alternate site

Follow the steps shown earlier to remove the domain from the original SMS site. Then wait until the Site Configuration Manager at the original site has completed the removal of the SMS components from the target domain before you add it to the alternate site. You can check on the progress by looking at the Domain Properties dialog box for the original site and marking the Current Properties button. If the changes have been completed, the dialog box will not display the domain you removed as part of the site. If the changes have not taken place, the dialog box will still reflect the previous settings.

Managing SMS Site Configurations

In order to build the SMS hierarchy of sites, you'll need to be able to add both secondary and child sites to the central SMS site. A child site is a primary site that attaches, and then reports its inventory to another primary site called the parent site. The parent and child are shown in the Sites window in the standard Desktop Management Task Force (DMTF) compliant hierarchical view, with the parent sites appearing at the top of the tree (see fig. 15.3).

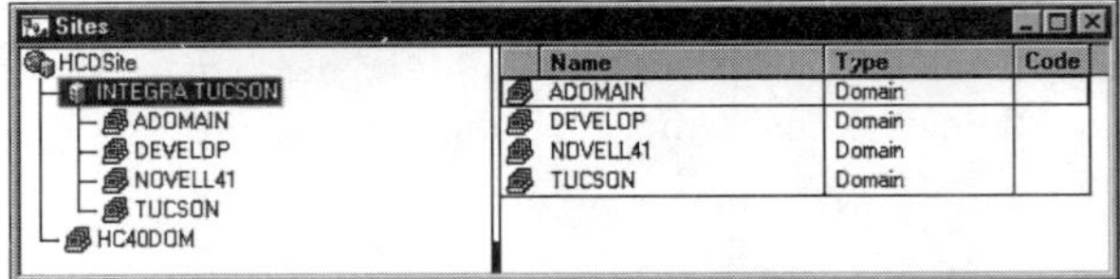

FIG. 15.3
A view of the parent-child relationship in the Sites window.

The child site, in turn, may have other child sites (primary sites) reporting to it, and the parent site may itself be a child site that reports its inventory to another primary (or parent) site. This action of attaching primary sites to other primary sites in a parent-child relationship is the basis for the SMS hierarchical structure.

NOTE Don't get the terms secondary site and child site confused. A secondary site is installed using a primary site server. It contains no site database, and cannot have any child sites attached to it. Technically, the secondary site can be considered a child site, because it reports all of its inventory to a primary site. In fact, all sites can be considered child sites except for the central site, because it's the only site that does not report its inventory to another site. On the other hand, the term "child site" refers to a full primary site that has been attached to another primary site. This site is then instructed to forward its inventory information, along with any information from its own child sites, to the primary (or parent) site above it in the site hierarchy.

This section will cover the configuration and management of primary sites within the site hierarchy, including the removal of secondary sites. We'll also review some of the communications methods used when connecting sites together. Later, you'll see how to detach a primary site from the SMS hierarchy.

The full instructions for the setup of a secondary site are given in Chapter 5, "Server Installation, Part I," and Chapter 19, "Installation Overview."

Attaching a Child Site to a Parent Site

The terms "child" and "parent" refer to the relationship between the two sites after they have been attached to each other. Since both of the sites we are attaching are primary sites, it's easier to identify them during the course of the text if we refer to each in their prospective roles of child and parent.

Child sites are attached to parent sites using one of the six Senders used by SMS. An Address is then set up on each primary site for the attaching site, using the appropriate Sender. Before we go any further, let's review the Senders and Addresses.

There are six different types of Senders that can be installed on a site server, as follows:

- MS_LAN_SENDER—the LAN Sender is used when the destination site can be accessed over an established LAN (or WAN with high-speed links).

- MS_ASYNC_RAS_SENDER—utilized when asynchronous modems and dial-up phone lines are being used for connecting sites.
- MS_ISDN_RAS_SENDER—used when ISDN connectivity exists.
- MS_X25_RAS_SENDER—used when X.25 connections exist between sites.
- MS_BATCH_SNA_SENDER—used when the SNA communication configuration uses LU pairing set to #BATCH mode.
- MS_INTER_SNA_SENDER—used when the SNA communication configuration uses LU pairing set to #INTER mode.

The one you use will depend on the method of connectivity being used to connect the sites together. Each physical method of connection between sites has a specific Sender that must be used with it. For example, on a Local Area Network where site servers are connected directly via high-speed network lines, the LAN Sender would be used. On sites being connected over dial-up phone lines, the ASYNC RAS Sender would be used. Each of the Senders and its properties are described in the section covering creating addresses in Chapter 6, "Server Installation, Part II."

By default, the LAN Sender is always installed on each site. If you're attaching a site that can be accessed directly via a high-speed network connection, there is no need to install another Sender. If your sites are not connected via a LAN or WAN link, you'll have to install an appropriate Sender on both the parent and child sites before they can be attached.

Once the Senders have been set up at each site, an Address must be set up for the attaching site. This Address will be used to designate the Sender and logon connection information that's used when establishing communication between the two sites.

TIP See Chapter 6, "Server Installation, Part II," for full installation information on Senders and Addresses.

Establishing connectivity between a parent and a child site is a relatively simple process. Just create the proper Address in the Site Properties window at each site, and you're attached. The connection process gets slightly more complicated when connecting several levels of parent and child sites together to form a complex hierarchical structure. The point to remember is that a site must be able to address all of its direct descendants, as well as its parent site. This is necessary to keep the information flowing from the site at the bottom of the site hierarchy all the way up to the primary central site at the top of the hierarchy.

To attach a child site to a parent site, perform the following steps:

1. Set up the Address at both the child and parent site. At the child site, set up the Address (and Sender if needed) for the parent site. At the parent site, set up the Address (and Sender if needed) for the child site.
2. At the child site, start the SMS Administration program and open the Site window.
3. In the left window pane, highlight the current site (marked with a globe icon). From the File menu, choose Properties to display the Site Properties dialog box.
4. Click the Parent Site button to display the Parent Site dialog box, as shown in figure 15.4.

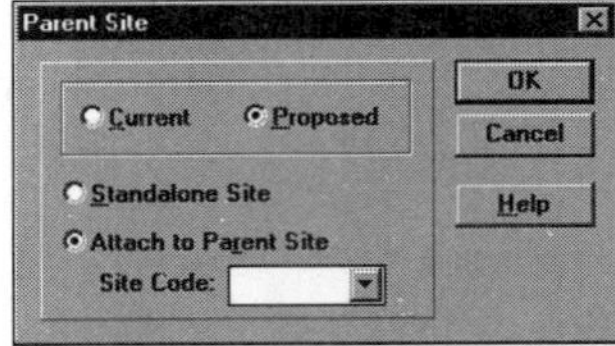

FIG. 15.4
Use the Parent Site dialog box to attach to primary site.

5. Mark the Proposed button and the Attach to Parent Site button.
6. If you have already defined an Address for the parent site, you'll be able to choose it from the Attach to Parent Site box drop-down list. If you haven't defined the Address yet, type in the Site Code of the parent site. The Site Code is the three-letter alphanumeric designation given to every site during its creation. Click the OK button when you've designated a Site Code. If you have already defined an Address for the parent site, you can skip to step 11.
7. The SMS Administrator dialog box, shown in figure 15.5, will appear, indicating that communication cannot be established with the parent site. Click the Yes button to create an Address for the parent site.

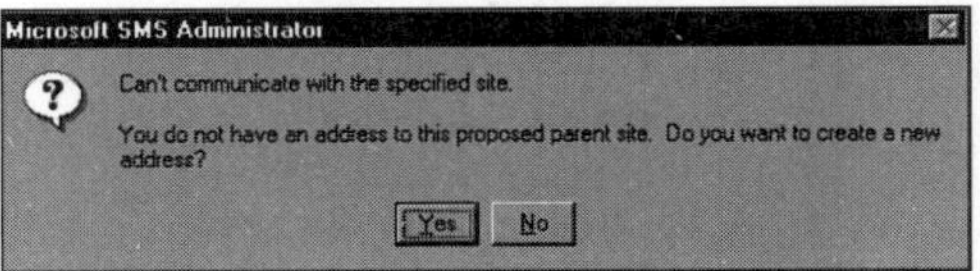

FIG. 15.5
Click Yes to create an Address.

8. The Address Properties dialog box will appear with the Site code already in the Destination Site Code box. In the Type box, select the Sender to be used from the drop-down list.
9. Click the Details button to open the Sender Address From child sitecode To parent sitecode dialog box. This dialog box will vary depending on the type of Sender you have selected. Each dialog box will prompt you for information specific to making a connection using that particular Sender. For example, the dialog box used with the LAN Sender is shown in figure 15.6.

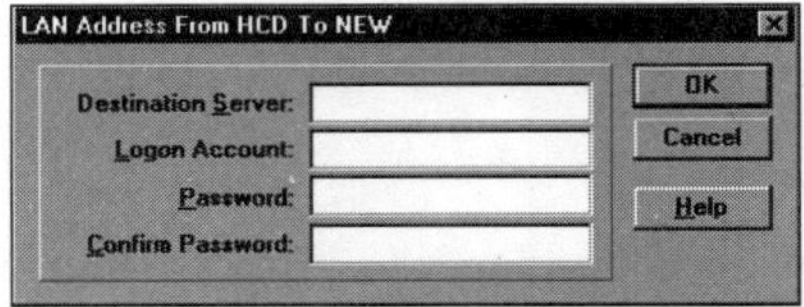

FIG. 15.6
Complete this dialog box when using a LAN Sender.

Figure 15.7 shows the dialog box that appears when using the ASYNC RAS Sender.

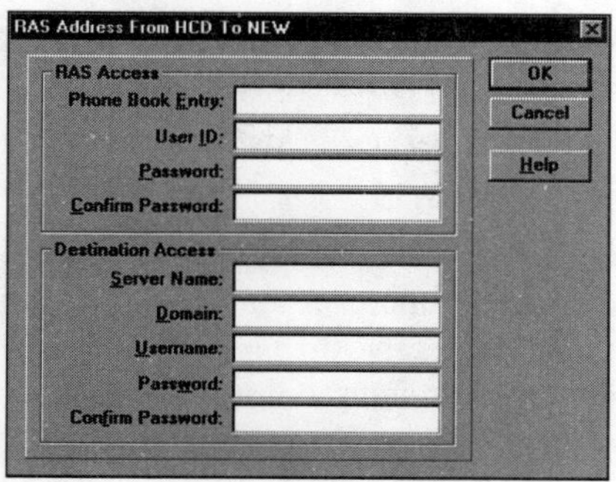

FIG. 15.7 Complete this dialog box when using an ASYNC RAS Sender.

Supply the connection information and click the OK button to close the dialog box and return to the Address Properties dialog box.

10. Click the OK button to return to the Parent Site dialog box. Click the OK button once again to close the Parent Site dialog box.
11. Click the OK button in the Site Properties dialog box to bring up the Site Update Confirmation box. Click the Yes button to confirm the change.

The Site Hierarchy Manager at the child site will detect the change to the site database caused by the administrative modification to the site hierarchy. It will then create a system job to report the information contained in its site database to the parent site. In addition, a system job will be created for each child site contained within the current child site's database. These jobs, called control jobs, are used to update the parent site's database. If the parent site itself has a parent site that it reports to, each of the control jobs are forwarded on to that parent site for inclusion in its database. The control jobs will be forwarded all the way up to the central site database.

Detaching a Primary Site

You can detach a child primary site from a parent site and then attach it to another parent site. Or you can detach it and make it the central site of its own SMS hierarchy. Any child sites that report to the child site will continue to report to the detached child site. They are detached from the parent site along with the child site, but remain connected to the child site.

Detaching a site does involve some extra cleanup of the parent site's database to remove the remaining inventory associated with the detached site and its child sites. This cleanup will have to be performed at the detached parent site and any parent sites it may have, all the way up to the central site database. Perform the following steps to detach a child site from a parent site:

1. At the child site, start the SMS Administration program and open the Site window.
2. In the left window pane, highlight the current site (marked with a globe icon). From the File menu, choose Properties to display the Site Properties dialog box.
3. Click the Parent Site button to display the Parent Site dialog box, as shown in figure 15.4.

4. Mark both the Proposed button and the Stand-alone Site button, then click the OK button to return to the Site Properties dialog box.
5. Click the OK button in the Site Properties dialog box to bring up the confirmation box. Click the Yes button in the Confirmation dialog box to initiate the changes.

After the change has been initiated, the Site Hierarchy Manager will sense the change in the site database caused by the administrative modification, and will create a system job to detach from the parent site. The parent site will receive the instructions contained in the system job, and will then update its site database accordingly. If the detached parent site has a parent site it reports to, the job will be forwarded to that site, and all the way up the hierarchical chain to the central site.

The additional cleanup of the parent site(s) database involves the removal of the child site's inventory information. This must be done on the detached parent site. If the detached parent site has a parent site of its own, the inventory information must also be removed from that site. In fact, the inventory information must be removed on any parent site, all the way up to the central site. This can be accomplished in a couple of different ways. With the first, a query is created to search for all machines with the detached child site's sitecode. The query results are then used to designate the machines that are to be deleted from the site database, as follows:

1. Start the SMS Administration program.
2. From the File menu, choose Execute Query to display the Execute Query dialog box.
3. Make sure that Ad Hoc Query is showing in the Query box, and click the OK button.
4. Set the Architecture to Personal Computer and click the Add AND button to display the Query Expression Properties dialog box.
5. Scroll down to the Identification Group, find the line containing the Attribute named Site and highlight it.
6. In the Operator box, choose the relational operator "is like" from the drop-down list.
7. In the Value box, type the three-letter sitecode of the detached child site. The completed Query Expression Properties dialog box should look similar to figure 15.8.

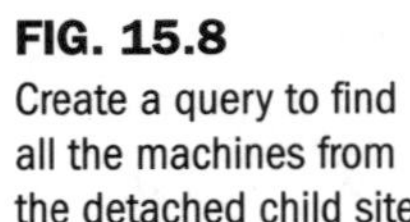

FIG. 15.8
Create a query to find all the machines from the detached child site.

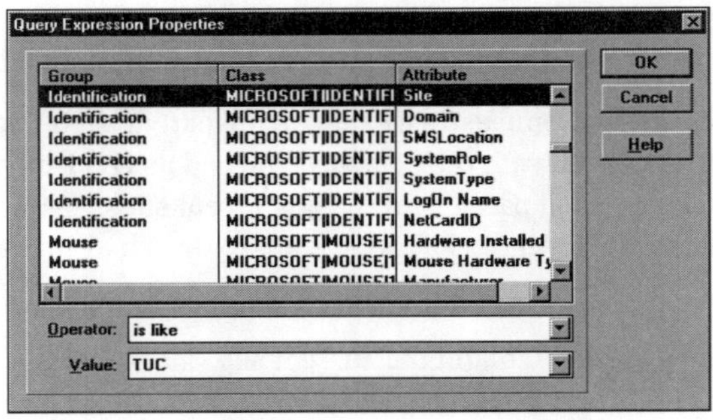

8. Click the OK button to begin to return to the Query Properties dialog box, then click OK again to start the query.
9. The Query Results window will then display all the Personal Computer inventory objects for the detached child site. Highlight all the entries in the Results window, and delete them.

The second method of removing the detached child site's inventory involves using the PREINST.EXE utility, found in the SMS*SITE.SRV*\platform directory. This utility is run from the command line on the detached parent site's site server. The syntax for the command is as follows:

```
PREINST /DELSITE {childsitecode parentsitecode}
```

where *childsitecode* is the three-letter sitecode of the detached child *site and paren*tsitecode is the three-letter sitecode of the parent site.

NOTE Deleting the computers using the SMS Administration program removes the inventory objects from the site window, but it does not remove the database records for the inventory object in the site database (or any other databases that may exist at a higher position in the site hierarchy). To remove computer records from the site database(s), the SMS Database Utility must be used. For complete instructions on running the DBCLEAN (SMS Database Utility) program, see Appendix B, "SMS System Files and Utilities." ■

If you want to remove a child site completely from the site hierarchy (to the point of performing a deinstall of the SMS components), perform the following steps:

1. Ensure that the site has been completely detached from the parent site by starting the SMS Administration program at the child site that's being detached.
2. Choose Properties from the File menu to display the Site Properties dialog box.
3. Click the Parent Site button to display the Parent Site dialog box. The site has been detached from the parent site when the Current and Proposed properties both indicate a stand-alone site.
4. Detach any child sites that belong to the detached child site using the steps given earlier for detaching a child site from a parent site.
5. Remove any Addresses associated with the site you're deleting from any sites that may have maintained communications with it.
6. Reattach any child sites (the ones that have been detached from the site we're removing) to new parent(s).
7. Perform a deinstallation on the site using the SMS Setup program.

Moving a Primary Site

You can move a primary site from one area of a site hierarchy to another area of the site hierarchy by performing the following steps:

- Follow the steps for detaching a primary site given earlier in the chapter. Check the Parent Site dialog box to verify the site has been detached before proceeding.
- Use the procedure given earlier for attaching a child site to a parent site to relocate the current site.

Removing a Secondary Site

Secondary sites cannot be detached; they can only be removed. This is done using the SMS Administration program at the site directly above the secondary site that's being removed, as follows:

1. Start the SMS Administration program and open the Sites window.
2. Highlight the icon that represents the secondary site you want to remove in the left window pane. Choose Delete from the Edit menu. The secondary site's icon changes into a wrecking ball, indicating the site is being removed.
3. If the clients of the secondary site will be logging on to another SMS site, the inventory for the clients will automatically be moved when the false logon count has been exceeded. If the clients are to be completely removed from the SMS system, the inventory objects must be removed on the parent site (and any other sites above it in the hierarchical structure). The procedure for this was outlined earlier in the chapter. Any inventory objects that are not removed from parent sites will become orphaned objects in the database.

Client Configuration and Removal

The SMS Administration program allows you to specify which client components will be installed during the Client Setup. It also allows you to designate the startup mode used if the component is installed. Clicking the Clients button in the Site Properties window brings up the Clients dialog box. This box enables you to view and set the properties associated with the SMS client configurations at your site.

The Client Software portion of the Client dialog box lets you specify which of the client components will be installed at the user's machine when the SMS Client Setup program is run. It also allows you to specify if the installed components will be started automatically during logon. We'll take a look at the properties available for configuration using this dialog box.

Package Command Manager (Clients)

Check this box to install the client Package Command Manager (PCM). This is a program used by SMS to run package commands on the SMS clients. Package commands are commands placed in an SMS object called a package. A package is created by the SMS Administrator to distribute and install software programs on the client machines within the site or its subsites. The package contains all the information needed to identify and install a specific software application on a client platform.

When a package is distributed to a client workstation for installation, the Package Command Manager allows the user to view the package and its description. Two types of packages are distributed to the client workstations.

If the package is an optional package, users can choose to skip the installation if they wish. If a user decides to accept the package, the installation can be performed at a convenient time. If the package is a mandatory package, it must be executed before the user will be allowed to continue working on the computer.

Clearing the box next to Package Command Manager will prevent the PCM from being installed on the client workstations during the SMS client installation. If the PCM components were already installed on the clients, clearing the box will cause the SMS system to remove the components from any client workstation in the site they are currently installed on.

Checking the Automatically Start This Component option will cause the PCM to start automatically when the workstation is started. The PCM for Windows 3.1, Windows for Workgroups, Windows 95, and Windows NT will start when the Windows environment is initialized. On MS-DOS workstations, the PCM is started as a program in the AUTOEXEC.BAT file.

Program Group Control (Clients)

Check this box to install the Program Group Control (PGC) components (APPCTL and APPSTART) on the user workstations. This feature can be installed only on Windows 3.1, Windows for Workgroups, Windows 95, and Windows NT clients. PGC enables network applications so they can be run over the network from distribution servers.

Clearing this box will prevent the PGC from being installed on the client workstations during the SMS Client Setup. It will also deinstall any PGC components currently installed on any client workstations in the site.

When the PGC components are installed, checking the Automatically Start This Component option will cause the PGC to start automatically when the Windows environment is started.

Remote Troubleshooting

When this box is checked, the Remote Troubleshooting support components are installed on the client workstations. Remote Troubleshooting support is required to be running on the client when using the remote help desk and remote diagnostic features of the SMS Administrator. Remote Troubleshooting support can be installed on computers running MS-DOS, Windows 3.1, Windows for Workgroups, Windows 95, and Windows 3.51 and later.

Deselecting this box will instruct the SMS system to remove the Remote Troubleshooting support from the computers the next time the Client Setup program is run.

Selecting the Automatically Start This Component option will cause the Remote Troubleshooting support to start automatically when the workstation is started. MS-DOS, Windows 3.1, Windows for Workgroups, and Windows 95 workstations will run the Remote Troubleshooting agent (USERTSR.EXE) from the computer's AUTOEXEC.BAT file. Remote support is then available when the Windows environment is initialized and started. Windows NT machines run the Remote Troubleshooting agent as a service that is configured with the Auto Start option enabled.

MIF Entry Program (Clients)

SMS installs the MIF Entry Program on all client computers in the site when this box is checked. MIF is an acronym for Management Information Format, a standard for accessing desktop information across different hardware and software platforms using an ASCII file that complies to a set of standard formatting rules. This program allows clients to enter information on forms that can then be kept in the SMS database for future reference. The forms can be generated using the MIF generator that's included with SMS software. The forms can be distributed automatically to be filled out by the users of the network's workstations. Forms can be created for a wide variety of purposes. Anything from user information to computer serial numbers can be stored in the database using these forms.

Clearing the MIF Entry Program check box will cause the SMS to deinstall the MIF Entry Program from all workstations at the site.

The Automatically Start This Component option will start the MIF Entry Program when the workstation is started. On clients running Windows 3.1, Windows for Workgroups, Windows 95, and Windows NT, the program will start when the Windows environment is started. MS-DOS machines start the program from the AUTOEXEC.BAT file during startup.

The Automatically Configure Workstation Logon Scripts (Clients) Option

Checking this box will allow you to have SMS automatically set up and maintain user workstations in the site. It does this by configuring the user logon scripts in LAN Manager and Windows NT domains to run the SMSLS script file as the user's logon script. In NetWare domains, the system logon script is modified on all servers in each domain. If the user already has a logon script, a call to the SMSLS batch file will be placed in the user's existing logon script. You can designate the location of the call statement in the user logon script by marking the Insert at Top of Logon Script button or the Add to Bottom of Logon Script button.

CAUTION

Before enabling this option, consider the number of users that may potentially be loading the SMS client components at the same time over your network. This can cause a strain both on network bandwidth and on network support personnel. Consider using a phased approach by adding clients to the system in smaller groups that are more manageable and will cause less impact on both network and support resources.

Setting the Package Command Manager Polling Interval

This property allows you to set the default polling interval that the client Package Command Manager uses when polling the logon server for new packages. The default polling interval is 60 minutes. This means that every 60 minutes, the PCM will check with the logon server to see if any new packages are available for installation.

Client Component Removal

The removal mode of the Client Setup program is invoked using the /r command line option. As its name implies, it is used to remove the client components from a computer. This command can be run from the SMS logon server's SMS_SHR share. Before you run the Client Setup command from the command line, make sure you are in the proper logon server directory for the client operating system or platform you are working from.

Client removal can also be accomplished by running the DEINSTALL batch file from the logon server share. DEINSTALL will detect the operating system type (and processor architecture if needed) and run the correct version of the Client Setup program with the /r switch for you automatically. Regardless of how the Client Setup program is invoked, the removal mode still performs the same steps.

On DOS-based machines that do not have Windows installed, the removal process is performed in one pass. In this phase, all the SMS files are removed from the client, and all SMS-related entries are deleted from the system files. Like the Client Setup program running in upgrade mode, removal mode on Windows-based clients is also performed to two phases as follows:

> The first phase modifies the SMS.INI file's [Local] section SetupPhase entry to equal DEINSTALL as follows:
>
> ```
> [Local]
> SetupPhase=deinstall
> ```
>
> The second phase requires a reboot of Windows clients and a log off/log on of NT clients.

During the second phase of the client removal process, the following will happen:

1. The SMSRUN file scans the SMS.INI file and detects the DEINSTALL phrase.
2. SMSRUN continues the process by starting the SMSSRV program with the /c switch.
3. SMSRUN then exits, leaving SMSSRV to call the Client Setup program to complete the removal process.
4. Once the user has logged back on, SMSSRV invokes the Client Setup program with the /k switch.
5. The Client Setup program then removes any SMS components from the computer.
6. The Client Setup program completes the removal process by eliminating any SMS-related statements from the computer's system files.

Configuring the SMS Services

In order to relieve some of the load on your site server, you can move some of the SMS Executive service components to other Windows NT servers within the site. The following listed components can be moved.

Scheduler

Initially located on the site server during installation, the Scheduler (SMS_SCHEDULER) service can be moved to a helper server. It is located on both primary and secondary sites.

The Scheduler processes both system and administrative jobs. It becomes very CPU-intensive when compressing packages.

Inventory Data Loader

This is another component that is originally installed on the site server, but may be moved off onto a helper server.

The Inventory Data Loader (SMS_INVENTORY_DATA_LOADER) is responsible for maintaining user group, inventory, job status, and event information within the SQL SMS database. It takes Delta-MIF (DEL*.MIF) files created by the Inventory Processor and uses them to update the site database. The process used by the Inventory Data Loader for updating the site database is outlined below.

If you move this service to an alternate server, it is recommended that the server be the SQL Server that contains the site database. This is because the Inventory Data Loader is the service that updates the site database. Placing it on the same server that contains the SQL database allows for more efficient performance.

Inventory Processor

The Inventory Processor (SMS_INVENTORY_PROCESSOR) runs on all site servers. It uses the *.RAW files created by the Inventory Agent to create Delta-MIF (DEL*.MIF) files.

Despooler

By default, the Despooler (SMS_DESPOOLER) component is installed on the site server in both primary and secondary sites. It can be moved to a helper server to ease the processing load on the site server.

The Despooler acts as a control agent for package files by reading the associated instruction file and processing the package according to the instructions. Since this service decompresses packages, it also places a heavy load on the CPU.

To move this service, or one of the other services mentioned here to another server, follow these steps:

1. At the child site, start the SMS Administration program and open the Sites window.
2. In the left window pane, highlight the desired site. From the File menu, choose Properties to display the Site Properties dialog box.
3. Click the Services button to display the Services dialog box.
4. Mark the Proposed Properties button. This will allow you to modify the Service Locations area of the dialog box.
5. Enter the server name of the target server in the Server Name box next to appropriate service. In the example shown in figure 15.9, we are moving the Despooler service components to the server named MARS.

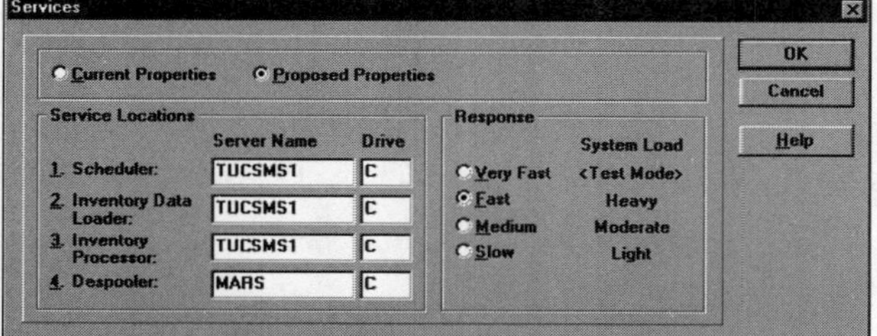

FIG. 15.9 Designate a new location for service components using the Services dialog box.

6. In the Drive box, enter the drive letter of an NTFS partition on the target server. This is the location to which the service components will be moved.
7. Click the OK button to return to the Site Properties dialog box, and click the OK button once again to display the confirmation box. Click the Yes button in the confirmation box to verify the changes.

You'll notice that the Services dialog box also allows you to set the frequency at which the services monitor the site database. This allows you to adjust the load placed on the server(s) by the SMS services.

Setting the Monitoring Frequency

This portion of the Services dialog box allows you to set the response time used by the services when monitoring the site. SMS services monitor the site database, SMS directories, and the system files on both the site server and logon servers. The faster the response time, the more frequently the services monitor the site. The more a service monitors a site, the more the service uses server resources, thus placing a heavier load on the server.

The Response setting controls the polling period that is used for each of the services. Table 15.1 shows the services that are affected by the response property, along with the polling period (in minutes) used for each response rate setting.

Table 15.1 The Polling Time (in Minutes) for Each Response Rate Setting Will Vary Depending on the Service

Service Name	Slow	Medium	Fast	Very Fast
Site Hierarchy Manager SMS Alerter SMS Scheduler Applications Manager	30	15	5	1
Maintenance Manager	360	180	60	12
Site Configuration Manager Despooler	720	360	120	24

Each of the services will perform certain actions at each polling period that contributes to the operation of the SMS system. A brief description of the actions taken by each service follows:

- Maintenance Manager—verifies that the correct and most current files are installed on all the site's logon servers.
- Site Configuration Manager—checks active logon servers to ensure all SMS services are running.
- Site Hierarchy Manager, SMS Alerter, SMS Scheduler, and Applications Manager—check the site database for any changes.
- Despooler—setting the response rate for the Despooler controls the retry rate at which the Despooler will attempt to process failed Despooler instructions.

CAUTION

Setting the Response rate at Very Fast will place a very heavy load on the server, especially in a large site. This setting is usually reserved for testing purposes only.

Configuring the Default Servers Machine Group

The Default Servers machine group is created during the site installation, and initially contains only the site server. This machine group is used to designate the machines that will be used as target distribution servers for jobs when Default Servers is selected as the target. When a job is created, the SMS Scheduler builds a list of target servers based on the Default Servers machine group. The information for each site's Default Servers machine group is retrieved from the database where the job was created. It will therefore include only servers for the target site's machine group that were present the last time the target site reported its inventory.

It is recommended that the site server be removed from the Default Servers machine group. This is done to conserve disk space and reduce the load on the site server. You can replace the site server with one or more of the following computers:

- Any Windows NT SMS logon server
- Any LAN Manager SMS logon server
- Any NetWare SMS logon server
- Any Windows NT Workstation

The computers do not need to be part of the SMS system to be designated as a distribution server. Note that if you're using a Windows NT Server or Workstation, you must ensure that the SMS Service Account is a member of the Administrators local group. In addition, clients that will be accessing packages from these machines must have adequate access privileges to the directories containing the distribution files for the package.

Follow these steps to add a server to the Default Servers machine group:

1. At the child site, start the SMS Administration program and open the Sites window.
2. In the left window pane, highlight the desired site. From the File menu, choose Properties to display the Site Properties dialog box.
3. Click the Servers button to display the Servers dialog box.
4. Mark the Proposed properties button, then click the Add button to display the Server Properties dialog box.
5. Type the name of the server you want to add to the Default Servers machine group in the Server Name box, then click the OK button.
6. Select Default Package Server from the Server Type drop-down list (see fig. 15.10) and click the OK button.

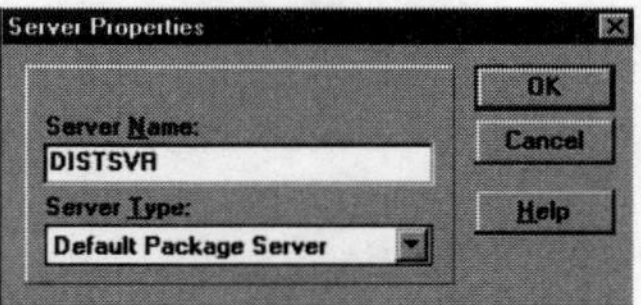

FIG. 15.10
Configure the Default Servers machine group.

7. The new distribution server is now added to the Servers at Site dialog box. Click the OK button to close the Servers dialog box and return to the Site Properties dialog box. Click the OK button to bring up the confirmation box, and click Yes to confirm the changes.

Changing the SMS Service Account

The Accounts dialog box appears when you click on the Accounts button in the Site Properties window. This allows you to change the SMS Service Account used by SMS services.

Changing this dialog box affects only SMS Services and not the actual user account. It does not actually configure the logon domain user account or password. This dialog box specifies only a user account name and password for the SMS Services to use.

The dialog box contains the following information:

- Username—the ID of the user account that will be used for running SMS services. This account must be a member of both the local Administrators group and the Global Domain Admins group.
- Password—password for the user account designated for running SMS services.
- Confirm Password—password confirmation for the SMS Service account.

CAUTION

It is suggested that when changing the Account properties, you do not change just the password, but change both the username and password.

Assigning the SMS Services to a new user account will prevent problems if the site server happens to get restarted during the configuration changes. By changing only the password, you risk the chance that the Site Configuration Manager will not be able to restart. This can happen because the new password may not have been processed by the time the server gets restarted. Because the Site Configuration Manager will try to use the old password to log on, the service logon will fail, which, in turn, will prevent the service from starting.

When a new account is created, the Site Configuration Manager service is still able to logon using the old account (and password) in the event the new account information has not been processed. Once logged in under the old service account, the Site Configuration Manager can continue to process the transition to a new account and password.

The SMS Setup program can also be used to set the SMS Service Account, and to change the SQL Server logon ID used by SMS services. The advantage of setting the SMS Service account information using the Setup program is that the Setup program will verify the existence of the domain account being used. It will also verify that the account has the proper permissions on the domain. This is not done when using the SMS Administration program to change the account information. The only restriction to using the SMS Setup program to configure the service account is that it can set up an account only on the current site.

From Here...

This concludes the chapter covering modification of the site configuration. Further information concerning the topics discussed here can be found in the following:

- Chapter 6, "Server Installation, Part II," covers the Site Properties dialog box and its options in detail. It also covers the details of a secondary site installation.
- Chapter 16, "Monitoring the SMS Site," examines the techniques and tools used within SMS to monitor the site.
- Appendix B, "SMS System Files and Utilities," looks at the files and utilities that are used in the daily maintenance of the site.

CHAPTER 16

Monitoring the SMS Site

In this chapter you will learn how to:

- **Configure SQL Alerts**
- **Use SQL Performance Monitor**
- **Use Network Monitor**
- **Set up a Network Trace**

As captain of the SMS ship, at times you will have to look at the compasses, gauges, and meters on the console. The SMS Administrator is your console. You can also use NT and SQL Event Viewer and Performance Monitors for monitoring your operation. ■

Setting Up SQL Server for Mail Alerts

You can configure Mail SMS Alerts with a Microsoft Mail Account. This will allow you to monitor alerts via a mail account when SQL Server generates alerts. Mail is built into Windows NT, and these alerts help you to manage the SQL facet of SMS operations.

To configure Mail SMS Alerts, perform the following steps:

1. Click the SQL Setup icon and choose Set Server Options.
2. Choose the Mail Login button and enter a Mail Login Name and Password(you should have a Microsoft Mail Account set up on the NT Server).
3. Choose Auto Start Mail Client so that Mail will start automatically when SQL starts up (recommended).
4. Choose the Change Options button to complete.

It is important to monitor SQL database activity.

Setting Up the SQL Performance Monitor

In the SQL Server group on the NT Server, notice that there is an SQL Performance icon. This is similar to NT Performance Monitor, but is specifically geared to show you what the SQL database is doing. In the bottom window are the following five types of activity:

- Cache Hit Ratio—tells you whether you have enough cache memory allocated to SQL Server and Windows NT. If you have to page out memory to the hard disk, your cache is not big enough. A cache hit ratio of 85 percent to 95 percent is ideal.
- I/O Transactions/sec.—hard disk I/O.
- Page Reads/sec.—SQL memory page reads.
- Single Page Writes/sec.—SQL page writes.
- User Connections—SMS can often leave phantom user connections. If the maximum connections are 25, the default, you can see the last value, the minimum value, and the maximum value of the number of user connections. You can use this monitoring counter to track what the optimum user connection value should be. The default value for the figures to be updated is every five seconds, and it can be changed.

One unique counter is Log Space Used (MB). You may want to see how large the log file gets for SMS and tempdb. SQL keeps all transactions in a log until a checkpoint, and then clears the log. SMS uses the tempdb log for queries.

Try bringing the SQL Server down and back up during off hours to lose phantom user connections. Do this in the SQL Service Manager by pressing Stop and then Start/Continue. SMS will run continuously through this process.

If you want to see a graphical representation of your five counters in the bottom window, use the `Edit, Add to Chart` command to choose which counters you want to see in graph form—for example, cache-hit ratio—and which color line in the graph should correspond to that particular counter. The Explain button will explain every counter in detail.

The default view in Performance Monitor is a chart view, and your counters will be added to the chart immediately.

Saving Your Chart

Your chart options will not be saved unless you choose File and Save Settings. Try exporting your chart with a .TSV or .CSV file. The .TSV files are tab-delimited, the .CSV files are comma-delimited.

Configuring Alerts in Performance Monitor

Under Options menu is an Alert option. There are three interesting options available for setting up a system alert, as follows:

- Switch to Alert View
- Log Event in Application Log
- Send a Network Message

Let's say that you want to get an alert if the SMS log is greater than 80MB. You would choose Options, Alert, find the counter SMS Log Space Used, alert if over "80."

If you choose the View, Alert option in Performance Monitor, you will see the Alert entry in an Alert log in Alert view. However, if you choose the Send Network Message option in the Alert Options window, you will get an NT message alerting you to SMS log > 80.

Improving Performance

Consider the following for improving performance:

- Add CPU
- Mete out SMS Services to helper servers
- Place the SQL Server on a separate machine
- Upgrade CPU

Systems Management Server provides the Help Desk and Diagnostics features which offer the ability directly to control and monitor remote clients running MS-DOS, Windows 3.1, Windows for Workgroups, and Windows 95.

The information below can help you determine a hardware configuration that maximizes performance for your site.

Although this discussion focuses on CPU, RAM, and disk resources, thorough hardware planning also considers factors such as cache memory, throughput to the network, and bus speed for adapter cards.

The *Systems Management Server Administrator's Guide* recommends this minimum site server configuration:

- 66-MHz 80486 processor
- 28 MB of RAM
- 100 MB of free disk space

Although these minimums are adequate for some sites, larger sites may require additional hardware for satisfactory performance. The sections below examine the specific factors to consider when planning your site server hardware.

In general, most sites dedicate the most powerful CPU (or even multiple-CPUs) to Systems Management Server. For most sites the CPU does not become a bottleneck, so a single, fast 80486 or Pentium processor is adequate as a site server. Site servers running Microsoft SQL Server in addition to Systems Management Server are more likely to become CPU-bound, in which case you can add CPUs or move SQL Server to a dedicated computer. You can check CPU usage with Microsoft Windows NT Performance Monitor.

During normal operation, the Systems Management Server site server at a primary site runs a set of Systems Management Server Services consuming at least 18 MB of RAM on the server and 16 MB on secondary site servers at startup. Systems Management Server requires about 8 MB of RAM on each Systems Management Server Logon Server.

Systems Management Server requires a great deal of disk space on the site server and the computers running SQL Server. You need to carefully monitor the free disk space available on both types of computers: a site can stall if the SQL Server database is full, or if the Systems Management Server site server runs out of disk space. When this happens, Systems Management Server cannot send or receive any new packages, warning events, or status. All of the Systems Management Server services continue to run, but Systems Management Server Administrator displays no new information.

Systems Management Server files can be installed to several different drives and directories, as described below (numbers supplied are for x86 systems):

- The Systems Management Server system files are copied to the Systems Management Server root directory (specified by the user at installation). This directory requires the most disk space—typically about 60 MB for a default x86 installation, and another 17 MB if the site has any child secondary sites.
- Note that after Systems Management Server has been installed it writes many other types of files, such as inventory and event MIFs, into this directory. In a large, busy site, this can account for 20-40 MB of associated files in the Systems Management Server root directory; in a complex site experiencing performance problems (for instance, generating a lot of events and resyncs), there may 100 MB or more.

- Files used by the local client processes running in the local user context are installed to the \MS directory. This directory may or may not be installed on the same drive as the site files, depending on free-space conditions. Typically these files take about 1 - 3 MB of disk space.
- Files that are used during the user logon process are copied to the NETLOGON and EXPORT shares in the Windows NT Server directory tree. Typically these files take about 1 MB of disk space.
- If the site server is also being used as a package source server, or as a package distribution server, then multiple copies of the package exist on the server. Although two of the copies are compressed (the sent and received copies), the copies take up to four times as much disk space as the original package.

A default software unit installation consists of:

- x86 Client
- x86 Network Monitor
- x86 Server
- x86 Systems Management Server Administrator
- Scripts
- Systems Management Server Books Online

An All Software Units installation consists of the default list plus:

- Alpha Client
- Alpha Server
- Macintosh Client
- MIPS Client
- MIPS Server

Disk space requirements roughly double when you include all software units.

Disk throughput is one of the most important factors to consider when selecting an Systems Management Server site server. Systems Management Server can run on a site with Windows NT Server, SQL, and Systems Management Server installed on the same disk, but it runs very slowly if there is much of a load on the site.

You can use Performance Monitor to observe disk throughput and if it proves to be a performance bottleneck you can increase disk I/O capacity by using faster disk drives, multiple disk drives, or a faster bus. An array of disks with a cached, fast SCSI, bus-mastered controller dramatically increases Systems Management Server system performance.

Systems Management Server makes heavy use of SQL Server, and the interface to SQL Server is frequently a performance bottleneck. For instance, it typically takes the Systems Management Server Data Loader Service one or two minutes to process and load a complete hardware inventory MIF into the database; loading 1,000 MIFs may take more than a day.

Because of this and other factors (described below), the SQL Server used for Systems Management Server should be dedicated to Systems Management Server if possible, and SQL Server should not be run on the Systems Management Server site server, if possible.

Microsoft recommends at least 32 MB of RAM dedicated to SQL Server for Systems Management Server. The SQL Server configuration lists the minimum SQL Server memory requirement. This is a key Systems Management Server performance factor, and increasing the amount of RAM dedicated to SQL Server is frequently one of the easiest ways to speed up Systems Management Server performance. At a central site, or even at very busy primary sites, 64 to 128 MB of RAM can boost performance by allowing SQL Server to cache the database.

Help Desk

Using the SMS management tools from a Windows NT Server or Windows NT Workstation console, an administrator or technician can take control of a remote computer running Windows 95, MS-DOS or NT (with 1.2 and above) to perform management or troubleshooting tasks.

From a single seat an administrator, with or without the user being present, can do the following:

- Check the memory map, interrupts, and other system parameters.
- Monitor the state of the remote computer, including resource utilization.
- Remotely execute commands.
- Reboot the remote computer.
- Install software.
- Transfer data.
- Remotely chat with two-way text messaging between the administrator and the client computer.
- View the remote computer's screen and guide the user through a difficult task.

When the Help Desk option is run, Systems Management Server verifies that the client computer is running and connected to the network. If not, Help Desk attempts connection using various protocols installed on the server, until the server successfully connects to the client computer. Users can control the degree of access they want to give the administrator by setting the following options:

- Remote boot
- Remote file transfer
- Remote execution of commands
- Remote takeover
- Remote viewing

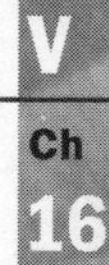

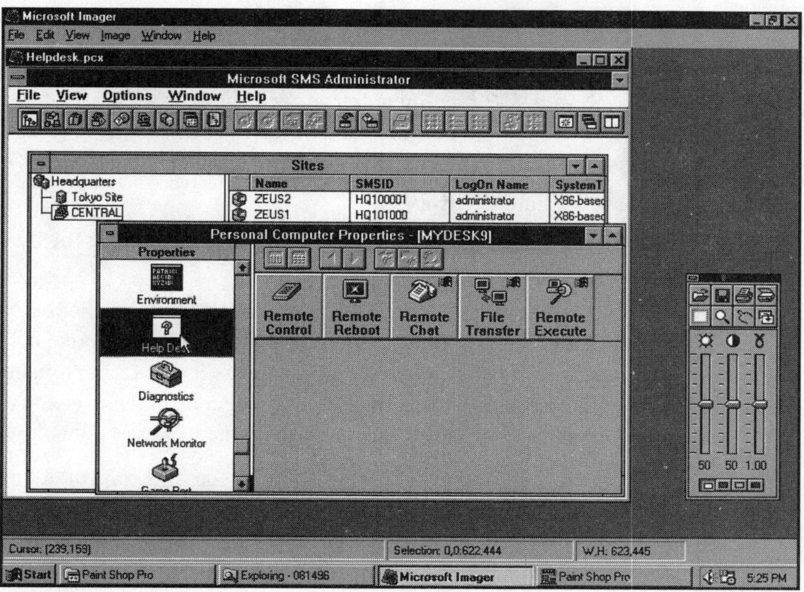

FIG. 16.1
Help Desk options.

Remote file transfer and remote execution of commands must be enabled for the client to participate in software distribution through Systems Management Server.

If you are viewing the properties of a Windows-based client and you have already enabled the remote control features on the client, you can start working with the remote features of Systems Management Server. As you explore the inventory details, in the Personal Properties you will see two options: Help Desk and Diagnostics. Each feature detects whether or not the machine is running, and then starts either a remote help session (Help Desk) or a remote diagnostic session (Diagnostic).

The Help Desk option allows you to troubleshoot and support individual computers remotely. From the Systems Management Server administration console, a support technician can take control of a remote MS-DOS or Windows-based computer, and access the Windows NT Workstation and Windows NT Server management tools to perform management tasks—all from one central location, across either a LAN or WAN. A support technician can:

- Guide the user through a difficult task or perform the task directly, with or without the user being present
- Remotely execute commands
- Check the memory map, the status of interrupts, and other operating system parameters
- Transfer files and install software
- Restart the computer

To remotely access the client from the primary site server, follow these steps:

1. From the Properties list of the Personal Computer Properties dialog box, choose Help Desk. Systems Management Server will check whether the machine is running and attached to the network. This action will try the various protocols that are installed on the server until it successfully connects to the client machine.
2. Choose Remote Control.
3. The Quick Windows Viewer window appears, displaying the desktop of the remote client.
4. Notice that the site server has shared control with the client during the remote control session; if you move the mouse at the site server, the mouse pointer moves on the remote client. Likewise, either you or the user at the client machine can enter text with the keyboard. You also can use the remote control features to run an application on the client machine from the Systems Management Server console.

By remotely accessing the client it is possible to take full control of the client and work on the machine just as if you were there—the cost savings are obvious. It is worth noting that these features can work across X.25, ISDN, or standard asynchronous phone lines, as well as any normal routed network. Once you have worked with the remote control feature, try some of the other features of the Help Desk option, such as File Transfer or Remote Execute.

In addition to Help Desk, there are a number of tools available using the Diagnostics option. The following picture shows the amount of Windows Memory available on the machine being viewed. All of these tools provide the ideal solution for help desk operators by enabling them to resolve users' problems from one central location, thus minimizing the need for individual trips to users' machines.

Diagnostics

The diagnostics utilities allow you to view the current hardware and software configuration of a workstation. Table 16.1 shows diagnostic utilities for Windows 95 clients.

Table 16.1 Diagnostic Utilities for Windows 95 Clients

Item	Description
CMOS Info	Displays the CMOS data, which is used during startup to configure the client computer.
Device Drivers	Provides information about the device drivers.
DOS Memory	Lists the programs currently loaded in conventional memory.
GDI Heap	Lists and describes the characteristics of memory objects in the local memory storage for the graphical device interface.

Item	Description
Global Heap	Lists the addresses of memory objects in the remote client's global memory storage, along with various characteristics associated with each object.
Interrupt Vectors	Lists the MS-DOS interrupt vector table.
Ping Test	Sends packets between the administrative console and the client; verifies the accuracy of transmission.
ROM Info	Provides detailed information about all installed read-only memory chips.
Window Classes	Provides information about Windows classes used in programs.
Windows Memory	Provides information about memory and available memory resources.
Windows Module	Provides information about active code modules.
Windows Tasks	Provides information about programs listed in the Task List.

These tools provide the ideal solution for help desk operators, allowing them to resolve many user problems from a central location.

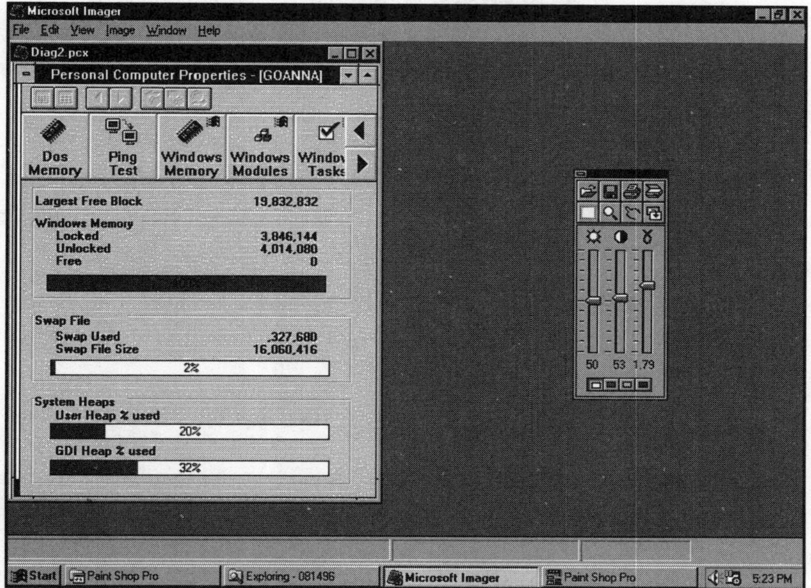

FIG. 16.2
The SMS diagnostic tools.

Alerts

Anything you can set up a query about, you can set up an alert for. Would you like to be alerted if client's workstations' hard disks are full? If server hard disks are full?

Creating an alert involves the process of specifying the alert query, the threshold for reporting, and the actions to be performed.

To create an alert, perform the following steps:

- Open the Alerts window in SMS Administrator.
- Choose New from the File menu. The Alert Properties dialog box appears.
- Type the following requested information in the appropriate boxes:
    - Name—used to save and reference the alert.
    - Comment (optional)—used for additional reference information about the alert.
    - Query Opens the Execute Query—dialog box where the query used by this alert is defined.
    - Actions—opens the Alert Actions dialog box where the alert actions are defined. You will specify alert conditions with thresholds that are required to trigger the alert's actions. For each alert, the Alerter process executes a query against the site's database at an interval that you specify. The Alerter compares the query's hit count to the alert's threshold. If the condition is true, the alert actions are per formed. You must execute a query to set up your alert. The following lists options in the Execute Query dialog box:
    - Query—the name of the query to be executed.
    - Limit to Sites—the sites on which to execute the query.
    - Include Subsites—specify if the alert will apply to the site's subsites.
    - Repeat Query Every—the time interval between executions of the query.
    - Generate Alert—six comparison operators that can be used in creating the alert.

Defining Actions to Be Performed by an Alert When conditions specified by the alert query cause the hit count to cross the threshold, SMS performs the actions set for the alert. An alert can perform any or all of the following actions:

- Log an Event—logs an event in the SMS Database and the Windows NT Event Log at the site server.
- Execute Command Line—specify the commands you want entered when this alert is triggered. It will execute from the computer where the SMS Alerter is installed.
- Notify Computer or Username—sends a network message to the computer and/or users specified. The message box includes the alert time and the date and time that the alert was detected.

Viewing, Modifying, and Deleting an Alert After you have created an alert, you can view and edit the alert's properties from the SMS Administrator Alert Properties dialog box.

If the alert query changes, SMS will automatically run the query again. The SMS Alerter monitors the database for any changes made to alert properties. When a change is detected, the Alerter implements the changes.

You can delete an alert from the Alerts window by using the Delete key or the Delete command from the Edit menu, and removing it from the system database. When the Alerter detects that an alert has been removed from the database, it stops all processing of an alert. However, if a query is being executed by the Alerter, it will be allowed to complete, but it will not trigger an action.

Monitoring a Multi-Site Environment

In a multi-site environment, the Systems Management Server Hierarchy Manager service manages the multiple-site hierarchy when the user has multiple sites.

Multiple-site hierarchies are constructed in two ways: by connecting primary sites together, and by creating secondary sites beneath primary sites.

All primary sites are created by running Systems Management Server Setup. Secondary sites are created using the SMS Administrator. Primary sites have a Systems Management Server Administrator and an SQL database. Secondary sites have no Systems Management Server Administrator or SQL database.

The terms parent and child, when applied to SMS sites, are subject to the following rules:

1. A site can have only one parent. A strict tree structure is observed, where each node can have only one parent and an arbitrary number of children. The site tree cannot contain any kind of circular references, and sites cannot have more than one parent.
2. Secondary sites cannot report to each other in a parent-child relationship. Each secondary site must report to a primary site as its immediate parent. There is no mechanism at secondary sites to forward information to another site in this way.
3. Primary sites are added to the tree from the bottom up. A parent site does not acquire a primary child site. A primary child site must decide to report to a parent and attach to the parent site after creating an address to that site.
4. Primary sites can decide to detach themselves from their parent site and become a top-level site with no parent. When they do this, the parent receives instructions to eliminate that site and all its children from its hierarchy tree. The primary site can then reattach to a different parent, if needed. The primary site can also simply switch to a new parent site in one operation.
5. Secondary sites are deleted through their parent site. The site is physically deinstalled when this happens.

6. The structure of the site tree can be altered by changing parent site codes for the various sites. A primary site can detach from its current parent and attach to a new one or become independent, as stated in point four above. Secondary sites can also have their parent code altered to another site.

Using the Network Monitor

Network Monitor lets you capture and view raw network frames across the network. The protocol parser in Network Monitor checks the raw frame for a particular protocol (for example, NetBIOS or SMB) and returns data properties about that protocol. You can then use these properties to query for specific frames from the entire set of acquired frames.

Network Monitor provides a full API set for controlling the capturing, querying, and displaying of frames from Windows applications, ensuring support for internal and third-party developers.

Network Monitor runs in the background. A user can run other applications while Network Monitor is capturing or filtering the network traffic. It runs on Windows NT-based and Windows for Workgroups-based computers.

NOTE To use Network Monitor, network cards must support promiscuous mode. Luckily, most newer cards do. Network Monitor is compatible with NDIS 2 or 3. NDIS is the Network Driver Interface Standard that allows Microsoft Networking to support a multitude of network cards, and makes network topology transparent to the upper layers of the network operating system. ■

Starting Network Monitor

SMS includes Network Monitor agents for Windows NT, Windows 95, and Windows for Workgroups.

When you want to analyze traffic on a network segment, a capture agent puts your network card into promiscuous mode. The agent makes a copy of all frames that pass your computer on the network for as long as you want the capture. Network Monitor stores the frames and sends the summary statistics to the Network Monitor application.

You can start Network Monitor from the SMS Administrator under the PC Properties dialog box, under the SMS program group on the SMS Server, or from the client. If you start it from the client, it will capture only the frames relevant to that client, making it a useful tool if the client is having connectivity problems.

You can set password options for Network Monitor, believe it or not, by going into Windows NT Control Panel. Under your Monitoring Agent icon, you can set Network Monitor to start in one of the three following ways:

- Full access for capturing and displaying data, no password requested.
- Partial access only for displaying data, requires a display password
- Full access with a password.

NOTE Display-only access only allows you to view previously captured files.

Capturing Network Traffic Data

The Network Monitor user interface has the following four sections:

1. The bar graph displays current activity on the network.
2. The Session Statistics section displays statistics about individual sessions on the network.
3. The Station Statistics section displays statistics specifically on the computer running Network Monitor.
4. The Summary Statistics section includes all graphs of total network utilization, including frames, bytes, broadcasts, and multicasts per second, as well as statistics for individual computers.

Network Monitor automatically builds an address database of "friendly names" to help you identify individual stations. You can filter captures based on computer address (or address pairs), protocols, or data patterns within the frame. These friendly names appear in the Station Statistics and Session Statistics sections in place of the network adapter card addresses.

Network Monitor capture triggers allow you to start capturing when a specific frame pattern is received, and then execute specific programs or batch files when the capture agent receives a frame containing a pattern you specify. You can also edit and retransmit frames you have already captured to reproduce network problems or to generate network activity to simulate specific test conditions.

To capture and display data from the network, perform the following steps:

1. From the Capture menu, choose Start.
2. To stop collecting data, from the Capture menu choose Stop.
3. To pause the data capture, from the Capture menu choose Pause.
4. To display collected data, from the Capture menu choose Stop and View.
5. Or from the Capture menu, choose Stop and then choose Display Captured Data.

The Network Monitor interface has three windows or panes—the Summary pane, the Detail pane, and the Hex pane. You can use the toolbar's `zoom` command to maximize or reduce each pane.

Summary Pane The Summary pane will show you all the types of frames that have been captured in a given amount of time—for example, NetBios Broadcast.

There are columns in the Summary pane. These columns include the following:

- Frame—all frames are listed with a frame number and a capture time here. You can set a filter to see only a certain type of frame.

- Time—frames here are listed according to the time they were captured. You can set the display to see the frame according to the time of day, or relative to the last time a similar frame was captured.
- Source Address—shows the hardware address for the machine originating the frame.
- Destination Address—shows the hardware address of the computer receiving the frame.
- Protocol—the protocol used to transport the frame.
- Description—a summary of the frame's contents. The summary information can include all protocols used in a frame.

Detail Pane The Details pane displays protocol information for any frame highlighted in the Summary pane.

If you select a protocol in the Detail pane, the associated hex strings for the current frame are highlighted in the Hex pane. If a protocol has a "+" beside it, you can get more information in the Detail pane by clicking the protocol. You can also specify colors to use in displaying the various protocols.

Hex Pane The Hex pane displays the content of the selected frame in hexadecimal and also lets you edit frames.

If you highlight information in the Detail pane, the hexadecimal data appears highlighted in the Hex pane. The Network Monitor displays each byte in the frame as two hexadecimal characters, 00 to FF. The corresponding ASCII characters appear on the right.

If you clear the Read Only menu option in the Edit menu, you can edit a frame's content by changing hexadecimal values or by editing text in the ASCII section.

Reporting a Network Problem

Microsoft suggests you take certain steps if you are having a problem with SMS, either to report a bug or to report an unusual problem to their support center.

To report a network problem, you should do the following:

- Turn on tracing to a file or console for the tracking of processes.
- Use the REGDMP utility to dump the Registry to a file.
- Provide a listing of the SMS installation directory. Use the `dir/s` command. Example: `dir c:\sms/s>DIR.TXT`.
- Provide a listing of the currently running services. Use the `Net Start` command to display services. Example: `net start>SERV.TXT`.
- Provide a copy of the pertinent files (SITECTRL.CTO,*.SRQ,*.INS, and so on) and any input files used that might have caused the problem, such as .MIF or .RAW files.

Network Monitor Architecture

- Network Monitor's layered architecture consists of four major components, as follows:
- Network Monitor User Interface (UI)—the Network Monitor UI is just one example of an application that uses the Network Monitor Kernel. When used to control a Remote Agent, the Network Monitor UI is often called the Manager (because it manages the remote session).
- Network Monitor Kernel—supports the Network Monitor Kernel APIs.
- Support Modules (DLLs)—supports various Network Monitor functions, such as protocol parsing and Capture of Display Filter.
- Network Abstraction Layer (NAL)—consists of a Network Driver Interface Specification (NDIS) device driver.

User Interface (UI) The most of the UI focuses on capturing data and manipulating the display of previously captured data (setting display filters, stipulation search criteria, making property queries). It does this by using the extensive API set provided by the Kernel. The UI controls the Network Abstraction Layer (NAL) indirectly through the Kernel, and tells it when to place the network in promiscuous mode and begin the capture sequence.

Network Monitor Kernel The main tasks of the Network Monitor Kernel are to communicate with the protocol parser modules using a parser interface; to control the support modules and the Network Abstraction Layer (NAL); and to provide application programming interface (API) support to applications such as the User Interface.

Support Modules (DLLs) Network Monitor supplies various support modules, such as protocol parsers, filters, and toolbars. The most important of these are the protocol parsers and the filter manager. Parsers analyze captured raw data, recognizing and decoding a particular protocol (or suite of protocols), and identifying properties of interest. After it identifies them, the parser attaches properties to the raw data via APIs that the Kernel provides. The Kernel stores property information for all parsers and isolates the parser from the UI. This design approach makes it easy to replace the UI and change or add parsers without drastically affecting other modules.

Network Abstraction Layer (NAL) The Network Abstraction Layer (NAL) driver implements the Network Driver Interface Specification (NDIS) driver that emulates an NDIS-compliant protocol stack. This driver manipulates the adapter and acquires the network information by communicating with an NDIS-compliant network card driver. By creating a different NAL for each network interface specification, Network Monitor can take advantage of many drivers and cards. In the first release, Network Monitor supports NDIS 3.0. Future versions might support other network specifications.

Remote Agent Architecture When running on Windows NT, the Network Monitor Manager can connect to Remote Agent drivers. This allows the Network Monitor User Interface to display data captured on a computer running the Network Monitor Agent, even if it was on a different subnet.

The Network Abstraction Layer concept allows Network Monitor to perform captures on remote machines running the Remote Agent, much like local captures.

The Manager Remote NAL (RNAL) communicates over the network with the Agent RNAL using Network Monitor's own RMB (RNAL Message Block) protocol. The agent captures data on its network through an appropriate NDIS Network Abstraction Layer.

As the preceding paragraph indicates, a manager can connect to the remote machine via a direct LAN link or through a modem and a Remote Access Server (RAS). If the remote computer contains multiple network cards, the user specifies which card to use in capturing frames. ●

CHAPTER 17

Troubleshooting SMS Components

An SMS troubleshooting specialist will be a treasure in the MIS department of the future. With the SMS package saving ten times the time of deploying software distribution and inventory methods of yesterday, one of the important members of a corporate MIS team is the SMS specialist. Knowing how to troubleshoot SMS is worth big bucks, for you and your company.

In this chapter, you will learn:

- **Using SMS Troubleshooting Utilities to Troubleshoot and Solve Problems**
- **Collecting a Network Monitor Trace**
- **Listing and Troubleshooting the Most Common SMS Problems**
- **Tracing the Operation of Each SMS Process**
- **Using the Windows NT Event Viewer to Look at SMS Error Messages**

Understanding Services

One of the first things you will learn as an SMS troubleshooting specialist is that you should know all the services necessary to run SMS. View services by starting the SMS Services Manager tool in the SMS program group. The following five services and nine SMS_EXECUTIVE components must appear and be running:

SMS_HIERARCHY_MANAGER

SMS_SITE_CONFIG_MANAGER

SMS_INVENTORY_AGENT_NT

SMS_PACKAGE_COMMAND_MANAGER

SMS_EXECUTIVE

Processes started by SMS_EXECUTIVE are the following:

Maintenance Manager

Inventory Processor

Site Reporter

Scheduler

Despooler

Inventory Data Loader

Applications Manager

Alerter

LAN Sender

SMS_HIERARCHY_MANAGER and SMS_SITE_CONFIG_MANAGER startup should be set to Automatic. The SMS_EXECUTIVE's service startup is set to Manual. The SMS_SITE_CONFIG_MANAGER will start up the other manual startup services—no administrator intervention is required.

SMS will give an error message if a key service is not started. At times you will have to check the SMS Services Manager tool's window to check which service isn't running. If a service is missing, go into NT's Control Panel Services applet and try starting the service needed. If that doesn't work, shut down and restart the Windows NT (Site) Server. If the missing services or components do not appear, you must do a Site Reset. This can be done by running SMS Setup, and choosing the Operations option and then the Reset Site option.

Checking Shares

From time to time, you may want to check to make sure the SMS required shares are created and in order. To do this, you would use the File Manager (or Explorer in NT 4.0) to determine whether all of the required shares are shared out and working.

SMS_SHRd—the SMS root directory, *d*:\SMS, will be added on your NTFS installation partition, indicated by *d*:\. The following subdirectories will appear under the SMS root directory:

SMS_SHR—the directory SMS\LOGON.SRV on every logon server. The main directory accessed by the client, it contains SMSLS.BAT and other files used for client operations.

SMS_SITE—the location to which a remote site connects when transmitting data to the local site.

The following shares are created on the site server during the setup process:

SMS_SHR*d*, SMS_SHR, SMS_SITE.

Understanding SMS Error Reporting

Systems Management Server reports events, warnings, errors, and information to both the Windows NT application event log and the SMS site database. In addition, the SMS processes report their errors to individual trace files.

Once SMS generates these events, the Windows NT Event Viewer or SMS Administrator can be used to view them. In an SMS site hierarchy, all the events flow up the hierarchy to the central site.

When an SMS event is reported by an SMS process, it performs the following two tasks:

1. An event is written to the local Windows NT event log. If the process is running on a computer other than the site server, an event is also logged at the site server.
2. The Inventory Data Loader places the event in the SMS database at the primary sites. The originating process creates a Delta-MIF file in the SITE.SRV\DATALOAD.BOX\DELTAMIF.BOX directory. If there is a parent site, the Inventory Data Loader passes the Delta-MIF file to the Site Reporter. This is how system events are reported all the way up to the central site.

Using the Events windows of the SMS Administrator, you can view events for the site where you are logged on and all sites below it.

Troubleshooting General Problems

Regardless of the function being carried out, most SMS errors fall into one of four categories: database, disk errors, network, and security, as follows:

- Database Errors Processes fail because the database is shut down or is corrupted.
- Disk Errors Processes fail because they do not have enough disk space, or files are too corrupted to perform their tasks.

- Network Errors Processes cannot move data reliably between servers on the network.
- Security Errors Processes fail because they do not have the appropriate permissions to files, directories, or the database.

It is also helpful to divide troubleshooting concerns into major categories of actions within SMS, as shown in table 17.1.

Table 17.1 Major Troubleshooting Categories

Actions	Difficulty
Installing a primary site	The SMS processes will not start.
Installing a secondary site	The remote site installation never completes.
Inventory and MIF files	Expected inventory is not displayed correctly in SMS Administrator.
Running commands on SMS	Client application packages and their command lines are not being distributed or run correctly on the SMS client.
Shared applications	The shared application is not running correctly on the SMS client.
Remote Control	The administrator is unable to perform remote control correctly on an SMS client.
Alerts	Expected alerts are not occurring.

Troubleshooting Site Configuration and Installation

Configuration of a Site Server is a fairly simple thing to accomplish. There are, however, some things to keep in mind while working within the Site Properties window.

The following steps review the installation and configuration process:

1. Generate a site configuration and update the SMS database with the proposed change.
2. The Hierarchy Manager monitors the database for configuration changes.
3. Hierarchy Manager produces a site control file with the .CT1 extension, listing proposed changes.
4. The Site Configuration Manager reads the .CT1 file and carries out changes.
5. The Site Configuration Manager produces a site control file with a .CT2 extension, listing actual changes made.
6. The Hierarchy Manager reads the .CT2 file.

7. Hierarchy Manager updates the SMS database with the actual changes.
8. SMS Administrator now reflects the configuration changes in the Site Properties window.

Inventory collection can be broken down into two general areas. The first is the definition and distribution of inventory collection information to the site's Logon Servers, so that it may be read by the inventory agent running on the clients. The second phase of inventory collection involves the client agent writing collected inventory data to the Logon Server where it is then picked up by and processed at the Site Server. It is also the Site Server which finally adds the inventory information into that site's SMS database, and, if it has a parent site, passes the inventory information up the SMS Hierarchy until it reaches the Central Site. The following information will help clarify various aspects of the inventory collection process.

Inventory Collection

The actual inventory collection process starts at the client machine. This is where the Inventory Agent runs and performs its hardware and software scan. Inventory collection continues at the site server where the inventory information is collected and processed.

There are different Inventory Agents for each of the supported client operating systems located on the logon servers in the *d*:\SMS\LOGON.SRV\X86.BIN subdirectory. For troubleshooting purposes, the /V switch should be used when running the agent. This causes the agent to go into verbose or trace mode while running a hardware and software scan. This can be accomplished by modifying the SMSLS.BAT file on the logon server. The output should be piped to a text file, because the information will probably scroll off the screen too fast to read. An example using the NT 32-bit inventory agent is the following:

```
INV32.EXE /V > SCAN.TXT.
```

The text file can then be read to determine if the agent encountered any problems.

For troubleshooting the remainder of the process, use File Manager to follow the movement of the files described below, use the trace logs of the components involved, and finally check the SMS Administrator tool's Events window for any error messages.

The following steps review the inventory collection process:

Configuring Inventory

1. SMS Administrator is used to configure inventory collection and place the configuration information in the database.
2. The appropriate processes on the site server get the information from the database and then create configuration files on the logon servers.
3. The Inventory Agent on the client uses the configuration information to determine which software to inventory and whether inventory is being resynchronized.

▶ **See** Appendix D, "A Detailed Look at the Data Flow," for more information.

Don't use the Collect This File option in a package setup unless you really need to. Each file collected that is found on a client will be moved to the logon and site servers every time a software scan is performed on the client. This can slow down performance at the client and take up disk space at all primary and secondary site servers.

Reporting Inventory

Inventory is collected by the Inventory Agent at each client and reported all the way up the site hierarchy, as follows:

1. The agent writes the inventory information (*.RAW) to an SMS logon server; this file includes the collected files.
2. The Maintenance Manager collects the files from the logon server.
3. The *.RAW file is converted to a *.MIF file, a text file approximately 20 to 40 Kb in size.
4. Data is read into the database.
5. The change information is reported to a parent site if applicable.

Software Distribution

The following steps review the process of configuring an application for distribution:

- The administrator uses SMS Administrator to create a package and a job, which are placed in the SMS database.
- The Scheduler compresses the .SRC source files and creates the package instruction and send request .SRQ files.
- The Scheduler gives the files to the Sender, to be sent to the destination sites for each job.
- The Despooler at the destination site receives the package and stores a master copy in its \STORE directory.
- The Despooler decompresses the master copy and then copies these files over to the job's distribution servers. After placing the files on the distribution servers, the Despooler creates .IOO instruction files for the SMS clients, telling them what package is available and from which distribution servers it can be run.
- The Package Command Manager (PCM) on the client runs the `package` command that has been sent to it. After the `package` command is run, status is reported back to the Despooler, which passes the information to the Inventory Data Loader to update the SMS database.

Check SMS.INI for Job Status— it will tell you whether a job has executed. Type=Workstation, Status=None means that the job's Command Line has not yet been executed at the client.

NOTE The workstation's Domain | SMS UID entry in SMS.INI is used as identification, not the machine name. ■

TIP Check the Inventory This Package option when Creating Packages. This is disabled by default. Unless this box is checked, this package's information will not get compiled into the master inventory list (PACKAGE.RUL) at the site server for later analysis.

NOTE Don't forget to look in the SMS Administrator tool's Events window. ■

Sharing Applications

The following is a summary of steps configuring an application as a shared application that can be run at SMS clients:

1. The administrator configures an application for sharing, which includes:
   Setting up a software package.
   Defining program items.
   Setting up a Share Package on Server job.
2. The administrator configures the program group for the clients.
3. The Scheduler, Sender, and Despooler send application groups to the distribution servers. The Maintenance Manager places configuration information on the logon servers.
4. When a user logs on, the Program Group Control (PGC) application gets shared application and user group information from the logon server.
5. Program Group Control gives a program manager group and icon to the user for each available shared application. After creating the desktop icons, Program Group Control runs any configuration scripts.

After the shared application group and icons are configured, the user can run the application. Make sure you check the following items:

- Database—Check that SMS Administrator can connect to the SMS database to create the job.
- Disk—Check that there is disk space for the packages and that the disk is reading and writing properly.
- Network—Check network protocols, or use the Network Monitor utility to view how data is crossing the network.
- Security—Check that the client has access to the files on the distribution server.

The Administrator account must be able to connect to \\SQL_Server\IPC$ (Named Pipes).

The Sender copies files to *destination site_server*\SMS_SITE, using the account that corresponds to the destination site's address. If this account is not valid or has expired, or the password has to be changed, the Sender will fail. The Scheduler uses the SMS service account. The Despooler must be able to access \\distribution_server\SMS_SHR.

- Use caution with the Run Local Copy if Present option. If checked, it will look for a file matching the Command Line entry. For example, the program item is setup to run Excel 5.0 off a Distribution Server; the Run Local Copy if Present box has been checked. A user executes the program item on the client machine, where a local copy of EXCEL.EXE is found. The local copy executes, but unfortunately it is Excel 4.0.
- Do not forget to pick the Supported Platforms option or the program item will not show up on the appropriate desktops.

Check the C:\MS\SMS\PCMHIST.REG file to see a job's execution history.

Remote Control

The remote control process allows the administrator to take control of an SMS client's keyboard and mouse. This is done using SMS Administrator and a corresponding client TSR program. These two applications communicate over a NetBIOS or IPX session.

Troubleshooting at the Client

Here are some tips for avoiding problems at the client workstation.

- Don't forget that by default the Remote Viewer Options at the client are disabled, meaning remote control will not be possible. Use the Help Desk Options tool in the SMS Client program group at the client to enable remote control. Remote control over TCP/IP requires that the stack have NETBIOS support.
- Reboot the machine after it is scanned for the first time to allow USERxxx.EXE to load, and the SMS Client program group to be created.
- The `USERTSR` or `USERIPX` command is located in C:\MS\SMS\BIN\CLIENT.BAT. CLIENT.BAT is called from AUTOEXEC.BAT.
- The client agent, USERTSR.EXE, uses the first loaded protocol. By default USERIPX.EXE uses IPX/SPX.
- Do not forget to start WUSER.EXE on Windows 3.1 and Windows for Workgroups 3.11 machines. Use the Remote Control tool in the SMS Client program group at the client to start it.
- To troubleshoot, use USERTSR.EXE with the /L switch to choose a protocol stack other than LANA 0, that is, the one loaded first. For example if NetBEUI is the second protocol that is loaded (LANA base=2), then the line must read USERTSR /L2.

Tracing SMS Processes

When the problem has been narrowed down to a specific process or program, then you can look at the trace file to see exactly what is wrong.

Each SMS process has the ability to place trace information in a log file in real time. The trace information describes the different operations the process is performing and whether the operation has succeeded or failed.

Tracing is configured by the SMS Service Manager application. System tracing is on by default when you install SMS. For performance reasons, tracing can be turned off or on for the whole system or for individual processes. The location and size of the log files for each process can also be configured. By default, the maximum size of a log file is 128Kb.

Each SMS process makes log entries for significant actions that it performs or errors that it encounters. These entries are written to one or more log files.

The log files are ASCII text files that you can view with a text editor. All the server component log files are located in \SMS\LOGS except the Setup and Site Configuration Manager log files. The Setup log is located in C:\, while the Site Configuration Manager log is in the root directory of the partition on which SMS is installed.

You can use the log files to help you diagnose problems, follow the progress of actions within the system, or simply monitor the SMS processes.

Understanding the Hierarchy Manager Steps

The Hierarchy Manager keeps track of the Site Hierarchy in SMS. The Hierarchy Manager monitors the database for proposed site configuration changes, creating .CT1 files for such changes. It monitors the SITE.SRV\SITECFG.BOX directory for .CT2 site control files that reflect new configuration changes from the Site Configuration Manager. If a .CT2 file appears in the above directory or when its polling interval expires, it will begin action.

Each time the Hierarchy Manager is activated, it performs the following tasks:

- Reads the Registry for SQL Server information. This information includes the SQL Server account, database name, and SQL Server name needed for the Site Hierarchy Manager to connect to the SMS database.
- Checks for disk space. If there isn't at least 512Kb free disk space, the Hierarchy Manager goes dormant until the next processing cycle occurs.
- Looks for changes to the local site and each subsite in the site table. If changes have been made in SMS Administrator, it takes the unposted records and performs appropriate actions, such as creating a .CT1 file.
- Updates the database with information from the .CT2 file.

- Checks the addressability of the local site to itself and all subsites. Heirarchy Manager is normally the first to know about new sites. If an address is not found, it generates an error event.
- Reads the Registry for the Polling Interval and goes dormant until next interval for Polling occurs.

Understanding the Site Configuration Manager

The Site Configuration Manager runs on the site server. It waits for .CT* files to be copied to the SITECFG.BOX inbox directory in the SMS install directory. Site control files define the site configuration options you want, such as domains in the site or services to install. Site Configuration Manager does the following:

- Updates the Local Registry with Site Control File Information (.CT0)

  The Site Configuration Manager retrieves the data in the site control file (.CT0) and writes this data to the Registry as Pending Install if they are new to SMS.
- Updates the List of Logon Servers in the Domains within the Site

  The Site Configuration Manager reads the list of domains for the site from the Registry. It enumerates the servers in each domain to find all logon servers. The logon servers are added to the Registry and marked as Pending Install if they are new to SMS.
- Verifies the Values Specified in the Registry

  The Site Configuration Manager uses the Registry as the definition for the site installation, and proceeds with verifying that the actual installation of domains and servers exists as defined. It removes any domains or servers that are marked as Pending Deinstall, and it installs any that are marked as Pending Install. If any are marked as Active, it verifies the installation.
- Reports Back Any Changes to the Hierarchy Manager

  The Site Configuration Manager reports the installation status of the site by creating a site control file (.CT2) and writing this file to the Hierarchy Manager's directory. If this is a secondary site, a system job is used to send the file.
- Configures User Scripts for Automatic Inventory Collection

  The Site Configuration Manager adds the SMSLS.BAT users' logon scripts or a NetWare server's system logon script when Automatically Configure Logon Script is selected. It copies the logon files into the REPL$ share of the primary domain controllers for the Windows NT, LAN Manager, or LAN Server domains in the site for replication to the backup domain controllers.

The Scheduler Steps

Scheduler reads configuration information from the Registry and saves the current SQL Server time for later use in cleaning up the Job Details table.

The Scheduler performs the following tasks in its main task of processing jobs:

- Checks for a scheduled job's source. At a primary site this is the database, and at a secondary site this is the SCHEDULE.BOX directory.
- If the Scheduler finds any jobs that have to be repeated, it creates a new job and schedules its start time to current time plus the repeat interval. The repeat status of the original job is marked complete.
- Sends a cancel message with the job ID to the trace file, and then performs the necessary actions for the type of job to cancel that job.
- Prints current job, send, and work status in the trace file.
- At secondary sites, deletes completed mini-jobs.

The Scheduler is also responsible for determining which Senders are available and which one is most appropriate for a given send request.

The Scheduler performs the following functions:

- Keeps a list of available sender outboxes.
- Loads the current outbox schedules.
- Updates the Send Request list.
- Gets the Outbox Capabilities from the *.CPB file for each outbox.
- Builds the Outbox Send Request lists.

Run the net time `\\`*`server_name`* `/SET /Y` command at the client to synchronize its clock with that of the server. Scheduler operations require good time.

Understanding Sender and Despooler

The most common reasons for failure by the Sender are network problems and lack of disk space on the target machine. Account problems can also block access. Be careful entering the password in sender properties: once it is in there it is encrypted and never again displayed as text. If there is a problem with the sender password, the only option is to enter the current password as an update and wait until the change is propagated. To check the connection, use the NT command:

```
NET USE \\destserver\ipc$ /u:UserAccountName  Password
```

The Sender uses the user account name listed in the Addresses window under Site Properties for the target site. Note that there can be multiple addresses to one site. Check the account name for all addresses to the site. Consider using the domain name as part of the account name (that is, CentralDom\smsadmin) to help resolve ambiguity about which domain to use to verify the account.

How to find the entries about your job in the sender.log:

1. Start with the SCHED.LOG. When the Scheduler sends the job to the Sender, it assigns a send request to it. Find the job id (in the Jobs window in the Admin UI).
2. You can find the job by searching in the lansend.log file on 30008DPW.

Messages from different threads are intermingled and the file can be confusing if multiple threads are sending at once. Read the thread at the end of the line to keep things straight.

1. By default, the LAN Sender can spawn up to five threads to send packages, but no more than three to any one target site. If the Sender has four packages to go to the same site, it sends the three with the highest priority first, then sends the fourth job as soon as one of the first three is finished. If five packages are going different sites, it sends all five simultaneously.

   This is the only part of the process that uses the "Priority" field from the Job Schedule screen. If there are three sends to one site in progress and a higher priority send for that site arrives, the Scheduler suspends a low priority job and starts the new, higher one.
2. The number of threads for LAN senders can be configured with the registry key \\hkey_local_machine\software\microsoft\sms\components\sms_lan_sender\.
   Maximum Concurrent Sendings (the total number of threads, five by default)
   Maximum Concurrent Site Sendings (the maximum sends to a site, three by default).
3. In the example above, notice that the file name the Sender is writing to is a combination of the Package ID (not the job ID or the send request number) plus .w[two numbers]. The .w indicates a Workstation Install job; an .s indicates a Shared Application.
4. If sending is interrupted the Sender can resume from where it left off. If the connection cannot be re-established, the Sender reports this to the Scheduler, which postpones the send and retries later—repeatedly over several days before canceling the job as Failed.

The Despooler processes the package. The Despooler does not use polling cycles; Windows NT notifies it whenever a file is placed in its directory and the Despooler begins processing. If jobs fail, the Despooler wakes itself up periodically to retry them.

This says the Despooler has started processing the package. The instruction file that the Scheduler created for this Despooler has the send request number as the instruction filename. The Despooler also reports the job ID and package ID.

This directory is off the root and starts with _S as the directory name. The Despooler completely re-creates the directory structure of the original source tree, tries to establish a connection to the first distribution server to receive the package, chooses an "appropriate" volume on that server, and copies the files. It always follows this process, even if it is going to distribute the package to itself.

If multiple servers are to receive the files, the Despooler at this point would copy them from the temp directory to the other servers.

Next the Despooler creates the instructions that client Package Command Manager reads and places them in site.srv\maincfg.box\pcmdom.box\<domain>.000. The Maintenance Manager section (next) explains how these files get to where the client can read them.

With distribution complete, the Despooler deletes the temp directory and the job is done.

The Despooler sends back status MIFs during processing: decompression successful (Arrival MIF), distribution to a server successful(Server MIF), distribution complete (Completion MIF). If the Dataloader is backlogged, it make take a while for these entries to be loaded into the database.

1. The most common cause for failed distribution to a server is lack of disk space.
2. The next most common cause is a failed connection. The Despooler attempts to connect to the servers using the account specified under "Account" in the Site Properties window for the site where Despooler is running.
3. Another cause is that the target servers don't support that type of package being distributed. For instance, the source directory contains Macintosh files but the distribution server does not have Services for Macintosh installed, or the source directory contains long filenames and the target server is running NetWare.
4. If the distribution to any of the servers fails, the Despooler retries frequently and creates a descriptive error MIF that shows up in the Systems Management Server Events window.
5. If the distribution does not succeed with all servers, the Despooler still creates the client instruction files (ins files), but only lists in them the servers to which distribution succeeded, and the clients try only those servers.

Senders

The six Senders (LAN, RAS-ASYNC, RAS-ISDN, RAS-X25, SNA-Batch, SNA-Interactive) all operate in the same manner; they check for a send request instruction file (.SRQ) in their appropriate directory and follow its instructions. The Sender then moves two files: the instruction file for the destination Despooler, and a compressed package file.

As the Sender moves the files, it updates status and changes the file extension. The file extension changes from .SRQ to .SRS, because they are now status files.

Despooler

The Despooler monitors the arrival of the SITE.SRV\DESPOOLR.BOX\RECEIVE instruction files .INS. When an .INS file arrives, the Despooler immediately wakes up and begins processing the instructions.

Troubleshooting the Maintenance Manager

Clients report inventory and status information to the logon server. The Maintenance Manager collects this data and moves it to the site server. The Maintenance Manager also manages data related to software distribution. Maintenance Manager tasks are as follows:

- Collects ISV MIF files from the LOGON.SRV\ISVMIF.BOX. This will also collect the inventory reported by the Macintosh and OS/2 Inventory Agents. Collected files from these clients are moved from the ISVMIF.BOX*.CFD directory to the site server.
- If the PACKAGE.RUL file on the site server has changed, the Maintenance Manager updates the software scanning rule file PKG_16.CFG at the site server in the SITE.SRV\MAINCFG.BOX\CLIENT.SRC.
- Reads the site server's local registry for the DOMAIN.INI parameters (SMS\Components\SMS_MAINTENANCE_MANAGER).
- Copies the SMS client instruction files and gives the Inventory Agent an instruction for resynchronization. The resynchronization instructions for all clients of one domain are kept in the file RESYNC.CFG in the MAINCFG\INVDOM.BOX\domain _name directory. The RESYNC file for each domain is replicated to all the logon servers in that domain.
- Copies the files used by the Inventory Agent:*.UID, PKG_16.CFG, DOMAIN.INI, SMSLS.BAT.
- Copies the client application .RAW and .MIF files. All the binary files are placed in LOGON.SRV*Platform*.BIN.
- With Macintosh clients, updates the DOMAIN.TMP file with Mac information. If the logon server has Services for Macintosh on it, the InvMacIniInfo parameter is set to the path of the DOMAIN.INI file. This parameter will be blank if DOMAIN.INI is in the root of the SMS_SHR volume (default). The [AppleServers] section is also updated with the Zone and logon server name.

NOTE If the logon server is running Services for Macintosh Zone, MM will look in its Registry for the default Zone name. If the default Zone name has been left blank (or has the * character), SMS will not function properly.

NOTE Maintenance Manager checks for inventory on NetWare servers every 24 hours, because there is no Inventory Agent or SMS inventory service running on the NetWare servers.

Using SMS Diagnostic Tools

Like most other areas of SMS, there is a wealth of tools and techniques for troubleshooting. Many of these can be found on the SMS CD-ROM and have been developed by or as a result of PSS. They are located in the PSSTOOLS directory. Below is a sample of some of the most useful utilities.

Like most other areas of SMS there is a wealth of tools and techniques for troubleshooting. Many of these can be found on the SMS CD and have been developed by or as a result of PSS. They are located in the PSSTOOLS directory.

Network Monitor

This utility is used to diagnose network problems between two computers or general problems with the network. It is also discussed in Chapter 16, "Monitoring the SMS Site."

Network Monitor is used to collect and view raw network frames in real time. After the frames have been captured and stored, they are broken into their separate protocol entites by modules known as protocol parsers. The protocol parser's job is to determining if the raw frame contains a particular protocol (for example, NetBIOS or SMB) and returns properties about that protocol. These properties are then used to query for specific frames from the entire set of acquired frames. Network Monitor provides a full API set for controlling the capturing, querying, and displaying of frames from Windows applications.

Starting Network Monitor

Network Monitor is entirely software-based; the only special hardware you need is a network card (with a supporting NDIS driver) that supports promiscuous mode. SMS includes the Network Monitor console, agents for Windows NT, and Windows for Workgroups.

When you want to analyze traffic on a network segment, a capture agent (a program running on a computer attached to that segment) puts its network card into promiscuous mode. The agent makes a duplicate of frames that pass that computer, stores the frames in a buffer, and sends the session summary statistics to the Network Monitor console (either local or remote).

Capturing Network Traffic Data

To capture and display data from the network, perform the following steps:

1. From the Capture menu, choose Start.

   To stop collecting data, from the Capture menu choose Stop.

   To pause the data capture, from the Capture menu choose Pause.

2. To display collected data, from the Capture menu choose Stop and View.

   Or from the Capture menu, choose Stop and then choose Display Captured Data.

CLEANSMS.BAT

Use this to clean SMS files off clients workstations. The syntax is "cleansms d," where "d:" is the drive where your MS\SMS\BIN directory resides.

DUMPSEND.EXE

The Dumpsend utility is used when diagnosing problems with sending data between two sites. It will show the status of the send request; for example, how much data has been sent, and whether the send has failed. The syntax is Dumpsend *Filename*.

MIFCHECK.EXE

MIFCHECK.EXE is an MIF syntax checker for use in verifying text MIFs before submitting them to SMS. It is designed to help those who are writing MIFs for new components to report.

This is a MIF parser/syntax checker for use in verifying text MIFs before submitting them to the system. It reports syntax and semantic errors. It is designed to help ISVs who are writing MIFs for new components for SHIC to report.

DumpNAD and ViewNAD

DumpNAD is used to look at application and group settings and their files .HAF and .HGF. This is useful in determining the exact settings for shared applications and their program groups, as stored in the NAD configuration files.

ViewNAD is used to view the shared applications from a client machine that are located on servers and are available to be used by clients. This utility should be run from the LOGON.SRV\APPCTL.BOX\DATABASE directory.

ViewNAD provides a text based graphical display of the current SystemsManagement Server Network Applications Database (NAD) for review.

SMSTrace

SMSTrace is a graphical application that can load multiple trace log files at a time. It formats and displays each log file in real time as it is updated by an SMS process. SMSTRACE.EXE is located in \SMS\SITE.SRV\platform.BIN. ●

CHAPTER 18

Providing Fault Tolerance and Data Recovery

In this chapter, you will learn:

- **Back Up and Restore the SQL Server Database**
- **Learn SMS Survival Skills**

Like a lot of other, newer, client-server products in the BackOffice Suite, SMS "self-heals" in different situations. The transaction logging feature in SQL, for one thing, will ensure a much cleaner, quieter database operation than the databases of yore.

However, it is good to plan your backup and disaster recovery. Following are a few good reasons:

- Accidental or malicious use of commands like drop database, and so on
- Viruses
- Hard disk failure
- Natural disasters
- Software failure
- Theft

For example, a friend of mine in the Los Angeles area was in the practice of taking copies of SQL Server database backup tapes home every weekend, a practice that paid off after the Northridge earthquake. ■

Backing Up and Restoring the Database

Making sure that the SMS database is fully backed up and can be brought back up live very quickly in the event of a system crash is critical to the operation of the SMS Management Server.

Backup and Recovery

SMS does not provide a backup and restore utility. To perform the backup or restore operation, you need the SQL Administrator utility.

The good news is that Microsoft SQL Server 6.0 delivers robust backup advantages, as follows:

- 60Kb read/write blocks—larger read/write block size maximizes tape and disk throughput.
- Browsable header information—an administrator can browse backup headers to track database and log dumps.
- Data compression—boosts data throughput to devices and optimizes storage.
- Parallel striped backup—SQL database and log backups can be striped across 32 backup devices (tape or disk) at a time, attaining as much throughput as 20GB per hour.
- Single table backup/restore—allows individual table back up and restores independent of the database. Critical for DDS systems with large static tables.

Backup Strategy

We don't want to nag, but you should have a solid backup plan in place before any application is ever moved from production.

It is also unimaginable not to test your backup strategy.

NOTE I like to keep a hot spare server online with a test backup restored to it every so often. Not only does that provide for a spare server, it tests the backup restoral regularly. ■

The following are some items for consideration:

- How often should the backups be done?
- How often does your data change?
- Will you use full database dumps versus transaction log dumps?
- What medium will you want to use? Tape, diskette, disk?
- Will the backups be done online (while users are working) or after-hours?
- Will the backups be done manually or by an automatic scheduling facility?
- If the backups are automated, how will they be verified?
- How long will the backups be saved before reusing the medium?
- How long will it take to restore to the last backup?
- What is an acceptable amount of downtime?
- Where will the backups be stored, and do the necessary people have access to them?
- Who is responsible for seeing that the backups are done and done correctly?
- If the system administrator is gone, is there someone else who knows the proper passwords and procedures to do backups and, if necessary, restore the backups?
- Then there's my favorite, who's going to do backup?

Creating a Device

In order to perform backup and restore operations with SQL Administrator, a device called a dump device must be created. This device is created in the same way as a SQL Server database device (see fig. 18.1).

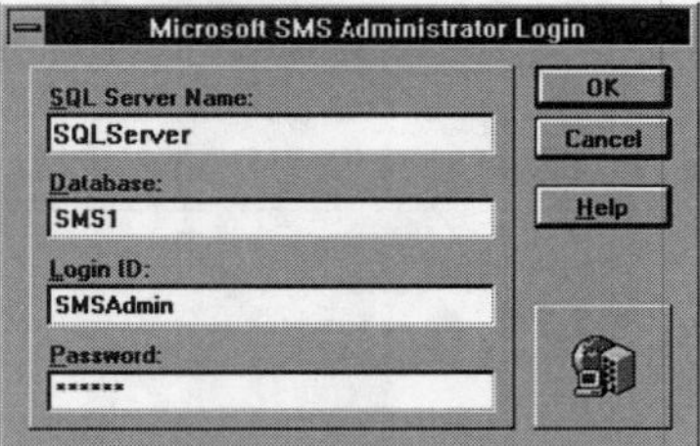

FIG. 18.1 Creating a device with SQL Server.

From the SQL Enterprise Manager, log on using the **sa** account (or a Windows NT Administrator account, if you are using integrated security). The account you use must have the ability to create SQL devices. The **sa** account is the default account for SQL administration.

From the main screen, select the Database Devices Icon. Click the right mouse button, and select New Device, as shown in the following illustration.

From the New Database Device menu, enter in the details of the first device (typically SMSData), as shown in the following illustration.

If the device were created on the computer used for the SMS primary site, the Name would default to SMSData, and the Path would default to \win32app\SQL60\DATA\SMS.DB. You might choose to use these values in creating the database on a separate computer. The Size for SMSData should generally be set at 45 MB. See SMS online Help for additional information on setting the Size.

Once the first device has been created, do the same for the second device (SMSLog). For the log device, the recommended size is 8 MB.

When you are installing SMS and the following screen appears, enter the details of the remote SQL Server that you just worked with and the name of the database that you would like SMS to create.

For more information about working with Microsoft SQL Server, please refer to the SQL Server documentation.

For each additional SMS administrator account, a separate SQL Server client license is required. The first comes with the SQL Server license itself, but additional licenses must be purchased if more than one SMS administrator account is to be used.

Under the Manager, Devices command in SQL we can create a device. If the logical name was SMSBackup, the physical name would be SMSBACKUP.DAT with the correct path would pop up.

The type of device would be a diskdump device.

NOTE Also create a device to dump the MASTER.DAT that would back up the master database and five other databases associated with the bare bones operation of SQL. ■

I can just hear Microsoft howl as I say this, but the Master Database file in SQL is MASTER.DAT. I've seen people backup this file simply by copying it somewhere else and then restoring it back when needed. The same is true for other SQL database files.

Backing Up and Restoring the SMS Database

Here are the broad range of steps to follow when you want to backup or restore the SMS database:

1. Determine the method of backup or restore: floppy disk, tape, or hard drive.
2. Confirm that the corresponding device exists.
3. From the SQL Administrator toolbar, select the DB button. The Database window appears.
4. Select the database that you want to back up or restore.
5. From the Manage menu, choose Backup/Restore. A submenu appears.

6. Choose Backup/Restore from the submenu. The Backup/Restore Database dialog box appears.
7. Indicate the device to be used for the operation.

Specifying a Device to Backup or Restore a Database

To back up or restore a SQL database, you must specify the device to be used (see fig. 18.2).

FIG. 18.2
Specifying a device in SQL Server.

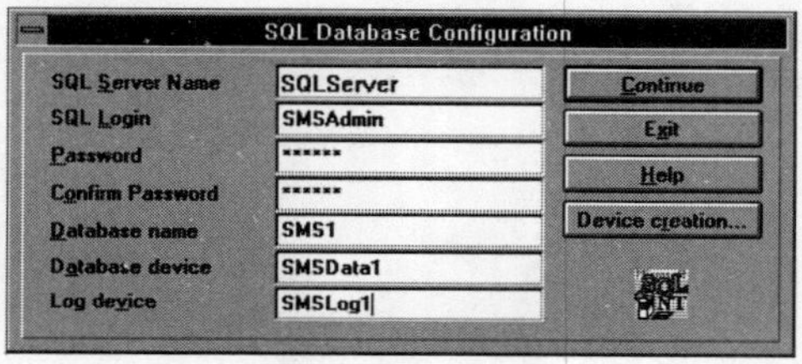

To specify the device to be used for the backup or restore operation, take the following steps:

1. From the Dump Device list, choose a dump device.
2. If you want to restore your database, choose Load Database.
3. If you want to perform a backup, choose Dump Database.
4. After making the appropriate selection, choose OK. The operation will commence.

It is not necessary to dump (back up) the transaction log, because SMS truncates the transaction log at checkpoint.

If you are backing up a database, verify the dump device used for data after performing the backup.

If you are restoring a database, view the data using SMS Administrator for correct data.

Checking Consistency of the SMS Database in SQL

There are utilities in SQL that you can run after you dump a database for backup. DBCC CHECKDB, DBCCCHECK TABLE, DBCC CHECKALLOC, and DBCC CHECKCATALOG check the logical and physical consistency of the database.

You may want to check the database especially if backing up online, because transactions can occur during or after the DBCC but before the dump. You may want to dump the database and then run the DBCCs to ensure that the database was consistent at the time it was dumped.

Scheduling Backup

There is a schedule backup option under the Backup/Restore command in SQL Administrator. You might want to schedule nightly backup this way. There is also an option where you can get e-mail reporting the status of the backup.

You can create a different subdirectory for each day of the week and put a different backup file into each every night. This ensures that you have numerous backups, and you may want to keep older backups in case the newer ones are faulty.

SMS Fault Tolerance Features

The SMS system itself requires minimal maintenance. It also provides its own brand of fault tolerance: if any portion of the system besides the central database goes down, minimal functionality is lost. Notice how each SMS management functions when part of the network is down.

Site Server Down

If a site server goes down and the central database stays up, most management functions run uninterrupted. The SMS Administrator utility can be run from any Windows NT machine (workstation or server).

Inventory Reporting

Inventory reporting, while collected locally at every user logon, is made to the central site only once a day. Changes in inventory are infrequent, and it is not critical to maintain up-to-the-minute inventory data.

Once a downed server comes back online, it automatically begins collecting inventory again, and is brought back in line with the central database during the next synchronization.

Remote Control

As long as the central database is running, help desk staff can still remotely control users—even users in a site with a downed server.

Package Distribution

Package distribution features load-balancing across many domain controllers, so users in a site with a downed server can still execute any jobs that have already been sent, and will see an interruption in current jobs only if the downed server is the only distribution server targeted for that package. Otherwise, other distribution servers are used until the downed server is restored. New distribution jobs must wait for the site server to come back online.

Program groups controlled by SMS continue to work if a site server is down, but distribution of new Program Groups must wait for the site server to come back online.

The Windows NT Performance Monitor should be used regularly to assess performance of various system components for returning as needed.

From Here...

For related information, refer to the following chapters:

- Chapter 23, "Investigating Remote PC Problems," for desktop PC troubleshooting.
- Chapter 24, "Investigating Network Problems," for more information on identifying and fixing Network troubles.

PART VI

Putting It All Together—A Step by Step Example

CHAPTER 19

Installation Overview

This is the first chapter in this book's step-by-step guide to using SMS. It, and the rest of this guide, are meant to be used as a quick reference for procedures related to installing and maintaining SMS. Here's what we'll cover in the chapter. ■

The installation of Microsoft Windows NT Server

We'll start the chapter with the setup of NT version 4.0, including a section on creating a network boot disk to use in the installation process.

The installation of Microsoft SQL Server version 6.5

The next section of the chapter covers the setup of SQL Server. You'll get easy-to-reference step-by-step instructions for installing the SQL Server component.

The primary site server installation of SMS

Next, we show you how to set up the initial SMS site server for your organization.

The installation of a secondary SMS site server

The section on the primary site server installation is followed with an example of a secondary site server installation.

The installation of the client components

In the final portion of the chapter, you'll see how to configure the system to automatically set up the SMS client components and take workstation inventory. We'll also cover the manual installation of logon scripts and the client components.

Creating the Site Server

This section deals with the steps required when setting up an SMS primary site server. The section starts with an illustration of how to create a network installation disk.

Creating a Network Installation Disk

With this method, you make a DOS boot disk containing the proper network card drivers for the machine on which you are installing NT Server. You then use this disk to boot the computer and make a network connection to a share containing the NT distribution files.

This option can be used if you already have a Windows NT server online that has the Network Client Administration utility, and you have one of the network cards found in the utilities Network Adapter Card list of choices. The machine you're loading as a server must have one of the cards on the list. This listing includes Ethernet and Token Ring drivers for most of the popular adapter cards found in use.

This example uses an existing Windows 4.0 server to create an installation disk with the appropriate network interface drivers needed to make a connection to the network distribution point. These installation disks are intended for use in distributing various Microsoft products, such as Windows for Workgroups, LAN Manager clients, and RAS clients, by using a network share.

▶ For a complete discussion on the installation of SMS and its supporting software, **see** Chapters 5, 6, and 7, "Server Installation" Parts I and II, and "Installing Client Sites."

The Network Client Administration utility inherently does not allow the creation of installation disks for the purpose of installing NT server. But we can create an installation disk for Windows for Workgroups, then modify it to use an installation point containing the NT distribution files, instead of the Windows for Workgroups files. Make sure you observe any licensing requirements before installing software using this method (or any other method, for that matter).

Follow the steps below to create and configure a network startup disk.

1. Make a note of the configuration settings (IRQ, I/O Address) of the network adapter you will be using in your new NT Server.
2. If the existing NT Server you're using to create the startup disk has a CD-ROM drive, place the NT installation CD-ROM in the drive. If your current server does not have a CD-ROM drive, you'll need to be able to connect to a CD-ROM drive on another computer that contains the NT Server installation CD-ROM.
3. Begin by starting the Network Client Administration utility, as shown in figure 19.1.

   Mark the Make Network Installation Startup Disk radio button and click Continue. Figure 19.2 shows the Share Network Client Installation Files dialog box when the NT installation CD-ROM is found in the local CD-ROM drive.

FIG. 19.1
Use the Network Administration Utility to create a startup disk.

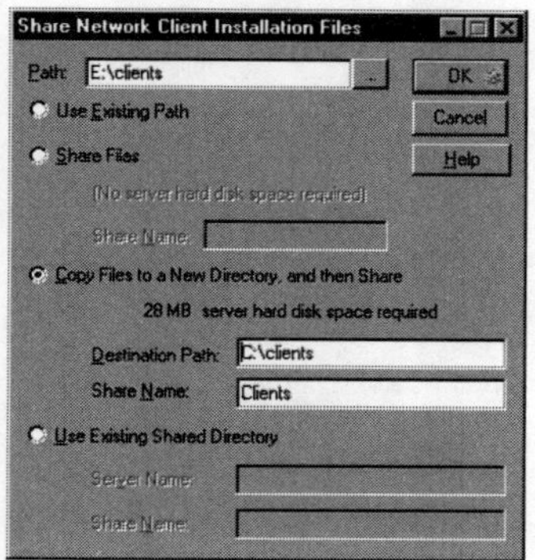

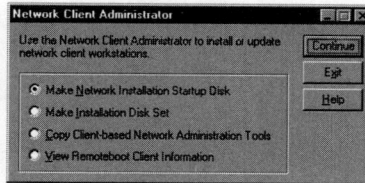

FIG. 19.2
Supply the path to the Windows NT CD-ROM's client distribution files.

NOTE Normally, when an installation disk is created, information regarding the location of the source files must be provided in the installation disk's startup files. This, in turn, requires that the source files be available at some shared installation point on the network.

The Client Administration utility does this by allowing you to share the distribution files for the various products (Windows for Workgroups, LAN Manager Clients, RAS service, and others) directly from the CD-ROM, or it allows you to copy them to a network drive and share them. If the client distribution files are already installed on your network, you can designate that share by marking the Use Existing Shared Directory radio button. Then, supply the name of the source server and its share name that contains the distribution files. ■

4. For the purpose of making the required shared directory, mark the Share Files radio button and click OK. You can remove the Clients network share on your server after the creation of the installation disk if you want.
5. After the client directory is shared, the Target Workstation Configuration dialog box appears, as shown in figure 19.3. From here, choose the proper media type for the floppy drive in your system by marking the appropriate radio button in the Floppy Drive box.
6. In the Network Client box, make sure the Network Client v3.0 for MS-DOS and Windows option is highlighted.
7. From the Network Adapter Card drop-down menu, choose the proper NIC driver for the network card installed in the machine that is designated to be your new server. In our example, we have chosen the Intel EtherExpress 16 or 16TP driver, as shown in figure 19.4.

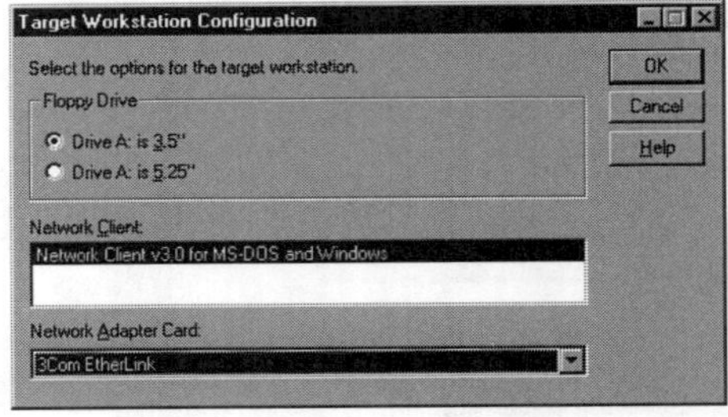

FIG. 19.3
Choose the MS-DOS and Windows client version 3.0 option.

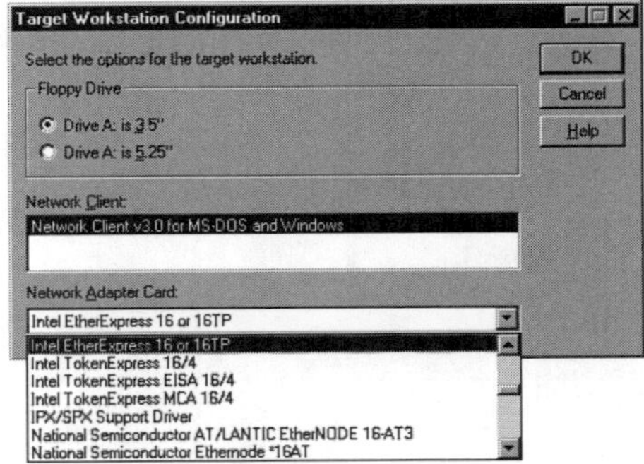

FIG. 19.4
Pick the adapter card you're using from the listing.

NOTE If you don't find the driver for your network adapter, either use the CD-ROM method shown later, or see the sidebar entitled "Creating Startup Disks for Unlisted Network Cards."

8. Insert the DOS-formatted floppy system disk that you created earlier into your NT Server's A: drive and click the OK button. The Network Startup Disk Configuration dialog box, shown in figure 19.5, will appear. Fill in the Computer Name box with a name to be used as the network name of the computer. This name is used only temporarily while installing software from an installation disk, and can be any name you want, as long as it meets naming standards.

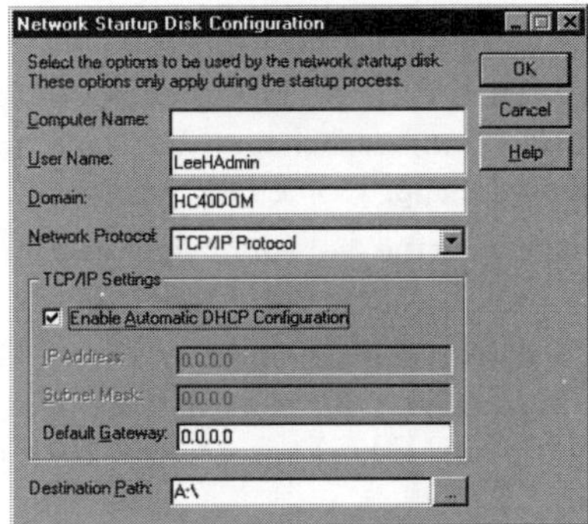

FIG. 19.5
Specify the protocol type you wish to use.

9. Fill in your network user id in the User Name box. Your current user logon name should already be shown in the box.
10. Fill in the name of the Windows NT or LAN Manager domain that you normally log into in the Domain box.
11. Choose the appropriate network protocol for your network from the Network Protocol drop-down box. You need to make sure the protocol you choose is the same protocol being used on the server that contains the installation share point. For our example, we'll use NetBEUI. If you use another protocol, such as TCP/IP, choose it and fill in the appropriate fields. The completed Network Startup Disk Configuration dialog box is shown in figure 19.6.

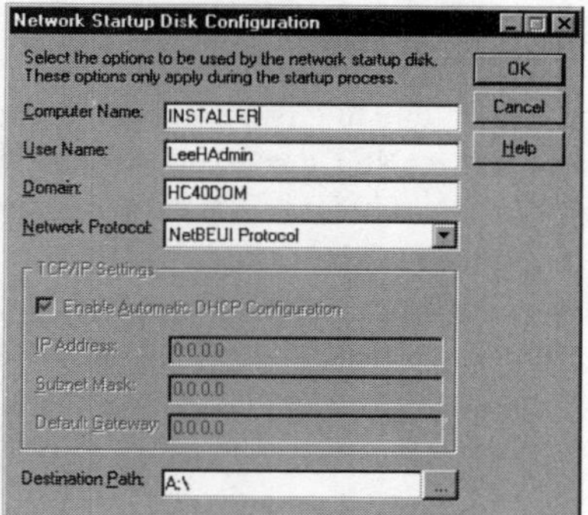

FIG. 19.6 The completed Configuration dialog box.

12. Ensure the Destination Path (the drive path to your DOS-formatted floppy) is correct and click the OK button. The confirmation box, shown in figure 19.7, will appear. Ensure the information shown is correct and click the OK button. If you need to change the information, click Cancel to take you back to the previous dialog box to make corrections.

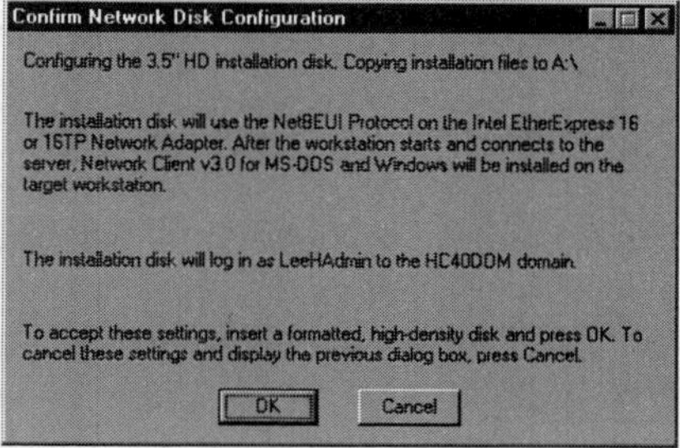

FIG. 19.7 Confirm the installation options you selected.

13. The Copying Files window appears, showing the progress of the disk creation. When the disk copying is finished, click the OK button to return to the Network Client Administrator dialog box. From here, click Exit.

14. Review the information contained in the dialog box that appears (see fig. 19.8). Take special note of the information regarding the network adapter card settings, and click OK.

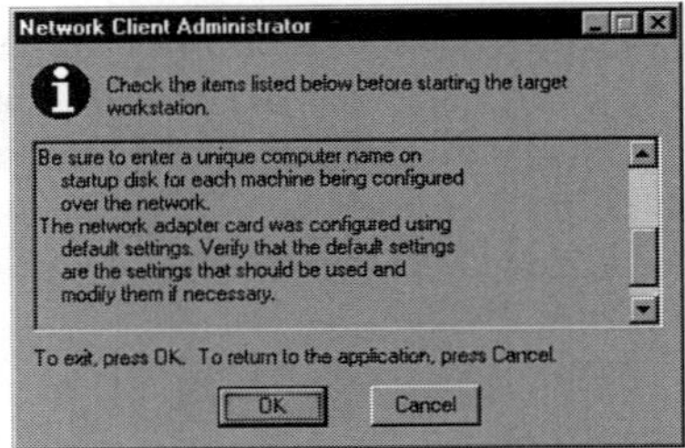

FIG. 19.8
Review the information contained in the dialog box.

15. Use the information gathered in step one to ensure the correct settings are specified in the PROTOCOL.INI file located in the \NET directory of the newly created startup disk. A partial listing of the PROTOCOL.INI file for our startup disk (which used an Intel EtherExpress 16 driver) is shown later. This section contains entries for the network card's IRQ and I/O address. The section for your specific network card may have a different name, but will have similar entries. The settings and options will vary in this section, depending on the network card you've installed. The default configuration values are shown as commented out.

```
 [ms$ee16]
drivername=EXP16$
; IRQ=3
; IOADDRESS=0x310
```

    Supply the proper values for each one of the configuration settings that are appropriate to your adapter (the NIC settings gathered in step 1) and remove the comments designation (;) from each line. The network card being used in our example has an IRQ setting of 10 and an I/O address of 300. In the listing below, we have modified the appropriate entries to work with our network card.

```
[ms$ee16]
drivername=EXP16$
IRQ=10
IOADDRESS=0x300
```

16. The newly created startup disk has been configured with CONFIG.SYS and AUTOEXEC.BAT files that will load the appropriate network drivers, make a network connection to the distribution share, change to that share, and then begin the setup procedure for Windows for Workgroups. Since our intention is to create a startup disk for loading Windows NT Server, we must edit the AUTOEXEC.BAT file to connect to a network share containing the NT installation files, not the Windows for Workgroups installation files.

    The original AUTOEXEC.BAT file on our installation disk is as follows:

```
path=a:\net
a:\net\net start
```

```
net use z: \\HC40SERV\Clients
echo Running Setup...
z:\msclient\netsetup\setup.exe /$
```

In its current form, the AUTOEXEC.BAT will make a connection to the client share on the server named HC40SERV. Modify this entry to make a connection to a share containing the NT Server installation files instead. This can be a share created using the original setup CD-ROM, or it can be a directory that you've copied the installation files into and then shared.

In our example, we have copied the i386 directory from the NT Server setup CD-ROM to a drive on the server named HC40SERV. We then shared the directory as i386 and modified our AUTOEXEC.BAT file as follows:

```
path=a:\net
a:\net\net start
net use z: \\HC40SERV\i386
echo Running Setup...
z:\
cd i386
winnt /b
```

This modification to the AUTOEXEC.BAT file will start the NT Server installation using the /b command line option. This option prevents the boot disk set from being created during installation.

The creation of the network installation disk is now complete. Partitioning and formatting of the hard drive on the target machine can be accomplished by additionally placing the fdisk and format utilities on the installation disk.

Creating Startup Disks for Unlisted Network Cards

If the correct driver for your network card is not found, it is still possible to still create a startup disk. However, you may find this to be more trouble than it's worth if you're not familiar with network initialization files (and their format). If you wish to create a custom disk, you must have the LAN Manager drivers for the network card you're using. Simply install your card's driver files on the new installation disk's NET directory. Then, edit the appropriate lines in the PROTOCOL.INI file and substitute the name of your driver for the name of the current driver.

As an example, in our current illustration we have created a startup disk for a computer that has an Intel EtherExpress 16 network card installed. The driver used for that card is named EXP16.DOS, and has been placed in the \NET directory of the installation startup disk.

By looking at the current PROTOCOL.INI file found in the \NET directory of the installation disk, you will see that this driver (EXP16.DOS) is designated in the [ms$ee16] section of the file as the current driver. You can now customize your disk by placing your unlisted network card driver in this same directory (\NET), and by modifying the PROTOCOL.INI file to include this new driver's name.

Following is a complete listing of the original PROTOCOL.INI file as created by the Network Client Administration utility, and next to it is a modified version used with an Inter Etherlink Pro adapter.

Table 19.1 A Comparison of PROTOCOL.INI Files

The Original PROTOCOL.INI	The Modified PROTOCOL.INI
[network.setup] version=0x3110 netcard=ms$ee16,1,MS$EE16,1 transport=ms$ndishlp,MS$NDISHLP transport=ms$netbeui,MS$NETBEUI lana0=ms$ee16,1,ms$netbeui lana1=ms$ee16,1,ms$ndishlp	[network.setup] version=0x3110 netcard=epro_nif,1,EPRO_NIF,1 transport=ms$ndishlp,MS$NDISHLP transport=ms$netbeui,MS$NETBEUI lana0=epro_nif,1,ms$netbeui lana1=epro_nif,1,ms$ndishlp
[ms$ee16] drivername=EXP16$; IRQ=3 ; IOADDRESS=0x310 ; IOCHRDY=Late ; TRANSCEIVER=Thin Net version=0x3110	[epro_nif] DRIVERNAME = EPRO$ IOADDRESS = 0x210 IRQ=9
[protman] drivername=PROTMAN$ PRIORITY=MS$NDISHLP	[protman] drivername=PROTMAN$ PRIORITY=MS$NDISHLP
[MS$NDISHLP] drivername=ndishlp$ BINDINGS=ms$ee16	[MS$NDISHLP] drivername=ndishlp$ BINDINGS=epro_nif
[ms$netbeui] drivername=netbeui$ SESSIONS=10 NCBS=12 BINDINGS=ms$ee16 LANABASE=0	[ms$netbeui] drivername=netbeui$ SESSIONS=10 NCBS=12 BINDINGS=epro_nif LANABASE=0

Copying Driver Files.

Ensure that the proper driver files are copied to the \NET directory of the boot diskette. The preceding example required the EPRO.DOS file be copied into the \NET directory. You may also need to edit the adapter card settings in the PROTOCOL.INI file to match those of the adapter you're using.

Installation Steps for Microsoft NT Server 4.x

To install NT 4.x from a CD-ROM or from a network share point, follow these steps:

Before you begin to install any software on the computer, make sure you set and record the configuration settings (I/O address, IRQ, Transceiver Type, and so on) for the network adapter card(s) in the machine.

1. Create a DOS (version 5 or higher) bootable floppy disk using format a:/s command.
2. Use this disk to create a bootable startup disk containing the appropriate network card driver

   or Use the newly created boot disk to create a startup disk containing the appropriate CD-ROM drivers that will allow the use of a CD-ROM for the NT Server installation.
3. After creating a bootable startup disk, copy the fdisk and format utility programs to it. The utility versions must match the version of DOS the disk was formatted under.
4. Boot the target server using the startup disk that you've just created.
5. From the DOS command prompt, run the fdisk utility to partition the computer's hard disk, and then reboot the computer.

NOTE A partition must be created that is large enough to contain the NT Server OS files, the system paging file, and a temporary copy of the NT source files. A partition of at least 120MB is recommended. ■

6. After the system reboots, use the format utility on the startup disk to format the hard drive partition that you created in step five. The use of the /s switch with the format command is not required when running the utility.
7. Once the formatting is complete, reboot the system if needed. Then, connect to the installation point containing the NT Server source files by changing to the appropriate CD-ROM or network drive.
8. Move into the setup directory (appropriate for the platform you're installing NT Server on) and run the following command from the DOS prompt:

   ```
   drive:\i386>winnt /b
   ```

   This will start the text-based portion of the NT Setup program . The /b command instructs the Setup program not to make the three NT setup disks that are normally made during the setup process.

9. You will next be prompted to verify the path to the installation point. Confirm that the drive and directory are correct, and press the Enter key to continue. Temporary installation files are then copied to your local hard drive. Process time can vary from 2 to 30 minutes, depending on method of transfer. During this period, you'll see a yellow progress bar, and the percentage of files copied will be displayed.
10. The file copy process will stop with a message instructing you to remove any floppy disk that may be in the diskette drive. Remove the startup floppy disk and press the Enter key. This will restart your computer.
11. After rebooting, the computer will display a message indicating its hardware configuration is being inspected. It will then load the appropriate startup drivers, load the NT Kernel, and boot the operating system. Next, the Welcome to Setup screen appears.
12. The Windows NT server setup will then display a list of the mass storage devices it has found in your computer. Follow the onscreen instructions to add any devices that were not detected. When you've finished adding devices, press the Enter key to continue.
13. Follow the instructions to change any of the options listed. When you're finished, highlight the option for No Further Changes and press the Enter key to continue.
14. The next message to appear will instruct you on choosing the destination partition on which to install the NT operating system files.

    The bottom of the screen contains a box that shows the available disk devices, the drive space of the device, the remaining space on the device, and how they are currently partitioned. Use the arrow key to highlight the desired destination partition, and press Enter.
15. If the drive was formatted as a FAT drive, you will be given the opportunity to have Windows automatically convert the drive to NTFS during installation. The screen will display the chosen partition format type, size, remaining space, and device information. Highlight Convert the Partition to NTFS option, and press the Enter key to continue.
16. You will be prompted for confirmation of the FAT-to-NTFS conversion. Press C to convert the drive to an NTFS format. This conversion will not take place until after the computer has been rebooted.
17. Before Setup installs the Windows NT files onto your hard disk, you must choose the location where you want these files to be installed. The default is to place the operating system files in the \WINNT directory of the boot drive. To change the suggested location, press the BACKSPACE key to delete characters and then type the directory where you want Windows NT installed. When finished, press the Enter key to continue.
18. The next screen prompts the type of hard disk examination you would like to have performed on your destination drive. Your drive has just been formatted and is relatively clean. Go ahead and press the Enter key and perform the exhaustive examination. This process usually won't take very long for even the largest drive. If it does, you may have reason to suspect a problem with the drive or the controller hardware. On our example 515 MB drive, the inspection took less than 20 seconds.

19. After the drive has been examined, the file transfer process of moving and expanding the source files into the destination directory begins. A progress bar will be shown, along with the percentage of files that have been copied. When the copy process has been completed, a dialog box will appear to notify you. Press the Enter key to conclude the text-based portion of the setup, and restart the computer.
20. At this point, the computer will reboot and continue with the Windows-based portion of the setup. At this phase of the setup, some preliminary files are copied, followed by the appearance of the first in a series of Windows NT Setup screens that are used in guiding you through the rest of the installation.

    "Welcome to the Windows NT setup Wizard, which will guide you through the rest of Setup. To continue, click Next.

    The next three parts of Setup are:

    1) Gathering information about your computer

    2) Installing Windows NT Networking

    3) Finishing Setup."

    Click or press the Next button.
21. The message "Please wait while NT prepares the directory for installation" will briefly appear, followed by the dialog box prompting you for name and organizational information. This information is then used to personalize your installation of Windows NT. Complete the informational fields and then click or press the Next button.
22. The licensing mode screen will appear next, prompting you to select the licensing mode you wish to use. Two modes are available, as follows:
    - Per Server—each concurrent connection to this server requires a separate Client Access License.
    - Per Seat—each computer that accesses Windows NT Server requires a separate Client Access License. Use License Manager (located in the Network Administration program group) to record the number of Client Access Licenses purchased and avoid violation of the license agreement.

    Choose the method of licensing that is appropriate for your installation by marking the button next to your choice.
23. The next screen will prompt you for a machine Name for the new server with the following message:

    "Windows NT needs a computer Name to identify your computer. Please enter a name of 15 characters or less.

    NOTE: You must ensure that the name you enter is unique on your network. Ask your network administrator if you are not sure what name you should enter."

    Enter the name of your choice, then click or press the Next button.
24. You will next be asked to select a server type with the following message:

    "Please select a type for this server."

Your SMS server must be a primary (PDC) or backup (BDC) domain controller. The SMS server cannot be a stand-alone server. You may choose BDC if you already have a domain in place with a PDC. If you are starting a new domain, you must choose PDC. In our example, we chose our server to be the PDC.

25. Since we chose to configure the server as a PDC, the next screen will prompt us for the password for the default Administrator account, as follows:

    "Please enter a password of 14 characters or less to use for the Administrator account. Reenter the same password in the Confirm Password field.

    The Administrator account allows maximum access to your computer's resources. Therefore, the administrator password is an important piece of information which you should guard carefully.

    Note: Take special care to remember the password you supply. It is recommended that you write the password down and store it in a safe place."

    Enter the administrator password of your choice in both boxes and click or press the Next button to continue.

26. The next screen prompts you to make a repair disk for your system. You may wish to do this step now, or you may wait until later, after your system has been completely configured with accounts and devices.

    "Setup can create an emergency repair disk, which is a floppy disk that can be used later to repair Windows NT should it become damaged. (In some cases Windows NT can be repaired without an emergency repair disk.)

    Note: You can create an emergency repair disk at any time by using the RDISK utility. Would you like to create a repair disk during setup?"

    Make your selection and click or press Next. In our example, we will choose to skip this step. The RDISK utility will be used later to construct a more up-to-date repair disk.

27. The Setup program will now allow you to select the components you want to have installed. The screen allows you to select if you want the Microsoft Exchange Client software to be installed on the server. Because we want to reduce our use of disk space and won't be using the server as a client workstation, we won't load the e-mail client software.

    "To add or remove a component, click the check box. A shaded box means that only part of the component will be installed. To see what's included in a component, click Details."

    Leave the Exchange client box unchecked and click or press Next to continue.

28. We now begin the Setup phase that deals with the network components and their configuration. The following message will be displayed:

    "Setup is now ready to guide you through installation of Windows NT Networking. If you want to review or change any settings before continuing, click Back.

    To begin installing Windows NT Networking, click Next.

    1) Gathering information about your computer
    2) Installing Windows NT Networking

3) Finishing Setup"

Click or press Next to continue.

29. The message "Setup is preparing to initialize the NT network installation" will appear briefly, followed by:

    "Windows NT needs to know how this computer should participate on a network.

    Wired to the network: Your computer is connected to the network by a ISDN Adapter or Network Adapter.

    Remote access to the network: Your computer uses a Modem to remotely connect to the network."

    Assuming that your computer is wired to a LAN (as we are in our example) check the box for Wired to the Network, and click or press Next to continue.

30. Setup will then display the following message:

    "To have Setup start searching for a Network Adapter, click Start Search button."

    Go ahead and click on the Start Search button to have Setup automatically detect your network interface card. If you have additional cards, you can have Setup scan for them also. If your adapter is not detected, you can choose the Select from List button to manually specify an adapter. You can choose from a list of supplied drivers or you can supply drivers using a disk containing the adapter board OEMSETUP.INF and other setup files for the card.

    Any network adapters that are found will be displayed. After all the network adapter drivers have been installed, choose the Next button to continue.

31. The next screen will allow you to choose the network protocol(s) you want to use by displaying the message:

    "Select the networking protocols that are used on your network. If you are unsure, contact your system administrator."

    This then gives the following protocol choices:

    - TCP/IP Protocol
    - NWLink IPX/SPX Compatible Transport
    - NetBEUI Protocol

    By default, both NWLink and NetBEUI are marked. Modify the choices, if needed, to reflect the protocol appropriate to your network environment. When finished, click Next to continue.

32. Now we are shown the services that will be installed on the system, and given a chance to add or change the choices. The screen displays the following message:

    "Listed below are the services that will be installed by the system. You may add to this list by clicking the Select from list button."

    The Network Services shown by default are the following:

    - Remote Access Service
    - RPC Configuration

- NetBIOS Interface
- Workstation
- Server

All but Remote Access Service (RAS) are actually installed by default. Add additional services if desired, and click Next to continue.

33. Setup gives us the opportunity to go back and make changes before installing the network components by displaying the following message:

    "Windows NT is now ready to copy and install networking components that you selected and others required by the system.

    This process will allow individual components to install themselves and raise dialogs so they may install correctly.

    Click Next to continue.

    Click Back to make changes to your selections."

    Go back and make changes if needed; otherwise, choose the Next button to continue with the installation.

34. Your adapters will now be installed. Depending on the adapter, a dialog box will usually appear, asking you to set or confirm the adapters' configuration settings (I/O address, IRQ, Transceiver Type, and so on). Choose the proper settings for your adapter and click the OK button.

    Setup will install the protocols and services at this point. You may be asked to provide additional information, depending on the protocols and services you have selected. For example, if you chose TCP/IP as one or your protocols, you'd be asked for IP address information. If you had selected to install the Remote Access Service, you'd be asked to choose a COM port and modem to use.

    After the configuration of the protocols and services is completed, the next screen that appears is the following:

    "Windows NT is now ready to start the network so that you can complete the installation of networking.

    Click Next to continue.

    Click Back to stop the network if it is running and make changes to your selections."

    This is another chance to go back and reconfigure anything you may have missed. If you're finished, click the Next button to continue.

35. Since we have chosen to configure the server in our installation example to be a primary domain controller, the following screen will appear:

    "You have requested that Windows NT create a Primary Domain Controller.

    You must supply the name of the domain that this Primary Domain Controller will manage."

    Supply the name for the new domain, and click the Next button to continue.

36. The final phase of the NT Server will begin with the following message:

    "Setup is almost finished. After you answer a few more questions, Setup will complete installation. If you want to review or change any settings before continuing, click Back. To continue, click Finish.

    1) Gathering information about your computer

    2) Installing Windows NT Networking

    3) Finishing Setup

    Click the Finish button to start the last phase of Setup."

37. The brief message "Setup is configuring your computer to run Windows NT." is then followed by the screen that enables you to set the properties for the date, time, and time zone. It is important to set this information accurately, particularly if your SMS sites are spread across different time zones.

    First, choose the correct time zone for your area from the drop-down scroll box. After that, move to the Date & Time tab, and verify that the settings are accurate. If they aren't, adjust them as needed so they reflect an accurate time.

    Click OK when you're done.

38. Next, you will be able to choose the display properties of your screen, based on the video adapter detected by the Setup program. The system will display the adapter type it has detected. You can then set and test the Screen Resolution, Color Palette, Font, and Refresh Frequency appropriate for your video adapter. Once you've tested the screen properties, press the OK button to continue the installation process.

39. The final Setup screens will start by displaying the message "Setup is configuring your computer to run Windows NT." Setup then saves the configuration information to the registry hives and removes the temporary installation files. When it's finished, the Setup program will display the restart message, as follows:

    "Windows NT 4.00 has been installed successfully.

    Remove disks from floppy drives and choose Restart Computer."

    Click the Restart Computer button to reboot your machine.

Congratulations—you have completed the installation of the NT Server software. The following events take place after the restart of the computer:

- The FAT file system will be detected. This will be followed by the check disk utility (chkdsk) being automatically run on the FAT partition prior to NTFS conversion.
- The FAT partition is converted to NTFS. This is followed by an automatic reboot of the computer.

Installation Steps for Microsoft SQL Server 6.5x

For our example, we have chosen to install SQL on the same server that will be acting as the SMS primary site server.

Perform the following steps to install Microsoft SQL 6.5:

1. Connect to the CD-ROM drive or the network installation point for SQL 6.5. Change to the proper directory (I386, Alpha, or MIPs) according to the hardware platform you're installing on. Run the Setup program located in this directory.
2. The SQL Server Setup Welcome screen appears. Click the Continue button to proceed with the installation.
3. The next screen prompts you for your Name, Company, and Product ID. Enter the appropriate values and click the Continue button. The Product Identification number can be found on the back of the SQL CD-ROM jewel case.
4. Verify that the correct values were entered, and click the Continue button.
5. On the next Setup screen, verify that the button for Install SQL Server and Utilities is marked, and click Continue.
6. The next screen will prompt you for the licensing mode you want to use. Fill in the appropriate values and click the Continue button.
7. The next screen prompts you for the installation destination path. Choose an appropriate drive that has sufficient space for the installation, and click Continue.
8. The MASTER Device Creation screen will appear. Verify the target drive and directory for the SQL database MASTER device. Also, specify the size of the database. In most cases, the default of 25MB will work if the SQL Server is to be used for only SMS. Click Continue to proceed.

You can save steps later if you create a MASTER device with a size of 45MB. This extra space will be used when we expand the SQL temporary database (TempDB) from its default size of 2MB to the minimum 20MB size required by SMS.

9. You are then prompted for the SQL Server Books Online installation options. The files may be installed to the local hard disk (15MB of disk space is needed) or run from the CD-ROM (1MB of disk space is needed), or you may choose to skip the online book installation entirely. Choose an option and click Continue.
10. Next, you're presented with the Installation Options dialog box. From here, you can set the Character Set, Sort Order, Additional Network Support, and SQL Startup options. Begin by clicking the Sets button to choose the Character Set.
11. In the Select Character Set dialog box, choose the appropriate character set for the language you're working with. The default is ISO (International Standards Organization) Character Set, which is appropriate for most installations. When the correct character set is highlighted, click the OK button.
12. Click the Orders button to view the sort order options. The most important thing to remember is that if you have multiple SQL Servers in your organization, they should all be consistent in the Sort Order that they use. In our example, we have chosen Dictionary Order, Case-Insensitive, Uppercase Preference. Highlight the desired sort order and click the OK button.

13. To view the network options, click the Networks button. This screen will enable you to select which Net-Libraries will be installed. By default, Named Pipes is selected as the communications mechanism.

CAUTION

You may choose additional mechanisms, but DO NOT deselect Named Pipes at this time. Setup uses Named Pipes during the installation process. If you desire to remove Named Pipes as a communications mechanism, run the Setup program after the initial setup and remove the Named Pipes support.

For our example, we have chosen to include the Multi-Protocol Net-Libraries. When you have made your choice(s), click the OK button to continue.

14. Make sure the boxes for both Auto Start SQL Server at Boot Time and Auto Start SQL Executive at Boot Time are checked. When you're finished, click the Continue button.
15. The dialog box for the SQL Executive Log On Account information will be presented next. Ensure that the button for Install The SQL Executive Service To Log On To Windows NT As is marked. In the Account box, provide the name of the SQL Service Account. Click the Continue button to proceed.
16. In our example, the Multi-Protocol Net-Libraries were selected earlier, so we are now presented with a dialog box that will allow you to enable Multi-Protocol Encryption on Multi-Protocol connections. The default of no encryption was chosen.

Installation Steps for Microsoft SMS 1.x

1. Log on to the server under an administrative account (this account must belong to the NT local Administrators Group, and the Global Domain Administrators Group). Find the proper installation directory on the CD-ROM for your server platform type (Alpha, MIPS, or X86), and run the Setup program it contains. Note that you can use the following optional switches with the setup command:

   /TRACING:on—will cause tracing to be started on all Windows NT computers running SMS services in the site.

   /noacctcheck—used to bypass the verification of the SMS Service Account. If this switch is not used, the Setup program will by default verify that the SMS Service Account and SMS SQL login ID both exist, and that they both have the required account permissions.

2. Click the Continue button when the Welcome screen appears. SMS build and setup version information is then displayed followed by the Registration screen. Type in the required information and click the Continue button twice.
3. The next screen will present the installation options available. Click the Install Primary Site button.
4. Read the software licensing information, check the I Agree That box, and click the OK button. The next dialog box contains information on the prerequisites that must be

completed prior to installing SMS. If you've been following our example, you'll have seen that these requirements have been met and you can click the Continue button. If the prerequisites have not been met, you must cancel the Setup and complete them before attempting to install SMS again.

5. The next dialog box will prompt you for the installation directory. Accept the default or enter the location of your choice. Make absolutely sure before proceeding that your target destination has a minimum of 100MB of available space and is located on an NTFS partition. We'll accept the default destination in this example, and click the Continue button.
6. The Setup Install Option dialog box will then display the default components that will be included in the installation. You can add or remove components by clicking the Custom button to display the Software Installation Options dialog box. We accept the default for our example, and click the Continue button.
7. The dialog box will prompt for information on the SQL Server to be used with SMS. If you've installed SQL on the same server, as we did in our example, the SQL Server name box will default to the local server name. If you set up SQL Server on a separate computer, type in its name and make sure you've created the database devices required by SMS on that SQL Server in advance. Because we are installing SMS on the same server on which we've installed SQL, the SQS Database Configuration dialog box will allow us to create the SMS-related database devices at this time.
8. Click the Device Creation button to bring up the SQL Device Creation dialog box. The defaults shown here (see fig. 19.9) will provide adequate space for storing the inventory information for approximately 2,200 PCs.

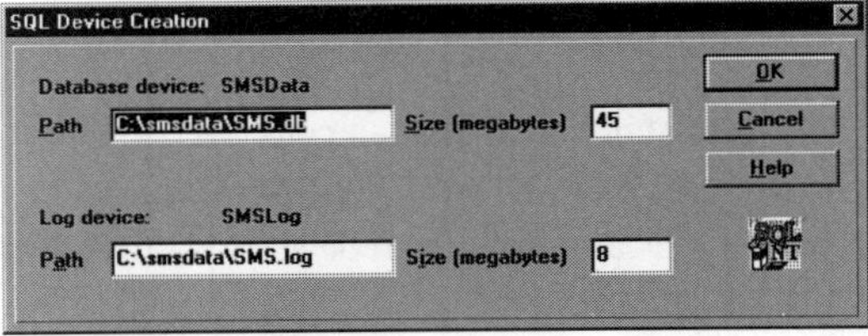

FIG. 19.9 Create the SMS database and log devices.

The general rule for estimating the size of the different devices is as follows:

- SMSData device—allow at least 20Kb for every PC that will be on the SMS System.
- SMSLog device—20% of the SMSData device size, with a 5MB minimum size.
- TempDB device—20% of the SMSData device size, with a 20MB minimum size.

This dialog box also allows you to choose the location of the devices. Accept the defaults or modify them to suit your installation, then click the OK button to return to the SQL Database Configuration dialog box.

9. Confirm that the SQL Login box contains the name "sa" and that password boxes are blank, and click the Continue button.

10. The Primary Site Configuration Information dialog box appears, prompting you for the Site and Service Account information. Begin by entering the Site Code, which can be any three-letter combination of alphanumeric characters; special characters are not allowed.
11. Enter an appropriate name for your SMS site in the Site Name box. This can be any descriptive name you like.
12. Ensure that the name of your server appears in the Site Server box.
13. Ensure that the correct domain name is present in the Site Server Domain box.
14. Check the Automatically Detect All Logon Servers box.
15. Enter the name and password of the SMS service account in the appropriate boxes. When you're finished, click the Continue button.

    At this time, the service account and password will be validated, the file installation will take place, and the database devices will be created.
16. If you chose to install the Network Monitor, the screen shown in figure 19.10 will appear.

FIG. 19.10 Follow the instructions in the dialog box to install the Network Monitor.

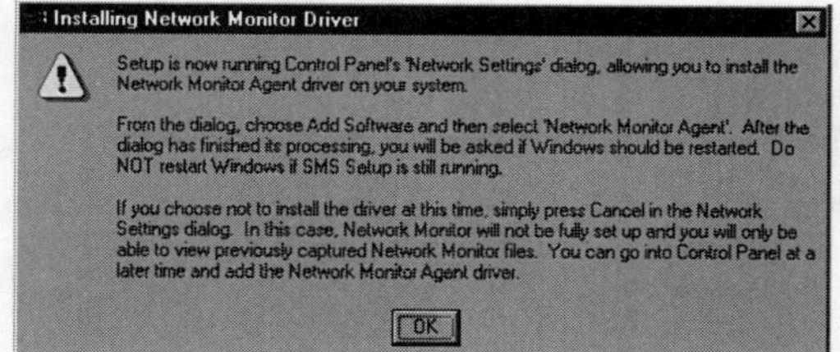

    This dialog box gives you the option of installing the Network Monitor components now or at a later time. For our installation example, we will install the Network Monitor now. Read the screen and click the OK button to add the Network Monitor. The SMS Setup program will continue to run in the background while you set up the Network Monitor. When the Setup completes, a message will appear to indicate the Setup was successful.

17. To add the Network Monitor, choose Add from the Services tab, then select Network Monitor Agent and Tools from the Network Service option list (see fig. 19.11), and click the OK button and then the Close button.

FIG. 19.11 The Network Service options.

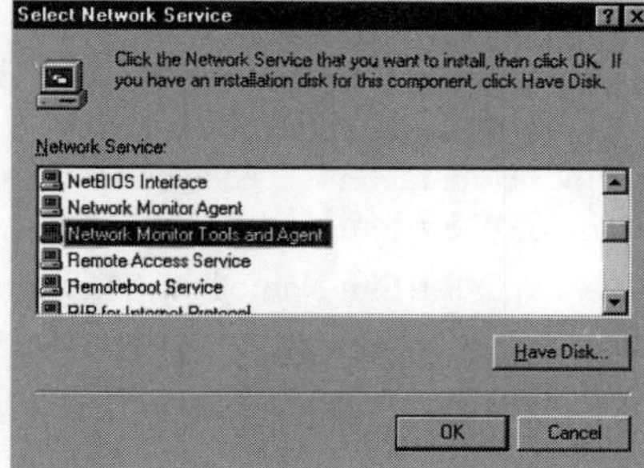

The service installation will take place, followed by the Restart message. DO NOT restart Windows if the SMS Setup program is still running in the background. Note that the Setup program will continue to run in the background while you set up the Network Monitor. If the SMS Setup program completes by the time you get the Restart message, you can go ahead and click Yes to restart Windows without any problems. If the Setup program is still running, click No and restart the server after the SMS Setup program completes.

After restarting the server, log back on under the same administrative account you used previously. You will now find a new program group, called SMS Administration Utilities, that contains icons for the SMS components you've installed.

Installing a Secondary Site Server

Follow these steps to configure a secondary site server:

1. Log on to the SMS site server using an administrative account and start the SMS Administrator program.
2. Open the Sites window in the Administrator program. On the left side of the Sites window, highlight the name of the current site (indicated by the globe).
3. From the File menu, choose New. The New Secondary Site dialog box will appear, as shown in figure 19.12.

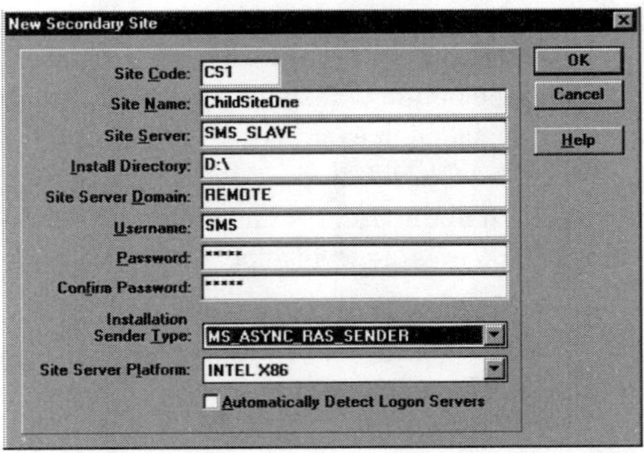

FIG. 19.12 Specify the secondary site properties in this dialog box.

4. Enter the Site Code for the new site. This is the unique three-character code used to identify the site. This code is used in site-to-site communications. It can be any three-letter combination of alphanumeric characters; special characters are not allowed. This code must be unique within the SMS System.
5. Next, type a name for the new site in the Site Name box. This name can be any text you want up to a maximum length of 255 characters (including spaces). Short but descriptive site names usually work the best.

6. In the Site Server box, enter the computer name of the Windows NT Server designated to be the secondary site server. This server must be available using the SMS Sender type you designate in step 12.
7. Enter the target drive letter and directory path on the secondary server that will receive the SMS components and shared directories in the Install Directory box. The drive you designate must be running an NTFS partition.
8. Supply the name of the domain that the target server belongs to in the Site Server Domain dialog box.
9. Next, in the Username box, supply the name of the user account that will be used as the SMS Service Account at the new site. This user name may be one of the following:
   - Local Domain Account—specified simply by typing the local user account ID (the local ID designated as the SMS Service Account) in the Username box. The user account must have the appropriate privileges that will allow the SMS Site Configuration and Maintenance Managers to access and maintain the local domain's logon servers.
   - Trusted Domain Account—precede the user name with the name of the trusted domain in which the SMS Service Account resides. For example, if the SMS Service Account we wanted to use was an account from a trusted domain named CORPHQ, we would type the name as CORPHQ*username*. Keep in mind that this trusted user account must have the appropriate privileges that will allow the SMS Site Configuration and Maintenance Managers to access and maintain the local domain's logon servers. It must also have the appropriate rights to any subsequent domains that are added to the site. Also, bear in mind that the trusted account will be used for any further domain additions to that site, even if a duplicate account with exactly the same name and password exists on the local domain. This implies that if you're using a trusted SMS Service Account, the trusted account must have the proper privileges in all subsequent domains that are added to the site.
10. Supply and confirm the password for the designated SMS Service Account in the Password and Confirm Password boxes.
11. Choose the type of Sender that will be used to link the primary and secondary servers together from the Installation Sender Type drop-down box. You may choose from the following Sender types:
    - MS_LAN_SENDER—the LAN Sender is used when the destination site can be accessed over an established LAN (or WAN with high-speed links).
    - MS_ASYNC_RAS_SENDER—utilized when asynchronous modems and dial-up phone lines are being used for connecting sites.
    - MS_ISDN_RAS_SENDER—used when ISDN connectivity exists between site locations.
    - MS_X25_RAS_SENDER—used when X.25 connections exist between sites.

- MS_BATCH_SNA_SENDER—used when the SNA communication configuration uses LU pairing set to #BATCH mode.
- MS_INTER_SNA_SENDER—Used when the SNA communication configuration uses LU pairing set to #INTER mode.

The one you choose will depend on the type of connectivity currently in place between your site locations. In our example, we have picked the ASYNC RAS Sender.

CAUTION

The use of the ASYNC RAS Sender for installing a secondary site server is not recommended. Even at high asynchronous baud, the installation done over dial-up phone lines can take many hours to complete. It is used here for example purposes only.

12. Specify the target server's platform type in the Site Server Platform box. The default, which is set to INTEL X86, specifies that SMS components for Intel-based platforms should be installed on the target server.
13. Check the Automatically Detect Logon Servers box if you want the secondary server to detect logon servers in its domain.

    When this box is checked, all of the site server domain's logon servers will automatically be enumerated and added to the SMS site. This includes Windows NT Servers acting as primary domain controllers (PDCs), backup domain controllers (including LAN Manager version 2.x BDCs), and servers in the domain. LAN Manager PDCs and BDCs will be enumerated, but LAN Manager members and stand-alone servers will not. All Netware version 3.x and 4.x (running bindery emulation) servers will be detected and enumerated. Detection of Novell Servers can take place over as many as 16 router hops. Checking this box will also cause the Site Configuration Manager continuously to monitor for any new logon servers being added to the network. If any are detected, the new logon server is automatically configured and added to the SMS site.

    If this box is cleared, the only server added to the site is the site server itself. All other servers will have to be manually added to the site using the Site Properties dialog box.

CAUTION

Do not check the Automatically Detect Logon Servers box if you're using several SMS sites that have servers belonging to the same domain. In other words, clear this box if the NT (or LAN Manager) domain spans several sites.

14. When you're finished supplying the properties for the secondary site server, click the OK button.
15. No further configuration is needed if the default LAN Sender was used as the Sender type. If a RAS or SNA Sender was picked, additional dialog boxes will appear. They require that you supply the addressing information for the RAS or SNA Sender to use.

NOTE You must supply the connection information for each server, not just the current server. This means that the RAS or SNA address information dialog box will appear twice. The first time you will specify the Secondary Site To Primary Site connection information. In the subsequent address dialog box, you specify the Primary Site To Secondary Site connection information.

16. For the ASYNC RAS Sender used in our example, we must first provide the Secondary Site To Primary Site addressing information in the RAS Address From *secondary sitecode* To *primary sitecode* dialog box shown in figure 19.13. This means that we will be designating the values used by the secondary site server to connect to the primary.

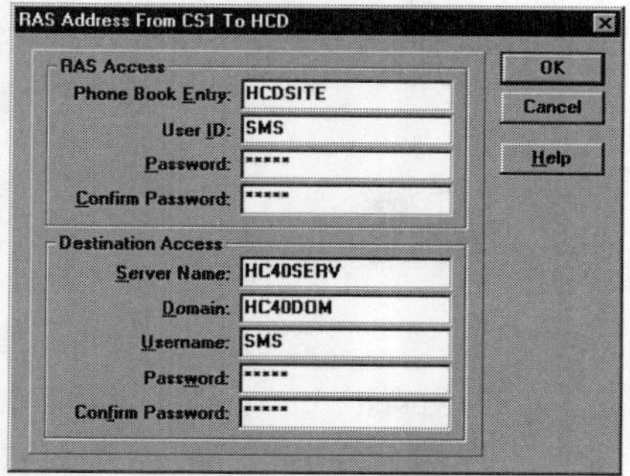

FIG. 19.13 First, specify the child-to-parent communication properties.

- Phone Book Entry—the name of an entry defined in the secondary site server's RAS phone book. This entry will be used when making a connection to the primary site. Each phone book entry contains the information needed to dial up or connect to the RAS Server at the primary site. When specifying a phone book entry, make sure that you use the proper phone book for the Sender Type you are using. For example, if using an ISDN RAS Sender, you must choose a phone book entry from the ISDN phone book.
- RAS User ID—the RAS user account specified here is used when making the connection to the primary site's RAS Server. You must make sure that this account has RAS dial-in permissions on the destination site's RAS Server.
- Password/Verify Password—provide and verify the password for the RAS User ID account.
- Server Name—identifies the name of the site server in the destination site.
- Domain—specifies the name of the domain in which the primary server resides.
- Username—the account name that will be used when accessing the primary site. It must have the appropriate privileges to the primary site server's directory structure and files. Change or Full Control permissions are required on the primary site server's SMS_SITE share. In addition, Read and Write permissions are required on its SITE.SRV\DESPOOLR.BOX\RECEIVE directory.
- Password/Confirm Password—provide and confirm the password for the Username user account.

After completing the addressing information for the secondary site server, click the OK button to be presented with the next addressing dialog box (see fig. 19.14). This dialog box will allow you to specify the Primary Site To Secondary Site connection information. You supply the same values but, this time, they are appropriate to the primary site server.

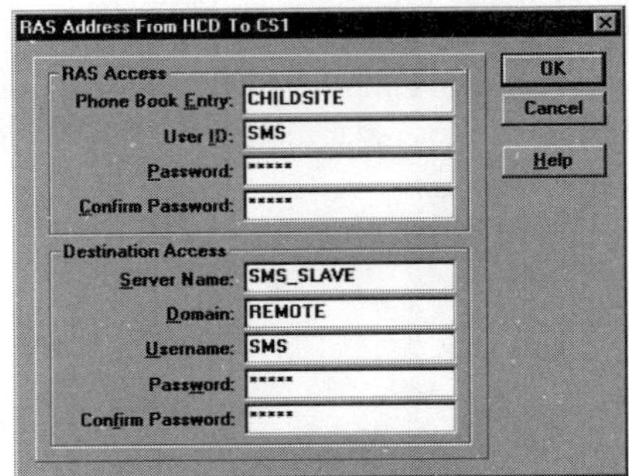

FIG. 19.14
Next specify the parent-to-child communication properties.

- Phone Book Entry—the name of an entry defined in the primary site server's RAS phone book. This entry will be used when making a connection to the secondary site server. Each phone book entry contains the information needed to dial up or connect to the RAS Server at the secondary site. When specifying a phone book entry, make sure that you use the proper phone book for the Sender Type you are using. For example, if using an ISDN RAS Sender, you must choose a phone book entry from the ISDN phone book.
- RAS User ID—the RAS user account specified here is used when making the connection to the secondary site RAS Server. You must make sure that this account has RAS dial-in permissions on the secondary site RAS Server.
- Password/Verify Password—provide and verify the password for the RAS User ID account.
- Server Name—identifies the name of the secondary site server.
- Domain—specifies the name of the domain in which the secondary site server resides.
- Username—the account name that will be used when accessing the secondary site server. It must have the appropriate privileges to the site server's directory structure and files. Change or Full Control permissions are required on the secondary site server's SMS_SITE share. In addition, Read and Write permissions are required on its SITE.SRV\DESPOOLR.BOX\RECEIVE directory.
- Password/Confirm Password—provide and confirm the password for the Username user account.

Had we picked the SNA Sender, you would have been required to supply the following address information for each server:

- Destination LU Alias—the name of the target site's LU alias. Each target site must have an SNA server running the SMS SNA Receiver with an LU alias defined. In addition, the current site must have an SNA Sender LU alias defined that is paired with that target site's LU alias.
- Username—the account name that will be used when accessing the destination site. It must have the appropriate privileges to the site server's directory structure and files. Change or Full Control permissions are required on the destination site's SMS_SITE share. In addition, Read and Write permissions are required on its SITE.SRV\DESPOOLR.BOX\RECEIVE directory.
- Password/Confirm Password—provide and confirm the password for the Username user account.

NOTE When SNA Sender is used, the SNA Receiver service must be installed and started on the SNA Server used at the secondary site. This installation will be covered later in the chapter. ■

17. When you've finished supplying any supplemental addressing information, click the OK button. Click the Yes button to begin the secondary site server installation process.
18. A dialog box will then appear, verifying the successful initiation of the secondary site installation. This does not indicate a successful completion of the installation, only the initiation. During the initialization phase, the new secondary site will be indicated by an Under Construction icon with the new secondary site's name next to it in the Sites.

Automatically Adding Clients

To add all the DOS, Windows 3.1, Windows for Workgroups, Windows 95, Windows NT Workstation, and NT Server machines residing in an NT or LAN Manager domain system to the SMS site, follow these steps:

1. Log on to the SMS site server using an administrative account, and start the SMS Administrator program.
2. Open the Sites window and highlight the SMS site you wish to configure. From the File menu, choose Properties to display the Site Properties dialog box.
3. Click the Clients button to display the Clients dialog box.
4. Mark the Proposed Properties button at the top of the dialog box.
5. Mark all the features of the client software you wish installed during the automatic installation under the Client Software section of the dialog box.
6. Mark the box next to the Automatically Configure Workstation Logon Scripts option.
7. Next, decide where you would like the call to the SMS logon script to be placed in any preexisting domain logon script. If no logon script exists, the SMSLS batch file will

become the logon script. If a script does exist, the Insert at Top of Logon Script and Add to Bottom of Logon Script options allow you to place the SMSLS batch file call where you want.

Often an existing logon script will be used to synchronize the workstation's time with that of a server. If this is the case, the set time call should be left at the beginning of any logon script that is presently being used. The SMSLS batch file call should follow it. If a logon script is not currently being used for synchronizing time between servers and workstations, it's a wise idea to create one, since SMS relies heavily on time synchronization for the distribution of software. Use the following command line:

net time *servername* /DOMAIN:*domain name* /s /y

at the beginning of the logon script and choose Add to Bottom of Logon Script option to place the SMSLS batch file call after it.

8. When you've finished making your selections, click the OK button twice and then verify the update by clicking the Yes button in the Microsoft SMS Administrator dialog box.

In the next monitoring cycle, the Site Configuration Manager will initiate the changes to the site.

Manually Setting Up Logon Scripts

Follow the steps below to configure the SMS login scripts on your network manually.

1. Copy the files listed in Table 19.2 from the site server's SMS_SHR share (*drive*:\sms\logon.srv directory) into the NETLOGON share (*drive*:\winnt\system32\RepNImport\Scripts) directory on each logon server in the domain.
2. Copy the SMSLS.INI file located in the *drive*:\sms\site.srv\maincfg.box into the NETLOGON share (*drive*:\winnt\system32\RepNImport\Scripts) directory on each logon server in the domain.
3. Copy the platform-specific version of SETLS into the proper *platform*.bin directory (*drive*:\winnt\system32\RepNImport\Scripts*platform*.bin) on each logon server.
4. Copy the files listed in Table 19.3 from the SMS_SHR shares *platform*.bin directory into the proper *platform*.bin (*drive*:\winnt\system32\RepNImport\Scripts*platform*.bin) directory on each logon server.

Table 19.2 Copy the Files Listed to Each Logon Server's NETLOGON Share

Files copied from SMS_SHR share (*drive*:\sms\logon.srv directory)
CLRLEVEL.COM
DOSVER.COM
NETSPEED.COM

Files copied from SMS_SHR share (*drive*:\sms\logon.srv directory)
NETSPEED.DAT
SMSLS.BAT and SMSLS.CMD
SMSLS.INI

Table 19.3 Copy the Files Listed to Each Logon Server's NETLOGON Share's Appropriate .BIN Directory

Files copied from SMS_SHR share (*drive*:\sms\logon.srv*platform*.bin directory)
NLSMSG16.EXE
NLSMSG32.EXE
NLSMSGO2.EXE
NLSRES.INI
SETLS16.EXE
SETLSOS2.EXE

The version of SETLS you copy will depend on the hardware platforms in place at your site. Different versions of SETLS exist for different NT hardware platforms. You'll find the version of SETLS you need under the processor-specific subdirectory (X86.BIN, ALPHA.BIN or MIPS.BIN) of the SMS_SHR share. You need to copy the file SETLS32.EXE from this directory to the NETLOGON share.

- Intel processors—copy SETLS32.EXE from the SMS_SHR share's X86.BIN directory to X86.BIN\SETLS32.EXE on the NETLOGON share of the logon server.
- Alpha processors—copy SETLS32.EXE from the SMS_SHR share's ALPHA.BIN directory to ALPHA.BIN\SETLS32.EXE on the NETLOGON share of the logon server.
- MIPS processors—copy SETLS32.EXE from the SMS_SHR share's MIPS.BIN directory to MIPS.BIN\SETLS32.EXE on the NETLOGON share of the logon server.

Manually Adding Clients

If you don't want to configure logon scripts to take inventory automatically when a user signs on, you can manually run the client setup and inventory agent from the site servers SMS_SHR share (*logonserver\volume*\sms\logon.srv on NetWare servers). Then, the file name RUNSMS is executed instead of the SMSLS batch file. The RUNSMS batch file does not contain the NETSPEED.COM program to detect slow network links. Otherwise, its content is the same as the SMSLS batch file that's normally run in logon scripts.

To manually take inventory on a client machine, connect to the logon server's SMS_SHR share (or NetWare volume and drive) and type RUNSMS at the command prompt.

Adding Macintosh Clients

Services For Macintosh must be running on the site logon server that will be used by the Macintosh clients. Once SFM is running, you can follow these steps to add a Macintosh client to the SMS system:

1. At the Macintosh machine, connect to the SMS_SHR volume that SMS created.
2. Open the MAC.BIN folder in the SMS_SHR volume.
3. Find the Installer program and start it.
4. When the SMS Script dialog box appears, click on Install.
5. You will be prompted to close any open applications. If you agree, the Setup program will close any open programs and proceed to install the SMS client components on the computer. A message will appear after the installation is complete.
6. Click Restart.

From Here...

This finishes the step-by-step chapter on installing your site servers and clients. Other site configuration tasks are discussed in the step-by-step chapters:

- Chapter 20, "Taking the Hardware and Software Inventory," takes you through the inventory configuration process.
- Chapter 21, "Sharing Applications," follows with the information you need to start distributing and sharing application across your network.
- Chapter 25, "SMS Management Tasks," shows you the steps needed to maintain a site configuration.

CHAPTER 20

Taking the Hardware and Software Inventory

The SMS inventory collection process is a lot more important than it seems. It provides the entire infrastructure for SMS operations. It collects and stores all the hardware and software inventory for all clients in the site, and this data plays a key role for most features in SMS. If you are to use software distribution or remote troubleshooting, the client information must be inventoried in the SMS database.

A veritable ocean of data can transport across SMS's architecture. Systems Management Server can collect hardware and software data, as well as copies of client files for analysis. By default, data is collected whenever users log on. That is a lot of potential data traffic. ■

How to collect the Hardware and Software Inventories

Accurate collection of information about the hardware and software systems will enable you to use key features of the SMS sortware.

How to Configure the Directory Replicator Service

The Directory Replicator Service allowss you to transfer logon scripts other servers.

How to expand SMS' functionality

Learn how to create a custom MIF Form, use the SMS Data Entry Application, and more.

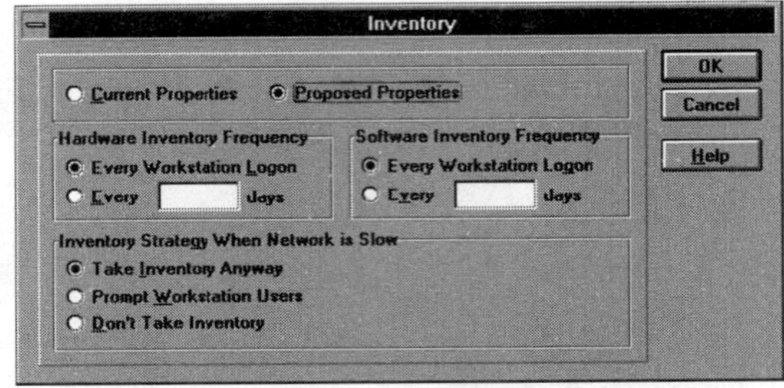

FIG. 20.1
Taking the hardware and software inventory.

Let's take a look at some of the data collected for SMS inventory information, as follows:

- Hardware Configuration Data—The configuration information about client's RAM, BIOS data, hard disk space, and many other hardware configuration details.
- Software Inventory Data—The administrator specifies which software packages to include in the software inventory. He or she defines software inventory queries in the form of packages, searching clients' computers for WINWORD.EXE for instance.
- File Collection—The administrator can make copies of a client's AUTOEXEC.BAT and other files, copying them automatically to the site server, where they can be analyzed.

All data is passed up through the SMS hierarchy to the central site, where the main SMS database is kept.

Collecting Hardware, Software, and File Inventories

The installation of software using Systems Management Server starts with the collection of inventory information from machines. This hardware and software inventory information is stored in the Systems Management Server database and is used to plan and control the installation process.

Hardware Inventory Collection and Reporting

With hardware inventory, SMS knows how to collect data without much configuration needed.

The system component responsible for hardware inventory collection and reporting is called the Inventory Agent. Inventory is collected and reported by each client. By understanding the Inventory Agent's path through the SMS architecture, you can understand the whole SMS inventory process.

The actual collection process starts at the client machine. This is where the Inventory Agent runs and performs its hardware and software scan. Inventory collection continues at the site server, where the inventory information is collected and processed.

Inventory can be manually run from a client by connecting to the logon server \SMS_SHR and running the appropriate Inventory Agent for the client. The inventory applications will be in the \X86.BIN, \MIPS.BIN or \ALPHA.BIN directory.

NOTE The clients supported by Systems Management Server are: MS-DOS 5.0 or later, Windows (all versions), and Mac System 7. The network operating systems supported for inventory are Microsoft Networking (supporting SMBs), Novell NetWare, and Appletalk. ■

Table 20.1 gives the Inventory Agent command files for the different types of clients.

Table 20.1 Inventory Agent Command Files

Client	File Name
DOS	INVDOS.EXE
Windows NT, Windows 95	INV32.EXE
OS/2	INVOS2.EXE
Macintosh	INVMAC

The different Inventory Agents for each of the supported client operating systems are located on the logon servers in the *d:*\SMS\LOGON.SRV\X86.BIN subdirectory.

Normally, the inventory code runs an INVDOS, INVMAC, INVWIN32, or INVOS2 executable. The first thing the inventory .EXE does is to determine if inventory should be taken. This is done by comparing the time of the last inventory scan, which is stored in the SMS.INI file, to the rule entry in the DOMAIN.INI file at the server. This means the inventory executable will be run every time even if inventory is not actually going to be taken. However, inventory may not be collected even though the .EXE runs.

The following is a list of steps the Inventory Agent executes:

1. The Inventory Agent determines the computer name in the SMS database. With MS Networking, a NetBIOS name is used. With Netware systems, a network card ID and IPX network number are concatenated to produce an identifier number. In any other system, the user is prompted for a computer name.
2. The Inventory Agent opens a temporary file on the logon server as a computer identification to the file. Hardware and software inventory information is then added to the temp file. This inventory is collected only when the inventory frequency set by the administrator has passed.
3. It then closes the temp file and renames it with the appropriate extension. MS-DOS and Windows NT clients create a .RAW file in the \Inventory.Box directory on the logon server; .RAW files are later processed and turned into .MIF files.
4. Windows NT Inventory Agent generates a lot of the same code and also produces a .RAW file.
5. The Inventory Agent updates the local SMS.INI file with the last count of inventory. It also updates SMS.INI for any changes from DOMAIN.INI, additional logon servers, and any failed tests from running the hardware check safety routine.

NOTE For troubleshooting purposes, the /v switch should be used when running the Inventory Agent. This causes the agent to go into verbose or trace mode while running a hardware and software scan. The output should be directed to a text file for easy viewing. An example using the DOS/Windows agent:

INVDOS /V > SCAN.TXT.

The text file can then be read to determine if the agent encountered any problems.

For troubleshooting the remainder of the process, use File Manager to follow the movement of the files described above, use the trace logs of the components involved, and finally check the SMS Administrator tool's Events window for any error messages. (There's a further discussion of troubleshooting in Chapter 17, "Troubleshooting SMS Components.")

Software Inventory Collection and Reporting

When configuring inventory collection in Systems Management Server, you make use of the SMS Administrator tool and three components of the SMS_Executive service that work behind the scenes: Application Manager, Maintenance Manager, and Site Configuration Manager. The following shows you how the process is begun:

1. With software inventory, the Administrator sets up an Inventory package to set up scanning rules.
2. The text file PACKAGE.RUL is compiled by Application Manager Service, a master file for software scanning rules.
3. PACKAGE.RUL is converted to a binary file, PKG_16.CFG.
4. PKG_16.CFG is transported onto every logon server in the site by the Maintenance Manager service.
5. SMS Configuration Manager creates an internal SMS job to send the package information to the child sites.

The Inventory Package is something the SMS Site Administrator defines to configure software inventory. For instance, if you wanted to see which clients had WINWORD.EXE loaded, you would create a package file to collect that data. When an Inventory Package is added, deleted, or modified, the file PACKAGE.RUL is recompiled, as it is the master file. There is only one such file per site. It is converted to a binary file, PKG_16.CFG, to be placed on every logon server in the site by the Maintenance Manager.

Later in this chapter, in the section "Inventory Collection Configuration," we'll see how software inventory collection can be configured by the Administrator.

Reporting Inventories

Inventory reporting is the way the SMS process brings inventory collection data to the central SMS database and the central site.

Once SMS inventory collection is configured and is underway, inventory reporting begins. Workstations post inventory files to site servers in the site. Inventory files collected on the secondary site server are passed to the primary site server, which posts inventory changes to SQL Server, which passes them to the central and primary sites.

The steps to inventory reporting are as follows:

1. The Agent writes the inventory information (*.RAW) to an SMS logon server; this file includes the collected files.
2. Maintenance Manager collects the files from the logon server.
3. The *.RAW file gets converted to a *.MIF file; text file, approximately 20 to 40 Kb in size.
4. The .MIF file is read into the SQL database.
5. The change information gets reported to a parent site if applicable.

With the steps outlined above, inventory collection data is brought back to the central SMS database.

File Collection

The Inventory Agent adds collected files (and extended inventory information, discussed later in this chapter) to the temp files for MS-DOS and Windows NT clients. For OS/2 and Macintosh clients, temp files are not created. Instead, the collection information is placed on separate files on the logon server. Systems Management Server keeps track of all collected files by writing a record for each one in a local file called COLFILE.HIS. Collected files are collected again only when they change, not every time the inventory is run.

Inventory Collection Configuration

In this section we'll see how software inventory collection can be configured by the Administrator:

- Automatic Inventory Collection
- Collection Frequency
- Software Packages
- Configuring the Directory Replicator Service

Most companies will want to configure Systems Management Server to start automatic inventory collection whenever the user logs on. Figure 20.2 shows the Automatic Configure Workstation scripts. Automatic inventory collection is possible on a Windows NT network, Lan Manager, or Novell Netware Network. Automatic inventory collection is started when you add the SMSLS.BAT file to the user's logon script. This can be set automatically in the SMS Administrator program, under Site Properties, Clients. Choose the Automatically Configure Workstation Logon Scripts option. This process will also install SMS client software on the client computer.

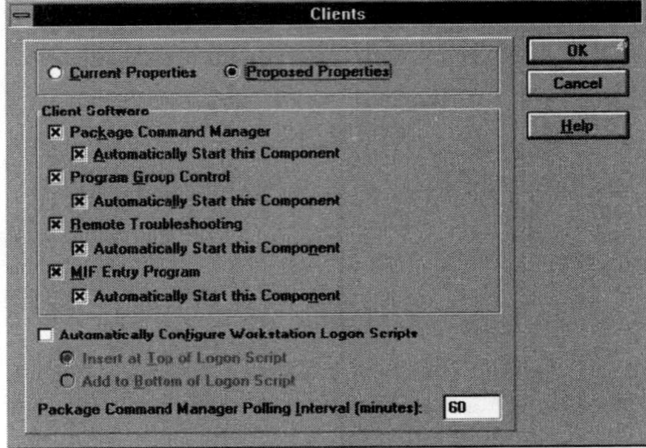

FIG. 20.2 Using SMS to configure inventory collection automatically.

In an NT Server domain, changes are made to the logon scripts on the logon server at the site. In a Novell Netware environment, changes will be made to the system logon script.

In a Macintosh environment, the client starts inventory when a user logs on to a server running Services for Macintosh. Because they do not have logon scripts, user runs the Installer application in the MAC.BIN folder. The Installer places the Mac Inventory Agent into the Mac system folder.

NOTE The Automatically Configure Workstation Logon Scripts option will work only for user accounts that have no logon scripts or for logon scripts with an extension such as USERPREF.BAT. A file with no extension, such as USERPREF, will not be modified.

Inventory Collection Frequency

Although the default is to collect inventory every time a user logs on, you may want to adjust this to reduce network traffic, especially if equipment configuration does not change very much.

To set the frequency, choose Site Properties, Inventory.

Notice that, as shown in Figure 20.3, you can set the inventory collection for hardware and software separately. You can set collection to happen at logon, or every few days. You can also set what happens if the link is slow. A slow network link is defined as a link where 1Kb of data takes more than 500ms to be transferred.

The Inventory Frequency for software and hardware is copied to the logon server's DOMAIN.INI file and then transferred to SMS.INI on the clients.

FIG. 20.3
Setting the frequency of inventory collection.

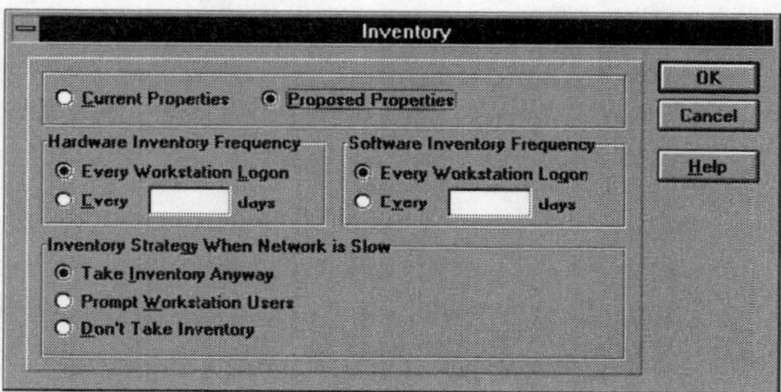

Configuring Software Packages

Software inventory is useful for a variety of reasons, as follows:

- You can keep track of your software licensing.
- You can define whether the wrong type of software is installed; for example, screen savers and Internet files.
- You can check to see whether files are installed that may be necessary for an upgrade. You may need to check that the right version of software is installed on a workstation.

To audit software, the administrator creates a software inventory package for a particular software application. The administrator's inventory software package specifies a specific file (for example, WINWORD.EXE) from the software application, as well as other information such as checksum, size, and date. Size and date of a file are relatively self-explanatory; checksum refers to a calculation that detects the sum of all values stored at a specific set of bytes and compares the sum to a specified value. If no additional properties are specified, the filename alone is used.

Under the File Properties object you can configure the Collect This File feature. This configures the inventory process to copy the file to the site server for your review.

Configuring the Directory Replicator Service

With NT networks, the Directory Replicator Service can be used to transfer copies of user logon scripts to their local logon servers.

To make sure the Directory Replicator Service is running, check the Control Panel, Services applet and look for Directory Replicator Service. Make sure it is configured for automatic startup.

Use Server Manager to configure Replication from your site server to other logon servers. In Server Manager, enable exporting from your site server's \REPL$\Scripts directory and importing from your logon servers' \REPL$\Scripts directory.

Planning an Inventory Strategy

The base of good inventory strategy is to reduce excess network traffic. Inventory frequency is a large part of this strategy. You will have to ask yourself how often you need to poll for hardware or software inventory.

Software inventory is used to control software installation and upgrades. Hardware inventory is important to installing or upgrading software as well, as you will need to check that enough disk space exists, enough RAM, and so on. You may want to check that no one is removing hardware. On the other hand, your environment may be relatively static and unchanging.

Once every one to two weeks may be a good setting to start with for software or hardware collection frequency.

One factor you should consider is the Every Workstation Logon option for hardware and software inventory. When this option is selected, every time the inventory executable is run, inventory will be collected.

The following are the Inventory Strategy When Network is Slow options:

- Take Inventory Anyway
- Prompt Workstation Users
- Don't Take Inventory

When configuring inventory collection over a slow WAN link, do the following:

- Limit the amount of software being inventoried. If you have a permanently slow link, you really need to keep the inventory times low by not trying to inventory too many software packages.
- If the workstation will be across slow links only occasionally, as with portables, then select the Don't Take Inventory option. The Prompt Workstation Users option requires manual intervention and puts the strategy into the hands of the users.
- If workstations will be part of a site and are running across a slow link, then you will need to select the Take Inventory Anyway option to make sure that they are getting inventoried.

Extending Inventory Collection

Wouldn't it be nice to have serial numbers and asset tag numbers entered into the SMS database the first time you put a new PC out at a user's station? Besides the usual inventory elements, such as RAM, ROM, and so on, you may want to keep track of the keyboard and monitor serial numbers, or non-PC equipment such as dictation equipment, VCRs, and so on. Hence the need for extending inventory collection.

Hardware components or other components that are not inventoried by SMS can be added to the SMS database by using a custom MIF file. The MIF form resides at the user's station and can contain any field that you find useful. Once collected, the inventory data can then be viewed using SMS Administrator.

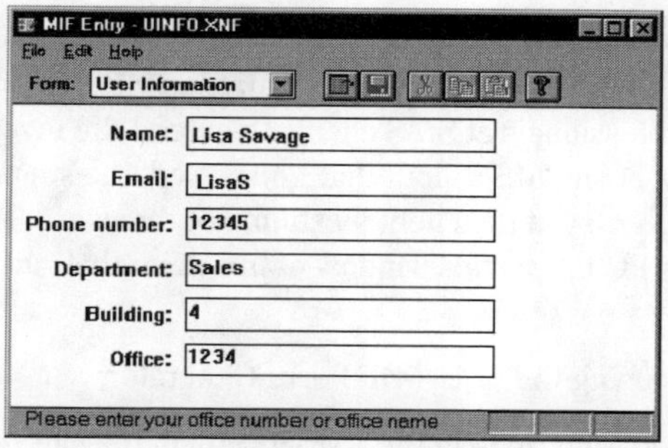

FIG. 20.4
Extending inventory collection.

There are two ways to add custom inventory. One is to create a custom MIF file, the other (and easiest way) is to use the MIF Data Form Generator.

Creating a Custom MIF Form

The following are steps to create a custom MIF file:

1. Create an MIF file with the custom data and any necessary SMS information, such as identification and architecture information. Syntax in a custom MIF file can get pretty hairy. You may want to stick with the MIF Data Entry Form Generator, discussed later in this chapter. To check syntax for custom MIF files, look in the SMS Administrator's guide.

   The following is the basic custom MIF file structure:

   ```
   Start component
   Name = "Workstation"
   Description = "Inventory information about a PC"
   <Path Definitions> (Optional)
   <Enumeration Definitions> (Optional)
   <Group Definitions>
   <Attribute Definitions>
   <Table Definitions> (Optional)
   End Component
   ```

2. Place the MIF file in a collection directory at any of the following locations:

   An SMS client: \MS\SMS\IDMIFS

   A logon Server: \LOGON.SRV\ISVMIF.BOX

   The site server: \SITE.SRV\ISVMIF.BOX

3. If the collection directory is on a client, the Inventory Agent must be run to report the MIF data.

4. The data is then processed by the Inventory Processor and the Inventory Data Loader, and added to the database.

Using the MIF Form Generator

Using the SMS MIF Form Generator and the SMS Data Entry Form Application, you can enable users or support professionals at SMS clients to extend the inventory information of their local clients. Recently, at an SMS rollout that I observed, the support professionals installing client PCs did MIF data entry at the client location, not the users. The custom data will appear as a new icon in the PC Properties window of the client that ran the SMS Data Entry Form.

Following are the steps for using the SMS MIF Form Generator:

1. Locate the Forms Generator icon in the SMS group on the site server. Start the SMS MIF Form Generator.
2. The administrator distributes the form to the SMS clients using the Run Command on Workstation job.
3. The form is filled out in the MIF Entry Application (MIFWIN.EXE), and a MIF file is generated.
4. The Inventory Agent runs and collects the MIF file. This data is eventually passed back to the site server and placed in the SMS database.

Creating Forms with the SMS MIF Generator

Once you use Forms Generator for custom data entry forms, users or support professionals can open the forms at client workstations to help with form fill-in.

The Form Generator is installed automatically on site servers at primary sites. The SMS Setup program also creates a program item for the Form Generator in the Microsoft SMS Program Group. The Form Generator runs only on Windows NT.

When you create a form, the Form Generator saves the form as a file with the .XNF extension. The form is later used by the SMS Data Entry application.

A form consists of items which the user will fill in. There are three types of items, as follows:

- Numbers—for placing a numeric entry into the database.
- Text—for placing a text string into the database.
- List—for presenting a list of options from which the user can select.

The list of items displays all the current items in the form. It also determines the order in which the user fills in the data. The items can be moved around by cutting and pasting them into the proper place. Any number or combination of these items can be put on an SMS form.

For each of these items, there are some user-specified options, such as length, read-only, and storage type. Numeric items are limited to 32-bits. Read-only items are automatically put into the output MIF and do not appear on the form. They appear as data when viewed in SMS Administrator.

The storage space for each item can be set to either SPECIFIC or COMMON. If an item's value will be the same for many users, it should be stored as COMMON data. Multiple users share

COMMON data, and redundant data is thus avoided in the database. If the item's value varies from component to component, use SPECIFIC to assign a separate storage space in the database.

Using the SMS Data Entry Application

The MIF Entry application (entitled SMS Data Entry Form) reads the Form data file (.XNF) and then presents a dialog box in which the user can fill in the fields of the form. This application runs on the MS_DOS (MIFDOS.EXE), Windows 3.x, Windows 95, Windows NT (MIFWIN.EXE), and Macintosh (MIFMAC) platforms. After the data is entered, it generates an .MIF file.

Loading a Form (.XNF File)

By default, when the Data Entry application runs, it looks in the \MS\SMS\BIN directory for SMS forms (.XNF files) and presents a list of available forms. If a form is specified on a parameter on the command line for the Data Entry application, it loads that specific form and displays the list of available forms.

Using the Default User Information Form

After the form is loaded, the user is prompted to enter the data for each of the items. SMS sends out a default form to every client to collect user information. If you edit this file, you should copy the edited form to the \SITE.SRV\MAINCFG.BOX\CLIENT.SRC*platform*.BIN directory. Maintenance Manager then copies this file to the logon servers in the site. If you do not want this form distributed to users, delete the UINFO.XNF file in the site server and in any logon servers and clients to which the file has been distributed.

Generating the MIF File

When the user chooses Save in the Data Entry application, a MIF file is generated and placed in the MachineISVMIFPath directory (specified in the client's SMS.INI file). By default, the Machine ISVMIFPath is the \MS\SMS\NOIDMIFS directory. The form is then collected when the Inventory Agent runs on the client. The generated MIF file is always part of the local client's inventory.

Dealing with Hardware Failures during Collection

When the Inventory Agent runs, it creates an SMSSAFE.TMP file to keep track of hardware failures during collection. Failed hardware tests are written into this file while the Inventory Agent is scanning the hardware.

When inventory is complete, Inventory Agent writes the change to the [workstation] status section in the SMS.INI file, using the FailedHardwareChecks keyword. After the failed tests are written to the SMS.INI file, SMSSAFE.TMP is deleted. Next time Inventory Agent runs, it will see the failed tests in SMS.INI and skip those tests.

You can log on again once the hardware component is working and the inventory will update itself to include the working component.

Final Considerations

With hardware inventory, SMS knows how to collect data without much configuration needed. The Inventory Agent steps described earlier are responsible for hardware inventory.

With software inventory, the Administrator sets up an inventory package to set up scanning rules. The text file PACKAGE.RUL is compiled by Application Manager Service, a master file for software scanning rules. PACKAGE.RUL is converted to a binary file, PKG_16.CFG. That file is transported to the central database and site.

With File Collection,the administrator can make copies of client's AUTOEXEC.BAT and other files, copying them automatically to the site server, where they can be analyzed.

The Inventory Agent adds collected files to the temp files for MS-DOS and Windows NT clients. For OS/2 and Macintosh clients, the collection information is placed on separate files on the logon server. SMS keeps track of all collected files by writing a record for each one in a local file called COLFILE.HIS. Collected files are collected again only when files change.

The following is a checklist to help with successful inventory collection:

- Ensure all Inventory Agents/services are running on server.
- Configure SMSLS.BAT in logon scripts, manually or automatically.
- Establish software and hardware inventory settings, resulting in client settings in SMSLS.INI (domain, workgroup, and so on).
- Check timing of each inventory reporting phase.
- Test file collection or custom inventory collection if necessary.
- Change workstation configuration and reinventory (check inventory history).
- Modify Windows NT Registry settings for SMS event timing as appropriate.

From Here...

- For more information about using the SMS Administrator, see Chapter 5, "Server Installation, Part I."
- To gain a better understanding of the way SMS processes all of the information, see Appendix D, "A Detailed Look at the Data Flow."

CHAPTER 21

Sharing Applications

In this chapter, you'll learn how to:

- **Describe the process of distributing shared applications**
- **Create and configure a shared application package**
- **Create a job to send a shared application package**
- **Create program groups and icons for shared applications**
- **Identify changes made to Program Manager when it receives a shared package**
- **Identify the tasks that can be performed by shared application scripts**
- **Describe the difference between shared application and installation scripts**
- **Identify where the shared application process failed in a given situation**

After we bucked the trend of host-based systems in the 70s and the trend of distributed systems in the 80s, we are now moving back to a mode of application sharing. Following are some reasons why the vision of shared applications with SMS is the vision of the future:

Shared applications can be attached to user profiles in Microsoft Networking; therefore, if you log on as yourself, you can use the applications from any station.

New multithreaded network applications are more robust, allowing more simultaneous users.

Applications can be removed or upgraded at any time.

Licensing is easily resolved.

Dynamic Resource Allocation—if one distribution server is busy, another one will be used. ■

Understanding Shared Applications

A shared application is one that is stored on a distribution server for multiple users to run. When it is started by a user, it is loaded over the network into the local computer's RAM and is run at the local computer.

The process of configuring an application as a shared application is described in the following five steps:

1. The administrator:
   - Sets up a software package with sharing properties.
   - Defines program items.
   - Sets up a Share Package on Server job.
2. The administrator configures the program group that will be displayed to users at the their computer, including program items, commmand line, and source directory.
3. The application files are placed on distribution servers by a process called the Despooler. The configuration information is placed on logon servers by a process called the Maintenance Manager.
4. When a user logs on, the Program Group Control (PGC) application retrieves the list of available shared applications and user's group information from the logon server.
5. PGC installs a Program Manager Group on the user's desktop, making an icon for each available shared application. After creating the desktop icons, PGC will also run any specified configuration scripts to set up the local registry for application dependency information and OLE.

After the shared application program group and icons are configured for the user, the user can run the application.

Working with Shared Application Supported Clients

For application sharing, the list of supported clients is smaller than with other features.

Supported clients are Windows 3.x-based including Windows for Workgroups, Windows 95-based, and Windows NT 3.x-based computers only.

MS-DOS, Macintosh, and OS/2 computers are not supported. OS/2 computers are not supported because OS/2 does not have network support for Windows applications.

NOTE It is possible to use SMS to distribute the shared version of an application to a Macintosh client. This is done by creating a Workstation package and a Run Command on Workstation Job for the application. A command should be sent to the Macintosh to run the installer for the application and install a network version of the application. ■

Macintosh clients cannot have security on shared applications so that specific groups of users can run an application, nor do they have the ability to run a shared application from one of multiple distribution servers. On the Macintosh, the installer always uses the distribution server from which the application was installed.

Creating User Groups

In the SMS system, shared applications are assigned to a group or multiple groups of users. These groups are not created by SMS; they are created within the security system of the servers on which the application will be shared. Valid groups are Windows NT Server global groups, LAN Manager 2.x user groups, and NetWare user groups. Windows NT Server local groups are not valid.

Adding User Groups

The Site Configuration Manager monitors all the logon servers within the site. It verifies directories, updates logon scripts, and reads the groups from each of the servers at periodic intervals. The Site Verification interval is based on the site's Service Response Time configuration. The Logon Script Updates and User Group Reporting intervals are every 24 hours. These intervals can be configured under the Site Configuration Manager key in the Windows NT Registry on the site server.

When the User Group Reporting interval has elapsed, Site Configuration Manager will do the following:

- List the Global User Groups for each Windows NT domain, the user groups for each LAN Manager domain, and the groups for each NetWare domain. For each domain, the domains that it trusts will be analyzed for global user groups.
- Create a Delta-MIF file to report the groups that are enumerated.
- Copy the Delta-MIF file to the Data Loader inbox for processing.

Groups from additional domains that are not in the SMS site can also be added to SMS by running the UGMIF.EXE utility. This program, located on the SMS CD-ROM under \PSSTOOLS, reads the groups from a domain and creates a Delta-MIF file. The file is then placed in the Data Loader directory and added to the SMS database. The user group is then available to be used in the SMS Administrator.

Creating a Shared Application Package

A shared application package is configured through the Setup Package for Sharing dialog box.

To create a shared application package, perform the following steps:

- Open the Packages Window.
- From the File menu, choose New.
- In the Name box, type a package name.
- Choose the Sharing button to produce the Setup Package for Sharing dialog box.

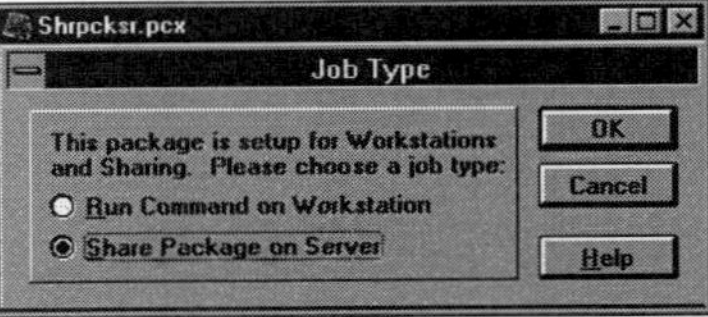

FIG. 21.1
Set the preferences of your package by using the Share Package on Server dialog box.

The following three key pieces of information have to be entered here in the dialog box shown above:

1. The Source Directory for the software application;
2. The Share Name to be used on the distribution servers;
3. Program item information for the program item(s) associated with the application.

Preparing the Source Directory

Before a package can be configured, the application source files must be installed. Keep in mind the following considerations when installing an application to be shared.

The source directory can be located on the site server or on any server which the Scheduler can access with Read privilege. The Scheduler uses the SMS Service Account to connect to other servers, and it should be granted the Read privilege.

A shared application package requires that the application files be installed and configured in the source directory. That is, the files must be in an uncompressed state and ready to run.

If there is a version of an application that is designed to run from the network, that version should be used. These applications normally place all the files required to run the application in a specific directory or subdirectory.

Some applications do not have a true network version. Instead they have a workstation version that places some of the application's files on the server and commonly used files in the local \WINDOWS and \SYSTEM directories to reduce the network traffic. If this is the case, place the commonly used files in the source directory with the network application, or run the Setup program for the workstation version at each target computer.

If an application has an embedded application, such as the Microsoft Draw package for Microsoft Word for Windows, you have to create a separate package for the embedded application with a separate share. For example, for Microsoft Word for Windows, you must install a package and program item for the MSAPPS embedded applications.

Defining the Share Name

The Source Directory specifies the location of the source files. The Scheduler builds the compressed package from these files. The share name should be a UNC name for Scheduler access.

The share name is the actual share (or NetWare volume name) and directory on your distribution servers that the application would be shared as. For example, the share name could be

SERVER\APPS\WORD. If the directory is not specified, the Despooler creates a directory (under the root directory of the largest available drive) with the same name as the share name, and creates a share to make the application available on the network. This is used for servers running Windows NT or LAN Manager.

On Novell NetWare servers, the Despooler cannot create shares, so it uses existing server volumes. If an existing volume is not specified as part of the share name, the Despooler uses the default SMS volume on the NetWare server. If only a volume name is specified as a share name, the Despooler puts the package on that volume in a subdirectory of the volume's root directory. The subdirectory name will be the package ID number.

NOTE The share name should be C$, D$, or any other administrative share, because of the way packages are removed. All the files under the package share are deleted. It would be catastrophic to delete all the files on a partition. ■

Setting the Share Access

After the Despooler creates the share on a Windows NT or LAN Manager computer, it sets read and write permissions to it. These permissions are assigned for only two groups: Users and Guests. They correspond to the Domain Users and Domain Guests global groups of a Windows NT Server computer and to the User and Guests groups of a LAN Manager server.

Creating Program Items

To configure program items, choose the New button in the Setup Package for Sharing dialog box. Complete the Program Item Properties dialog box using the following information:

- Description—this text is displayed under the program item icon on the client.
- Command Line—this is the command that will be run by PGC at the target computer.
- Registry Name—this name is used as an entry for the application in the local client registry. Registry names enable an application to call another application by its registry name. An example of this is Microsoft Word calling the Draw program.
- Configuration Script—this optional entry specifies a script to configure the application when its icon is installed on the target computer. It should contain the full path to the Microsoft Test script. This path should also be accessible to the Scheduler. SMS makes this script available to PGC to use. It is useful for configuring the local registry and initializations file so that the application can run correctly from the network. Sample configuration scripts are provided with SMS in the PRIMSITE.SRV\IMPORT.SRC directory.
- Don't Display Icon in Program Group—if this check box is selected, the program item is not displayed in the Program Manager group.
- Run Minimized—if this check box is selected, the program is automatically minimized when it is started.
- Run Local Copy if Present—if this check box is selected, PGC searches the path for a local copy of the application. If it does not find a copy, it uses the one on the server.

- Drive Mode Select—the appropriate connection option. The default selection is Runs with UNC Name. Some applications cannot run from a UNC connection. Select Requires Drive Letter to direct PGC to connect a drive letter and run the shared application from that drive. If Requires Specific Drive Letter is selected, and that drive is already in use on the target computer, PGC prompts the user to use the first available drive or to cancel the operation.
- Supported Platforms—select the platforms on which an icon will be made available to run. PGC creates and displays icons only if the program is configured for the target computer's platform. Uncheck those platforms that don't apply, for example, MIPS or Alpha.

SMS will update your package at all site distribution servers. You can then see your packages in the SMS Administrator under the Packages icon.

Setting Random Selection of Servers

When a user initiates the Program Group Control application, it gathers a list of available application servers from the logon server. From this list, a random selection produces a server which the Program Group Control application will use for the shared application.

If a global group spans an entire domain of users, the distribution servers distributing applications could cover the whole domain, including some slow WAN links. A user could end up using a slow link to connect to a server when one is sitting on the same segment as the user.

In understanding the way SMS randomly selects distribution servers, and in understanding the way that groups control the distribution, you can ideally configure distribution to maximize efficiency and suit your needs.

Creating a Share Package on Server Job

The Job Setup dialog is very similar to the setup details of software distribution described earlier (see fig. 21.2). In fact the same guides apply that were suggested in the section on software distribution for the Send Phase and Distribute Phase. The difference is the Job target section. In a Share Package On Server job, the package is moved only to a site and distribution servers, so there is no need to define individual workstations. Taking this a step further, shared applications are not controlled by workstation information, but rather by user information.

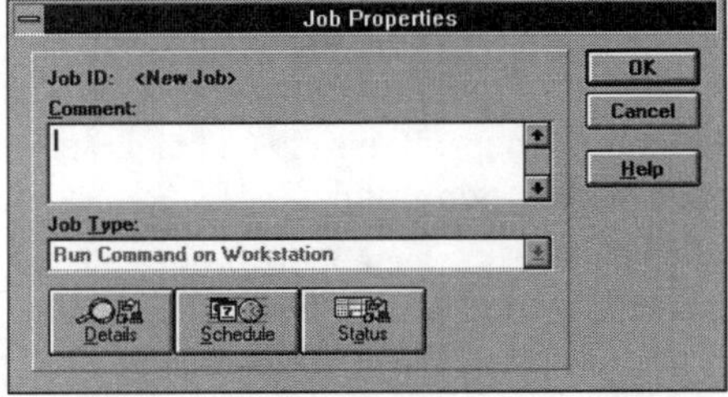

FIG. 21.2 The Job Properties Setup dialog box.

Assigning the Global Groups

When the user logs on to a workstation and runs the Program Group Control application, it determines which shared applications the user should have. It then creates program groups or deletes old groups on the desktop for the user. The fact that global groups define access to the applications means something interesting happens: the user's desktop view of shared applications follows the user to any workstation on the network. This can also present an adverse side effect: if the user logs on to a workstation in a site where the application was not sent to a distribution server, the desktop will still be set up as if the application is available. This is an issue that needs to be understood when sending the application to distribution servers, especially when the Master Account Domain model is used.

A Share Package on Server job is used to distribute and install shared packages. It can be created by dragging a package, with the share properties defined, onto a site. Share packages can be dragged only onto sites or Site Groups, not machine groups, machines, or domains. This kind of job can also be created by opening the Jobs window, choosing New from the File menu, and selecting the Share Package on Server job type.

Creating a Share Package on Server job is very similar to creating a Run Command on Workstation job, except that no target computers or commands are defined. Only the package, its destination sites, and the distribution servers are defined.

The Send and Distribute phases operate in the same way as the Run Command on Workstation Job. The package is compressed and sent to the target sites, and then it is decompressed and placed on the target distribution servers. However, when a shared package is placed on a distribution server, it is located in its own share instead of being placed in the SMS_PKGd share.

Share Package on Server packages, like Run Command on Workstation packages, are tracked by the Despooler service. It keeps a list of both master (stored) packages on the site server and of distribution servers on which a package is stored. These lists are stored in the Windows NT Registry under SMS\Component\SMS\DespoolerMaster Packages or Transfer Packages for distribution servers. Share Package on Server packages are labeled with an S_packageID name, while Run Command on Workstation packages are labeled with a W_packageID name.

The Share Package on Server job is carried out in almost the same manner as the Run Command on Workstation job.

The Scheduler activates the job and creates the following files:

> Package File (\SENDER.BOX\TOSEND*.S00);
> Despooler instructions
> (SENDER.BOX\TOSEND*.I00);
> Send request file (SENDER.BOX\REQUESTS\sender*.SRQ).

The Despooler at the target site receives the package file and instructions.

The instruction file tells the Despooler that this is a Share Package on Server job.

The Despooler stores a master copy of the package (DESPOOLR.BOX\STORE) and decompresses the package in a temporary directory under the root directory of the disk with the most available free space. If the package contains any long filenames or unique characters, the package is decompressed on the NTFS drive with the most available space.

After the files are decompressed, they are copied to all the job's target distribution servers and shared with the name specified by the package details. If any of the distribution servers are NetWare servers, the GSNW software must be on the same computer as the Despooler component. After the distribution servers all have a copy, the temporary directory is deleted. The Despooler updates the Registry with the package storage locations.

The Scheduler also sends configuration script files to destination sites. The Despooler at the destination site places these files in the SITE.SRV\MAINCFG.BOX\APPCTL.SRC\SCRIPTS directory. From this directory the Maintenance Manager copies the files to all logon servers.

Creating Program Groups

The second step in configuring shared applications for SMS users is to create the program groups that will contain the icons for the shared applications. The Administrator configures the packages that will appear in a specific program group and the user groups that will see the program group on their desktop.

Configuring a Program Group Package

The available packages for the program group are those that were set up for sharing in the Setup Package for Sharing dialog box. After a package has been made (see fig. 21.3) a member of the program group, specific items (commands or executable files) from the package can be selected. These items will show up as individual icons in the program group. The available program items were configured in the Package Sharing Properties dialog box.

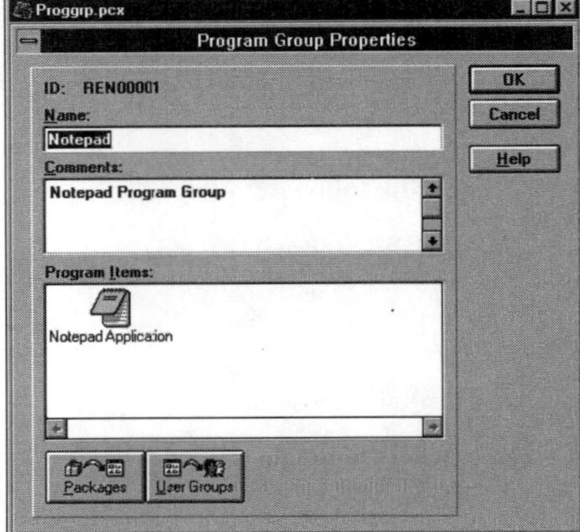

FIG. 21.3
Creating a program group package.

Configuring the User Groups

Select the User Groups button. The User Group Properties identify the list of users who will have the program group added to their desktop when running Program Group Control (see fig. 21.4). The list of user groups is made available by the Site Configuration Manager that enumerates the groups on Windows NT Server computers, LAN Manager 2.x servers, and Novell NetWare 3.x or 4.x servers (with 3.x binary emulation turned on).

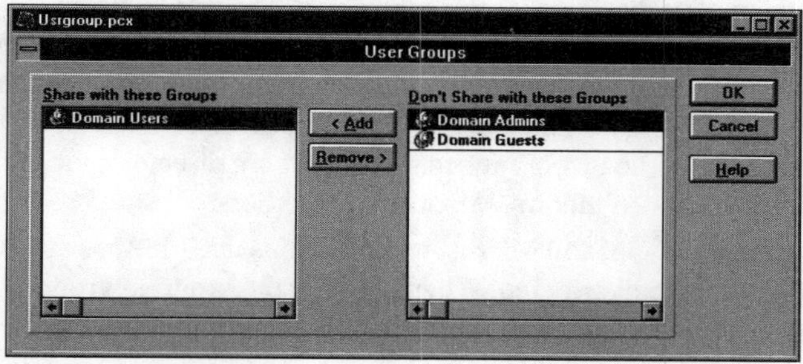

FIG. 21.4
Use the User Groups dialog box to add users and groups to your package.

Configuring the Program Group Distribution

When the Program Group has been configured, the following process occurs to distribute the information to the user group client computers.

The Applications Manager monitors the Program Group table in the SMS database for changes. As changes occur, the Applications Manager generates program group configuration files. The configuration files are split into program group files (.HGF) and program item (application) files (.HAF).

After these files are created, they are placed in the SITE.SRV\MAINCFG.BOX\APPCTL.SRC\DATABASE directory.

The Maintenance Manager copies the files to all the logon servers, copying them to the LOGON.SRV\APPCTL.BOX\DATABASE directory.

Finally, the files are used by the Program Group Control application on target computers. All these files are maintained in a Network Application Database (NAD). This database is simply a file with a .NAD extension which contains references to the .HGF and .HAF files. Program Group Control reads the .NAD file and uses the appropriate group and application files to build the desktop.

Using Microsoft Shared Applications

The shared versions of Microsoft Office and Works applications use the ACME Setup program to install. SMS provides some utilities to automate the installation, along with a proxy application for each of the shared applications for OLE compatibility. Whenever an OLE object is activated, the proxy application is called, and SMS connects to a distribution server to run the shared application.

Follow these steps when installing a Microsoft shared application:

- Create the source directory for the shared application using SETUP/A.
- Copy the SMSPROXY directory (and subdirectories) to the source directory for the application.
- For example, for Word for Windows 6.0c, copy \SMS\PRIMSITE.SRV\IMPORT.SRC\WWD60C\SMSPROXY and its subdirectories to source_dir\SMSPROXY.
- Create an SMS package for the application. This is easily done by loading one of the Package Definition Files (*.PDF) that have been included with SMS for Microsoft applications. It loads the correct program items and configuration for the applications using SMS Setup for initial configuration. SMS is loaded with .PDF files for easy software distribution in the SMS\Primsite.srv\Import.src directory, including ones for Word, Excel, DOS and Windows, MSOffice, and others.
- Distribute MSApps. All Microsoft applications use MSApps and will not run unless MSApps is also distributed. When creating the program group for the shared application, add the MSApps icons to the program group.

The Program Group Control Application

The Program Group Control (PGC) application runs at the client. It consists of two other programs: APPCTL and APPSTART.

APPCTL

APPCTL builds the appropriate network application program groups, based on information in the .NAD file. This occurs when Windows 3.x, Windows 95, or Windows NT is started.

If any SMS program groups do not belong on the desktop because of changes in the user groups, they are deleted.

Any program groups to which the user has access are added to the desktop. If a program group definition contains program items that are not valid on the client platform, the icons are not created for those applications.

APPCTL configures the local Registry with Program Group Control information about each application. In the Registry there is a key for Groups and Applications.

APPSTART

When the user starts a network application, the APPSTART application finds a server and creates a connection. APPSTART gets its configuration information from the .NAD file on the logon server. It then uses DDE to send that information to Program Group Control. This is the connection that PGC uses to run the application. If the application has a configuration script, it is run the first time the application is started.

If a connection already exists to a distribution server, APPSTART uses that distribution server for the shared application, instead of randomly selecting another one.

Every time the Program Group Control runs, it determines which logon server to connect to by reading the SMS.INI file. It also finds the directories where the .NAD file, .INI files, and configuration script files exist.

The following is a sample SMS.INI file:

```
[Servers]
 Domain=ABC
 Current Logon Server=LOGON
 Server1=LOGON
[Share]
 CurrentLogonServer=SMS_SHR
 Server1=SMS_SHR
[Program Group Control]
 directory=appct1.box\database
[AppCtrlIniFiles]
 directory=appct1.box\inifiles
[AppCtlScripts]
 directory=appct1.box\scripts
```

Troubleshooting Shared Applications

Program Group Control logs several different types of errors in the \Windows_Directory\ SMSLOG.TXT file. Common errors logged by Program Group Control include the following:

- Invalid permissions for application database—Indicates client doesn't have valid server permissions
- Invalid server reported by application database—server is offline or not registered in the SMS database
- Network error occurred while accessing the application database—Network error
- Out of memory while accessing application database—not enough RAM available
- Program Group Control cannot find server, share, or directory information in SMS.INI—Server, share or directory not available
- Server not found by Application Control program—Server could not be found

Methods for Troubleshooting Shared Applications

The following is a checklist of possible solutions for shared application problems:

If shared applications are not appearing on the desktop:

> Check that the share application instructions are correct. Run the SMS ViewNAD from the APPCTL.BOX\DATABASE directory on the logon server. It shows the program groups and applications available to clients. It also lists the user groups necessary to make the application available.

If this is not the problem, verify that the application package has been shared correctly with a Share Package on Server job, and that the correct program groups have been created in SMS Administrator. Also verify that the user is a member of the correct groups.

If shared applications are not running correctly:

Check that the server is accessible to the client. Also verify that the local Registry is configured correctly for the application.

Check that the share has been successfully created at the distribution server.

A Remove Package from Server job removes packages that have been placed on servers with Run Command on Workstation or Share Package on Server jobs. The site's master copy is also removed, but the original source directory and packages on SMS clients are not removed.

Removing a Package

SMS maintains a database of all the packages that are installed on distribution servers at each site called PackageLocations. The table contains the names of the distribution servers, the package IDs for packages installed, and the type of package, among other things. You can view the distribution servers where the packages are installed by using the query screen and choosing PackageLocations in the Architecture field. Based on this list, you can create a machine group with the list of specific distribution servers from which you want to remove the package.

To remove a package, choose the Remove Package From Server job type in the New Job dialog box and define the job's details.

These include the package, the sites, and distribution servers that are used by the job. For distribution servers, specify whether to remove the package from all distribution servers at a site or from a specified group of servers. If the Remove From All Distribution Servers option is selected, the master package at the site server is also deleted.

When the job is completed, all files are removed from distribution servers, and any shares created for Share packages are removed. The only copy not removed is the copy in the SITE.SRV\SENDER.BOX\TOSEND directory. It is kept there in case you want to add new distribution servers in the future and copy the package to them. It must be deleted manually.

From Here...

This chapter covers Application Sharing and Creating program groups. For more information read the following chapters:

- Chapter 10, "Software Inventory and Audit"
- Chapter 11, "Software Distribution"
- Chapter 17, "Troubleshooting SMS Components"

CHAPTER 22

Retrieving System Data

In this chapter, you will learn how to:

- **Define and Execute a Query**
- **Format Query Results**
- **See a Sample Deployment Query**
- **Use related tools**

SMS delivers ease of use in its query function. To create a query, there are user-friendly drop-down lists that show you the Boolean operators, such as ADD and OR. To run the query, you just click the query in your list of queries and drag it to the icon of the site on which you want to run the query. Even a network engineer can use SMS query function.

Groups of objects in the SMS database are called architectures. Before you can begin defining a query, you need to choose which architecture you are using. There are five architectures in the SMS database: Personal Computer, PackageLocation, UserGroups, JobDetails, and SMSEvents. In most cases you will be querying the Personal Computer architecture, but sometimes you may want to query the other architectures as well.

An architecture defines one or more groups of objects. The Personal Computer architecture consists of the following groups:

Disk
Environment
Identification
IRQ Table
Mouse
Netcard
Network
Operating System
Parallel Port
PC BIOS
PC Memory
Processor
Serial Port
Services
Video
Workstation Status

In addition, the Personal Computer architecture group Workstation Status could work to query the status of Packages, Collected Files, Audited Software, or custom PC BIOS data. ■

Understanding Queries

A query allows the user to search for information in the SMS database (see fig. 22.1). All database information pertaining to sites, jobs, and packages can be queried.

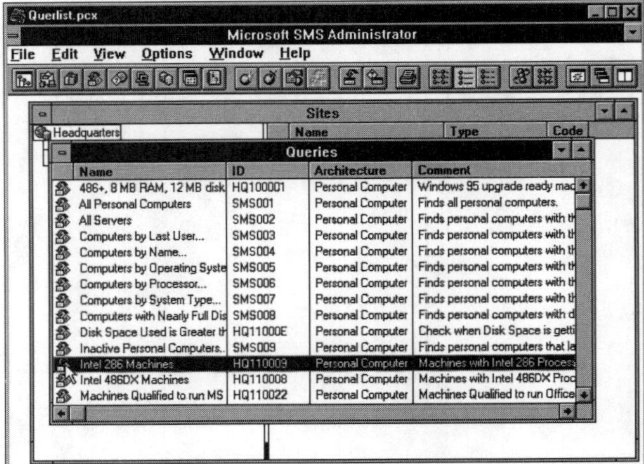

FIG. 22.1
Seeing a List of Queries.

A query contains an expression or set of expressions that defines the subset of items for which the database is searched.

In figure 22.2, you see the dialog box to create your query expression. A query expression consists of an attribute of the database, a Boolean operator, and a comparison value. An attribute is the item that you are looking up, for example, MachineName. Relational operators that can be used include "greater than," "less than," "equal to," and so on. The specific relational operators available depend on the type of attribute. The comparison value is a target value of the attribute for which the query searches.

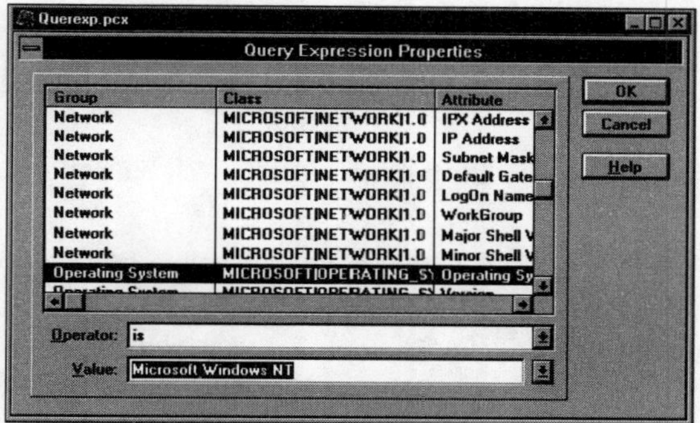

FIG. 22.2 Use the Query Expression dialog box to implement SMS queries.

For example, a query could be set up to search the database for all computers that have Windows for Workgroups as the operating system. In this example only one expression is required. The attribute would be OperationSystemName, the relational operator would be "is," and the comparison value would be "Window for Workgroups 3.11." The query result would list all computers in the database that are running Windows for Workgroups.

Expressions can be combined to form more complex queries. An example of a complex query is a query to search for all computers that are running Windows NT and that do not have a 3COM Etherlink II net card. In this example the expressions could be read as "OperatingSystemName is Windows NT" AND "Netcard is not Intel Ether Express 16." The expressions are combined using AND to result in a list of all computers in the database that are running Windows NT and do not have Intel Ether Express 16-bit cards.

Defining Query Properties

A query is defined using the Query Properties dialog box in SMS Administrator. To display the Query Properties dialog box, open the Queries window and, from the File menu, choose New.

These are the main elements of the Query Properties dialog box:

- Add AND—the logical AND operator.
- Add OR—the logical OR operator.
- Architecture—determines which set of objects the query will be performed against.
- Comment (Optional)—a place for comments about the query.

- Properties—shows a Query Expression dialog box where you can edit the selected query expression.
- Query Name—the name used to save the query so that it can be executed as needed.

A typical query expression might be CPU equals '486' AND OperatingSystemName equals 'DOS'. We will setup a sample query later in this chapter.

Defining a Query Expression

A query expression determines whether a record will be selected from the database.

To define a query expression, do the following:

1. Under Group, select a group. A group is an element of the selected architecture, such as "NetCard."
2. Under Attributes, select an attribute. An attribute is a subset of a group, such as "3 Com II Etherlink."
3. In the Operator box, select a relational operator. An example is "AND."
4. In the Value box, type a value, depending on the data type of the attribute. Values can be Boolean, numeric, or string. For example, if the attribute is %DiskFull, then the value should be numeric. Values are often available in a drop-down list.

For string values, case sensitivity is determined by the sort order ID as configured in SQL Server, usually Dictionary Order, Case-Insensitive for SQL Server 6.x.

Using Multiple Expressions

A query can consist of multiple expressions linked together with a logical operator. SMS gives the AND operator priority over the OR operator. Therefore, the order in which expressions are entered will matter.

For example, suppose you want to know how many computers on your network have an 80486 processor and are running either MS-DOS or Windows for Workgroups. "MS-DOS OR Windows for Workgroups AND 80486" produces a list which includes all MS-DOS computers, regardless of processor type, and 80486 computers with Windows for Workgroups.

The good news is that you can group expressions in the Query dialog box with parentheses in a similar way to using parentheses in Algebra: N*N-1 is different from N*(N-1).

Grouping expressions using parentheses helps give clarity in assembling a set of expressions. Grouping expressions makes a more complex query easier to follow and helps clarify the search order. In the example, "80486 AND (MS-DOS OR Windows for Workgroups)," parentheses would change the search order and yield the proper result.

Editing a Query

You can change individual elements of a query through editing. Query editing is done through the Query Properties dialog box, which offers several editing options.

From the Query Properties dialog box, you can do the following:

- Edit a single expression by selecting it and then choosing Properties.
- Change a logical operator (AND, OR) by selecting it and choosing Toggle. When you select only a logical operator, the Properties button changes to a Toggle button.
- Delete a single expression by selecting the expression and its logical operator, and choosing Delete. This ensures that there is always a valid multiple expression.
- Copy an expression by selecting a valid expression and choosing Copy. You can copy complex expressions as long as the syntax is correct.
- Paste an expression by selecting either an expression or a logical operator.

Viewing Query Result Formats

When a query executes, you can choose from a variety of formats to display your results. You can view each target machine in a form view, or see many machines at once in a table view. This format is created with the Define Query Result Formats dialog box.

The Query Results Screens provide a lot of flexibility (see fig. 22.3). For example in Table View, you can drag-and-drop columns or adjust the width of the columns.

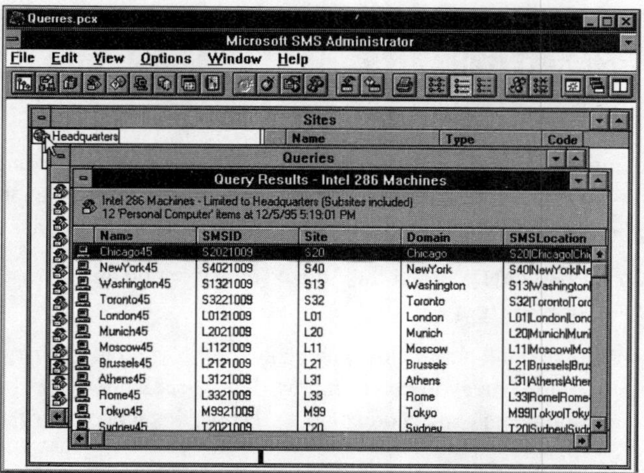

FIG. 22.3
Results from your query are displayed in the Query Results dialog box.

Like with many database view features, SMS offers a variety of formats to view your query results. For involved queries with many fields, you may want to use a form view; for a "big picture" view, a table view.

To define the Query Result format, take the following steps:

1. From the File menu, choose Define Query Result Formats.
2. From the list box, select Architecture. The available formats appear.
3. Choose New to define a new format.

   Each architecture generally has a default format that is used. The default format can be changed by selecting the format and choosing Set As Default Format.

NOTE Column widths are not saved in query results, unlike a program like Excel, which remembers your column widths. ■

Executing a Query in SMS

After a query has been defined and a query result format created, you can run the query against the database. This is called executing a query.

To execute a query, take the following steps:

1. From the File menu, choose Execute Query. The Execute Query dialog box appears.
2. In the Query box, highlight the name of the query to be executed.
3. In the Query Result Format box, choose the format in which you want the results to be displayed.
4. Select the site for the query.
5. Select whether subsites should be included in the query.
6. Choose OK.

Understanding the Ad Hoc Query

An Ad Hoc query is a query not saved in the SMS database. It is for one-time-only queries that are executed immediately. After an Ad Hoc query has executed, the query criteria used are lost. A good example of an Ad Hoc query is to check to see if a job has run.

To create an Ad Hoc query, select the Ad Hoc query option and proceed as if you were creating a permanent query.

It is also possible to build an Ad Hoc query after running an existing query. To do this, run the existing query. In the Query Results window, double-click the Query Status bar. The Query Properties dialog box appears. Modify Query Properties if necessary and execute.

Using Drag-and-Drop Shortcuts

Queries for the Personal Computer architecture can be done through drag-and-drop.

To execute a query using drag-and-drop, drag a query about the Personal Computer architecture from the Query window to the Sites window, and drop it on the site you want to query.

Viewing the Database with Other Tools

SQL Server databases can be accessed by a variety of tools. Commonly used tools include the SQL Server Administrative applications, Microsoft Access, Microsoft Excel, and Microsoft Visual Basic.

Microsoft SQL Server provides two applications for viewing the SMS database: SQL Administrator and SQL Object Manager. These tools are used for querying and administering the database.

Microsoft Access provides a user-friendly environment for interfacing with SQL Server databases. Access can be used to perform queries as an alternative to SQL Server. Viewing an SQL Server database using Access involves linking the SQL Server tables to an Access database.

Microsoft Excel, like Access, provides a user-friendly environment for interfacing with SQL Server databases.

Microsoft Visual Basic offers a programming interface alternative to working within the SQL Server environment. Visual Basic can be used to create a user interface to perform queries on the database.

CAUTION

Making changes to the SMS database with tools external to SMS can result in database corruption that will require restoration or reinstallation. Changes to the database made with products external to SMS are not supported by SMS. Always back up your database before accessing it with other tools.

To use products such as Microsoft Access and Visual Basic with SQL Server, an interface was developed called ODBC (Open Database Connectivity). When you install Access or Visual Basic, you have the option of installing the ODBC libraries. Install these libraries if you want Access or Visual Basic to interface with a SQL Server database.

SMSVIEW Utility

Using the SMSVIEW program, you can create views of the SMS database. Using ODBC, you can use these views in other applications (such as Microsoft Word) to view the computer inventory and generate reports. SMSVIEW creates views for all Personal Computer groups that exist in the site database at the time SMSVIEW is run. The SMSVIEW program is automatically installed on the primary site server.

Perform the following steps to start the SMSVIEW program:

1. From \SMS\SITE.SRV\X86.BIN, start SMSVIEW. The Create Views dialog box appears.
2. Make the following settings:
   - Server Name—specifies the name of the SQL Server that contains the site database.
   - Login Name—specifies a login ID on the SQL Server that has database owner (dbo) permissions on the site database.

- Password—specifies the password for the login name.
- Database—specifies the name of the site database.

3. Select the Drop Only check box if you want to drop any existing views on the site database.
4. Choose OK.

If this is the first time that SMSVIEW has been run against the site database, SMSVIEW creates views for all groups in the Personal Computer architecture.

If SMSVIEW has previously been run against the site database, SMSVIEW creates views for any new groups that have been added to the site database since the last time that SMSVIEW was run.

After SMSVIEW completes, it displays a message box telling you that it succeeded or failed in creating the view. SMSVIEW also logs an event to the Windows NT event log. If SMSVIEW fails, the event gives a brief explanation of the cause (for example, if one of the command line parameters was invalid).

Using a Sample Windows 95 Deployment Query

You may want to implement a query that determines which workstations could have Windows 95 successfully installed and which do not.

The query will look like the following:

```
Free Storage (MByte) is equal to '80' AND
Disk Index is 'C' AND Total Physical Memory (KByte) is greater than or
equal to '8000'
AND Processor Name is like '486'
OR Processor Name is like 'PENTIUM'
```

NOTE SMS queries are directed at the SMS database, not the target computers themselves. For the results to be meaningful, allow time after the job is run for the database to be updated before you query for successful deployment. The time intervals for hardware inventory frequency and software inventory frequency are set for each SMS site in the Site Properties window. By default, the inventories are performed each time the user logs on.

Modification of these two queries is probably unnecessary, unless you wish to add additional criteria to the definitions of a successful Windows 95 installation. For example, you might want to add the criteria Free Disk Space greater than 10MB. Any of the query options can be altered through the Queries Properties in the SMS Administrator.

The Successful Windows 95 query is as follows:

```
OperatingSystemName equals'MS Windows 95'
```

The Not Successful Windows 95 query is as follows:

```
Operating System Name equals 'MS_DOS' AND Version IS NOT '7.00'
```

If you want to deploy Windows 95 and Office for Windows 95 in one pass, you'll also need to run the queries provided to help you select target computers for both Windows 95 and Office for Windows 95.

Depending on your organization, you might want to use a modified version of this query. This particular query will include the following criteria: A PC running Windows for Workgroups, with 40MB of free disk space on drive C, using either a 486 or Pentium processor and with 8MB of physical memory.

A predefined query included in Systems Management Server examines the CPU, the operating system, the available hard disk space, the installed RAM, and so on. If you want to create a query called, for example, Windows 95-Capable PCs, follow these steps:

- In the Query Properties dialog box, enter the appropriate comment, such as PCs Capable of Installing Windows 95, and the Architecture (for example, Personal Computers.
- Select the Personal Computer items, in this case:

  (Processor Name is like '486' or Microsoft|Processor|1.0: Processor Name is like 'Pentium') AND Operating System Name equal to (MS-DOS OR Windows for Workgroups) AND Disk Space greater than 80 MB AND Memory Available greater than 8MB.
- Choose the Group command so the disk information will be moved to the top of the query.

From Here...

This chapter familiarizes you with Queries, configuring and using them. For more information read the following chapters:

- Chapter 12, "Queries and Reports"
- Appendix E, "Deploying Software"

CHAPTER 23

Investigating Remote PC Problems

In this chapter, you'll learn:

- **How to identify the clients that support Remote Control**
- **How to identify the requirements for remotely monitoring and controlling SMS clients**
- **Listing the SMS utilities that monitor and control SMS clients**
- **Remote Control Utilities**
- **Using each remote controlling function**
- **SMS utilities that monitor and control SMS clients**
- **Which clients support remote control**
- **Requirements for remotely monitoring and controlling SMS clients**
- **Procedures to use each remote controlling function**

Anyone who has closed help desk tickets vaguely knows the satisfaction of using a remote network management tool. The challenge is getting into the habit of using these tools rather than walking out to visit a client at every turn.

In the future we may not have a choice. Visiting a user every time he or she has a support issue is becoming a thing of the past. Already, more help desks are becoming centralized, with administrators covering many more sites at once.

With tools like SMS Help Desk Utilities, help desks will become increasingly more remote and more outsourced. A single-seat administration desk is too efficient for help desks of the past to compete. ■

An SMS Administrator can directly monitor and control inventoried clients in real time from the SMS Administrator computer. At the client's workstation, the user can control the level of the administrator's rights for remote control.

When the administrator has access, he or she has the ability to access remotely and support all clients in the inventory, parent, and child sites.

With the Diagnostic utilities, an administrator can see configurations of client computers. With the Help Desk utilities, the administrator's keyboard and mouse can control the client's computer.

The Diagnostic and Help Desk utilities for SMS version 1.2 support a client running MS-DOS and Windows, Windows for Workgroups, Windows 95, and Windows NT.

Diagnostic Utilities

Using the SMS Diagnostic utilities, the administrator can view the hardware and software configuration of an SMS client in real time.

The following are the steps to using Diagnostic utilities:

1. Open the PC Properties window for the client whose configuration you want to view.
2. Choose the Diagnostic group and the specific utility.

The Diagnostics icon under Personal Computer Properties has some information that can help troubleshoot a server or client PC. The following is a list of the different categories under the Diagnostics feature :

- CMOS Information—this shows the CMOS settings in the memory used at the computer's start time. At some companies, there is a problem with people getting into their CMOS setup screens and saving information. On some types of PCs, IBM PS/2s for instance, it is really easy for the user to get into the CMOS settings at startup and to change settings, especially if there is a problem on startup, because there is an option to get into the CMOS.

NOTE Remember that PCs before the AT model (1986) did not have a CMOS. If you have original IBM PCs (and compatibles) or PC/XT's, no CMOS information can be displayed. ■

- Device Drivers—shows all the device drivers loaded at the client. You can see at a glance if a client has the right driver installed, such as a CD-ROM driver, mouse driver, and so on.
- ROM Strings—provides information about ROM (Read-Only Memory) in the client computer. More detailed information can be obtained by selecting a specific ROM entry from choices in a list box.
- Interrupt Vectors—a convenient master table of IBM interrupts. Helps determine interrupt conflicts between hardware components.

- DOS Memory—not only shows you free conventional and upper memory, but also shows you all programs loaded in conventional and upper memory. DOS Memory does not map beyond upper memory. Check for memory available or for conflicts between TSRs.
- Ping Test—not to be missed! The Ping Test utility tests the TCP/IP network connection between the server and the client workstation, complete with a "thermometer" showing you the packets per second. The ping test sends 1,000 packets between the site server and the client as rapidly as possible. The packets per second will show in text and meter form.

For people who want to do more ambitious analysis of the network, there are other types of features among the SMS Diagnostics utilities, as follows:

- Windows Memory—Windows Memory shows the largest amount of contiguous linear memory as well as the amount of locked, unlocked, and free memory. Swap file usage is also displayed, which is great information for supporting 95 and NT clients. Locked memory is the amount of memory in use by a program or system process; free memory is memory not allocated; unlocked memory is memory that can be swapped to disk if necessary.
- Windows Modules—Windows Modules lists drivers and DLLs, among other things. When you have DLLs that are out of date with the rest of software files, there can be a conflict.
- Windows Tasks—this utility provides information about all open windows that appear in the Task List window of Program Manager.
- Window Classes—this utility lists the window classes currently in use. If two applications try to use a window class of the same name, there will be a conflict.
- Global Heap—the global heap is all the free memory available to Windows applications.
- GDI Heap—GDI heap is memory reserved by Windows for the graphical device interface (GDI). If client performance is slow but there is ample space in the global heap, it could be that GDI space is getting used up.

Help Desk Utilities for MS-DOS and Windows Clients

With remote control of your servers and key workstations, you will be prepared to troubleshoot and maintain any machine in your SMS site. With SMS 1.2 you can remotely control your NT servers as well as your workstations. Your Help Desk utilities like Remote Control and Remote Reboot are your tools to remote troubleshooting.

Remote Control

Remote Control allows you to take control of the client's screen with your keyboard and mouse. You have a view of the client screen through the Quick Windows Viewer. The Quick Windows Viewer has an easily identifiable, moving, yellow-and-black border that separates this window from other open windows on the desktop.

Once a Remote Control session has been established, the current settings of the client are passed to the site server—for example, Caps Lock. All keystrokes and mouse actions are passed to the client, and the client processes these actions as if they were controlled locally.

While the client is being controlled, the client's keyboard and mouse are still active. If both the administrator and the client use their keyboards simultaneously, the results could produce a garbled screen.

NOTE CTRL+ALT+DEL will not work from the Administrator computer. To restart a client remotely, use the Remote Reboot utility. ■

The Remote Reboot utility is useful if the administrator has changed a startup procedure, loaded a new configuration, and so on. Once the client has been rebooted, it becomes accessible after remote agent software is reloaded (USER.EXE or USERIPX.EXE).

Help Desk Utilities for Windows Clients

There are two utilities that are unique to clients running Windows 3.x, as follows:

1. File Transfer—using the File Transfer utility, the administrator can initiate a file transfer between the administrator computer and the client.
2. Remote Execute—this utility enables the administrator to start an application on a Windows-based client. For an MS-DOS-based application, an MS-DOS window opens to run the application.

Requirements for Using Remote Utilities

Remote Control, Remote Reboot, Remote Chat, and Remote Execute are the "remote utilities," found under the Help Desk icon in Personal Computer Properties in SMS Administrator. Not all machines can be remotely controlled, however. Before you set out to use these options, the following is a list of requirements for using the remote utilities:

1. Client must be in the site inventory—if the site server is configured for automatic inventory collection, a client will be inventoried when a user logs on to an SMS domain. If not, the SMSLS.BAT file can be started at the client to initiate the inventory collection process.
2. The right Remote Agent software must be started on the client.
3. The server and client must use a common protocol—either the same NetBIOS protocol (NetBEUI or TCP/IP) or IPX. SMS can use the Diagnostic and Help Desk utilities to remotely monitor and control clients that are connected to the network locally or on a wide area network (WAN). SMS supports all Windows NT protocols, such as NetBEUI, NWLink (IPX), and TCP/IP. SMS can also perform Help Desk functions for a client on a remote network that is connected using RAS. Support is not available across an SNA link.

Automatically Configuring Client for Remote Help

Remote Control software is configured to install automatically on Client machines upon initialization. With this default setting, SMS modifies the client AUTOEXEC.BAT to include the CLIENT.BAT file. CLIENT.BAT starts the remote agent software.

Loading Remote Agent Software To load the Remote Agent software onto a client, you must choose Site Properties, Clients in SMS Administrator. You can install the Remote Troubleshooting software to be installed on client computers. This software can be set to start automatically when the client initializes by selecting Automatically Start This Component. Remote Agent is not installed onto the client workstation by default.

Once this setting is chosen, SMS will alter the client's AUTOEXEC.BAT file to include the CLIENT.BAT file (located in the \MS\SMS\BIN directory). CLIENT.BAT starts the remote agent software. Clients might use different remote agents, depending on the protocol they are using.

Microsoft MS-DOS network clients use a protocol with NetBIOS interface (NetBEUI, NWLink, TCP/IP) and USERTSR.EXE remote agent software.

NetWare clients use Novell's IPX protocol and USERIPX.EXE remote agent software.

On Windows clients, the remote agent must be loaded by CLIENT.BAT before running Windows. After Windows is loaded, the user at the client has to run Remote Control (WUSER.EXE), which is located in the SMS Client group. This icon can be added to the Startup group, so that it is started automatically.

After the remote agent software and the client's network drivers are loaded, the administrator can remotely view and diagnose MS-DOS clients.

Manually Starting the Remote Agent at the Client If you clear the check box for Automatically Start This Component in the Site Properties, Client dialog, you must start the remote agent software manually at the client if you want the client to participate in remote control, as follows:

1. From a command prompt, change to the MS\SMS\BIN directory.
2. Type usertsr or useripx (depending on the client protocol).

NOTE For a list of command-line options, type usertsr -?. ■

Setting Remote Control Options at the Client For security reasons, remote control is disabled on all clients. Although the remote agents can be started, the user at the client must choose what level of remote help will be allowed.

To modify Remote Control options for Windows and Windows for Workgroups clients, use the Help Desk Options icon in the SMS Client group.

To configure remote control options for MS-DOS clients, you must edit the [SIGHT] section of the SMS.INI. The [SIGHT] section of the C:\SMS.INI file should be modified with Help Desk preferences. The C:\SMS.INI file is hidden by default. It can be made visible to the `dir` command by using the MS-DOS `attrib` command or Windows File Manager.

NOTE If the user does not set Help Desk options correctly, the administrator will connect to the client, but the Help Desk options will be unavailable. The options are unavailable because the administrator does not have permission to perform those Help Desk functions.

Table 20.1 defines the options available. Set variables to YES or NO as you prefer.

Table 20.1 Remote Control Options

Allow Takeover	Enables or disables the SMS Administrator computer from remotely controlling the client.
Allow Reboot	Determines whether a client can be restarted remotely by the SMS Administrator.
Allow File Transfer	Determines whether the SMS Administrator can initiate a file transfer between itself and the client.
Allow Remote Execute	Determines whether the SMS Administrator can start applications (processes) at the client.
Visible Signal	When viewed, determines whether the client displays a Being Accessed icon when being remotely controlled.
Audible Signal	When viewed, determines whether an audible signal sounds at the client to notify the user that it is being remotely controlled.

Configuring Multiple Protocols To use the Diagnostic and Help Desk utilities, the same NetBIOS or IPX protocol must be on the SMS Administrator computer and the client. The SMS Administrator can control different clients using different protocols. To support these clients, the SMS Administrator must be running each of the different protocols.

When the SMS Administrator has to connect to a client, it searches through the first five loaded protocols (LANA 0-4) to find a common protocol for connecting to the client. To add to or edit these five protocols, the administrator runs REGEDT32.exe. The values are kept under SMS\Components\SightNT\Lana. There are five default values; additional default values can be added.

The LANA number for any of the remote control protocols can be changed. For example, a RAS connection might be at LANA 8—to find clients over this LANA, the administrator would have to modify an existing protocol entry or add a new one for remote control. A time-out value can also be set for each protocol, which might be useful in the event of a slow RAS link.

Client Uses First Loaded Protocol The SMS client does not search for a protocol, but uses the first protocol that was loaded. If the client has more than one protocol loaded, you can designate which protocol it will use for remote control. This is necessary, for example, if the client has NetBEUI and TCP/IP (NetBEUI loaded first), and the SMS Administrator computer has TCP/IP. In this case, by default SMS Administrator will use TCP/IP, but the client uses NetBEUI, which will prevent communications from being established. The client should designate TCP/IP as the remote control protocol. The LANA number for TCP/IP can be specified when starting the remote agent software. For example: usertsr/L1.

This command can be done manually or it can be added to the CLIENT.BAT file.

NOTE The PROTOCOL.INI file lists the designated LANA numbers.

Clients in a WAN environment are supported over TCP/IP or IPX. Special considerations are required in a routed IP environment.

Using SMS in a TCP/IP Environment

SMS Help Desk utilities communicate over NetBIOS. The utilities register NetBIOS names to communicate between the SMS Administrator computer and the remote client.

Help Desk utilities initialize communication with each other by doing a broadcast to find each other. Using broadcasts is not a problem for the NetBEUI or IPX protocols, but it does affect TCP/IP when the communication occurs between two different segments or networks.

Most routers connecting multiple networks are not configured to forward broadcasts. You can forward NetBIOS broadcasts if you enable port UDP 137 on most modern routers; however, you probably wouldn't want to—enabling broadcasts opens the floodgates for lots of traffic across the WAN. Therefore, you want to employ the Windows NT WINS service for naming services, or use the manual LMHOSTS file for a static naming table.

Understanding the LMHOSTS File

Windows NT 3.x and LAN Manager both contain a file called LMHOSTS, a text file that resolves remote NetBIOS names. For using remote control and file transfer, there are some special commands that should go into LMHOSTS.

Certain entries must be added to LMHOSTS on both the SMS Administrator computer and the SMS client. Each entry must be exactly 16 characters long, and the last character (C,D,E, or F) must be the sixteenth character.

LMHOSTS entries for the SMS Administrator computer are as follows:

```
<IP address><tab>"<client name> C" (Letter C enables remote control)

<IP address><tab>"<client name> E" (Letter E enables file transfer)
```

Example (at the SMS Administrator computer):

"SMS_Client C"

"SMS_Client E"

LMHOSTS entries at the client are as follows:

```
<IP address><tab>"<SMS Administrator name> D" (Letter D enables remote control)

<IP address><tab">"<SMS Administrator name> F" (Letter F enables file transfer)
```

Example (at the SMS client):

```
128.20.60.31 ADMIN_PC D

128.20.60.32 ADMIN_PC F
```

Configuring the LMHOSTS File

The LMHOSTS file is simple to configure. It is a merely a text file located in the winnt_system_root\SYSTEM32\DRIVERS\ETC directory. If your LMHOSTS file has never been configured, it will be LMHOSTS.SAM. This is a combination sample file and a "read.me type" file with good information about the syntax for different LMHOSTS commands.

If LMHOSTS is already in use, take great care not to replace the LMHOSTS file already in use, but rather to add the entry you need to the end of the list of LMHOSTS entries with a text editor. Steps to configuring the LMHOSTS file are:

1. Locate the LMHOSTS file in the winnt_system_root\SYSTEM32\DRIVERS\ETC directory on your SMS Administrator computer.
2. Add a remote IP address and client name to the file. For example:

   128.20.60.32 ADMIN_PC D
3. Save the file.

NOTE On Windows NT 3.5, the LMHOSTS file is named LMHOSTS.SAM. Edit and save the file as LMHOSTS. ■

Specific RAS Requirements

Many installations employ RAS in their overall SMS plan. RAS allows ISDN and asynchronous phone dial-up, as well as X.25 switching protocol.

The following are the steps required for file transfer and remote control over RAS:

1. Install the RAS component on the SMS Administrator computer.
2. A RAS server must also be located in the same site as the remote client.

3. The SMS Administrator computer, the RAS server, and the remote client must be running the same NetBIOS transport.
4. To use the Help Desk utilities, it is suggested you use a RAS communications link of 9600 baud or higher. At lower baud rates, the communications link might time out during Help Desk operations.

Automatic RAS Connections to Remote Sites

SMS uses GATEWAY.DLL to make an automatic RAS connection to a site and access the client. GATEWAY.DLL initiates the RAS connection to the remote LAN and authenticates the user by communicating with a RAS server that exists on the same LAN as the client. When a Remote Control utility terminates, the GATEWAY.DLL closes the session and frees up the port and modem. The GATEWAY.DLL disconnects the target LAN when Remote Control is terminated.

NOTE Since SMS Remote Control utilities support only NetBIOS transports across RAS, NetWare clients are not supported. In addition, GATEWAY.DLL does not support the SNA sender and will return the message "Can't connect via RAS" to the SIGHTNT.DLL for SNA links. ■

Troubleshooting Remote Control Utilities

The following list shows some Remote Control utility problems and their possible solutions:

Client is not in the inventory

- Inventory the client. The client must be in the SMS database to be accessed remotely.

Client is in the inventory, but can't establish connection

- Check for common protocols. The client and SMS Administrator computer must use same protocol.
- Check to see whether the client has changed its NetBIOS name. There might be two entries in the inventory for one physical client.
- If multiple protocols are used, make sure that both have specified which LANA number to use for remote communications.
- If the client is on a remote TCP/IP network, make sure you can resolve the client's NetBIOS name to its IP address using LMHOSTS file.
- Use MEM/C to verify that the client has its Remote Control agents loaded.
- Verify that the client has Remote Control allowed in the [SIGHT] section of SMS.INI.

Working with Microsoft Network Client 3.0 for MS-DOS

The Microsoft Network Client 3.0 software is provided with Windows NT 3.5x Server. Remote Troubleshooting does not work correctly in the following circumstances:

- When using NWLink as the primary Protocol—with this configuration, Remote Troubleshooting will not work.
- When using TCP/IP and WINS—you will have to add entries manually to an LMHOSTS file at the administrator's computer before doing Remote Control to a client on another network. This is because this network client does not register its NetBIOS names with WINS. Clients on the local subnet are not affected, but you must use LMHOSTS if any remote subnets are involved.

Working with NetWare Clients

The following files are required for remote troubleshooting of NetWare clients using IPX/SPX:

NWCALLS.DLL

NWIPXSPX.DLL

NWNETAPI.DLL

These files are normally provided with your NetWare client software. They are also available from Novell or public forums such as CompuServe.

Without these files, NetWare clients running Windows 3.x will display an error message when launching remote control.

If you see this message, you must ensure that the listed files are installed on the client. NWCALLS.DLL and NWIPXSPX.DLL are normally installed on a NetWare client running Windows 3.x. Most likely, the NWNETAPI.DLL will be missing from the client.

You can use SMS to install the NWNETAPI.DLL file on NetWare clients. Place the file in the SITE.SRV\MAINCFG.BOX\CLIENT.SRCC/X86.BIN directory on the site server. The Maintenance Manager will replicate the file to all NetWare logon servers. The file will be installed to the MS\SMS\BIN directory of all NetWare clients when users run the Client Setup program.

From Here...

This chapter familiarizes you with Remote Utilities, configuring, and using them. For more information read the following chapters:

- Chapter 13, "Using Help Desk and Diagnostics on a Remote PC"
- Chapter 24, "Investigating Network Problems"

CHAPTER 24

Investigating Network Problems

- Start Network Monitor
- Install Network Monitor Agent
- Install Network Monitor Agent as a Service

The network monitor utility provides a full featured software sniffer. The program is launched from a personal computer properties screen. With this as the starting point for the network monitor program it will be configured, via the filter capability, for monitoring all traffic to and from that workstation. After the network monitor program is running it can be manipulated as a stand alone software sniffer. The network monitor utility is a powerful troubleshooting tool in the hands of an experienced user.

One caveat is that for the network monitor to work you need a network adapter card that supports a promiscuous mode.

As you know from other chapters in this book, the Network Monitor utility provides a full-featured software sniffer. A sniffer is a term for a monitoring program.

Network Monitor is launched from a personal computer properties screen. The Network Monitor program can be configured, via the filter capability, for monitoring all traffic to and from that workstation. The Network Monitor utility is a powerful troubleshooting tool.

NOTE You need a network adapter card that supports promiscuous mode to use Network Monitor. ■

You can start and stop the agent as an executable application, or you can run the Network Monitor agent as a service. ■

Launching the Network Monitor

SMS has a Network Monitor user interface, which enables network administrators to detect and troubleshoot problems on LANs or WANs. Network Monitor can work with your LAN protocols or with Microsoft Remote Access Service (RAS).

Using the Network Monitor user interface and Network Monitor Agent, you can do the following:

- Capture frames directly from the network.
- Capture frames from a remote computer and then display the captured statistics on the local computer at intervals that you specify.
- Display and filter captured frames.
- Edit and transmit captured frames onto the network to test network resources or to reproduce network problems.

The Network Monitor Agent significantly enhances the scope of Network Monitor by enabling it to capture data across more than one network. In addition, when you install the Network Monitor Agent, counters are added to the Windows NT Performance Monitor. You can use the counters for limited monitoring of network performance. Network Monitor Agents can be password protected to prevent unauthorized access.

The Systems Management Server Network Monitor allows you to analyze network traffic and pinpoint problems or potential bottlenecks. With Network Monitor you can:

- Capture frames (also called packets) directly from the network.
- Display and filter captured frames.
- Edit and transmit captured frames onto the network to test network resources or reproduce network problems.
- Capture frames on a remote computer and display the capture statistics on the local computer at intervals you specify.

Network Monitor is entirely software-based. The only special hardware you need is a network card (with a supporting NDIS driver) that supports "promiscuous" mode. (Promiscuous mode enables the network adapter card to be directed by a device to pass on all frames that pass over the network to the operating system.) When you want to analyze traffic on a network segment, a "capture agent" (a program running on a computer attached to that segment) puts its network card into the promiscuous mode. The agent makes a duplicate of frames that pass through that computer, stores the frames in a buffer, and sends the session summary statistics to the Network Monitor console (either local or remote). The summary statistics include: graphs of total network utilization and statistics of frames, bytes, broadcasts, and multicasts per second, and statistics for individual computers.

Network Monitor automatically builds an address database of "friendly names" to help you identify individual stations. You can filter captures based on computer address (or address pairs), protocols, or data patterns within the frame. From the Network Monitor console, you can display each of the individual frames captured, including details of the protocols used to send it, and hexadecimal and ASCII representations of the captured data. The frames can also be filtered for display based on address, protocol, or contents.

Network Monitor capture triggers allow you to execute specific programs, or batch files, when the capture agent receives a frame containing a pattern you specify. You can also edit and retransmit frames you have already captured to reproduce network problems or to generate network activity to simulate specific test conditions. Systems Management Server includes Network Monitor console and agents for Windows NT Workstation, Windows NT Server, and Windows for Workgroups.

The following steps demonstrate how to capture and save network frames using Network Monitor. You can capture data from a remote computer by running the Network Monitor Remote Agent.

Setting a trigger to stop capture when the buffer is full:

1. From the Systems Management Server Administrator tool, open the Sites window.
2. Open the Personal Computer Properties window for your site server.
3. Under Properties, select Network Monitor.
4. Select Start Network Monitor as shown here.
5. From the Capture menu, select Trigger and choose the following options:

In this box	Select
Trigger On	Buffer Space
Buffer Space	100%
Trigger Action	Stop Capture

6. Choose OK to return to the Network Monitor Capture Window.

Capturing Network Broadcast Frames

1. From the Capture menu, select Start. Network Monitor allocates buffer space for network data and begins capturing frames.
2. Place the cursor anywhere in the 1—>2 column, and click the right mouse button.
3. Select Sort Column. Network Monitor sorts the contents of the Session Statistics window pane by the frames sent.
4. When the Trigger dialog box appears, stating the specified amount of buffer that has been filled, choose OK.

5. Place the cursor anywhere in the 1<—2 column, click the right mouse button, and select Sort Column. Network Monitor again sorts the frames that were sent. The first address in this list shows the source of the most frames.

Highlighting the captured data

In the following steps, you will change the color of all NetBIOS protocol frames. This is useful in selecting frames of a particular protocol for viewing.

1. From the Display menu, select Colors.
2. Under Name, select NetBIOS.
3. Under Colors, set Foreground to Green.
4. Choose OK.

Filtering the captured data

In the following steps, you will create a display filter to view only the frames that represent the conversation between your two servers.

1. From the Display menu, select Filter.
2. Select the ANY<—>ANY line.
3. Under Edit, select the Expression button.
4. Under *ANY <—> *ANY, select the Address tab.
5. Under Station 1, select the primary site server name.
6. Under Station 2, select the secondary site server name.
7. Choose the OK button to return to the Display Filter dialog box.
8. Choose the OK button. The Network Monitor Capture Summary window appears, displaying all frames in the conversation between your primary and secondary site servers.

Using the Network Monitor on Remote Subnets

Network Monitor has the ability to capture traffic on another subnet by connecting to a LAN running the Remote Agent software on that subnet. The Network Monitor Agent software is shipped with Windows NT Workstation and Windows NT Server. In Network Monitor, choosing Networks from the Capture menu displays Remote as one of the options. You can provide the remote agent's computer name to connect with that machine.

For Network Monitor to connect to a remote agent across a router, the remote agent's computer name needs to be resolved. If the name cannot be resolved, you'll get the following error message:

```
Failure connecting to <computer name of Agent>
```

The remote agent registers a NetBIOS name which is 16 characters long or less. It consists of the computer name followed by 0xBE (extended characters).

So a machine named REMOTEAGENT would be REMOTEAGENT\0xBE\0xBE\0xBE...

Connecting to the Agent across a Router

Here are details on connecting across a Router

1. Ensure that the Manager and the remote agent systems have a routable protocol such as TCP/IP or NWLINK installed.
2. Start the Network Monitor Agent service from the Control Panel Services applet by selecting Network Monitor Agent in the list of services, and choosing Start. You can also use the Windows NT command line, NET START NMAGENT.
3. If TCP/IP is the protocol that is used, then there are two ways to resolve a NetBIOS name to an IP address: WINS Server, or LMHOSTS. If both the management station and the remote agent are using WINS (Microsoft Windows Internet Naming Service), the name will be resolved via WINS, and WINS locates the agent machine. If not, then the LMHOSTS file on the management station must contain a special entry for the remote agent.

   Following are some examples from an IMHOSTS file:

   "REMOTEAGENT\0xBE\0xBE\0xBE\0xBE\0xBE"#PRE

   #PRE entry is common to preload the IMHOSTS table entry into the NT Server's cache.

   The computer name should be all caps.
4. The NBTSTAT command can be used to flush and reload the LMHOSTS cache after modifying the LMHOSTS file. To reload the cache, type "nbtstat - R". To view the cache, type "nbtstat -c."
5. Once the cache has been updated, it should be possible to connect to the remote agent.

With NWLINK protocol, routing should succeed because most routers are configured to forward broadcasts on packet type 20.

Installing the Network Monitor Agent

Here are the steps to install the Network Monitor Agent

1. In the Windows NT Program Manager, open the Main program group.
2. Choose the Control Panel, Network icon.
3. Choose Add Software.
4. The Add Network Software dialog box appears.
5. In the Network Software box, select Network Monitor Agent.
6. Choose Continue and OK.

A message reminds you to restart your computer for the changes to take effect.

Starting the Network Monitor Agent

From the File, Run or Start, Run prompt, type "nmagent."

The Network Monitor Agent is removed from the system each time you log off, and must be restarted every time you log on.

You can run Network Monitor agent continuously if you run it as a service.

Running the Network Monitor Agent as a Service

As mentioned before, you can run the Network Monitor agent as a service. Here are the steps :

1. In Windows NT Registry Editor (Regedt32), select the following Registry key:

   Hkey_Local_Machine\Software\Microsoft\Windows\ CurrentVersion\RunServicesOnce
2. Choose Edit, New, and then click String Value.
3. Type a label for the value name, such as "nmagent," and then press ENTER.
4. Choose Edit menu, Modify.
5. In the Value Data box, type:

   NMAGENT.EXE
6. Click OK.

The Network Monitor agent will continue to run after a user logs off if it is started as a service. You can, however, type a command to stop running the agent, whether the agent was started as a service or run from the command prompt.

To Stop the Network Monitor agent, do the following:

1. Choose File, Run or Start, Run.
2. Type "nmagent - close."

From Here...

- For more information, see Appendix D, "A Detailed Look at the Data Flow."
- For more information about monitoring, see Chapter 17, "Troubleshooting SMS Components."

CHAPTER 25

SMS Management Tasks

In this chapter, you will learn:

- SMSVIEW
- SMS Database Manager
- Monitoring Disk Usage
- SMS Service Manager
- NT Event Viewer
- SQL Error Logs

This chapter is a hodge-podge of topics that didn't quite fit into the other chapters. ■

Using the SMSVIEW Utility

SMSVIEW is a unique utility that lets you see SMS data in other database front-end tools, such as Excel, Access, Word, or other ODBC-compliant applications. Using ODBC, you can use these applications to view the computer inventory and generate reports.

Microsoft ODBC database connectivity technology is an open and vendor-neutral application programming interface (API) for database connectivity that provides access to a variety of personal computers, minicomputers, and mainframe systems, including the Microsoft Windows operating system and the Apple Macintosh personal computer.

ODBC is Microsoft's strategic interface for accessing data stored in a wide variety of formats—in personal databases such as ACCESS, dBASE and Paradox, SQL database servers such as MS SQL Server, ORACLE, and even data stored in EXCEL spreadsheets.

SMSVIEW makes the SMS data available to ODBC. By using ODBC users can view, query, and report upon SMS data from their favorite tool—Excel, Access, and so on.

SMSVIEW creates views for all Personal Computer groups that exist in the site database at the time SMSVIEW is run. The SMSVIEW program is automatically installed on the primary site server.

To start the SMSVIEW program, perform the following steps:

- From \SMS\SITE.SRV\X86.BIN, start SMSVIEW. The Create Views dialog box will come up.
- Fill in the following settings:

  Database—specifies the name of the site database.

  Login Name—specifies a login ID on the SQL Server that has database owner (dbo) permissions on the site database.

  Password—specifies the password for the login name.

  Server Name—specifies the name of the SQL Server that contains the site database.
- Check the Drop Only check box if you want to use any existing views on the site database.
- Choose OK.

If this is the first time you've run SMSVIEW on the site, it creates views for all groups in the Personal Computer database.

When SMSVIEW has finished, it displays a dialog box telling you that it's completed the view. SMSVIEW also logs an event to the Windows NT event log. If SMSVIEW fails, the event gives a brief explanation of the cause (for example, if one of the command line parameters was invalid).

Because SMS data is kept in a SQL database, you can include the data in reports you generate using Microsoft Access or Microsoft Excel. These reports can be used in scheduling the tasks for different phases of the deployment. Microsoft (according to Microsoft Technet) apparently used this technique when it deployed Windows 95 to its European offices. This section tells you how to do the same in your organization.

By using the SMSVIEW utility included with SMS, you can modify the SMS database on a given SMS primary server so that Microsoft Access can retrieve the information. The steps to modify the database need to be done only once for each SMS primary server. The "hooks" into the database are then built via the ODBC drivers available from Microsoft.

SMSVIEW is installed automatically on the computer used as an SMS primary site server. To start the utility, enter SMSVIEW at the command line. The Create Views window appears, as shown in the following screen.

Enter the server name and database name in the boxes provided. Use "sa" as the login name, and supply the password you have assigned to that account. Leave the Drop Only check box clear, unless you want to drop existing views on the site database.

The first time you run SMSVIEW, it creates views for all groups in the Personal Computer database. If you add new groups later, run SMSVIEW again to create views for those groups. For more information on SMSVIEW, see the *Systems Management Server Administrator's Guide*, Appendix I, "Using Computer Inventory Information in Other Applications."

To build the "hooks" into the SMS database, run the ODBC Administrator. This will build the links used by Microsoft Access to gain entry to the SMS database tables.

With the links set up, you are ready to build queries in Microsoft Access 2.0 to extract the data. These will be specific to your organization. The discussion that follows describes the process used in Microsoft's ITG Europe.

To build queries in Microsoft Access for the ITG Europe deployment, first a list of "eligible" users at each site was created from a master database. This gave each SMS site administrator a starting point from which to select the users who would receive the upgrade.

The extraction of the data from the data source SMSEUROPE had to be done in three stages. Because of the complex nature of the queries, ITG Europe found it easier to build two "static" tables. These two tables were built within Microsoft Access and contained all user information that met the client selection criteria they had established.

Once these two tables were built, a third stage was used to extract the data that was wholly compliant with the selection criteria. The resulting lists of user names, machine names, and SMS Uid's were then exported to Microsoft Excel spreadsheets for presentation purposes.

The completed Microsoft Excel spreadsheets were then distributed to the SMS primary site administrators for use in the rollouts to their respective sites. The list proved useful in giving the site administrators a starting point from which to build their machine groups. The lists were sent out once a week to allow the site administrators time to prepare for the next week's likely candidates.

Understanding the SMS Database Manager

The SMS Database Manager is used to perform general housekeeping of your SMS database. This tool, DBCLEAN.EXE, is found in \SMS\SITE.SRV\X86.BIN. Unnecessary data, such as old events or completed jobs, are removed by this application.

Using the SMS Database Manager

Microsoft's documentation (MS SMS Server Capacity Planning and Performance Guidelines) suggests the use of DBClean to do cleanups both weekly and monthly.

Weekly :

> Check for duplicate machines in the Systems Management Server database by using the DBCLEAN utility. Delete older duplicates, and fix any problems that may be causing duplicate machines to appear.

Monthly :

> Use the DBCLEAN utility to check for and delete Unused Records and Abandoned Collected Files.

The following is a detailed list of items that can be removed from the database:

- Completed Jobs—this will delete all jobs that have been inactive for a specified amount of time, or all jobs before a certain date. The administrator can use the Database Manager to delete these completed jobs or can select jobs in the Jobs window of SMS Administrator and delete them.
- Machines—Database Manager can remove computers that have been inactive for a specified amount of time. This is useful for removing computers that have moved to another site or have gone offline. Inventory history and duplicate computers can also be removed by the Database Manager. History data are kept every time a computer reports inventory and builds up over time. The Database Manager cleans up history data before a specified date so that less database space will be used.
- Old History Data—history data are kept every time a computer reports inventory, and they build up over time. After a while you will not need to keep the old history files. The Database Manager cleans up history data before a specified date so that less database space is used.
- Abandoned Collected Files—Database Manager will find and delete any collected files that are not associated with the inventory of a computer in the SMS database. Abandoned collected files appear when a computer is deleted from the database.
- Old Events—Events before a specified date can be removed by Database Manager or in SMS Administrator.

- Group Classes—Database Manager can delete unused groups and specific group classes. This must be done when using the Software Auditing feature. Before running a software audit a second time, the Software Auditing class must be deleted by Database Manager. Otherwise SMS will not update the audited software for the computer.
- Set Display Preferences—Database Manager lets you control the way groups are displayed in the database. Each group can be configured to display automatically as a column or as a table of information.

Watching Disk Usage

An easy way to see the disk usage of the SMS Database is by going into SQL Administrator (you can use the SQL Enterprise Manager or the SQL Server Administrator utilities to do this) and clicking the Database Management button. (You can see the amount of disk space available for each database in comparison to its device. Each database must be contained within its device.)

Under Manage, Backup/Restore you can set backup for SMS database. Choose the dump device to start backing up. It is a good idea to backup the master device as well.

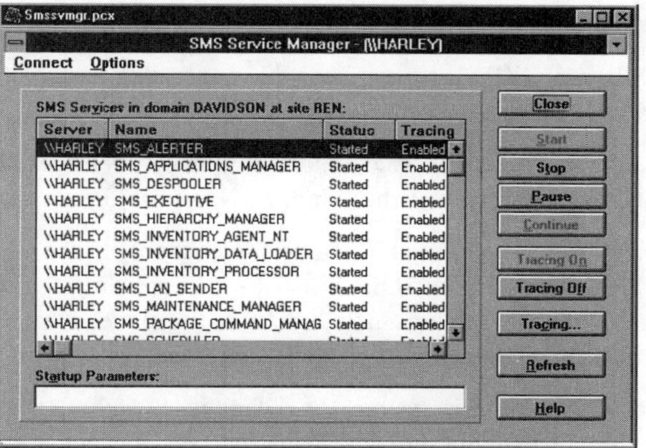

FIG. 22.1
SMS Service Manager.

You will use Service Manager for many things, including the following:

- **Trace files**—every SMS Administrator should become familiar with the trace file. Each SMS service can be monitored via a trace file. Tracing can take some system overhead, but it is a great tool.

  First, set the trace file size, and then trace information is logged until that size is reached. A backup of the file is created, and logging begins again until the maximum size is reached. This provides a history equivalent to two times the maximum size set.

  Use Server Manager to control the stopping and starting of trace files. Service Manager provides the capability needed to control the SMS system services and the trace files.

- **Stop and Start Services**—Service Manager can start and stop each service individually. SMS Service Manager also controls the nine "sub-services" or threads started by the SMS Executive Service.
- **Remote Systems**—Service Manager can control any remote SMS systems.

Using the NT Event Viewer

All messages are logged to the NT Event Viewer as well as the SMS database. In fact, the message format is identical for both SMS and NT Event Viewer. Since messages can be viewed through the administrator, there is little reason to use the NT Event Viewer to look at SMS messages.

Understanding SQL Error Logs

SQL Server error messages are written to the SMS database. Error logs are accessible through SQL Server Event Viewer. SQL is 50% of SMS, and troubleshooting SQL will be an extremely important skill in your skill set.

If you encounter a problem while running Microsoft SQL Server, the first thing you should do is check the log for entries that might help identify the cause.

How you start Microsoft SQL Server and on which operating system it is running determine where SQL Server events are logged.

After you start SQL Server as a service under the Windows NT operating system, events are logged to the SQL Server error log, the Windows NT event log, or both.

Both the error and event logs record the same information, but the SQL Server error log contains only SQL Server messages and the Windows NT event log contains messages for all activities on the computer. Both logs include informational messages (such as startup data) and both automatically record the date and time of all events.

With the Windows NT operating system, the default is to use both the Windows NT event logging service and the SQL Server error log. However, you can set certain installation options to log SQL Server events to only one log.

Other Management Tasks

There are several other tasks that are critical to the operation of the System Management Server. In this section we will discuss those tasks.

Monitoring the SMS Unique ID

The machine's UID is assigned the first time SMSLS.BAT is run from the SMS_SHR. Every machine in the SMS Hierarchy has an SMS.INI (hidden) file in the root of its primary partition.

The SMS.INI file contains the SMS Unique ID entry, the number that uniquely identifies each machine in the SMS Hierarchy.

These UIDs are permanent, and the values are not reused. The first three characters represent the site code of the domain from which the machine was initially inventoried. The remaining five positions represent an incrementally assigned number tracked by the site server. In addition to the SMS UID, SMS also uses the machine name and net card ID to help uniquely identify a machine. The SMS UID takes precedence. These three values are used by SMS to track the machines in the SMS Hierarchy.

Dealing with Duplicate SMS UIDs

If you delete SMS.INI from your root directory, the machine name and net card ID remain the same, and the next time you start SMSLS.BAT, a new SMS.INI file will be created. Then a new SMS UID will be created. This will cause a new inventory record to be written in the SMS database.

A warning message will appear in the Events windows saying that a new machine has been added to the inventory, but the machine name and/or net card ID values match those in another record. It is up to the administrator to resolve the conflict.

There may be no conflict if the machine's original SMS.INI file can be recopied, if it was ever collected at the site server or backed up. Then the new inventory record can be deleted from the Sites window.

The other alternative is just to delete the original inventory record from the Sites window. However, any Run Command on Workstation jobs that are pending for the machine will not run.

Moving Clients to Different Domains

Clients can be moved from a domain in one site to a different domain in the same or a different site. This is accomplished by running SMSLS.BAT, either through logon scripts or manually, from a logon server in the new domain. After three consecutive times (default), the client's SMS.INI file will be updated to reflect the new domain information, and the client's inventory information will now appear under its new domain. The original SMS ID, stored in the SMS.INI file on the client, will be retained, however.

The [LogonHistory] section of the client's SMS.INI file tracks the number of consecutive times the SMSLS.BAT file has been run at the particular domains. If a different domain is used before the False Logon Limit (default=3) is reached, then the counter is set back to 1. The False Logon Limit setting is stored in the site server's registry and is passed to the DOMAIN.INI file on all the site's logon servers under the [SMS] section where the entry reads as follows:

```
InvAgtFalseLogonCount = x.
```

Whenever a client runs SMSLS.BAT in a new domain, or the Logon History counter is less than **x-1**, where **x** is the False Logon Limit, then a hardware/software scan will not occur. This fact is displayed on the client's screen when SMSLS.BAT is run, but it usually flies by too fast to read. This means that if the user keeps logging on to different domains without hitting the limit, a scan will not occur, and the client's inventory information will not be updated. The information in the SMS.INI file can, of course, be edited to change the counter value. Set the False Logon Limit to a large value if there will be large numbers of clients logging on to other domains for limited periods of time—for example, laptops being used at another site during a business trip.

Please note that there is no utility to do bulk movement of inventory information from one domain to another, nor to move a domain from one site to another.

Managing Package Definition

Here are some hints about package distribution in SMS.

When defining the Inventory Package, make sure that the package name is descriptive, because this is what will show up in the client's Software Inventory window. For example, use Excel 5.0a, not XL. When defining the search criteria, wildcards are not supported. Looking for "*.EXE" will not produce results.

Do not forget to check Inventory This Package; this is disabled by default. Unless this box is checked, this package's information will not get compiled into the master inventory list (PACKAGE.RUL) at the site server. Use Collect This File sparingly. Each file targeted for collection that is found on a client will get moved to the logon and site servers each time a software scan is performed on the client. These collected files are also stored on the site server and are passed up the SMS hierarchy to the site server's parent, and so on. These files take up space! So do not collect EXCEL.EXE and PPTVIEW.DLL. Collect files such as SMS.INI, AUTOEXEC.BAT, or WIN.INI.

Inventory Packages defined at a parent site are automatically passed down the SMS hierarchy to its children, grandchildren, and so on, the effect being cumulative. For example, if there are three sites in a parent-child-grandchild relationship, and an Inventory Package for Excel 5.0a has been created at each site; then after the parents have sent their definitions to their children, the parent would have one Excel 5.0a Inventory Package, the child site two, and the grandchild three (all with different SMS IDs). Note the three occurrences of Excel 5.0c. The Excel 5.0c package will show up three times in the inventory information for a client in this site that was found to have Excel 5.0c.

Keep in mind that it takes time for the inventory instruction file (PKG_16.CFG) to get out onto the logon servers for the agents to read them. So when new Inventory Packages are created at the site, note the date and time and then use File Manager to check the logon servers and note when the instruction file is modified; this date/time stamp will be later than the date and time when the new package(s) were created. If this is not the case, then the new package information has not yet been received at the logon servers, and will not be scanned for at this time. ●

Appendixes

APPENDIX A

SMS Components and Terminology

The following is an alphabetical glossary of some SMS terms:

Applications Manager—An SMS process that manages the shared applications. If there is a proposed change, the Applications Manager transfers the information to all the sites, and creates configuration files for the shared application groups.

Central Site—The central site is a primary site where all other sites in the SMS system report their inventory and events. This is the top site in the Systems Management Server architecture. All sites and computers in the hierarchy can be administered from this site. There can be an unlimited number of subsites below the central site. The central site must be a primary site, and must have a SQL Server database. The central site must be running Windows NT Server.

Child Site—Automatically reports pertinent site information to its respective parent sites in the SMS hierarchy.

CLEANSMS.BAT—Used to clean SMS files off clients.

\CLIENTS.SRC—Directory containing all the files used for client setup.

COLFILE.HIS—SMS keeps track of all collected files by writing a record for each one in a local file called COLFILE.HIS. Collected files are collected again only when they change, not every time that inventory is run.

.CTx files—Control files that reflect pending changes in a site. .CT0 files are pending changes before verification by SMS, .CT1 files are pending changes after verification by SMS, and .CT2 files list actual changes to a Site.

Despooler—The Despooler is the SMS process that receives, decompresses, and distributes a package during software distribution.

Distribution Server—Distribution servers are used during software distribution and shared application packages. Distribution servers are used as a distribution point when sending applications for clients to install or run. This way the system administrator sends only one copy of the software to each group of computers connected to the distribution server, reducing traffic on the network. A distribution server can be a Windows NT, LAN Manager, or Novell NetWare server.

Domain—A Systems Management Server domain is a set of servers and client computers that have been grouped together. A domain is primarily used to organize servers and clients into manageable groups and to provide logon validation, inventory collection, report generation, and package distribution. Valid domains are Windows NT, NetWare, LAN Manager, and LAN Server. In SMS, the three types of Domains are Windows NT, LAN Manager, and Novell NetWare.

DOMAIN.INI—Master SMS profile used by all clients in the domain. It resides on the logon server and serves as a template for the SMS.INI file on each client.

Helper Server—Helper servers are used to offload some of the processing from the site server. They must be running Windows NT Server.

Hierarchy—Made up of one or more sites which are organized in an inverted tree structure.

Hierarchy Manager—Hierarchy Manager is an SMS process that is in charge of the SMS Site Hierarchy. It verifies the addressability of the local site and all sub-sites on a polling interval. Processes site table looking for changes. If changes are proposed, i.e., a new sub-site is created, Hierarchy Manager will carry out the change.

Inventory Agent—Inventory Agent is an SMS process that collects inventory. Places entries in the SMS.ini and SMSSAFE.TMP files while it is collecting inventory to show when inventory was last collected.

Inventory Data Loader—Inventory Data Loader is an SMS process that adds inventory changes to the SMS database. Checks for Delta-MIF files to find these changes. If MIF files are not correct, it adds them to the BADMIFS directory. Writes a record of collected changes to the local file Colfile.his.

\INVDOM.BOX—\INVDOM.BOX directory contains instructions for clients that need to resynchronize their inventory.

INVDOS.EXE—Inventory agent application for DOS.

Inventory Package—Defines what software to look for on the clients.

Invmac—Inventory agent application for Macintosh.

INVOS2.EXE—Inventory agent application for OS2 clients.

Job—An instance of a Package (except inventory) which is targeted at a specific set of client machines (software distribution), or sites (shared applications), including start time, priority, and repetition.

Logon server—Each domain must contain at least one logon server. The logon server is a server which supports client logon and other services within its domain. It is a repository of instructions for the client agents, as well as the initial point of collection for SMS client inventory information. A logon server can be a Windows NT, LAN Manager, or Novell NetWare server.

In a small Systems Management Server site it is possible for the site server also to be the logon server, the distribution server, and the SQL Server. Once a server has been added, it is considered an SMS logon server.

Maintenance Manager—The Maintenance Manager is an SMS process that manages inventory and status information between the SMS clients and the site server.

.MIF File—After hardware and software inventory collection, the (*.RAW) files get converted to (*.MIF) files—text files approximately 20 to 40 Kb in size. The .MIF file is read into the SQL database.

Package—A group of instructions for software scanning and auditing, or software installation or deinstallation.

PACKAGE.RUL—The software scanning rules file.

Parent Site—Will contain all the pertinent information about its child sites, as well as having the ability to control many operations at the child sites.

Netlogon—Logon share for NT logon server.

Network Monitor—The Network Monitor utility is a full-featured software sniffer. Its capabilities include monitoring all traffic to and from that workstation. The Network Monitor utility is a powerful troubleshooting tool in the hands of an experienced user. For the Network Monitor to work, your network adapter card should support promiscuous mode.

Package Command Manager—An SMS client application that runs package commands sent to it.

Program Group Control—An SMS client application that gets the available list of shared applications when the user logs on. It also runs and configures the user's desktop with the Program Manager group and icon for each available shared application.

PKG_16.CFG—Software audit rules file, binary.

Primary Site—A Systems Management Server site that has its own database, which contains all of the hardware and software inventory information for the site and its subsites. Local administration can be performed for the site server and all the sites below it in the hierarchy. A primary site must be running Windows NT Server. It has an associated SMS database in which it stores its system, inventory, package, job, and status information. A primary site can be a parent only (in which case it is called the central site), a parent and child simultaneously, or a child site only.

Program Group—Used to create collections of program items defined in Sharing Packages and associate them with groups of users.

.RAW File—After collecting hardware and software inventory, MS-DOS and Windows NT Clients create a .RAW file in the \INVENTORY.BOX directory on the logon server. Closes the temp file and renames it with the appropriate extension. MS-DOS and Windows NT Clients create a .RAW file in the \INVENTORY.BOX directory on the logon server.

Replicator Service—NT Service that automates replication of logon scripts and other key files between the central site servers and other logon servers in the SMS site.

**\REPL$\Scripts**—Use Server Manager to configure Replication from your Site Server to other logon servers. Enable exporting from your Site Server's \REPL$\Scripts directory and importing from your logon servers' \REPL$\Scripts directory.

Scheduler—Scheduler checks SQL Server time, then processes jobs ready to be activated on a processing cycle.

Sender—The sender is an SMS process. There are six senders (LAN, RAS-Async, RAS-ISDN, RAS-X25, SNA-Batch, SNA-Interactive) all operate in the same manner: moving compressed application files to their destinations during software distribution.

Secondary Site—A Systems Management Server site that does not have a SQL Server database or Systems Management Server Administrator tool. This site is administered from any site above it in the hierarchy and does not have subsites. Its site information is reported to the site above it. A secondary site must be running Windows NT Server. Performs the same functions as a primary site, except that it does not have an associated SMS database which it controls. Its site information is stored in the SMS database of its immediate parent site. Since it does not have an associated SMS database, a secondary site cannot have any child sites. A secondary site is created by its immediate parent.

Sharing Package—Defines the software and program items that will be used by the clients.

Site—The basic SMS Hierarchy's organizational unit. It is made up of one or more domains.

Site Configuration Manager—Site Configuration Manager is an SMS process that enumerates the domain, server or services options of the SMS site. It also adds SMSLS command to user's logon scripts when Automatically Configure Logon Scripts is selected.

Site Server—Each site in the SMS system must have a site server. A site server contains the SMS components needed to monitor and manage the site and its domains. The site server is the computer which controls the SMS site. It handles the coordination of information and services within the site. Each site has one and only one site server. This computer must be a Windows NT Server V3.5. A site server is a computer running Windows NT Server that contains Systems Management Server components needed to monitor and manage the site, its domains, and its computers. The site server also serves as a collection point for instructions and inventory information. Sites are organized into an SMS Hierarchy by setting up parent-child relationships between the sites.

Site.Srv\SiteCfg.Box—Storage location for PACKAGE.RUL file, software scanning rule file.

SMS.INI—A hidden file located in the root directory of drive C on every SMS client. It contains configuration information for the inventory agent, package command manager, and program group control. The inventory agent keeps this file updated with any changes. When inventory collection is complete, the inventory agent writes new configuration information into this file.

SMS_Executive—The Master NT Service for SMS.

SMS_SHR—Share that clients need to run SMS and assorted commands.

SMSLS.BAT—Automatic inventory collection is started when you add the SMSLS.BAT file to the user's logon script.

SMSLS.CMD—Runs on Novell Networks to modify the System Login Script.

SMSLS.INI—This file is used to map a workstation to an SMS logon server. Used to establish other software and hardware inventory settings (domain, workgroup, and so on).

SQL Server—Each primary site must have a SQL Server. Systems Management Server uses Microsoft SQL Server to store the site database. SQL Server can be installed on the site server or on a separate server. Although each site must have its own database, different sites can share the same SQL Server. It is, however, more efficient for the SQL Server to be on the same LAN as the sites using its databases.

.UID file—Unique identifier that SMS uses for the client.

Workstation Package—Defines the software and command lines that will be distributed to the clients. You can choose to add automatically the other servers in the site server domain to the site's computer inventory. (The site server is always added to the computer inventory.) Or you can add them manually.

X86.BIN, also \ALPHA.BIN and \MIPS.BIN—Contains .EXE files for SMS operation.

APPENDIX B

SMS System Files and Utilities

- Two of the service manager programs used by SMS: the Site Hierarchy Manager and the Site Configuration Manager. We'll take a view at how they work together to manage site configurations within the SMS hierarchy.
- The SMS Executive service and how it acts as the controller for several other SMS components. These components perform some of the basic tasks within the SMS system. Each of the components and its associated functions are then explained.
- Two more SMS services are reviewed: the Inventory Agent service and Package Command Manager service for NT.
- A listing of the startup batch files, SMSLS and RUNSMS, followed by the listing for the client removal program DEINSTAL. As each file is listed, key sections are examined.
- The three initialization files, SMS.INI, SMSLS.INI, and DOMAIN.INI, are then covered. A listing of each file statement and associated statement variable is presented, followed by a description of the function for each. Then a comparison is given between the SMS.INI and the DOMAIN.INI file entries.

In this appendix, we take a look at the programs and files that comprise SMS.

The major SMS components and services are explained, along with their supporting files. We'll look at the program files and any associated command line options they may have. One of the more important topics covered here will be the SMS Database Maintenance Utility. We'll go over its different uses and see how it can be used to keep your SMS database from having problems.

Why do you need to know this? Because someday the system won't work correctly, or at least the way you believe it should. When it's time to look under the hood, you need to be able to tell what you're looking at. Remember, just because you can drive a car doesn't mean you can fix it. The information offered here is intended to give you an idea of what you're looking at, and hopefully some insight into troubleshooting the SMS system. ■

Understanding the Site Hierarchy and Configuration Managers

Two of the most important services within the SMS system are the Site Hierarchy and and the Configuration Managers. We'll take a look at each one and see what it does, then we'll see how they work together to manage the site properties.

What Is the Site Hierarchy Manager?

The Site Hierarchy Manager (SMS_HIERARCHY_MANAGER) is one of the two SMS services started automatically by the NT operating system on startup. It exists only on primary site servers, and is located in the \\SMS\SITE.SRV*platform* directory with the file name PREINST.EXE.

One of its jobs is to monitor for any proposed changes in the SMS database. A change to the database is caused by the SMS administrator making a proposed change to the SMS site configuration while using the Administration program. A proposed change is just that—proposed. The change does not take effect immediately and will not become the "current" configuration until SMS performs a series of specific actions. The proposed change can be at that site or any subsite. An illustration of a proposed change is shown in figure B.1. In this illustration, the DEVELOP domain has just been added as a secondary server. Figure B.2 shows the change after SMS has processed the configuration change.

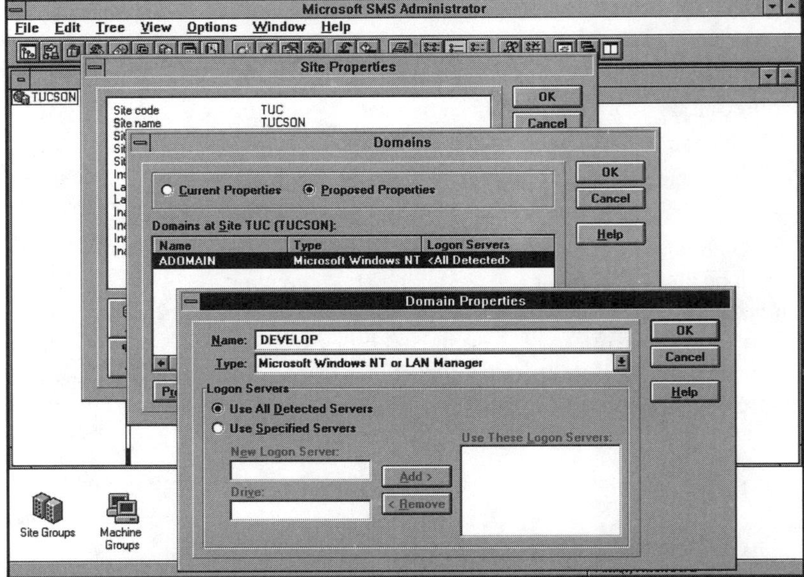

FIG. B.1
A proposed change to the site configuration.

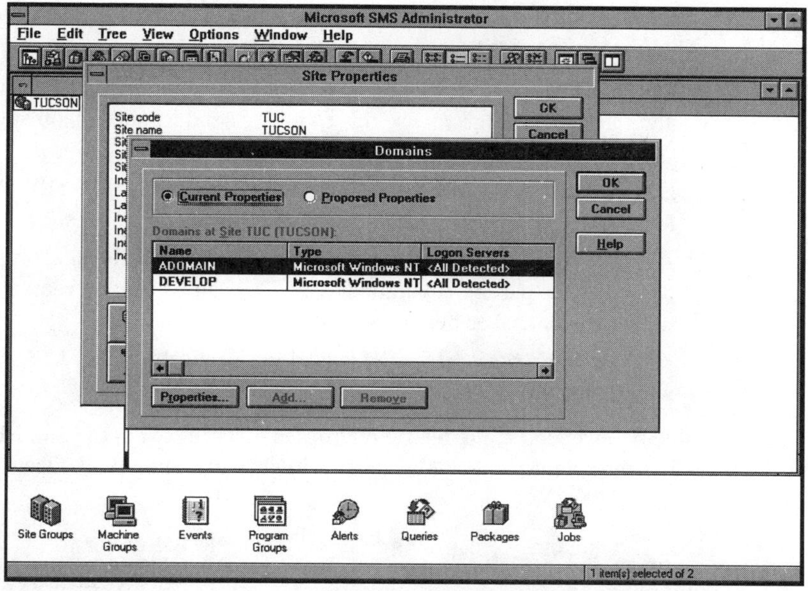

FIG. B.2
The change has gone into effect when it is shown as the "current" configuration.

The events that take place between the change being proposed (Fig. B.1) and the change becoming current (Fig. B.2) start with the Site Hierarchy Manager.

Once a proposed change has been entered by an administrator, it is stored in the SQL SMS database on the primary site. Any changes to a site are detected and saved by the Site Hierarchy Manager to a site control image (*.CT1) file. The *.CT1 file is then used by the Site Configuration Manager to update the NT registry, and to modify the site configuration if needed.

After updating the NT registry, the Site Configuration Manager passes another file called the site control (*.CT2) file back to the Site Hierarchy Manager. This file is used by the Site Hierarchy Manager to update the SQL SMS database.

▶ **See** Appendix D, "A Detailed Look at the Data Flow," for further reference concerning the *.CT1 and *.CT2 files data flow path through the SMS system.

The Site Hierarchy Manager can also be passed commands by specifying its executable name with certain program switches from the command line. This is a very useful tool for diagnosing and fixing site-related problems. A summary of the available program options for PREINST.EXE follows:

> **/DELSITE:**{**sitecode,parentsite**}—this option can be used to remove sites that were removed without first being detached from their parent site. The sitecode indicates the target site to be removed. The parentsite parameter ensures that the target site is removed from the correct parent site in the SMS tree. This is in case the target site has actually been moved to another parent site within the SMS tree, during a tree reorganization for example. This will prevent the moved site (with the same name as the target site) from being removed from the site tree instead of the intended target site. In other words,

if a site with the same sitecode exists in two places in the SMS tree, this parameter makes sure the right one gets deleted.

/DEINSTALL:{*sitecode*}—if you have difficulty removing a secondary site using the administration program, use this switch to send a deinstall job to the secondary site. The target of the job is indicated by the *sitecode* parameter.

/DUM—places control images for all the sites in the SITE.SRV\SITECFG.BOX directory. These images are useful for troubleshooting purposes.

/SYNCPARENT—forces any control file images for the site, or any of its subsites, to be passed to the parent site immediately. This can be used to remedy problems that are due to the site databases being out of synchronization.

/UPGRADE:{*sitecode*}—can be used to specifically target a site for upgrading when a global upgrade has failed.

In Table B.1, we look at the files and libraries that are part of the Site Hierarchy Manager. The table lists the primary executable along with its supporting .DLL files.

Table B.1 Binary Files Associated with the Site Hierarchy Manager

Primary Executable	Dynamic Link Library	File Directory Location(s)
PREINST.EXE		SMS\SITE.SRV*platform*.BIN
	BASE.DLL	SMS\SITE.SRV*platform*.BIN
	BASE2.DLL	SMS\SITE.SRV*platform*.BIN
	BASE3.DLL	SMS\SITE.SRV*platform*.BIN
	BASE4.DLL	SMS\SITE.SRV*platform*.BIN
	BASE5.DLL	SMS\SITE.SRV*platform*.BIN
	SMSINST.DLL	SMS\SITE.SRV*platform*.BIN
	SMSMFC.DLL	SMS\SITE.SRV*platform*.BIN
	NTWDBLIB.DLL	SMS\SITE.SRV*platform*.BIN
	MSVCRT20.DLL	SMS\SITE.SRV*platform*.BIN
	NADAPI32.DLL	SMS\SITE.SRV*platform*.BIN
		SMS\logon.srv*platform*.BIN
		SMS\SITE.SRV\MAINCFG.BOX\CLIENT.SRC*platform*.BIN
	EHISMSG.DLL	SMS\SITE.SRV*platform*.BIN\00000409
	CPPS32.DLL	SMS\SITE.SRV*platform*.BIN
		SMS\SITE.SRV\MAINCFG.BOX\CLIENT.SRC*platform*.BIN

Primary Executable	Dynamic Link Library	File Directory Location(s)
	SMSNET32.DLL	SMS\SITE.SRV*platform*.BIN
		SMS\logon.srv*platform*.BIN
		SMS\SITE.SRV\MAINCFG.BOX\CLIENT.SRC*platform*.BIN
	SMSMS32.DLL	SMS\SITE.SRV*platform*.BIN
		SMS\logon.srv*platform*.BIN
		SMS\SITE.SRV\MAINCFG.BOX\CLIENT.SRC*platform*.BIN
	DBNMPNTW.DLL	SMS\SITE.SRV*platform*.BIN

The Site Configuration Manager

The Site Configuration Manager (SMS_SITE_CONFIG_MANAGER) exists on both primary and secondary site servers. During the installation of SMS, it's the Site Configuration Manager that sets up the domain shares and starts the major services. It monitors to make sure the site configuration information is kept up-to-date in the NT registry. It works with the Site Hierarchy Manager to do this.

Any site control image (*.CT1) files created by the Site Hierarchy Manager are detected by the Site Configuration Manager. It uses the site control image (*.CT1) file's data to modify the NT registry. Then, based on the NT registry information, it performs several actions related to maintaining the site configuration. These actions include enumerating servers, adding SMS components to new logon servers, and adding or deleting domains and their associated components. The Site Configuration Manager then reports any actions it performed back to the Site Hierarchy Manager in the form of a site control(*.CT2) file.

The Site Configuration Manager performs its actions during a period called the *watchdog* cycle. This watchdog cycle is divided into four stages: stage 1 through stage 4. The tasks carried out during each stage of this cycle are recorded in the SCMAN.LOG file. Unlike the other log files, which are located in the SMS\LOGS directory, this file is located in the root directory of the site server. If you take a look at the SCMAN.LOG file, you'll see the sequence of events that take place during the different stages of the *watchdog* cycle. Let's take a look at the different stages of the watchdog cycle as they are recorded in the SCMAN.LOG file.

Stage 1a of the watchdog cycle checks for expired polling intervals.

```
~~Waiting on site control files (*.ct1) in directory C:\SMS\site.srv\sitecfg.box
➥...   $$<SMS_SITE_CONFIG_MANAGER>< Sun Apr 21 04:09:21 1996~><thread=9D>
~Directory monitor: Done waiting; stopped due to time interval up of 7200 seconds
$$<SMS_SITE_CONFIG_MANAGER>< Sun Apr 21 04:09:21 1996~><thread=9D>
~Stage 1a   $$<SMS_SITE_CONFIG_MANAGER><Sun Apr 21 04:09:21 1996~><thread=A9>
~Service startup at: 04/19/96 17:28:54;
Watchdog interval=120 min.;
Logon script interval=1440 min.; previous=1442 min. ago;
Status file interval=1440 min.; previous=1442 min. ago;
```

```
User group MIF interval=1440 min.; previous=1442 min. ago
$$<SMS_SITE_CONFIG_MANAGER><Sun Apr 21 04:09:21 1996~><thread=A9>
```

Stages 1b - 1e are performed only if a site control image (*.CT1) file is detected by the Site Configuration Manager.

```
~Stage 1b   $$<SMS_SITE_CONFIG_MANAGER><Sun Apr 21 04:09:21 1996~><thread=A9>
~Stage 1c   $$<SMS_SITE_CONFIG_MANAGER><Sun Apr 21 04:09:21 1996~><thread=A9>
~Stage 1d   $$<SMS_SITE_CONFIG_MANAGER><Sun Apr 21 04:09:21 1996~><thread=A9>
~Stage 1e   $$<SMS_SITE_CONFIG_MANAGER><Sun Apr 21 04:09:21 1996~><thread=A9>
```

In stage 2, the Site Configuration Manager checks the domain list for new logon servers and tags any new servers found as a "pending-install."

```
~Stage 2   $$<SMS_SITE_CONFIG_MANAGER><Sun Apr 21 04:09:21 1996~><thread=A9>
~NetServerGetInfo server: ADMSERV type: 4122f platform id: 500 version 3.50
➥$$<SMS_SITE_CONFIG_MANAGER><Sun Apr 21 04:09:21 1996~><thread=A9>
~Constructing Domain (ADOMAIN)  Status(SUCCESS) NetProv() NetDLL(NETMSLM.DLL)
~NetServerEnum server: AMO_SERVER platform id 500
➥$$<SMS_SITE_CONFIG_MANAGER><Sun Apr 21 04:09:34 1996~><thread=A9>
~NetServerEnum server: FEARLESS platform id 500   $$<SMS_SITE_CONFIG_MANAGER><Sun
➥Apr 21 04:09:36 1996~><thread=A9>
```

In the third stage, the Site Configuration Manager verifies that the domains and their components exist as specified in the NT registry.

```
Stage 3   $$<SMS_SITE_CONFIG_MANAGER><Sun Apr 21 04:09:40 1996~><thread=A9>
~CWNetEnum::Expand() Enum Finished on DEVFILERO hEnum=0
➥$$<SMS_SITE_CONFIG_MANAGER><Sun Apr 21 04:09:40 1996~><thread=125>
~NetUserEnum domain: DEVFILE, entries read 29, total entries 29 return: 0
~Stage 3 before site FindRemovals()   $$<SMS_SITE_CONFIG_MANAGER><Sun Apr 21
➥04:09:47 1996~><thread=A9>
~Server TUCSS_SMS has 11 shares   $$<SMS_SITE_CONFIG_MANAGER><Sun Apr 21 04:09:47
➥1996~><thread=A9>
~Server TUCSS_SMS status Active role 0xa   $$<SMS_SITE_CONFIG_MANAGER><Sun Apr 21
➥04:09:47 1996~><thread=A9>
~Server TUCSS_SMS has 29 inboxes; 4 domain master inboxes; 14 components
```

During stage 4 of the cycle, a new *site control* (*.CT2) file is created.

```
~Stage 4   $$<SMS_SITE_CONFIG_MANAGER><Sun Apr 21 04:10:46 1996~><thread=A9>
~~Waiting on site control files (*.ct1) in directory C:\SMS\site.srv\sitecfg.box
➥...   $$<SMS_SITE_CONFIG_MANAGER><Sun Apr 21 04:11:17 1996~><thread=A9>
~Directory monitor: Done waiting; stopped due to file created, deleted, or
➥renamed in directory C:\SMS\site.srv\sitecfg.box
➥$$<SMS_SITE_CONFIG_MANAGER><Sun Apr 21 04:11:17 1996~><thread=A9>
```

Our listing showing the SCMAN.LOG file gives us some idea of the watchdog cycle and its various stages. The file is actually quite long but worth examination if you'd like a better understanding of the complete watchdog cycle. Use Notepad or another text editor to open the SCMAN.LOG log file and look at its contents. Remember that this file is located in the root directory of the site server and not in the SMS\LOG directory. Let's continue by looking at the watchdog cycle and its stages in more detail.

As you saw in the SCMAN.LOG file listing, Stage 1 of the process is actually divided into five smaller subprocesses. They are stages 1a through 1e. The stage 1a actions taken by the Site Configuration Manager are outlined in greater detail as follows:

Checking for Expired Registry Intervals As the watchdog cycle begins, the Site Configuration Manager checks the registry to see if the following polling intervals have expired. You can see this activity listed under stage 1a in the previous SCMAN.LOG file listing. If the intervals have expired, the Site Configuration Manager will take the appropriate actions. These actions can be initiated either by the expiration of a polling interval or by the processing of a site control image (*.CT1) file by the Site Configuration Manager.

Logon Script Configuration Interval During the start of the watchdog cycle or when a site control image (*.CT1) file begins to be processed, the logon script configuration polling interval is checked on all domains. This polling interval defaults to 1440 minutes (24 hours). This interval, as well as the other intervals discussed here, can be modified by using the NT registry editor.

User Group Reporting Interval During the start of the watchdog cycle or during the processing of a site control image (*.CT1) file, the list of User Groups for all domains in the site is collected. The list is then reported to the site database in the form of an .MIF (Management Information File). The default interval is 1440 minutes (24 hours).

Site Configuration Reporting Interval This is the time interval between the creation of the site control(*.CT2) files by the Site Configuration Manager. This interval defaults to 1440 minutes (24 hours). The site control files are then used to update the site database.

You can configure the values for these properties in the NT registry key:

```
HKEY_LOCAL_MACHINE\SOFTWARE\Microsoft\SMS\Components\SMS_SITE_CONFIG_MANAGER
```

Two other registry settings are also found in this key, as illustrated in Fig. B.3, and need to be mentioned.

NOTE In the example illustrated in Fig. B.3, the default values for the Logon Script Configuration Interval, User Group Reporting Interval, and Site Configuration Reporting Interval have been changed from 1440 minutes to 120 minutes.

Restart After Shutdown Delay Interval The Site Configuration Manager is responsible for starting the SMS services after a site server has been shut down and restarted. The value specified in this key determines the amount of time (in minutes) that the Site Configuration Manager will wait after a restart before starting the SMS services. The default value for this property is 5.

Watchdogging Interval This is the frequency in minutes between the initiation of a new watchdog cycle. This is the cycle of events that this section on the Site Configuration Manager is covering. At the beginning of this cycle, the Site Configuration Manager checks to see whether any of the other four registry intervals have expired. The cycle continues with the Site Configuration Manager performing the actions that are described later in this section, starting with the conditional update of the registry. The default value for this property is 120 minutes (2 hours).

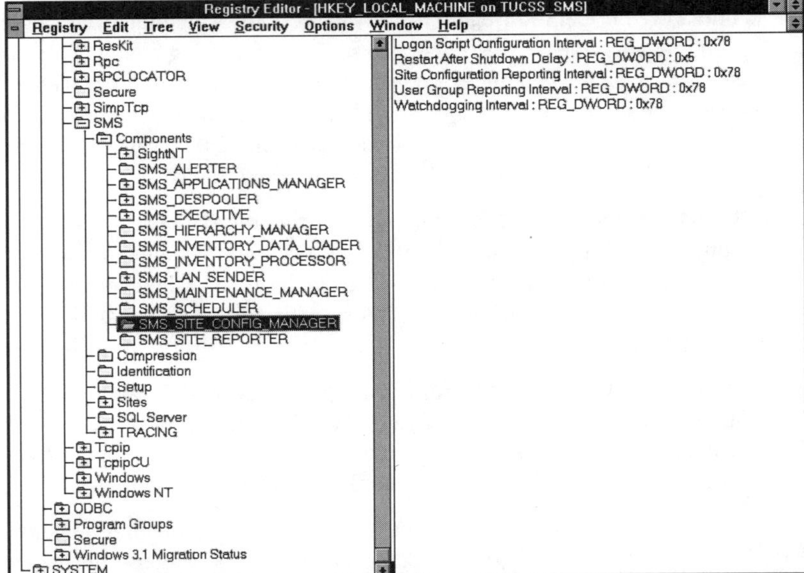

FIG. B.3
Use this NT registry key to alter the default interval values.

Updating the Registry Information The last four steps (1b to 1e) of stage 1 take place only if a site control image (*.CT1) file is detected. A site control image (*.CT1) file is created by the Site Hierarchy Manager whenever a proposed change to the database takes place. At this stage, the Site Configuration Manager writes information to the NT registry based on the data contained in the site control image (*.CT1). The type of SMS data entered in the registry includes the following:

- Information regarding the site's identification.
- Domain and logon server information.
- Address, site account, and other miscellaneous configuration values.
- Information regarding the SQL server.

New Domain Logon Servers Are Found Next, in stage 2, the Site Configuration Manager reads the registry's list of SMS domains and checks each domain for new logon servers. If a new logon server is found, it will be entered in the registry as a "pending-install."

Site Verification and Changes In stage 3 of the cycle, the Site Configuration Manager verifies that the domains and their components exist as specified in the NT registry. Any domains, servers, or components marked for pending-uninstall are removed, and any marked for pending-install are added. Existing components that are marked as active are verified. An outline of the actions taken by the Site Configuration Manager when installing an NT or LAN Manager domain into a site is as follows:

- Logon servers for the new domain are detected.
- SMS shares (SMS and SMS_SHR) are installed on the logon server's NTFS drive containing the most free space.
- The SMS_SHR share is installed on the site server.
- The Inventory Agent is installed and started on NT or LAN Manager servers.
- The Package Command Manager is installed and started on NT servers.
- The Executive service is installed and started.
- If the Automatically Configure Workstation Logon Scripts option is enabled, the following occurs:

  The SMSLS batch files, associated script files (DOSVER.COM, NETSPEED.COM, and so on), and supporting system platform directories (containing the SETLS program files) are copied to REPL$\SCRIPTS directory on the **primary domain controller**.

  The SMSLS command is added to the user's logon script if a logon script already exists. If no script exists, the SMSLS logon script is added to the user's profile.

It is possible to exclude a user from having to run the SMSLS batch file even if the Automatically Configure Workstation Logon Scripts option is enabled. This is done by designating a logon script name in the user's profile that does not have an extension. An example would be a script named "NOSCRPT."

On NetWare servers, the system login script is modified to install and run the SMS client software and Inventory Agent.

- The SMS directory is created on NetWare servers when a NetWare domain is added.

The Site Control File Is Created During stage 4 of the cycle, a new *site control* (*.CT2) file is created by the Site Configuration Manager and sent back to the Site Hierarchy Manager. On remote sites, the file is sent back to the parent as a mini-job. The Site Hierarchy Manager then uses this file to update the SQL SMS database with the latest site configuration information.

Table B.2 shows the files and libraries that are associated with the operation of the Site Configuration Manager.

Table B.2 Binary Files Associated with the Site Configuration Manager

Primary Executable	Dynamic Link Library	File Directory Location(s)
SITEINS.EXE		SMS\SITE.SRV*platform*.BIN
	BASE.DLL	SMS\SITE.SRV*platform*.BIN
	BASE2.DLL	SMS\SITE.SRV*platform*.BIN

continues

Table B.2 Continued

Primary Executable	Dynamic Link Library	File Directory Location(s)
	BASE3.DLL	SMS\SITE.SRV*platform*.BIN
	BASE4.DLL	SMS\SITE.SRV*platform*.BIN
	BASE5.DLL	SMS\SITE.SRV*platform*.BIN
	SMSINST.DLL	SMS\SITE.SRV*platform*.BIN
	SMSMFC.DLL	SMS\SITE.SRV*platform*.BIN
	NTWDBLIB.DLL	SMS\SITE.SRV*platform*.BIN
		SMS\logon.srv*platform*.BIN
		SMS\SITE.SRV\MAINCFG.BOX\ CLIENT.SRC*platform*.BIN
	EHISMSG.DLL	SMS\SITE.SRV*platform*.BIN\ 00000409
	CPPS32.DLL	SMS\SITE.SRV*platform*.BIN
		SMS\SITE.SRV\MAINCFG.BOX\ CLIENT.SRC*platform*.BIN
	SMSNET32.DLL	SMS\SITE.SRV*platform*.BIN
		SMS\logon.srv*platform*.BIN
		SMS\SITE.SRV \MAINCFG.BOX\ CLIENT.SRC*platform*.BIN
	SMSMS32.DLL	SMS\SITE.SRV*platform*.BIN
		SMS\logon.srv*platform*.BIN
		SMS\SITE.SRV\MAINCFG.BOX\ CLIENT.SRC*platform*.BIN
	DBNMPNTW.DLL	SMS\SITE.SRV*platform*.BIN
	NETMSLM.DLL	SMS\SITE.SRV*platform*.BIN
	NETNVNW.DLL	SMS\SITE.SRV*platform*.BIN

Using the Sendcode Utility The PSSTOOLS directory on the SMS CD-ROM contains a utility called sendcode. This utility can be used to force the Site Configuration Manager to perform specific tasks outside its normal watchdog cycle.

The command line syntax for the sendcode utility is:

```
sendcode sms_site_config_manager svccode
```

where svccode represents the service code number listed in Table B.3.

CAUTION

Make absolutely sure you enter the correct service code number on the command line. By using service code 255 with this tool, you will initiate the complete deinstallation of all SMS components, including all files and shares, located on all SMS servers. This includes the site server, all logon servers, and all helper servers.

Table B.3 Descriptions for Service Codes Passed to the Site Configuration Manager by the Sendcode Utility

Code Number	Service Code Name	Service Code Description
192	watchdog	The code can be used to start a normal watchdog cycle.
193	status	Starts the watchdog cycle and writes a *site control*(*.CT2) file.
194	upgrade	Used after sending the shutdown service code to initiate the watchdog cycle as an upgrade.
195	usergroups	Starts the watchdog cycle and writes a user group Management Information File (.MIF).
196	logon_scripts	If the Automatically Configure Workstation Logon Scripts option is enabled, the logon scripts will be modified after this code initiates the watchdog cycle.
234	shutdown	This code is used to stop and deinstall all services at the site. This includes the site server and any logon or helper servers.
255	site_deinstall	This code will perform the same function that code 234 performs. In addition to deinstallation of the SMS services, code 255 also causes all other SMS components, files, and shares to be removed from any servers in the site.This includes the site server and any logon or helper servers.

How They Work Together

The Site Hierarchy Manager and the Site Configuration Manager work together to keep the NT registry and the SQL SMS database updated. The interaction that takes place between the two management services as follows:

1. Proposed changes made to the site properties in the administration program will be written to the SQL SMS database.

2. The Site Hierarchy Manager monitors the SQL SMS database for any proposed changes to site properties. When changes have been detected, the Site Hierarchy Manager will use the change information it finds in the SQL SMS database to create a site control image (*.CT1) file.
3. The Site Configuration Manager detects the site control image (*.CT1) file, then updates the NT registry and performs any specified configuration tasks on the site.
4. A site control (*.CT2) file containing site installation status information is then created by the Site Configuration Manager and passed back to the Site Hierarchy Manager.
5. The SQL SMS database is updated by the Site Hierarchy Manager using the information contained in the site control (*.CT2) file.
6. The proposed site changes then become part of the current site configuration, and are displayed by the administration program as part of the current configuration for the site.

Now that we've taken a look at both the Hierarchy and Configuration Manager services, it's time to turn our attention to a service that acts as a control program for several other SMS components. This service is called the SMS Executive.

The SMS Executive Service

This service is started by the Site Configuration Manager during setup, and it, in turn, starts several other SMS *components*. The SMS Executive service (SMS_EXECUTIVE) reads the NT registry on site, logon, and helper servers to determine which components to start on each. By default, the following nine components are started on the site server (although each component is controlled by the SMS Executive, each still functions as an independent service):

- Alerter
- Applications Manager
- Despooler
- Inventory Data Loader
- Inventory Processor
- LAN Sender
- Maintenance Manager
- Scheduler
- Site Reporter

The view of the registry keys shown in Fig. B.4 reveals that each of the components runs a thread under the Executive service.

To control these services, you must use the SMS Service Manager program. The standard service control manager in NT will allow you to control only the five main SMS services components, as shown in figure B.5.

FIG. B.4
Each of these components runs as a thread under the control of the Executive service.

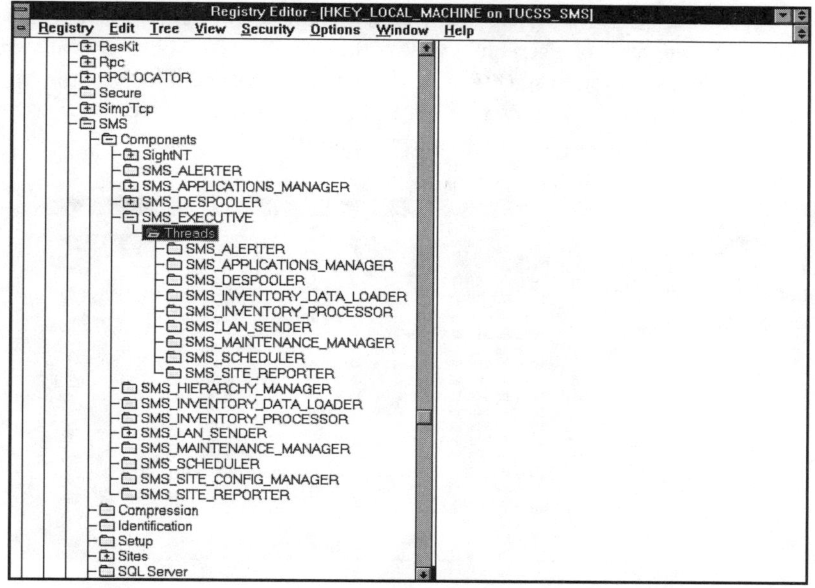

FIG. B.5
The standard service control manager allows you to control the five main components.

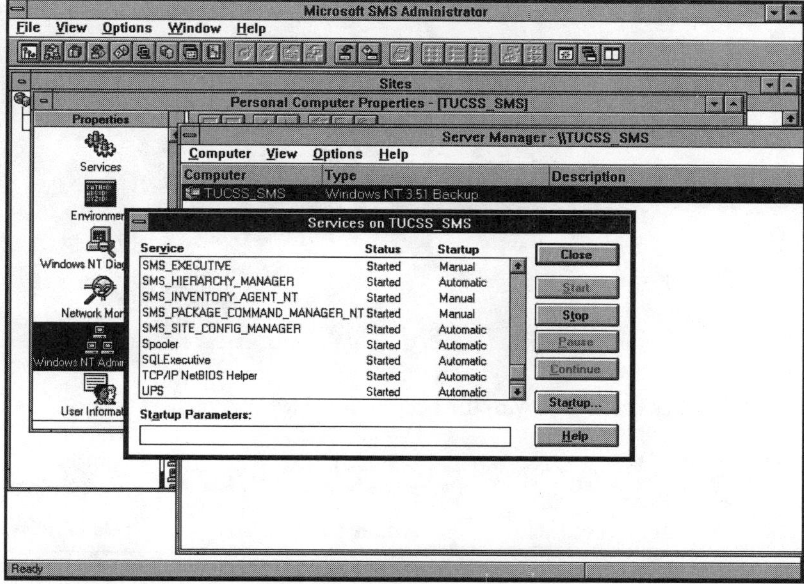

The SMS Service Manager will allow you to control all of the SMS services on all the servers in your site from one screen. A view of the SMS Service Manager is shown in Fig. B.6. This program allows you to start, stop, and pause services and to control the *tracing* (or logging) of the various services. You can specify the trace log file name, location, and maximum size using the Trace Properties window, as shown in figure B.7.

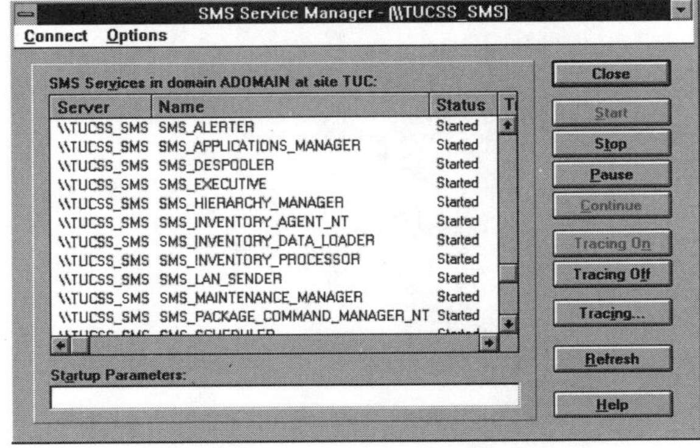

FIG. B.6
The SMS Service Manager allows you to control all of the SMS service components.

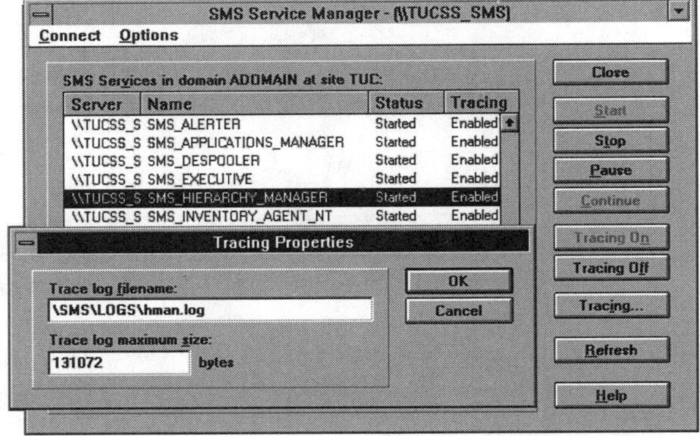

FIG. B.7
You can configure trace file properties in the SMS Service Manager.

The files associated with the operation of SMS Executive service are listed in Table B.4.

Table B.4 Binary Files Associated with the SMS Executive Service

Primary Executable	Dynamic Link Library	File Directory Location(s)
SMSEXEC.EXE		SMS\SITE.SRV*platform*.BIN
	BASE.DLL	SMS\SITE.SRV*platform*.BIN
	BASE2.DLL	SMS\SITE.SRV*platform*.BIN
	BASE3.DLL	SMS\SITE.SRV*platform*.BIN

Primary Executable	Dynamic Link Library	File Directory Location(s)
	BASE4.DLL	SMS\SITE.SRV*platform*.BIN
	BASE5.DLL	SMS\SITE.SRV*platform*.BIN
	SMSINST.DLL	SMS\SITE.SRV*platform*.BIN
	SMSMFC.DLL	SMS\SITE.SRV*platform*.BIN
	NTWDBLIB.DLL	SMS\SITE.SRV*platform*.BIN
		SMS\logon.srv*platform*.BIN
		SMS\SITE.SRV\MAINCFG.BOX\CLIENT.SRC*platform*.BIN
	EHISMSG.DLL	SMS\SITE.SRV*platform*.BIN\00000409
	CPPS32.DLL	SMS\SITE.SRV*platform*.BIN
		SMS\SITE.SRV\MAINCFG.BOX\CLIENT.SRC*platform*.BIN
	SMSNET32.DLL	SMS\SITE.SRV*platform*.BIN
		SMS\logon.srv*platform*.BIN
		SMS\SITE.SRV\MAINCFG.BOX\CLIENT.SRC*platform*.BIN
	SMSMS32.DLL	SMS\SITE.SRV*platform*.BIN
		SMS\logon.srv*platform*.BIN
		SMS\SITE.SRV\MAINCFG.BOX\CLIENT.SRC*platform*.BIN
	DBNMPNTW.DLL	SMS\SITE.SRV*platform*.BIN
	SMSZIP.DLL	SMS\SITE.SRV*platform*.BIN
	SMSUNZIP.DLL	SMS\SITE.SRV*platform*.BIN
	NETMSLM.DLL	SMS\SITE.SRV*platform*.BIN
	NETNVNW.DLL	SMS\SITE.SRV*platform*.BIN

Now, we'll take a look at each component individually to see what duties it performs.

Alerter

The Alerter (SMS_ALERTER) component exists only on primary sites. It monitors the SQL SMS database for new alert conditions and any changes to current alert conditions. When the Alerter detects a true *trigger condition,* it can do the following:

1. Send a message to an administrator or computer with a notification of the alert.
2. Execute a command line in response to a true trigger condition. This command is executed from the system path of the server that Alerter is installed on.
3. Log the SMS event.
4. Create an entry in the Windows NT event log.

Alerts are generated by comparing current query result information with the alert criteria. If the results of the query meet the alert criteria, the trigger related to the alert is set to a true condition.

Applications Manager

This component can exist on both primary and secondary sites. When changes (additions, deletions, or modifications) are made to a package or program group via the SMS Administration Program, the SQL SMS database is modified to reflect the changes, and then the following occurs:

- The Applications Manager (SMS_APPLICATIONS_MANAGER) then detects the changes to the database and distributes network package and program group configuration information from the site database to other components.
- It distributes this information to the current site components and to any components in sites beneath the current site.
- The configuration information is then used to update the Program Group Control database at the site. This database contains configuration files that are used by the client-based Application Control program.

Despooler

By default, the Despooler (SMS_DESPOOLER) component is installed on the site server in both primary and secondary sites. It may be moved to a helper server to ease the processing load on the site server.

The Despooler acts as a control agent for package files by reading the associated instruction file and processing the package according to the instructions, as follows:

- Despooler instruction files and package files created by the Scheduler are detected and processed by the Despooler.
- The instruction file contains information on how to process the associated package file. The Despooler will read the instruction file, decompress the package, and distribute the contents of the package according to the instructions.

The Despooler also maintains the client Package Command Manager instructions on all the client machines that are the targets of a Run Command On Workstation job. In addition, it will report the status of any Run Command On Workstation job back to the site where the job was created.

Inventory Data Loader

This is another component that is originally installed on the site server but may be moved off onto a helper server.

The Inventory Data Loader (SMS_INVENTORY_DATA_LOADER) is responsible for maintaining user group, inventory, job status, and event information within the SQL SMS database. It takes Delta-MIF (DEL*.MIF) files created by the Inventory Processor and uses them to update the site database. The process used by the Inventory Data Loader for updating the site database is as follows:

- Delta-MIF files are placed in the SITE.SRV\DATALOAD.BOX\DELTAMIF.COL directory by the Inventory Processor.
- The Inventory Data Loader uses the data contained in the Delta-MIF.
- The Inventory Data Loader reads the data contained in the Delta-MIF and attempts to locate the object computer in the site database. It tries to find the computer based on the SMS ID and on key attributes of its ID group.
- If the object computer exists in the site database, it is updated or deleted according to the instructions contained in the Delta-MIF.
- If the object computer does not exist in the site database, the Inventory Data Loader will initiate a resync command to update the database on the computer that generated the Delta-MIF file. For more information on the resync command, see the sidebar "How SMS Uses the resync Command."

The Inventory Data Loader is responsible for sending the Delta-MIFs to the site reporter after processing them. Jobs are then created by the site reporter to forward the Delta-MIFs on to any parent sites if they exist. During the initial installation when a parent/child hierarchy is being established, the Inventory Data Loader moves the inventory up to the parent site. It also gets the task of cleaning up any temporary Delta-MIFs that remain in the SITE.SRV\DATALOAD.BOX\DELTAMIF.COL directory.

How SMS Uses the resync Command

We learned earlier in this Appendix that a resync command will be issued by the Inventory Data Loader if a Delta-MIF (DEL*.MIF) file is received for a computer that does not exist in the site database. In Chapter 6, we also learned that removing a computer from a site was a four-step process. One of the steps involved in the process is the removal of any references to the SMSLS batch file from the computer user's logon script.

The resync command is a result of removing a computer from a site database without modifying the reporting status of the computer. In other words, you removed the computer from the site, but the user of the computer still ran the SMSLS batch file from his logon script the next time he logged on to the network.

In this situation, the Inventory Agent will run on the user's computer and send a *.RAW file to the Inventory Processor. The Inventory Processor will compare history records for the computer that might

continues

continued

still remain in the database with the current *.RAW file, and create a Delta-MIF. Or, it won't find any history file records and so will simply write the entire *.RAW file out to a Delta-MIF.

Either way, the Inventory Data Loader will fail to find a matching object computer in the site database and will then initiate the resync command. The phases of the resynchronization process are as follows:

1. A system job with a command line for the specific object computer is created by the Inventory Data Loader.
2. The Scheduler receives the system job and creates the resynchronization instructions.
3. The Sender sends the resynchronization instruction to the object computer.
4. The Despooler executes the instructions and initiates a domain resynchronization instruction.
5. The Despooler places a resync command in the SITE.SRV\MAINCFG.BOX\INVDOM.BOX*domainname*.000\RESYNC.CFG file on the site server.
6. The RESYNC.CFG file is replicated to the LOGON.SRV directory on all logon servers by the Maintenance Manager.
7. When the Inventory Agent for the target computer executes the next time, it reads the RESYNC.CFG file and looks for the computer's SMS ID. If the ID is found, the Inventory Agent looks for a CMNDHIS.* history file on the computer with a resync stamp from a later time than the current resync time.
8. If no later resync history is found, the Inventory Agent will do a complete hardware and software scan of the computer.
9. The Inventory Agent then sends a new *.RAW file to the Inventory Processor.
10. The Inventory Processor tags the *.RAW file as a resync file and creates a Delta-MIF with a *pragma:resync* attribute.
11. The Inventory Data Loader updates the site database with the computer's inventory, and the computer once again appears in the site window.

Inventory Processor

The Inventory Processor (SMS_INVENTORY_PROCESSOR) runs on all site servers. It uses the *.RAW files created by the Inventory Agent to create a Delta-MIF file. The *.RAW files sent by the Inventory Agent are compared to the image of the computer's last *.RAW file. This image of the last *.RAW file is known as the history file. The Inventory Processor compares the current *.RAW file to the history file and creates a Delta-MIF file. If this is the first time the Inventory Agent has run, or if no history files exist, the entire *.RAW file is converted to a Delta-MIF file. The Inventory Processor also converts *.MIF files from Macintosh and OS/2 computers to Delta-MIF files.

The Delta-MIF files are then used by the Inventory Data Loader to update the site database.

In order to cut down on network overhead, a four-day reporting interval that filters out redundant Delta-MIF files has been implemented. Redundant Delta-MIFs can cause undue overhead. By having a four-day reporting interval, any Delta-MIF is filtered unless changes occur outside the Identification Group and Workstation Status group.

You can adjust this interval using the registry key:

```
HKEY_LOCAL_MACHINE\SOFTWARE\Microsoft\SMS\Components\SMS_INVENTORY_PROCESSOR\
Inventory Update Reporting Interval (Days).
```

The minimum value for this entry is one day. Beware: You may increase the system overhead by decreasing this value from its default of four days.

LAN Sender

Sites communicate with one another using one of six SMS Sender (SMS_LAN_SENDER) services. These Senders transmit SMS files and instructions between the sites. They are absolutely necessary if the sites are to transfer information between one another. The Sender will monitor the outbox directory for any compressed files and despooler instruction files that need to be sent to another site. If the request is valid, the Sender will transfer the files to the target site.

The type of Sender used will depend on the communications method you use to link your sites. The six different Senders and their descriptions are illustrated in Table B.5.

Table B.5 The Type of Sender You Use Depends on Your Communication Method

TYPE OF SENDER	DESCRIPTION	LOG FILE
LAN Sender	This Sender is installed by default and is used when a direct network connection is available between sites.	LANSEND.LOG
RAS Sender X.25	This Sender is used when an X.25 frame relay network connection is available between sites.	RASX25.LOG RASSEND.LOG
RAS Sender ISDN	The ISDN Sender is used when ISDN connectivity is available between sites.	RASISDN.LOG RASSEND.LOG
RAS Sender Asynchronous	RAS asynchronous communications Sender is used to allow site communication with dial-up lines and standard modems.	RASSYNC.LOG RASSEND.LOG SNABATCH.LOG SNASEND.LOG
SNA Batch	Used with SNA Batch Mode links. Requires the SNA Server communications service.	

continues

Table B.5 Continued

TYPE OF SENDER	DESCRIPTION	LOG FILE
SNA Interactive	Used with SNA Interactive links. SNAINTER.LOG requires the SNA Server communications service.	SNAINTER.LOG

SMS will allow you to have multiple addresses and multiple Senders between sites. This gives you the ability to create a fault-tolerant environment with redundant site links. Senders will work automatically to make and break connections as needed. They also provide fault tolerance in the form of transaction tracking and rollback capabilities should a link fail. This guarantees that instructions will be delivered intact to the target site or a retransmission of the data will take place.

You can control different parameters for each Sender. They determine time-out or retry values for broken links and the number of concurrent outbound communications channels available. The registry entries available for the LAN Sender are listed in Table B.6.

```
Key Name:          SOFTWARE\Microsoft\SMS\Components\SMS_LAN_SENDER
```

Table B.6 The Configurable Registry Values for Controlling the LAN Sender Service

	VALUE 0	VALUE 1	VALUE 2	VALUE 3	VALUE 4	VALUE 5	VALUE 6
NAME	Enable Bandwidth Control	Maximum Concurrent Sendings	Maximum Concurrent Site Sendings	Number of Retries	Retry Delay in Minutes	Sender Capability ID	Update Timeout in Minutes
TYPE	REG_ DWORD	REG_ DWORD	REG_ DWORD	REG_ DWORD	REG_ DWORD	REG_ SZ	REG_ DWORD
DATA	0 0 0	0x5	0x3	0x2	0x1	00000000	0x5

Value 1, the Maximum Concurrent Sendings key, controls how many threads will be allocated to service send request (*.SRQ) files at one time. Number of Retries designates the number of retries to be performed when a connection fails. The Retry Delay in Minutes determines the delay between retries.

Maintenance Manager

By default, the Maintenance Manager (SMS_MAINTENANCE_MANAGER) is installed on every site and performs a variety of tasks, as follows:

- It collects and forwards *.RAW and *.MIF files from the logon servers to the SMS site server according to the current polling intervals. The Maintenance Manager collects the client inventory files (*.RAW files) from LOGON.SRV\INVENTRY.BOX directories on all logon servers at the site. The Maintenance Manager polls the INVENTRY.BOX directory on Netware servers. It forwards the files in these directories to the SITE.SRV\INVENTRY.BOX directory on the site server.

- The Maintenance Manager also installs and maintains the SMS client components on the logon servers. It replicates any configuration changes made in the site server's SITE.SRV\MAINCFG.BOX directory to the REPL$ share on all NT and LAN Manager servers.
- It monitors for changes in the package rule file.
- It maintains history files in the SITE.SRV\INVENTRY.BOX\HISTORY directory.
- It creates a unique identifier (*.UID) file for the logon server. This file is used to derive the client's unique SMSID.
- It checks for any missing files on logon servers and replaces them if needed.
- It performs an inventory on NetWare servers and creates corresponding MIF files by querying the NetWare bindery. It sends the inventory text MIF to the site server's SITE.SRV\INVENTRY.BOX, where the MIF is processed by the Inventory Processor.
- The Maintenance Manager takes files created by the INVMac program from the Services for Macintosh logon server's LOGON.SRV\ISVMIF.BOX directory, and moves them to the SITE.SRV\ISVMIF.BOX on the site server. This is also how it handles IDMIF files created by OS/2 clients (which are also placed in the LOGON.SRV\ISVMIF.BOX directory).The Inventory Processor will then process the files and place them in the SITE.SRV\DATALOAD.BOX\DELTAMIF.COL directory.
- It creates a copy list from the SYSTEM.MAP file. This list is used to instruct the client setup program on where to place client files.

Scheduler

Initially located on the site server during installation, the Scheduler (SMS_SCHEDULER) service can be moved to a helper server. It is located on both primary and secondary sites.

The Scheduler processes both system and administrative jobs. A system job would be one created by the system inventory process. In this circumstance, the job would be a result of the Site Reporter creating a job for the transfer of inventory (Delta-MIF) files to the parent site. A Run Command on Workstation job would be an example of an administrative job. In each case, the Scheduler is responsible for the same general task.

An example of the Scheduler process follows, showing the distribution of Delta-MIF files to a parent site as part of the overall system inventory process:

1. The Delta-MIF files are compressed into a single file. The file's name is in the form of *jobid*.P*, where *jobid* represents an eight-character job ID.
2. The *jobid*.P* file is put into the SITE.SRV\SENDER.BOX\TOSEND directory.
3. A despooler instruction file is created with a corresponding job ID name. This file's name takes the form of *jobid*.I*, where *jobid* is the same eight-character identifier that was used

for the compressed file (*jobid*.P*). The despooler instruction file contains instructions used by the parent site when decompressing the *jobid*.P* file. These instructions also tell the parent site how to process the decompressed Delta-MIF files.

4. The *jobid*.I* file is put into the SITE.SRV\SENDER.BOX\TOSEND directory along with the *jobid*.P* file.
5. A send request file (*.SRQ) file is created by the Scheduler containing instructions for sending the *jobid*.P* and *jobid*.I* files to the parent site. It is placed in the appropriate outbox directory, as determined by the type of Sender being used. For example, if the RAS sender were being used, the target would be SITE.SRV\SENDER.BOX\REQUESTS\RAS_ISDN.000.

The Scheduler can also prioritize and manage send requests. Its management ability allows it to suspend lower-priority jobs in favor of higher-priority ones. A suspended job resumes after the higher-priority job is finished.

Site Reporter

The Site Reporter (SMS_SITE_REPORTER) is located on both primary and secondary sites. It is responsible for forwarding Delta-MIF (DEL*.MIF) files to the parent site. It is also responsible for deleting Delta-MIF files if no forwarding takes place (because there is no parent site or because the Delta-MIF contains only job information). A general outline of the Site Reporter's actions follows:

1. The Inventory Data Loader updates the site database with the Delta-MIF files.
2. After the current site database has been updated, each Delta-MIF file is moved to the SITE.SRV\SITEREP.BOX directory, where it is held in a queue of Delta-MIF files. These files will temporarily remain queued in this location while they are waiting to be transferred to the parent site.
3. The Site Reporter detects the Delta-MIF files that are queued and creates a system job (*.JOB) file in the SITE.SRV\SCHEDULE.BOX directory. This system job file contains instructions for the delivery of the Delta-MIFs to the parent site.
4. The inventory files for each specific site are moved into the appropriate SITECODE* directory or the SITE.SRV\DATALOAD.BOX directory.
5. The Scheduler processes the system jobs and sends the queued Delta-MIF files to the parent site.

The most resource-intensive service in SMS is the Executive service. For this reason, the following components of the Executive service may be moved to helper servers to ease the overhead on a single-hardware platform:

- Scheduler
- Despooler
- Inventory Data Loader

continues

continued

- Inventory Processor
- Senders

In some cases, you may also want to tune the memory usage of an SMS Executive Working Set manually to increase server performance. The Working Set refers to the memory pages in physical RAM that are currently available to an application process without triggering a page fault. By adjusting the size of the Working Set, you can set up a predetermined amount of physical RAM on reserve for an application. Adjusting the Working Set size will affect the behavior of the virtual paging process and possibly improve performance by reducing the number of page faults incurred. Setting the Working Set values will not guarantee that memory will always be available, but the system will allocate the memory whenever possible. During certain low-memory conditions or when the process is idle, the memory may be allocated to other processes. In Table B.7 below, you can see the default values for the SMS Executive Working Set based on physical RAM in the system.

Table B.7 The SMS Executive Working Set Default Values Are Based on the Physical RAM Installed on the System

SMS Executive Working Set Size	Physical RAM Installed on the System
3.5MB	28MB or less
4.5MB	29MB to 33MB
5.5MB	33MB to 41MB
6.5MB	41MB or more

Setting the SMS Executive Working Set manually involves using the NT registration editor. Always use caution when using the NT registration editor. Mistakes can cause you to spend many hours recovering your system. Always perform a backup of the system (including the NT registry), and have a current copy of the NT system rescue disk on hand in case of problems.

The registry key you need to edit is:

```
HKEY_LOCAL_MACHINE\SOFTWARE\Microsoft\SMS\Components\
SMS_Executive[Working Set Limit]
```

At the default value of zero, the Working Set is autotuned to the default values shown in Table B.7. If you set the limit manually, the smallest Working Set allowed is 2MB (200000hex). This value (set in bytes) has no upper limit; values greater than 7MB (700000hex) are not recommended. Restart the SMS Executive service for any changes to take effect.

File Names and Locations

Each of the Executive's components has its associated dynamic link libraries. Table B.8 shows you the DLL file names and locations for each of them.

Table B.8 Binary Files Associated with the SMS Executive Service Components

Primary Component	Sub Component	Dynamic Link Library	File Directory Location(s)
SMS Executive	Alerter	ALERTER.DLL	SMS\SITE.SRV*platform*.BIN
	Applications Manager	APPMGR.DLL	SMS\SITE.SRV*platform*.BIN
	Despooler	DESPOOL.DLL	SMS\SITE.SRV*platform*.BIN
	Inventory Data Loader	DATALDR.DLL INVUPD.DLL	SMS\SITE.SRV*platform*.BIN SMS\SITE.SRV*platform*.BIN
	Inventory Processor	INVPROC.DLL	SMS\SITE.SRV*platform*.BIN
	LAN Sender	SENDER.DLL	SMS\SITE.SRV*platform*.BIN
	LAN Sender Async RAS	SENDER.DLL CONNRAS. DLL	SMS\SITE.SRV*platform*.BIN SMS\SITE.SRV*platform*.BIN
	LAN Sender ISDN RAS	SENDER.DLL CONNRAS.DLL	SMS\SITE.SRV*platform*.BIN SMS\SITE.SRV*platform*.BIN
	LAN Sender X.25 RAS	SENDER.DLL CONNRAS.DLL	SMS\SITE.SRV*platform*.BIN SMS\SITE.SRV*platform*.BIN
	LAN Sender Batch SNA	SENDER.DLL CONNSNA.DLL	SMS\SITE.SRV*platform*.BIN SMS\SITE.SRV*platform*.BIN
	LAN Sender Inter SNA	SENDER.DLL CONNSNA.DLL	SMS\SITE.SRV*platform*.BIN SMS\SITE.SRV*platform*.BIN
	Maintenance Manager	MAINTAIN.DLL	SMS\SITE.SRV*platform*.BIN
	Scheduler	SCHED.DLL	SMS\SITE.SRV*platform*.BIN
	Site Reporter	SITEREP.DLL	SMS\SITE.SRV*platform*.BIN

Other Important Services

There are two other important SMS service components that must be mentioned. These components are not one of the SMS Executive's thread services, but are independent services which are designed to serve a specific role.

The Bootstrap Service The Bootstrap service is a temporary service that's used by SMS when setting up secondary site servers. It is used to begin the installation process on a new secondary server. The primary site will detect the new secondary, and will send instructions to create the SMS directory and start the Bootstrap service. This service will then take over the secondary installation by decompressing a package sent from the primary site to create the SMS directory structure and install the various components in it. After the primary sends a site control(*.CT2) file to the secondary, the SMS Site Configuration Manager starts and removes the Bootstrap service. This is the only other service besides the Site Configuration Manager that has its log file located outside the SMS\LOGS directory. The Bootstrap log file is named BOOT.LOG and is located in the root directory of the secondary server.

SNA Receiver The SNA Receiver is used in conjunction with the SNA Sender for communications between sites utilizing an SNA link. The SNA Receiver is automatically installed when the SNA Sender is installed on a server. Unlike the SNA Sender service, which is started by the SMS Executive, the SNA Receiver is started by the Site Configuration Manger. Table B.9 lists the files associated with the SNA Receiver.

Table B.9 Files Associated with the SNA Receiver Service

Primary Executable	Dynamic Link Library	File Directory Location(s)
RCVSNA.EXE		SMS\SITE.SRV*platform*.BIN
	BASE.DLL	SMS\SITE.SRV*platform*.BIN
	BASE2.DLL	SMS\SITE.SRV*platform*.BIN
	BASE3.DLL	SMS\SITE.SRV*platform*.BIN
	BASE4.DLL	SMS\SITE.SRV*platform*.BIN
	BASE5.DLL	SMS\SITE.SRV*platform*.BIN
	SMSINST.DLL	SMS\SITE.SRV*platform*.BIN
	SMSMFC.DLL	SMS\SITE.SRV*platform*.BIN
	MSVCRT20.DLL	SMS\SITE.SRV*platform*.BIN
	NADAPI32.DLL	SMS\SITE.SRV*platform*.BIN
		SMS\logon.srv*platform*.BIN
		SMS\SITE.SRV\MAINCFG.BOX\CLIENT.SRC*platform*.BIN
	EHISMSG.DLL	SMS\SITE.SRV*platform*.BIN\00000409
	CPPS32.DLL	SMS\SITE.SRV*platform*.BIN
		SMS\SITE.SRV\MAINCFG.BOX\CLIENT.SRC*platform*.BIN
	SMSNET32.DLL	SMS\SITE.SRV*platform*.BIN
		SMS\logon.srv*platform*.BIN

continues

Table B.9 Continued

Primary Executable	Dynamic Link Library	File Directory Location(s)
		SMS\SITE.SRV\MAINCFG.BOX\CLIENT.SRC*platform*.BIN
	SMSMS32.DLL	SMS\SITE.SRV*platform*.BIN
		SMS\logon.srv*platform*.BIN
		SMS\SITE.SRV\MAINCFG.BOX\CLIENT.SRC*platform*.BIN
	DBNMPNTW.DLL	SMS\SITE.SRV*platform*.BIN

This concludes the section on the SMS Executive and its related components. As we've seen, the SMS Executive and its components perform many of the tasks associated with the background operation of SMS. Data flow through the system was introduced briefly as we described each service. For a full understanding of the data flow associated with these components (and the SMS system in general), see Appendix D, "A Detailed Look at the Data Flow."

In the next section, the Inventory Agent and Package Command Manager for NT are examined. These are background services on NT servers that work with the components we've just seen to report inventory and perform unattended package installation.

The Inventory Agent Service and the Package Command Manager Service for NT

The Inventory Agent service and the Package Command Manger (PCM) service for NT are both services that run on NT servers. The Inventory Agent can also run as a service on OS/2 servers. Let's take a closer look at each one and see what it does.

The Inventory Agent Service

Collecting inventory at the server level is the job of the Inventory Agent (SMS_INVENTORY_AGENT_NT) service. This service is started by the Site Configuration Manager during SMS installation and collects inventory on all Windows NT servers, including site, logon, and helper servers. The OS/2 version of the Inventory Agent (SMS_INV_OS2LM) runs on LAN Manager OS/2 servers. The Inventory Agent does not collect inventory on NetWare servers—that task is left to the Maintenance Manager in a NetWare environment.

In order to run the Inventory Agent on a server, the SMS service account must be a member of the local administrators group and have "log on as a service" rights to the server.

▶ To learn how to set up the Inventory Agent as a service on a Windows NT Workstation, refer to the Sidebar "How to Install the Inventory Agent as a Service on NT Workstations" in Chapter 6, "Collecting the Hardware Inventory."

The server Inventory Agent service (INVWIN32.EXE on NT servers, INVOS2.EXE on OS/2 servers) performs the same function as the DOS or Windows Inventory Agent (INVDOS.EXE); the only difference is that the Inventory Agent service is just that—a service—and is not called by the SMSLS or RUNSMS batch file.

The Inventory Agent does the job of collecting hardware and software inventory during client logon. In the case of DOS and Windows machines, the inventory information that's collected is sent to the logon server in the form of *.RAW files. They're placed in the LOGON.SRV\INVENTRY.BOX directory, where the Maintenance Manager collects them. The OS/2 Inventory Agent places an ASCII MIF file (instead of a *.RAW file) in the logon server's LOGON.SRV\ISVMIF.BOX directory.

App B

The default collection interval for this service is 1440 minutes (24 hours). This essentially means that the user will be scanned every time he or she logs on (assuming logon once a day). If you double the interval, the scan will occur every other time the client logs on. The interval can be adjusted in the Site Properties box of SMS Administration or by editing the following registry key:

```
Key Name:          SOFTWARE\Microsoft\SMS\Components\SMS_MAINTENANCE_MANAGER
Value 10
Name:              Inventory Agent Service Interval
Type:              REG_DWORD
Data:              0x5a0
```

The data string 0x5a0 hex represents the value of 1440 minutes. By increasing this time period, you will minimize the system overhead by decreasing the frequency of inventory collection. For large sites with hundreds (or thousands) of clients, this can dramatically cut both network and SMS System resource overhead.

▶ Inventory Agent command line options are presented later in Appendix B section titled "Client Components."

The Package Command Manager for Windows NT

The Package Command Manager (SMS_PACKAGE_COMMAND_MANAGER_NT) service, PCM for short, is installed on all site, logon, and helper servers. PCM (PCMSVC32.EXE) is a service that runs on Windows NT servers and allows for the unattended installation of software packages. As long as the package conforms to certain rules, it will be installed automatically without a user being required to be logged on. These rules are as follows:

1. The package must be configured for automatic installation in background mode.
2. The package installation does not require user input.
3. The package does not display windows during installation.

The SMS.INI file contains a [Package Command Manager] section that can be used to view the *administrative* polling period. This polling period is specified in minutes; in the example below, the polling interval is set for 60 minutes.

```
[Package Command Manager]
InstructionSharePoint=pcmins.box
```

```
ResultSharePoint=despoolr.box
LocalRegistryLocation=C:\MS\SMS\DATA\pcmhist.reg
PollingInterval=60
```

As mentioned, the polling interval listed here is the administrative default that is installed during client setup. The user of the computer can always override this value by configuring a different polling interval using the PCM program dialog box. The values specified in the PCM program are written to the [Local] section of the SMS.INI file and take precedence over any value listed in the [Package Command Manager] section.

The PCM operates by polling the designated logon server's SMS_SHR\PCMINS.BOX for binary PCM instruction files. These instruction files are targeted to a specific computer by using the target computer's SMS ID appended with the .INS extension as their file name. The File Manager display in Fig. B.8 shows an instruction file targeted for a computer located in the DEVELOP domain with an SMS ID of TUC0D00F. If the PCM finds a file name that is the same as the local computer's unique SMS ID, it will read the file. The information parsed from this binary file provides the instructions for carrying out a package installation on the target computer.

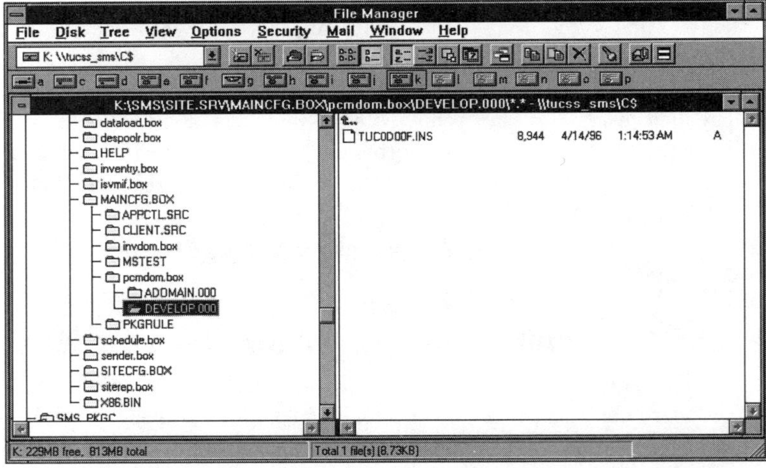

FIG. B.8
Notice that the file name of the instruction package matches the computer's SMS ID.

You can troubleshoot PCM problems using PCMDUMP, a Win32 utility located in the PSSTOOLS directory of the SMS CD-ROM. This utility dumps the contents of the PCM instruction file out to a text file that can be examined for errors.

During its poll, the PCM checks the SMS.INI for the location of the PCMHIST.REG file. This file contains the package history information for that computer. After each package installation, the PCMHIST.REG file is updated with new information to indicate the package has been executed.

Take note that this discussion has been related to the PCM (PCMSVC32.EXE) service on NT servers. There are three other PCM programs that do the same thing, but are not services. These programs are the PCM for DOS, the PCM for both Windows 3.1 and WFW, and the PCM for Macintosh. They are reviewed a little later in the Appendix B section titled "Package Command Manager". Now we'll go on to look at the three of the batch files that SMS uses.

▶ A complete overview of the client PCM program and its options are given in Chapter 7, "Installing the Client Sites," under the section entitled "SMS Client Program Options."

The Batch Files SMSLS, RUNSMS, and DEINSTAL

When you enable the Automatically Configure Workstation Logon Script option, the SMSLS batch file is automatically installed as the default login script for all users in the domain. If a user already has a logon script, a statement is inserted into the current logon script that calls the appropriate SMSLS batch file.

Three versions of the SMSLS batch file exist. The first one, SMSLS.BAT, is for DOS, Windows, WFW, Windows 95, and NT clients; the second one, SMSLS.CMD, is for OS/2 clients; and the third, SMSLS.SCR, is for use with NetWare clients, and is run from the NetWare server's system login script. They will be collectively referred to as the SMSLS batch file, and they all perform the same basic function. The location of the SMSLS batch file(s) is the NETLOGON share of the logon server (except for SMSLS.SCR, of course).

Another version of the SMSLS batch file exists in the *logonserver*\SMS_SHR. It's the RUNSMS.BAT and the OS/2 client RUNSMS.CMD file. The primary difference between the SMSLS and RUNSMS batch files is the addition of the netspeed command in the SMSLS files. This executable is called from the SMSLS batch file to detect slow network links. If a slow link is detected, certain parameters are set to determine if client inventory should be taken. According to Microsoft, the RUNSMS batch file should not be used in the logon script. Instead, this file is run when the user connects to the SMS_SHR and manually executes the file.

In the last part of this section we'll look at the DEINSTAL.BAT file. This file is used to remove the SMS components from a client computer. As we discussed in Chapter 9, "Collecting the Hardware Inventory," there are two methods of removing client components from a computer. The first is to move manually to the correct logon server directory for the platform you're working on and run the client setup program with the remove option. The second way is simply to run the DEINSTAL.BAT file. A listing of the file will be given in the DEINSTAL section and its operation will be examined.

SMSLS/RUNSMS

In this section we look at the listing for the SMSLS.BAT file. The file is well documented with remarks that give a good explanation of how the file operates. Comments have been added between the different sections to supplement the information contain in the remark statements. Note that this listing also applies to the RUNSMS batch file. They are basically the same file, with a couple of exceptions, as follows:

- The SMSLS file contains a call to the executable netspeed. It calls netspeed in order to determine the speed of the network link to the NETLOGON share.
- The RUNSMS batch file contains sections that handle NetWare clients operating in a pure netx environment.

Now let's take a look at the file.

The first *if* statement of the file will determine whether the verbose mode is enabled. The verbose mode comes in handy when troubleshooting client problems. By invoking the verbose mode, you can see detailed information regarding the operation of the different client setup programs.

```
REM If the SMSLS environment variable is set on the workstation (e.g.,
REM set SMSLS=1), verbose output will be enabled for SETLS16, CLI_DOS,
REM and INVDOS or SETLS32, CLI_NT and INVWIN32.

if "%SMSLS%" == "" goto START
set SMS_VERBOSE=/v
echo Executing SMS logon script.
goto START
```

This section of the file determines if enough environment space is available for the *path* to the proper version of SETLS and NLSMSG to be appended to the *current* path statement.

```
REM Determine the binary files directory on the SMS logon server by
REM checking environment variables for operating system and processor
REM architecture. Set environment variables for this directory and
REM for the OS type. The directory this file exists in and the platform
REM specific directory beneath it are added to the path so that the proper
REM version of SETLS and NLSMSG can be called.

:START

REM Check to see if we can save path and reserve the neccessary environment
REM space before continuing.
set SMS_P=%PATH%

set SMS_TEMP=12345678901234567890123456789012345678901234 5
if "%SMS_TEMP%"=="123456789012345678901234567890123456789012345" goto FIND_OS
goto LOW_ENV
```

The execution of the batch file will branch to the appropriate label based on the operating system that is detected on the client. Batch file execution stops if OS/2 version 1.3 or greater is detected.

```
:FIND_OS
set SMS_TEMP=
if "%OS%" == "Windows_NT" goto NT_BIN

REM Determine the DOS version and exit if OS/2 1.3 or greater.
%0\..\dosver
if errorlevel 13 goto OS2
```

The DOS variables are set.

```
:DOS_BIN
set SMS_OS=16
set SMS_BIN=x86.bin
goto RUN_FROM
```

The file execution branches to the proper code based on the type of processor architecture.

```
:NT_BIN
if "%PROCESSOR_ARCHITECTURE%" == "ALPHA" goto NT_ALPHA
if "%PROCESSOR_ARCHITECTURE%" == "MIPS"  goto NT_MIPS
if "%PROCESSOR_ARCHITECTURE%" == "x86"   goto NT_X86
```

If the batch file is not able to determine the operating system or the processor architecture, it will display a failure message and terminate.

```
echo.
echo Unable to determine operating system or processor architecture.
echo.
echo Consult your network administrator.
echo.
pause
goto END
```

The variables are set for ALPHA architectures.

```
:NT_ALPHA
set SMS_BIN=alpha.bin
set SMS_OS=32
goto RUN_FROM
```

Variables are set for MIPS architectures.

```
:NT_MIPS
set SMS_BIN=mips.bin
set SMS_OS=32
goto RUN_FROM
```

Variables are set for Intel architectures.

```
:NT_X86
set SMS_BIN=x86.bin
set SMS_OS=32
goto RUN_FROM
```

The run path is set based on the operating system type.

```
:RUN_FROM
if "%OS%" == "Windows_NT"     set PATH=%PATH%;%0\..\%SMS_BIN%
if not "%OS%" == "Windows_NT" set PATH=%0\..;%0\..\%SMS_BIN%;%PATH%
```

Netspeed is run to determine if a slow network connection exists to the NETLOGON share. Clients can be configured to exit the batch file at this point if a slow network is detected. This prevents the inventory process from executing over slow links. Taking inventory over a slow link can cause the time required to complete an inventory at the client to increase dramatically.

Note that this section of the SMSLS batch file containing the netspeed statement does not exist in the RUNSMS batch file. RUNSMS is intended to be run manually from the SMS_SHR directory. It is assumed that anyone manually executing the command over a known slow link will be aware that the processing time may be lengthy.

```
REM Check for a slow network connection to the NETLOGON share and
REM possibly exit.  If not, the SETLS program is run during NET LOGON to
REM a Windows NT or LAN Manager server and is used to find the correct
REM SMS logon server and spawn the executable files for CLI_DOS and
REM INVDOS or CLI_NT and INVWIN32 located on this server.

netspeed
if not errorlevel 1 goto RUN_SETLS
if not errorlevel 2 goto RESTORE
if errorlevel 2 NLSMSG%SMS_OS% 6 /C YN /T Y,30 /M "Slow network detected.
Continue"
if not errorlevel 2 goto RUN_SETLS
goto RESTORE
```

The program branches to the proper SETLS command lines based on the operating system type. SETLS reads the SMSLS.INI file to determine the logon server from which to run the Client Setup and Inventory Agent. The SETLS, Client Setup, and Inventory Agent programs are covered in more detail later in this appendix.

```
:RUN_SETLS
if "%OS%" == "Windows_NT" goto RUN_NT

:RUN_DOS
setls%SMS_OS% -m:E -i -p:%SMS_BIN%\CLI_DOS.EXE -pa:/p:%%SMS_UNC%%\ -
pa:%SMS_VERBOSE% %SMS_VERBOSE%
setls%SMS_OS% -m:E -i -p:%SMS_BIN%\INVDOS.EXE  -pa:/l:%%SMS_UNC%%\ -pa:/i -
pa:%SMS_VERBOSE% %SMS_VERBOSE%
goto RESTORE

:RUN_NT
setls%SMS_OS% -m:E -i -p:%SMS_BIN%\CLI_NT.EXE   -pa:/p:%%SMS_UNC%%\ -
pa:%SMS_VERBOSE% %SMS_VERBOSE%
setls%SMS_OS% -m:E -i -p:%SMS_BIN%\INVWIN32.EXE -pa:/l:%%SMS_UNC%%\ -pa:/e -pa:/
t0 -pa:/i -pa:%SMS_VERBOSE% %SMS_VERBOSE%

goto RESTORE

:OS2
echo.
%0\..\x86.bin\NLSMSGo2 5 /M "Please run SMSLS.CMD from an OS/2 window"
echo.
pause
goto END
```

This section of the batch file attempts to increase the amount of space for environmental variables if the required amount is not already available.

```
REM SMSLS was unable to reserve the neccessary amount of environment space
REM and was unable to complete successfully. Increase the available environment
REM space and repeat logon.

:LOW_ENV
```

```
set SMS_TEMP=

REM Try to start a new command shell to procure more env space
REM but only once to avoid extra recursion.
if "%1" == "" goto newshell

echo.
%0\..\x86.bin\NLSMSG16 7 /M "Not enough environment space"
%0\..\x86.bin\NLSMSG16 8 /M "Use the /E parameter on the shell= command in
config.sys"
%0\..\x86.bin\NLSMSG16 9 /M "to increase the amount of environment space
available."
pause
goto END

:newshell
command /e:2048 /c %0 retry
goto END
```

The last section restores the path and removes any environment variables that may have been set. CLRLEVEL.COM is called to reset the DOS errorlevel flags.

```
:RESTORE
REM Restore the previous path setting.
PATH=%SMS_P%
goto END

REM Clean up the environment variables and reset the errorlevel.
:END
set SMS_P=
set SMS_OS=

set SMS_BIN=
set SMS_VERBOSE=
if errorlevel 1 if     "%OS%" == "Windows_NT" clrlevel
if errorlevel 1 if not "%OS%" == "Windows_NT" %0\..\clrlevel
```

How Does SMSLS Set a Correct Path to the Executable Files?

When a logon script executes from the NETLOGON share, the script file must be able to determine the correct path to the executable files that it calls. On Windows NT machines, the NETLOGON share is automatically included in the path. Since the executables will be in the search path on NT systems, there is no problem finding location of the files. This is not true for other operating systems.

To overcome this problem, a hard-coded drive letter could be used, but that's not the most desirable way of referencing the files. Instead SMSLS gets around the problem by using the DOS path statement %0\..\ in the command line for the executable files. This path statement is taken from the ARG[0] value at the time the batch file is run.

Look in the SMSLS batch file listing for the %0\..\ statement to get a better idea of how it's used to reference the executables.

DEINSTAL

The version of the Client Setup program you need to run is specific to the operating system installed on the client computer. This batch file automates the process of connecting and running the correct version of the Client Setup program in the removal mode. You'll notice that the same method used to determine the client operating system in the SMSLS batch file is used in the DEINSTAL batch file.

Notice the similarity to the SMSLS batch file in determining the current operating system.

```
@echo off

if "%OS%"=="Windows_NT" goto NT
goto DOS

:NT

if "%PROCESSOR_ARCHITECTURE%" == "ALPHA" goto NT_ALPHA
if "%PROCESSOR_ARCHITECTURE%" == "MIPS" goto NT_MIPS
if "%PROCESSOR_ARCHITECTURE%" == "x86" goto NT_X86

echo.
echo Unable to determine operating system or processor architecture.
echo.
echo Consult your network administrator.
echo.
pause
goto DONE
```

After the operation system has been determined, the batch file changes to the appropriate directory for the operating system and then jumps to the NT RUN label.

```
:NT_ALPHA
cd alpha.bin
goto NT_RUN


:NT_MIPS
cd mips.bin
goto NT_RUN


:NT_X86
cd x86.bin
goto NT_RUN
```

The batch file then executes the CLI_NT program with the /r switch to remove the client SMS components. Note that the correct version of the Client Setup program will always be executed. This is because the batch file is executing from the directory that is specific to the operating system or processor architecture of the client machine.

```
:NT_RUN
echo.
echo This batch file will cause all SMS client software to be deinstalled
echo from this machine.  The deinstall process will require 2 phases to
```

```
echo complete.
echo.
echo About to run phase 1.
echo.
pause
echo Running CLI_NT /R
cli_nt /r
echo.
echo Phase 1 of Client deinstall complete.  You must now restart Windows NT
echo for the deinstallation to complete.
goto DONE
```


This is the section that is executed if a DOS-based operating system is detected. As you see, it calls the Client Setup program from X86.BIN directory.

```
:DOS
cd x86.bin
echo.
echo This batch file will cause all SMS client software to be deinstalled
echo from the client machine.  If Windows is installed on this machine,
echo the deinstall process will require 2 phases to complete. Otherwise,
echo the complete deinstallation will be done now.
echo.
echo About to run phase 1.
echo.
pause
echo Running CLI_DOS /R
cli_dos /r
echo Phase 1 of Client deinstall complete.  If this is a Windows machine, you
echo must start or restart Windows now for the deinstallation to complete.
goto DONE


:DONE
echo.
pause
```

Later in the appendix we examine the Client Setup program's removal mode in more detail.

SMS.INI, DOMAIN.INI, and SMSLS.INI

Three initialization files are used by SMS to set the client environment, as follows:

- The SMS.INI file is a hidden file located on the boot partition of client computer. It contains all the configurable property values required for the specific computer it resides on.
- The DOMAIN.INI acts as the template for SMS.INI file during the SMS client component installation.
- The SMSLS.INI file is located on the logon server. It is an optional file used to map computers to specific domains.

Most of our attention will be focused on the SMS.INI file and DOMAIN.INI file. The use of the SMSLS.INI file is covered in detail in Chapter 9, "Collecting the Hardware Inventory," but a file listing is included here for your reference.

SMS.INI and DOMAIN.INI Comparison

All clients that are inventoried by the SMS system have the SMS.INI file installed. It contains information that the various SMS components use as they are executed on the client. Fourteen sections with more than 60 entries can be present in the file. Descriptions for each one of the SMS.INI file's entries are documented both on-line and in the administrative manual. For this reason we won't repeat the list of descriptions here.

Instead we'll take a look at an actual SMS.INI file located on a client computer. This file is maintained by the Inventory Agent and requires no manual configuration. The entries contained in this example are typical of the ones you'll encounter when looking at the SMS.INI file.

Our example is from a Windows 95 client computer named HADFIELD. This computer is currently one of three machines inventoried in the DEVELOP domain (see figure B.9). The other two machines shown in the site window are logon servers for the DEVELOP domain.

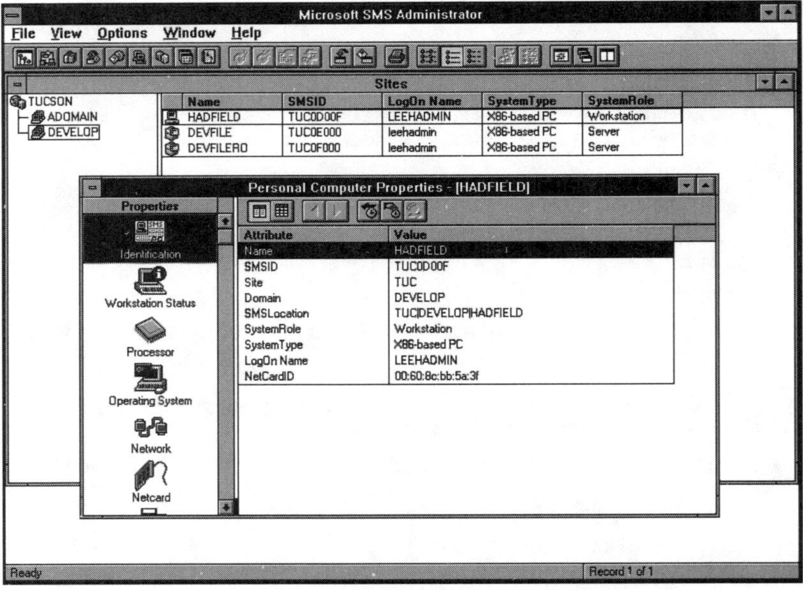

FIG. B.9 Properties displayed here correspond to the values listed in the computer's SMS.INI file.

As mentioned, the DOMAIN.INI file acts as a template for the SMS.INI file during client installation. Many of the SMS.INI file statements are copied directly from the DOMAIN.INI file during installation. The location of the DOMAIN.INI file is in the SMS_SHR share of the logon server. Table B.10 lists the DOMAIN.INI file for the DEVELOP domain; next to it we list the SMS.INI file for the client computer HADFIELD. Any SMS.INI entries derived from the DOMAIN.INI are shown next to each other.

Table B.10 SMS.INI Uses DOMAIN.INI as a Template

DOMAIN.INI a	SMS.INI
[Package Command Manager] InstructionSharePoint=pcmins.box ResultSharePoint=despoolr.box LocalRegistryLocation=C:\MS\SMS \pcmhist.reg PollingInterval=60	[Package Command Manager] InstructionSharePoint=pcmins.box ResultSharePoint=despoolr.box LocalRegistryLocation=C:\MS\SMS\DATA \pcmhist.reg PollingInterval=60
[Servers] Domain=DEVELOP CurrentLogonServer=DEVFILE Server1=DEVFILE Server2=DEVFILERO	[Servers] Domain=DEVELOP CurrentLogonServer=DEVFILE Server1=DEVFILE Server2=DEVFILERO
[Share] CurrentLogonServer=SMS_SHR Server1=SMS_SHR Server2=SMS_SHR	[Share] CurrentLogonServer=SMS_SHR Server1=SMS_SHR Server2=SMS_SHR
[Program Group Control] directory=appctl.box\database	[Program Group Control] directory=appctl.box\database
[AppCtlIniFiles] directory=appctl.box\inifiles	[AppCtlIniFiles] directory=appctl.box\inifiles
[AppCtlScripts] directory=appctl.box\scripts	[AppCtlScripts] directory=appctl.box\scripts
[MSTest16.20] directory=mstest	[MSTest16.20] directory=mstest
   Components=PCM APPCONTROL REMOTE_CONTROL MIFENTRY AutoStart=PCM APPCONTROL REMOTE_CONTROL MIFENTRY	[WorkstationStatus] SysFilesNotModified= FilesNotDownloaded= InstalledComponents=PCM, MIFENTRY, REMOTE_CONTROL AutoStartComponents=PCM, MIFENTRY, REMOTE_CONTROL
[SMS] UniqueIdPath=\\DEVFILE\SMS_SHR\S MSID\ INIFileVersion=66228 SiteCode=TUC	[SMS] BuildNo=692 INIFileVersion=66228 CopyListVersion=824252840 SiteCode=TUC SMS Unique ID=TUC0D00F

continues

Table B.10 Continued

DOMAIN.INI a	SMS.INI
SMSPath=C:\MS\SMS	SMSPath=C:\MS\SMS
	SMSBinPath=C:\MS\SMS\BIN
StandaloneISVMIFPath=C:\MS\SMS\idmifs	StandaloneISVMIFPath=C:\MS\SMS\idmifs
MachineISVMIFPath=C:\MS\SMS\noidmifs	MachineISVMIFPath=C:\MS\SMS\noidmifs
	LocalWindowsPath=C:\WIN95
	SharedWindowsPath=C:\WIN95
	SMSLogPath=C:\MS\SMS\LOGS
	SMSDataPath=C:\MS\SMS\DATA
	SMSTempPath=C:\MS\SMS\TEMP
	SMSLocalTempPath=C:\MS\SMS\TEMP
	SharedWindowsBinaries=No
	SharedSMSBinaries=No
	ModifyAutoexecBat=Yes
	LogonRoot=
LastLogonServerPath=\\DEVFILERO\SMS_SHR\	
UniqueIdPath=\\DEVFILERO\SMS_SHR\SMSID\	
LastSoftwareScan=19960418121126.000000+000	
LastHardwareScan=19960418121126.000000+000	
SoftwareScanInterval=1	SoftwareScanInterval=1
HardwareScanInterval=1	HardwareScanInterval=1
InvAgtFalseLogonCount=3	InvAgtFalseLogonCount=3
inventoryCollectionPoint=inventry.box	InventoryCollectionPoint=inventry.box
	SlowNetFlag=no
	OS=5
ISVMIFCollectionPoint=isvmif.box	ISVMIFCollectionPoint=isvmif.box
InvAgtServiceWakeupInterval=1440	InvAgtServiceWakeupInterval=1440
CompanyName=Integra Technology	CompanyName=Integra Technology
NetworkType=2	NetworkType=2
	[Local]
	SetupPhase=installed
	LanguageCode=00000409
	SystemType=X86-based PC
	SystemRole=WorkStation
	MachineName=HADFIELD
	NetCardID=00:60:8c:bb:5a:3f
	ShowPCMIntroDialog=FALSE
	LastPCMFileTime=829466094
	LastPCMFileTime=829466094
	LastPCMFileTime=829466094
	UserName=Lee Hadfield
	CompanyName=Integra Technology

DOMAIN.INI a	SMS.INI
[SIGHT] Allow Takeover=No Allow Reboot=No Allow File Transfer=No Allow Chat=No Allow Remote Execute=No Visible Signal=Yes Audible Signal=Yes Allow Ping Test=No Allow DOS Diagnostics=No Allow Windows Diagnostics=No Permission Required=Yes	[Sight] Allow Takeover=No Allow Reboot=No Allow File Transfer=No Allow Chat=No Allow Remote Execute=No Visible Signal=Yes Audible Signal=Yes Allow Ping Test=No Allow DOS Diagnostics=No Allow Windows Diagnostics=No Permission Required=Yes
InventoryOnlyFlag=1 FileTime=31694986 SectionMatch=machine KeyMatch=HADFIELD Domain=develop	[SMSLSIni] FileName=Z:\smsls.ini
[LogonHistory] Entry= Counter=0	
[UserName] Counter=0	

SMSLS.INI

Modifying the SMSLS.INI file allows us to map a computer to a domain that is not the logon domain of the user. The section entitled "How to Control Domain Mapping" in Chapter 9, gives an explanation of how to use the SMSLS.INI file to map computers to non-logon domains.

We continue our previous example with a listing of the SMSLS.INI file from the TUCSON SMS Site. Note the previous SMS.INI file listing has a section named [SMSLSIni]. This section has derived its entries from the SMSLS.INI file. In this case, entries were placed in the SMSLS.INI file's [machine] section to map the computer named HADFIELD to the DEVELOP domain. The following [SMSLSIni] section entries were added to the SMS.INI file as a result.

```
SectionMatch=machine
KeyMatch=HADFIELD
Domain=develop
```

This causes the inventory for the computer HADFIELD to be reported in the DEVELOP domain (as illustrated in figure B.9), even though the user of the computer logs on to the domain named ADOMAIN. You can use this as a tool to organize your site's inventory reporting structure to represent better the actual resource groups in which people most often work. In our example, the computer HADFIELD is represented as using the resources of the DEVELOP domain the most.

Here's the listing of the SMSLS.INI file. Notice the remarks placed in the listing give you a good idea of how to use the file. It begins with an explanation of SETLS and how it uses the SMSLS.INI file.

```
; SMSLS.INI is an initialization file used by the SETLS program.
;
; SETLS is called by the SMSLS batch file. When you run SMSLS.BAT or
; SMSLS.CMD as part of a logon script, the SETLS program (which is run
; within the SMSLS batch file) uses the SMSLS.INI to find a server in
; the domain where the workstation should be added to a site.
;
; SETLS evaluates SMSLS.INI from top to bottom. It will use the first
; successful match in the list. After it has found a match, it will use
; the mapped domain as the workstation's SMS domain and attempt to find
; a server within that domain randomly. SETLS then connects to that
; server and runs Client Setup and Inventory Agent programs from that
; server. This adds the workstation to the mapped domain.
;
; The SMSLS.INI file enables you to map existing configurations on a
; workstation to a domain that is part of an SMS site. By using these
; mappings, a workstation will appear in the specific domain that you
; want—regardless of which domain that the workstation actually logs
; on to. You can map the following workstation configurations to a SMS
; domain:
```

It continues with the [WIN.INI] section. This section is for reference and contains only comments.

```
[WIN.INI]

; This section enables Windows workstations to use the domain specified
; by the [SMS] section in the workstation's WIN.INI file. The [WIN.INI]
; section in the SMSLS.INI file requires no entries. At Windows
; workstations, you create an [SMS] section in WIN.INI and add the
; domain entry to that section to set the workstation's SMS domain. For
; example, you would add the following lines to WIN.INI to set the
; workstation's SMS domain to CSUEDOMAIN:
;      [SMS]
;         domain = CSUEDOMAIN
```

Read this section if you plan on incorporating LAN Manager 2.x Enhanced workstations in the SMS system.

```
[other domain]

; This section enables LAN Manager 2.x Enhanced workstations to use
; the domains in the OTHDOMAINS entry of the WORKSTATION section in
; the workstation's LANMAN.INI file to map to an SMS domain. The SETLS
; program tries to map a domain in the OTHDOMAINS entry starting with
; the first domain in the OTHDOMAINS entry. In the SMSLS.INI file, you
; add the [OTHER DOMAIN] section with entries that map the domain
```

```
; entries for the OTHDOMAINS in the workstations' LANMAN.INI to SMS
; domains. The entries in the section have the following form:
; otherdomain = SMSDomain
; where otherdomain is the name of the domain from the workstation's
; OTHDOMAINS entry that you want to map to an SMS domain. SMSDomain
; is the name of the domain to which the domain is mapped.
; Example:
; [other domain]
;    CSUESOUTH=CSUEDOMAIN
;    CSUENORTH=CSUEDOMAIN
;    *=CSUETEST
```

This section comes in very handy if you would like to organize the computers in your SMS domain by the workgroup they belong to.

```
[workgroup]

; This section enables Windows NT, Windows for Workgroups, and MS-DOS
; Workgroup Connection workstations to map the workgroup set on the
; workstation to a SMS domain. The entries in the section have the
; following form:
; workgroup = SMSDomain
; where workgroup is the name of the workgroup that you want to map to
; an SMS domain. SMSDomain is the name of the domain to which the
; workgroup is mapped.
; Example:
; [workgroup]
;    ACCOUNTING=admindom
;    SALES=admindom
;    MAINTENANCE=helpdom
;    *=testdom
```

Use this section if you would like to completely remap an entire logon domain to a specific SMS domain.

```
[domain]

; This section enables Windows NT, Windows for Workgroups, MS-DOS
; Workgroup Connection, and LAN Manager 2.x Enhanced workstations to
; map the domain where the workstation user is currently logged on to an
; SMS domain. The entries in the section have the following form:
; logondomain = SMSDomain
; where logondomain is the name of the domain that you want to map to
; a SMS domain. SMSDomain is the name of the domain to which the domain
; is mapped.
; Example:
; [domain]
;    admindom=admindom
;    masterdom=admindom
;    *=testdom
```

This section allows you to map an individual machine to the SMS domain of your choice. Notice the entry "hadfield=develop" in the [machine] section listed below. This statement will cause the computer to be inventoried in the DEVELOP domain even though the user logs into the domain named ADOMAIN.

```
[machine]

; This section enables Windows NT, Windows for Workgroups, MS-DOS
; Workgroup Connection, and LAN Manager 2.x Enhanced workstations, to
; map individual computers to an SMS domain. The entries in the section
; have the following form:
; computername = SMSDomain
; where computername is the name of the computer that you want to map to
; an SMS domain. SMSDomain is the name of the domain to which the
; computer name is mapped.
; Example:
; [machine]
;    *=admindom
hadfield=develop ; modified to place machine hadfield in develop domain
```

The use of the asterisk (*) as a wildcard is permitted to allow the mapping of all workgroups, domains or machines to a single domain. Take note of the last statement if you intend on using the wildcard with other mappings in the same section.

```
; OTHER OPTIONS
; For the Workgroup, Domain, Other Domain, and Machine sections, you
; can specify an asterisk (*) on the left side of an entry to specify
; that all items are mapped to the domain on the right side. For
; example, the following entry for Workgroup would map all workgroups
; to CSUEDOMAIN:
; [WORKGROUP]
;      * = CSUEDOMAIN
;
; Note that the asterisk specifies all items; therefore, when you have
; a section with entries with specific mappings, you should place the
; entry that uses the asterisk at the end of that section.
```

Client Components

To this point we have been focusing on the various services and server-side components found in the SMS system. Just as important to the operation of SMS are the client-side components. SMS wouldn't function without these assorted client programs and files. The different client programs work in conjunction with the server services to provide the features that make SMS a powerful network administration tool.

The following is a list of the different functions that the client components are responsible for:

- Inventory collection at the client
- Package distribution using the client's Package Control Manager program
- Network application group control
- Remote troubleshooting of the client computer
- The user interface for entering MIF form information
- Component setup on client platforms

The functions listed above are not available on all client platforms. Look at Table B.11 to see which features are supported for the different client operating systems. After we review the different client components, we'll examine the SETLS command and see how its used within the SMSLS batch file to call the Client Setup and Inventory Agent programs. Then, in the last part of this section, the Client Setup program and its various command line options are discussed.

Table B.11 The Different Client Types and Their Supported Features

Client Platform	Supported Features	Features Not Supported
Windows 95	Inventory Package Command Manager Remote Troubleshooting MIF form entry	Network Application Group
Windows for Workgroups	Inventory Network Application Group Package Command Manager Remote Troubleshooting MIF form entry	
Windows Version 3.1	Inventory Network Application Group Package Command Manager Remote Troubleshooting MIF form entry	
DOS	Inventory Package Command Manager Remote Troubleshooting MIF form entry	Network Application Group
Windows NT	Inventory Network Application Group Package Command Manager MIF form entry	Remote Troubleshooting
Macintosh	Inventory Package Command Manager MIF form entry	Network Application Group Remote Troubleshooting
OS/2 1.3 and 2.0	Inventory	Network Application Group Package Command Manager Remote Troubleshooting MIF form entry
OS/2 2.1x	Inventory Package Command Manager MIF form entry	Network Application Group Remote Troubleshooting

Now we'll look at each one of the client components and see what programs and files are required to support it.

Inventory

We saw earlier in the appendix that NT servers have an Inventory Agent that runs as a service. The Inventory Agent is run as an executable on non-NT platforms, and provides exactly the same functions as the version that runs as a service. This Inventory Agent is responsible for collecting inventory from the servers and then for sending the information to the proper server directory in the form of *.RAW files (ASCII .MIF files for Macintosh and OS/2 systems), so that the Maintenance Manager can process them.

The actual executable file name of the Inventory Agent will vary, depending on the operating system it's associated with. Table B.12 lists the executable file names of the Inventory Agent and the operating systems it works with.

Table B.12 The Inventory Agent Executables Are Specific to the Operating System of the Client Computer

Program Executable Name	Supported Operating System
INVWIN32.EXE	Windows NT
INVDOS.EXE	Windows 95 Windows for Workgroups Windows 3.1 MS-DOS (version 5.0 or later)
INVMac	Macintosh (system 7.0.0 or later)
INVOS2.EXE	OS/2 (versions 1.3 and 2.x or later)

If the user is on a Windows NT or LAN Manager network, the Inventory Agent program is invoked when the client runs the SMSLS logon script batch file. If the client machine is logged on to a NetWare environment, the Inventory Agent is called from the system login script. For Macintosh machines, the Inventory Agent (INVMac) is run locally from the Macintosh startup folder when the Macintosh is started.

Inventory Agent command line switches can be used for several purposes, such as forcing certain actions to be performed or displaying verbose progress information on the status of the agent. Modifications can be made to the appropriate command line in the SMSLS, or RUNSMS, batch file to configure the Inventory Agent to use these switches.

Table B.13 lists the various switches.

Table B.13 Inventory Agent Command Line Switches

Command Line Switch	Description
/a:*architecture*	Allows you to specify the architecture of the client.
/e	Used with INVWIN32.EXE and INVOS2.EXE to allow them to be run as executables on server platforms.
/f	Forces the Inventory Agent to perform a software and hardware scan regardless of the scan interval.
/i	The Inventory Agent will not perform any tasks except inventory collection.
/l:*uncpath*	Allows you to specify the UNC path to the logon server's SMS_SHR share.
/n	Tells the Inventory Agent to request a unique computer name.
/p:*collectionpoint*	The client's collection point is specified by the UNC pathname being placed in the switch.
/t:*timeoutinterval*	Allows you to specify the INVWIN32.EXE timeout interval in minutes.
/v	Specifies that detailed progress information will be displayed for the Inventory Agent while it is executing. The information displayed can scroll past the screen before you can read it. To remedy this problem, pipe the output of the command to a text file: invdos /v >info.txt.
/?	Displays command line help.

Later, during our look at the SETLS program, you will be able to see how the correct version of the Inventory Agent is determined. You'll also see how to pass arguments to the Inventory Agent using the SETLS command line.

Network Application Group Control

Network Application Group Control actually refers to two separate activities. Each activity has its own executables that perform part of the application group control task. Three operating systems currently support Network Application Group Control; they are as follows:

- Windows 3.1
- Windows for Workgroups
- Windows NT

The first task is accomplished by the executable files SMSRUN16.EXE or SMSRUN32.EXE.

SMSRUN The SMSRUN executable is used to create program groups and start applications on the client computer. On Windows 3.1 and Windows for Workgroups clients, the WIN.INI file is modified to include the following statement:

```
load=c:\ms\sms\smsrun16.exe
```

This statement calls the SMSRUN16.EXE program.

On NT machines the following registry key:

```
HKEY_Current_User\Software\Microsoft\WindowsNT\CurrentVersion\Windows\Load
```

is modified to start SMSRUN32.EXE. Both of these files read and parse their associated initialization file (SMSRUN16.INI or SMSRUN32.INI) to determine what program groups to create and which applications to start. In figure B.10 we show the location of the SMSRUN32.INI file, followed by a listing of its contents.

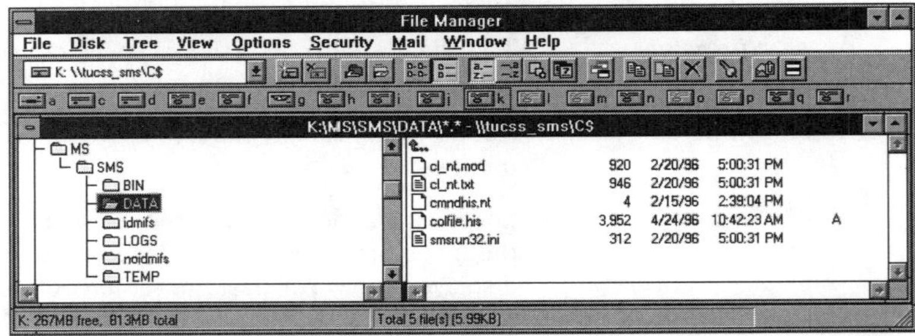

FIG. B.10 The location of SMSRUN32.INI on a Windows NT client.

```
[SMS Client]
SMS Client Help=C:\MS\SMS\BIN\sm32.hlp
Package Command Manager=C:\MS\SMS\BIN\pcmwin32.exe
Program Group Control=C:\MS\SMS\BIN\appctl32.exe
MIF Entry=C:\MS\SMS\BIN\mifwin.exe

[startup]
load=C:\MS\SMS\BIN\pcmwin32.exe
load=C:\MS\SMS\BIN\appctl32.exe
load=C:\MS\SMS\BIN\mifwin.exe /SMSLS
load=APPSTA32.EXE msoffpro+word
```

The SMSRUN16 and SMSRUN32 files reside on the logon server's directory, as follows:

SMS\logon.srv*platform*.BIN

They originate from the site server's directory, as follows:

SMS\SITE.SRV\MAINCFG.BOX\CLIENT.SRC*platform*.BIN

when the components for the logon server are first installed.

APPCTL and APPSTART The second task is to ensure that the proper environment information is supplied to any program groups that have been created and to automatically start any program applications that are desired. This is accomplished by the Program Group Control (PGC) agents APPCTL and APPSTART.

The APPCTL (APPCTL32 or APPCTL16) or Application Control program starts by getting the required environment information from the Network Application Database (NAD). The list of servers in the [Servers] section of the SMS.INI file is used by the Application Control program randomly to choose a server containing NAD database. The NAD is created in the site server directory as follows:

```
SITE.SRV\MAINCFG.BOX\APPCTL.SRC\DATABASE
```

in the form of configuration files. The following two types of files make up the database:

- Configuration files that contain information about the program groups. These program group configuration files have the file extension .HGF.
- Configuration files that contain information about the program group items or applications. These application configuration files have the file extension .HAF.

If the required program configuration files are not found on the first server, it will randomly choose another server in the list in order to find the NAD database. APPCTL then uses the NAD database information to set up the Windows environment for the specific application, so that it will run correctly.

You can dump the contents of the NAD database to a text-based graphical display for troubleshooting purpose using the VIEWNAD.EXE utility. This utility is one of many found in the SMS CD's PSSTOOLS directory.

The general steps taken by the APPCTL program are as follows:

1. The NAD database is checked for new program groups and shared applications. The registry is updated for any new items that are found.
2. Obsolete shared applications are deleted and removed from the PGC internal data structures.
3. Permissions are checked for the shared packages. The database removes the shared applications object from the Insert Object dialog menus for any users that no longer have permissions to the shared application. It adds the application object back into the Insert Object dialog menu if permission is returned to a user.
4. Program group icons are verified and updated. Icons are added for any new groups, and removed for any applications that are no longer shared.

Once the server has been located, and the environment has been set, the APPSTART program (APPSTA32 or APPSTA16) is then responsible for starting the application. The SMSRUN32.INI file listed earlier gives us an example of an APPSTART command located under the [startup] section.

```
load=APPSTA32.EXE msoffpro+word
```

This line will start a shared application of MS Word on the client.

After the application program is shut down, APPCTL will clean up the environment and terminate any unused network connections.

Certain command options, listed in Table B.14, can be used to control the APPCTL program.

Table B.14 APPCTL Command Line Switches

Command Line Switch	Description
/stop	Terminates the current APPCTL session.
/hide	Can be used after the /stop switch to hide the program group control window.
/deinstall	Clears the Program Manager of any SMS program groups and will also clean the NT registry of any groups. This switch is incorrectly identified in the Administrators manual as the / delete switch.

The APPCTL32.EXE, APPCTL16.EXE, APPSTA32.EXE, and APPSTA16.EXE files reside on the logon server's directory, as follows:

`SMS\logon.srv\`*`platform`*`.BIN`

They too are replicated from the site server's directory, as follows:

`SMS\SITE.SRV\MAINCFG.BOX\CLIENT.SRC\`*`platform`*`.BIN`

when the components for the logon server are first installed. APPCTL32.EXE and APPCTL16.EXE are also installed locally on client computer in the directory as follows:

`MS\SMS\BIN`

Package Command Manager

Earlier we discussed the Package Command Manager for Windows NT and how it runs as a service on NT servers. Four other versions of the Package Command Manager (PCM) are used by SMS; each version works with a specific client operating system, as shown in Table B.15.

Table B.15 The Version of the PCM to Run Will Depend on the Client's Operating System

Program Executable Name	Supported Operating System
PCMWIN32.EXE	Windows NT
PCMWIN16.EXE	Windows for Workgroups Windows 3.1

Program Executable Name	Supported Operating System
PCMDOS.EXE	MS-DOS (version 5.0 or later)
PCMMac	Macintosh (system 7.0.0 or later)

The PCM will check the servers for new packages during the client logon and at each polling interval after that. This polling interval can be set using the Package Command Manager program or by editing the PollingInterval entry in the SMS.INI file. Remember, the values specified in the PCM program are written to the [Local] section of the SMS.INI file and take precedence over any value listed in the [Package Command Manager] section. An example of the SMS.INI entries pertaining to the PCM follows:


```
[Package Command Manager]
InstructionSharePoint=pcmins.box
ResultSharePoint=despoolr.box
LocalRegistryLocation=C:\MS\SMS\DATA\pcmhist.reg
PollingInterval=60
```

In this example, the polling interval has been set to 60 minutes.

The SMS.INI file is checked and provides the PCM with the polling interval, share point information, and the history file (PCMHIST.REG) location.

The PCM checks to see if any new packages are waiting at the server. The PCM operates by polling the designated logon server's SMS_SHR\PCMINS.BOX for binary PCM instruction files. These instruction files are targeted to a specific computer by using the target computer's SMS ID appended with the .INS extension as their file name.

When the PCM checks for new packages it takes the following actions:

- The PCM will display in the foreground whenever a new package is detected. The user can install the package then, or can choose to wait before installing the package. The user's options will depend on the type of the package.
- The PCM runs the package installation commands that install the package on the client.
- The PCM then stores the package information in the history file to indicate that the package has been executed.

The PCM executable files exist in several different locations, like the APPCTL programs. They are located in the directory as follows:

SMS\logon.srv*platform*.BIN

which is replicated from the site server's directory, as follows:

SMS\SITE.SRV\MAINCFG.BOX\CLIENT.SRC*platform*.BIN

They are also installed locally on the client computer in the directory as follows:

MS\SMS\BIN

Remote Troubleshooting Agents

The files USERTSR.EXE and USERIPX.EXE are files referred to as client agents. They are used on the client machine to enable remote diagnostics. USERTSR.EXE utilizes the first network protocol loaded at the client as its default to communicate with the Administrator Machine. The Administrator Machine must be running the same NetBIOS or IPX protocol as the client in order to communicate.

If the client machine has several protocols loaded on it, the client agent, USERTSR.EXE, uses the first loaded protocol specified by the *lana0* entry in the PROTOCOL.INI. A partial listing of a WFW PROTOCOL.INI file is shown below. In this example, NETBEUI is bound to lana0, while TCP/IP is bound to lana1.

```
[network.setup]
netcard=ms$elnk3,1,MS$ELNK3,2
lana0=ms$elnk3,1,ms$netbeui
lana1=ms$elnk3,2,tcpip-32n

[NETBEUI]
BINDINGS=MS$ELNK3
LANABASE=0

[MSTCP32]
BINDINGS=MS$ELNK3
LANABASE=1
```

In this case, USERTSR.EXE would use NETBEUI to communicate with the Administrator Machine. This does not apply to the client agent USERIPX.EXE since it supports only IPX/SPX.

The Administrator Machine may have one or more protocols loaded on it. When attempting a remote connection with a client, the Administrator Machine will try to connect using the first four of its loaded protocols. The order in which they are attempted is determined by the binding order in the Network Binding configuration.

At times the client stations may be running a lana0 protocol that is not the same as a protocol running on the Administrator's machine. In this situation, several options exist to create a common protocol, as follows:

1. Load the lana0 protocol that the client machine is using on to the Administrator Machine, and bind it as one of the first four loaded protocols.
2. Change the client's lana0 protocol to a protocol that is compatible with the Administrator Machine.
3. If the client is running multiple protocols, with a compatible protocol being loaded as lana1, lana2, or higher, use the /Lx switch on the USERTSR command line to force the client agent to use a common protocol. For example, if NETBEUI was the common protocol but was being loaded as lana2, you could edit the USERTSR line of the CLIENT.BAT file to include the switch /L2.

The AUTOEXEC.BAT file calls the CLIENT.BAT file, which is located in the MS/SMS/DATA directory of the client machine. A listing of a modified CLIENT.BAT file for our example follows:

```
REM SMS 1.1
C:\MS\SMS\BIN\SMSWORK.EXE
C:\MS\SMS\BIN\USERTSR.EXE /L2
```

Besides the /L switch, several more command line options are available to use with USERTSR and USERIPX. Table B.16 lists them for you.

Table B.16 USERTSR and USERIPX Command Line Options

Command Line Switch	Description
/L	Used with USERTSR.EXE to specify a lana number other than the default lana number (lana 0) as the protocol to be used to communicate with the administrator's machine. On WFW machines this switch must be used in conjunction with the /W switch.
/N	Disables mouse support between the administrator and client. Mouse activity is not captured and sent to the administrative program. This will save over 700 bytes of memory when used.
/0	Can solve problems experienced with older VGA cards having unreadable registers. Try this switch if remote support does not work correctly.
/S	Eliminates snow on older CGA adapters.
/U	Can be used to unload the USERTSR or USERIPX from memory, but only if outside the Windows environment.
/W	Causes USERTSR to wait until WUSER.EXE is started before initializing on the network. Used only with USERTSR.EXE on WFW 3.11 machines.
/v*flag* or /vNO*flag*	Can be used to set the remote access flags. Preceding the flag with NO will disable the function. This flag may be used while USERTSR is already loaded. The flags you can set are: *VIEW*—allows remote viewing of the client *CHAT*—allows the remote chat utility *FILEXFER*—enables remote file transfer ability *EXECUTE*—enables the remote execution of programs *REBOOT*—to reboot the client computer remotely *DOSDIAG*—allows MS-DOS diagnostics to be per formed on the client *WINDIAG*—allows Windows diagnostics to be performed on the client *PING*—enables ping testing.

continues

Table B.16 Continued

Command Line Switch	Description
/y*flag* or /yNO*flag*	The switch refers to local flags that can be set. Like the /v switch, the prefix NO can be added to the flag to disable the option. This flag may also be used while USERTSR is already loaded. The local flags are: *AUDIBLE*—causes an audible signal to be heard when the administrator is viewing the client *VISIBLE*—causes a visual signal to appear on the client screen when being viewed by the administrator *PERMISSION*—presents a dialog box to the user when an administrator attempts to view the client. The dialog box will prompt for user permission to be viewed by the administrator.
/?	Displays command line help.

Note that multiple command line switches may be used at once.

Another file used on the client computer is WUSER.EXE, known as the Remote Client Agent. This file must be started before any Help Desk functions can be performed on the client. The file icon can be placed in the Windows startup group for automatic execution during startup, or the program can be started manually from the Remote Control tool located in the SMS program group. Make sure this program is not running on the client computer before performing any upgrade of the SMS client components.

NOTE If you plan to use a TCP/IP protocol stack for communication between the client and administrator machines, you must make sure that the TCP/IP protocol stack you use supports NetBIOS. Remote control will not work properly unless the stack supports this.

The location of the WUSER.EXE file is referenced by the remote control entry in the SMSRUN16.INI file. Following is an example of the SMSRUN16.INI file on a WFW machine:

```
[SMS Client]
Package Command Manager=C:\MS\SMS\bin\pcmwin16.exe
Program Group Control=C:\MS\SMS\bin\appctl16.exe
Remote Control=C:\MS\SMS\bin\wuser.exe
Help Desk Options=C:\MS\SMS\bin\editini.exe
MIF Entry=C:\MS\SMS\bin\mifwin.exe
SMS Client Help=C:\MS\SMS\bin\sm16.hlp

[startup]
load=C:\MS\SMS\bin\pcmwin16.exe
load=C:\MS\SMS\bin\appctl16.exe
load=C:\MS\SMS\bin\mifwin.exe /SMSLS
```

You'll notice that the SMSRUN16.INI file shows the file locations of the other client components we have discussed. Three files that we haven't discussed are also referenced in the initialization file. They are MIFWIN.EXE, SM16.HLP, and EDITINI.EXE. MIFWIN.EXE is one version of the MIF form utility, which will be reviewed in the next section. The SM16.HLP is a standard MS help file for the SMS client. EDITINI is used to configure the SMS.INI file's [Sight] section entries from within Windows without having to edit manually the SMS.INI file with a text editor. The entries that can be changed are as follows in a [Sight] section excerpt from the SMS.INI file.


```
[Sight]
Allow Takeover=No
Allow Reboot=No
Allow File Transfer=No
Allow Chat=No
Allow Remote Execute=No
Visible Signal=Yes
Audible Signal=Yes
Allow Ping Test=No
Allow DOS Diagnostics=No
Allow Windows Diagnostics=No
Permission Required=Yes
```

You can see that the parameters listed here match those you can control in the Help Desk Option window of the EDITINI.EXE program shown in figure B.11. Changing a setting in the Help Desk Options will change the corresponding SMS.INI file entry. You may also notice that these are the same options that can be controlled with the USERTSR/USERIPX command line switches discussed earlier.

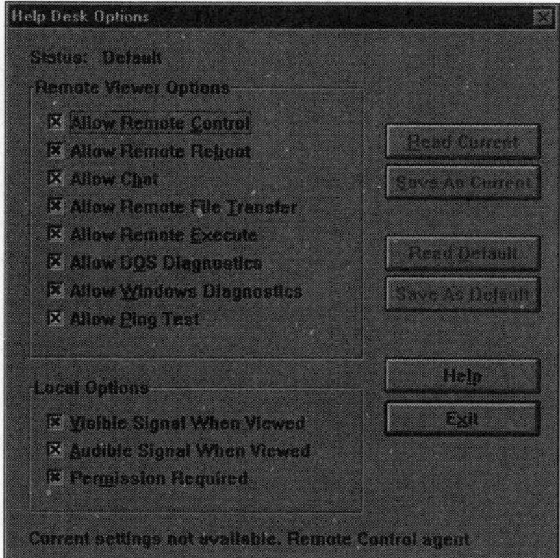

FIG. B.11
The Remote Control Help Desk Options that are configurable by the user match the SMS.INI entries.

MIF Form Utility

The MIF form utility allows the user of the workstation to fill in electronic forms (eforms) with specific information. Eforms can be used to gather information such as user names, telephone numbers, computer location, and so on. The information gathered in these forms can be added as an inventory object that can be displayed via the administration utility. A default form is installed on all SMS clients and appears the first time a new client logs on. The default form can used as it is or can be modified, or a completely new form can be made using the MIF Form Generator.

The actual MIF form utility program file will vary depending on the operating system of the client, as follows:

MIFDOS.EXE is used with MS-DOS clients that are not running Windows.

MIFWIN.EXE is used on clients running in the Windows environment.

MIFMAC.EXE is used on Macintosh clients.

The default form UINFO.XNF (located in the MS\SMS\bin directory) will automatically come up if the utility program is started and there are no other forms available. If other forms are available, the user is given the option of choosing which form to use.

When a MIF form is saved, the MIF utility creates a file with a .SEV extension. This file contains all the entries that were made to the form, and is saved to the path designated by the MachineISVMIFPath entry in the SMS.INI file, as follows:

```
MachineISVMIFPath=C:\MS\SMS\noidmifs
```

When the .SEV file is saved, a MIF file is created with the same name as the .SEV file but with a .MIF extension. This file is used to report the .SEV entries to the SMS system. As an example, if you look in the MS\SMS\noidmifs subdirectory on the client, you will see the .SEV and .MIF files for the default form file UINFO.XNF. The information contained in the .SEV file remains available to the user anytime he or she opens that form with the MIF form utility.

SETLS

During user logon, SETLS(xx) is called from the SMSLS batch file. SETLS is used to call, execute, and pass parameters to the Client Setup and Inventory Agent programs. A specific version of SETLS is required for each operating system and processor architecture. The SMSLS batch file determines the operating system and processor architecture, and calls the proper version of SETLS. Two versions of SETLS can be called: SETLS16 or SETLS32. We'll see how the correct version is determined shortly.

During SMSLS batch file exectution, SETLS scans the SMSLS.INI file. Scanning the SMSLS.INI file determines the correct logon server from which to run the client setup and inventory agent programs. The pertinent lines of the SMSLS batch file are shown below. Notice the way the SETLS file is called using the %SMS_OS% variable.

```
:RUN_DOS
setls%SMS_OS% -m:E -i -p:%SMS_BIN%\CLI_DOS.EXE -pa:/p:%%SMS_UNC%%\ -
pa:%SMS_VERBOSE% %SMS_VERBOSE%
setls%SMS_OS% -m:E -i -p:%SMS_BIN%\INVDOS.EXE  -pa:/l:%%SMS_UNC%%\ -pa:/i -
pa:%SMS_VERBOSE% %SMS_VERBOSE%
goto RESTORE

:RUN_NT
setls%SMS_OS% -m:E -i -p:%SMS_BIN%\CLI_NT.EXE   -pa:/p:%%SMS_UNC%%\ -
pa:%SMS_VERBOSE% %SMS_VERBOSE%
```

```
setls%SMS_OS% -m:E -i -p:%SMS_BIN%\INVWIN32.EXE -pa:/l:%%SMS_UNC%%\ -pa:/e -pa:/
t0 -pa:/i -pa:%SMS_VERBOSE% %SMS_VERBOSE%
```

The %SMS_OS% variable will determine which SETLS file to execute. Table B.17 shows the SETLS file name for each specific operating system.

Table B.17 The Version of SETLS Called Depends on the Operating System of the Client

Program Executable Name	Supported Operating System
SETLS16.EXE	DOS Windows for Workgroups Windows 3.1 Windows 95
SETLS32I.EXE	Windows NT Intel clients
SETLS32A.EXE	Windows NT Alpha clients
SETLS32M.EXE	Windows NT MIPS clients
SETLSOS2.EXE	OS/2 clients

The SMSLS batch file can be modified to include command line switches for the SETLS command. These switches can be used to set various parameters such as the default logon share, an initialization file other than SMSLS.INI, specific logical drive letter connections, and so on. In order to understand better how SETLS works, let's first look at the command line syntax and command line options following:

```
{setls16¦setls32¦setlsos2} [-m:E] [-p:programfile] [-pa:argument [-pa:argument]]
[-sh:sharename] [-sn] [-v:[on]] [-i[:inifile]]
{setls16¦setls32¦setlsos2} [-m:C] [-d:drive] [-dr:driverange] [-sh:sharename] [-
i[:inifile]] [-v[:on]]
{setls16¦setls32¦setlsos2} [-m:D] [-d:drive] [-v[:on]]
```

Table B.18 The Command Line Switches for the SETLS Program

Command Line Switch	Description
/m:C	Uses a logical drive letter to make the network connection.
/m:D	Deletes the network connection using a logical drive letter.
/m:E	Executes a program on a remote server without making a logical drive connection.
/sn	Prevents programs from running under slow network situations.
/d:*drive*	Specifies the specific drive letter, defaults to next available drive letter.

continues

Table B.18 Continued

Command Line Switch	Description
/dr:*driverange*	Can be used to limit the search for the next available network drive.
/sh:*sharename*	Specifies a share other than the default of SMS_SHR to connect to.
/i:*inifile*	Specifies an initialization file other than the default of SMSLS.INI.
/v[:on]	Can be used to specify the output message level, defaults to off.
/p:*programfile*	Specifies a file name or the relative path to a .EXE or .COM file.
/pa:*argument*	Passes a command line argument to a program when it is executed.

If we take one of the command lines for SETLS found in the SMSLS batch file and compare it to the command line syntax, we can begin to see how SETLS works. Let's examine the line calling the Client Setup program for NT operating system running on an Intel platform. Note that the information here also applies to the Inventory Agent program when it is called by the SETLS command.

The syntax for the SETLS command is as follows:

```
{setls16¦setls32¦setlsos2} [-m:E] [-p:programfile] [-pa:argument [-pa:argument]]
[-sh:sharename] [-sn] [-v:[on]] [-i[:inifile]]
```

The actual command line found in the SMSLS batch file that calls the NT Intel version of the Client Setup program is as follows:

```
setls%SMS_OS% -m:E -i -p:%SMS_BIN%\CLI_NT.EXE   -pa:/p:%%SMS_UNC%%\ -
pa:%SMS_VERBOSE% %SMS_VERBOSE%
```

Remember, each of the SETLS command lines has the specific operating system version of the Client Setup and Inventory Agent program hard-coded into it. In the example above, the CLI_NT.EXE (the Client Setup program for the NT operating system) will be called. Which version (Intel, MIPS, or Alpha) of the NT Client Setup program is called is determined by the variable %SMS_BIN%. We'll see that this variable is set at the same time the %SMS_OS% variable is set.

Finding the Version of SETLS to Run The version of SETLS that is called is determined by the value present in the variable %SMS_OS%. The following is the portion of our command line containing the %SMS_OS% variable:

```
setls%SMS_OS%
```

Let's follow the batch file execution as it determines the value of the variable. %SMS_OS% is determined by the following lines in the SMSLS batch file:

```
:FIND_OS
set SMS_TEMP=
if "%OS%" == "Windows_NT" goto NT_BIN
```

If the operating system variable %OS% equals "Windows_NT," the file execution jumps to the :NT_BIN label. If it doesn't equal "Windows_NT," the file execution will continue with a check of the DOS version using the DOSVER.COM program, as follows:

```
REM Determine the DOS version and exit if OS/2 1.3 or greater.
%0\..\dosver
if errorlevel 13 goto OS2
```

If dosver.com determines that the operating system is OS/2, it will jump program execution to the OS2 label. If DOSVER.COM does not produce an errorlevel 13 code it is determined that DOS is the current operating. Had the NT operating system not been detected, the value of %SMS_OS% would have been set here to the value of 16 as follows:

```
:DOS_BIN
set SMS_OS=16
set SMS_BIN=x86.bin
goto RUN_FROM
```

Since the NT operating system has been detected, file execution will jump to the :NT_BIN label, as follows:

```
:NT_BIN
if "%PROCESSOR_ARCHITECTURE%" == "ALPHA" goto NT_ALPHA
if "%PROCESSOR_ARCHITECTURE%" == "MIPS"  goto NT_MIPS
if "%PROCESSOR_ARCHITECTURE%" == "x86"   goto NT_X86
```

The file execution branches to the proper code base on the type of processor architecture.

If an Alpha, MIPS, or Intel architecture is detected, the %SMS_OS% variable is set to 32. Notice, however, that the *%SMS_BIN%* variable will be different for each one. If the Alpha processor is detected, the %SMS_BIN% variable is set to "alpha.bin" as follows:

```
:NT_ALPHA
set SMS_BIN=alpha.bin
set SMS_OS=32
goto RUN_FROM
```

If a MIPS architecture is detected, the value is set to "mips.bin" as follows:

```
:NT_MIPS
set SMS_BIN=mips.bin
set SMS_OS=32
goto RUN_FROM
```

And if the Intel architecture is detected, the variable is set to "x86.bin" as follows:

```
:NT_X86
set SMS_BIN=x86.bin
set SMS_OS=32
goto RUN_FROM
```

The value of this variable determines the directory location of the Client Setup and Inventory Agent programs. Both of these programs are located in directories that are specific to each of the operating systems (Intel, MIPS, Alpha, DOS, and so on). In our example the value of the variable was set to "x86.bin".

The Other Command Line Variables The next part of the command line is as follows:

```
-m:E -i -p:%SMS_BIN%\CLI_NT.EXE
```

This specifies that it is to execute [-m:E] the program CLI_NT.EXE from the directory specified by the %SMS_BIN% variable.

The -pa: %%SMS_UNC%% argument will pass the path of the logon server to the CLI_NT.EXE program, as follows:

```
-pa:/p:%%SMS_UNC%%\
```

The -pa:%SMS_VERBOSE% argument will pass the /v switch to CLI_NT.EXE program if the set SMS_VERBOSE statement in the beginning of the SMSLS batch file has been set to equal one, as follows:

```
-pa:%SMS_VERBOSE%
```

Following is another look at the beginning of the SMSLS batch file and the section that determines the value of the %SMS_VERBOSE% variable:

```
REM If the SMSLS environment variable is set on the workstation (e.g.,
REM set SMSLS=1), verbose output will be enabled for SETLS16, CLI_DOS,
REM and INVDOS or SETLS32, CLI_NT and INVWIN32.

if "%SMSLS%" == "" goto START
set SMS_VERBOSE=/v
echo Executing SMS logon script.
goto START
```

As you can see, if the SMSLS variable is null, then the set SMS_VERBOSE=/v statement is skipped. When the SMSLS variable has been set equal to 1, the set statement shown above will cause the %SMS_VERBOSE% environmental variable to be set equal to /v. The /v will then be passed as an argument to the CLI_NT.EXE program. This in turn will cause the CLI_NT.EXE program to display verbose information to the screen when it is executed from the SETLS command line.

This information may scroll across the screen too quickly to read. To make the output easier to read, edit the SETLS command line in the SMSLS batch file to redirect the output to a text file. You may not want to make these modifications to the SMSLS.BAT or SMSLS.CMD, since these files run on all clients. Instead, edit the RUNSMS.BAT or RUNSMS.CMD, which can be run from the command line on a specific client during troubleshooting.

Just add the switch -pa:>*filename*.txt to the SETLS command line to pipe the output to a file with a .TXT extension. Then you can use a text editor to review the contents of the file and see the verbose output from the CLI_NT.EXE program. This same method can be used to pipe the output of the Inventory Agent to a text file.

Client Setup Program

Our next subject is the Client Setup program. It performs several important tasks related to client setup. The following is an overview of what it does:

- The Client Setup program will determine the current state of the client installation and will then setup, upgrade, or remove client components as required.
- If the SMS.INI file does not exist at the client computer, a new installation of the client components will be performed on the computer.
- The program updates the client installation when needed. It reads the DOMAIN.INI file and updates the SMS.INI as required, and also uses the information found in the DOMAIN.INI to add or remove files from the client installation.
- The program removes client components from the client computer when run in removal mode.

This program can be run manually, but is normally executed by the SETLS command in the SMSLS or RUNSMS batch file (or from the system login script on NetWare clients). It can be executed in the removal mode by running the DEINSTAL batch file.

The Client Setup program will run each time a user logs on if the SMSLS batch file is added as, or is called by, the user's network login script. It will also run if the RUNSMS batch file is manually executed from a client computer.

The Client Setup program is operating system-specific. The SMSLS (or RUNSMS) batch file determines the version and location of the Client Setup program to run for each specific client platform. Five versions of the Client Setup program are used: three are NT versions, one is an OS2 version, and the other version works with DOS, Windows 3.1, Windows for Workgroups, and Windows 95-based clients. Table B.19 shows the file name, location, and associated operating system for each version.

Table B.19 The Client Setup Program Executable File Name and Its Location for Each OS Version

Program Executable Path and Name	Supported Operating System
LOGON.SRV\X86.BIN\CLI_DOS.EXE	DOS Windows for Workgroups Windows 3.1 Windows 95
LOGON.SRV\X86.BIN\CLI_NT.EXE	Windows NT Intel clients
LOGON.SRV\ALPHA.BIN\CLI_NT.EXE	Windows NT Alpha clients
LOGON.SRV\MIPS.BIN\CLI_NT.EXE	Windows NT MIPS clients
LOGON.SRV\X86.BIN\CLI_OS2.EXE	OS/2 clients

Before we look at the Client Setup program's different modes of operation, we'll take a look at the various command line options available to it. Table B.20 gives a list of these options.

Table B.20 Command Line Options for the Client Setup Program.

Command Line Switch	Description
/d:*drive*	By default, SMS installs the client components to the drive with the most free space. Use this switch to override the default.
/f	Can be used to verify that all client components are installed and configured correctly.
/p:*path*	Used to designate a specific path for the logon server share (SMS_SHR) either by a drive letter or UNC pathname.
/q	Allows you to override the default language set by the country code.
/r	Designates that the Client Setup program is to be run in "removal" mode. This option will stop all SMS client components, require a reboot, and then remove the client components from the computer.
/u	Specifies that the client components are to be stopped and the client computer rebooted, and that the client components are to be updated.
/v	Instructs the Client Setup program to run in verbose mode, displaying status messages to the screen as it executes. Used in troubleshooting client problems.

Now we'll go over the different modes of operation, starting with some of the standard tasks that the Client Setup program performs each time it's run.

Client Setup Program Standard Tasks The following tasks are normally performed each time the Client Setup program is run:

1. A check is made to determine if the SMS.INI file exists on the client. If no SMS.INI file is found, the Client Setup program will consider this a new installation. See Client Setup program installation tasks in the next section.
2. The operating system that the client is running is detected, and the language used on the computer is determined. Once the Client Setup program has established which operating system is being used on the client, it will use the appropriate copy-list and modification files for that platform to perform any file updates that are needed on the client.
3. The program reads the DOMAIN.INI file to determine if any updates need to be performed on the local SMS.INI file. Comparing the Components and AutoStart entries in the [SMS] section of the DOMAIN.INI file to the InstalledComponents and AutoStartComponents entries in the [WorkstationStatus] section will determine which client components need to be installed or removed from the client.

4. The program determines if a local copy of the copy-list file (CL_x.TXT) exists. The list of files in the copy-list file is compared to the files that are actually installed on the client. It does this to determine if older files that need to be deleted exist on the client. If a local copy of the CL_x.TXT file is not present, the Client Setup Program uses the copy-list file found on the logon server to do this.
5. Checks the FilesNotDownloaded entry of the [WorkstationStatus] section of the SMS.INI for any files that were not previously downloaded, and attempts to recopy them before exiting.

Client Setup Program Installation Mode Tasks The requirement for a new client component installation is detected by the absence of the SMS.INI file on the client computer. After the standard tasks are completed, the following additional actions are taken by the Client Setup program:

1. A temporary SMS.INI file is created on the root of the client's boot drive.
2. The copy-list (CL_x.TXT) file and the components entry of the [SMS] section of the DOMAIN.INI file are use to determine which files get copied to the client computer.
3. The files determined in step 2 are then copied to the drive with the most free space. The exception to this being if the /d:drive option was specified on the Client Setup program command line. In that case the files would be copied to the drive specified by the option switch.
4. The names of any files that are designated to be copied to the client but can't be because they are missing or in use are placed in the SMS.INI file's FilesNotDownloaded entry. The Client Setup program will attempt to recopy these files the next time it is run.
5. The program creates a local copy of the CL_x.TXT file in the MS\SMS\DATA directory on the client computer.
6. The program uses the modification files found in the LOGON.SRV\X86.BIN*language_id* (*.MOD) and the [SMS] section of the DOMAIN.INI file to modify the client computer's configuration. This includes the modification of registry keys, initialization files, DOS startup files, and so on.

The type of operating system (NT, Windows, or DOS) being run on the client computer will determine what unique modifications need to be made to the client configuration. After the OS specific modifications have taken place, the SetupPhase entry of the SMS.INI file's [Local] section is modified to reflect an installed state, as follows:

```
[Local]
SetupPhase=installed
```

Let's take a closer look at the modifications that take place for each one of the client operating system types.

NT Clients Here's a list of events that take place during the installation of an NT Client.

1. The SMSRUN32.INI file is created on the client computer's MS\SMS\BIN directory using information derived from the logon server's CL_NT.MOD file. It specifies which

applications to start automatically and what program groups to create on the client computer.

2. SMSRUN32.EXE is started by the Client Setup program. It reads the newly created SMSRUN32.INI file and runs the programs specified in the file's [Startup] section.
3. Client Setup modifies the registry key HKEY_CURRENT_USER\Software\Microsoft\WindowsNT\CurrentVersion\Windows\Load to start the SMSRUN32.EXE file automatically on startup. From this point on, the Client Setup program will not run SMSRUN32.EXE unless for some reason the load statement is missing from the registry key.

Windows 3.1, Windows for Workgroups, and Windows 95 Clients Here's the list of events that take place during the installation of a Windows 3.1, WFW or Windows 95 Client.

1. The SMSRUN16.INI file is created on the client computer's MS\SMS\BIN directory using information derived from the logon server's CL_WIN.MOD file. It specifies which applications to start automatically and what program groups to create on the client computer.
2. The WIN.INI file's LOAD= line is modified to include the SMSRUN16.EXE statement. Windows then uses this statement to run SMSRUN16.EXE, which in turn automatically starts any specified applications and creates any specified groups.
3. A file called CLIENT.BAT is created in the MS\SMS\BIN directory on the client computer. The AUTOEXEC.BAT file is modified to call the CLIENT.BAT file.
4. Certain settings in the [386Enh] section of the SYSTEM.INI file are modified if remote control is to be used on the client. The following modifications take place:

    Modifies the line: Device=vuser.386;

    Modifies the line: NetHeapSize=24 (set to 24 if the current value is less than 24, not modified if the value exceeds 24);

    Attempts to recopy any files that failed to copy during the original file copy process;

    The CLIENT.BAT file is modified to run the USERTSR.EXE or USERIPX.EXE. Which one of the files is run is determined by the network type.

The following is a look at the modification file CL_W95.MOD for a Windows 95 client. The first section contains the instructions to modify the CLIENT.BAT file:

```
[STANDARD]
mod client.bat              ADD_CLIENT_LINE REM SMS 1.1
mod client.bat              ADD_CLIENT_LINE %SMSBIN%\SMSWORK.EXE
```

The next section adds the Package Command Manager to the configuration and sets it to start automatically when Windows 95 loads, as follows:

```
[PCM]
mod %SMSDATA%\smsrun16.ini  ADD_IF_NOT_SET  "SMS Client"  "Package Command
Manager"   %SMSBIN%\pcmwin16.exe
[AUTOSTART_PCM]
```

```
mod %SMSDATA%\smsrun16.ini  ADD_IF_NOT_SET  "startup"  "load"
%SMSBIN%\pcmwin16.exe
```

The [REMOTE CONTROL] section adds the WUSER.EXE and EDITINI.EXE programs to the client configuration. It continues with modification instructions for the SYSTEM.INI file, as follows:

```
[REMOTE_CONTROL]
mod %SMSDATA%\smsrun16.ini  ADD_IF_NOT_SET  "SMS Client"  "Remote Control"
%SMSBIN%\wuser.exe
mod %SMSDATA%\smsrun16.ini  ADD_IF_NOT_SET  "SMS Client"  "Help Desk Options"
%SMSBIN%\editini.exe
[REMOTE_CONTROL_386]
mod system.ini              ADD_IF_NOT_SET  "386enh"  "device"
%WINBIN%\VUser.386
mod system.ini              ADD_OR_REPLACE_IF_LESS_THAN "386enh"  "NetHeapSize"
24
```

The following section gives Client Setup program modification instructions that will update the CLIENT.BAT file to call the USERTSR.EXE file. This file (or USERIPX.EXE) is required for communication between the client and the Administrator Machine:

```
[AUTOSTART_REMOTE_CONTROL_LANMAN]
mod client.bat              ADD_CLIENT_LINE %SMSBIN%\USERTSR.EXE /w
```

The following entry instructs the Client Setup program to add the MIF program to the configuration and automatically start it during Windows 95 startup:

```
[MIFENTRY]
mod %SMSDATA%\smsrun16.ini  ADD_IF_NOT_SET  "SMS Client"   "MIF Entry"
%SMSBIN%\mifwin.exe

[AUTOSTART_MIFENTRY]
mod %SMSDATA%\smsrun16.ini  ADD_IF_NOT_SET  "startup"   "load"
%SMSBIN%\mifwin.exe /SMSLS
```

The second [STANDARD] section instructs the Client Setup program to place a call to the CLIENT.BAT file in the client computer's AUTOEXEC.BAT file. In addition, it includes instructions for adding the load SMSRUN16 statement to the WIN.INI file. Then it adds the instructions needed to include the SMS client help file in the configuration, as follows:

```
[STANDARD]
mod autoexec.bat            ADD_CLIENT_CALL  call %SMSDATA%\client.bat
mod win.ini                 ADD_TO_LIST     "windows"  "load"
%SMSBIN%\smsrun16.exe
mod %SMSDATA%\smsrun16.ini  ADD_IF_NOT_SET  "SMS Client"   "SMS Client Help"
%SMSBIN%\sm16.hlp
```

DOS Clients not Running Windows Here are the actions that take place for a DOS only client:

1. A file called CLIENT.BAT is created in the MS\SMS\BIN directory on the client computer. The AUTOEXEC.BAT file is then modified to call the CLIENT.BAT file.

2. If remote control will be used, the CLIENT.BAT file is modified to run the USERTSR.EXE or USERIPX.EXE. Which one of the files is run is determined by the network type.
3. The CLIENT.BAT is modified to run the Package Command Manager.

Client Setup Program Upgrade Mode Tasks You can upgrade a current client installation by running the Client Setup program using the /u command line option. This causes the appropriated client component files to be replaced with newer versions. It also makes any system file modifications that are required by the upgrade. Before you run the Client Setup command from the command line, make sure you are in the proper logon server directory for the client operating system and/or platform you are working from.

On DOS-based machines that do not have Windows installed, the upgrade process is performed in one phase. In this phase all the necessary files are replaced and system files modified. On Windows-based clients this upgrade is performed to two phases as follows:

> The first phase modifies the SMS.INI file's [Local] section SetupPhase entry to equal UPGRADE, as follows:
>
> ```
> [Local]
> SetupPhase=upgrade
> ```
>
> The second phase requires a reboot of Windows clients and a logoff and logon of NT clients.

During the second phase of the client upgrade the following will occur:

1. The SMSRUN file scans the SMS.INI file and detects the UPGRADE phrase.
2. SMSRUN continues the process by starting the SMSSRV program with the /c switch.
3. SMSRUN then exits, leaving SMSSRV to call the Client Setup program to complete the upgrade process.
4. Once the user has logged back on, SMSSRV invokes the Client Setup program with the /k switch.
5. The Client Setup program then removes any files required for the proper completion of the upgrade.
6. Then the Client Setup program modifies any SMS-related statements in the system files and copies any new client component files that are needed from the logon server.
7. SMSSRV then uses the SMSRUN16 or SMSRUN32 initialization files to set up the SMS Client program group. Then it starts the client components that are configured to start automatically. When it has completed starting the client components, SMSSRV exits.

Client Setup Program Removal Mode Tasks The removal mode of the Client Setup program is invoked using the /r command line option. As its name implies, it is used to remove the client components from a computer. Once again, before you run the Client Setup command from the command line, make sure you are in the proper logon server directory for the client operating system and/or platform you are working from.

Client removal can also be accomplished by running the DEINSTAL.BAT batch file from the logon server share. DEINSTAL.BAT will detect the operating system type (and processor architecture if needed) and automatically run the correct version of the Client Setup program with the /r switch. Regardless of how the Client Setup program is invoked, the removal mode still performs the same steps

On DOS-based machines that do not have Windows installed, the removal process is performed in one pass. In this phase, all the SMS files are removed from the client, and all SMS-related entries are deleted from the system files. Like the Client Setup program running in upgrade mode, removal mode on Windows-based clients is also performed to two phases, as follows:

The first phase modifies the SMS.INI file's [Local] section SetupPhase entry to equal DEINSTALL, as follows:

```
[Local]
SetupPhase=deinstall
```

The second phase requires a reboot of Windows clients and a logoff/logon of NT clients.

During the second phase of the client removal process, the following occurs:

1. The SMSRUN file scans the SMS.INI file and detects the DEINSTALL phrase.
2. SMSRUN continues the process by starting the SMSSRV program with the /c switch.
3. SMSRUN then exits, leaving SMSSRV to call the client setup program to complete the removal process.
4. Once the user has logged back on, SMSSRV invokes the client setup program with the /k switch.
5. The Client Setup program then removes any SMS components from the computer.
6. Then the Client Setup program completes the removal process by eliminating any SMS-related statements from the computer's system files.

The SMS Database Manager DBCLEAN

The SMS Database Maintenance Utility can be used to delete most types of old or unused records from the SMS database. The actual file name of the SMS Database Maintenance Utility is DBCLEAN.EXE. It is located in the SITE.SRV*platform*.BIN directory on all computers that have the SMS Administrator installed.

CAUTION

Before you use the SMS Database Maintenance Utility, note that the SMS Database Maintenance Utility is a very powerful tool and should be used by experienced SMS systems administrators only. It contains no help files and can be confusing to the novice administrator. In addition, it is always wise to have a current backup of the database before performing any maintenance tasks on it.

The SMS Database Maintenance Utility allows you to perform several maintenance tasks on the SMS database. You can use the utility to delete or merge duplicate machine records, delete unused database records, delete Group Classes, and remove collected files that are no longer referenced to the SMS database.

Let's examine the utility by looking at examples of the tasks that can be performed using the database maintenance utility.

CAUTION
Before you use the database maintenance utility take note—database problems can result if the SMS Database Maintenance Utility is used to remove or alter objects in the database while that database is currently opened by another administrator using the SMS Administration program.

Setting up the Database Maintenance Utility and Logging on

The easiest way to make the utility available is to open File Manager and drag the executable file DBCLEAN.EXE from the SITE.SRV*platform*.BIN directory to SMS Administrators Group. The Database Maintenance utility will appear in the Administrator's Program Group, as shown in figure B.12.

FIG. B.12 The Administrators Program Group after adding the DB Maintenance Utility Icon.

Once in the program group, you can easily start the utility with a double-click of the mouse.

You start the maintenance utility by logging into the SQL database. This is done in exactly the same way you log on to the database when starting the SMS Administration Program. Figure B.13 shows the logon screen that the maintenance utility displays.

Once you've successfully logged on, you can start to use the utility. The utility will display a rather plain window with a pull-down menu, as shown in figure B.14.

From this screen you can perform several database maintenance tasks, including the following:

- Deleting duplicate machine records from the SQL SMS database.
- Merging duplicate machine records in the SQL SMS database.
- Setting Machine Group preferences.
- Deleting group classes.
- Deleting unused records.
- Deleting abandoned collected files.

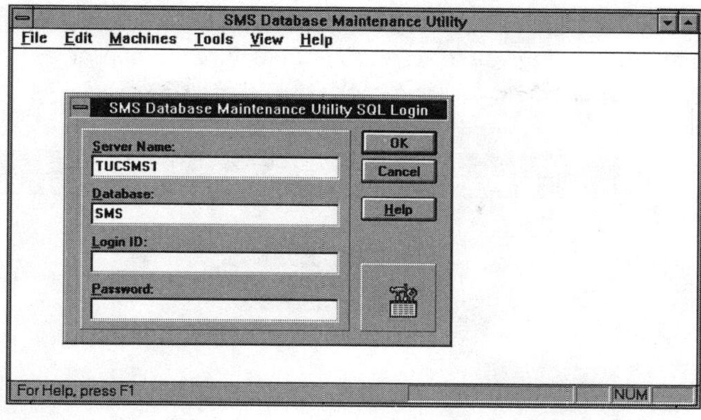

FIG. B.13 The SMS Database Maintenance Utility logon screen is exactly the same screen you see when logging in to the SMS Administration Program.

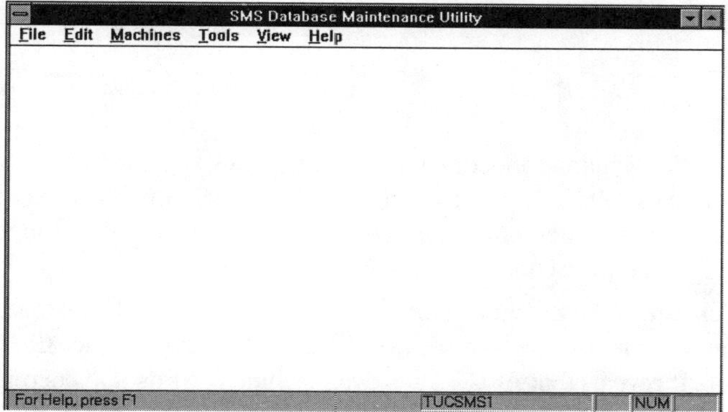

FIG. B.14 The SMS Database Maintenance Utility screen.

Follow along as we use the utility to perform each of the maintenance tasks listed above.

Deleting Duplicate Machines from the SQL SMS Database

At times you may notice that a machine name appears more than once in the inventory listing for a site domain. Each of the duplicate names listed within the Sites window the SMS Administrator program will display a different SMSID. The reason for this is because the hidden SMS.INI file located on the SMS client has been deleted. This causes the SMS Inventory Agent to create a new SMS.INI file with a new SMSID issued by the system. The result is duplicate machine records in the site database, and duplicate machine names in the Sites window display.

You can remove the duplicate records from the site database, and in turn remove the duplicate names that appear in the domain inventory listing by using SMS Database Maintenance Utility. For our example we've noticed that the computer named ARCOS (along with a couple of other computers, named MACLEOD and NAKANO) is listed twice in the Sites window for our domain. To remove the duplicate name for ARCOS (and its duplicate machine records), start the SMS Database Maintenance Utility and follow the steps listed below.

1. Click Delete Duplicates from the Machines pull down menu (found on the toolbar).. A window requesting you to select an architecture will appear, as shown in figure B.15. Select Personal Computer and click OK.

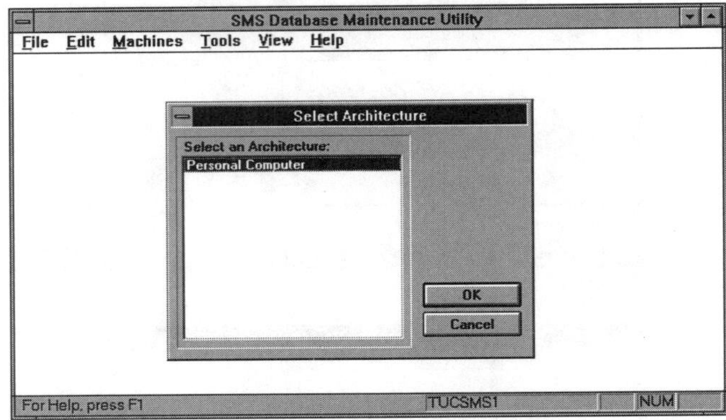

FIG. B.15
The Select Architecture window appears. Highlight Personal Computer and Click OK.

2. In the left windowpane, the duplicate machines are listed under the Name and NetCardID attributes. Expanding the Name attribute in our example shows three machines that each have multiple machine records listed in the SMS database, they are: ARCOS, MACLEOD, and NAKANO.
3. Click one of the machine names to expand a list of duplicate machine records in the right windowpane. In our example we clicked the machine name ARCOS, as shown in figure B.16. It reveals that ARCOS has two machine records that currently exist in the SMS database under its name. The first record carries the SMSID of TUC0200M. The second carries the SMSID of TUC02009.

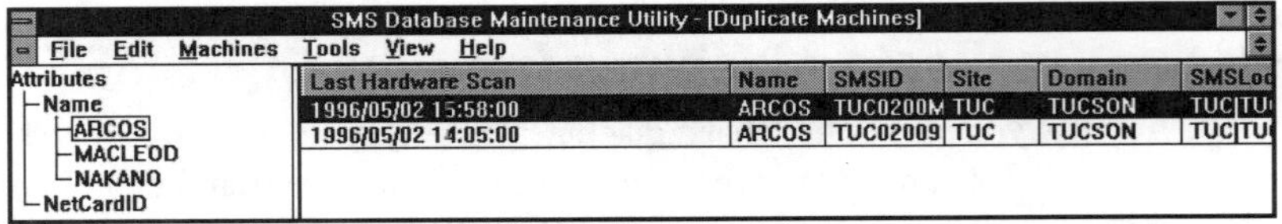

FIG. B.16
Clicking the duplicate name ARCOS reveals the duplicate machine records for that machine in the right windowpane.

4. We can delete a duplicate record by highlighting the record(s) in the right windowpane that you want to delete, and then choosing Edit from the toolbar. Then choose Delete Selected, as shown in figure B.17. In our example we choose to delete the duplicate record that carried the SMSID of TUC0200M.
5. Answer Yes to the confirmation box shown in figure B.18. After a short period, the spinning hourglass will disappear. At this point, when we refresh the screen (as shown in figure B.19), the machine named ARCOS will no longer be listed as a duplicate under the Name attributefigure. The servers named MACLEOD and NAKANO are still listed

because they still have duplicate records in the SMS database. They will continue to appear as machines with duplicate records until we perform the same process on them that we performed on ARCOS.

FIG. B.17
Choose Delete Selected from the Edit menu.

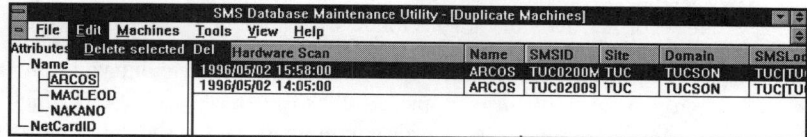

FIG. B.18
Answer Yes to the confirmation box to delete the duplicate machine.

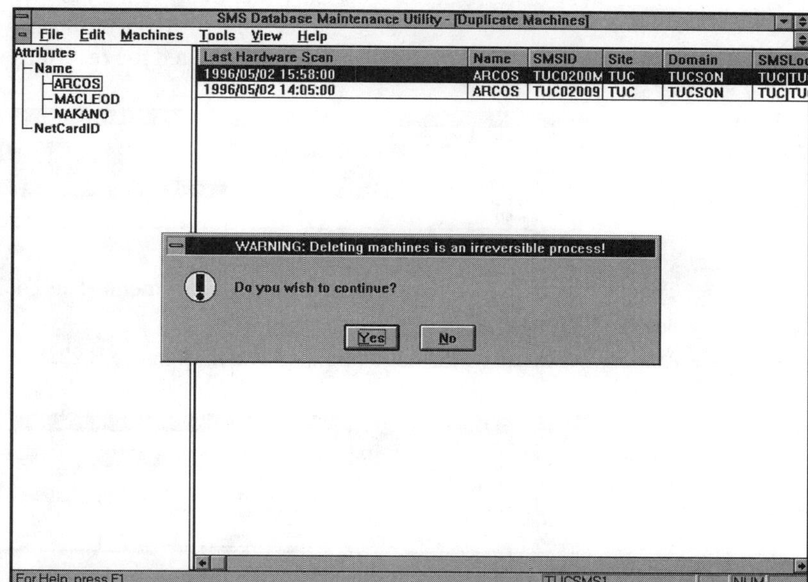

FIG. B.19
ARCOS is no longer listed as a duplicate under the Name Attribute.

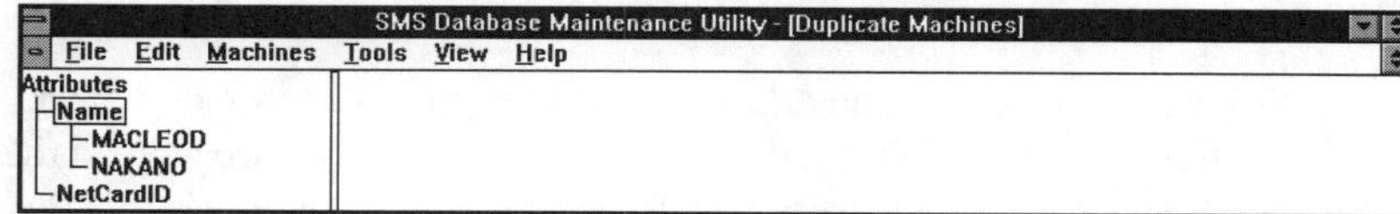

Now if we looked at the Sites window in the SMS Administrator program, we would see only one machine listed for the domain with the name of ARCOS. However the other two machines, named MACLEOD and NAKANO, would still show up multiple times in the domain inventory listing since we didn't remove their duplicate records using the SMS Database Maintenance Utility.

In the next example we'll show you how to merge a duplicate machine record into another machine record, instead of deleting it. This gives you the opportunity to retain the inventory information for the machine that exists within a duplicate record.

Merging Duplicate Machine Records in the SQL SMS Database

Instead of deleting duplicate machine records, we can merge the duplicates into history records for a single machine. In our example we have to duplicate records for the computer named MACLEOD. Instead of deleting the extra record, we can merge it into the other machine record as a history file, as follows:

1. Click the attribute Name or NetCardID of the machine you want to merge duplicate records on. In our example, we click the name MACLEOD which opens up the associated list of duplicate records currently located in the database, as shown in figure B.20.
2. Highlight all of the folders except the folder that you want to merge the other into. In the example, we are going to merge the record from 1996/04/30 into the record from 1996/05/01. Figure B.20 shows that we have highlighted the record from 1996/04/30.

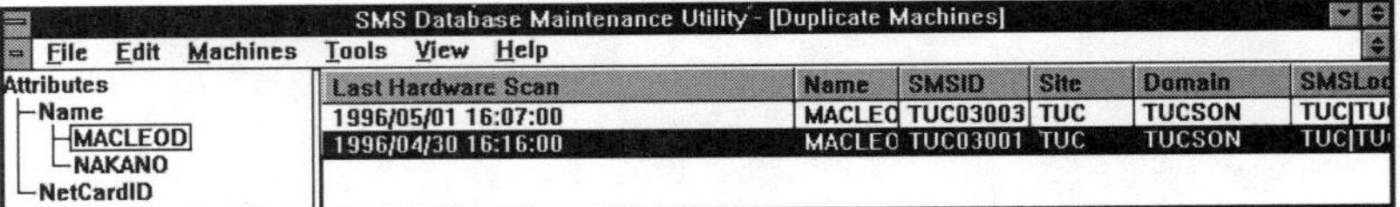

FIG. B.20 Highlight all folders except the one you want to merge the others into.

3. Choose Merge Selected Machines from the Tools menu. The Tools menu is illustrated in figure B.21.
4. Answer Yes to the confirmation box, as shown in figure B.22.

FIG. B.21 The SMS Database Maintenance Utility Tools menu.

5. Refreshing the screen will reveal that the computer named MACLEOD is no longer listed as a duplicate machine. The updated screen is shown in figure B.23.

Now when you look in the Administration Program's site window, it will show only one machine named MACLEOD in the TUCSON domain. When we deleted the duplicate record for ARCOS we got the same result. However the difference here is that the current inventory record for MACLEOD will reflect the merged duplicate machine record as a history file.

Figure B.24 shows the Inventory information for the machine named MACLEOD. Note the current record is dated 5/1/1996 16:07, corresponding to the record we saw in the database utility with a date of 1996/05/01 16:07, and in fact it is the record we merged the duplicate record into.

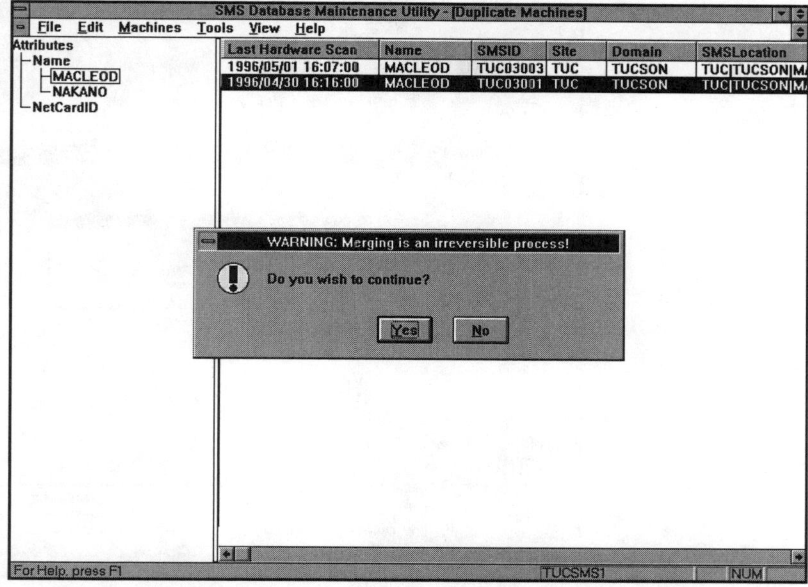

FIG. B.22
This warning message will appear before any actions are performed on the database. You must answer Yes to proceed.

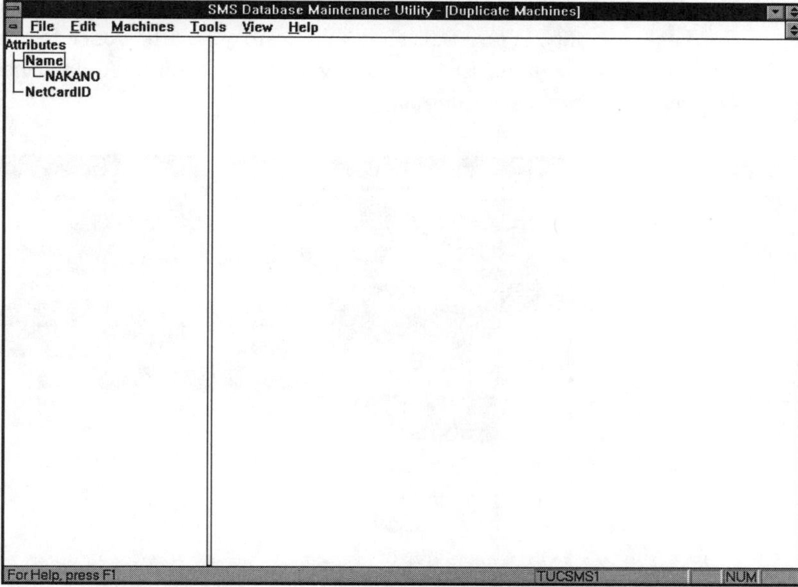

FIG. B.23
MACLEOD no longer appears as a duplicate machine under the Name attribute.

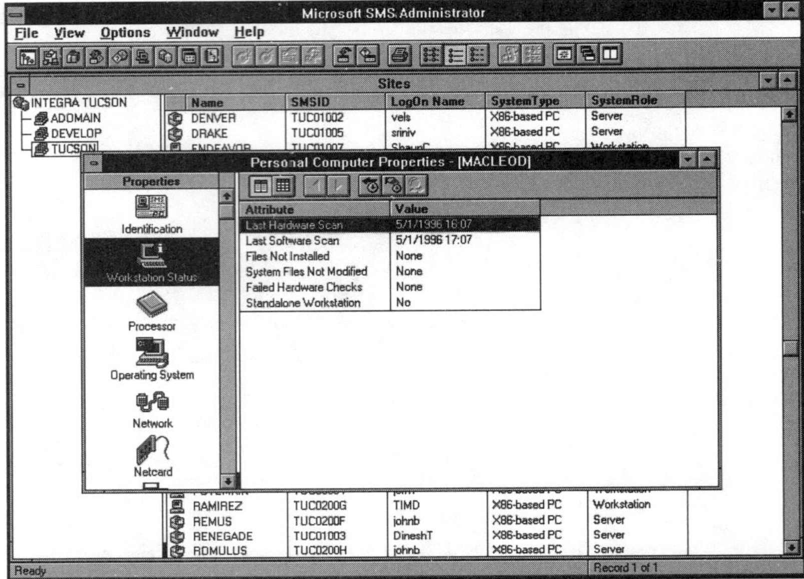

FIG. B.24
The Inventory record for the computer MACLEOD.

Now if we look at the history of MACLEOD, we will see the history record we merged using the database utility. Figure B.25 shows the history record. Notice that the record's date and time matches that of the record we merged in the database. And in fact it is the same record. Our record merge was successful.

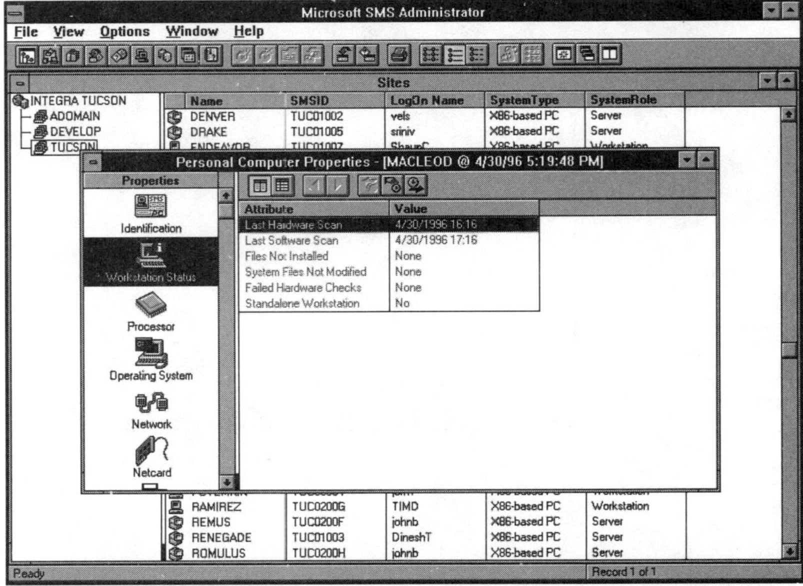

FIG. B.25
This duplicate record now shows as a history record for the computer named MACLEOD.

Setting Machine Group Preferences

Setting the Machine Group preferences allows you to specify the format in which the Machine Group objects are displayed by the Administration Program. The two formats to choose from are the column and table formats. These formats can also be specified in the Administration Program when viewing any Machine Group object. This lets you set a default format if you wish.

To set the Machine Group preferences, do the following:

1. From the Tools menu, choose the Machine Groups Preferences option, as shown in figure B.26.

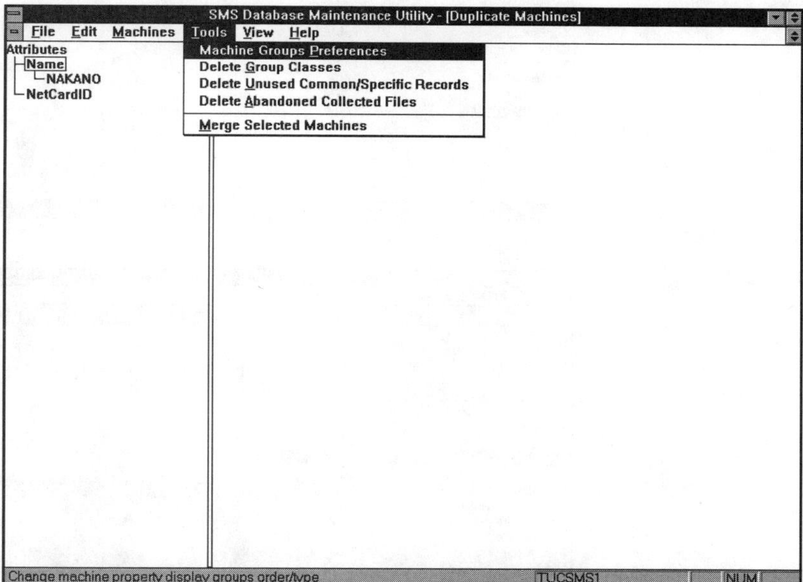

FIG. B.26
Choose the Machine Groups Preferences from the Tools menu to set the viewing format.

2. After you choose the "personal computer" architecture, the Machine Property Display Preferences screen appears. It lists the current format settings for the different Machine Groups. A typical screen is shown in figure B.27.
3. To change the viewing format, double-click the name of a machine group listed in the left windowpane. In our example, shown in figure B.28, we are changing the Disk view from a table format to a column format.
4. Choose the Save Changes item under the File menu before exiting.

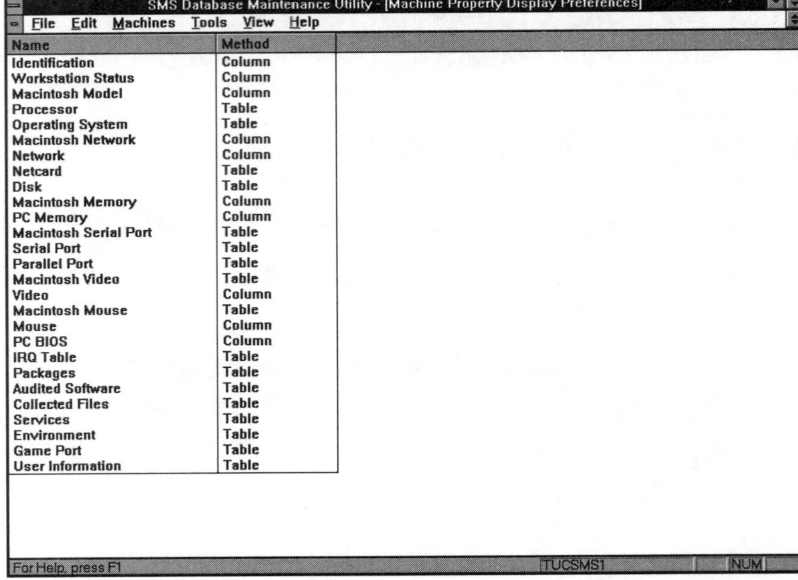

FIG. B.27 The Machine Property Display Preferences screen.

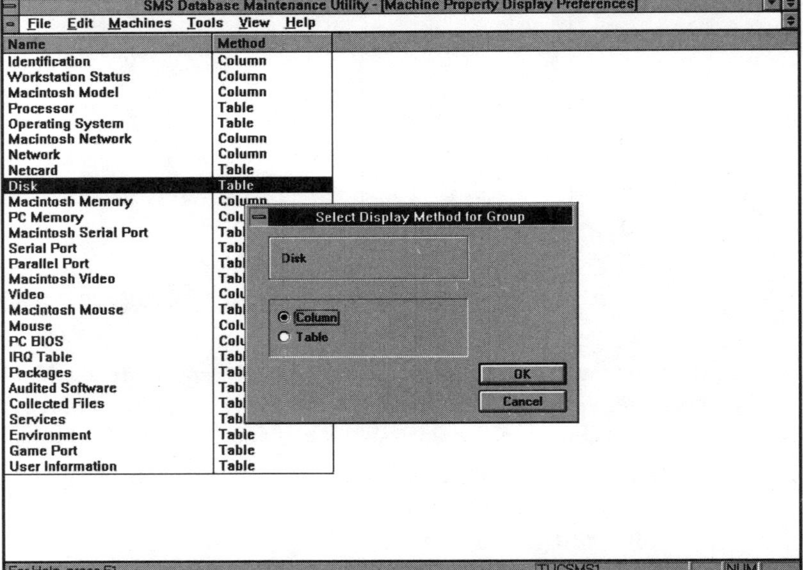

FIG. B.28 Changing the default Disk view.

Deleting Group Classes

The Database Maintenance Utility also allow you to completely delete group classes. This allows you to remove any group, as shown in figure B.29.

CAUTION

Since the DB Utility does not prevent an Administrator from deleting any of the groups listed in figure B.29, it is possible to delete the identification class for any architecture. If you delete the identification class for ANY architecture, YOU WILL ALSO AUTOMATICALLY DELETE THE IDENTIFICATION CLASS FOR THE "PERSONAL COMPUTER" ARCHITECTURE. This could render your SMS database useless.

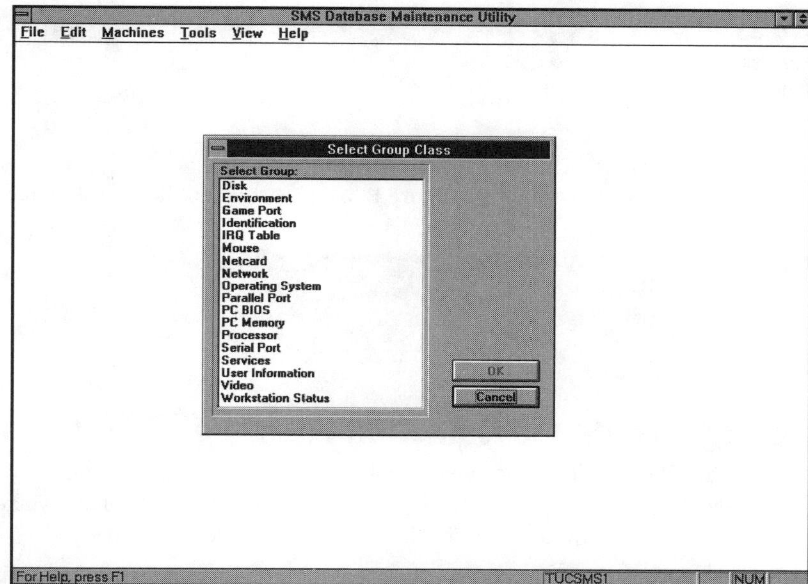

FIG. B.29 Any of the these Group Classes may be deleted. Be very careful not to delete any of the identification group classes!

Follow the instructions below to delete a group class:

1. To delete a group class, choose Delete Group Classes from the Tools menu, as shown in figure B.30.

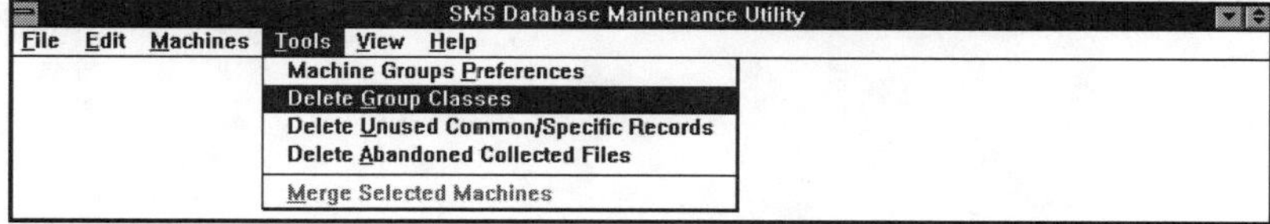

FIG. B.30 Choose Delete Group Classes to view the groups available for deletion.

2. Highlight the group that you want to delete and click the OK button.

Deleting Unused Records

Unused records are left in the SQL SMS database when a machine is deleted from the site inventory without having its associated history records purged. The records take up valuable database space and can easily be removed, as follows:

1. Choose the Delete Unused Common/Specific Records from the Tools menu.
2. The confirmation box appears, as shown in figure B.31, asking you to verify your choice.

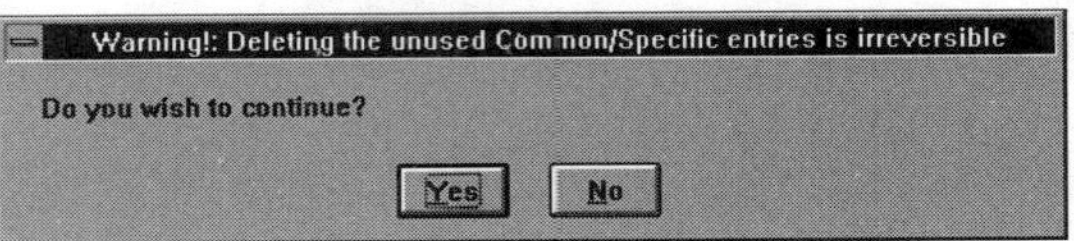

FIG. B.31
You are asked to confirm the deletion of unused records.

3. The window shown in figure B.32 appears when the operation has been completed.

FIG. B.32
The deletion process is completed.

Deleting Abandoned Collected Files

Often files that have been collected by the SMS system will become "no longer referenced" to any computer currently in the site inventory. The DB Utility allows you easily to clear these files from your system and regain valuable disk space, as follows:

1. Choose Delete Abandoned Collected Files from the Tools menu. Refer to figure B.30.
2. The message shown in figure B.33 appears if the system is free of abandoned files.

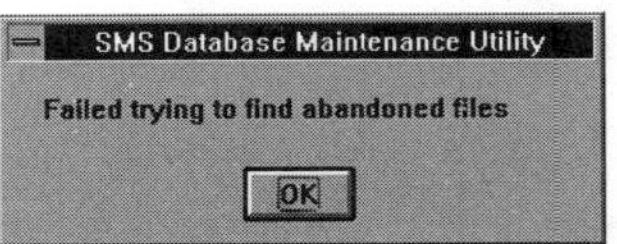

FIG. B.33
The following message appears if the system is free of abandoned files.

APPENDIX C

SQL Server Basics and Installing NT Services

SMS uses SQL Server to store configuration and inventory information. SQL is the engine of the SMS data storage, and to date only Microsoft SQL is supported for this function. When running SMS 1.x on Windows NT 3.5x, SQL Server 4.21a or greater is required. A SQL Server client license is not required for running SMS.

Even a SQL Server beginner can use SMS. For example, SMS will create the appropriate databases and database devices automatically when the system is first installed. However, there are times when you want to adjust the SQL Server configuration.

The SQL Server that will hold the SMS site database can be located on the same computer as the SMS site server. Or, to reduce the load on a single computer, the SMS site server and the SQL Server that holds the SMS database can be on different computers. In the latter case, slower response times between the SMS site server and the SMS database can occur because of increased network traffic.

A primary site's database contains system and inventory information for itself and the sites below it. A central site's database contains the system-wide inventory and configuration information for all sites in the SMS system. ■

Pre-installation Considerations: NT and SQL Server

There are some considerations before the SQL Server can be installed. The author is describing below how the logon account is created.

Before installation can proceed, the SMS Service Account must be created. When creating this account, make sure that it is part of the global Domain Administration group and that it has the Logon As A Service Right. If you are using Windows NT trust relationships, make sure that any trusting domain controllers that will participate in the SMS site have added the SMS Service Account to their local Administrators group.

NOTE If your server has a previous SMS installation, either as an SMS Server or an SMS client, make sure that the old SMS.INI file (hidden) is removed from the C:\ directory. Also, remove any remaining SMS keys from \HKEY_LOCAL_MACHINE using the Windows NT registry editor (REGEDT32.EXE). Choose the Find Key option in the View menu, and search for all occurrences of SMS. Make sure that the Match Whole Word Only check box is not selected.

Installing SQL Server

Once pre-installation steps are out of the way, the installation itself is quite simple.

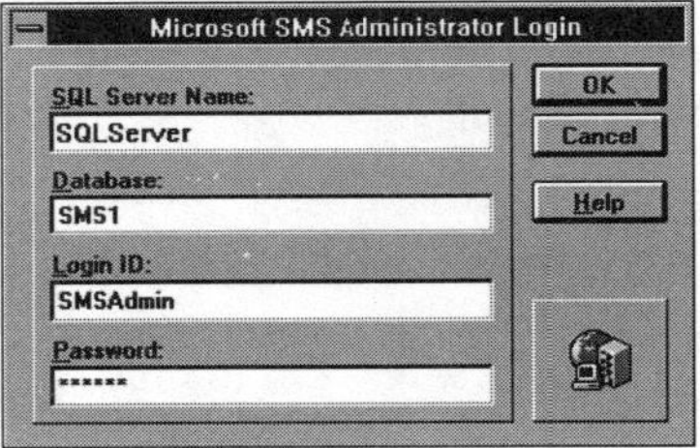

FIG. C.1
Installing SQL Server.

Notice that you have the option to install administration tools. This choice gives you the opportunity to install the SMS Administrator tool on any Windows NT 3.x machine. This allows an SQL site to have multiple administrators. Their access permissions can be set using the SQL Security Manager tool. If you want to be able to control clients remotely from this machine, you must have a common protocol, with the target client as well as the SQL Server housing the SMS database containing the client's information.

The following are steps for installing SQL Server version 6.x:

1. Create a SQL Server Service Account in NT.
2. Create a database device and transaction log device in SQL.
3. Make sure that the SQL Server has been set with the current time.
4. Create a Database Name.

NOTE After setup you may see a message on the screen telling you that there was a failure to install the SMS service. If this occurs and you are given the options Retry or Continue, do so. Many times the retry will work and the setup process will continue. If the setup process fails, check the C:\SMSSETUP.LOG file, to see why. If reinstallation is necessary, remove SQL and try again.

Let's take a look at each of these steps in detail.

Creating a SQL Server Service Account

When installing SQL, you must create a SQL service account so that SMS can accomplish the following tasks:

Create Database	Defines Space for Database.
Dump Database	Backs up Database.
Dump Transaction	Backs up Transaction Log.

You can use the default SQL "sa" account for SMS (it stands for service account), or you can create a new SQL account. The permissions are applied on the master database. They comprise the minimum set of permissions that allows SMS to create and maintain the SMS database. After setup is complete, this account is used by SMS services to access the SMS database. The SMS Administrator utility then does all of its work in the SMS database. When you start the SMS Administrator, you are prompted for the SQL Server user account.

Creating the SQL Logon ID Account in NT Make sure you have an SMS SQL logon ID to use when you install the site database (you will need to specify this logon ID when you run the SMS Setup program). This is also the logon ID you use to log on to the site database when you start the SMS Administrator. Changing the SMS SQL logon ID affects only SMS services—not the actual SMS SQL logon ID account. The SMS Setup program sets SMS services only so that they will use the specified account and password. To change, modify, or delete a logon account or a logon account's password on the SQL Server, you must use the SQL Administrator (or an ISQL command). You can also change the SMS SQL logon ID through the Accounts dialog box for the site (from the Site Properties dialog box). However, the SMS Setup program verifies the account (checks that the SMS SQL logon ID exists and has the proper permissions). When you change the SMS SQL logon ID with the Accounts dialog box, Setup does not verify the account.

Type the SMS SQL logon ID that you want the SMS services to use to access the site database.

The SQL Server must have a corresponding logon ID with the same name and password specified in this box, and that logon ID must have database owner (dbo) privileges on the site database.

Password Type the password for the SMS SQL logon ID that you specified for Logon ID.

Confirm Password Retype the password that you specified for Password.

Creating the Site Database Device and Transaction Log Device

A SQL device is a predefined hard disk storage area. SMS requires two devices: one for the SMS site database, and the other for the transaction log.

The transaction log device stores all changes made to data in the database. The transaction log is used to recover database events in case of a system failure. This log does not have to be very large because SQL clears (truncates) it after each transaction has been successfully written to disk.

If you run SQL Server and SMS on the same server, SMS gives you the opportunity to create the SQL devices and databases during Setup automatically. If you choose to install the site database on a SQL Server on another server (not the site server), you must manually create the device for the site database and the device for the site database's transaction log. The SMS SQL logon ID specified in the SMS Setup program must have Create Database, Dump Database, and Dump Transaction permissions on the Master database. This enables the SMS Setup program to create and maintain the site database. If you create the SQL logon ID as part of the SMS Setup process, the appropriate permissions will be added to your account automatically.

We will cover how to create the SQL devices automatically, as a part of SQL Server setup.

You must have a site database device and a transaction log device. If you choose to install the site database on the SQL Server on the site server, the SMS Setup program can create the devices for the site database and its transaction log, as well as create a database for the site database.

CAUTION

If you use an existing device for the site database or the transaction log, the SMS Setup program will delete all objects in the site database and transaction log devices. The SMS Setup program uses the entire site database device for the site database and the entire transaction log device for the transaction log.

NOTE You should be able to use the SMS Service Account to make a network connection to the SQL Server. If you plan to install the site database on a server different from the site server, make sure the SMS Service Account has access to the SQL Server. ■

Make Sure the SQL Server Is Set with the Current Time

The SMS Scheduler uses the SQL Server time to determine when to perform jobs.

Creating a Database Name

If you have restored the site database using a different database name, you can specify the new database name. You should fill in this box only if you are restoring the site database under a different database name.

The Setup program verifies that the SQL Server exists, the SMS SQL logon ID exists on the SQL Server, and the specified database is an SMS site database. The program then makes the changes to the site.

You can also elect to use the Auto Start Server and SQL Executive. When the SQL Server Setup for Windows NT Installation Options dialog box appears, make sure you select Auto Start SQL Server at boot time and Auto Start SQL Executive at boot time. This way you don't have to start SQL manually every time you shut down and restart the server.

Post-installation Considerations: SQL Server

The following parameters affect the performance of SMS and should be configured by the SQL Server Administrator:

CAUTION

You should change the name of the site database or the SQL Server only if you have restored the site database for the site to a database with another name, or if you have restored the site database to another SQL Server.

- If you are using 500 or fewer computers, the SQL default values are acceptable; however, you must increase your Tempdb size to at least 20MB no matter what.
- Temporary Database (Tempdb) Make sure the temporary database is large enough. The default size for the Tempdb is 2MB. 4Kb per PC is recommended. For 2000 SMS clients, the Tempdb must be 8MB or greater. A larger Tempdb improves the performance of queries containing sorts.

NOTE The Tempdb is stored on the master device. You may want to create a new device for the Tempdb instead of sharing it with the master device.

- User Connections—The SMS installation program requests 25 SQL connections during installation. This is the default value. More user connections will probably be required. The SMS services running on the Site Server require approximately five connections to the SMS database SQL Server. In addition, each administrator for that site requires five more connections while running SMS Administrator. With multiple administrators connecting to the same SQL Server, it is possible to run out of connections. If this happens it is possible that the SMS services will be unable to perform their tasks, resulting in errors at the site.

  In addition to the connections required by the SMS services, you should allow at least five connections per administrator on that SQL Server. Also, keep track of how many administrators are out there. They should close the SQL or SMS Administrator tools when done, releasing the connections.

When SQL Server is used for the site database only, you can use the number or user connections recommended above, maybe 40 or 50 in a large site. If you have other databases, you should add five or more to the existing number of connections for each database.

If you are using SMS tools such as the SMS Security Manager and the SMS Database Manager, or if you have installed the SMS Administrator on another Windows NT computer, you may need additional user connections so that those applications can access the site database.

- Memory SQL Server allocates memory for its use in 2kb pages. By default this number is 3,072 units or 6MB of RAM. This number should be increased to at least 5,000 units. This will give SQL Server about 10MB of memory to use. Increasing this number will improve SQL performance, although you may draw down on the system resources for other products such as NT or SMS.
- Open Objects Tune the open objects option in the system configuration for the SQL Server. The number of open objects determines how many tables, views, or stored procedures can be open at a time. The default number of open objects is 500. It is recommended to set this value to 5000 or greater for SMS.

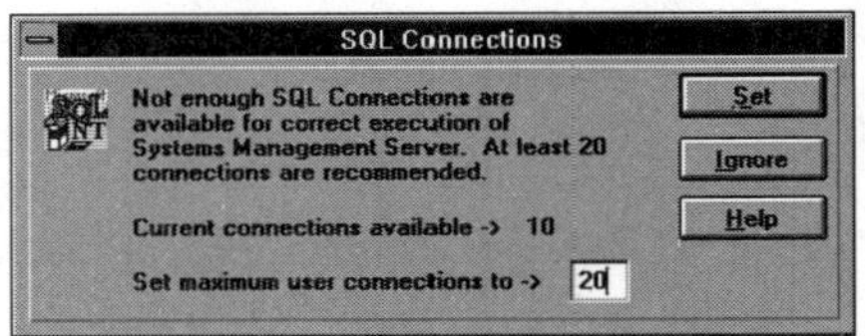

FIG. C.2 User Connections dialog box.

NOTE It is recommended that you allow at least 20Kb per computer in the SMS Database (SMSData) for data. The Database Log (SMSLog) should be at least 20 percent of the data size and Tempdb should be at least 4Kb per computer (20MB minimum) for the Temporary Database (Tempdb). For example, for 10,000 computers in your SMS database, you should allocate at least 200MB total for SMSData, at least 40MB for SMSLog, and 40MB for Tempdb.

NOTE In addition to the configuration parameters above, the SQL Server administrator should synchronize the time of the SQL Server and SMS site server, because SMS will use the SQL Server's time when scheduling its tasks. The SMS Scheduler uses the SQL Server time to determine when to perform jobs.

NT Issues

Before you can proceed with the SMS installation, the following must be completed in NT:

- Install Windows NT Server 3.51 or higher. Do not install it as a server (the default) since it must contain the domain user account database. Make sure that it is either a primary or a backup domain controller.
- Install NT with at least one NTFS partition which is at least 100MB in size to operate the site server. This does not take into account space required for the SMS database, applications, or working space. 500MB would be a reasonable minimum for all site server needs. This number can grow depending on how much software distribution and application sharing you plan on doing.
- When installing site servers in an environment utilizing Windows NT trust relationships, care has to be taken when entering the SQL Service Account information during the Setup process. If the target site server's machine account is in a trusting domain, and the SQL Service Account is in one of this domain's trusted domains, the Service Account name entered during Setup must be prefixed by the trusted domain name followed by a backslash.

  For example: \\ABC\Smssa where Smssa is the trusted domain in which the SMS Service Account, Apollo, is defined. Do not forget to give \\ABC\Smssa the Logon As A Service right, and add this account to the local Administrators group in the trusting domain.
- Finally, check the NT Event Viewer for any service, component, permission, or database errors. Be sure to look at the Event's details for a complete description of the problem. Also remember to check the application log as well as the system log.
- Double-check that the SQL Server is installed and started in NT:

  MSSQLServer

  SQLExecutive

NOTE Regarding Windows NT Server, if you have trust relationships established between domains, the SMS Service Account should be added only to the master trusted domain.

If trust relationships do not exist in a multiple-domain environment, a common SMS service account must be added to all domains.

APPENDIX D

A Detailed Look at the Data Flow

One of the most important functions you will have as an administrator is tracing the flow of files through the SMS hierarchy for troubleshooting and maintenance. This way you'll be able to do the following:

- See how fast a proposed change is being made.
- Delete old files for hard disk storage maintenance.
- Troubleshoot stopped processes.

This appendix serves as reference for all the key directories and files involved with every major SMS function and process. A review of each major SMS function and its data flow will show you how to retrace the flow of files through directories for each of the functions you are trying to accomplish in SMS.

This appendix is divided into the following three parts:

- The Major SMS Functions: Key Files and Directories.
- The Major SMS Processes: Key Files and Directories.
- Diagnostic Tools: Key Files and Directories. ■

The Major SMS Functions: Key Files and Directories

The Major SMS functions covered include the following:

- Primary site configuration
- Inventory
- Software distribution
- Sharing applications

Primary Site Configuration and Installation

Key files include the following:

- .CT1 files
- .CT2 files

The following is the data flow for the site configuration process:

- The SMS Administrator changes site properties, and the SMS database is updated with the proposed change. Hierarchy Manager produces a site control file with .CT1 extension listing proposed changes.
- The Site Configuration Manager reads the .CT1 file and carries out changes. The Site Configuration Manager produces a site control file with a .CT2 extension, listing actual changes made.
- The Hierarchy Manager reads the .CT2 file. Hierarchy Manager updates the SMS database with the actual changes. SMS Administrator now reflects the configuration changes in the Site Properties window.

Inventory

The installation of software using Systems Management Server starts with the collection of inventory information from machines. This hardware and software inventory information is stored in the Systems Management Server database and is used to plan and control the installation process.

Systems Management Server automatically retrieves detailed information about both the hardware and software for every machine within your enterprise, and then stores all the information in a standard SQL Server database. You can select, sort, and view the data, or you can extract the data and create custom reports with popular desktop applications, such as Microsoft Access or Lotus 1-2-3.

Inventory Collection The key files are the following:

- .CT1 files
- .CT2 files

The following steps review the inventory collection process:

- The Administrator configures inventory collection and configuration information that is put into the SMS database.
- Processes on the site server get the information from the database and then create configuration files on the logon servers. The Inventory Agent on the client uses the configuration information to determine which software to inventory.

Inventory Processes In this section we will look at the key files and directories significant to the Inventory processes.

Inventory Agent The key files are the following:

- .CT1 files
- .CT2 files
- SMS.INI
- SMSSAFE.TMP

The Inventory Agent places entries in the SMS.INI and SMSSAFE.TMP files while it is collecting inventory. Check these files to determine exactly when the inventory was last collected and whether or not there were any problems during the collection process.

Inventory Processor The key files and directories are the following:

- .MIF files
- .RAW files
- \ISVMIF.BOX
- \SITE.SRV\INVENTRY.BOX
- \SITE.SRV\ISVMIF.BOX

The Inventory Processor monitors the \SITE.SRV\ISVMIF.BOX and \SITE.SRV\INVENTRY.BOX directories for inventory files. As soon as a new file is detected in one of these directories, this process prepares the inventory for the Inventory Data Loader by comparing the current inventory information to its history file.

The Inventory Processor handles three types of files, as follows:

- .RAW files—inventory collected from Windows NT and MS_DOS clients which is placed in the \INVENTRY.BOX directory of the logon server.
- .MIF files—inventory collected from OS\2 and Macintosh clients which is written directly to .MIF files. The .RAW files are converted to .MIF files, which are text files approximately 20 to 40 Kb in size. These files are placed in the \ISVMIF.BOX directory.
- .MIF files—custom files created to extend the inventory information in the SMS database. These can be "hand-written" by the administrator or created by users running MIF Data Entry.

Inventory Data Loader The key files and directories are the following:

- .MIF files
- \BADMIFS
- COLFILE.HIS
- Delta-MIF files

The Inventory Data Loader periodically checks for Delta-MIF files to add changes to the inventory data of the SMS database. If any of the .MIF files are incorrect, they are placed in the \BADMIFS directory.

SMS keeps track of all collected files by writing a record for each one in a local file called COLFILE.HIS.

Site Reporter

The key files and directories are the following:

- \SITE.SRV\SITEREP.BOX
- Delta-MIF files
- .MIF files

The site monitors the \SITE.SRV\SITEREP.BOX directory for files. When a Delta-MIF file is placed in the directory, the Site Reporter waits an hour, then sends all the .MIFs in the directory to the parent site.

Applications Manager

The key files and directories are the following:

- \MAINCFG.BOX\PKGRULE
- PACKAGE.RUL file

The Applications Manager monitors the SMS database for changes to packages. If it detects a change, the Applications Manager communicates package and program group configuration information from the site database to all sites.

The Applications Manager manages the shared application program groups and the inventory rules for an application sharing package. It creates the configuration files for these and also creates an internal SMS job to push them to the correct child sites.

It creates the PACKAGE.RUL file in \MAINCFG.BOX\PKGRULE for software inventory packages.

Reporting Inventory

The key files are the following:

- .CT1 files
- .CT2 files

Inventory is collected by the Inventory Agent at each client and reported up the site hierarchy. Inventory is collected at each client computer, using the information in the inventory configuration files, and is then copied back to the logon server. The site server copies the information from the logon server to the site server.

Information is transferred to the SMS database. If there is a parent site, the inventory information is passed to the parent site.

Software Distribution

The key files and directories are the following:

- \STORE
- .SRC files

The following six steps describe the process of configuring an application to be run or installed at SMS clients:

The administrator creates a package and a job, which SMS Administrator adds to the SMS database. The Scheduler compresses the source files (.SRC)and creates the package instruction and send request files. The Scheduler gives the files to the correct sender, to be sent to the destination sites for the job. The Despooler at the destination site receives the package and stores a master copy in its \STORE directory.

The Despooler decompresses the master copy and then copies these files over to the job's distribution servers. After placing the files on the distribution servers, the Despooler creates instruction files for the SMS clients, telling them which package is available and from which distribution servers it can be run.

The Package Command Manager (PCM) on the client runs the package command that has been sent to it. After the package command is run, status is reported back to the Despooler, which passes the information to the Inventory Data Loader to update the SMS database.

Sharing Applications

The key file and directory are the following:

.PGC (Program Group Control)

The following three steps describe the process of configuring an application as a shared application that can be run at SMS clients:

The administrator configures an application for sharing, which includes:

- Setting up a software package
- Defining program items
- Setting up a Share Package on Server job

The administrator configures the program group that will be displayed to users on the client workstations.

The application files are distributed by the Scheduler, senders, and Despooler to the distribution servers. The configuration information is placed on the logon servers by the Maintenance Manager.

When a user logs on, the Program Group Control (PGC) application gets the list of available shared applications and user group information from the logon server.

Program Group Control runs and configures the user's desktop with a program manager group and icon for each available shared application. After creating the desktop icons, Program Group Control will also run any specified configuration scripts to set up the local registry for OLE and application dependency information.

After the shared application group and icons are configured, the user can run the application.

The Major SMS Processes: Key Files and Directories

In this section, we will discuss the crucial SMS Processes that are part of any SMS Server installation.

The Hierarchy Manager

The key directories and files are the following:

- SITE.SRV\SITECFG.BOX
- .CT1 files
- .CT2 files

The Site Hierarchy Manager monitors the database for proposed site configuration changes. .CT1 files reflect such changes. It also monitors the SITE.SRV\SITECFG.BOX directory for .CT2 site control files. It is activated whenever a .CT2 file appears in this directory or when its polling interval expires. The Hierarchy Manager uses a polling interval because it is not alerted when changes occur to its site tables in the database.

Each time the Hierarchy Manager is activated, it performs the following tasks:

- Reads the Registry for SQL Server information. This information includes the SQL Server account, database name, and SQL Server name needed for the Site Hierarchy Manager to connect to the SMS database.
- Checks for disk space. If there is not at least 512Kb free disk space, the Hierarchy Manager goes back to sleep until the next processing cycle occurs.
- Processes site table looking for changes (for the local site and each subsite). If changes have been made in SMS Administrator, it takes the unposted records and performs appropriate actions, such as creating a .CT1 file.

- After changes have been completed, the Hierarchy Manager updates the database with information from the .CT2 file.
- Checks the addressability of the local site to itself and all subsites. The reason for this is that the Hierarchy Manager is the first to find out about new subsites when it receives the configuration information. If an address is not configured, it generates an error event.
- Reads the registry for the Polling Interval and goes back to sleep for Polling Interval seconds. The interval depends on the response mode of the processes (Very Fast = 1 minute, Fast = 5 minutes, Medium = 15 minutes, Slow = 30 minutes).

The Site Configuration Manager

The key directories and files are the following:

- SITE.SRV\SITECFG.BOX
- .CT0 files
- .CT2 files
- \REPL$ share

The Site Configuration Manager waits for site control files to be copied to the \SITECFG.BOX directory in the SMS install directory. Site control files define the site configuration options such as domains, server, or services options.

The Site Configuration Manager retrieves the data in the site control file (.CT0) and writes this data to the Registry as "Pending Install."

The Site Configuration Manager reads the list of domains for the site from the Registry. It enumerates the servers in each domain to find all logon servers. The logon servers are added to the Registry and marked as "Pending Install" if they are new to SMS.

The Site Configuration Manager uses the Registry as the point of definition for the site installation. It verifies that the actual installation of domains and servers exists as defined. It removes any domains or servers that are marked as "Pending De-Install," and it installs any that are marked as "Pending Install." If any are marked as "Active," it verifies the installation.

The Site Configuration Manager reports the installation status of the site by creating a site control file (.CT2) and writing this file to the Hierarchy Manager's directory. If this is a secondary site, a system job is used to send the file.

Configures User Scripts for Automatic Inventory Collection The Site Configuration Manager also adds the SMSLS command to user's logon scripts (or a NetWare Server's system logon script) when Automatically Configure Logon Script is selected, and copies the logon files into the \REPL$ share of the primary domain controllers for the Windows NT, LAN Manager, or LAN Server domains in the site for replication to the backup domain controllers.

App D

The Scheduler

The key directories and files are the following:

- SCHEDULE.BOX
- Minijob inbox
- Send Request inbox
- .CPB files

The Scheduler is crucial to the functioning the System Management Server. Here are the key tasks performed by the Scheduler:

1. Scheduler reads configuration information from the Registry and saves the current time from the SQL Server.

   At the start each processing cycle, Scheduler reads configuration parameters from the Registry. It reads the SQL Server information (server name, database name, account, and password), and it reads the name of the SMS site's Site Server. Then, connecting to the Registry of the Site Server, Scheduler reads the locations of the Minijob inbox and the Unscheduled Send Request inbox, and reads the Polling Interval.
2. Scheduler begins processing jobs and send requests.
3. Manages jobs.

   The Scheduler performs six tasks in processing all current jobs in the SMS system. Steps two through four are dependent on job type.
4. Determines where to find the jobs.

   The Scheduler determines the primary source of jobs. At a primary site, this is the database, and at a secondary site, this is the SCHEDULE.BOX directory. If it finds any minijobs at a primary site, they are moved to the database. If the Scheduler cannot find a primary source of jobs, an error is logged, and the Scheduler exits this task.
5. Processes jobs ready to be activated.

   The Scheduler prints an activating job message in the trace file and then calls the appropriate function for the type of job. Other pertinent information, such as Job ID, priority, destination site, and instruction type, is also listed.
6. Processes jobs to be repeated.

   If the Scheduler finds any jobs that have to be repeated, it creates a new job and schedules its start time to current time + repeat interval. The repeat status of the original job is marked complete.
7. Processes jobs to be canceled.

   The Scheduler prints a cancel message with the Job ID in the trace file and then performs the necessary actions for the type of job.

8. Updates active jobs.

   The Scheduler prints an updating job message in the trace file and then calls the specific routine to update that type of job. After updating the job, it also prints the current job/send/work status in the trace file.

9. At secondary sites, deletes completed minijobs.

10. Manages and schedules outboxes and send requests.

    The Scheduler is responsible for determining which senders are available and which one is most appropriate for a given send request.

11. Updates the current list of available sender outboxes.

12. Loads the current outbox schedules.

13. Updates the send request list.

14. Gets the outbox capabilities from the *.CPB file for each outbox.

15. Builds the outbox send request lists.

    The Scheduler builds a list of send requests for each outbox in memory. These lists are sorted by priority and start time.

16. Checks all send requests.

    The Scheduler examines all the send requests in all the outboxes (not including the unassigned outbox). It checks to see that the send requests have started on time and that a sender has not stopped the send request. It handles any processing needed when a send request has completed (either by finishing, failing, or being canceled or suspended).

17. Schedule all send requests.

    This schedules all unscheduled send requests. This includes any new jobs in the unassigned outbox and any send requests that have not started sending.

    To select the outbox, the Scheduler determines what the estimated start and finish times would be if the send request were placed in each of the outboxes. Based on the earliest finish time, an outbox is selected and the send request is moved to that outbox.

    If no outbox is available for seven days, it will try again with the backup outboxes.

Sender and Despooler

In order for one site to communicate with another site, each one must have a Sender. A Sender is a Windows NT service that Systems Management Server uses to transmit instructions and data from one site to another. Systems Management Server provides three basic types of Senders: LAN, RAS, and SNA. It is possible to create additional senders for other communication methods, such as MAPI.

Once you have a Sender (the LAN Sender is installed as default), you can set up communication with other sites that use the same communication method. In order for one site to be able to communicate with another site, the sending site must have an address which contains specific information about the site and is defined for the receiving site.

Systems Management Server design allows you to have multiple Senders and multiple addresses between sites, giving you the flexibility to create a communication structure that works for your environment and provides all the fault tolerance you need. Once you have configured a Sender to communicate with another site, the Sender makes the connection automatically whenever it processes a request to send instructions or data to that site. The Sender also ensures that instructions and data are transferred intact from one site to another, and provides roll back capabilities if the link goes down. After the Sender has carried out the request, it breaks the connection.

Senders The key files are the following:

- .SRQ files
- .SRS files
- .WOO files

The six senders (LAN, RAS-Async, RAS-ISDN, RAS-X25, SNA-Batch, SNA-Interactive) all operate in the same manner. They each receive a send request instruction file (.SRQ) in the appropriate directory (SENDER.BOX\REQUESTS\LAN_DEFA.OOO for the LAN Sender) and follow its instructions. This file contains the names of the files to be moved and the name of the destination site. The two files moved by the sender are the instruction file, .IOO, for the destination Despooler, and a compressed package file, .WOO. The compressed instruction file (.IOO) is in the \SITE.SRV\SENDER.BOX\TOSEND directory. The .WOO file is also placed in the \SITE.SRV\SENDER.BOX\TOSEND directory.

As the sender moves the files, it updates the send request file, .SRQ, with current status. The file extension changes from .SRQ to .SRS, since it is now a status file. The Scheduler uses this file to monitor and handle any problems with sending the data to the destination site.

Despooler The key directories and files are the following:

- \DESPOOLER\STORE
- \LOGON.SRV\PCMINS.BOX
- \S_xxxxx.TMP
- \SITE.SRV\DESPOOLR.BOX\RECEIVE
- \SITE.SRV\MAINCFG.BOX
- \SITE.SRV\MAINCFG.BOX\PCMDOM.BOX
- .INS
- SMSID.INS

The Despooler does the following:

- Creates PCM instruction files for a Run Command on Workstation job.
- Deletes PCM instruction files when canceling a job.
- Places software on distribution servers.

The Despooler monitors the \SITE.SRV\DESPOOLR.BOX\RECEIVE directory while waiting for .INS instruction files to arrive. When an .INS file arrives, the Despooler immediately begins processing the instructions.

The Despooler receives, decompresses, and distributes the package. The Despooler monitors its inbox (\SITE.SRV\DESPOOLER.BOX\RECEIVE) for compressed instruction files (.I*).

The Despooler completes the following tasks:

1. Copies the compressed package file to the \DESPOOLER\STORE directory. In doing so, it follows the instructions regarding whether or not to overwrite an existing package.
2. Decompresses the package. The Despooler decompresses the package on the drive with the most available free space and creates a temporary directory (S_xxxxx.TMP). This might reside on the site server or on a helper server. A master copy of the package is kept on the site server.
3. Creates a list of servers to copy the decompressed package. The Despooler decides whether or not to overwrite copies of the package on the distribution servers. The Despooler keeps a list of package locations in the Windows NT Registry, in HKEY_LOCAL_MACHINE under \Software\Microsoft\SMS\Components\SMS_Despooler.
4. Creates the distribution server share for the package directory and copies the files to the distribution servers. The share name is SMS_PKGx, where x is the NTFS partition with the most free space. If no NTFS partition exists, the drive with the most free space is chosen. The directory name is SMS_PKGSx, with subdirectories named after the SMS Package IDs.
5. Deletes the temporary directory and all its files.
6. Adds a record to each target client's Package Command Manager instruction file (SMSID.INS) in the SMS\SITE.SRV\MAINCFG.BOX\PCMDOM.BOX directory. The record includes the run command instructions, package information such as path and server type (Windows NT, LAN Manager, or NetWare servers), and zone information if the server is running Services for Macintosh. The Maintenance Manager moves the .INS files to the SMS\LOGON.SRV\PCMINS.BOX directory on the logon servers for the target client computers.

The Maintenance Manager

The key directories and files are the following:

- \\logon_server\SMS_SHR
- \LOGON.SRV\INVENTRY.BOX
- \LOGON.SRV\ISVMIF.BOX
- DOMAIN.INI
- PACKAGE.RUL
- PKG_16.CFG
- RESYNC.CFG

The Maintenance Manager manages the inventory and status information data that flows between the SMS clients and the site server through the logon servers.

Clients report inventory and status information to the logon server. The Maintenance Manager collects this data and moves it to the site server. The Maintenance Manager also manages data related to software distribution.

The Maintenance Manager keeps a master copy of client configuration information in the \SITE.SRV\MAINCFG.BOX directory. This master copy is built by Maintenance Manager and then replicated to the logon servers.

The Maintenance Manager creates or updates the software scanning rule files. If the PACKAGE.RUL file on the site server has changed, it will update the software scanning rule file PKG_16.CFG at the site server in the \SITE.SRV\MAINCFG.BOX\CLIENT.SRC directory.

After collecting data on the logon servers, the Maintenance Manager places the client configuration information on each server on \\logon_server\SMS_SHR.

The Maintenance Manager copies the SMS client instruction files. The Inventory Agent currently receives one instruction, which is for resynchronization. The resynchronization instructions for all clients of one domain are kept in the file RESYNC.CFG in the \MAINCFG\INVDOM.BOX\domain _name directory. The appropriate RESYNC file for each domain is replicated to all the logon servers in that domain.

The Maintenance Manager copies the files used by the Inventory Agent: *.UID, PKG_16.CFG,DOMAIN.INI, SMSLS.BAT.

The Maintenance Manager copies the client application binary files. All the binary files are placed in LOGON.SRV\X86.BIN for MS-DOS-based and Intel-based Windows NT clients.

NOTE Maintenance Manager checks for inventory on NetWare servers every 24 hours, because there is no Inventory Agent of SMS inventory service running on the NetWare servers.

Diagnostic Tools: Key Files and Directories

Here are some useful utilities, and important files that help in troubleshooting problems.

DumpNAD and ViewNAD

The key files and directories are the following:

- .HAF
- .HGF
- \LOGON.SRV\APPCTL.BOX\DATABASE

DumpNAD is used to look at application and group (.HAF and .HGF) files. This is useful in determining the exact settings for shared applications and their program groups, as stored in the NAD configuration files.

ViewNAD is used to view from a client machine the shared applications that are located on servers and are available to be used by clients. This utility should be run from the \LOGON.SRV\APPCTL.BOX\DATABASE directory.

Tracer

The key files and directories are the following:

- \SMS\SITE.SRV\platform.BIN
- SMSTRACE.EXE

Tracer is a graphical application you can use to display log files. Whenever the log file is updated, Tracer places the information in its application window. This allows a process to be traced as it is working. Multiple instances of Tracer can be run so that more than one SMS process can be traced simultaneously.

SMSTRACE.EXE is located in \SITE.SRV\platform.BIN.

APPENDIX E

Deploying Software

Systems Management Server allows you to perform an automatic upgrade with no intervention from you or the user.

There are two issues to address with an SMS deployment software. One is planning and the other is the actual deployment procedure. We will cover both in this appendix. ■

Planning for Deployment

In planning for a distribution of software, you should consider the following:

- Planning the project and team foundation
- Configuring and installing
- Preparing a test lab
- Identifying your target computers
- Assembling installation and support teams
- Developing the user training plan

Let's take a look at these considerations in more detail.

Planning the Project and Team Foundation

The following are some suggestions for team formation:

- Choose a project manager or manager(s). This function may be shared among several people.
- Enumerate the skills needed for the planning team.
- Evaluate what resources you have in-house, and which people you will have to search for outside your company.
- Gather a meeting to discuss the project.
- Assign roles and responsibilities to team members.
- Set a timeline for the project, planning, test, and rollout phases.
- Gather the tools and resources necessary to support the project.

Configuring and Installing

Following is a partial list of configuration and installation considerations:

Company Policies—review department policies concerning standard configurations and individual user control.

Hardware and Network Requirements—you need 28MB of hard disk space for a compact installation of Microsoft Office Standard, 55MB for a typical installation, and 89MB for a custom installation. For Office 95 Professional, you need 40MB of hard disk space for a compact installation, 87MB for a typical installation, and 126MB for a custom installation.

There are no RAM guidelines for installing Office 95, although for Windows 95, you should have 8MB RAM minimum. With Exchange loaded, you should count in at least 4MB RAM more. Research the documentation to understand what your minimum hardware requirements will be and to decide whether any of your computers need to be upgraded.

Hardware Configuration—a predefined query included in Systems Management Server lets you see the CPU, the operating system, the available hard disk space, and the installed RAM for your user inventory.

Installation Media—Office for Windows 95 can be installed from the compact disc, floppy disks, or a network server.

Installation Options—three methods can be used to perform an Office 95 installation: Batch, Interactive, and Push. Batch provides a preset installation script for the user *.STF. Interactive allows the user to make all installation decisions, and Push "pushes" the installation without need for user intervention. For Office 95 installation, you can customize your own .STF file for installation to be run in batch mode.

Laptops Versus Desktop Computers—enlist your laptop experts to review the laptop configurations needed.

Local Versus Shared Office Files—Office for Windows 95 can be shared. See the advantages of shared applications in Chapter 21, "Sharing Applications." Office for Windows 95 offers the additional option of putting some files on the local hard disk and some files on the server.

Migrating Existing Configurations—with an established user community, you will have to address issues such as migrating existing data, macros, and add-on programs.

Network Access—users without network access will need to have Office for Windows 95 software installed locally from compact disc or floppy disks. You may want to plan to inventory them somehow as well, probably by creating a custom .MIF file in SMS.

Network Bandwidth—if you intend to install Office for Windows 95 over the network, or if you intend to share applications, you need to evaluate performance over your existing bandwidth.

Network Operating Systems—you need to consider how your particular network operating system (NOS) affects your installation Office for Windows 95. Issues include client network drivers, permissions, and so on.

WAN Connections—for client computers connected over a slow-link network, either installing or running Office for Windows 95 remotely over the network may not be practical.

Preparing a Test Lab

Not testing is not an option! There have been companies that have rolled out an NOS and then realized there was a fundamental incompatibility between their new NOS and their homegrown mission-critical applications, rendering all the users helpless on the first day of production.

Similar things can happen when rolling out a new software platform. If you have homegrown Access applications and so on, you will want to check things out in a lab first.

You must test Office on different hardware platforms, on multiple network operating systems, over slow WAN links, with homegrown applications, and so on.

Identifying Your Target Computers

You may want to query who has a system with at least a 486, 8MB RAM, 75MB hard disk space available. Using Systems Management Server, you can query the SQL Server database to locate all computers that match upgrade requirements. A predefined query included in Systems Management Server examines the CPU, the operating system, the available hard disk space, the installed RAM, and so on.

Developing the User Training Plan

Use company training resources to come up with a training plan for your users. It is great to give everyone in the company Excel; however, if they've been working for years in Lotus 2.x, they will not be very productive or happy until they get some training.

A network-based, computer-based training program can be a good resource for users, who can have self-paced training at their desktop.

Assembling the Rollout Team

Assemble staff who are skilled for rollout. You may have to train staff to make sure they have the skills to install and support the new Office 95 environment. Training is important, because relying on outside contractors long-term or having staff using the "learn as you earn" method may be more expensive than getting training for your people.

Defining the Ideal Client Configurations

The preferred configuration is likely to vary for different groups of users. Some companies have as many as 75 different "standard configurations." However, a good generic standard configuration is invaluable, and help desk support staff, group managers, and your rollout planning team should all meet to come up with a solution for a standard configuration.

Deploying Office for Windows 95: The Steps

In this section, we will discuss Office 95 installation options with Systems Management Server.

The following steps show how to distribute Office for Windows 95 software for local installation on client machines:

- Create an administrative installation point for Office for Windows 95 (run setup /a to a server location).
- First, create a network installation server share by performing an administrative setup of Office for Windows 95 from the Office Installation compact disc or floppy disk set. By using the Network Installation Wizard, you can modify the files in this share to customize the client installations, including whether clients will run Office for Windows 95 locally or on the network. Be sure to document how you customized the installation.
- In the SMS Administration program, create a package using the Office for Windows 95 .PDF that will reference your installation point.

- Give SMS the command to distribute the package to your users.
- SMS copies all the files in the MSOffice folder on the administrative installation point to your target servers for distribution to the clients.
- Users run the package on their computer and SMS runs Setup from the copy of MSOffice residing on the distribution server. All the main and shared Office for Windows 95 components are accessed from this server.

Because SMS copies Office for Windows 95 files to a distribution server, a server that has been designed to service users, users can install Office for Windows 95 onto their local hard disk using the SMS client software.

Distributing Office for Windows 95 for Shared Installation

In this section, we will discuss Office 95 installation options, specifically how to install a shared version of Office 95.

- Start setup using SETUP /a. This copies source files into a directory you specify, and creates a SETUP.STF file for use in network installations.

NOTE Do not use the SETUP.STF file located on the installation disks—it is not for networks or customized installations.

- Create the \MSAPPS32 directory for shared files. MSAPP components are required for all Office Applications.
- Set permissions for access on your network installation point.
- The computer on which you will be running SETUP.EXE must be running Windows 95, Windows NT Workstation 3.51 or later, or Windows NT Server 3.51 or later.
- To share MSAPPS, create an administrative installation point and define where the shared MSAPPS folder will be placed on the network; this location is written into the SETUP.STF file. When a user installs Office for Windows 95 to run shared components from this MSAPPS folder, the MSAPPS location defined in the SETUP.STF file is written into the user's registry.

NOTE SMS will distribute the Office for Windows 95 installation package to the distribution server that is defined for a particular user, but it will not change the shared MSAPPS location defined in the .STF file. This means that, even though a particular package may be sent to multiple distribution servers, all users of that package will share the same MSAPPS network location definition.

Creating the Office for Windows 95 Package

Microsoft Office for Windows 95 includes a sample Package Definition File (.PDF) for use with SMS: OFF95STD.PDF in the Office 95 Standard product, or OFF95PRO.PDF in the Office 95 Professional product.

The .PDF has command line definitions in it for the standard types of client setup: Typical, Compact, Custom, Complete (the same as Custom but with all options selected), and Workstation (called Run From Network Server in Setup). For example, the command line for Typical is: CommandLine=setup.exe /q1 /b1. There's a setup command line for every specific installation type (except for Custom, for which Setup is run interactively).

The /q1 option directs Setup to run with no user interaction; the /b1 option directs Setup to use the Typical installation type. When this command is run from this SMS package, Setup automatically installs Office for Windows 95 using the predefined options for the Typical installation type.

NOTE It is not always easy to get information for batch installations. With Windows 95, there are utilities in the 95 Resource Kit or Microsoft Plus for batch installation. With Office, you can pull numerous white papers from **http://www.microsoft.com** on batch installation of Office and deployment SMS. ■

Remember that you should not remove a package from the distribution server, because that is where users share the application from.

Adding Custom Commands to the .PDF

Using the Packages window in the Systems Management Server Administrator, you can create a new command in the Office for Windows 95 package that will run your custom command line for Setup.

Use the following procedure to add your command to the Office 95 .PDF file:

- In the Packages window, choose File menu, New.
- In the Package Properties dialog box, click Import.
- In the file browser, select the .PDF file OFF95STD.PDF or OFF95PRO.PDF, included with Office for Windows 95. It is located in the administrative installation point in the folder containing the main Office for Windows 95 application files, not on the diskettes.
- In the Package Properties dialog box, click Workstation if you want to install Office for Windows 95 on the user's local hard disk.
- In the Setup Package dialog box, specify the location of the administrative installation point for Office for Windows 95 as the "source folder."
- To define the new command line, click New. In the Command Name box, type a name for the new command; for example, type "Office Install for New York Site Ver 2.0."

- In the Command Line box, type the command to run your custom Setup; for instance, to run SETUP.EXE from the administrative installation point with the SETUP.STF file setup file, in quiet mode, type SETUP.EXE /t SETUP.STF /qt. Setup files, .STF, are described later in this chapter.

Here are the details on the Setup command line options :

Setup has several command line parameters. Following are the parameters most valuable for a Systems Management Server installation.

- **/q1** or **/qt**—Quiet mode, **q1** does not request any user input; **qt** hides the setup display, including the blue background and the percent done bar. The **qt** switch prevents users from canceling the installation.
- **/b#**, where # is 1, 2, 3, or 4—Specifies the type of installation: typical, compact, custom, run from server.
- **/g "c:\off95log.txt"**—Generates the log file to record the details of the setup process. This file can then be collected in the next inventory and reviewed.
- **/t filename.stf**—Gives the name of the customized .STF file.
    - Select the Automated Command Line check box, so no user input is necessary.
    - If you will be installing on Windows NT, you can also select the System (Background) Task check box to indicate that you want the package to run in the background. This will work if no user input is necessary.
    - In the Supported Platforms box, select the appropriate platforms: Windows 95, Windows NT, or both. Click OK, and then click Close.

You can now create a Run Command On Workstation job and distribute your Office 95 package.

When SMS sends the MSOffice package to a distribution server, it places the entire MSOffice folder and subfolders in an internal location on the distribution server. When the user package is executed on a user system, Setup is run from within this copy of MSOffice. If the user selects the Run From Network Server installation type, Setup will install Office for Windows 95 so that the user will share the Office for Windows 95 executables from this location on the distribution server.

Using Setup Scripts to Install Windows 95 and Office for Windows 95

Windows 95 and Office for Windows 95 allow the use of special information files: .INF files for Windows 95 and .STF files for Office for Windows 95.

Command lines in Office 95 give the user of a target computer different installation options, such as Typical, Compact, Complete, and Custom.

The package's command line definitions can be created manually by the SMS administrator, or they can be automatically created by using a Package Definition File (.PDF) A .PDF file is a text file that contains all the required SMS package information, including the command line definitions. A package to deliver source files to a site server can use the compressed .CAB file to minimize traffic across links.

If you want to use a .PDF file for Office 95 Installation and, say, the SMS administrator wants to set up the "Office 95 Package" definition, the administrator opens a new Package Properties window and uses the Import feature. This will import the .PDF file that is included with this guide. This file then inserts the required information for installing Office 95 in the Package Properties window, including command line definitions.

The administrator then needs only to enter the path information to Office 95 source files on a network server, and the package definition is complete. This completed package can be used to create an SMS job that installs Office 95 on the target computers. ●

APPENDIX F

Third-Party Add-On Products for SMS

While Microsoft did a good job of addressing the management of popular PC operating systems and LANs, it also left a number of holes just waiting to be filled by third-party vendors. UNIX, for example, is a big area where SMS falls short. Fortunately, SMS is built around standards such as DMI and SNMP that ease integration with other products. The fact that SMS maintains information about itself and information that it has collected in SQL Server makes it straightforward to use that information in other applications. Additionally, Microsoft provides the SMS Software Development Kit, enabling solution providers and developers to create direct links to SMS services.

This appendix contains a representative, but not all-inclusive, sample of the software vendors who are providing products that complement or provide some degree of integration with SMS. For convenience, this list is sorted both by product category and by company name. ■

By Company Name

Company	Product Category	Product Name
ABC Systems and Development 011-441-952-271-000 **http://www.pcug.co.uk/~akcsl/abc.htm**	Admin	Lan Admin ABC Lan Admin is a tool that is designed to do two things: First, it draws all day to day admin tasks for the entire network to a single point; allows an administrator to add or modify users, groups, printers, resources, install applications, and so on from his or her desktop; second, the product enables the administrator to provide the user with a fully mobile, customized Windows desktop.
ABC Systems and Development 011-441-952-271-00 **http://www.pcug.co.uk/~akcsl/abc.htm**	Metering	Lan Licenser Lan Licenser has been designed to automate the collection and storage of information about the usage of applications on the LAN; Lan Licenser then provides the reporting tools to enable this information to be reported upon, allowing the information to be used to build a cohesive management strategy for application licenses on the LAN. Lan Licenser also gives the ability for the network administrator to set the maximum number of concurrent licenses for an application in use on the LAN at any one time, helping you to comply with your license agreements. Lan Licenser has been designed for the larger LAN and includes a PDF (Package Definition File) that enables it to be installed by Systems Management Server across the entire network. Lan Licenser can automatically query Microsoft BackOffice Systems Management Server for its software inventory. Microsoft Systems Management Server and Lan Licenser 2 both use Crystal Reports as their report engine (Lan Licenser 2 ships with example reports already in place). This means that a generated report can contain data from both Microsoft Systems Management Server and Lan Licenser.

Company	Product Category	Product Name
American Power Conversion 401-789-5735 **http://www.apcc.com/**	Power	PowerChute Plus PowerChute Plus for Windows NT (4.2.2 and above) supports Microsoft Systems Management Server (SMS). This capability allows network managers to view basic information for all UPSs attached to NT servers running PowerChute Plus. The information is useful in a variety of ways: Determining inventory (for example, what UPSs are available on the network); System planning (for example, based on UPS capacity, what additional equipment may be plugged into it); Preventive maintenance planning (for example, tracking the age of a UPS and when its battery was last replaced).
Apsylog 415-812-7700 **http://www.dfc.com/apsylog.htm**	Asset	Apsylog Asset Manager Asset Manager is an asset management system that relies on popular database products such as Oracle and Sybase to store collected information and can use SMS as an auto-discovery tool.
Apsylog 415-812-7700 **http://www.dfc.com/pcgalaxy.htm**	Asset	PC Galaxy for Windows NT PC Galaxy is an asset management tool that enables you to: establish a detailed inventory of hardware and software assets; simplify equipment maintenance; track Help Desk calls and create a technical knowledge base; reduce procurement costs (estimates, orders, receiving, stock); monitor expenses and bill them to cost centers; prepare advanced reports using SQL queries.

continues

continued

Company	Product Category	Product Name
ASI Corporation 613-723-7374 **http://www.assetpro.ca/**	Asset	AssetPRO AssetPRO 2.0: Enterprise Asset Management combines all the features of traditional life-cycle asset management with automatic data collection, integrated Help Desk, and electronic asset procurement. AssetPRO is aimed at assisting MIS in reducing workloads, tracking and identifying hardware and software, issuing asset responsibility to users, and solving user issues via Help Desk. AssetPRO integrates with SMS events.
BateTech Software 303-763-8333 **http://www.batetech.com/**	Help Desk	Customer One Customer One is a Windows NT-based Help Desk solution with business rules that define your customer service levels and automatic escalation of service requests. It has links to a variety of systems, including SMS.
Bay Networks **http://www.baynetworks.com/**	Network	Bay Networks Embedded routing in Windows NT Server allows the local office administrator to use Microsoft's System Management Server for NT to control all aspects of the local network, including BayRS components, through a PC server-based network management interface.
BMC Software **http://www.bmc.com/**	Application	PATROL PATROL provides automatic alert capabilities for applications databases, messaging, middle-ware, operating systems, and other underlying resources. The PATROL data management family of products automates many of the manual, error-prone steps associated with data

Company	Product Category	Product Name
		management. PATROL integrates with SMS events and alerts.
Cheyenne Software, Inc. 516-629-4413 **http://www.chey.com/**	Backup	ArcServe for Windows NT ArcServe 6, a network backup solution for Windows NT, offers full support for Microsoft BackOffice, including "hot," online backup of Microsoft SQL Server and Microsoft Exchange Server, protection and integration of Microsoft Systems Management Server, and mainframe connectivity through Microsoft SNA Server.
Cheyenne Software, Inc. 516-629-4413 **http://www.chey.com/**	Virus	InocuLAN for Windows NT 1.0 InocuLAN 1.01 for Windows NT is an anti-virus solution designed to protect your entire network with support for Windows 3.x, Windows 95, DOS, Macintosh, and Windows NT workstations. InocuLAN is fully integrated with SMS—Microsoft's standard for software management.
Comma Soft 0228/9770-0 **http://www.comma-soft.com/**	Help Desk	HelpLINE HelpLINE is a Help Desk software product. A HelpLine Integration Pack for the Microsoft Systems Management Server adds SMS integration.
Comma Soft 0228/9770-0 **http://www.comma-soft.com/**	Setup	Remote Package Command Manager Remote Package Command Manager provides laptop support for the SMS Package Command Manager.

continues

continued

Company	Product Category	Product Name
Compaq Computer **http://www.compaq.com/**	Device	Insight Manager Compaq Insight Manager is a comprehensive management tool that monitors the operation of Compaq servers and Compaq Deskpro PCs. Insight Manager provides inventory MIFs that make extensive inventory information available to SMS. Additionally, Insight Manager can launch from the SMS toolbar.
Computer Associates (CA) 206-451-2900 **http://www.cai.com/**	Console	CA-Unicenter CA-Unicenter provides administration of client/server networks featuring enterprise software delivery, intelligent control of RDBMSs and applications, distributed hierarchical storage management, and Help Desk functions.
Computing Edge Corporation 206-788-4828 **http://www.computingedge.com/**	UNIX	Proxy Domain Services Proxy Domain Services from Computing Edge extends the management capabilities of Systems Management Server. With Proxy Domain Services, Systems Management Server can control branch office Novell NetWare or LAN Manager UNIX LANs across Wide Area Network links. Supported platforms include NetWare 3.x and 4.x, Digital UNIX, HP-UX, LINUX, and NCR.
Crystal, a Seagate company 604-893-6313 **http://www.crystalinc.com/**	Report	Crystal Reports for Systems Management Server Reporting Package bundled into Systems Management Server.

Company	Product Category	Product Name
Crystal, a Seagate company 604-893-6313 **http://www.crystalinc.com/**	Report	Crystal's 101 Reports for Microsoft BackOffice Microsoft SMS (SQL Server) Reports capture your hardware and software inventory information, distribute software, and provide troubleshooting with SMS. Crystal Reports for SMS provides reports sorted and subtotaled by product type or user. SMS (SQL Server)reports include: Computers with duplicate IP addresses; Operating system in use by domain; Systems ready for Windows 95 upgrade; Free disk space of PCs by domain.
Datawatch 800-988-4739	Asset	Q-Support/Quetzal Corporation Q-Support is a comprehensive, flexible Help Desk automation and asset management package capable of managing every aspect of support center operations. It interfaces SMS for inventory, alerts, and software distribution.
Digital Equipment Corporation 603-881-0390 **http://www.digital.com**	Network	POLYCENTER NetView for NT POLYCENTER Manager on NetView for Windows NT is integrated with POLYCENTER AssetWORKS and Microsoft's Systems Management Server. Through the use of bidirectional launch capabilities, these products provide a comprehensive approach to managing enterprisewide, multivendor hardware, software, and network resources. From POLYCENTER Manager on NetView for Windows NT, the network manager can launch Microsoft's Systems Management Server and POLYCENTER AssetWORKS to display a Systems Management Server property sheet for a network or system object.

continues

continued

Company	Product Category	Product Name
Digital Equipment Corporation 603-881-0390 **http://www.digital.com**	UNIX	POLYCENTER AssetWORKS POLYCENTER AssetWORKS operates in conjunction with Microsoft's Systems Management Server to provide a broad range of configuration management capabilities for multivendor computer systems across the network. From the Systems Management Server and POLYCENTER AssetWORKS, the network and system manager can launch NetView to find a network object, diagnose it, show its properties, and graph network traffic.
Distributed Technologies Corporation 617-684-0060 **http://www.dtcorp.com/**	Asset	GlobalAUDIT GlobalAUDIT is an application with LAN and Web components which automatically discovers and tracks distributed computer system resources across multivendor LANS and WANs. GlobalAUDIT delivers a profile of about 300 distinct data elements from each desktop system.
Express Systems 206-728-8300 x414 **http://www.express-systems.com/**	Metering	Express Meter Express Meter manages your concurrent software licenses and can prevent more than the licensed number of copies from running. It comes preconfigured with metering information on over 100 of the most popular applications.
Fujitsu Ltd. 81-559-24-7246	Network	MpWalker MpWalker is a systems and network management product that is integrated with SMS.

Company	Product Category	Product Name
Hewlett Packard 408-553-3783 **http://www.hp.com/**	Network	HP OpenView for Windows HP OpenView for Windows is a distributed, scalable network management product that allows for multiple operator consoles and distributed collection stations.
Intel **http://www.intel.com**	Virus	LANDesk Virus Protect LANDesk Virus Protect for Windows NT utilizes server-based technology, providing centralized virus protection of vital data as it passes through the server, and preventing viruses from passing to client workstations.
Intel Corporation **http://www.intel.com**	Device	LANDesk Server Manager Intel LANDesk Server Manager Pro gives LAN administrators and network managers a nonproprietary hardware and software management solution for NetWare and Windows NT servers. It is DMI-enabled for management from any DMI Management Console, and includes DMI Service Layers for NetWare and NT.
Janus Technologies 412-787-3030	Asset	Argis Argis is a Windows-based IT asset management tool that focuses on reducing a company's IT asset budget through its cost, contract, and inventory management facilities. Argis provides extensive online help, security features and interfaces to leading automatic inventory management tools.

continues

continued

Company	Product Category	Product Name
Novadigm, Inc. **http://www.novadigm.com/**	Policy	EDM Adapters for Microsoft SMS The NOVADIGM Enablement Initiative is a formalized effort to take advantage of the flexibility of EDM's object-oriented infrastructure to rapidly integrate complementary third-party products. The initiative provides customers, ISVs, and IT service providers with an extended portfolio of objects and methods that serve as Snap-In Adapters that automatically establish working interfaces between EDM and industry-leading client/server development, desktop tools, and systems management environments. An EDM Adapter is now available for SMS.
OnDemand Software 941-261-6678 **http://www.ondemand.com/**	Setup	WinINSTALL WinINSTALL totally automates software distribution and makes quick work of adding new applications or upgrading installed applications to the latest release. WinINSTALL Version 5.1 is tightly integrated with Systems Management Server. It is a simple matter to create System Management Server Run Command on Workstation jobs which use the power of Systems Management Server to determine target machines, to distribute files to servers throughout the enterprise, and to launch WinINSTALL as the install process on the user's desktop. This approach combines the strengths of both products to provide an extremely effective network management combination.

Company	Product Category	Product Name
Seagate EMS 919-489-6300 **http://www.seagate.com**	Schedule	AshWin Seagate AshWin provides mainframe-like unattended background processing for heterogeneous client/server environments. It allows you to use all your enterprise computing power 24 hours a day, eliminating the need to purchase additional workstations. AshWin is "Designed for BackOffice" and is certified as such by Microsoft. Seagate AshWin can use Systems Management Server's machine inventory information to group workstations into user-definable sets for scheduling specific applications.
Seagate Software (formerly Arcada Software) 206-936-5660 **http://www.arcada.com/**	Backup	Backup Exec Backup Exec for Windows NT is a 32-bit backup program that protects the entire Windows NT network. Backup Exec provides true client/server integration for Microsoft BackOffice, including SMS capabilities to manage software distribution, licensing, and network operations.
Software Spectrum Technology Services Group 214-864-5946 **http://www.swspectrum.com/gr/tsg/tsg.htm**	Service	Systems Management Server Alliance Software Spectrum delivers solutions based on Microsoft Systems Management Server and Symantec Norton Administrator for Networks (NAN) to help manage distributed PC environments using cost-efficient approaches. Each of these solutions provides three major capabilities to increase the control and data available to information technology professionals: Auto-discovery of hardware and software inventory across the network; Electronic software distribution and installation; Centralized remote network administration and support of both servers and the desktop.

continues

continued

Company	Product Category	Product Name
Stirling Technologies, Inc. **http://www.installshield.com/**	Setup	InstallShield InstallShield3 is a comprehensive installation system that lets you create complete window software installations, including Windows 95.
Tally Systems 603-643-1300 **http://www.tallysys.com/**	Asset	NetCensus NetCensus enhances the level of inventory within Systems Management Server with the most detailed and accurate hardware and software inventory available. Supported platforms include DOS, Windows, Windows 95, and Windows NT.
Tally Systems 603-643-1300 **http://www.tallysys.com**	Metering	CentaMeter CentaMeter supplies comprehensive software metering and usage tracking to Systems Management Server. CentaMeter provides Systems Management Server with the information needed to manage and control software usage enterprisewide. Supported platforms include DOS, Windows, Windows 95, and Windows NT.
Tally Systems 603-643-1300 **http://www.tallysys.com**	Multifunction	Cenergy Cenergy offers complete desktop asset management functionality within the Systems Management Server environment and feeds information into the Systems Management Server database.

By Product Category

Product Category	Company	Product Name
Admin	ABC Systems and Development 011-441-952-271-000 **http://www.pcug.co.uk/~akcsl/abc.htm**	Lan Admin ABC Lan Admin is a tool that is designed to do two things: First, it draws all day-to-day admin tasks for the entire network to a single point; this allows an administrator to add or modify users, groups, printers, resources, install applications, and so on from his or her desk top; second, the product enables the adminis trator to provide the user with a fully mobile, customized Windows desktop.
Application	BMC Software **http://www.bmc.com/**	PATROL PATROL provides automatic alert capabilities for applications, databases, messaging, middleware, operating systems, and other underlying resources. The PATROL data management family of products automates many of the manual, error-prone steps associated with data management. Patrol integrates with SMS events and alerts.
Asset	Distributed Technologies Corporation 617-684-0060 **http://www.dtcorp.com/**	GlobalAUDIT GlobalAUDIT is an application with LAN and Web components which automatically discovers and tracks distributed computer system resources across multivendor LANS and WANs. GlobalAUDIT delivers a profile of about 300 distinct data elements from each desktop system.

continues

continued

Product Category	Company	Product Name
Asset	Apsylog 415-812-7700 **http://www.dfc.com/apsylog.htm**	Apsylog Asset manager Asset Manager is an asset management system that relies on popular database products such as Oracle and Sybase to store collected information and can use SMS as an auto-discovery tool.
Asset	Apsylog 415-812-7700 **http://www.dfc.com/pc galaxy.htm**	PC Galaxy for Windows NT PC Galaxy is an asset management tool that enables you to: establish a detailed inventory of hardware and software assets; simplify equipment maintenance; track Help Desk calls and create a technical knowledge base; reduce procurement costs (estimates, orders, receiving, stock); monitor expenses and bill them to cost centers; prepare advanced reports using SQL queries.
Asset	ASI Corporation 613-723-7374 **http://www.assetpro.ca/**	AssetPRO AssetPRO 2.0: Enterprise Asset Management combines all the features of traditional life-cycle asset management with automatic data collection, integrated Help Desk, and electronic asset procurement. AssetPRO is aimed at assisting MIS in reducing workloads, tracking and identifying hardware and software, issuing asset responsibility to users, and solving user issues via Help Desk. AssetPRO integrates with SMS events.

Product Category	Company	Product Name
Asset	Janus Technologies 412-787-3030	Argis Argis is a Windows-based IT asset management tool that focuses on reducing a company's IT asset budget through its cost, contract, and inventory management facilities. Argis provides extensive online help, security features, and interfaces to leading automatic inventory management tools.
Asset	Tally Systems 603-643-1300 **http://www.tallysys.com/**	NetCensus NetCensus enhances the level of inventory within Systems Management Server with the most detailed and accurate hardware and software inventory available. Supported platforms include DOS, Windows, Windows 95, and Windows NT.
Asset	Datawatch 800-988-4739	Q-Support/Quetzal Corporation Q-Support is a comprehensive, flexible Help Desk automation and asset management package capable of managing every aspect of support center operations. It interfaces SMS for inventory, alerts, and software distribution.
Backup	Seagate Software (formerly Arcada Software) 206-936-5660 **http://www.arcada.com/**	Backup Exec Backup Exec for Windows NT is a 32-bit backup program that protects the entire Windows NT network. Backup Exec provides true client/server integration for Microsoft BackOffice, including SMS capabilities to manage software distribution, licensing, and network operations.

continues

continued

Product Category	Company	Product Name
Backup	Cheyenne Software, Inc. 516-629-4413 **http://www.chey.com/**	ArcServe for Windows NT ArcServe 6, a network backup solution for Windows NT, offers full support for Microsoft BackOffice, including "hot," online backup of Microsoft SQL Server and Microsoft Exchange Server, protection and integration of Microsoft Systems Management Server, and mainframe connectivity through Microsoft SNA Server.
Console	Computer Associates (CA) 206-451-2900 **http://www.cai.com/**	CA-Unicenter CA-Unicenter provides administration of client/server networks featuring enterprise software delivery, intelligent control of RDBMSs and applications, distributed hierarchical storage management, and Help Desk functions.
Device	Compaq Computer **http://www.compaq.com/**	Insight Manager Compaq Insight Manager is a comprehensive management tool that monitors the operation of Compaq servers and Compaq Deskpro PCs. Insight Manager provides inventory MIFs that make extensive inventory information available to SMS. Additionally, Insight Manager can launch from the SMS toolbar.
Device	Intel Corporation **http://www.intel.com**	LANDesk Server Manager Intel LANDesk Server Manager Pro gives LAN administrators and network managers a nonproprietary hardware and software management solution for NetWare and Windows NT servers. It is DMI-enabled for management from any DMI Management Console, and includes DMI Service Layers for NetWare and NT.

Product Category	Company	Product Name
Help Desk	BateTech Software 303-763-8333 **http://www.batetech.com/**	Customer One Customer One is a Windows NT-based Help Desk solution with business rules that define your customer service levels and automatic escalation of service requests. It has links to a variety of systems, including SMS.
Help Desk	Comma Soft 0228/9770-0 **http://www.comma-soft.com/**	HelpLINE HelpLINE is a Help Desk software product. A HelpLine Integration Pack for the Microsoft Systems Management Server adds SMS integration.
Metering	ABC Systems and Development 011-441-952-271-00 **http://www.pcug.co.uk/~akcsl/abc.htm**	Lan Licenser Lan Licenser has been designed to automate the collection and storage of information about the usage of applications on the LAN; Lan Licenser then provides the reporting tools to enable this information to be reported upon, allowing the information to be used to build a cohesive management strategy for application licenses on the LAN. Lan Licenser also gives the ability for the network administrator to set the maximum number of concurrent licenses for an application in use on the LAN at any one time, helping you comply with your license agreements. Lan Licenser has been designed for the larger LAN and includes a PDF (Package Definition File) that enables it to be installed by Systems Management Server across the entire network. Lan Licenser can automatically query Microsoft BackOffice Systems Management Server for its software inventory. Microsoft Systems Management Server and Lan Licenser 2 both use Crystal Reports as their report engine (Lan Licenser 2 ships with example reports already in place). This means that a generated report can contain data from both Microsoft Systems Management Server and Lan Licenser.

continues

continued

Product Category	Company	Product Name
Metering	Express Systems 206-728-8300 x414 **http://www.express-systems.com/**	Express Meter Express Meter manages your concurrent software licenses and can prevent more than the licensed number of copies from running. It comes preconfigured with metering information on over 100 of the most popular applications.
Metering	Tally Systems 603-643-1300 **http://www.tallysys.com**	CentaMeter CentaMeter supplies comprehensive software metering and usage tracking to Systems Management Server. CentaMeter provides Systems Management Server with the informa tion needed to manage and control software usage enterprisewide. Supported platforms include DOS, Windows, Windows 95, and Windows NT.
Multifunction	Tally Systems 603-643-1300 **http://www.tallysys.com**	Cenergy Cenergy offers complete desktop asset management functionality within the Systems Management Server environment and feeds information into the Systems Management Server database.
Network	Bay Networks **http://www.baynetworks.com/**	Bay Networks Embedded routing in Windows NT Server allows the local office administrator to use Microsoft's System Management Server for NT to control all aspects of the local network, including BayRS components, through a PC server-based network management interface.

Product Category	Company	Product Name
Network	Digital Equipment Corporation 603-881-0390 **http://www.digital.com**	POLYCENTER NetView for NT POLYCENTER Manager on NetView for Windows NT is integrated with POLYCENTER AssetWORKS and Microsoft's Systems Management Server. Through the use of bidirectional launch capabilities, these products provide a comprehensive approach to managing enterprisewide, multivendor hardware, software, and network resources. From POLYCENTER Manager on NetView for Windows NT, the network manager can launch Microsoft's Systems Management Server and POLYCENTER AssetWORKS to display a Systems Management Server property sheet for a network or system object.
Network	Fujitsu Ltd. 81-559-24-7246	MpWalker MpWalker is a systems and network management product that is integrated with SMS.
Network	Hewlett Packard 408-553-3783 **http://www.hp.com/**	HP OpenView for Windows HP OpenView for Windows is a distributed, scalable network management product that allows for multiple operator consoles and distributed collection stations.

continues

continued

Product Category	Company	Product Name
Policy	Novadigm, Inc. **http://www.novadigm.com/**	EDM Adapters for Microsoft SMS The NOVADIGM Enablement Initiative is a formalized effort to take advantage of the flexibility of EDM's object-oriented infrastructure to rapidly integrate complementary third-party products. The initiative provides customers, ISVs, and IT service providers with an extended portfolio of objects and methods that serve as Snap-In Adapters that automatically establish working interfaces between EDM and industry-leading client/server development, desktop tools, and systems management environments. An EDM Adapter is now available for SMS.
Power	American Power Conversion 401-789-5735 **http://www.apcc.com/**	PowerChute Plus PowerChute Plus for Windows NT (4.2.2 and above) supports Microsoft Systems Management Server (SMS). This capability allows network managers to view basic information for all UPSs attached to NT servers running PowerChute Plus. The information is useful in a variety of ways: Determining inventory (for example, what UPSs are available on the network); System planning (for example, based on UPS capacity, what additional equipment may be plugged into it); Preventive maintenance planning (for example, the age of a UPS and when its battery was last replaced).

Product Category	Company	Product Name
Report	Crystal, a Seagate company 604-893-6313 **http://www.crystalinc.com/**	Crystal Reports for Systems Management Server Reporting Package bundled into Systems Management Server.
Report	Crystal, a Seagate company 604-893-6313 **http://www.crystalinc.com/**	Crystal's 101 Reports for Microsoft BackOffice Microsoft SMS (SQL Server) Reports capture your hardware and software inventory information, distribute software, and provide troubleshooting with SMS. Crystal reports for SMS provides reports sorted and subtotaled by product type or user. SMS (SQL Server) reports include: Computers with duplicate IP addresses; Operating system in use by domain; Systems ready for Windows 95 upgrade; Free disk space of PCs by domain.
Schedule	Seagate EMS 919-489-6300 **http://www.seagate.com**	AshWin Seagate AshWin provides mainframe-like unattended background processing for heterogeneous client/server environments. It allows you to use all your enterprise computing power 24 hours a day, eliminating the need to purchase additional workstations. AshWin is "Designed for BackOffice" and is certified as such by Microsoft. Seagate AshWin can use Systems Management Server's machine inventory information to group workstations into user-definable sets for scheduling specific applications.

continues

continued

Product Category	Company	Product Name
Service	Software Spectrum Technology Services Group 214-864-5946 **http://www.swspectrum.com/gr/tsg/tsg.htm**	Systems Management Server Alliance Software Spectrum delivers solutions based on Microsoft Systems Management Server and Symantec Norton Administrator for Networks (NAN) to help manage distributed PC environments using cost-efficient approaches. Each ofthese solutions provides three major capabilities to increase the control and data available to information technology professionals: Autodiscovery of hardware and software inventory across the network; Electronic software distribution and installation; Centralized remote network administration and support of both servers and the desktop.
Setup	Comma Soft 0228/9770-0 **http://www.comma-soft.com/**	Remote Package Command Manager Remote Package Command Manager provides laptop support for the SMS Package Command Manager.
Setup	OnDemand Software 941-261-6678 **http://www.ondemand.com/**	WinINSTALL WinINSTALL totally automates software distribution and makes quick work of adding new applications or upgrading installed applications to the latest release. WinINSTALL Version 5.1 is tightly integrated with Systems Management Server. It is a simple matter to create System Management Server Run Command On Workstation jobs which use the power of Systems Management Server to determine target machines, to distribute files to servers throughout the enterprise, and to launch WinINSTALL as the install process on the user's desktop. This approach combines the strengths of both products to provide an extremely effective network management combination.

Product Category	Company	Product Name
Setup	Stirling Technologies, Inc. **http://www.installshield.com/**	InstallShield InstallShield3 is a comprehensive installation system that lets you create complete window software installations, including Windows 95.
UNIX	Computing Edge Corporation 206-788-4828 **http://www.computingedge.com/**	Proxy Domain Services Proxy Domain Services from Computing Edge extends the management capabilities of Systems Management Server. With Proxy Domain Services, Systems Management Server can control branch office Novell NetWare or LAN Manager UNIX LANs across Wide Area Network links. Supported platforms include NetWare 3.x and 4.x, Digital UNIX, HP-UX, LINUX, and NCR.
UNIX	Digital Equipment Corporation 603-881-0390 **http://www.digital.com**	POLYCENTER AssetWORKS POLYCENTER AssetWORKS operates in conjunction with Microsoft's Systems Management Server to provide a broad range of configuration management capabilities for multivendor computer systems across the network. From the Systems Management Server and POLYCENTER AssetWORKS, the network and system manager can launch NetView to find a network object, diagnose it, show its properties, and graph network traffic.

continues

continued

Product Category	Company	Product Name
Virus	Cheyenne Software, Inc. 516-629-4413 **http://www.chey.com/**	InocuLAN for Windows NT 1.0 InocuLAN 1.01 for Windows NT is an anti-virus solution designed to protect your entire network with support for Windows 3.x, Windows 95, DOS, Macintosh, and Windows NT workstations. InocuLAN is fully integrated with SMS—Microsoft's standard for software management.
Virus	Intel http://www.intel.com	LANDesk Virus Protect LANDesk Virus Protect for Windows NT utilizes server-based technology, providing centralized virus protection of vital data as it passes through the server, and preventing viruses from passing to client workstations.

Index

Symbols

A

E

F

J-K

L

M

N

Q

R

S

T

U-V

W-X-Y-Z

Check out Que® Books on the World Wide Web http://www.mcp.com/que

As the biggest software release in computer history, Windows 95 continues to redefine the computer industry. Click here for the latest info on our Windows 95 books

Make computing quick and easy with these products designed exclusively for new and casual users

Examine the latest releases in word processing, spreadsheets, operating systems, and suites

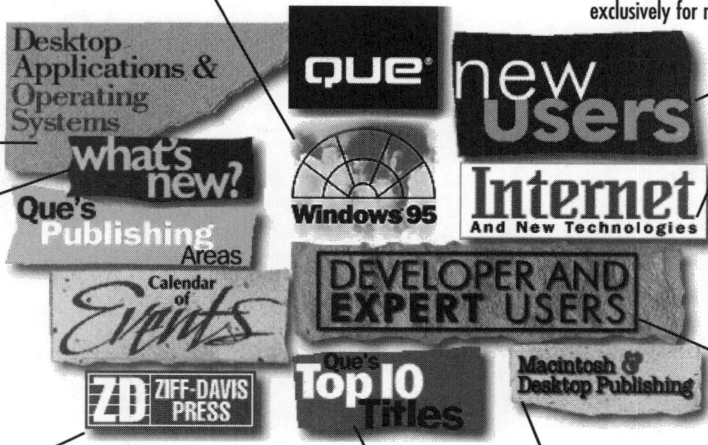

The Internet, The World Wide Web, CompuServe®, America Online®, Prodigy®—it's a world of ever-changing information. Don't get left behind!

Find out about new additions to our site, new bestsellers and hot topics

In-depth information on high-end topics: find the best reference books for databases, programming, networking, and client/server technologies

A recent addition to Que, Ziff-Davis Press publishes the highly-successful *How It Works* and *How to Use* series of books, as well as *PC Learning Labs Teaches* and *PC Magazine* series of book/disk packages

Stay on the cutting edge of Macintosh® technologies and visual communications

Find out which titles are making headlines

With 6 separate publishing groups, Que develops products for many specific market segments and areas of computer technology. Explore our Web Site and you'll find information on best-selling titles, newly published titles, upcoming products, authors, and much more.

- Stay informed on the latest industry trends and products available
- Visit our online bookstore for the latest information and editions
- Download software from Que's library of the best shareware and freeware

Que®

Complete and Return this Card for a *FREE* Computer Book Catalog

Thank you for purchasing this book! You have purchased a superior computer book written expressly for your needs. To continue to provide the kind of up-to-date, pertinent coverage you've come to expect from us, we need to hear from you. Please take a minute to complete and return this self-addressed, postage-paid form. In return, we'll send you a free catalog of all our computer books on topics ranging from word processing to programming and the internet.

Mr. ☐ Mrs. ☐ Ms. ☐ Dr. ☐

Name (first) ______ (M.I.) ☐ (last) ______

Address ______

______

City ______ State ______ Zip ______ ______

Phone ______ ______ ______ Fax ______ ______ ______

Company Name ______

E-mail address ______

1. Please check at least (3) influencing factors for purchasing this book.

- Front or back cover information on book ☐
- Special approach to the content ☐
- Completeness of content ☐
- Author's reputation ☐
- Publisher's reputation ☐
- Book cover design or layout ☐
- Index or table of contents of book ☐
- Price of book ☐
- Special effects, graphics, illustrations ☐
- Other (Please specify): ______ ☐

2. How did you first learn about this book?

- Saw in Macmillan Computer Publishing catalog ☐
- Recommended by store personnel ☐
- Saw the book on bookshelf at store ☐
- Recommended by a friend ☐
- Received advertisement in the mail ☐
- Saw an advertisement in: ______ ☐
- Read book review in: ______ ☐
- Other (Please specify): ______ ☐

3. How many computer books have you purchased in the last six months?

- This book only ☐
- 3 to 5 books ☐
- 2 books ☐
- More than 5 ☐

4. Where did you purchase this book?

- Bookstore ☐
- Computer Store ☐
- Consumer Electronics Store ☐
- Department Store ☐
- Office Club ☐
- Warehouse Club ☐
- Mail Order ☐
- Direct from Publisher ☐
- Internet site ☐
- Other (Please specify): ______ ☐

5. How long have you been using a computer?

- ☐ Less than 6 months
- ☐ 6 months to a year
- ☐ 1 to 3 years
- ☐ More than 3 years

6. What is your level of experience with personal computers and with the subject of this book?

	With PCs	With subject of book
New	☐	☐
Casual	☐	☐
Accomplished	☐	☐
Expert	☐	☐

Source Code ISBN: 0-7897-0820-5

7. Which of the following best describes your job title?

Administrative Assistant .... ☐
Coordinator .... ☐
Manager/Supervisor .... ☐
Director .... ☐
Vice President .... ☐
President/CEO/COO .... ☐
Lawyer/Doctor/Medical Professional .... ☐
Teacher/Educator/Trainer .... ☐
Engineer/Technician .... ☐
Consultant .... ☐
Not employed/Student/Retired .... ☐
Other (Please specify): ______________ ☐

8. Which of the following best describes the area of the company your job title falls under?

Accounting .... ☐
Engineering .... ☐
Manufacturing .... ☐
Operations .... ☐
Marketing .... ☐
Sales .... ☐
Other (Please specify): ______________ ☐

9. What is your age?

Under 20 .... ☐
21-29 .... ☐
30-39 .... ☐
40-49 .... ☐
50-59 .... ☐
60-over .... ☐

10. Are you:

Male .... ☐
Female .... ☐

11. Which computer publications do you read regularly? (Please list)

____
____
____
____
____
____
____
____

***Comments*:** ______________________________
____
____

Fold here and scotch-tape to mail.

NO POSTAGE NECESSARY IF MAILED IN THE UNITED STATES

BUSINESS REPLY MAIL
FIRST-CLASS MAIL PERMIT NO. 9918 INDIANAPOLIS IN

POSTAGE WILL BE PAID BY THE ADDRESSEE

ATTN MARKETING
MACMILLAN COMPUTER PUBLISHING
MACMILLAN PUBLISHING USA
201 W 103RD ST
INDIANAPOLIS IN 46290-9042

Before using any of the software on this disc, you need to install the software you plan to use. If you have problems with *Special Edition Using Microsoft Systems Management Server*, please contact Macmillan Technical Support at (317) 581-3833. We can be reached by e-mail at support@mcp.com or by CompuServe at GO QUEBOOKS.

Read this Before Opening Software